R
CULTURAL GEOGRAPHY

RE-READING CULTURAL GEOGRAPHY

Edited by **KENNETH E. FOOTE**

PETER J. HUGILL

KENT MATHEWSON

JONATHAN M. SMITH

University of Texas Press, Austin

Royalties from the first printing of *Re-reading Cultural Geography* will be donated to the Association of American Geographers to establish the Wagner and Mikesell Award in cultural geography. This award, honoring Philip Wagner and Marvin Mikesell, will be made yearly for the best student paper in cultural geography presented at the annual meetings of the Association of American Geographers.

LIBRARY OF CONGRESS
CATALOGING-IN-PUBLICATION DATA

Re-reading cultural geography / edited by Kenneth E. Foote
. . . [et al.] — 1st ed.
    p.   cm.
    Includes bibliographical references and index.
    ISBN 0-292-72483-7 (alk. paper)
    ISBN 0-292-72484-5 (pbk. : alk. paper)
    1. Human geography.   I. Foote, Kenneth E., 1955–
GF43.R4   1994
304.2—dc20   93-40072

CONTENTS

IV. WHAT THE WORLD MEANS

V. FUTURE WORLDS OF CULTURAL GEOGRAPHY

PREFACE AND ACKNOWLEDGMENTS

R e-reading *Cultural Geography* has been designed to be more at home in a student backpack than on a library shelf. It should be viewed less as an anthology than as a collection of resources for teaching cultural geography in a number of ways at both the undergraduate and graduate levels. Eighteen accessible, but sometimes challenging, articles touching on the major themes of contemporary cultural geography form the core of this volume. These articles have been reprinted in their entirety as exemplars of sound empirical and theoretical investigation; many of them have been revised and updated by their authors for republication here. In addition, each article now includes an annotated list of supplementary readings that expand on the relevant issues. Over two hundred articles and books have been abstracted in these lists. Finally, the articles are framed by thirteen introductory articles, commentaries, and essays written especially for this collection. These pieces inventory and assess major developments in cultural geography over the last thirty years. The book's bibliography of approximately fifteen hundred citations is one of the largest and most comprehensive ever compiled on cultural geography.

These features offer four resources for teaching. The core articles form a primary reading list. The annotated bibliographies provide a supplementary reading list. The introductory articles, commentaries, and essays outline a course syllabus and suggest topics for classroom discussion. Finally, the comprehensive bibliography provides a point of departure for in-depth study. These resources can be used as needed to suit the needs of different audiences and the interests and points of view of different instructors.

As an aid to the use of these materials, the editors' introductory essays outline fourteen themes that can serve as individual units of instruction, perhaps of a week in length. In a fifteen-week semester, the fourteen themes can be used in sequence following a one-week introduction. In many cases, however, instructors will prefer to focus on a subset of these themes and dwell on each for a longer interval. In my own department, a few of these fourteen themes are closely examined in courses other than cultural geography, so I abridge my discussions of these themes and develop instead those that are less well represented in our curriculum.

Re-reading Cultural Geography thus can be adapted to serve several audiences. In lower-division introductory courses that employ one of the many fine cultural geography textbooks available, *Re-reading Cultural Geography* can be used as a supplementary text for in-depth readings on selected topics. In upper-division courses, it can be used as a primary textbook or in combination either with one of the major books listed in the annotated bibliographies or with several of the articles. In graduate-level courses, the volume can be supplemented with ten to twenty of the articles listed in the annotated bibliographies or with excerpts from the books. In all cases, *Re-reading Cultural Geography* should be viewed as an intellectual buffet suited to many tastes rather than as a *menu à prix fixe* of instruction. The authors hope that, used in this way, this book will whet the taste of the new generation of cultural geographers just as effectively as Philip Wagner and Marvin Mikesell's *Readings in Cultural Geography* whetted the taste of a previous generation.

ACKNOWLEDGMENTS

Valery Billingsley of the Department of Geography at the University of Texas was instrumental in converting many of the reprinted articles into digital form for stylistic revision and editing. Lissa Alspach, Shannon Crum, and Alyson Greiner, all graduate students in cultural geography at the University of Texas, provided assistance far beyond the call of duty as voluntary research assistants on this project. Their command of the literature of cultural geography proved to be an invaluable resource in the checking and cross-checking of references and quotations and in compiling the index. Students in Geography 605 at Texas A & M University and Geography 336 at the University of Texas provided many helpful suggestions.

Thanks must also be extended to all the authors, commentators, and essayists who often worked extra hours on this project on very short deadlines. Special note should be made of those individuals who gave willingly of their time to revise both new and reprinted articles, to compile annotated bibliographies, and to answer my frequent queries: Dan Arreola, Jim Blaut, Jacquelin Burgess, Karl Butzer, Alfred Crosby, Mona Domosh, Carville Earle, Barbara Rubin Hudson, Terry Jordan, Peirce Lewis, Marvin Mikesell, Bernard Nietschmann, James Parsons, Douglas Pocock, Robert Riley, Isobel Stevenson, and Karl Zimmerer.

Publication of this volume would not have been possible without the support and encouragement of Shannon Davies of the University of Texas Press. Many thanks also to Phil Wagner for instigating this project and spurring it on to completion.

KENNETH E. FOOTE

I
THE WORLD
OF CULTURAL
GEOGRAPHY

PHILIP L. WAGNER | 1

FOREWORD:
CULTURE AND GEOGRAPHY:
THIRTY YEARS OF ADVANCE

More than thirty years ago I sat in a hut in a Mexican village and labored over the texts that Marvin Mikesell and I contributed to our *Readings in Cultural Geography*. Now I am planted in a small German town, confronting a similar task. The circumstances dictate that I proceed very tentatively to characterize the work of a long generation that has sped past like one of these trains traveling down the Rhine, origin and destination unknown—their sounds familiar but their contents always concealed. But separated as I am from *Readings in Cultural Geography*—both in time and space—I can nonetheless try to recall and reflect on the broader conceptual foundations, and sometimes unuttered assumptions, that go together inseparably with active empirical investigations to constitute the discipline of cultural geography.

Just as one might profitably fall back on a good understanding of geography to guess where the roaring trains are going to and coming from, and hence what freight they might be carrying, one may aspire to discern the "whence and whither" and the substance of the current traffic in cultural geographic ideas by mapping the intellectual terrain through which they move. A map is a moment, yet traffic restlessly moves. The temporal aspect imposes itself, as in any valid geography. This landscape of ideas, then, has a history that will clarify its present structure and its dynamism. It presents a problem of cultural diffusion.

OUR OWN DIFFUSION PROBLEM

Like the concept of regionalization, the theme of cultural diffusion lies close to the hearts and minds of all cultural geographers. It informs the work of postmodern practitioners of the disciplines, such as those working on cities or gender relationships, as surely as that of the previous generations, as I shall explain.

Cultural geography itself is an outspoken diffusion phenomenon. Moving from multiple centers of innovation and undergoing constant modification, an impulse toward understanding has grown, spread, and differentiated. What, indeed, could better typify the process of cultural diffusion than the progress of this single unifying concept through its many diverse transformations and translocations?

The widely differing and sometimes seemingly disconnected efforts of cultural geographers make patent both constancy and change. No diffusion totally dominates: all recipient realms are suffused with competing and discordant voices, and the field that is subject to the influence of any inspiration must always accommodate dissimilar input from alternative centers. Cultural geography responds to multiple stimuli, internal but also external to its leading authorities. Robert Platt, Alfred Meyer, Vaughan Cornish, Maximilien Sorre, Fred Lukermann, and Fraser Hart count as progenitors as fully as did Carl Sauer, who himself brought our European models to our attention. Many voices join in our harmony and construct our fruitful dissonance.

Likewise, the messages, like rumors, suffer transformations in the process of transmission. No diffusion is immune to reinterpretation, which often lends new life to old ideas.

What I invite you, the reader, to appreciate, then, is the diversity of original contributions, the mutability of messages, and yet the community of commitment that allows us to recognize our modest subdiscipline as a persistent, permissive, and open quest for a shared understanding, acknowledging multiple precedents and allowing for numerous metamorphoses within the diffusional universe that constitutes our common territory.

DELIGHT IN DIVERSITY

The world's diversity has always fascinated the geographer and invited exploration and interpretation. The distinctiveness of distant places stimulates comparison, which can increase awareness of the special character of what has seemed familiar and obviously necessary in the home surroundings of the sensitive observer; this new view of what was previously commonplace and unexamined counts as one of the geographer's most treasured rewards. We share it in teaching.

The individuality of place or landscape, though, however striking and illuminating, consists of a particular conjunction and relationship among a host of spatially extended elements, both natural and cultural or artificial. Although each local complex expresses only given forms and magnitudes of these elements in its dynamic character, each element in turn belongs to some comprehensive and orderly system of distribution and interaction that can be appreciated in its own right.

The geographer attends to more than just the specific "personality" of places and landscapes and the general order of natural energy cycles and historical progressions. Temporal aspects are also crucial; the regular rhythms of nature, as well as their shifts and interruptions, render distributions dynamic rather than static, and the developmental interplay among a multitude of agencies, both natural and cultural, constructs and constantly transforms particular localities. As so many geographers have insisted, both space and place must be considered. The key to their conceptual integration is temporal: the processual and the historical vision are essential in comprehending the natural order and the multitudes of local manifestations of its great complexity, which is differentiated further by the agency of human beings, whose cultural diversity contributes so much to the world's unending novelty and color. Geography both celebrates variety and seeks to understand it systematically.

DEFINITION BY DEFAULT

In prizing and proclaiming the particular, cultural geography appears perhaps devoid of general conceptions and theoretical foundations. Although the recognition of contrasting regions, or spatial differentiation, inheres essentially in all geography, most geographers agree that it can no longer fully describe, much less justify, the practice of geography. It cannot be its rationale. Similarly, culture history, although a crucial feature of the subdiscipline, chronicles change without explaining it and constitutes within itself no adequate foundation for a separate systematic and explanatory science. These considerations, however, do not mean that cultural geography has no intrinsic unity and no consistent intellectual validity.

In *Readings in Cultural Geography,* Marvin Mikesell and I proposed identifying the subject as "the application of the idea of culture to geographic problems." I now consider that identification to be faulty. Critical appraisals by Claval, Harvey, Brookfield, Duncan, and others have exposed the weakness in our conception of culture, which was taken for granted and invoked in an ad hoc, unsystematic fashion. Yet I do not now believe that cultural geography has much need of a concept of culture as such. It instead deserves a much deeper, clearer, more operational conception of human behavior and development, as do its sister disciplines of archaeology and anthropology.

Although such a grand, new conception still may be lacking, the longtime practice of the cultural geographers prefigures it, precisely through rejecting physical determinism and its economic counterpart and insisting that some other model of human motivation and action, however dimly yet discerned, is required to adequately explain the world's diversity and dynamisms. In its present stage of development, then, cultural geography may be best defined by what it is *not*.

My private predilection is for a far more biological orientation, placing cultural geography within the wider ambit of biogeography but according strong emphasis at the same time to communicative action (itself a biological phenomenon), which would imply a firm linkage with the humanities. Furthermore, the communication viewpoint, which I have advocated at length elsewhere, would call for a much greater emphasis on social relationships and institutional processes. Thus, I find it gratifying to detect certain signs of all these tendencies within this present collection, even if they still await an explicit and harmonious integration.

A LANDSCAPE ANTHROPOLOGY

Whereas the notion of the region is just as essential to physical and economic as to cultural geography, that of landscape is most at home in the cultural context. Humanity has appropriated so much of the earth's surface that pristine physical landscapes scarcely exist, and what could be called economic landscapes are simply partial aspects of the total locality as modified by human action.

In fact, though, any apperception of a landscape encompasses no more than a partial aspect of a local reality. Such an apperception has its own unique standpoint and scale. It construes a concrete experience and incorporates something of the individual who observes the landscape, which lends the place a humane significance, as many of the articles collected herein attest.

Such a significantly anthropological implication of landscape may authorize considering cultural geography as a sort of "landscape anthropology." Whereas professional anthropologists and archaeologists for the most part have until recently neglected to pay close attention to the landscape aspect of the places they worked in, cultural geographers have shown no corresponding reluctance to envision their physical sites of field research in very human terms and to assess the social and cultural characters of these sites. They have frequently gone further, evaluating the localities studied in terms of their bearing on human welfare and asking what their conditions might reveal regarding the essential character of the human species. In this respect they contemplate humanity reflected in its own creations and concern themselves with the consequences and costs of varied systems of human intervention in nature. Cultural geographers thus pursue an important kind of philosophical anthropology that possesses humanistic relevance and ethical implications.

WORLD AWARENESS

Everyone seems to acknowledge that geographers study such things as countries, areas, regions, and landscapes. Some people also know that the much discussed "environment" has long lain within our province, although we have perhaps wrongly neglected to assume the leadership this might imply. But the geographer, the cultural geographer particularly, studies something else important, too: a world.

Geography at the planetary scale is manifested in climatology, for instance, and in studies of commerce, but nowhere is it more central to interpretation than in the cultural subdiscipline. Both the comparative appreciation of the many types of cultural adaptation practiced throughout the world and the tracing of human movement and spatial diffusions of innovations that together inspire those adaptations constitute basic concerns of the cultural geographer. Whereas the idea of a "world system" as propounded by economists and historians such as André Gunder Frank and Immanuel Wallerstein may count as novel in their disciplines, it has existed in cultural geography from the beginning. The unity of humankind and the importance of distant contacts, exchanges, influences, and migrations are emphases central to our subdiscipline, and it could not carry on its work unmindful of them.

Thus, although attentive to the particularity of place and the always subjectively appreciated distinctiveness of landscapes, cultural geography also maintains a complementary universalizing outlook and depends for its interpretations on a comprehensive scheme of a single world order forever varying in time and conveying influence from each place and people to others at far remove. Likewise and simultaneously, developments and influences progressing through time, whether reconstructed for a single locality or tracked across the wider spaces of the world, command the attention of cultural geography wherever it is practiced and irrespective of the

given topic addressed. This characterization applies as fully to recent urban work, semiotic analyses of landscapes, or activist approaches to social problems as it does to the older culture history.

MORPHOLOGY, MECHANISM, MEANING

The editors of this collection have elected to arrange its contents under three rubrics representing morphology, mechanism, and meaning. Like the five themes that organized the earlier *Readings in Cultural Geography,* these three focal groupings are by no means mutually exclusive or antagonistic. Physical description is presupposed, for example, by any discussion of function, and phenomenological interpretation responds to concrete and dynamic stimuli. In this respect, whatever its mutations and amplifications, cultural geography has always retained a holistic outlook. Nothing less would properly respect and accord with the great complexity of all the cases it studies and problems it addresses.

Furthermore, the field experiences justifying our pronouncements tend to inundate us with unsorted and disparate bits of information that have to be sifted and shifted about to construct a coherent account of anything at all. Acutely aware of a wider world with all its turbulences and transformations, its energy exchanges and information diffusions, we reflect on our raw field experience to situate it in space and in time. But then we must see it in place, as it is—or rather, as we and our local informants have been able to perceive it. We contemplate the site in all its immediacy, seeking first simply to show it, to render a faithful description in terms of our purposes. Then we attempt to envision it more abstractly as an instant within the eternal flux of an infinitely complex and dynamic reality, reasoning as best we can from images of ordered systems and principles of cause and consequence.

But the yield of our indispensable fieldwork depends at least as much on our educated vision, which we owe to teachers and friends, as it does on the inherent features of the sites we confront. We see in part through the eyes of our mentors. Thus, in a sense, one may recognize a cultural geographer as a person whose outlook and alertness have been shaped by previous cultural geographers, among others, and who is loyal to the disciplined canons of his or her craft. Our practice both continues and contributes to a worthy heritage.

WE DISCOVER AMERICA

Cultural geography owes a vast debt to the help, guidance, and testimony of the ordinary local folk on whom so much of fieldwork depends. We should regard our literature as, among other things, a lasting memorial expressing our gratitude to these often anonymous informants.

Cultural geographic writings convey meanings both derived from the scholar's upbringing and professional training and imparted by field informants. It is altogether proper and important that we attend to the conceptions, opinions, and feelings of the inhabitants of an area we study. Hence, the respect and attention given to this class of meanings, often manifested in this volume, must be welcomed and valued. It is also good to discover something of the meaning of America in this book, and to see it through the eyes of the people.

But what comfort and benefit do we in turn confer on those local interlocutors, so frequently impoverished and overburdened, from whom we garner information that will bring us rich careers? Alas, but little. What contributions, furthermore, to human welfare generally do we make? Again, too little. The problems with which cultural geography has dealt have often been and still are momentous and timely ones. The urgent relevance of our time-honored theme of the degradation of environments, for example, is obvious to everyone by now, but what service have we rendered toward arresting harmful practices? Again, with all our vaunted sensitivity to culture and to ethnic differences, what help have we given to a world now plagued by bitter intertribal and intercommunal strife?

At least, as this volume indicates, some cultural geographers have finally discovered their own homelands, their troubled cities and the movements of their restless mainstream cultures, and they even seek to help in dealing with the pressing human problems these present. We ar-

rive in this land of our own, astonished and even alarmed at its state, with eyes widened by years in alien places, with sympathies conditioned by distant experience. And thank God, we try to be of some use.

NEW PERSPECTIVES

Just as the Columbian discovery of a new world in 1492 galvanized vast alterations in the thought and practices of Europeans, cultural geography's discovery of its own American, English, and other urbanized, "developed," Western homelands cannot fail to overturn established ways of thinking and to challenge us to reconsider our priorities and procedures. Let us hope that it will not result in such disaster for the natives of the older cultural tradition as befell indigenous Americans. And let us hope that these new discoverers show a far greater measure of compassion, respect, help, and equity in interacting with the people whose worlds they begin to explore than Columbus and his successors used.

Cultural geography can help to analyze and attack the human problems in our own societies that attach to race and poverty, age and gender, ethnicity and alienation. Spatial imagination, historical awareness, cultural sensitivity, and ecological insight, as well as that observational gift on which fieldwork depends, can all play a part in rendering service, and committed engagement will enrich our vision as well.

During the last three decades I have watched with wonder as cultural geography homed in ever more on its metropolitan targets and as simultaneous advances in technology endowed the discipline with eyes out in space (hence the powerful instrument of GIS, or geographic information systems). Our fields of vision and concern have thereby doubly increased. Rapid and enormous gains in information from the planetary scale to that of urban neighborhoods now challenge cultural geography not only to improve its technical procedures but above all to refine, clarify, and integrate its concepts and apply them in more useful ways.

As I have observed our subdiscipline expanding and developing its new perspectives, it became clear to me as a longtime proponent of cultural geography, as it may have to others, that a reappraisal of our accomplishments and directions had become desirable. Nevertheless, I considered myself less qualified to render an informed and fair account of current interests and aspirations than younger colleagues would be. I therefore approached the present editors, proposing that they undertake the selection and presentation of a collection of articles to represent the recent trends in cultural geography. The decisions and all the hard work have been theirs; I have done no more than watch and encourage their enterprise. And they have done well.

Cultural geography continues to flourish. Its locus of interest has changed, but not its logic of inquiry, as I hope these introductory remarks have been able to show.

PETER J. HUGILL AND
KENNETH E. FOOTE

2
RE-READING
CULTURAL
GEOGRAPHY

Cultural geography today has reasserted its claim to a central position in the discipline of geography. The claim stems from a recognition that the wealth of issues and ideas now under debate in cultural geography unites rather than divides research being pursued across the entire discipline. The debates themselves—however cantankerous and contentious—are direct evidence of vitality, for from the clamor of competing claims has emerged the realization that scholars working at the research frontiers of cultural geography continue to share ideas and interests more conducive to concord than to discord. These common, unifying ideas are the subject of this book. They have arisen from a variety of sources and represent a combination of longstanding intellectual traditions and more recent research excursions. Further, they have developed in both revolutionary and evolutionary ways since their last comprehensive inventory thirty years ago in Philip Wagner and Marvin Mikesell's *Readings in Cultural Geography* (1962). Regardless of their source and pedigree, these ideas outline a subdiscipline capable of addressing the central concerns of contemporary pluralistic geography.

Wagner and Mikesell's *Readings in Cultural Geography* was published at a similarly important moment in the development of modern geography. As Mikesell (1992) has written, geography in the late 1950s and early 1960s was dominated by three major concerns: cultural and historical processes, the spatial dynamics of urban and economic phenomena, and environmental processes. *Readings* took stock of the first of these. The volume was international in scope, but its main achievement was to define cultural geography one generation after its launch. *Readings* outlined five themes: culture, culture area, cultural landscape, culture history, and cultural ecology. The articles reprinted in the book were grouped somewhat differently under four headings: orientation, cultural areas and distributions, cultural origins and dispersals, and landscape and ecology.

The discipline has changed greatly since 1962, and other factors have replaced those that made *Readings in Cultural Geography* such an important statement for its time. Today, Wagner and Mikesell's five topics encompass only a portion of what cultural geographers profess and practice. Research on cultural landscapes and cultural ecology has generated more debate; investigations of cultural areas and distributions rather less. The topics of cultural origins and dispersals and of cultural history have held their own. As a consequence, we claim that the present volume is a sequel to *Readings* only in spirit. We assess an intellectual world that is far different from the one in which cultural geography held such a focal position thirty years ago. One of the major differences in *Re-reading Cultural Geography* is our singular focus on Anglo-American research. Whereas Wagner and Mikesell drew articles from much of the world, we have confined our selections to those by British, American, and Canadian scholars. This reflects, as much as anything else, Wagner and Mikesell's success in persuading a whole generation of anglophone geographers that the themes of cultural geography were, indeed, important.

We identify fourteen distinct research themes, which we have grouped under the following three headings: "How the World Looks," "How the World Works," and "What the World Means." These headings were selected to highlight the distinctions cultural geographers make in their use of the term *culture*. The papers in each section exemplify research on one or more of the fourteen themes while drawing attention

to larger bodies of scholarship. These fourteen themes are introduced below and in the introductory essays that preface this book's three main sections.

Our method of organization is also based on other considerations. The literature of cultural geography is now so extensive that a single-volume international survey of the entire field would be impracticable. At the time of its publication, *Readings in Cultural Geography* could serve as both an introductory textbook and a guide to advanced research. These roles can no longer be subsumed in a single volume. The introductory audience is served by several outstanding textbooks (English and Miller 1989; W. A. D. Jackson 1985; Jordan and Rowntree 1976 et seq.), but the research frontiers remain the province of special collections of papers stressing specific topics (Agnew and Duncan 1989; Barnes and Duncan 1992; Birks et al. 1988; Cosgrove and Daniels 1988; Hugill and Dickson 1988; Kniffen 1990; Ley and Samuels 1978; Lowenthal and Bowden 1976; Meinig 1979b; M. Richardson 1974, 1984; C. Riley et al. 1971; B. L. Turner et al. 1990; Wong 1992). Our aim is to interweave the wide range of related themes found at the research frontiers in a way useful to advanced students and scholars alike.

Despite these advances, cultural geography no longer stands out from other disciplinary concerns as it did thirty years ago. The hallmark of contemporary geography is its methodological and philosophical pluralism, and today's cultural geography gains its strength from blending with and supporting research spread across a wide range of topics. Indeed, to assert that cultural geography can still be assessed as an independent subdiscipline seems almost to contravene conventional wisdom, yet we believe that good can come of refocusing geography's pluralistic concerns on key ideas and issues. Pluralism offers certain intellectual freedoms, but it also draws attention away from the commonalities of interest that unite geographers into a discipline (B. Berry 1980; Palm 1986). *Re-reading Cultural Geography* addresses the themes that unite, rather than divide, Anglo-American cultural geography. We reach out to the work of scholars strung along geography's research frontiers. All can be bound together within the explicitly catholic view of cultural geography we espouse, which maintains that cultural geography should not be divided by its own common interests.

A PLURALISTIC PUZZLE

Like many American social sciences, geography fragmented into a large number of subdisciplines in the 1970s. The Association of American Geographers began the formation of specialty groups in 1979, and most members now belong to several of them. By 1992 there were thirty-nine such groups, four of which were oriented toward cultural geographic themes: cultural geography, cultural ecology, environmental perception and behavioral geography, and historical geography, with other groups claiming the allegiance of varying numbers of cultural geographers. Despite the large number of scholars publishing on topics that can be broadly described as cultural geography, the subdiscipline was one of the last to organize a specialty group, waiting until 1988 to do so. Rather than seeking the consensus needed to create an effective specialty group, cultural geographers avoided confrontation by working in groups of smaller size. The disagreements within cultural geography during the 1970s and 1980s had the positive effect of widening the range of topics and theories debated within geography as a discipline, while having the drawback of fragmenting the subdiscipline into intellectually self-contained, self-sufficient constituencies.

Given the trend toward intellectual pluralism, tracing the ideas that unify cultural geography is a difficult task. Reviewing the origins and history of a subdiscipline is always controversial, but all the more so in the case of today's cultural geography, where historiography is akin to assembling the pieces of a complex intellectual puzzle. The issues that enliven contemporary debates have been shaped by many ideas and many scholars. Some pieces of this puzzle fit together more readily than others, but even the most recalcitrant fit into place when set in the context of the subdiscipline's origins, its position within the discipline of geography, and a variety of revolutionary and evolutionary developments that have

shaped the goals of geography as a whole over the last thirty years.

BERKELEY SCHOOL ORIGINS

Cultural geography developed as a distinctive subdiscipline within American human geography in the 1920s and 1930s, for the most part at the University of California at Berkeley under the leadership of Carl Sauer, and it enjoyed this position until the mid-1960s. Sauer and the Berkeley school have been both eulogized and attacked, but no one denies their early and ongoing influence on cultural geography (M. Price and M. Lewis 1993). The subdiscipline's development was, in part, a response to the prevalence of environmental determinism in human geography in the first decades of this century, but its specific boundaries were a product of the personality of Sauer, who directed his attention and that of his students to premodern cultures (Hooson 1981; Kenzer 1987; Leighly 1963; 1976; 1978; Speth 1981; Robert West 1979; 1982; M. Williams 1983). The most comprehensive expression of Berkeley school themes appeared in 1956: *Man's Role in Changing the Face of the Earth* (Thomas 1956).

By the early 1960s Berkeley school cultural geography was at its apogee. Sauer's thirty-three doctoral students and, increasingly, his students' students (Vicero 1976) were established in almost all the major graduate schools in the United States and Canada. Two of Sauer's students, Wagner and Mikesell, then at the University of Chicago, published *Readings in Cultural Geography* in 1962. The collection was a fresh appraisal of the research themes that defined the Berkeley school. Wagner and Mikesell touched on European humanistic research traditions in geography and marked the beginnings of what might have been, under different circumstances, a quantitative turn in cultural geography, if not a revolution.

At the time that *Readings* appeared, the quantitative revolution in social science in the late 1950s and early 1960s was beginning to have a marked impact on geography (Billinge, Gregory, and Martin 1984; Burton 1963). One effect of the quantitative revolution in geography was an emphasis on its spatial orientation, whether in physical or human geography. By the mid-1960s this development was threatening the continued existence of the humanistic research tradition represented by cultural geography, and the sub-discipline was forced to regroup and restructure. Fragmentation resulted. Some themes, such as cultural ecology, sustained large and productive constituencies throughout the period. Other themes gradually lost adherents. At the same time, other humanistic concepts were discovered, rediscovered, and developed within the contexts of both Berkeley school cultural geography and the discipline at large (Entrikin 1976; Tuan 1976b). During the 1980s the pieces and fragments of cultural geography began once again to coalesce around a "new cultural geography" (Cosgrove and Jackson 1987), yet this coalescence was new only insofar as it suggested the value of a unity of focus across a broad range of themes. Wagner and Mikesell prefigured these developments as much as they defined the end of the *ancien régime* of the Berkeley school, hence both the importance of their work and the need to place it in historical context.

THE DISCIPLINARY CONTEXT

Cultural geography was more advanced in its theories than was the rest of human geography in the 1920s and 1930s (Leighly 1937). Increasing disapproval of environmental determinism as an explanation of human behavior at the individual level caused human geography to regroup around the regional concept, though this concept never acquired the explanatory power enjoyed by environmental determinism in its heyday (Wagner 1977). In the 1920s and 1930s only cultural geography maintained a search for universal processes in human spatial behavior, in particular through what became its central tenet, diffusionism (Dodge 1937; Sauer 1927). For cultural geographers, diffusion was the key to explaining the process by which human phenomena became distributed through space.

In *Agricultural Origins and Dispersals* (1952) Sauer went even farther, inquiring into the origin of the first great revolution to shape human societies, the agricultural. He developed the thesis that agriculture most likely originated in particularly favored environments—the hilly, riverine terrain of the humid tropics. Here, rather than on the drier riverine plains of the subtropics, simple hunting and gathering societies had the leisure to experiment with the domestication of plants—most of which Sauer regarded as genetically quite distant from their wild forebears—in a wide variety of soils and climates. Sauer thus made clear what should be the second of cultural geography's prime concerns, the origins of cultural systems. As he noted in *Agricultural Origins*, once the idea of the domesticated plant was developed in such a propitious environment, the process of diffusion would take over. The idea of agriculture would then spread by human agency—specifically, "contagious diffusion"—as part of a package of cultural ideas (Blaut 1977; Dickson 1988; C. Reed 1977; Zelinsky 1973). This separation of provenance from process, origins from dispersal, is one of the central and most unremarked on tenets of Berkeley school cultural geography.

Sauer's contributions have been addressed by many commentators since his death in 1975 (Entrikin 1984; Hooson 1981; Kenzer 1987), but whatever the merits of Sauer's argument (and it has attracted plenty of detractors as well as supporters), his work defined cultural geography in the American academy, and his students ensured its dispersal from Berkeley. In separating origins from dispersals, however, provenance from process, Sauer and his students retained for the physical environment a powerful role in the matter of origins of key cultural items while they rejected it as a universal causal factor in the routine behavior of individual human beings. Provenance thus came to be concerned with relatively rare events, such as the emergence of agriculture, civilization, science, commerce, capitalism, industry, and democracy (Blaut 1976). These were not inventions triggered by a simple cause but phenomena that originated in a limited number of very specific places. Process concerned much commoner events, such as the spread of these complex inventions throughout humankind, and could be regarded as universal.

Two other characteristics expressed in *Agri-*

cultural Origins were a concern for macroscale rather than microscale events and an inclination to consider these events over relatively long spans of time. The Berkeley school was always one of cultural *historical* geography, a point Sauer (1941a) noted in his "Foreword to Historical Geography." From the late nineteenth century to the 1930s, macroscale accounts were still common in social science, and theory was not a suspect word in history. Continuing in the traditions of inquiry established still earlier by Montesquieu, St. Simon, Hegel, and Marx, Toynbee's cycles of history went around, Weber gave a spirited account of the origins of capitalism, and the frontier had not yet closed on the Turner thesis. Yet the period saw the decline of all these projects as the certainty of progress was called into question by world events. The social sciences, following the path of economics, entered a period characterized by microscale and ahistorical theories.

Cultural geography and anthropology, almost alone among the social sciences, resisted these trends, staying true to the macroscale and the long time line. Historians, who had shown a strong interest in theory earlier in the century, almost totally abandoned such efforts to Marxists. Non-Marxist theories, such as Toynbee's cycles, simply could not coexist with Marx's stages of historical development. The search for long-run, macroscale theories thus moved to the social sciences that were in a sense furthest removed from economics. This is not to imply that the search was thorough or even conscious. Human geography was heavily influenced by these changing currents of thought in the social sciences. In the United States, beginning in the late 1950s, the quantitative revolution took hold in the subdiscipline of economic geography. This subdiscipline was revitalized by imported German ideas about the spatial structure of economy and society through the writings of von Thünen, Lösch, and Christaller. British geographers began to follow this trend in the early 1960s, but those working in a more humanist tradition also began to look to Europe for Marxist explanations of the historical dynamics of human institutions. Marx's theories of stages of historical development and, in particular, the primacy of the class struggle in historical change seemed much better suited to a relatively class-stratified society such as Britain than to the United States, where society is stratified along different lines of income, race, and ethnicity.

The quantitative revolution was a revolution not so much in the substance of geography or the data that geographers collected as it was in the techniques employed to analyze that data and in the power of the theories that were brought into play. Geographers had long collected quantitative data on many natural and human phenomena in their attempts to describe regions on the earth's surface. The region remained the unifying concept regardless of the phenomenon under scrutiny. Three major subdisciplines of American geography operated on this principle from the 1920s through the 1960s. Physical geographers enumerated and classified climates, soils, and landforms. Economic geographers enumerated and classified populations and the production and distribution of crops, goods, and services. Cultural geographers enumerated and classified the material artifacts of culture. All geographers mapped the phenomena they had enumerated and classified, and all sought to define regions based on some quantifiable constellation of traits.

Economic geographers tended to be the most mathematical because they worked with uniform data sets. Physical and cultural geographers were oriented toward fieldwork in which they collected at least some of their own data. Physical and cultural geographers also considered the past more than economic geographers did, because they dealt more with the real world than with the world of statistics. Even such simple concepts as the Davisian cycle of erosion stressed the long-term sequence of events in the physical realm. Cultural geographers looking at the landscape were immediately aware of the persistence of such artifacts as field types and boundaries, as well as building materials, house types, and town plans.

In Berkeley school cultural geography, such historical awareness was compounded by the conditions of its intellectual origins. Sauer was by predilection an antimodernist (Entrikin 1984;

Mathewson 1987), and his students studied pre-industrial societies almost exclusively. Since Kroeber and his anthropology students at Berkeley were already engaged in describing and classifying vanishing Native American societies, Sauer left this enterprise to them. Sauer and his students turned outside the United States, mostly to Mexico, occasionally elsewhere in Latin America, and sometimes further afield. This intense focus on the preindustrial world has obscured the importance of Berkeley school cultural geography in social science. Its contributions, in particular its separation of provenance and process, were attended to only by those interested in premodern societies.

The successful adoption by economic geographers in the 1960s of new theories and analytic techniques affected the position of Berkeley school cultural geography within the discipline. Cultural geography ceased to be the most theoretically informed of the subdisciplines and embarked on a long search for theory that is still underway. In 1962, when Wagner and Mikesell published *Readings in Cultural Geography*, this was not yet clear, and the subdiscipline was still defined by the work of Sauer, his students, and their collaborators and sympathizers.

REVOLUTIONARY CURRENTS OF THOUGHT

The publication of *Readings in Cultural Geography* corresponded closely with the appearance of a number of works that signaled the success of the early phase of the quantitative revolution (B. Berry 1967; Bunge 1962; Hägerstrand 1967; Haggett 1966). During this period a number of graduate programs, first in the United States and then in Britain, reorganized to assume the lead in promoting quantitative methodologies, much as the Berkeley department had been the focus of cultural geography in the 1920s and 1930s. By the late 1960s few programs remained unchanged. Early casualties in the United States were regional and physical geographers, who seemed to have no place in what was essentially an econometric social and spatial science. Regional geography, because it was particularistic and unable to produce universal, lawlike statements, was

demoted in most programs—even in Britain, where it was more firmly entrenched (Thornthwaite 1961). Physical geographers, however, had always maintained a reasonably strong theoretical stance. In Britain physical geography adapted quickly to the quantitative revolution and remained a central part of academic geography, propounding sophisticated mathematical models of physical processes. Although there was some common interest in general systems theory in the 1960s (Chorley and Haggett 1967) and in environmental protection in the 1970s (Marcus 1979), physical and human geography grew increasingly estranged over this period. This merely aggravated a longstanding condition of which Sauer (1956b) had strenuously disapproved.

In some departments cultural geographers were powerful enough to remain dominant, but most of the major graduate programs embraced the quantitative revolution. By reason of mutual concern for environment, cultural geographers had always valued the contributions of physical geographers, and in departments with strong cultural leanings, physical geography often survived. Even so, geography in the United States, with its focus on human rather than human and physical geography, found itself increasingly polarized into economic and cultural geography. The theoretical interests of geography in the United States, which for cultural geographers had been historical and macroscale, became for the remainder of the field ahistorical, microscale, and mathematical. Some theorists, such as Bunge, were quite willing to write time—and by implication, historical geography—out of the discipline (Bunge 1962).

If the work of Berry, Bunge, Hägerstrand, and Haggett signaled a peak in the quantitative revolution by 1967, Harvey's *Explanation in Geography* (1969) marked the dawning of the realization that the quantitative revolution consisted of more than statistical analysis, and that such analysis was not intrinsically explanatory. Harvey viewed explanation in geography as the rigorous application of scientific method to geographic problems. He followed Haggett (1966) in identifying five major themes around which geographers organized their thoughts at the time: areal differentiation; landscape; relationships between people and their environments; spatial distributions; and geometrics (Harvey 1969, 114–15). Harvey recognized one of these themes—landscape—as an overtly cultural geographic theme that evolved from Sauer's introduction of German ideas in his article "The Morphology of Landscape" (1925). He linked a second theme, the "man-environment relationship," to human ecology on the British model exemplified by Brookfield (1964) and Eyre and Jones (1966), rather than to Barrows's (1923) article "Geography as Human Ecology." Though slighted by Harvey, the theme of the relationships between people and their environment was, of course, at the heart of the Berkeley school.

Cultural geographers felt obligated to respond to criticisms that their subdiscipline lacked theoretical goals. In some ways, this was ironic, since Sauer had long subscribed to Chamberlin's (1890) notion of multiple working hypotheses (Entrikin 1984, 401). Sauer never doubted the importance of the iron law of distance and its impact on human behavior, he just did not believe it was the only process at work. In *Readings in Cultural Geography*, Wagner and Mikesell translated into English Edgar Kant's 1953 article "Classification and Problems of Migrations," with its plea for "new methods of cartographic analysis and description" (Wagner and Mikesell 1962, 354). They went on to introduce to a much wider audience one of the first great examples of such new methods, Hägerstrand's (1962) mathematical cartographic analysis of diffusion, the process central to the interests of cultural geographers. Ironically, this article was called to the attention of cultural geographers just as they began to retreat from the quantitative revolution. The mathematical modeling of diffusion was instead subsumed by the quantifiers, as if it were just another element of German econometric geography. Hägerstrand's analysis could have been adopted just as easily by cultural geography in the early 1960s. Hägerstrand himself was somewhat neutral in the matter of advancing the quantitative revolution, and his later work has certainly been as much in the tradition of cultural geography as in that of spatial theory (Hägerstrand 1978; 1988). In retrospect, the preoccupations of Sauer and his students with premodern societies and with fieldwork stood in the way of an adequate response.

EVOLUTIONARY CURRENTS OF THOUGHT

Since 1962 cultural geographers have had to define their interests in contrast to prevailing notions of geography as a spatial science. Nonetheless, it would be a mistake to overlook other currents of thought that followed evolutionary rather than revolutionary trajectories through the same period. Most of this evolutionary thinking focused on Wagner and Mikesell's theme of cultural landscape. Berkeley school geographers became interested in the landscape at an early stage, either as a study in morphology, as evidence of the diffusion of material culture, or as communication. Some nongeographers became interested in ordinary landscapes, and some geographers with no connection to the Berkeley school began to be concerned with the human perception of order and meaning in the environment. In "Learning from Looking" (1983) P. Lewis balances Sauer's contribution to the study of cultural landscapes with those of Fred Kniffen, J. B. Jackson, and J. K. Wright, each of whom initiated new lines of research into these topics.

Kniffen was an early Berkeley graduate who turned his well-honed field skills to understanding the morphology and diffusion of material culture. Although the work of Kniffen (1936; 1965; 1974; 1990) and his students is sometimes derided for its exhaustive cataloging of house types and other material artifacts, particularly in the rural American South, the insights generated by this tradition have been profound (Mathewson 1993; Wyckoff 1979). Behind the careful tracing of "streams" of house types and artifacts is the view that these are "keys to diffusion," a process central to cultural geographic inquiry. In this view types of folk houses and assemblages of material traits indicate the movement of cultural ideas through time and space. The influence of Kniffen's subtle analysis can be seen in the work of Glassie (1975; 1982), Jordan (1978; 1989a; 1989b; Jordan and Kaups 1987; 1989), P. Lewis

(1975), Newton (1974), and Stilgoe (1982). Another Berkeley graduate, Wilbur Zelinsky, produced an impressive series of articles on the diffusion of material and nonmaterial traits, such as place names and religions (Zelinsky 1951; 1955; 1961; 1967; 1970b; 1973).

J. B. Jackson's writings and his work as founding editor of *Landscape* magazine have also been broadly influential both inside and, even more importantly, outside cultural geography (J. B. Jackson 1970; 1972a; 1972b; 1984). Jackson called attention to every facet of the cultural landscape, no matter how ordinary or common, but rather than rushing to some abstract theoretical formulation or some quick judgment of beauty and value, he sought to understand varied landscape elements as the product of human values and aspirations. Jackson founded *Landscape* in 1951, and although the magazine was not widely read by geographers until after the publication of *Readings in Cultural Geography*, it is now considered a major forum for interdisciplinary excursions into the themes of cultural geography. In Britain W. G. Hoskins (1955) analyzed the historical development of the English landscape as, in Macaulay's famous words, a "marvellous palimpsest." Meinig (1979b) summarized the contribution of both writers to our understanding of ordinary landscapes in similar terms, while noting Hoskins's regrettable avoidance of industrial landscapes, a topic that would not gain attention until later (Coones and Patten 1986; Trinder 1982).

J. K. Wright's contributions are of a different order, for his writings challenged geographers to look beyond the visible landscape and to consider how humans perceive meaning and order in environment (J. K. Wright 1966a). His articles "*Terrae Incognitae:* The Place of Imagination in Geography" (1947) and "Notes on Early American Geopiety" (1966b) developed hermeneutics still not fully realized by geographers. The influence of these humanistic and perceptual ideas can be seen in some of Wright's contemporaries (S. Jones 1952; B. Floyd 1961; 1962), in Tuan's *Topophilia* (1974b) and many of his other writings (Tuan 1974a; 1975; 1976a; 1977; 1979b), in Lowenthal's "Geography, Experience, and Imagination: Toward a Geographical Epistemology"

(1961), in Meinig's "Geography as an Art" (1983), and in the volume of articles edited by Lowenthal and Bowden (1976) as a tribute to Wright.

David Sopher was the Berkeley-trained geographer who probably moved furthest from the precepts of the Berkeley school. He willingly embraced a more mathematical style of cultural geography and attempted to reunite cultural geographers with spatial-analytic human geographers (Sopher 1972, 321). Perhaps his greatest legacy is the project of "deciphering the palimpsest" of the cultural landscape, carried out for the most part by his students (Sopher 1972, 327). This comes down to the issue of whether the landscape should be read as text (Duncan 1973) or viewed as a form of communication (Hugill 1975). Wagner (1972, 43–61) also stressed the central importance of communication in cultural geography, not only through the cultural landscape but also through such major institutional forms as religion and language, which have a clearly geographic distribution. Sopher's (1967) *Geography of Religions* was central to Wagner's analysis of communication through religion. Sopher's (1972, 327) concern with such alternatives to positivism as phenomenology also prefigures more recent inquiry in the humanistic tradition.

Not all the changes that have occurred in cultural geography over the last thirty years can be attributed to the influence of individual scholars. Other themes and theories important to contemporary cultural geography have arisen within the context of broader disciplinary debates. The topics most noticeably absent from *Readings in Cultural Geography* but important today were historical materialism, environmental perception, and humanistic geography.

Marxism's importation to America was closely tied to the exodus of British academicians to the United States from the late 1950s to the present. The exchange between North America and Britain was, of course, also important to the diffusion of the quantitative revolution, which was just getting under way as this exodus began. Although the concerns of cultural geography do not lend themselves overtly to Marxism, the issues of historical materialism, class struggle, and ideology have had an influence on contemporary debate. Cosgrove recast the process of landscape formation in Marxist terms (Cosgrove 1984), and Harvey (1985; 1989) has shown how Marxist theory can yield insight into topics traditionally of concern to cultural geography. British geographers drew their notions of cultural processes from what they call cultural studies rather than anthropology, and many were influenced by Marxist writers such as Raymond Williams (1961; 1965; 1973) and Roland Barthes (1972; 1979). The result is an emphasis on culture as repressive and hegemonic and a concern for disfranchised minorities (P. Jackson 1989). The applicability of Marxist theory seems greatest in areas where cultural and social geography overlap, a situation that arises more often in the British literature (P. Jackson and Smith 1984).

A new research frontier in cultural geography in the 1960s was that of environmental perception. Early research sought to explain variability in human response to natural hazards and disasters, but differences in beliefs and values rapidly came to be viewed as keys to understanding divergent adaptive strategies among various populations. Through the 1970s and 1980s, the precepts of environmental perception research spread through human geography and came to be applied in a wide range of subdisciplines. Perception research offered a means of tracing human behavior to long-lived, underlying beliefs and values. Apart from directly borrowing these ideas, cultural geographers gained indirect guidance from earlier influential writings in historical geography addressing related topics (R. Brown 1943; 1948; Sauer 1971). Common interests included immigrants' perceptions of their new environments, the cultivation of landscape values and tastes through time, and the emergence of regional identity.

Cultural geography was also influenced—and challenged—by human geographers' adoption of humanistic philosophies and methodologies. Set against the background of American society of the 1960s and 1970s, the call for humanistic research in geography echoed the questioning of prevailing priorities in national political and social life (Zelinksy 1975). This questioning was not all of a kind, and what came to be known as "humanistic geography" emerged less as an integrated subdiscipline than as a loose federation based on philosophical critique, methodological experiment, and programmatic challenge comparable to other radical challenges being voiced at the same time and that together served as criticism of prevailing research values (Entrikin 1976). British and Canadian scholars helped urge these challenges forward and can be credited with introducing to debate many of these new ideas. But most British-trained scholars lacked direct experience with the traditional themes of the Berkeley school, and this lack of contact slowed the emergence of an Anglo-American research tradition. If humanistic philosophy celebrates human intellectual potential and creative ability, humanistic geography quickly came to pay tribute to human development of emotive bonds with environment as expressed creatively in landscape, social life, and artistic media. In turning toward a humanistic understanding of the geographical experience of human beings, the subdiscipline gave preference to questions of environmental meaning and human experience over issues of spatial patterning and economic prerogatives.

Humanistic geography is occasionally characterized as an antipositivist critique of human geography that stresses subjective experience over objective scientific observation. This is not entirely accurate, because scientific positivism is itself very much a product of humanistic currents of thought and is based on the supposition that humans hold the power to understand nature and culture through systematic scientific inquiry (Gregory 1978). Early work in humanistic geography nonetheless criticized the prevailing research program in human geography and questioned the goals and motives of geographers who were searching for generalizations and laws of human spatial behavior and interaction with environment. In the face of the social upheavals of the 1960s and 1970s, humanistic geographers sensed a need to study the human condition more directly, in terms not of abstract spatial analysis but of human values, beliefs, and perceptions (Buttimer 1974).

The questions raised by humanistic geographers had been asked before, but the work of scholars such as J. K. Wright only hinted at a broader research agenda. To outline a more encompassing program of research, humanistic geographers quickly began to look outside geography. They turned to such philosophies and methodologies as ethnomethodology, existentialism, idealism, phenomenology, symbolic interactionism, and transactionalism. In retrospect, successful applications of each of these can be found in the geographical literature, but none captured the imaginations of more than a handful of geographers at a time. This is still the case today. Even so, Ley and Samuels's (1978) anthology, *Humanistic Geography*, was clearly an attempt to define a "new" cultural geography.

The failure of this attempted coup explains some of the contentions that shape contemporary debate (M. Price and M. Lewis 1993; Duncan this volume). The most serious obstacle lay in the fact that a large number of geographers had continued to cultivate the traditional themes of the Berkeley school defined by Wagner and Mikesell in 1962 and rearticulated by Mikesell in 1978. These geographers felt little need to accept humanistic geography and resented its new agenda. Humanistic research had little to say about traditional concerns. The unfortunate mismatch between American cultural geography and British social geography compounded problems of assimilation. Although the two fields are very close, subtle differences in the two traditions sometimes prevent ready intellectual exchange. The contributions of British social geography to recent advances in humanistic cultural geography have been increasing (P. Jackson 1989), but the overlap is slight.

RE-WORKING THE THEMES OF CULTURAL GEOGRAPHY

Though still bound loosely to the topics developed by Wagner and Mikesell, contemporary cultural geography encompasses a wider range of themes. Writing independently, both Wagner and Mikesell have reflected on their original classificatory scheme (Wagner 1975; Mikesell 1978; 1992). We extend this reassessment to fourteen themes grouped within three categories. Our categories are based, in part, on different orientations toward culture and process but also on differing goals and points of emphasis within the

literature. The research of the last three decades has greatly extended cultural geography's scope and enhanced its interpretive power. A reawakening of interest in cultural geography has arisen from the sources discussed above: the literature of humanistic geography; the study of environmental perception and behavior; well-developed research departures in cultural ecology; and new ideas in social, economic, and historical geography. For some time now these varied ideas have been converging with the traditional themes of cultural geography identified by Wagner and Mikesell to bring into being the broadened range of themes we identify.

Central to all fourteen themes is the problem of identifying what is meant by *culture*. Our categories of orientation toward culture, provenance, and process arise from our struggle with that problem. Culture is and has been one of the most difficult concepts to define in the social sciences (Kroeber and Kluckhohn 1952; R. Williams 1976). This is not to suggest that social scientists and humanists have avoided trying to come to terms with culture as a concept or have shunned attempts to develop working definitions of culture. As early as 1952 Kroeber and Kluckhohn assembled a critical review of cultural concepts and definitions based on hundreds of sources. The volume cited only two geographers—Friedrich Ratzel and Dmitry Anuchin—even though the term *cultural geography* had then been in circulation for a century and the subdiscipline had been a going concern for at least half a century. German geographers were the first to develop their research around the concepts of culture in the late nineteenth century, and by the 1920s, Sauer had begun to use these concepts to organize his investigations.

Sauer initially elaborated his concept of culture in conjunction with his interest in the morphology of landscape (Sauer 1925). Putting it in memorable epigrammatic form, he stated that "culture [through time] is the agent, the natural area is the medium, the cultural landscape is the result." In the absence of more elaborate conceptions, this formula became the basic program for much of the work in cultural geography over the next several decades, although other cultural geographers offered working definitions of culture from time to time, usually borrowing or adapting concepts derived from anthropology. At root, culture in these contexts implies no less and no more than a group's way of life, or *genre de vie*. This notion of culture places particular emphasis on the group's customary or traditional way of doing things, especially those activities associated with human transformations of the natural world. Cosgrove (1983) has pointed out that Marx's concept of *mode of production* and the Vidalian notion of *genre de vie* have strong parallels.

Other working definitions of culture can be discerned in the literature of cultural geography—hence the grouping principle employed in this volume. "How the World Looks" views culture as revealed in the regularity and patterning of cultural traits and material artifacts. The stress on how the world "looks" emphasizes the cultural geographer's concern for tangible and visible features of cultural life, but not to the exclusion of such less tangible traits as religion, language, and ethnicity. As it has with Kniffen, a concern for patterns of cultural traits and material artifacts has inspired some of the finest work in cultural geography. Although pattern is a starting point, the best work in this area inevitably entails concern for process.

"How the World Works" develops the view of culture as *genre de vie*. Emphasis is placed on the relationship between humans and environments as expressed in the ways in which humans work to make use of the earth and to maintain and propagate their *genres de vie* from generation to generation. The themes of this section address the human use of the earth and the cultural values and forces woven into social, economic, and political systems.

"What the World Means" analyzes culture as a system of shared values and collective beliefs. These values and beliefs are studied as they are expressed or represented in the ways in which humans perceive and ascribe meaning to environments; interpret the world through artistic and creative representation in film, literature, and the visual arts; develop attachments to place; and adopt moral, ethical, and ideological principles to guide their actions.

From these three general orientations toward the term *culture*—and to the tasks of cultural geography itself—follow fourteen more specific themes. As introduced below, these themes both inventory the major areas of contemporary research and divide the field into a suggested syllabus for the teaching of cultural geography, each theme balanced against the others in a semester's course.

HOW THE WORLD LOOKS

In 1962 Wagner and Mikesell noted that the cultural landscape was one of the most poorly occupied salients of cultural geography. That is no longer true. Studies of the cultural landscape are central to Anglo-American cultural geography and appear in both the first and the third sections of this book. The articles in the first section pertain to the visible artifacts of culture, phenomena that have long served as a staple of inquiry in cultural geography. They are generally the product of original fieldwork and analyze real rather than represented landscapes, places rather than pictures. Fresh interpretive strategies continue to disclose new aspects of material culture worthy of study and thereby to demonstrate the undiminished viability of this fundamental tradition. The articles are not catalogs of material culture: each places its subject in an explanatory framework as well as in the larger geographical context. Cultural geographers have attributed variability in the appearance of the landscape to many facets of culture, including individual identity, social class, gender difference, ethnicity, religion, and political economy. Each article is also noteworthy for its demonstration of the various geographical scales at which the phenomena of the visible landscape can be perceived, conceptualized, and analyzed.

In this section, the articles are discussed in the context of four specific themes: (1) Learning from Looking; (2) Ordinary Landscapes; (3) Emblems of Authority; and (4) The Dynamic Region. These themes combine a recognition of the continued importance of traditional interests in material culture with indications of fresh sources of vitality. Together they provide an important foundation for the following section in two ways. First, the visible landscape serves as a fundamental pedagogical device in virtually all courses in cultural geography. Second, by showing how material forms can both express cultural values and guide human action, these articles provide a defensible explanation of the transfer and transformation of ideas and material culture. Within this section the landscape is viewed as a text that the inhabitants emboss on the natural environment over time, a text that cultural geographers can read and interpret. Much research has revolved around interpreting landscapes as collections of signs or symptoms of underlying generative processes. Following Kniffen, this view stresses the ways in which traits and artifacts can be used to make inferences about the dynamic relationship between humans and the natural environment. A variation on this strategy, pioneered by J. B. Jackson, seeks understanding of particular, ordinary features of the cultural landscape in their own terms, irrespective of whether these landscape features illustrate general processes or local, idiographic variants.

More recently, other methods of analysis have emerged. In "Landscape Taste as a Symbol of Group Identity," Duncan drew his method from American pragmatism and its offshoot, symbolic interactionism (Duncan 1973). If humans mediate their interpersonal interactions symbolically with words and gestures, then landscapes can be used to mediate sociospatial interaction among groups. Duncan showed how groups with almost identical incomes in a Westchester County village produced different residential landscapes—texts—on the basis of ethnicity and their respective social networks. Hugill later focused on the communication process inherent in landscapes and the way in which landscape elements cue appropriate responses from social groups, including examples in which elite groups constructed landscapes to engage in generations-long communication with other groups (Hugill 1975; 1984).

Another development has been to view the landscape as embodying relationships of power and authority among social groups. Meinig noted the blatantly imperial symbolism of Fort Douglas in Salt Lake City, Utah, "established in the 1860s on a high terrace overlooking the city, as a tangible symbol of the supremacy of the federal government over Mormondom" (Meinig 1965, 212). Harvey (1979) analyzed the Basilica of the Sacré-Coeur in Paris and noted how it became a powerful symbol of a resurgent Catholic monarchism on the skyline of revolutionary Paris.

This work has been extended by Cosgrove (1984) and Cosgrove and Daniels (1988). Further extension of these ideas can be found in recent discussions of postmodernism. Drawing heavily on French linguistic theory and Marxism, such discussions have taken the view that signs embody power relationships and must be deconstructed if social change is to occur (R. Harris 1991; Harvey 1989; Short 1991; Soja 1989).

This body of work on the landscape as a material construct of human action is a central issue in modern cultural geography with broad roots in American and British geography. Landscapes are both a means of communication and texts to be read. The questions that provoke debate are what it is that the groups are communicating and by whom these texts are meant to be read, or perhaps whether cultural landscapes can be regarded as either "unwitting autobiographies" (P. Lewis 1979a) or coercive tools of cultural hegemony.

HOW THE WORLD WORKS

The section on how the world works is concerned with the dynamics of human organizations in interaction with physical and social environments. Emphasis is placed on how humans make use of the earth and on the cultural values woven into social, economic, and political systems. When investigating the workings of the world, cultural geographers have generally sought out premodern, traditional, and, especially, small-scale societies. The themes of cultural diffusion, human agency in landscape transformation, and the impress of European cultures on non-European peoples have been central to depicting how particular aspects of the world work. The readings in this section identify processes as a central concern, but they do so from perspectives that suggest a greater awareness of the work of scholars in cognate disciplines. This interdisciplinary broadening of cultural geography's purview is particularly evident in recent innovations in ecological and economic analysis, though this has not weakened the field's traditionally strong ties with anthropology and history. These articles also demonstrate a shift toward macroscale analysis of heightened theoretical sophistication. This group of readings carries forward the traditional concerns of cultural geography but at the same time aligns this research more directly with contemporary currents in critical and historical social science. The readings are discussed in the context of five themes that have always been of concern to cultural geographers: (1) Technics and Culture; (2) Agency and Institution; (3) Contact, Conflict, and Change; (4) Innovation and Adaptation; and (5) Reproduction and Resistance.

The continued importance of these ideas owes much to the vitality of cultural ecology. Indeed, in the United States, a Cultural Ecology Specialty Group was formed within the Association of American Geographers before its Cultural Geography counterpart. Cultural ecology occupies a special place in the subdiscipline of cultural geography because of its direct links to Berkeley school traditions, although Butzer's (1989) recent review of cultural ecology makes clear the important advances that have been made during a period in which other cultural geographers grappled with problems of definition. This constancy of purpose may tempt some researchers to view cultural ecology as the whole of cultural geography. This position overstates the case, but cultural ecologists can be credited with continuously cultivating important research problems over a long period of time. These interests, which seek to analyze the relationships between people and their biophysical environment, are largely premodern in focus and heavily oriented toward fieldwork. The results of this concentration of attention are reviewed in more detail in the essay that introduces the section entitled "How the World Works" and are the subject of the articles in this book by Butzer, Nietschmann, Parsons, and Zimmerer.

Interest in the impress of European cultures on non-Europeans has grown, perhaps because cultural geography, as it came to confront modern as well as premodern cultures, was obliged to consider colonialism and imperialism. Work in this area was begun under one of Sauer's students, Andrew Clark, a Canadian with a strong sense of the change that accompanied the expansion of Europe overseas. Clark's students have continued that tradition even more thoroughly and have begun to develop theoretical structures to better explain colonization and expansion (Gibson 1978; Jordan 1989a; 1989b; R. Harris 1977). Although cultural geography is historical and, in most cases, materialist, most of the work in this area does not make explicit use of Marxist concepts; rather, the relevant issues are discussed as they arise. Earle's (1978) article, for example, refutes a central tenet of Marxism by demonstrating that agricultural labor systems in the United States were derived from ecological conditions and the choice of crops, a basically environmentalist argument. Earle's body of work is regarded as historical rather than cultural geography, but his sophisticated analysis of ecological conditions and human choices is central to many of the issues facing cultural geography. The collection of his major articles in a single anthology (Earle 1992) should bring his arguments to the much wider audience they deserve.

The concerns with Europe overseas implicit in Sauer's work but most effectively developed by Clark and his students have highlighted imperialism as a form of cultural contact unaddressed in *Readings in Cultural Geography*. We have selected articles on cultural imperialism and the impact of European cultures on the cultures they encountered during their expansion out of Europe during and after the age of exploration. This theme will continue to develop strongly in the future, as it has already in subsequent works by Meinig (1986), Crosby (1986), and Butzer (1992a; 1992b).

The theme of colonialism and imperialism has also been driven by the success of World System theory in macroscale, interdisciplinary social science. This represents a long overdue return to macrotheory and a break from the Marxist model of stages of historical development. Wallerstein's model of capitalist agriculture, first propounded in 1974 and subsequently developed in a large number of publications, is distinctly geographic in character (Wallerstein 1974; 1984). It retains a basically Marxist notion of the class struggle, but it exports that struggle to the periphery and recasts it as one between the periphery and the core. Controlled-cost labor systems are used in the periphery to produce cheap agricultural raw materials and foodstuffs to feed and clothe the wage labor population of the core. The core exports high-cost, high-value-added goods and services to the periphery. Other than its stress on power relationships, this is not fundamentally different from the theory of interdependent development propounded by the geographer Brookfield (1975). More recently, geographers have been involved with revitalizing the theory of long waves in the world economy, an idea first suggested by Kondratieff in the 1920s and elaborated by Schumpeter in the 1940s. P. Hall and Preston (1988) have noted that technological innovations cluster not only in time, in the manner suggested by long-wave theory, but also in space. Agnew (1987b) has applied long-wave theory to a regional geography of the United States, and B. Berry (1991) has demonstrated that the data previously dismissed by econometricians as inconclusive noise can be smoothed to demonstrate the regularities predicted by Kondratieff.

WHAT THE WORLD MEANS

The section entitled "What the World Means" develops the term *culture* as a set of shared values and collective beliefs that shape individual and group action within a community but that are themselves reshaped little from generation to generation. At issue are the many ways in which such values are expressed in everyday life and represented in landscape and environment. Although concern for these issues can be discerned in the work of cultural geographers over many decades, a recently reawakened interest has been particularly important in shaping contemporary debate in the subdiscipline. This debate has been grouped into five themes: (1) The Environment Perceived; (2) Privileged Views and Visions; (3) Sense of Place and Identity; (4) Ethical Senses of Nature; and (5) The Iconography of Landscape.

Geographers working in these areas have often turned to novel source materials for insight into the way in which humans perceive the environment, develop emotive attachments to

place, and interpret the world in artistic and creative media. The analysis of novels, poetry, art, and films has become common in the discipline and is well represented in the recent collection by Cosgrove and Daniels (1988). Less common, but perhaps more important to the future, is the interest by cultural geographers in alternatives to print media (Burgess and J. Gold 1985). On rare occasions geographers have used such alternative media themselves to represent places, such as Burgess's film of the Fens. The articles of this section address how meaning is perceived in, ascribed to, or imposed on places by human action. This action, whether conscious or unconscious, serves to construct worlds of meaning in which people develop strong positive and negative emotive bonds with place and environment.

Art is vital to the construction of meaning. The poet, playwright, novelist, painter, and filmmaker all construct places, imagined or real. A few cultural geographers have entered the realm of creativity by producing films and novels, as discussed by Burgess (1982), Meinig (1983), and P. Lewis (1985). More accurately, the best artistic visions represent a way of thinking about the present human condition and the future consequences of current actions. The imaginary worlds of literature have long attracted attention as visions of possible futures. There is also a developing tendency to look to the past for ways of imagining the future. Cultural geographers are also alert to ideologies that impose meaning on environment. This entails analyzing both the dominant groups in a given culture and those elements of ideology that sometimes come to be challenged. In the notion of the imposition of meaning there is a considerable crossover to ideas about how the world looks.

There are also places and worlds given meaning by the simple act of human habitation. Some of these are simple worlds; others have deep histories and complex meanings. These meanings are, however, essentially organic, having grown from within rather than having been imposed from without. In contemporary debate, the concept of place is one of the very few that has attracted a wide constituency throughout cultural geography.

INTO THE FUTURE

Philip Wagner and Marvin Mikesell made no claims of omniscience in looking from *Readings in Cultural Geography* into the future, and we are in no better position to anticipate developments in cultural geography in the next generation. Viewed as both inventory and prospect, however, the present discussion would be incomplete without some consideration of the direction of future research. We have relinquished this role to eight commentators and essayists. In addition to Philip Wagner's preface, each of the following three sections is closed by a distinguished researcher's commentary. The final section contains four new essays by other influential scholars, the last by Marvin Mikesell. These commentaries and essays serve to assess the present and, perhaps, to fathom the future.

II
HOW THE
WORLD LOOKS

3

INTRODUCTION

Many cultural geographers have an interest in the "look" of the land, in patterns immediately visible on the surface of the earth (Hart 1975, 13–14; Parsons 1986) and, just as importantly, in the discovery of previously unnoticed patterns. This section views culture as revealed in such patterns, in the ordering of cultural traits and material artifacts through areal distributions and distinctive morphological forms. The title of this section places stress on how the world appears, thus emphasizing a longstanding concern for the study of the material world's tangible and visible elements, although not to the exclusion of other, less tangible traits such as religion, language, and ethnicity.

Concern for patterns of cultural traits and material artifacts has inspired some of the finest work in cultural geography, both past and present. Nonetheless, the identification of pattern is only a starting point. The best research in this area also concerns processes. No matter how interesting patterns of cultural traits may be in their own right, their real value is as evidence of these processes—the movement of people and ideas, the modification of environments, or the rise or reinforcement of distinctive societies. The articles of this section reflect on the production of patterns at a variety of scales and on the forces that form them into hierarchies. In *Readings in Cultural Geography*, such concerns were placed under the themes of culture area and cultural landscape. Contemporary research has expanded to the point where the literature must be ordered into four themes: (1) Learning from Looking; (2) Ordinary Landscapes; (3) Emblems of Authority; and (4) The Dynamic Region.

To ask how the world looks seems to suggest an immediately sensible world apprehended through individual visual experience, but perception is largely a matter of intention and training (Meinig 1979a; Schumm 1991, 26–28; Jakle 1987). The perceptions of cultural geographers are guided by axioms, inspired by exemplars, and bound closely to source materials and the tools of camera, map, and sketchbook. J. B. Jackson describes such studies as "a *disciplined* way of looking at the physical world" (J. B. Jackson 1984, x). Two elements of this disciplined vision must be examined in detail: object and perspective. Object refers to the things that are observed; perspective, to the method of investigation and justification of purpose.

A QUESTION OF OBJECT

Some recent debate seems to be based on the belief that only a certain range of topics and perspectives falls within the domain of cultural geography. The debate is needlessly acrimonious, for it fails to admit that the range of topics investigated by cultural geography has varied greatly through time, as have the underlying research rationales. Cultural geographers working at the turn of the century were concerned with accounting for the patterning of world languages and religions. The geography of language and religion is a minor component of contemporary cultural geography, however, whereas much attention is focused on very small subcultures and how they express their identities in the landscape. Neither topic excludes the other from cultural geography, but such differences in subject matter necessarily imply different theoretical rationales and methods of investigation.

One need not look as far as the turn of the century to see how the subject matter of investigation has changed. Concern for patterns and distributions of cultural traits was a fundamental part of Berkeley school cultural geography. Such traits were fundamental to explaining the transmission and transformation of culture, historically and geographically. The traits of greatest concern were those most closely related to a society's way of life. Since *genre de vie* encompassed agricultural and economic production, conventions of exchange and trade, and systems of belief, kinship, and language, traits that provided evidence of these phenomena were of great interest. Tracking the diffusion of agriculture, for example, necessarily involved tracing the routes and distributions of innovations such as domesticated plants and animals and other indicators of agricultural technology. Yet Sauer made clear that investigating a people's way of life involved considering a far broader range of traits as indicators of cultural life (Sauer 1925; 1941a). Patterns on the landscape were indirect evidence of deeper economic, historical, and social processes. In Kniffen's (1936; 1965) work this broadening of purview encompassed house types and other elements of material culture as indicators of diffusion and change. In time, cultural geographers became willing to consider just about any trait that is distinctive—or diagnostic—of a group's identity or way of life: building types, methods of construction, fence types, types of agricultural implement, methods of cropping and husbandry, and even foods. As with so much Berkeley school research, however, these diagnostic indicators were centered on preindustrial and rural populations.

Much of the frustration voiced about these lines of investigation stems not from questions about the value of studying distributions of diagnostic traits but rather from the types of societies on which the investigations focused. The modern world is dominated by urban, industrial nations, and the diagnostic traits that catch the attention of many contemporary cultural geographers are very different from those that offer insights into rural enclaves and agrarian societies. In industrialized nations where less than 5 percent of a population is involved directly in primary economic activity, *genre de vie* appears to be an unsuitably rustic concept of culture. Cultural geographers must look to skyscrapers (Domosh 1988), not log buildings, and to mass culture rather than to folk culture (R. Riley 1980).

This expansion of interest in modern societies has caused undue friction within cultural geography over the last twenty years, because debate too often polarizes around misleading dichotomies between rural and urban, premodern and modern, and agrarian and industrial, as if cultural geography could concern itself with but one side of each issue.

THE ISSUE OF PERSPECTIVE

The changes in cultural geography's subject matter have been accompanied by changes in perspective and purpose. The rationale for many early studies of the distribution and regional classification of cultural traits was so widely accepted among researchers that justifications were more often implied than stated: patterns were traced insofar as they yielded insight into underlying cultural processes. The forces that spurred innovation, diffusion, migration, and movement could be read from the evidence left behind. Since the early 1970s, however, there have been more attempts to use this evidence to understand other cultural forces. Many of these interpretations derive from the metaphor of landscape as text (Sitwell 1981). The idea that the material evidence of cultural process can be read as a language is neither startlingly new to geography nor totally at odds with existing methods of interpretation. In the geography of Christian theology, the world was a "book of nature" that revealed God's word in a terrestrial mnemonic (Glacken 1967, 203–25). Contemporary appraisals of landscape as text draw their methods from recent theories of communication and language rather than from classical rules of grammar (Foote 1983, 1–42). Duncan (1973) was one of the first geographers to frame studies of landscape on a view of language as symbolic interaction. In this view, communication comprises not a language of sounds but a repertoire of actions that mediate human social behavior. Applying this idea to landscape yields the notion of people modifying the environment to control their interactions with one another. Such a view is particularly valuable in studying modern residential environments and the architectural form of contemporary cities (Domosh 1987; 1988; 1989;

1990; Duncan and Duncan 1984; Ford 1979; Hugill 1975; 1984; Ley 1987).

A second view of landscape as communication stresses the power of symbols in social life. Studies premised on iconographical and semiotic theories have stressed both the implicit and explicit symbolism that lies behind many landscape features. The idea is that landscape symbols can embody relationships of power and authority among social groups but also that such symbols influence human attitudes and behavior. In this view, cultural traits and material artifacts must be taken at more than their face value in registering the movement of people and the transformation of ideas. Such traits and artifacts must also be read as a record of human perceptions, values, fears, and aspirations. These questions of intention and value are very much a part of contemporary cultural geography, but they exist in a somewhat uneasy tension with interpretations that question the geographer's ability to fathom these problematic dimensions of landscape meaning.

A further development of these views of landscape as text lies at the heart of recent discussions of postmodernist geographies. Drawing on French literary criticism, recent structural theories of language and semiotics, and Marxism, these discussions develop the position that the spatial and material arrangements of contemporary societies embody ideological relationships that grant some social groups power over others. The study of these relationships involves deconstructing landscape and spatial arrangements into their component elements. These fundamental forms, stripped of their trappings, express the basic mechanisms through which social and economic power is exerted (Entrikin 1991; Harvey 1989; Shields 1991; Short 1991; Soja 1989). To take the critical technique of deconstruction seriously, we must allow that the text of the landscape will disintegrate if we interpret it in terms other than those of the dominant reading. Because deconstruction views culture as a zone of conflict rather than a product of consensus, it has not been widely accepted in cultural geography. Skepticism of it results from a sense that much of cultural process and form seems to stem from nonideological imperatives (Gale 1977; B. R. Hudson 1979; Sitwell 1990b).

Apart from these varied interpretive strategies, cultural geography's *disciplined* view of the world employs two points of view: from the ground, or some point very near to it, and from the air, which is the vantage point of those who draw and study maps (J. B. Jackson 1988). At ground level the cultural geographer sees a world composed of distinctive landscapes, whereas from the air the world appears as a patchwork of points, lines, and regions. In practice the two perspectives are used together to characterize, classify, and explain variations in both general and specific cultural traits.

The distinction between landscape and region is comparatively new. Among nineteenth-century German geographers, the term *landschaft* could be applied to a region and to the distinctive content of a region (P. James and Martin 1981, 178; J. B. Jackson 1984, 3–8). Some might argue that to insist on landscape as a ground-level view is to succumb to the artistic idiom of the landscape painter, which in turn invites distracting questions about the goals and scale of landscape analysis. Such objections can be overcome and the more comprehensive meaning of *landschaft* recovered by viewing "landscape as a cultural symbol, a pictorial way of representing, structuring or symbolizing surroundings" (Cosgrove and Daniels 1988, 1). In this sense, the difference between landscape and region is largely a matter of perspective. Both concepts can be used to divide the vast range of phenomena distributed across the earth's surface. Such phenomena can be interpreted and appreciated in their own terms or employed to explore processes of human use and occupation, past and present.

Thirty years ago Wagner and Mikesell placed much of the research bearing on these ideas under the categories of culture area and cultural landscape. Today the literature must be subdivided and regrouped differently to capture the spirit of contemporary research.

LEARNING FROM LOOKING

Despite differences of interpretation, cultural geographers seem to agree that looking is a fundamental means of learning about a culture (P. Lewis 1983). This is a view implicit in Sauer's distinction between human geography, whose principal interest is the relation of humans to their environment, and cultural geography, which in his words "directs its attention to those elements of material culture that give character to an area" (Sauer 1962, 30). But the term *material culture* is as difficult to define as *culture*. Glassie defines material culture as those objects that humans make to support their way of life, as well as the plans, methods, and reasons for producing things that can be seen and touched (Glassie 1968, 2–3). This definition of material culture is similar to the view of culture as a set of learned values. The emphasis in both definitions is on cultural ideas and values as the filter through which the realities of society and environment can be viewed, albeit imperfectly.

Interest in interpreting this evidence has always been an important part of cultural geography. As was noted above, however, since the early 1970s there have been far more attempts to expand the domain of these interpretations and to experiment with new methodologies. Attention has been recently directed toward the meaning of visible forms: the symbols, metaphors, and icons through which the landscape becomes a cultural text. This shift toward landscape meanings and values is a result of the partial and sometimes uneasy convergence of social and cultural geography. The recent literature demonstrates a heightened concern for social rather than material landscapes (Cosgrove 1984; 1985; Duncan and Duncan 1988; P. Jackson 1989; Penning-Rowsell and Lowenthal 1986; Sitwell and Bilash 1986). Long-subordinated subcultures are recognized as creating distinct landscapes based on distinctive perceptions of environment (Hebdige 1979). The persistence of ethnic identity within the United States has been studied (Conzen 1990), as have the effects of sexual preference (Weightman 1980), gender (Hayden 1981; J. Monk 1984; Norwood and Monk 1987; G. Pratt and Hanson 1988; Roberts 1991; L. Weisman 1992), and social class (Burns 1980; Duncan 1973; Hugill 1986). This reorientation has led to experimentation with research methods better suited to the study of urban, industrial societies (Cosgrove 1983; P. Jackson 1989). R. Riley (1980) raises the important issue of how to interpret modern mass culture and understand its power to reduce the variety that lent distinctiveness to local and regional landscapes. Mass culture can homogenize the landscape because design comes to be influenced more by the media than by tradition and more by the marketing strategies of large corporations than by the decisions of individuals and communities.

Perhaps equally important was the diffusion of continental European thought to North America. This has tended to divert American cultural geography from some of its traditional preoccupations. Ideas such as Gramsci's concept of hegemony reaffirm the fundamental importance of culture and check the tendency to reduce culture to a secondary symptom of the workings of society and economy (Cosgrove 1983). However, theoretical pile drivers are sometimes used to crack empirical walnuts. Even geomorphologists have begun to ask whether "breadth of experience in reality is more important than depth of theoretical abstraction" (V. Baker and Twidale 1991, 94). Nevertheless, tension remains between methods of seeing and knowing, and as has been said of art, geographic representation is a compromise between sight and concept, perception and convention (Berenson 1953; Tuan 1979b). Geographers increasingly recognize the physical limits of vision and the epistemological austerity of the world that it discloses (Entrikin 1991, 132–33). Some dismiss the fabled naked eye and the ideal of the field researcher working inductively from primary materials in favor of a more deductive approach to symbolism in the cultural landscape (Pudup 1988; Rowntree, Foote, and Domosh 1989).

Quite apart from its interpretive potential, landscape is an important and often underused pedagogic resource. Meinig (1971a, 5) has called for greater training in how to develop awareness of one's environment. P. Lewis (1979a) has called attention to axioms for reading the landscape that can be used to draw student attention to fascinating patterns of human behavior. The value of landscape as a pedagogic tool, the virtue of

learning from looking, has not been lost on the "new" cultural geography (Cosgrove 1989).

ORDINARY LANDSCAPES

A good deal of attention has been devoted to understanding the commonplace features of day-to-day life (Upton 1983). These are ordinary landscapes in the sense that they are created not by elite or powerful groups but by ordinary people to meet the needs of everyday life. As Stilgoe (1982, ix) makes clear, these landscapes are common not because they are rude or vulgar but rather because they belong to and reflect the needs and aspirations of a people. Canons of design are understood rather than stated and are passed from generation to generation by practical example rather than by abstract principle. The challenge of studying ordinary landscapes arises from the fact that the stories of such landscapes and of the people that build them are seldom recorded or celebrated, except in the landscape itself. Using a now-famous phrase, P. Lewis (1979a) describes the landscape as a people's "unwitting autobiography"; "like books," he continues, "landscapes *can* be read, but unlike books, they were not *meant* to be read" (P. Lewis 1979a, 12). Such unprepossessing creations are often overlooked and sometimes easily effaced. Given the paucity of written records bearing on the creation of ordinary landscapes, cultural geographers must use all the skills of a detective to make inferences from circumstantial evidence. In a variation on this idea, P. Lewis (1975) suggests that geographers are trackers of cultural spoor. Flora and fauna, street plans and house types, and survey patterns and toponyms can all be used to stalk cultural quarry.

The role of the geographer as detective or tracker can be traced to Sauer's studies of the transformation of Neolithic landscapes. His method of tracking plants, animals, and technologies along the paths of their diffusion around the globe remains important today (C. Riley et al. 1971; Hugill and Dickson 1988). Sauer used traits and artifacts to track prehistoric peoples, but his students applied the same techniques to track other populations, many of them unnoted in written history (Glassie 1975; Jakle, Bastian, and Meyer 1989; Jordan 1978; 1982; Jordan and Kaups 1987; 1989; Kniffen 1990).

Taking as his premise the deep affinity of humans for their houses, Lewis argues that individuals hold strong normative ideals as to the proper setting, appearance, and internal disposition of their houses and that these ideals constitute an unusually durable cultural inheritance. In a discussion of the houses built by Anglo-Americans on the Atlantic seaboard, he describes their divergence into regional styles and the coalescence of these regional styles (with the significant exception of the South) into a series of temporary national styles after 1865. Prior to 1865 these regions were broad bands spanning half a continent; after that date these regions gave way to rings, accretions of period architecture on the outer margins of expanding cities. Following Zelinsky's doctrine of first effective settlement, P. Lewis claims that the English influence was decisive for the future shape of American culture and its landscape (Zelinsky 1973, 13). This is not easily disputed (Fischer 1989), but the claim may overlook part of the story. Other nationalities have shaped the American landscape and continue to do so. Arreola and others have described what may be the most important extension of a cultural landscape to occur in the Western Hemisphere in the last century—the Hispanic re-shaping of the American Southwest—(Arreola 1981; 1984; 1987; 1988; Curtis 1980; Ford and Griffin 1981). San Antonio served as, in Arreola's words, "the corridor and the clearing house" for Mexican laborers, cultural practices, and political ideologies.

EMBLEMS OF AUTHORITY

Ordinary landscapes can be contrasted with extraordinary landscapes, which also have captured the attention of cultural geographers. Extraordinary landscapes are created and maintained by the most powerful groups and institutions within a society, often based on explicit principles of design. These landscapes are, in effect, coded to express messages of status, power, legitimacy, and authority and are intended to be read and responded to by other people (W. Nor-

ton 1989, 113–39). These emblems of authority can reflect power derived from many sources: social, economic, political, and religious.

Some of the most striking emblems of authority are based on religious and cosmographical principles. These are buildings, settlements, and landscapes that manifest theological and religious principles of design. Wheatley (1971; 1983) has considered in detail the question of urban origins, particularly in east Asia. With regard to a wide range of early civilizations, he has argued that the first cities evolved from ceremonial centers and were based on cosmographical principles. Fuson (1969) investigated the orientation of Mayan ceremonial centers, arguing that religion was the dominant factor and that celestial and geomagnetic knowledge shaped this theocratic landscape. Other students of New World civilizations have suggested that these religious canons of design extended across the landscape, far beyond the ceremonial centers themselves. In the words of Eliade (1959, 11), these ceremonial centers are the "manifestation of the sacred," and Stilgoe (1982, 56) uses the term *hierophany* to describe principles of design linking heaven and earth. Writers such as Tuan (1974b) and Scully (1979) have drawn further attention to these issues in traditional societies and classical civilization. In his study of Kandy, Duncan (1990) interprets landscape less as a text of religious belief and sacred power than as a means of exerting political power to suppress popular disbelief.

More attention has been directed toward understanding the elite landscapes of modern, urban societies, because, in secular societies, landscapes may still be oriented toward repositories of social, economic, and political power. Domosh (1987; 1989) and Harvey (1979) provide examples of how the economic and political elite can shape skyscrapers and architectural monuments to reflect their authority. Foote (1992) and J. Mayo (1988) reflect on the way national historical monuments are designed to convey nationalistic sentiments. Yet, in the words of one author, even "the house is oriented toward what it thinks is its chief source of power" (H. G. West 1951, 26). In "The Westward-moving House," J. B. Jackson (1953) attempts to link typical houses to the archetypal personalities of Nehemiah, Pliny, and Ray. Apparently influenced by the national character school of sociology, which gained notice through Riesman's *Lonely Crowd* (1950), Jackson interprets three ordinary landscapes as oriented toward perceived sources of power in the sacred community, economically productive land, and the mutable personality. This concern for the extraordinary landscape can be seen in later work on landscape tastes and elite residential landscapes (Lowenthal and Prince 1965; Duncan 1973; Duncan and Duncan 1984; Hugill 1986).

THE DYNAMIC REGION

Culture area was one of Wagner and Mikesell's five original themes and remains important today. In today's cultural geography, however, interest in culture areas implies a different range of concerns than it did thirty years ago. Originally, the demarcation of cultural areas was fundamental to tracing the origin and diffusion of cultural traits. Careful study revealed source areas of innovation and zones of influence around the periphery of these core regions. The changing nature of research in cultural geography has led not to the abandonment of this concern, but to a broadening interest in the ramifications of such areal differentiation and patterning. The spread of cultural influences and the creation of landscapes necessarily entail the disruption or obliteration of the supplanted landscape and the displaced society. No geographer has commented on this point more consistently than Meinig (1982; 1986, 65–76, 258–67). At the core of Meinig's approach is his concept of the dynamic area, "a culture, society and nation ever changing in areal extent, structure, functions and content . . . an areal phenomenon that can be traced from its tiny and complex origins to its present enormous and complex macrocultural dimensions" (Meinig 1978, 1188). This is an approach expressed in "American Wests" (1972) and other writings

(Meinig 1965; 1969b) as a generic scheme for the study of culture in terms of such dynamic areas. Imperialism is viewed as a process of cultural transformation, violent in its execution, pervasive in its impact, and deeply geographic in its causes and consequences. In "American Wests," Meinig sets out to demonstrate the manner in which geographers might use the concept of the region as a powerful and penetrating instrument of analysis.

Regional cultural change was also the concern of Sopher (1972), who attempted to elucidate the environmental and spatial factors that give rise to stability and instability. He considered adaptive success to be the first source of stability. Certain environments reward certain practices and attitudes while imposing penalties on any deviations; their power to encourage or discourage human activity will depend on the knowledge, technology, and social organization of their inhabitants. The second source of stability is the culture's sense of identity, which, when conserved, allows it to maintain spatial and temporal boundaries that act as screens filtering the flow of cultural information. Although tentative, Sopher's model is important for its emphasis on the geographies of communication and the attention it draws to information flows and the uneven spread of cultural knowledge.

In today's cultural geography, a new regional geography seems to be emerging, one that responds to many of the same issues that have spurred the revitalization of contemporary cultural geography. This new brand of regional geography reasserts the possibility of distinctiveness, if not the uniqueness of specific places and localities, and can be seen in the work of Arreola (1987), Wallach (1980; 1981), and others. This new chorology mirrors cultural ecology's recognition of individual agency, as well as other currents of thought in human geography (Lich 1992; Pudup 1988; Steiner and Mondale 1988; Thrift 1990, 1991).

DANIEL D. ARREOLA **4**

THE MEXICAN AMERICAN CULTURAL CAPITAL

San Antonio, Texas, is a special place. Early boosters bestowed on it a series of epithets like the City of Missions, the Metropolis of Texas, and the City of the Alamo. Currently it is touted as one of the most charismatic cities in the United States. In addition to a tourist image, San Antonio has a unique cultural position in the United States, because it is the only major city that ethnically is predominantly Mexican. This quality was apparent to early visitors, one of whom declared in 1877 that "San Antonio is, in fact, a Spanish town . . . and the only one where any considerable remnant of Spanish life exists in the United States" (Spofford 1877, 838–39; see also Everett 1975). The Mexican cultural heritage has earned the city a special identity in the twentieth century as indicated in references to it as "the old capital city of Mexican life and influence" or "the capital of the Mexico that lies within the United States" (Handman 1931; McWilliams 1941).

Los Angeles currently has the largest concentration of ethnic Mexicans in the United States. One writer dubbed it the capital of an emerging MexAmerica (Garreau 1981, 207–44). This shift illustrates one aspect of the rapidly changing social geography of the United States in the late twentieth century, because previously San Antonio had been relatively unchallenged as the focal point of Mexican culture in the United States. In this essay I reexamine the thesis that San Antonio is the primary focus of Mexican culture in the United States. The investigation provides an unusual opportunity to assess the role of historical patterns and their contemporary meaning as well as the importance of population numbers in determining cultural identifications.

BEGINNINGS

San Antonio was founded early in the eighteenth century on the northeastern frontier of New Spain. Between 1718 and 1731, five missions, a presidio, and a villa (civilian colony) evolved as the nucleus of the settlement. That concentration of varied institutions at one general location made San Antonio unique along the Spanish borderlands (Bolton 1915, 5). The missions were scattered along the San Antonio River, and the presidio and the villa were between San Pedro Creek and the river where it makes an ax-shaped eastward meander (J. Sánchez 1926).

The villa was known as San Fernando after 1731, but the presidio name, San Antonio de Béxar, usually shortened to Béxar, persisted throughout the Spanish period (Vidaurreta 1973–74). San Antonio began to serve as the capital of the province of Texas in 1770, but the function was not official until 1772. The granting of city status in 1811 made the villa the equal of Durango, Saltillo, and Monterrey. Throughout the colonial period, San Antonio remained a border town with a population hovering around 2,000 (Tjarks 1974; O. Jones 1979, 63). The settlement at San Antonio was the most viable rationale for Spanish and later Mexican tenuous claims to territory along the far-northeastern frontier of New Spain.

Between 1820 and 1850, sovereignty of San Antonio changed three times: from Spain to the Republic of Mexico in 1821, from Mexico to the Republic of Texas in 1836, and then to statehood in the United States in 1845. Population almost doubled to 3,500, and Mexicans became an increasingly significant part of this total. The settlement continued to comprise three distinctive, partially integrated communities: the secularized missions, a military garrison at the Alamo, and the civil colony at San Fernando (de la Teja and Wheat 1985).

Four neighborhoods or barrios evolved in the civil colony. Wedged between the San Antonio River on the east and San Pedro Creek on the west, barrios Sur and Norte flanked the main plaza. Established families dominated each barrio, all of which together made up the most prosperous area of the settlement. East of the river and south of the mission San Antonio de Valero (the Alamo) was barrio Valero, where military personnel lived. West of the creek was Laredo, a working-class neighborhood. By 1828 an official described the four areas as a single city.

Ethnic mixing accelerated as the four units coalesced. In 1820 persons of Spanish descent constituted 55 percent of the population, Indians 15 percent, and mixed bloods, predominantly mestizos, the remainder. A small group of Tlascalan Indians from Coahuila, Mexico, arrived in 1803 and readily mixed with the mestizo inhabitants as well as local Indians (Rodríguez 1913, 38; Tijerina 1977, 10–16).

It was reported in 1835 that the population of San Antonio was entirely Mexican, but in the years after independence from Mexico immigration was dominated by non-Mexican groups. From 1845 to 1860, German, American, French, and Irish immigrants became residents of the city. In 1837 all but one of the almost fifty candidates for municipal office were of Spanish-Mexican descent; a decade later there were only five (Almonte 1925; Remy 1968; Jordan 1969). Furthermore, ethnic separateness persisted as the city expanded. In 1850 only approximately 10 percent of all marriages among persons with Spanish surnames involved individuals with non-Spanish surnames, mostly upper-class women from Mexican families who married Anglo immigrants (Bean and Bradshaw 1970; Dysart 1976). Frederick Law Olmsted, during a visit to antebellum Texas, remarked, "We have no city, except New Orleans that can vie, in point of the picturesque interest that attaches to odd and antiquated foreignness, with San Antonio" (Olmsted 1978, 150), (figure 1).

Mexicans, numbering approximately 1,600, accounted for only 46 percent of the population of the city in 1850. By comparison, Santa Fe, with 4,041, had more Mexicans, but Los Angeles, with 1,229, fewer. Texas, however, counted 39 percent of its Mexican population as born in Mexico; the proportion for California was 15 per-

FIGURE I

A Mexican funeral procession, painted by a European immigrant in San Antonio circa 1850 (oil 30.5 × 25.5 cm). Source: *Entierro de un Angel* by Theodore Gentilz. Reproduced courtesy of the Daughters of the Republic of Texas Library at the Alamo, San Antonio.

cent and for New Mexico 2 percent. Although most of that Mexican-born group resided in the South Texas borderlands, their prominence signaled an important distinction between Mexicans in Texas and their brethren in California and New Mexico (Nostrand 1975; de León and Stewart 1983). Proximity and accessibility continued to bind San Antonio to that homeland well into the twentieth century.

EMERGENCE

The heritage of initial settlement and the proximity to Mexico became the principal factors that enabled San Antonio to emerge as the Mexican cultural capital in the United States. Although the Mexican group in the city continued to decline as a percentage of the total population into the twentieth century, San Antonio became the most significant center for Mexican immigrants entering the United States.

San Antonio vied with Galveston for position as the largest city in Texas between 1850 and 1900, but during the first two decades of the new century San Antonio was indisputably the chief urban center in the state. Strategic location proved advantageous as the state and the country were transformed during the railroad age. Situated at the inland margin of the Gulf coastal plains against the rim of the Edwards Plateau, San Antonio was a border town, poised at the southwestern edge of the eastern United States. Yet the city was also on a principal north-south route that linked the prairies and plains of north-central Texas and their extension to the Great Lakes with the central plateau of Mexico via the Rio Grande embayment (J. B. Jackson 1972a, 16).

Connections with Mexico during the nineteenth century were by way of Monterrey, founded in the sixteenth century as a service center for mining in northeastern Mexico. Monterrey during the second half of the nineteenth century achieved urban dominance in the area to serve as the regional trading center for most of northeastern Mexico (Canales 1971, 24). Blockades of ports, including Galveston and Brownsville, during the Civil War gave new significance to overland transportation, and stagecoach lines via Piedras Negras on the Rio Grande continued to link Monterrey and San Antonio after the war (Thonhoff 1971, 22, 34).

Those early connections are less significant to the cultural-capital thesis than the railroads of the late nineteenth century. They first forged and then kept vital the crucial economic and demographic linkages between San Antonio and Mexico on the one hand and the city and the rest of the United States on the other. Entering San Antonio in 1881, the International and Great Northern Railroad (IGN) connected it to St. Louis, Chicago, and points eastward. The IGN was extended from San Antonio to Laredo on the Mexican border the same year. In 1882 the Ferrocarril Nacional Mexicano was completed from Laredo to Monterrey. Financial troubles and a changed concession delayed completion of the long stretch between Monterrey and Mexico City until 1888 (S. Reed 1941, 320; McNeely 1964, 15–16; Canales 1971, 9–10) (figure 2). Additionally San Antonio became a pivotal point between Mexico and the American Southwest on the corridor of the Southern Pacific Railroad. It reached the city from the east in 1877 to be joined in 1883 by the western thrust from Los Angeles through El Paso (Everett 1961; Meinig 1971b, 38–52). San Antonio thus had two important geographical advantages over other cities whose heritage gave a claim to the role of Mexican cultural capital: proximity by rail to the central and eastern regions of the United States, and a direct rail connection to the heartland of Mexico.

Accessibility by railroad was a principal factor in the tripling of the city's population during the 1870s and the 1880s and then doubling between 1890 and 1910. The railroad line that brought Mexicans to the Rio Grande and beyond into San Antonio allowed them to retain ties to their homeland and kinsfolk. Yet the railroad was more than a mode of transportation. Ideas, dreams, and hopes as well as people moved along it. It was a conduit for new opportunities and for rapid diffusion of information about employment as well as other factors. For example, to develop retail ties, San Antonio merchants advertised in Monterrey newspapers with offers of a prepaid, round-trip railroad ticket to any resident of the city who purchased more than $1,500 worth of merchandise in their stores. The tactic was successful, for by the 1890s wealthy Mexicans from as far south as San Luis Potosí frequented San Antonio to shop (Coatsworth 1981, 75; R. Sánchez 1898, 21–24).

Early immigrants often did not venture far beyond San Antonio. A consequence was the concentration of Mexican immigrants in the counties between San Antonio and the border. During that period, the officials of the Mexican government actively used free land and tax exemption as inducements to lure emigrants back to their homeland (Santibañez 1930, 39; Barr 1971; Cortés 1979). Although the efforts were not always successful, they highlighted one aspect of the close ties that existed between emigrants and homeland.

Mexican laborers from both sides of the Rio Grande harvested cotton in the old productive regions of Texas. Migratory Mexican laborers played a key role in the transformation of the economy from cattle to cotton production that occurred across much of central Texas until 1910. To combat boll weevil, cotton growers switched from a variety that was harvested over many months to one that was reaped in a short period. That shift increased demand for Mexican workers, and San Antonio became the focal point for a new stream of emigrants (McWilliams 1949, 169–73; J. Walker 1984; Edward Davis 1940, 173–74).

Within the Southwest, Texas was by far the chief center of attraction for Mexican emigrants between 1910 and 1930. Texas contained more than one-half of all foreign-born Mexicans in the United States during the first two decades of the twentieth century as well as more than one-half

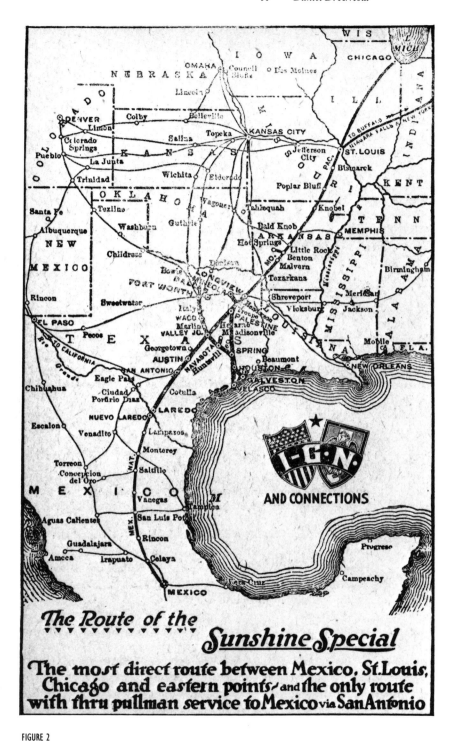

FIGURE 2

San Antonio was a transportation hinge between the eastern and western United States and central Mexico by 1888. Source: J. C. Sologiastoa (1924). Reproduced courtesy of the Barker Texas History Center, University of Texas, Austin.

of all the Mexican-stock population. Native-born and foreign-born migrant laborers were often grouped together under the term Mexican, although some contemporary observers recognized the distinctions within the ethnic Mexican population and referred to the native-born as Texanos and the immigrants as Mexicans or casuals. There was no dispute that Texas was the corridor and clearinghouse for most of the Mexican labor that entered the United States or that San Antonio was the primary node of dispersal. A labor agent there estimated that he had dispatched 200,000 Mexicans in one year during the 1920s, and an official of the San Antonio Chamber of Commerce reported that Mexican labor was rapidly becoming essential for the state (Grebler 1965, 51–56; Reisler 1976, 77).

The use of Mexican labor in Texas proved so successful that employers elsewhere began to tap the source, principally through labor contractors in San Antonio (figure 3). Mexicans, recruited through San Antonio, for example, replaced Belgian, German, and Russian laborers on sugar-beet farms in Michigan, Ohio, Indiana, Iowa, and North and South Dakota. The Mexican laborers often returned to San Antonio during the slack winter months to secure employment or to reside with relatives. In 1928 the Texas commissioner of labor testified that Mexicans performed as much as 75 percent of all unskilled construction labor in the state. The migrant streams sent north from San Antonio influenced the Middle West throughout the 1920s, despite a Texas law to deter shipment of emigrant laborers outside the state (P. Taylor 1933, 1–2; Rosales 1976; Reisler 1976, 88–97).

The growth of Mexican population in other American cities illustrates the role of numbers in cultural traditions. Los Angeles surpassed San Antonio as the American city with the largest Mexican population in 1930: 97,116 versus 82,373. However, the proportional influence of

FIGURE 3

A portion of a panoramic photograph of Mexican workers in San Antonio, 1924. Legend on sign in translation reads "Mexican Labor Contractors Office. Distributing to all parts of the United States." Source: E. O. Goldbeck. Reproduced courtesy of the Goldbeck Collection, Humanities Research Center, University of Texas, Austin.

the group continued to dominate in San Antonio. Mexicans accounted for 36 percent of its total population and only 8 percent in Los Angeles. As a ratio to the city population, the Mexican group had declined from almost one-half in 1850 but had revived from the less than 20 percent to which it had fallen in the 1880s and 1890s. The Mexican-born portion was higher in San Antonio than in Los Angeles: 35 percent to 20 percent for 1880, and 68 percent to 54 percent in 1920. Also San Antonio had the lowest rate of intermarriage with non-Mexicans for any major southwestern urban center during that period, a trend partly sustained by the inflow of emigrants (Griswold del Castillo 1984, 19, 61, 69; Camarillo 1979, 200; Longmore and Hitt 1943).

The internal structure of the old residential barrios was much altered during the early twentieth century. Mexicans had concentrated in the Laredo and Chihuahua neighborhoods that were located west of San Pedro Creek. Generally referred to as the Mexican Quarter, an area of slightly more than a square mile contained almost three-fourths of the Mexican population in the city by 1940. Observers noted that customs and practices there differed considerably from the rest of the city. The West Side had emerged as the core of Mexican San Antonio.

CULTURAL STRONGHOLD

San Antonio had become the principal Mexican cultural focus in the United States by the early twentieth century. The city was not only the chief repository of Mexican heritage in Texas but also the seedbed from which several Mexican cultural traditions dispersed to other Mexican American communities and to the country as a whole. Although the city displayed many Mexican customs and practices, intellectual and political innovation and contributions in cuisine and music especially distinguished San Antonio as the most influential center of Mexican culture in the United States.

San Antonio nurtured varied Mexican political ideologies in the early decades of the twentieth century, and the city has served as an important center in molding contemporary Mexican American political thought. Approximately 25,000 of the Mexican emigrants who came to San Antonio between 1900 and 1910 were political refugees (Woods 1949, 20–21). Many of that group were members of the Mexican upper class who used San Antonio as a temporary haven from which they intended to return to their homeland whenever political change there allowed. Two principal refugee groups in the city before and during the Mexican Revolution were plotters to overthrow President Porfirio Díaz and his exiled supporters after his downfall.

When a small group of intellectuals in San Luis Potosí began to agitate for liberal governmental policies, the position appealed mainly to persons opposed to the dictatorial Díaz government. A leader of that group was Francisco I. Madero, a native of Parras, Coahuila, who was related by marriage to a wealthy Monterrey family. Madero first fled to San Antonio in 1904. There he later issued his famous Plan of San Luis Potosí, a political manifesto that justified revolt and insurrection against the Díaz regime and helped ignite the Mexican Revolution. Although the proclamation and initial copies were dated and marked as if they had been published in Mexico, they were printed in San Antonio and smuggled across the border. A contemporary local newspaper estimated that three-fourths of the Mexican population in the city sympathized with Madero's cause, and a monument to this Mexican hero stands in the marketplace of the city (Ross 1955, 40–50, 112–14, 138; Cumberland 1969, 117–19).

Other refugees included wealthy Mexicans who supported the Díaz regime and went into exile when Madero and his followers came to power. It may seem politically ironic that the opposing parties found haven in the same city, though not concurrently, but the role illustrates the accessibility of San Antonio to central Mexico and the perceived importance of the city as a center of Mexican culture in the United States by emigrants. The Díaz exiles were sometimes called *los ricos* (the wealthy ones), although the same label identified established native-born Mexican families in the city.

One of the most prominent Díaz exiles was Ignacio E. Lozano, a native of Nuevo León, who

FIGURE 4
Printing room of *La Prensa,* circa 1928. Source: Mrs. Robert Rubio. Reproduced courtesy of the Institute of Texan Cultures, University of Texas, San Antonio.

came to San Antonio in 1908. He worked for a local newspaper until 1913, when he founded the influential Spanish-language *La Prensa,* which until 1954 remained the leading Spanish-language newspaper circulating in Texas (figure 4). It was also the most widely circulated Spanish-language newspaper in the United States for many years and had an international readership. In 1926, the demand for subscriptions from California prompted Lozano to open *La Opinión* in Los Angeles. Although Los Angeles had Spanish-language newspapers, none rivaled the country-wide scope of *La Prensa.* The headquarters for both newspapers remained in San Antonio, and editorial policy in each closely followed Lozano's political philosophy (Medeiros 1980).

La Prensa in its early years reflected the opinions of the wealthy exiles who favored Díaz, and its columns criticized and made proposals accordingly for Mexico. Lozano hired important exiled Mexican intellectuals to write for

the newspaper and to justify Porfirista policies such as strongman political stability, antisocialist proforeign economic intervention, and a united nationalistic society. Lozano contended that all Mexicans were the same and urged them to return and rebuild their homeland. One of his editors even published a book in which he asserted that Mexico should reconquer the American Southwest and other territory lost in the nineteenth century (Hinojosa 1940; Garcia 1978). While *La Prensa* articulated a narrow political viewpoint of a group of wealthy exiles, its pages contained news and features about the homeland and thus appealed to many Mexicans of other political persuasions in the United States.

In the context of the role that San Antonio played in internal Mexican politics, it is not surprising that the city was the center for development of early political consciousness among native-born Texas Mexicans and Mexican Americans. The first such organizations there date from

FIGURE 5
Untitled mural showing Patricio Flores, archbishop of San Antonio, by Juan Hernandez and Steve Adame at Cassiano Homes Housing Project, San Antonio, Texas. Photograph by author.

1875, were modeled on benevolent associations in Mexico, and typically catered to all Mexicans, whether born in Mexico or Texas. A small group of middle-class Texas Mexicans in San Antonio founded *La Orden Hijos de America* (The Order of Sons of America). The goal of the organization was to achieve for its members economic, social, and racial equality with other American citizens. Unlike previous mutual-aid societies, membership was exclusively for Mexicans who were native-born or naturalized citizens of the United States. A further emphasis was learning and speaking English. The ideal of the organization was to become national in scope by establishing local chapters with the primary council in San Antonio. During its initial years, the order became influential in several towns and cities in South Texas. Its philosophy and basic tenets were the model for the founding of the League of United Latin American Citizens (LULAC) at Corpus Christi in 1929. Currently LULAC has 240 active councils and more than 200,000

members across the country, but it is strongest in Texas (Meir and Rivera 1981, 191; Weeks 1929).

The Mexican American Youth Organization (MAYO) was founded in San Antonio in 1967 to promote civil rights among Texas Mexicans and to encourage political activity. Two members of MAYO were instrumental in forming La Raza Unida Party (RUP) in Texas in 1970. This party established branches in Mexican American communities throughout the Southwest and ran local candidates in local elections. It enjoyed the greatest success in areas where Mexican Americans had a voting majority as in San Antonio. Because the city is predominantly Mexican today, it has recently reversed the Anglo dominance of local politics. Mexican Americans now have a majority on the city council and the school board, and the mayor and the Roman Catholic archbishop are Texas Mexicans. Many neighborhoods in the predominantly Mexican American West Side formed Communities Organized for Public Service (COPS). Based largely on a network of Roman Catholic parishes, COPS has consistently lobbied in city hall for solution of problems like drainage, utility rates, and traffic in ethnic neighborhoods (Woodward 1985; Sekul 1983) (figure 5).

Mexican cuisine was a novelty among the Anglo-American and European residents, when the population of San Antonio was chiefly non-Mexican in the nineteenth century. Texas Mexicans quickly learned that their food tempted many non-Mexican visitors and residents and that a lucrative enterprise was possible. Because San Antonio was the first principal Mexican community encountered by Americans traveling westward along the southern route, the city's cultural features became the source of important impressions about Mexican Americans throughout the rest of the country. From plaza vendors through established eateries to food production and distribution, the popularity of Mexican cuisine in American food consumption originated in San Antonio (de León 1982, 94, 121). The most celebrated Mexican food attraction in the

city was the chili stands in the city plazas. Although early allusions to the spicy Mexican food existed, the first mention of the chili stands dated from the 1870s. The stands and the vendors, called chili queens, enjoyed enormous success. The ritual was mostly nocturnal as food vendors replaced the daytime marketing function of the plazas. Although the basic foods such as tamales, beans, tortillas, and even chili had an ancient Mexican Indian lineage, they gained a certain notoriety in nineteenth-century San Antonio (Bourke 1895; Steinfeldt 1978, 112–13).

The chili stands were a tourist attraction by the 1890s, but they were moved from their original locale in Military Plaza to other plazas, when a new city hall was erected. In 1900 chili vendors were still to be found on Milam Square at the western edge of downtown and on Alamo Plaza in front of the old federal building on the east (figure 6). Haymarket Square, adjoining the produce market on the western end of downtown, was the last plaza to accommodate the stands of benches and tables. By 1937 health officials dis-

FIGURE 6
Chili stands at the Alamo Plaza, San Antonio, circa 1900. Source: Jessie Thomson. Reproduced courtesy of the Institute of Texan Cultures, University of Texas, San Antonio.

couraged chili vending unless glass-enclosed carts were used. The demise of the chili stands strengthened the role of formal and informal dining establishments.

Many Mexican families provided neighborhood dining, often outside on benches and tables, but occasionally inside. By the early twentieth century, Mexican restaurants were being advertised in promotional tourist literature. The owners were often Anglo, but the kitchen crews were Texas Mexicans who prepared what some persons considered to be authentic dishes. A 1924 directory listed twenty-eight Mexican eateries in the city. Currently there are numerous fine Mexican restaurants in addition to hundreds of daily eateries. The Texas Mexican style of Mexican food appears to have spread largely to parts of New Mexico, Arizona, and the plains states, but recent infatuations with Texas regional specialties like *fajitas* (marinated flank steak grilled and wrapped in flour tortillas) have diffused as far west as California and as far east as Manhattan. One flamboyant San Antonio restaurateur has opened two Mexican-style eateries in Paris (Peyton 1946, 144; Sologiastoa 1924, 221–22; Richard West 1977; Hansen 1985; Patterson 1986).

San Antonio was also at the forefront of commercial Mexican food production for local, regional, and countrywide markets. A staple of Mexican cuisine is the tortilla, a pancakelike corn bread traditionally made by hand. The first *tortillería* or factory producing tortillas by machine allegedly started in San Antonio in 1924 with a maximum capacity of 50,000 a day. Every Mexican American community in the country now has its tortillerías. Although many produce tortillas of flour as well as corn, they employ the same technology that was pioneered in San Antonio. Pioneering distribution of Mexican American foods to a wide range of consumers was another advantage for San Antonio as a cultural capital. William Gebhardt, a German immigrant from New Braunfels, Texas, began to manufacture and sell chili powder in San Antonio in 1896. Gebhardt imported ancho peppers from Mexico, ground dried ones into a fine powder, and packaged the condiment in airtight containers. By 1911 Gebhardt was the first entrepreneur to produce canned Mexican foods like chili con carne or tamales. Although one might question the ethnic authenticity of such products, the success of Gebhardt's line meant that a non-Mexican public began to equate Mexican food with products from San Antonio. The firm now produces seventy-eight different items and markets them throughout the United States as well as in nineteen foreign countries (Federal Writer's Project 1938, 69; Landolt 1976, 166; Fehrenbach 1978, 210–11).

Conjunto, a type of Texas Mexican music, is especially popular in San Antonio and a surrounding region, bounded by Austin on the north, Corpus Christi on the east, and Alice on the south. In Spanish-speaking countries, including Mexico, the term *conjunto* simply means a musical group, but in Texas the word identifies a group in which the principal instrument is the accordion with bass, guitar, and drum accompaniment. The origin of the conjunto sound is unknown, but several folklorists ascribe it to one of three core areas: the south-central Texas region around San Antonio where it is most popular; the lower Rio Grande Valley where it has been largely displaced by a related style called Mexican *norteño;* or the Monterrey area in northeastern Mexico where norteño is also prominent (Peña 1985, 107; Reyna 1982).

A common trait in at least two of the proposed source regions, south-central Texas and Monterrey, was the presence of German and East European immigrants who were credited with introducing the accordion at mid-nineteenth century. According to one authority, the conjunto style emerged initially among working-class Texas Mexicans during the 1930s. San Antonio became the center for recording of Spanish-language music during the 1920s, when record companies dispatched units throughout the United States to acquire ethnic music. Company representatives sometimes set up recording facilities in local hotels, where Texas Mexican musicians performed their repertory, including accordion instrumentals that had been part of a *cantina* musical tradition (Schement and Flores 1977).

Several prominent accordion players during the 1930s combined that instrument with a *bajo sexto* (twelve-string guitar), stand-up bass, and vocals to create a distinctive ensemble. A founding member was Santiago Jiménez, Sr., who in 1936 was the first person to record conjunto in San Antonio. Conjunto gained widespread popularity among the working class in Texas Mexican communities during the 1940s, despite the popularity of orchestral music on radio broadcasts from Mexico. By the 1950s, Narciso Martínez, sometimes called the father of conjunto, was spreading the style on tours to New Mexico, Arizona, and California. The conjunto remains popular among Mexican Americans outside Texas, particularly in the Central Valley of California and in agricultural and urban districts in the Middle West, where Texas Mexicans have migrated (Gutierrez and Schement 1979, 6–17; Peña 1985, 53–71). A festival each spring in San Antonio perpetuates the distinctive sound and its performers (figure 7).

PERSISTENT CAPITAL

The Mexican population in California expanded more rapidly than that in Texas after 1920. Many persons attracted to California were migrants from Texas, New Mexico, and Arizona as well as directly from Mexico. The movement persisted after World War II: almost 60 percent of Mexican American interstate movers went to California between 1955 and 1960 in contrast with only 17 percent to Texas. California was preferred because of its high rate of economic development with its superior employment opportunities. Since the 1970s large numbers of Mexicans and Mexican Americans have immigrated to California, a partial result of changes in accessibility and perception of opportunity (Alvarez 1966; Grebler, Moore, and Guzman 1970, 109–11; Muller and Espenshade 1985, 37–54).

That San Antonio remains the distinctive center of Mexican culture in the United States can be validated by several measures. Studies of Mexican American intermarriage showed that 27 percent of the group in San Antonio married individuals from other ethnic groups during the 1970s, while in California 51 percent married exogamously. Analyses of language-maintenance patterns confirm what the data on intermarriage

FIGURE 7

Poster by Robert Sosa advertising the annual conjunto festival for 1985. Reproduced courtesy of Guadalupe Cultural Arts Center, San Antonio, Texas.

suggest about traditional behavior. Research conducted in California and Texas revealed decreasing facility in Spanish among Mexican Americans in Los Angeles and a heavy reliance on Spanish as the first language among Mexican Americans in San Antonio. Furthermore, a recent study of Mexican American youths in the urban Southwest concluded that language retention, religion, and social relationships were far more traditional among the study group in San Antonio than in Los Angeles (Murguía 1982, 47–50; Skrabanek 1970; D. Lopez 1978; Jankowski 1986, 75). San Antonio is the only American city with a permanent extension campus of the National Autonomous University of Mexico. This connection has existed since 1944, and the campus enrolls almost 400 students in cultural-heritage courses that range from Spanish language and literature to Mexican architecture and history.

Finally it cannot be too strongly emphasized that ethnically San Antonio as a place and a community is predominantly Mexican. In 1980 slightly more than one-half of the population of the city was Mexican, whereas the city of Los Angeles was only one-fifth Mexican. In addition, San Antonio has fewer ethnic groups and areas than Los Angeles, where black, Jewish, Japanese, Chinese, and Korean communities are prominent and distinctive. The future potential for ethnic homogeneity is much greater in San Antonio than in Los Angeles, and ethnicity in the Texas city equates almost invariably with the Mexican population.

The thesis of San Antonio as the cultural capital might suggest a rethinking of the doctrine of first effective settlement, especially in light of subsequent waves of immigration (Zelinsky 1973, 13). Settled more than a century after Santa Fe in the Spanish borderlands, San Antonio emerged as a center for Mexican, not Spanish, culture in the United States during the late nineteenth and early twentieth centuries, when its strongest links were forged with Mexico. Throughout much of its history, San Antonio culturally and geographically has been the chief stronghold of Mexican heritage and cultural innovation in the United States. That prominence is demonstrated in its roles as a focus for immigration and as a core of Mexican American political, culinary, and musical traditions. The city continues its cultural supremacy despite the fact that Los Angeles had almost one-quarter million more Mexicans in 1980. Mexican cultural dominance in San Antonio results from its homogeneous ethnic character and percentage rank among cities with large Mexican American populations.

San Antonio still receives and is assumed to contain the greatest number of undocumented Mexican aliens in Texas, a pattern reflecting the well-established connections by ground and air transportation with Mexico. As immigration from the homeland continues to infuse the city with Mexican ways and as resident Mexican Americans perpetuate traditional ethnic behavior patterns, San Antonio shows every likelihood of persisting as the Mexican cultural capital in the United States.

SOURCE

This article originally appeared in *The Geographical Review* 77 (1987): 17–34.

FURTHER READINGS

James P. Allen and Eugene J. Turner. 1988. *We the people: An atlas of America's ethnic diversity.* New York: Macmillan.

This atlas records the complex ethnic geography of the United States as recorded by the census of 1980. In addition to its detailed and provocative maps, the book contains interesting methodological chapters.

Daniel D. Arreola. 1984. Mexican American exterior murals. *Geographical Review* 74:409–24.
———. 1988. Mexican American housescapes. *Geographical Review* 78:299–315.
———. 1992. Plaza towns of south Texas. *Geographical Review* 82:56–73.

In his other writings, Arreola has explored many aspects of the impress of Mexican American and Hispanic culture on the landscapes of the Southwest. These three articles exemplify the diversity of Arreola's contributions and are useful supplements to the article reprinted here.

Molefi K. Asante and Mark T. Mattson. 1991. *Historical and cultural atlas of African Americans.* New York: Macmillan.

This atlas provides a geographically and historically comprehensive view of Africans in America.

Alvar W. Carlson. 1990. *The Spanish American homeland: Four centuries in New Mexico's Rio Arriba.* Baltimore: Johns Hopkins University Press.

This book examines the cultural and ecological basis for the persistence of the oldest rural European cultural region in the United States.

Michael P. Conzen. 1990. Ethnicity on the land. In *The making of the American landscape,* ed. Michael P. Conzen, 221–48. Boston: Unwin Hyman.

This chapter provides a good introduction to rural and urban landscapes that are the product of America's diverse population. Town plans, architecture, and "ersatz ethnicity" are discussed in their historical and geographical contexts.

Larry R. Ford and Ernst Griffin. 1981. Chicano Park: Personalizing an institutional landscape. *Landscape* 25 (2): 42–48.

This article reviews the story behind official recognition and preservation (in 1981) of painted walls on the supports of the Coronado Bridge to the Barrio Logan in San Diego. The park itself reflects a fading period of ethnic awareness, populism, and anxiety.

Richard V. Francaviglia. 1978. *The Mormon landscape: Existence, creation, and perception of a unique image in the American West.* New York: AMS Press.

Francaviglia describes another distinctive landscape of the American West. The Mormon church has left a distinctive imprint throughout the mountain West, in both the organization of its agriculture and farming settlements and the form of towns and cities.

Thomas D. Hall. 1989. *Social change in the Southwest, 1350–1880.* Lawrence: University Press of Kansas.

A social history of the Southwest, which is understood to extend from Texas to California, as interpreted from the vantage point of world-system theory.

Allen G. Noble, ed. 1992. *To build in a new land: Ethnic landscapes in North America.* Baltimore: Johns Hopkins University Press.

This recent volume is likely to become a standard work on ethnic landscapes of the United States.

Richard L. Nostrand. 1992. *The Hispano homeland.* Norman: University of Oklahoma Press.

This volume is a definitive study of the historical geography of one culture of the border region. Nostrand considers the Hispanos, who have lived for four hundred years in northern New Mexico and southern Colorado. This distinctive group comprises descendants of settlers who moved into this peripheral area of New Spain in the late sixteenth century and who gradually intermixed with Pueblo Indians, nomadic Indians, Anglos, and Mexican Americans. Nostrand traces the emergence of a unique sense of place and homeland among the Hispanos and relates this sense of place to the cultural, geographical, and environmental isolation this population faced through history.

Rob Shields. 1991. *Places on the margin: Alternative geographies of modernity.* London: Routledge Chapman Hall.

Two chapters in this book examine the rise of national and regional identity. Shields considers both the rise of Canadian national identity and the nature of the divide between Britain's north and south.

MONA DOMOSH **5**

THE SYMBOLISM OF THE SKYSCRAPER: CASE STUDIES OF NEW YORK'S FIRST TALL BUILDINGS

Why the skyscraper? The question that Jean Gottmann posed over twenty years ago remains vital today (Gottmann 1966). Perhaps no one landscape feature is more expressive of the modern world than the skyscraper; yet surprisingly few studies have attempted to analyze how skyscrapers as landscape artifacts became expressive of particular cultural meanings. Architectural historians have emphasized technological achievement and stylistic innovation in their explanation of that development (Condit 1960; Goldberger 1981; Webster 1959; W. Weisman 1970), and scholars of urban morphology have focused on the role of land values in promoting tall building development (Hurd 1903; Yeates and Garner 1976; Vance 1977). This article represents an alternative approach to answering Gottmann's question by examining the skyscraper as a symbolic element in the built environment.

Certainly many factors contributed to the emergence of the skyscraper. Technological innovations in building construction and design, including the passenger elevator; improved plumbing, heating, fireproofing, and lighting systems; and sophisticated framing techniques were necessary to the possibility of constructing tall buildings. In addition, increasing land values due to pressures to be close to the peak land value intersection provided sufficient profit motive for people to begin to expand vertically. This article does not attempt to assess the efficacy of these various factors in the history of skyscraper development, nor does it propose to analyze the complete history of skyscraper styles and building innovations (Condit 1960; Webster 1959; W. Weisman 1970; R. Stern, Gilmartin, and Massengale 1983). Rather, this article will examine the skyscraper within its broad cultural context in order to view it as a symbolic element in our built environment.

That the built environment can be understood as the reflection of social and economic processes is certainly not a novel idea. In his studies of the city in its historical context, Lewis Mumford continues to explore the links between culture and urban forms (Mumford 1938, 1961). The translation of religious conceptions into architectural form has been documented by such scholars as Sigfried Giedion, Paul Wheatley, and Mircea Eliade (Giedion 1967; Wheatley 1971; Eliade 1959). In the Western secular city, links between society, economy, and urban form are a bit more subtle. Denis Cosgrove (1984) has closely examined those links in Renaissance Italy, David Harvey (1985) in nineteenth-century Paris, and Carl Schorske (1981) in late-nineteenth-century Vienna. Most pertinent to this study, however, is Barbara Rubin Hudson's (1979) exploration of the role of culture and the culture elite in shaping modern American cities. In particular, her analysis of how the commercial imperatives of the nouveau riche class of late-nineteenth-century America found expression in the urban landscape will be explored in this essay.

To attempt such a synthetic study requires both an analysis of skyscraper location and design and a broad understanding of the more general economic and social trends into which that development fits. I have chosen, then, to present in the first section of the article a fairly brief examination of the cultural and spatial context of mid-nineteenth-century New York, focusing my discussion on the facts pertinent to an understanding of skyscraper development. The second section offers an analysis of several skyscrapers chosen as representative of the two industries that dominated the early history of tall buildings, the newspaper and the life insurance industry.

My insistence on a symbolic approach to examining the skyscraper is meant as a counterpoint to more traditional explanations that have focused on the skyscraper's functional attributes (Condit 1960; Gottmann 1966). I am using, then, a very broad definition of the word *symbol* that encompasses those aspects of the built environment that are not directly attributable to human needs. As symbols, skyscrapers embody the intentions of the particular group of people who built them. Donald Appleyard states:

> An environment becomes a social symbol when it is intended or perceived as a representative of someone or of some social group, when social meaning plays an influential role in relation to its other functions. There are thus two sides of the coin of social symbolism, (a) when an environmental action is intended by its proponent to convey social meanings, that is, as a symbolic action and (b) when the environment is perceived as a social symbol, whether this was intended or not. (Appleyard 1979, 144)

The study of symbolism in the built environment, then, is part of a more general study of what Appleyard calls environmental action. The commissioners—the people who initiate the action—do so in order to convey particular messages to an audience. By examining case studies of businesses that were the first to build tall, and placing those studies within a framework of the changing social and economic scene of nineteenth-century New York City, I hope to explain what types of messages the first generation of skyscrapers were meant to convey to the urban populace. To potential consumers of the goods and services offered by the establishments located in skyscrapers, the message was one of power and prestige. To the consumers of culture, that is, to the elite of New York who saw skyscrapers as aesthetic objects, the message was one of cultural legitimacy. I will argue here that the senders of these symbolic messages were the emergent merchants and entrepreneurs of New York City. It is this group of people who were looking for symbols of cultural legitimacy, social status, and economic power.

THE SOCIAL AND ECONOMIC SETTING

Although the debates as to the exact birthplace of the skyscraper as a technological advance continue (Condit 1960; Goldberger 1981; Webster 1959), it is clear that the impulse to build tall, and the subsequent evolution of the form, was most evident in New York City. That impulse was derived from a combination of certain economic, cultural, and spatial factors specific to mid-nineteenth-century New York City.

Since the early nineteenth century, New York had been not only the largest city in the United States but also the leading manufacturing center and seaport in North America (Haig 1927, 29–30). The city's location on the Hudson and East rivers with easy access to the Atlantic Ocean had established it as a prime commercial link to Europe, the completion of the Erie Canal provided the tie to the interior, and the railroads consolidated the initial advantage. Edward Spann points out:

> By 1860, New York was in direct contact by
> rail and telegraph with every major city of the
> North. By then, it had become the dynamo of
> the emerging urban system of cities and towns
> in the Northeast and Middle West which was
> working a fundamental change in American life.
> (Spann 1981, 417)

Between 1870 and 1890, the port of New York handled between 40 and 50 percent of the export trade of the country, and continued to dominate the import trade (T. Adams, Lewis, and Mc-Crosky 1929).[1] The city's access to natural resources, aided by improved transportation networks, and its access to a large supply, contributed to its development as a major manufacturing center. The combination of New York's dominance in trade and manufacturing eventually led to its supremacy in the financial world.

The economic primacy of New York City was both the result of and a major influence on the peculiar nature of its economic elite. That elite consisted of financiers, entrepreneurs, and professionals. Throughout the nineteenth century, the largest percentage of bankers and brokers in the United States was located in New York (Hammack 1982, 45). In addition, New York contained the "largest concentration of persons engaged in professional and financial services," and "in relation to its size New York had more technical

and professional experts than any large city in the United States" (Hammack 1982, 45). This business class, however, was far from staid and conservative. A comparative study of nineteenth-century elites in New York and Boston identifies three qualities that distinguish New York's merchants from those of Boston—"the New Yorkers were more inventive, their firms had shorter lives, and they were considered greater credit risks" (Jaher 1972, 32–33). The most important factors that accounted for this inventiveness were the diverse geographic origins of the population of New York, the constant infusion of new blood into the business community, and the resultant inability to maintain long-term family continuity (Jaher 1972, 33–35). New York's merchants had a long tradition of innovative policies on which to build, policies that ranged from the establishment of the first regularly scheduled freight and passenger lines to England, to the initiation of a market for commercial paper (Jaher 1972, 32–35). In other words, New York's economic elite were far more inventive than were the elite of other cities, particularly Boston, but they were also far less stable.

With such instability and lack of cohesiveness, New York's elite class was continually striving for appropriate material expression. That expression took the form of ornate private residences and commercial structures. This ambitious and upwardly mobile merchant and professional class helped to shape the changing physical environment of New York City. Until the 1840s, commercial activities were concentrated in plain four- and five-story brick buildings that lined Broadway south of Chambers Street; bankers and brokers were located in classical revival buildings surrounding Wall Street. Most of the real estate speculation and development had occurred in the newly developed sections of the city north of Chambers Street. New York's upwardly mobile merchants, by-products of New York's economic boom of the mid-nineteenth century, sought ways to express their newly found wealth and power. The European-revival-styled mansions of Fifth Avenue satisfied their desire to live in appropriately lavish structures, and the new commercial palaces of lower Manhattan satisfied their desire to work in fitting surroundings.

The 1846 Stewart Department Store on Broadway at Chambers Street signaled this development in lower Manhattan, and did much to popularize what has been called the palace style of architecture.[2] The style was inspired by the Italian Renaissance palazzo and was characterized by rusticated facades, ornate cornices, and elaborate decorative friezes (W. Weisman 1954, 285–302). An innovative businessman, Alexander T. Stewart was willing to experiment with a new design in order to express his break with tradition (W. Weisman 1954, 288). Other merchants followed Stewart's lead and constructed marble and granite buildings to house their expanding businesses. Department stores and insurance companies led the way in the new construction of the 1850s and 1860s (W. Weisman 1954, 295–300).

The result of this new construction was a city whose private sector had created one of the wonders of the modern world, the garish yet impressive avenue called Broadway. Although the city of 900,000 people could boast of few public monuments, the three-mile strip of Broadway from Union Square to Bowling Green provided sufficient ground for civic pride. It was the size of the street and the quantity of the wealth, above all, that attracted attention. In 1872, an observer commented:

> Some of the European cities contain short streets of greater beauty, and some of our American cities contain limited vistas as fine, but the great charm, the chief claim of Broadway to its fame, is the extent of its grand display. For three miles it presents an unbroken vista, and the surface is sufficiently undulating to enable one to command a view of the entire street from any point between Tenth Street and the Bowling Green. (McCabe 1872)

By the 1870s, the traditional brownstone of the five- and six-story commercial structures that lined the street had given way to marble, iron, and granite. The combination of this new architecture, the mass of signs and advertisements, and the throngs of people and animals in the street made Broadway an urban environment unsurpassed in its energy and dynamism (Lock-

wood 1976, 25–163). The 1854 description of Broadway in *Putnam's Monthly* still held true twenty years later:

> Broadway was "altogether the most showy, the most crowded, and the richest thoroughfare in America," declared *Putnam's Monthly* in 1854. It was "the most famous street in the United States, and perhaps the only one that has any European name and celebrity." But "the peculiarity of Broadway," continued the magazine, "consists in its being not only the main artery of the city, not only the focus [but also] the agglomeration of trade and fashion, business and amusement, public and private abodes, churches and theaters, barrooms and exhibitions, all collected into one promiscuous channel of activity and dissipation." (Lockwood 1976, 125)

The lower end of Broadway, marked by the small oval park, Bowling Green, was lined with offices of shipping companies, insurance companies, real estate agents, banks, and bankers' offices (McCabe 1872, 123–125). On the west side of Broadway, opposite Wall Street, stood Trinity Church, whose spire was recognizable from points all over the city. With the impressive French Renaissance revival city hall at its edge, the unfinished post office at its southern border, and its newly designed walkways, City Hall Park was the focus for social activity in lower Manhattan. The park was located on Broadway between Chambers Street and Park Row. Between the park and Union Square, Broadway was devoted to wholesale and retail activities, with several hotels and theaters located along the northern part of the street. Union Square, once a wealthy residential area, had become home to retail businesses, and Madison Square, at the intersection of Twenty-third Street, was dominated by large hotels and fashionable apartment houses. Broadway was fairly undeveloped above Thirty-fourth Street with a scattering of frame houses.

Most of the new commercial palaces of the 1850s and 1860s were located on Broadway (W. Weisman 1954, 295–300). Wall Street, Nassau Street, and Broad Street were all foci of economic activity and commanded high rents in their buildings, but Broadway became the center of the new and lavish architecture because it fulfilled certain symbolic needs. Weisman's analysis of the meaning of the palace style of architecture suggests what those demands were. Commercial palaces

> symbolized a reaction in taste on the part of a wealthy and elite social class against the staid austerity of the earlier republican period. This structure (Stewart's Department Store) mirrored the rise of a mercantile royalty who no longer were satisfied with shingles and homespun, but who yearned instead for the trappings of nobility. The palace movement was a reflection of this "calico aristocracy" as *Putnam's* called this group. The commercial palace, in other words, was the architectural symbol of the merchant prince. (W. Weisman 1954, 186)

The merchant princes chose to locate their symbolic structures on Broadway, because it was the widest, longest, and most centrally located street and therefore presented a succession of prominent sites in lower Manhattan. It would have made little sense for these merchants to locate their symbols on narrow streets where they would not have been noticed, or appreciated, by the public.

In retrospect, these commercial palaces can be seen as prototypes of the first tall buildings, and their locations as precursors to the pattern of tall building construction. Although the palace motif, as an architectural style, declined gradually after 1870 (W. Weisman 1954, 301–02), the motivation to build excessively ornate commercial structures grew stronger and reached its climax with the early skyscrapers of the 1870s and 1880s. With the development of the passenger elevator, and the subsequent improvements that made the tall building commercially viable in the 1870s, merchants could choose to house their enterprises in buildings that were tall as well as ornate. The possibility of building tall offered merchants and entrepreneurs a new form of expressing their rise to "nobility." The first skyscrapers, then, were located in order to be seen—first near City Hall Park and, later, along Broadway.[3] Two industries in particular were responsible for commissioning these first skyscrapers that were lo-

cated for display purposes—the newspaper and life insurance industries.

THE NEWSPAPER INDUSTRY

The earliest industry to translate its promotional needs and notions of corporate imagery into tall structures was the newspaper industry. Production of daily newspapers was a relatively new enterprise that relied on mass appeal to an urban audience, a result of nineteenth-century American "city culture" (Barth 1980; Crouthamel 1964).[4] It was also an industry that was dominated by a few strong magnates whose personalities were never opaque (Berger 1951; Churchill 1958; Elmer Davis 1921; Juergens 1966; Maverick 1970). These characteristics made the newspaper industry a likely exploiter of tall buildings. A more detailed look at the history of the industry will clarify its relationship to the urban economy and the decisions of some of its practitioners to build tall.

A large and competitive market for daily newspapers of general interest developed almost immediately after the *New York Sun* began publishing in 1834. The popularity of the metropolitan press was attributable to a new market created by the longing of urban masses for identity. The metropolitan press pioneered journalistic practices that satisfied people's needs for information about the bewildering place they found themselves in, the other inhabitants, and themselves (Barth 1980, 59). New York took the lead in that growth, and it is estimated that by 1856, almost every New York family bought a daily newspaper (Crouthamel 1964, 103). The national census of 1880 reported that the growth rate of the news industry was not equaled by "any other phase of industrial development in the United States" (quoted in Barth 1980, 59).

Three of the six structures that constituted the first tall building cluster on Park Row were directly associated with the newspaper industry. Park Row, which borders City Hall Park on the south, traditionally had been the site of the newspaper industry in New York. Prior to the advent of mass communication systems, an activity dependent on the rapid transmission of the news had to be located close to the sources of information. The newspaper industry, therefore, was located between the financial center at Wall Street and City Hall. Park Row was the most attractive location within this area, because it fulfilled these spatial demands and also satisfied particular promotional and symbolic needs of the newspaper business.

The tallest structure in this first cluster of tall buildings was the Tribune Building. The *New York Tribune* became a leading newspaper in the country shortly after its inception in 1841 (Crouthamel 1964, 101–02). It had occupied several different buildings on Printing House Square, but none gave such obvious evidence of the achievements of the paper as the 1875 Tribune Building. The building, designed by Richard Morris Hunt in the commercial neogrec style, measured 260 feet from the sidewalk to the top of its iron and granite tower (Landau 1986). In order to ensure the association of the newspaper with the tall tower, the words "The Tribune" were cut into granite blocks on all four sides of the building at the top level. The tower with its spire clearly proclaimed the supremacy of the *Tribune* in the work of New York journalism.

As a pioneer structure, the Tribune Building provoked strong reaction. Most often, the building was heralded as an architectural marvel. The noted architectural critic Montgomery Schuyler (1907, 161) commented, "The new Tribune Building was the wonder of New York that generations ago of which we were speaking. . . . The wonder by reason of its altitude." *Potter's American Monthly* in its article "The Palace-Building of the New York Tribune" (1875, vol. 5, 538) called it "the most convenient and well-appointed edifice in the country." The paper wasted no time in exploiting this attention. An advertising flier used by the paper is graphic evidence of the promotional use of the new Tribune Building (see figure 1).

The success of the Tribune Building as advertisement and image maker inspired other newspapers to build tall. One of the most powerful statements of prestige was delivered by the new home of Joseph Pulitzer's *New York World,* completed in 1889 on the corner of Park Row and Frankfort Street. Pulitzer had bought the paper in 1883 and changed the small press into an af-

fordable and popular newspaper that could boast a record-breaking circulation of 250,000 by 1886 (Bleyer 1927). Part of Pulitzer's successful formula was his switch to a sensational style of journalism and an expert handling of the visual qualities of the newspaper through the use of large headlines, illustrations, and political cartoons. Therefore, when the *World* outgrew its old quarters on Park Row, Pulitzer was more than willing to spend the extra money necessary to make a visual impact and construct a building both finer and taller than the Tribune Building. The result was the sixteen-story World Building, designed by George Post in the French Renaissance revival style (see figure 2). It towered six stories above any other building in the city and its gold dome, topped by a flagpole, ensured the distinctiveness and dominance of the *World* on the New York skyline.

Yet Pulitzer saw his building as more than mere advertisement and a sign of power. The prestige of creating the tallest structure in Manhattan was not sufficient for Pulitzer; he wanted his newspaper to be housed in a building that relayed a message more important than mere promotion. Pulitzer hoped that his World Building would serve as a monument to public service. In his message for opening-day ceremonies, he made clear his intentions:

> Let it ever be remembered that this edifice owes its existence to the public; that its architect is popular favor, that its moral cornerstone is love of liberty and justice, that its every stone comes from the people, and represents public approval for public services rendered. (*The New York World* 1890)

With its Renaissance revival style and classically inspired ornamented archways, columns, and pedestals, complete with four torchbearers representing Art, Literature, Science, and Invention, the World Building recalled the public structures of the nineteenth century and made it clear that the *World* was meant as a form of public "enlightenment." The World Building, therefore, succeeded as an advertisement to the mass market, as a monument to Pulitzer's success, and as a sign of the paper's legitimacy as a public in-

THE NEW YORK TRIBUNE.

FOUNDED BY HORACE GREELEY.

THE BEST AMERICAN NEWSPAPER.

DAILY, $10 PER YEAR; SEMI-WEEKLY, $3 PER YEAR; WEEKLY, $2 PER YEAR.

THE NEW
TRIBUNE BUILDING.

The largest newspaper office in the world.

The highest building on Manhattan Island.

Front on Nassau Street, 91 feet; on Spruce Street, 100 feet; and on Frankfort Street, 29 feet.

Depth of main building, 168 feet.

Height of main building, nine stories—150 feet.

Height of tower above foundations, 285 feet.

Materials, stone, brick and iron—the entire structure thoroughly fire-proof.

To be completed, front in 1874, main building in 1875.

Cost, exclusive of site, one million dollars.

TERMS
OF
THE TRIBUNE.

DAILY (by mail) one year..............$10 00

SEMI-WEEKLY, one year..............$ 3 00
Five copies   " 12 50
Ten copies (and one extra), one year.. 25 00

WEEKLY, one year...................$ 2 00
Five copies, one year............... 7 50
Ten   "   " 12 50
Twenty copies, one year............ 22 00
Thirty   "   " 30 00

Each person procuring a club of ten or more subscribers is entitled to one extra WEEKLY, and of fifty or more to a SEMI-WEEKLY.

Papers addressed separately to each member of Clubs will be charged ten cents additional to the above rates.

☞ Former subscribers to THE WEEKLY TRIBUNE, whose names do not appear on its books since February, 1873, can obtain the paper until January 1, 1875, by sending $2, subscription for one year, to this office.

ALL THE NEWS OF THE WORLD—FULL, FIRST AND INDEPENDENT.

THE TRIBUNE EXTRAS.

A LIBRARY FOR ONE DOLLAR.

No. 1.—23 Illustrations—Tyndall on Light. Price 5 cents.

No. 2.—Beecher's Compulsory Education; Phillips's Lost Arts; Bellows's Is there a God? Mark Twain's Sandwich Island Letters. Price 5 cents.

No. 3.—40 Illustrations— Prof. Wilder's Brain and Mind; Prof. Barker on the Spectroscope; Prof. Young on Astronomy, &c. Price 5 cents.

No. 4.—Six Shakespearean Studies, by John Weiss; Seven Art Studies; Parton's Pilgrim Fathers; Bret Harte's Argonauts of '49. Price 5 cents.

No. 5.—12 Illustrations—Three Lectures by Prof. Louis Elsberg on Sound and Hearing, Voice and Speech; Prof. Benj. Silliman's Deep Placer Mining in California; Parke Godwin on True and False Science, &c. Price 5 cents.

No. 6.—Beecher's Seven Lectures for Ministers. Price 5 cents.

No. 7.—Beecher's concluding Lectures, &c. "Creed Statements," by Thomas Starr King, &c. Price 5 cents.

No. 8.—62 Illustrations—The Method of Creation. Twelve Lectures, by Prof. Agassiz; Fossils found by the Yale College Expedition. Price 10 cents.

No. 9.—Credit Mobilier, Testimony, Debates and Votes. Price 10 cents.

No. 10.—10 Illustrations—Science for the Year. Proceedings and Discussions of the Annual Meeting of the American Association for the Advancement of Science, at Portland. Price 10 cents.

No. 11.—21 Illustrations—The Vienna Exhibition. Bayard Taylor's Letters. The List of American Awards. Price 5 cents.

No. 12.—The Evangelical Alliance. Meeting in New York. Papers, Discussions and Proceedings, complete. Thirty-two pages. Price 25 cents.

No. 13.—The Farmers' War. Letters from the Western States. The Rise, Progress and Purpose of the Farmer's Granges. Price 10 cents.

No. 14.—The Hayden Expedition. The Adventures and Explorations of Prof. Hayden in Colorado, during the season of 1873. Price 10 cents. Tribune extras Nos. 1 to 9 inclusive, or Nos. 6, 7, 8, 10 and 12 will be sent by mail to any address for 50 cents. The entire extra series now published sent by mail for One Dollar.

☞ Additional extra sheets containing the popular novels, "May," by Mrs. Oliphant, and "Lords and Ladies." Each by mail, 10 cents.

Address,

THE TRIBUNE, New York.

FIGURE 1
Advertising flier for the *New York Tribune.* Source: Warshaw Collection of Business Americana, Smithsonian Institution.

THE PULITZER BUILDING, THE NEW HOME OF THE NEW YORK "WORLD."—Drawn by Charles Graham.—[See Page 47.]

FIGURE 2
The World Building. Source: *Harper's Weekly* 39 (1890): 44.

stitution. As was made clear in a pamphlet published by the *World,* the building was indeed the embodiment of Pulitzer's ideal—its "dome was above the clouds" (*The New York World* 1890). The other leading newspapers joined the height competition, and their promotional motivations were only thinly disguised. As a commentator in *Scribner's* noted, "They [the newspaper buildings] rise, one above the other, in the humorous hope that the public will believe the length of their subscription lists is in proportion to the height of their towers" (R. Davis 1891, 588).

Newspapers continued to be a dominant exploiter of the tall building form for over twenty years. In 1881, three of the four new tall buildings were directly or indirectly associated with newspapers. The Evening Post Building housed the newspaper founded by W. C. Bryant, the Morse Building was owned by R. C. and S. E. Morse, founders of the newspaper *The Observer,* and the Bennett Building was owned by James Bennett, the owner of the *New York Herald.* The three tallest buildings that were constructed in the next ten years were owned by newspapers—the Times Building and the World Building on Park Row, and the Mail and Express Building on Broadway.

Although all of these first tall buildings represented some type of innovation in building technology, they were consistently designed in the eclectic revival styles popular at the time. These urban entrepreneurs attempted to fit their symbols of commercial power into what they considered to be the current aesthetic dictates, particularly the Italian Renaissance form, in order to create symbols of power and help impress an audience consisting of what Barbara Rubin Hudson (1979, 342) calls the "cultural elite." For example, Joseph Pulitzer made very clear to George Post his intention that his new building be considered an architectural marvel. In its report of the opening of its new building, the *New York World* stated that Mr. Pulitzer had insisted that

> the structure must be in every sense an architectural ornament to the metropolis; that it must be a magnificent business structure of the first order, embodying the very latest and best ideas in construction; that, to be worthy of the paper it housed, it must also be the best equipped newspaper edifice in existence. ("The Pulitzer Building" 1890)

Pulitzer was trying to legitimize his business enterprise by housing it in a building that impressed the arbiters of good taste.[5] Yet these entrepreneurs were also motivated to construct buildings as a form of advertisement for the general public. To fulfill their first goal, they attempted to have their buildings designed as commercial palaces; to fulfill the second goal, they built tall, individualized structures. As is evident from the following review of the World Building in the *Record and Guide,* these two goals often conflicted:

> But in a commercial building for a private owner who can tell whether the obstacles to architectural success come from the alterations of the architects or the freaks of the client? . . . It is not betraying anybody's secret to say that the dome is the obstacle to the architectural success of the World Building. The fact "jumps to the eyes" as the French have it, and it is fair to suppose that the client had imposed it. . . . But for thoughtful and refined design, one looks everywhere in vain, and the critic finds himself forced to follow the example of the designer—to "cuss the thing and quit it." (*Record and Guide,* 14 June 1890, "The New World Building")

The commercial impulse that led to individualized, tall buildings conflicted with correct aesthetic formulas. In other words, in order to please the cultural elite, the nouveau riche were going to have to forgo some of their commercial imperatives. That this did not happen is not surprising in light of the fact that the cultural elite in New York were only one segment of a fairly heterogeneous and fragmented elite class. As Jaher states:

> New York, unlike Boston or Philadelphia, retained no single nineteenth-century group with the generalized hegemony necessary to form an upper-class structure; nor did any group in that city develop into an aristocracy by perpetuating a multifaceted urban leadership over several generations. (Jaher 1973, 259)

The very fact that skyscrapers continued to develop without any checks to their spatial extent or height well into the twentieth century indicates that in New York the cultural elite had little, if any, real political power. The extent of the impact of the cultural elite on skyscraper development, then, seems to be limited to the design of the buildings, not to their form or locations.

Despite their apparent failure as forms of cultural legitimacy, these early skyscrapers can be thought of as successful forms of recognition and display. As one commentator noted:

> The commercial palaces grow more and more palatial with each decade. The little granite temples in which the banks of New York were housed forty years ago, and the iron sash frames which formed their facade twenty years ago, are alike giving way to buildings far larger and more luxurious, possessing, many of them, architectural individuality and interest. (*Harper's Weekly* 1880, 78)

The success of these early tall buildings as attention-catching devices seems to parallel their failure as signs of legitimacy.

THE LIFE INSURANCE INDUSTRY

The industry that took the place of newspapers as the leader in tall building construction was the life insurance industry.[6] Although built by newspapers, many of the first tall buildings housed insurance offices. Located in the early office buildings, such as the Bennett, Mills, and Potter buildings, were the headquarters of insurance companies. By the 1890s, some of those companies decided to build their own tall structures. Over 20 percent of the significantly tall buildings constructed between 1892 and 1896 were built by life insurance companies.[7] These included the American Surety, Home Life, Manhattan, Mutual Reserve, and New York Life insurance companies. Most of these buildings were located for functional and display purposes in the City Hall Park area,[8] not in the Wall Street district, where other types of insurance companies were located.[9]

Like the newspapers, the life insurance industry was a product of nineteenth-century urban culture (M. James 1947; Clough 1946; Buley 1959). The period of extreme growth of the life insurance industry coincided with the large waves of immigration that brought masses of people to the cities. These migrants, without family bonds and lacking security, provided an untapped market for the industry.[10] This new market, in combination with the more prosperous established urban dwellers who were willing to pay to insure their gains, explains the 12,000 percent increase in the assets of the life insurance companies in the second half of the nineteenth century (Keller 1963, 9).

With such wealth at stake, the competition among the leaders of the industry was fierce. The three big companies—Mutual Life, Equitable Life, and New York Life—were continually striving for primacy. Unlike other insurance companies, however, the life insurance industry felt a need to justify itself beyond the chase for profits. The executives of the maturing insurance companies shared an ideological commitment to public service. Equitable president James Alexander pinpointed that commitment with this statement, "assuredly, an institution which exists for the benefit of widows and orphans . . . is one which ought not to be conducted on a low plane of competition" (Keller 1963, 26).

The industry built on this theme of social responsibility, identifying itself with missionary work, and its leaders with prime ministers (Keller 1963, 27–31). This ideology of public service found appropriate expression in the home office buildings of the industry. Structures were required that could embody the tremendous economic power of the corporations, and their newly found public stature. As a historian of the life insurance industry points out:

> Men of great consciousness of place such as Hyde, McCurly, McCall, Dryden and Hegeman [presidents of life insurance companies] looked for—and found in elaborate home offices—the sort of physical expression that their un-material business otherwise denied them. (Keller 1963, 39)

Investments in real estate and elaborate architectural forms fulfilled that need for material expression. For example, the entryway of the classically inspired twelve-story annex of the New York Life Insurance Company was meant to resemble an ancient temple; it was, according to the company, a "Temple of Humanity" (Keller

1963, 39). When the Metropolitan Life Insurance Company moved into its new home at Madison Square in 1893, the structure was considered the most distinctive insurance building in New York. It "boasted a staircase inspired by the Paris opera, a president's office furnished at a cost of $90,000 and—by 1909—the famous tower then the tallest on earth" (Keller 1963, 39).

Metropolitan Life had been housed in three different structures in lower Manhattan before its move up to Madison Square. When the company began to outgrow its building at 32 Park Place, the president decided upon a new site for the expanded home offices—the corner of Madison Avenue and Twenty-third Street, facing Madison Square Park. In terms of real estate investments, the move was considered quite risky, since at the time Madison Square was known for its fashionable residences, not its business structures. In 1890, no office buildings were located north of Fourteenth Street (Dublin 1943, 49). Napoleon LeBrun, who had renovated the company's building on Park Place, was commissioned to design the new Madison Square structure and created an eleven-story marble edifice that opened in 1893. The Madison Avenue entrance led into a marble court with a vaulted ceiling three stories from the floor (M. James 1947, 112). Although the location of the building was considered a radical step, the building itself was rather conservative in form and design. The structure was more akin to the Italian Renaissance style commercial palaces of the 1860s than the skyscrapers of the 1890s. Since the location of the building was sufficient to warrant attention, the company could afford to choose a design that relayed a message of culture more than of commerce.

By 1905, however, the company was once again in need of more space. Metropolitan had grown enormously in the latter half of the 1890s, and in commissioning a new building the executives were seeking both more space and appropriate material expression for their new economic power. The sons of the deceased Napoleon Le-Brun were chosen as architects, and they designed a fifty-story tower to top the eleven-story building. The completion of the tower in 1909 gave Metropolitan Life Insurance Company the fame of having built the tallest structure on earth (see figure 3).

Apparently the idea of constructing a tower that would resemble the campanile of St. Marks in Venice was initially that of the president of the company, John Hegeman (M. James 1947, 174). The final design included a clock on the tower that was visible over a mile away and, at the top of the tower, a beacon that Haley Fiske, the vice president of the company, named "the light that never fails," a gesture that apparently was meant to compare the endurance and strength of the beacon with the company's new-found public stature (M. James 1947, 174). A pamphlet published by the company after the tower's completion makes the symbolic intent clearer:

> High and lofty, like a great sentinel keeping watch over the millions of policy-holders and marking the fast-fleeting minutes of life, stands the Tower, its completion marking the culmination of this series of building operations which, commencing with the construction during the years 1890 to 1893 of the southwesterly section of the structure fronting on Madison Avenue, ended in 1909. (*The Metropolitan Life Building* 1910, 1)

The enormous hands of the clock were illuminated at night and coordinated with the electric lantern at the top that, through a series of signals, flashed out the time (*The Metropolitan Life Building* 1910, 4). The image of the tower, with beams radiating from its top and the words "The Light That Never Fails" encircling the beams, became the logo for the company, and was placed on its advertising material as well as on the public service pamphlets that it published.[11] The executives of the Metropolitan Life Insurance Company, then, were very concerned with promoting the correct image for their business, an image that not only portrayed their economic power, but that conveyed a sense of their commitment to public service. A tower that in its style harked back to the precapitalist, civic values of medieval Venice and that was, in all aspects (even at night), quite prominent served those purposes.

Like the newspaper industry, insurance companies were concerned with more than mere promotion; they also hoped their buildings would

FIGURE 3
The Metropolitan Life Building.

represent their cultural and civic status. As Barbara Rubin Hudson states,

> The inventor-entrepreneur, on the other hand, despite his anarchic and individualistic approach to economic competition as manifested in his use of urban space in the late nineteenth century, entertained "cultural" aspirations commensurate with his wealth. (1979, 342)

The home offices of the life insurance industry were meant as opulent displays of wealth, but also as symbols of civic virtues and common values; they were to convey a message of innovation in the business world, but also one of stability and security. In other words, these first tall buildings need to be understood as attempts by this new economic class to fulfill two parallel goals—to find appropriate expression for its new power and to legitimize that power by placing it within the constructs established by the more traditional elite, thereby conveying a civic as well as a commercial message.

SPECULATIVE OFFICE BUILDINGS

By the turn of the century, speculative real estate companies had taken over control of the tall building industry.[12] Although the mammoth office structures they built in lower Manhattan were not expressions of individual entrepreneurs, speculators did continue to exploit the symbolism of height established by the first tall buildings. As the technology for tall building construction advanced, the financial risks decreased and many construction firms and developers invested in skyscraper development. The real estate corporations that undertook these schemes assumed that the symbolic importance of height would induce professional and corporate executives to pay more rent for a location in a tall office building, and they were eventually proven correct.

The pattern of tenancy of these new buildings reflected New York's changing economic position. New York's relative decline in manufacturing and trade near the end of the nineteenth century was more than compensated for by the increase in financial and professional service industries that concentrated in the city. By 1890, New York was the center for the offices of lawyers, engineers, and architects, as well as bankers and insurance men (Hammack 1982, 44–45). In addition, New York had become the capital of American corporate headquarters.

> By 1895 corporate offices were as disproportionately concentrated in the metropolitan region as were the banks and professionals. In that year Greater New York contained fully 298 mercantile and manufacturing firms worth more than one million dollars; Chicago, with a population about half as large, had only eighty-four, Philadelphia had sixty-nine, and Boston, sixty-four. (Hammack 1982, 46–47)

New York's economy experienced a shift in its work force from the productive to the nonproductive sectors. This large white-collar class occupied the offices of the speculative, new tall buildings. Yet the decision to locate in skyscrapers was based on the associations with height that had been established twenty years earlier. As the internal structure of business became increasingly more complex, and ownership became distanced from control, executives chose locations in tall buildings as reflections neither of themselves nor of their businesses, but because the symbolism of height had become established in American society.

That symbolism had developed out of New York's particular socioeconomic context in the late nineteenth century. Because New York's elite class was less cohesive than was the case in other leading cities, the need for its new commercial powers to find appropriate physical expression was far more essential. New York's new entrepreneurs of the late nineteenth century, seeing an opportunity to express their status, and a chance to lend an air of legitimacy to that status, did not hesitate to build the tall structures that the more staid elite classes called architectural aberrations. At an even broader level, New York skyscrapers can be understood as expressions of the shifting global economy that led to New York's rise as the capital of capitalism. From monuments of individual prestige, to symbols of corporate power, to speculative money-making ventures, skyscraper forms mirrored the changing economic role of New York City. The tremendous growth and competitiveness of New York's mercantile economy made skyscrapers feasible and desirable; the rise of modern business corporations and the availability of speculative capital that characterized New York's financial economy secured their continued desirability.

The answer to the question Jean Gottmann posed, Why the skyscraper? is far more complicated than that provided by urban economic theory. The skyscraper is a symbolic as well as a functional structure, and its original development and efflorescence need to be understood within the context of the social and economic setting of New York City. Part of the answer to Gottmann's question lies in an understanding of the messages that New York's business class wanted to convey to both the cultured elite and the urban populace. Certainly a wide range of factors shaped skyscraper development, and Gottmann's question cannot be fully answered until those have been explored. Yet it is hoped that this examination of the skyscraper as a symbolic structure has contributed to that answer and stimulated further exploration.

SOURCE AND ACKNOWLEDGMENTS

This article appeared originally in the *Journal of Urban History* 14 (1988): 321–45. The author wishes to express appreciation to Michael Steinitz, Paul Knox, and the two reviewers for their constructive criticism of the original manuscript of this article.

NOTES

1. Because of New York's supremacy as a port city, it attracted a large number of marine insurance companies, thereby establishing a strong link with the insurance industry that would continue throughout the century.

2. I am using here Winston Weisman's definition of the palace style. He states that "what made a building a palace was the richness of the architectural language and not its nationality. As we shall see, it seemed to matter little whether a building was done in the Italian, French, English, or German idiom; or whether the period was Ancient, Medieval or Renaissance. What counted was aristocratic appearance. If a structure had that, it was a palace" (W. Weisman 1954, 290).

3. City Hall Park is located on a triangular lot that is formed by Park Row intersecting Broadway at a forty-five-degree angle. The intersection of these two streets created the largest open space in lower Manhattan and, with the construction of the nearby Brooklyn Bridge in the 1870s, had become a focus of public attention. The park provided pedestrians with a place from which to view the encircling buildings, and the open space of the park allowed the full height of the buildings to be appreciated.

4. Newspapers prior to the 1830s in New York were mercantile newspapers that were sold by subscription and devoted entirely to news sought by merchants. It was only after the development of daily newspapers of general interest that newspaper companies required large buildings to house their staffs.

5. For the case of New York, those arbiters consisted of what Frederic C. Jaher calls the Old Guard, a group of economic elites that were losing power in the late nineteenth century. This group turned to cultural concerns as a way of combating the nouveau riche. "Aristocratic sponsorship became a weapon against materialistic vulgarity, a means of separating the Old Guard from the nouveau riche, and a compensation for displacement in other aspects of leadership" (Jaher 1982, 234).

6. The life insurance industry had been interested in material forms of display since the midcentury, as witness the various guises of the Equitable and Mutual Life buildings. The argument here is that the industry did not get involved in skyscraper (that is, buildings nine stories or more) development until after 1890.

7. Buildings were defined as significantly tall if they exceeded the general height level of the district in which they were located. For the exact heights, see Domosh (1985).

8. Unlike other types of insurance companies such as fire and marine insurance that needed to be central to financial activities, the life insurance industry was not directly linked to the financial district and could afford to move out of the area and seek lower-cost locations. As an already established display focus, City Hall Park became a desirable location.

9. From the 1890s on, life insurance companies were found in the tallest buildings in the city. In 1891, two life insurance companies were in the sixteen-story World Building, two in the eleven-story Potter Building, and one in the thirteen-story Times Building. In 1908, four life insurance companies were located in the twenty-six story St. Paul Building, and three in the fifty-six story Singer Building. Other types of insurance companies apparently felt no need to locate in the most prominent structures and located as close to Wall Street as was possible. For example, only three fire insurance companies were located in buildings over nineteen stories in 1908, and those buildings (the German American Insurance Building at 19 Liberty Street and the Kuhn, Loeb Co. Building at 52 William Street) were within the Wall Street district. Most of the fire insurance companies were located in medium-height structures. For example, in

1908, ten companies were in the sixteen-story Royal Insurance Co. Building at 84 William Street, thirteen in the ten-story building at 45, 49 Cedar Street, nine in the twelve-story building at 92 William Street, and seven in the thirteen-story Woodbridge Building at 1900 William Street. All of these buildings were in the Wall Street district.

10. The insurance needs of immigrants were originally served by cooperative fraternal societies that provided insurance for burial fees. Private enterprises responded with what was called industrial insurance that required only a small, fixed premium with weekly payments. This type of insurance vied with fraternal societies and was considered a step toward "Americanization" (Keller 1963, 9).

11. The company published a series of these pamphlets, on topics that ranged from first aid, to healthy cooking techniques. These pamphlets can be found at the Warshaw Collection of Business Americana at the Smithsonian Institution.

12. In 1896, eight of the twenty-four significantly tall buildings (that is, buildings that exceeded the general height level of the district in which they were located) had names that were neither personally nor institutionally associated. In 1902, that ratio was 15:21; in 1908, the ratio was 22:35. The assumption here is that buildings named without apparent association were built as speculative office buildings.

FURTHER READINGS

John A. Agnew and James S. Duncan, eds. 1989. *The power of place: Bringing together geographical and sociological imaginations.* Boston: Unwin Hyman.

This collection of essays focuses on the relationship between places and the sociological practices that give meaning to those places.

Laurel B. Andrew. 1978. *The early temples of the Mormons: The architecture of the Millennial Kingdom in the American West.* Albany: State University of New York Press.

This is a history of the way in which a new religion sought to create an architecture expressive of its theology. Andrew's study of the debate over architecture among Mormon leaders provides a fine counterpoint to Domosh's discussion of the rise of commercial architecture in New York.

Lois A. Craig. 1978. *The federal presence: Architecture, politics, and symbols in United States government building.* Cambridge: MIT Press.
Bates Lowry. 1985. *Building a national image: Architectural drawings for the American democracy, 1789–1912.* Washington, D.C.: National Building Museum.

These books by Craig and Lowry address the ways in which Americans grappled with the problem of developing architectural and design ethics expressive of democratic ideals. The relationship between national identity and architecture is also the subject of the books by Taylor and Vale listed below.

Mona Domosh. 1987. Imagining New York's first skyscrapers, 1875–1910. *Journal of Historical Geography* 13: 233–48.
Merrill Schleier. 1986. *The skyscraper in American art, 1890–1931.* Ann Arbor, Mich.: UMI Research Press.

Domosh and Schleier take up the issue of the representation of the skyscraper in artistic imagery of the American city. This representation took a variety of forms as the image of the skyscraper gradually came to assume an important role in American art, serving eventually as an icon of modern life.

Mona Domosh. 1992. Controlling urban form: The development of Boston's Back Bay. *Journal of Historical Geography* 18:288–306.

Here Domosh examines the relationship between the nineteenth-century construction of Boston's Back Bay and the ideology of that city's elite class.

James S. Duncan. 1990. *The city as text: The politics of landscape interpretation in the Kandyan Kingdom.* Cambridge: Cambridge University Press.

A study of the intertextual linkages of the religious center of Kandy and the two major traditions of Buddhist thought. The political elite sought to make Kandy reflect the tradition that was momentarily convenient, while the masses read the landscape in the light of their own interests.

David Harvey. 1979. Monument and myth. *Annals of the Association of American Geographers* 69:362–81.

In this account of the building of Paris's Sacré-Coeur, Harvey demonstrates how the built environment can serve as the focus of contested political meanings. In this case, the building of Sacré-Coeur by conservative religious and political factions came to symbolize their suppression of the Paris Commune.

Helen L. Horowitz. 1984. *Alma mater: Design and experience in the women's colleges from their nineteenth-century beginnings to the 1930s.* New York: Knopf.
Paul V. Turner. 1984. *Campus: An American planning tradition.* Cambridge: MIT Press.

Horowitz and Turner provide thorough studies of the ideologies that guided the design of American college and university campuses. The rise of higher education in America was accompanied by massive building campaigns throughout the nation. Many plans sought to make symbolically explicit the ideals invested in these new institutions. Horowitz's study of the "Seven Sisters" women's colleges is particularly interesting because of its careful interweaving of the architectural, academic, and social development of the schools. She demonstrates that, in some cases, conflicting demands were placed on the campus plans: cultivation of the students' intellects and control of the women's social worlds.

Thomas A. P. van Leeuwen. 1988. *The skyward trend of thought: The metaphysics of the American skyscraper.* Cambridge: MIT Press.

Leeuwen rejects the assertion that the skyscraper can be interpreted solely as the attempt by Americans to develop a commercially viable structure expressive of pragmatic values. Instead, Leeuwen develops the hypothesis that the skyscraper emerged out of a myth that Americans could create a new city and a new social order.

Robert R. Taylor. 1974. *The word in stone: The role of architecture in the National Socialist ideology.* Berkeley: University of California Press.

Architecture was an important part of the Nazi vision of the Third Reich. Taylor examines how Nazis sought to express their ideology in an explicitly "German" architectural aesthetic.

Lawrence J. Vale. 1992. *Architecture, power, and national identity.* New Haven: Yale University Press.

This book considers the connection between political power and use of the built environment both historically and cross-culturally. Vale concentrates on cities that were designed as national capitals, particularly the postcolonial government buildings of Papua New Guinea, Sri Lanka, Kuwait, and Bangladesh.

J. B. JACKSON 6

THE WESTWARD-MOVING HOUSE: THREE AMERICAN HOUSES AND THE PEOPLE WHO LIVED IN THEM

I. NEHEMIAH'S ARK

Three hundred years ago one Nehemiah Tinkham, with wife Submit Tinkham and six children, landed on the shores of New England to establish a home in the wilderness.

Like his forefathers, Tinkham had been a small farmer. He brought with him in addition to a few household goods those "needful things" which a catalogue for "Prospective New England Planters" had suggested several years before: 2 hoes, 2 saws, 2 axes, hammer, shovel, spade, augers, chisels, piercers, gimlet, and hatchet. These were all he had, these and a knowledge of certain traditional skills, necessary not only for building a house, but for clearing and farming new land. There were no nails on the list—nails being expensive—and no equipment for livestock.

Nehemiah soon acquired some 60 acres of virgin land at Jerusha, a new settlement a day's journey from Boston. He did not buy the land from a private owner, white man or Indian, still less appropriate a likely corner of the New England forest for himself. He bought it from the Jerusha town authorities who had obtained it from the Crown, and the town assigned him his land without giving him any choice of location.

Nevertheless his farm was as good as his neighbors'. It comprised three kinds of land: the smallest (and most valuable) section was the home lot, of about ten acres, that faced the green or common and was near not only other houses but the site of the future meetinghouse. The Massachusetts General Court had recently ruled that no dwelling was to be built farther from the meetinghouse than half a mile. The two other subdivisions of the farm were meadow and woodland. The meadow, located in the well-watered and protected valley, was gradually cleared of trees and planted to wheat and oats and corn, though some of it was left untilled for the cows which Nehemiah hoped to acquire. The woodlands on the rocky hills served to provide building materials and fuel.

The broadax which he had brought with him from England stood him in good stead; for though he and his neighbors had originally staked out their settlement in a thick forest, they cleared the land so rapidly of its trees that within a decade they had to go elsewhere for wood. While this cutting of trees lasted it concerned all men. Neighbors helped Nehemiah fell the largest trees—the oak and pine he intended to use for his house—and he in turn helped them. All joined forces to clear the common, to build a fence around it to prevent livestock from straying, to build a meetinghouse and a home for the minister. The Tinkhams had to live in a temporary half-underground shelter during the first winter, and all that Nehemiah could do was plant two acres of wheat—never a successful crop in New England and from the beginning overrun by barberry—plant some of the unfamiliar Indian corn, and set out a small apple orchard on the home lot.

Nehemiah never grew or tasted a tomato, an Irish potato, or a sweet potato. He never tasted either tea or coffee, and seldom tasted fresh beef or pork or lamb. The farm eventually provided the family with flour, a few fruits and vegetables, milk, butter, cheese, and eggs. These, together with game, made up most of their diet.

Nor did the Tinkhams possess a yoke of oxen or a workhorse until many years after they arrived in the New World. The fields, which Nehemiah cultivated in spite of the many stumps, were plowed for him by the one man in Jerusha who owned a plow. He harvested his wheat with a sickle, threshed it with a flail. He was fortunate to possess a crude two-wheeled cart for hauling loads, though whatever traveling he and his family did (it was little enough) was done on horseback. The few roads in the center of the village were rough and narrow; between villages there were no roads at all, merely trails through the woods.

FAMILY AND SUPERFAMILY

Had Nehemiah wanted to expand his farming activities, had he been interested in greater yields, and in selling to city markets and buying city goods in return, he would have resented these restrictions on movement and sought to improve his agricultural methods. But he was concerned first with keeping himself and his family alive, and then with maintaining an established way of life. It was a monotonous one, perhaps, but it provided him with food and clothes and shelter, and with the kind of sociability he wanted.

Poor communications with the outside world, a large degree of self-sufficiency, the pioneer custom of all men working together on certain undertakings, and lastly the grouping of all houses around the "Place for Sabbath Assembly" made for a very compact village. In our more charitable appraisals of early New England we speak of its democracy. Actually its guiding principle was something else. There was nothing particularly democratic about the social setup of proprietors, yeomen, and latecomers in descending order of importance and privilege. There was nothing democratic about the law which forbade those having less than a certain amount of money to wear expensive clothes. Nor were these latter-day backslidings from an earlier democracy; as early as 1623 it had been proposed that New England be settled by "Three sorts—Gentlemen to bear arms, handicraftsmen of all sorts, and husbandmen for tilling the ground." Likewise the Puritan church had its hierarchy of elders, deacons, and ministers. In the Jerusha meetinghouse the higher your social position the nearer you sat to the pulpit; when Nehemiah acquired a servant she was obliged to sit in the cold gallery with the children. The right to vote, the right to live within the township, the right to speak one's mind—these were jealously controlled by law.

Yet if Jerusha was not as democratic as a modern American town it had a quality which the

modern town has lost. It was a kind of super-family, more like the highest stage in a domestic hierarchy than the smallest unit of a nation, as it is now. Nehemiah found Jerusha a good substi-tute for the rural society he had left behind. He had never traveled much in England, and his fa-ther and grandfather had traveled even less. To generations of Tinkhams, family and village had been almost interchangeable terms. Nehemiah had been related to most of his neighbors in the Old World and had shared customs and tradi-tions with them all. The people who came to Je-rusha came, of course, from different places and from different walks of life; but like the Tink-hams they were all of them homesick, not so much for the safety and comfort of England as for the superfamily they had known. What could take the place of that? Nothing so impersonal as a social contract; what they created instead was the domestic village with its established hierar-chy and its working together on a common task.

Certainly the most obvious symbols of the urge for a superfamily were God the stern Father; the Jerusha meetinghouse as a sort of super-parlor where the family gathered for prayers; and the genealogical enthusiasm which still possesses New England. But the individual house was scarcely less important, and Nehemiah hastened to build his family as good a house as he could in order to reproduce still another aspect of the tra-ditional background. The completed article was naturally reminiscent of the house he had known

in England. It was of wood, of course, much of it unseasoned, with a stone foundation, and it was two stories high with a third story or attic under a steeply pitched roof.

THE HOUSE

As Anthony Garvan has pointed out in his *Architecture and Town Planning in Colonial Con-necticut* (1951), the early builders (Nehemiah in-cluded) used as a basic measurement in their houses the 16-foot bay—a span originally adopted in England because it was wide enough to house two teams of oxen. In America this was modified to the extent that almost every dimen-sion in the colonial house was divisible by 8—or half a bay. Another sign of Nehemiah's conser-vatism was the manner in which he built the house. The frame of oak which he laboriously constructed with the simplest of tools was a heavy and intricate piece of carpentry—unlike anything we see in contemporary construction. To quote Garvan (1951, 86, 89), "Such frames . . . not only carried the whole weight of the building but were also mortised and tenoned together so that they withstood any horizontal thrust of the elements. . . . The task of the frame was to carry the weight of the roof and ridgepole, not just to resist their outward thrust."

Thus Nehemiah's house was built to last, built to be inflexible, built to carry a load, and not built for easy alteration or enlargement. Like his theology, perhaps.

He never painted the house, nor sought to adorn it, but the passage of years has given it softness and beauty, and now we hear persons admire its functionalism. Hugh Morrison remarks in his *Early American Architecture* (1952) that the seventeenth-century builder was so far from being functionally minded that he never thought of inserting sheathing between the frame and the outside clapboards; never realized that the huge chimney was inefficient, or that the lighting in the house was atrociously bad. He never realized that the old-fashioned frame he took such pains with was needlessly slow and difficult to make.

The plan of the house was equally nonfunctional as we understand the term. The ground floor had two main rooms: a combination living room–workroom–kitchen with a large fireplace, and a parlor, also with a fireplace. The parlor was reserved for important guests and family religious observances. Between these two a flight of stairs led to the two bedrooms where the family slept, and above these, reached by a ladder, was the attic where slept the servant. There were in addition several outbuildings, including a barn, all near the house. Outside the back door there was a small garden chiefly devoted to vegetables and herbs, but containing a few flowers as well. The lawn which we always think of as in front of the Colonial house did not exist; a rail fence surrounded the place and kept out cows. The appearance of the house was for long bleak and graceless; its windows were small, the proportion of the rooms ungainly, and the furnishings scanty and of necessity crude. But Nehemiah and his wife Submit found little to criticize in it. It was solid, practical, and defensible against Indian assaults. If anyone dared mention its discomforts Nehemiah quoted Romans 5:3.

MEETINGHOUSE AS PARLOR

We cannot judge the house without knowing what functions it was supposed to serve and what functions it relegated to some other establishment. We are no more entitled to speak of the gloom of the Tinkhams' existence simply because their house lacked facilities for conviviality than a foreigner would be entitled to speak of the idleness of modern American existence because our houses do not contain places of work.

Nehemiah's home cannot be understood without some understanding of the importance of the meetinghouse, for the one complemented the other. If the dwelling sheltered the economic and biological functions of domestic life in Jerusha, the social and cultural functions belonged to the meetinghouse. That perhaps is why Nehemiah was almost as attached to the square edifice on the common as he was to his own home; not because he had helped build it with his own hands, not because he thought it beautiful, but because it was an essential part of his life.

It was school and forum for the discussion of civic affairs; it was his barracks and the place where he stored his weapons and ammunition. It was the spot for community gatherings and celebrations. Most important of all it was the image of the kind of world order that Nehemiah believed in. Here and here alone he felt that he was occupying his ordained place in the scheme of existence, even if that place was humble. He did not enjoy sitting for two hours in a cold building while the Reverend Jethro Tipping expounded the significance of the Tenth Horn of the Beast, but he believed that all was well while he did so. Dozing off during the exegesis he saw the world as an enduring and majestic pyramid, an orderly succession of ranks—yeomen, husbandmen, squires; elders, deacons, ministers; heathen, gentile, elect—each one indispensable to the solidity of the structure, and helping to bear the weight of the crowning stone. Apt as it was to thinking in allegories, Nehemiah's fancy saw the same spirit manifest in the landscape around him, in the ascending order of woodland, meadow, and home lot; in unredeemed wilderness, settlement, and meetinghouse on the common.

In this hierarchical view of the world he was a child of his age. What distinguished him, however, from his cousins in Europe was his conviction that the order could and should be simplified. Some of the steps in the pyramid ought to be eliminated, as it were, for communication between the highest and the lowest to be more direct and certain. If this world was but a preparation for the next (and the Reverend Jethro Tipping assured him that it was) men should organize it simply and efficiently. And in fact Nehemiah and his fellow colonists had already done this so well that in the eyes of their Old World contemporaries they passed for revolutionaries.

THE HOSTILE ENVIRONMENT

Nevertheless, Jerusha was aware that it was only a small beleaguered island of holiness in the midst of a hostile country. Almost within gunshot of the meetinghouse was an unredeemed wilderness inhabited by savages. A variety of factors prevented Nehemiah from venturing very far or very often into this hinterland. His farming methods were too primitive; labor was too scarce for him to exploit all the land he owned—much less acquire more. The absence of roads made settlement difficult in the more remote parts and again prevented him from selling to distant towns. Furthermore, neither he nor his friends were adventurous spirits; they were slow to adopt new ways and new ideas, since the old ones were backed by unimpeachable authority. Remembering the cultivated countryside they had left in England, they were appalled by the lawlessness of the New World environment. Emerson once said that the early settlers "do not appear to have been hardy men. . . . They exaggerate their troubles. Bears and wolves were many; but early, they believed there were lions. Monadnoc was burned over to kill them. . . . In the journey of the Reverend Peter Bulkley and his company through the forest from Boston to Concord they fainted from the powerful odor of the sweet fern in the sun" (Emerson 1904, 191–192).

No doubt much of this fear came from the hardships of pioneer life. A spiritual descendant of Nehemiah, Silas Lapham of Vermont, remarked almost two hundred years later: "I wish some of the people that talk about the landscape, and *write* about it, had to bust one of them rocks *out* of the landscape with powder. . . . Let 'em go and live with nature in the *winter* . . . and I guess they'll get enough of her for one while" (Howells 1971, 15).

But in fact, later generations of American pioneers had little or none of this hostility to nature; the sentiment was largely confined to Nehemiah and his time. What helped confirm it and make it almost an article of faith was the habit the early colonists had of comparing themselves to the Children of Israel in the Wilderness. "Thou hast brought a vine out of Egypt. Thou hast cast out the heathen and planted it" (Psalms 80:8). Such was the biblical inspiration of the motto of Connecticut and of the state seal adopted in 1644. How great is the contrast between such an emblem and those of the western pioneer states of two centuries later, with their rising suns and optimistic plowmen!

It is possible to interpret the landscape of Jerusha as the expression of pioneer economic conditions. The village centered on the common and meetinghouse, the houses turning their backs on the woodlands, the small fields surrounded by fences and walls—these are certain traits of a subsistence economy and of a society compelled to think in terms of self-defense. Even the nonexistent lions and the soporific ferns, in one form or another, are part of every pioneer environment. But we should not forget that Nehemiah thought of himself not as a pioneer but as an exile, that he strove throughout his life not only for security but for holiness, and his interests never wandered very far from that font of holiness, the meetinghouse. He never aspired to much more than establishing as firmly as he could a superdomestic order. He closed his eyes on this vale of tears in 1683, satisfied until his latest breath that two things at least were permanent: his own identity (which would rise in the flesh on the Day of Judgment) and the indestructible, unalterable house which he bequeathed to his widow Submit.

It was lucky he died when he did. Had he lived to see his grandson Noah come of age, he would have witnessed the beginning of the end of the old order. Noah was one of the first in Jerusha to start speculating in land values. He realized that there was no longer room near the common for more houses and that newcomers were not eager to belong to the church community; they were willing to live far away. It was Noah who persuaded the town selectmen to build roads into the forest five miles distant, and he made a substantial profit selling off some of his grandfather's unused woodland.

His was not so well behaved a world as Nehemiah's, but it was more extensive. It included the West Indies and Virginia and many new towns and frontier farms off by themselves in distant clearings. It included men who went about on horseback preaching a road to salvation much shorter and simpler than the one Nehemiah had so earnestly followed, and others who talked of a more direct relationship between people and government. Noah built himself a three-story house and furnished the parlor with mahogany and silver. The old house, now gray and in poor repair, was lived in by one of Noah's aunts. She prided herself on being loyal to the old ways, but she complained that the house was cramped, and put in larger windows on the ground floor; and she always referred to New England as home.

II. PLINY'S HOMESTEAD

The first time a member of the Tinkham family built a house outside of New England was when Pliny Tinkham moved west a little over a century ago and homesteaded near Illium, Illinois.

Pliny was young to be married and the father of three children, and young (his parents thought) to be going so far from Jerusha. But though he was not rich he had much more to start with than his ancestors had had two centuries earlier. He needed much more; he intended to farm on a larger and more complicated scale. Aside from money, Pliny and his wife Matilda took little with them, having been advised to buy whatever they needed near their destination. When they finally arrived at Illium they had bought (in addition to the same set of tools that Nehemiah had for pioneering) a team of horses, a yoke of oxen, a milch cow, a wagon, a plow, a pitchfork, a scythe—and ten pounds of nails. These were the articles listed as necessary in the Farmers' and Emigrants' Handbook which Pliny consulted.

PIONEERING IN THE PLAINS

Nehemiah, it will be remembered, had been assigned land by the township; land comprising three different kinds of terrain. Pliny, though no judge of prairie real estate, was obliged to choose the land he wanted and to bargain for it. He finally bought 120 acres from a man who had acquired it as a speculation, had done nothing to improve it, and now wanted to move even farther west. It was excellent land; gently rolling prairie with very rich soil; it contained a small amount of woodland, and was about ten miles

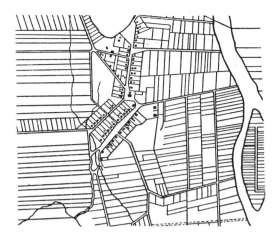

north of Illium on what would someday be a road. The nearest neighbor was a mile away.

Like Nehemiah, Pliny built a temporary shelter for the family first of all; only he built it out of logs and thus made it larger and more comfortable than that first underground Tinkham shelter. He did not have to cut down many trees to clear his land, for most of it was clear already, but he did have to cut them down for the log cabin, for a barn for the livestock, and for fences to keep the animals from wandering across the prairie. He soon saw that wood was not to be wasted in southern Illinois; there was too little of it. Again like his ancestor, Pliny hastened to plant the fields he had prepared; but instead of planting for family needs he planted twenty acres to wheat—in order to have a cash crop as soon as he could.

In many ways his pioneering was easier than that of Nehemiah. Pliny had no "hostiles" to deal with. The land was fertile and open, and he had the tradition of adaptability and self-reliance in a new country. He had a growing market not too far away, and a place where he could always buy to satisfy his needs. And then, finally, he and Matilda were optimistic and adventurous; the very fact that the purchase of the land had been a kind of speculation encouraged them to look at the whole enterprise of homesteading as speculative, for in a pinch they could always sell out and begin again.

On the other hand life during the first years was often harsh. Matilda had a recipe for bread made of powdered beechwood and another for

salad made of young pine needles, both to be used in times of near famine. She found herself having to practice a variety of domestic skills which the people of Jerusha had either never known or had been able to delegate to specialists within the village: the making of candles and soap and dyes, of sugar from corn and yeast from milk. She had to tend a much larger vegetable garden than Submit Tinkham had ever seen and preserve vegetables that Submit had never heard of. She had to nurse a family and keep it well according to methods which were scientific if rudimentary, whereas Submit had merely relied on traditional quackery and semimagic formulae or had turned to any neighbor who had had medical experience. As for Pliny, he was not only farmer, carpenter, mason, engineer, and blacksmith, he was also veterinarian, hunter and trapper, experimental agriculturalist, and merchant.

Moreover, the Tinkhams of Illinois were from the beginning much more on their own than the Tinkhams of Massachusetts. What neighbors they had were friendly, but they were remote and few. The Tinkham dwelling was several miles from Illium (and a good distance across prairie mud from the road leading to Illium), and once Pliny reached the town he discovered that no one there felt any responsibility for his welfare, spiritual or physical. The banker, the storekeeper, the shipper were all eager to do business with him, but they were not much interested in his personal problems. There was not one church in Illium; there were three. One of the ministers came out to see the Tinkhams, led a prayer, left a few tracts, and never came back. The population of Illium was constantly growing and changing. The rumor of a new railroad, of a packing plant, of a new county seat sent half of them scurrying elsewhere. In spite of his spending a good deal of time at the courthouse and in the bank, and of attending every fair, Pliny always felt like an outsider in the town.

FLIGHT FROM THE VILLAGE

To his forefather such a feeling would have been almost too humiliating to bear, but Pliny was a different person. He needed a different society, a different economy, and a different landscape, and he had left New England because he knew that he needed them. The reason given by the Tinkham tribe for the young man's defection was that there was more money to be made in farming out west, which was true, and that the old farm was exhausted after two hundred years of cultivation, which it was not. They also blamed the railroads, the cheap land, the growth of large cities—everything except themselves. But the fact is Pliny had rebelled against the old-fashioned farming methods of his father and against the old-fashioned domestic tyranny. The elder Tinkham, obsessed by the ancestral craving for security and solvency, and, like his ancestors, indifferent to the promise of wealth, had steadfastly refused either to enlarge the farm or improve it in keeping with new ideas. What had been good enough for Nehemiah was good enough for him. Furthermore, he firmly believed that as father, as representative of God in the home, he always knew best, that he was the apex of the established domestic order. He treated Pliny as a child of ten. Thus when Pliny moved west it was not so much in search of easy money as in flight from the Old Testament household, the old self-sufficient economy; in a way it might be said he was fleeing the New England village: common, meetinghouse, and all.

It was natural that the landscape which he and the other fugitives created in the West should have been in many respects the direct opposite of the landscape they had known as children. Instead of the cluster of farmhouses around the church there were farmhouses scattered far and wide across the prairie; instead of the land being fairly and equally apportioned by a benevolent authority, it was bought in the open market; and instead of the superfamily life of the New England village there was no village life at all. It was as if Pliny (like his remote ancestor) had set out in his turn to eliminate a few more steps in the hierarchy, some of the barriers between himself and immediate experience. Parents, clergy, aristocracy, township in the old sense were all abolished. And the chief artificer of the landscape was no longer the community but the individual. The independence that Pliny felt was expressed in a popular song:

I have lawns, I have bowers
I have fruits, I have flowers
The lark is my morning alarmer.
So jolly boys, now,
Here's God speed the plow
Long life and success to the farmer!

THE FUNCTIONAL
HOUSE — 1860

Most significant of all of Pliny's creations was his house, for it incorporated more revolutionary features than had any previous house in America. He placed it on a height in the center of the farm, where the air was fresh and the view wide, though he built at some distance from the highway and out of sight of neighbors. He and Matilda agreed that their house should be built primarily for the use of the family rather than for display or entertaining, and that it should be designed so that if need arose it could be easily sold. This was the advice that every home owner gave them, and it was in keeping with the speculative attitude they both unconsciously retained from the very first days on the farm. But that was only the beginning. After reading several useful handbooks on building, Pliny and Matilda decided that their home should be a place which could be added to in the future as the family grew and as they put aside more money; they planned for rooms which could be used as bedrooms now and later as storerooms, they planned for sliding doors which could divide a room in two.

A house with a flexible plan, a house designed so sensibly that it could be used by one family and then sold to another—a house, in short, that adjusted itself willingly to that outward thrust which Nehemiah's house had resisted so stoutly—was in itself a totally new concept. Equally new was the way Pliny built it. He abandoned the time-honored frame construction of his ancestors—and (significantly enough) the traditional dimensions based on the bay and the half bay—and used the latest method, the so-called balloon construction. Balloon construction is actually the type of construction we now use in every frame house in this country, but it was invented only a little over a century ago. Its principle, as Giedion defines it in *Space, Time and Architecture* (1967, 347) "involves the substitution of thin plates and studs—running the entire height of the building and held together only by nails—for the ancient and expensive method of construction with mortised and tenoned joints. To put together a house, like a box," he adds "using only nails—this must have seemed utterly revolutionary to carpenters." But to Pliny, who never prided himself on being a radical innovator, it was the logical procedure. It called for cheap and plentiful nails, and these he had.

So the house was inexpensive and fast to build, and it was larger, better lighted, and more convenient than the house in Jerusha. Its rooms were numerous, and whereas Nehemiah had thought chiefly in terms of the social function of each room—one for the family, one for ceremonies, one for the servant, and so on—Pliny thought in terms of domestic or practical function: kitchen, milkroom, pantry, living room, bedrooms, and of course a piazza. Just as he had promised, it was a house designed entirely for family life and not for show. What was the spiritual center of this dwelling? In Jerusha it had been the formal parlor with its Bible and hearth. But because of the scarcity of wood around Illium, and because of the more sensible arrangement of the rooms, Pliny had only Franklin burners and a cook-stove; two fires sufficed to heat the entire establishment. All that remained of the hearth was an open Franklin burner in the living room (or sitting room, as Matilda called it) and a small collection of books for family reading. Whittier and Longfellow and Household Words took their places alongside the Bible.

To say that the most important room in the Tinkham house was dedicated to family gatherings rather than to ceremonial occasions is to say that the house was designed for social self-sufficiency. None of the previous Tinkhams ever had so complete and independent a homelife as Pliny. This was chiefly because the house had to take the place of the church and meetinghouse and school—and sometimes even the tavern. Weddings, funerals, burials, business deals, and holidays gave it an importance that no Tinkham dwelling had ever had before or ever had afterward. It expanded to include almost every aspect of country living; it represented in its way the golden age of the American home.

THE FUNCTIONAL FARM

The farm which Pliny operated was not only larger than the one in Jerusha, it was far more efficient. Nehemiah had done everything by hand except haul stone and wood, and plow. On the farm near Illium every phase of the process of raising corn, except for husking, was done by horse power—and this long before the Civil War. Nehemiah had not owned one piece of farm machinery; Pliny had wagons, plows, cultivators, and harrows, and after ten years, when

the roads had been improved, he acquired a buggy. Gail Hamilton, a popular Boston essayist in the 1860s, compared the Midwestern farmer with his New England counterpart. The Midwestern farmers, she wrote, "do not go on there in the old ways in which their fathers trod for the very good reason they have neither ways nor fathers. . . . They make experiments, for they must make them. Indeed their farming is itself an experiment. Their broad lands necessitate broad vision. They farm with their brains as well as their hands. . . . Instead of taking his hoe and going to work, the (Midwestern) farmer harnesses his horse and takes a drive, but his drive does a good deal more hoeing than the Massachusetts man's hoe."

The Massachusetts man—to be specific, Nehemiah—had chiefly sought to satisfy his family needs from the proceeds of the farm, and as long as the family needs remained pretty much the same year after year, he saw no point in increasing the size of the farm or its yield. Pliny, on the contrary, gave up after the first few years any attempt to provide for the family in the traditional way; why raise sheep and spin wool and weave and dye and sew, when the railroad was bringing in ready-made clothes from the East? So he devoted more and more of his land to a cash crop—corn—which he could easily dispose of for ready money.

Once embarked on commercial farming, Pliny no longer had any reason for limiting the size of his farm; no matter how much he raised he could always sell it—or so it seemed; and as a result the farm started to expand. He bought other small farms, leased land, sold land, cleared land until he never quite knew how much he controlled. The expanding farm went hand in hand with the expanding house. Nehemiah had never changed the shape of his fields, bordered as they were with stone walls and each distinct as to soil and slope from the others. But Pliny, using wooden fences, could change his fields at will, and as he acquired large horsedrawn machinery he consolidated many small fields into a few big ones. Again, the flexible plan of the farm paralleled the flexible plan of the house.

From the beginning Pliny had never seen the wisdom of having a diversity of land; he had

PLINY'S HOMESTEAD

naturally wanted as much of the best as he could afford to buy, and a uniform topography was certainly most practical for a uniform crop. He never had any of Nehemiah's feeling that even the worst and least productive patch of land served some inscrutable purpose in an overall scheme. He spent much time and thought trying to modify the farm and increase its yield, thus making it impersonal and efficient, and easier to sell to another corn farmer.

It is unfortunately true that Pliny robbed the farm of variety and human association, and made it look more like a place of work than a traditional landscape; but it would be wrong to say that he did not love it. He probably never had that dim sense which Nehemiah had of being in partnership with a particular piece of earth. Pliny was indeed a strict and arbitrary master. Nevertheless he and Matilda and the children felt another kind of love which their colonial ancestor had never known. They enjoyed what in those days was called the grandiose spectacle of Nature. Pliny rode and hunted and fished in the remoter parts of the countryside, his children played in the woodlot and in the streams, and around the house Matilda planted a grove of locust trees and a romantic garden of wild flowers and vines. They belonged to a generation which believed that only good could come from close contact with Nature; like Thoreau they regarded Man "as an inhabitant or part and parcel of Nature, rather than a member of society" (Thoreau 1862). Never a churchgoer but always inclined to piety, Pliny was fond of saying that God could be worshipped in the great out-of-doors without the assistance of a preacher. As one of the emigrant handbooks put it (no doubt to reassure those pioneers who had always kept up their church attendance at home) "The church-going bell is not heard within his wild domain, nor organ, nor anthem, nor choir. But there is music in the deep silence. . . . He is indeed within a Temple not made with hands."

THE FAMILY AS A NATURAL SOCIETY

It is hard to realize that there was ever a time when such sentiments were new. But a century ago they not only represented a fresh approach to the environment, but a greatly simplified religious experience. Pliny loved the world of unspoiled nature for the same reason Nehemiah had dreaded it: it afforded him a direct and unimpeded glimpse of reality. Nehemiah had preferred to retain a hierarchy of Scripture and clergy between himself and the source of wisdom. Pliny liked to imagine that God was separated from him by little more than the thin veil of appearances.

The same sentiment inspired his concept of the ideal homelife. Remembering his family in Jerusha, forcibly subordinated to Old Testament law and parental authority, he chose to think of the household on the farm at Illium as a happy group of free individuals held together by common interests and affections, a beautifully natural society, independent of the outside world and unspoiled by artifice.

As he grew older Pliny had from time to time an uneasy suspicion that the house and the farm were no longer quite in harmony. The old domestic crafts had long since been abandoned, and increased contact with the national economy, increased dependence on hired help and semiprofessional skills, all tended to disrupt the ancient unity and self-sufficiency. But until his death in 1892 Pliny looked upon the homestead as the source of every virtue he admired: frugality and simplicity and independence. The free American farmer was the noblest of men, and to think of leaving the farm was to risk losing his identity. His solution to every problem, domestic or agricultural, was "add a new room" or "buy some more land." He insisted on a home burial (the last in the county) as a sort of final investment in the land, a final planting. He had no doubt that the proceeds would be profitable to everyone.

He never dreamt that his grandchildren would desert the place as soon as he vanished. They did, however. They could no longer enjoy the kind of life Pliny had arranged for them. They wanted less routine, more excitement; they took no pride in owning a large farm and having little cash, and they were bored with their identity as independent landowners. They rapidly went their several ways and the farm was eventually acquired by a Lithuanian immigrant with fourteen children, who raised onions, acres and acres of onions.

Pliny's way of life died with him, but Pliny's ghost and Pliny's home continue to haunt us. To many urban Americans they still embody a national ideal. Thanksgiving in Pliny's kitchen, fishing in the ole swimmin' hole on Pliny's farm, Pliny himself behind a team of plow horses now advertise beer and refrigerators and Free Enterprise. But the Tinkham family (who ought to have known what they were leaving behind, and why they left it) have long since moved on, and not all the persuasion of advertising copywriters and politicians can make them return to the farm near Illium.

III. RAY'S TRANSFORMER

The latest Tinkham house is not yet finished. It is being built at Bonniview, Texas, by Ray Tinkham, who hopes to have it completed sometime in the spring of 1953.

Meanwhile he and Shirley and the two children, Don and Billie-Jean, are still living out on the ranch with the Old Man. The Old Man, though a widower, does not want to leave the story-and-a-half frame house with its broad veranda that he built at the turn of the century. It is set in the midst of the cottonwoods which he and his wife planted, thinking of the grove of locusts around the house in Illinois. So he will stay there until he dies. Ray and he have a written partnership agreement by which the Old Man feeds a certain number of steers, while Ray manages the farm. It used to be a cattle ranch, but having discovered a vast underground supply of water Ray now plans to raise large crops of wheat or cotton or sorghum or castor beans, depending on the market. For the last month the bulldozers and earthmovers and Caterpillers of a contracting firm have been leveling part of the range, contouring slopes, building irrigation ditches and storage tanks, and installing pumps. "You'd never know the place," the Old Man says as he looks at the brand-new geometrical landscape. He often wonders how the venture is being financed—as well he might, for Ray Tinkham has little cash, and there is hardly a farm credit institution, public or private, that is not somehow involved. But Ray is not worried, and the Old Man has confidence in his son.

Now is the slack time of the year, and every afternoon the two men and Ray's boy Don, and once in a while a neighbor, go to work on Ray's new house. It is being built out of the best-grade cement blocks, brought by truck some two hundred miles, and it is to be absolutely the last word in convenience and modern construction. It is to be flat-roofed and one story high, with no artistic pretensions, but intelligently designed. It is located on a barren and treeless height of land on the outskirts of town. It has city water, of course, as well as city gas. Ray bought four lots on speculation when he came out of the Navy. From the large picture window in the living room there will be a view of prairie and a glimpse of a strange rock formation in the valley below. It will even be possible to see a corner of the ranch twelve miles away; the dust being raised by the Caterpillars is very visible when the wind is right.

PLANNING THE HOUSE

Twelve miles is an ideal distance. It means that Ray can get out to the headquarters (as he calls the old ranch house) in less than twenty minutes in his pickup, and leave his work far behind him at the end of the day. If the young Tinkhams were to continue to live out on the ranch the children would have to travel by bus to the new consolidated school in Bonniview, and even then miss the supervised after-school play period. As it is they will be able to walk the four blocks to school, and their mother will be near her friends after the daily trip to the supermarket and the foodlocker. She will be able to drop in on any of them for coffee. Ray approves all these arrangements and is counting the days until he and Shirley and the children have their own home.

He has even put up a rough frame where the picture window will eventually be, and Shirley never tires of looking out of it, over the vacant prairie and the strange rock formation below. Ray, who is a graduate of an agricultural college, pretends that he knows nothing about planning a house and leaves almost every decision to his wife. A very wise move, for she has not only pored over every home decorating magazine available, she has practical ideas of her own. She wants the house to be informal and not too big; easy to take care of, easy to live in, cheerful and comfortable. Styles and periods mean nothing to her, and since the place will be adequately heated by gas she suggests they save money by doing without a fireplace and chimney. She apparently knows the role the house can be expected to play in the life of the family, regardless of the role it might have played in the past. She knows that once in the new home the children will spend most of their time elsewhere and receive little of their upbringing in the house or from her. She will give them bed and breakfast, send them off to school, and in the late afternoon they will return in time to eat, having learned from their teachers how to sew, how to be polite, how to brush their teeth, how to buy on the installment plan—knowledge which Shirley herself acquired (after a fashion) from her parents. Eventually the two children will leave the house altogether, and their mother has already decided what to do with their bedrooms when that happens.

Ray, as a matter of principle, has never transacted any of his work at home, and even leaves the ranch books with an expert accountant in Bonniview. For the new house Shirley plans a small dressing room off the garage where her husband can wash and change his clothes after work. It is not that she feels that the home should be devoted exclusively to her interests, though the family recognizes her as the boss; indeed she is just as eager as anyone to reduce the functions of the house and to make it a convenience rather than a responsibility.

She wants as many labor-saving devices as they can afford; she wants to buy food which is already half-prepared—canned or frozen or pro-

cessed—and then entrust it to the automatic time controls of an electric range; she wants to have an electric dishwasher, and a garbage disposal unit and incinerator built into the wall of the kitchen; she wants thermostat heat control and air-conditioning. She wants an automatic washing machine. Confronted with these demands and with Shirley's reluctance to have a lawn or a vegetable garden—"who would water it?"—or a separate dining room for company—"just another room to take care of and more people to feed"—Ray is tempted to ask what she expects to do with her leisure. But he knows the answer; actually she will be lucky to have two free hours a day; and he himself thinks leisure—time spent away from routine work—a very desirable thing, though he cannot say precisely why, and he knows that Shirley is not lazy, that the house should not monopolize her time. It is not important enough to any of them for that.

THE FUNCTIONS OF THE HOUSE

He is right. It would be absurd to talk of the new Tinkham house as an institution, in the sense that the house near Illium was an institution, when it represents so little of permanent significance. What connection, for instance, can it possibly have with the process of earning the daily bread when it is twelve miles distant from the place of work? Its educational function will grow slighter every year; even homework has been done away with in the Bonniview public schools, and discipline is largely left to the teachers. Whoever falls sick goes to the hospital, for modern medical practice involves the use of complicated technical equipment. What social prestige is attached to the house that Ray is building? Neither he nor Shirley gave any thought to social or snobbish factors when they chose its site; convenience was all that mattered. They will sooner or later clamor for a paved road in front, but expensive and time-consuming landscaping they both consider superfluous until they know how long they will continue to live there. Although the Tinkhams have social ambitions like everyone else in Bonniview, they instinctively know that their standing depends more on the organizations they belong to, the car they drive, the clothes they wear, than on their house and its furnishings.

They have no illusions as to the permanence of the establishment they are about to set up. It does not occur to them that they will spend their old age in the house, much less that the children will inherit it and live in it after they have gone. As for the kind of family life that the Old Man knew back East in Illinois—reading out loud together, Bible instruction, games, large holiday dinners, winter evenings in the sitting room and so forth—the very mention of it makes Shirley impatient. The only time *her* family spends its leisure together—except for rapid meals—is when they are out in the car. And when the children *do* stay home they go to their separate rooms and listen to their favorite programs on their radios. The Tinkham house will have no provision for a permanent library of books, for a common literary heritage; an unending stream of newspapers and magazines, scarcely ever read, will pass through the living room. The Old Man regrets that the children have no religious instruction; has Shirley ever tried reading the Bible to them? "For pity's sake, Dad! Ray and me never go to church, so why should the kids?"

If such is to be the economic and social and cultural status—or lack of status—of the new Tinkham home, what will actually distinguish it from a motel—which indeed it promises to resemble, at least on the outside? Chiefly this: it is the one place where certain experiences, certain external energies are collected and transformed for the benefit of a group. This is clear in the design of the house itself: it is consciously planned to "capture" the sun, the breezes, the view, to filter the air, the heat, the light—even the distance, through the picture window, transforming them and making them acceptable to everyone. The kitchen is essentially a marvelous electric range which transforms raw or semiraw materials into food; the living room is the radio (and someday the television set) which transforms electronic impulses into entertainment; the dressing room transforms Ray from a workingman into a different person. The whole house exists not to create something new but to transform four separate individuals into a group—though only for a few hours at a time.

In a word, the Tinkham house is to be a transformer; and the property of transformers is that they neither increase nor decrease the energy in question but merely change its form. There is no use inquiring what this house will retain from the lives of its inhabitants, or what it will contribute to them. It imposes no distinct code of behavior or set of standards; it demands no loyalty which might be in conflict with loyalty to the outside world. No one will be justified in talking about the "tyranny" of the Tinkham home, or of its ingrowing other worldly qualities. Neither of the children will ever associate it with repression or wax sentimental at the thought of the days back in the Bonniview house. But still, it serves its purposes. It filters the crudities of nature, the lawlessness of society, and produces an atmosphere of temporary well-being where vigor can be renewed for contact with the outside.

THE FUNCTION OF THE FARM

It is no doubt significant that the house should be deliberately located at some distance from the farm and that it should have no connection with the farm setup. There are definite similarities, however, between the farm which Ray is creating and the house still under construction. Both of them, of course, disregard traditional form and layout, and the landscape which Ray will eventually produce will be as functional and as unencumbered as the house he is building. But how does he think of his farm? Does he, like Nehemiah, think of it as a fragment of creation which he is to redeem, support himself from, and pass on to his progeny? Or like Pliny, as an expanding organism, the victory of one individual over Nature? Does he look upon its produce as God's reward for work well and piously done, or as part of a limitless bounty given by a benevolent Nature to those who understand and obey her laws? Neither; Ray is the first of the Tinkhams to doubt the unending profusion of Nature, the first of ten generations to believe that the farm can and should produce much more than it has in the past, that much energy now being wasted can be put to use. Nehemiah, who saved every penny and never contracted a debt without examining his soul beforehand, would deny that Ray had any sense of economy; he turns in his grave at the thought of the mortgages and pledges and indebtedness, and of the small balance in the Bonniview bank.

But Ray knows something that Nehemiah never knew and Pliny never quite grasped: that work and time and money are interchangeable, and that the farm serves only to transform each of these several kinds of energy into another.

What does this knowledge of Ray's imply? Nehemiah was aware that his occasional small farm surplus could be converted into shillings and pence, but he never put those shillings back into the farm. Pliny, who disposed of most of his produce on the market, knew that in order to get money out of a farm you had to put money into it. Yet he never calculated the worth of his own labor or that of his sons, never kept account of the milk and eggs and meat the family took. He refused to make a distinction between the family and the farm; they belonged together. Finally it never occurred to him to expect the cost of certain improvements to be balanced by greater yields or lower overhead. If the price of corn was low, why bother to spend money on fertilizer? The farm, like the family, was not to be treated in terms of dollars and cents.

On the other hand Ray is organizing his farm along entirely different lines. As he sees it, it is to be an instrument for the prompt and efficient conversion of natural energy in the form of chemical fertilizer or water or tractor fuel or person hours or whatever into energy in the form of cash or further credit—into economic energy, in a word. There are still a few old-fashioned ranchers near Bonniview who accuse young Tinkham of being money-minded. Farming, after all, is a way of life, they say, and science and new ideas can be carried too far. They think that if he had not gone to agricultural college but had served an apprenticeship with his father on the ranch he would be more respectful of the old order.

THE IDENTITY OF
HOUSE AND FARM

Ray dismisses these criticisms as beside the point. He did not invent this kind of farming all by himself; his chief contribution is a willingness to accept certain definite trends. Labor is expensive and hard to get, so he has to mechanize and streamline his operations. Mechanization is expensive on a small irregular farm, so he has to expand and gamble on the results. The market fluctuates, so he must be ready to adjust the farm to other more profitable operations, or to sell it at a good price and get out. The farm is not a self-supporting economic unit; it depends on the outside world, so he must be assured of good roads and efficient transportation. Thus the new farm reproduces many of the characteristics of the new house: labor-saving devices, efficient and simplified layout, adaptability to and anticipation of change, and dependence on the proximity of a complex economy; on markets, super or otherwise. Like every other new house in rural America, the Tinkhams', in materials, method of construction, and location, has no organic relationship to its environment—weather or topography or soil. The Tinkham farm is of course something of a new departure, and its efficiency is yet to be proved. But it too is pretty much detached from the semiarid Southwestern landscape which surrounds it. Ray has changed the topography in no uncertain manner; his abundance of water for irrigation amounts to a change in the climate, and the soil—which even his father had always thought to be a constant factor—is being altered and improved in a variety of effective ways. Nothing more need be said of the infinitesimal cultural role which the home plays in the Tinkham family, but it is worth noting that the farm is, if anything, even less productive on that score. In the days when the Old Man ran the ranch and had several families of workers living on the place there was such a thing as a sense of unity among them all, and there was a distinctive way of life. Ray's few workers are paid well and treated well; but they check in and out like factory hands and think of their boss as an impersonal entity known as the Tinkham Land Development Company. And in fact Ray pays himself a salary as manager.

Two paint ponies stand in the corral waiting for Don and Billie-Jean to ride them. Once the farm is in operation they will be ridden on weekends only and in certain prescribed areas. Ray has made it clear that the farm is no place for Don to play at being farmer or rancher. "If he wants to learn this business he'll have to go to agricultural college the way I did, and study chemistry and engineering and accounting." Don, however, at present wants to be a jet pilot.

The ranch will not take every one of Ray's working hours. He hopes in time to be able to leave it to look after itself, not merely overnight but for weeks on end, while he and Shirley and the children take winter vacations in California.

He even dreams of having a small business in town to keep himself occupied. At present there are only two operations which he will delegate to no one: the preparing of the soil and planting of the seed, and the investment of the financial proceeds. The harvesting of the crop he has already contracted out to an itinerant crew which has its own machinery, and for several months of the year the Old Man's steers will be turned out into the stubble. In a sense all that interests Ray are the first process and the last—the energy which goes into the soil in the planting and fertilizing, and the energy which comes out of it in the form of money. How can he and the rest of the family help but think of the new farm as essentially an impersonal and flexible instrument of transformation? How can they help but be indifferent to the traditional aspects of farming? The farm at Bonniview is not and cannot be a way of life. It is not even negotiable property (since Ray can scarcely be said to own it); it is a process, a process by which grass is converted into beef, nitrogen into wheat, dollars into gasoline and back into dollars.

RAY'S IDENTITY

It would be fair to say that Ray is not a farmer at all, any more than his house is a farmhouse. Ray would be first to agree. Nevertheless there is a bond between him and the land that cannot be entirely overlooked. He himself is sub-ject to the same forces (however defined) which have modified so drastically the concept of the farm. For one thing, Ray's identity, like the identity of the land, has become alarmingly mobile and subject to rapid change. His remote ancestor Nehemiah (of whom he has never even heard) remained true to his identity of yeoman throughout his life—and even died believing he would some day rise again intact in every particular. But for some reason Ray is leery of any kind of permanent label. He will not call himself a farmer, for instance; he says he is engaged in farming. And who knows what he may not be doing ten years hence when he has made a success or failure of the Bonniview venture? Head of a trucking firm, oil well driller, owner of a farm equipment agency? They all cross his mind. He encourages his employees as well as his children to call him by his first name, as if he were reluctant to have any public status. He would probably explain this aversion of his to a permanent economic or social identity by saying that he merely wants to be himself. But even that identity refuses to be defined, just as it does to a lesser degree with his wife Shirley. Ray laughs at her incessant attempts to be someone different—now a peroxide blonde, now a redhead with a poodle haircut; following diets, mail-order courses in the Wisdom of the East, dressing up in slacks and cowboy boots and then reverting to femininity—never a dull moment when Shirley is trying to develop a new personality. But at the same time he is not always very sure of himself. Far more intelligent, far more sensitive than the first American Tinkham, he has inherited none of Nehemiah's tough integrity and self-assertiveness. It is easy for him to lose himself, as the phrase goes, and to become a totally different person; at a prize fight, or after two or three drinks, or at the scene of a bloody accident. "You should have seen yourself at the movie," Shirley says when they get home; "You sat there in the dark imitating every single expression Humphrey Bogart made on the screen."

Ray does not know the difference between hypnotism and amnesia and "getting religion," but he likes to talk about them; he likes to read in science fiction about brainwashing and thought control and transmuted identities. "It isn't scientifically impossible," he says, and he thinks of how he himself is radically changing the composition of the soil, how he is changing the face of the earth on a small scale. He thinks of the new house, not yet completed, ready to change its form, its owners, its function at a day's notice.

Bonniview is no more immune to the spiritual forces at large than were Illium and Jerusha. Ray is no less moved by an urge to apprehend truth than were Nehemiah and Pliny. If he has unconsciously destroyed the order which his father had established, and made his home a very different place, much freer, in many ways much poorer, it is chiefly because he has wanted to eliminate some of the stages between reality and himself as his predecessors tried to do. He sees the relationship in his own characteristic terms: he sees himself not as a child of God wishing to learn the parental command, not as a child of nature heeding the good impulse, but as an efficient and reliable instrument for transforming the invisible power within him into a power adapted to the world as he knows it.

SOURCE

This article originally appeared in *Landscape* 2 (Spring, 1953): 8–21.

FURTHER READINGS

James S. Duncan, ed. 1982. *Housing and identity: Cross cultural perspectives.* New York: Holmes and Meier.

This important collection contains essays on the psychological, anthropological, and sociological significance of domestic space and domestic architecture.

Dolores Hayden. 1981. *The grand domestic revolution: A history of feminist designs for American homes, neighborhoods, and cities.* Cambridge: MIT Press.

Hayden's survey stresses gender differences in the design and use of domestic space, an issue largely unaddressed in Jackson's essay. Here Hayden calls attention to designers and their ideas that are too often overlooked in the study of American architecture.

John B. Jackson. 1970. *Landscapes: Selected writings of J. B. Jackson.* Ed. Ervin H. Zube. Amherst: University of Massachusetts Press.
———. 1980. *The necessity for ruins, and other topics.* Amherst: University of Massachusetts Press.
———. 1984. *Discovering the vernacular landscape.* New Haven: Yale University Press.

These are three collections of J. B. Jackson's insightful essays on landscape form and history, many reprinted from *Landscape* magazine. Apart from reading these collections, another way to gain an appreciation of Jackson's remarkable work is to browse through the issues of *Landscape*, the journal he founded and then edited from 1951 to 1969. Under Jackson's management, *Landscape* became an intellectual meeting ground for writers and thinkers who shared Jackson's passion for the patterns that humans have wrought on the face of the earth. The magazine served as refuge for geographers fleeing the quantitative revolution and as a repository for splendid writing and thinking during a period when American academic geography was not noted for such qualities. Look especially for unsigned "Notes and Comments," written by Jackson, as well as for short pieces signed with his pseudonym, "Ajax." For an appreciation of *Landscape* and a bibliography of Jackson's work, see Lewis (1983) and Meinig (1979).

———. 1972. *American space: The centennial years, 1865–1876.* New York: Norton.

Jackson argues that, during these crucial years, American attitudes about the nature of space and environment underwent radical transformation. Landscapes were designed to facilitate the flow of energy through systems and the expectation of their perpetual transformation became the norm.

Anthony D. King. 1984. *The bungalow: The production of a global culture.* London: Routledge & Kegan Paul.

King presents a fascinating social history of a single house type, the bungalow. Tracing the origins of the bungalow is only the starting point for King's account of its rapid spread and the ways it was adapted to meet the demands of varying social and cultural situations.

Paul Oliver. 1987. *Dwellings: The house across the world.* Austin: University of Texas Press.

Oliver's work focuses on the dwelling as a key response to a society's physical, social, and psychological needs. This is one of Oliver's most recent books, and it examines the indigenous skills and building wisdom that lie behind the enormous range of dwellings found throughout the world. Oliver demonstrates how dwellings are shaped as much by belief systems and concepts of status, territory, and security as by economic, material, technological, and climatic considerations.

Amos Rapoport. 1969. *House form and culture.* Englewood Cliffs, N.J.: Prentice-Hall.

A classic and still provocative exploration of the relationship between buildings and cultural values. Rapoport draws on examples from around the world.

David Seamon and Robert Mugerauer, eds. 1985. *Dwelling, place and environment: Towards a phenomenology of person and world.* Dordrecht: Martinus Nijhoff.

A collection of essays that takes a different approach to the understanding of human habitation based largely on phenomenological theory and method. Here we see attempts to fathom how humans develop attachments to homes and environment, an issue to which Jackson alludes.

John R. Stilgoe. 1982. *Common landscape of America, 1580–1845.* New Haven: Yale University Press.

This volume is a survey of the elements of America's cultural landscape and the values and ethics that shaped them. Following the tradition of landscape interpretation pioneered by J. B. Jackson, Stilgoe carries the reader from the advent of American colonization to the time when settlers encountered the open prairies of the western Mississippi Valley. To Stilgoe, this was an era of a common landscape whose design belonged to the people and was shaped by widely understood and accepted cultural values.

Ervin H. Zube and Margaret J. Zube, eds. 1977. *Changing rural landscapes.* Amherst: University of Massachusetts Press.

This collection of essays, including eight by J. B. Jackson, is concerned with the cultural beliefs, human values, and technology as these interact to shape landscape. These are highly readable and stimulating essays that sharpen the reader's ability to see the landscape in new and different ways.

COMMON HOUSES, CULTURAL SPOOR

What people are within, the buildings express without; and inversely what the buildings are objectively is a sure index to what the people are subjectively.

— LOUIS SULLIVAN

For many people in many cultures, a house is the single most important thing they will ever build or buy. Certainly it is the most expensive. No physical possession receives more or graver attention than one's house—where it will be located and what it will look like. That is especially true in places like North America, with a long-standing tradition of owner-occupied single-family houses, set apart from other buildings on individual plots of ground—where the owner of a house is uniquely responsible for its appearance. In many parts of the world, the siting and building of a house are taken so seriously that they are attended by magical or religious ceremonies, and even in America, both Protestant and Catholic liturgies contain provision for blessing a house.

Most people avoid building or acquiring eccentric houses for the same reason they avoid eccentricity in haircuts, clothing styles, speech patterns, and table manners. Each is such a basic expression of unspoken cultural values that deviations from accepted standards are taken as evidence of unstable personality or dubious character, and invite unfavorable comment from one's neighbors. In communities where zoning laws are flouted in commercial and industrial districts, they are sacred in residential neighborhoods, and the person whose house trespasses on a building setback line or is painted an unseemly color risks not only legal reprisal but social ostracism.[1]

In short, one's house is more than mere shelter. It is a personal and social testament. Through their houses—whether great mansions in high style or the domestic shelter of common people—human beings etch their culture into the landscape.

This elemental fact is of high interest to geographers, historians, and others who delight in tracing cultural change across space and through time, and who have learned to their sorrow that written records are not necessarily dependable sources of information about vernacular—or even folk culture. To be sure, there is no dearth of written material, for humans are prolix creatures. Still, it is a lamentable fact—but a fact nonetheless—that humans are also vain, and loath to write unflattering things about themselves, their family, their culture, or anything else that they deem important. When common people assume the role of historians, the truth is often not in them. (Autobiographers, especially self-conscious about their subject, are notoriously unreliable.) But when people build houses—especially common, ordinary houses—they often "say" things unconsciously about themselves and their cultures which, simply because the statements are unconscious, are likely to be truthful. Common houses, in short, are cultural spoor.

If we accept the axiom that ordinary houses are tangible manifestations of common culture, several corollaries follow directly. First of all, domestic house types will change only as fast as culture itself changes, and since culture by its nature is conservative, common domestic architecture is also conservative, doggedly resisting fundamental change except under the most extreme duress. Such duress may be exerted by physical environment, as when traditional house types are hauled across an ocean and set down in a climate to which they are manifestly unsuited. Thus, gallons of eighteenth-century Virginian sweat were spilled before there was grudging admission that doors and windows that were well suited to the climate of Georgian London pro-

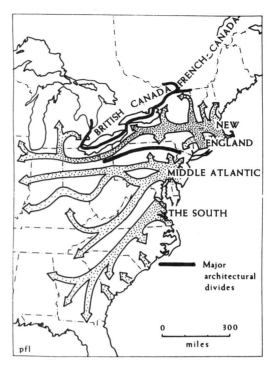

FIGURE I

The flow of architectural (and other) ideas westward from colonial culture hearths. Original version from Kniffen (1965) and Kniffen and Glassie (1966); modified on the basis of author's field observation.

vided inadequate ventilation for a Tidewater summer. (Much the same thing evidently happened when the English took their domestic house plans from foggy Devon to subtropical Australia.) Still, it was a long time before southerners could bring themselves even to attach porches to their Georgian townhouses (never mind that the colonial South had no towns to speak of; townhouses were suitable for people, and townhouses they got), and it took a hundred scorching midwestern summers to bring the Booth Tarkington veranda to its peak of comfortable eclectic magnificence. If America does begin west of the Alleghenies, the midwestern veranda may be architectural proof of it.

Cultural pressure is so strong that people will often adhere to familiar house types, even though their designs make no environmental sense at all. In isolated cultures, where architectural forms have evolved slowly in a given physical environment, conflicts seldom arise. But when environment and culture do collide—which often happens when one nation borrows faddish modes from another—culture usually wins, even though the result is highly uncomfortable. During the mid-nineteenth century in upstate New York, for example, Italian-style villas with flat or nearly flat roofs were built by the thousands in North America's most notorious snowbelt (see figure 20). The house was eminently suited to Italy, where flattish roofs served to catch rainwater for cisterns, but every winter in New York thousands of roofs leaked and some even collapsed. But fashion demanded Mediterranean roofs in defiance of New York State climatic facts and Yankee good sense. Indeed, the fashion spread widely across the North. When New Yorkers stopped building them, it was less because of collapsing roofs than the arrival of new modes that replaced the Italianate in popular approval. One of the new styles, for example, came equipped with crenelated turrets, a design which eases the task of pouring boiling oil on unwelcome visitors, but which poses problems to those who would explain house design in environmental terms.

Nor do technological innovations ordinarily have much effect on the basic form of common houses. Innovations, after all, are likely to make one's house look funny, as postmodern architects have demonstrated lately. (Significantly, new building technology gains quickest adoption in the design of factories, warehouses, and schools, where efficiency counts but looks do not. Both the local gasworks and the local junior college will be encased in purple styrofoam if that happens to be the cheapest suitable material available.) Thus, the Plastic Revolution of the 1930s and 1940s produced no enduring new forms of houses, its most important effect being conscious apings of antique materials—plastic pseudo-bricks, plastic Tudor half-timbering, and nonfunctional plastic shutters, glued to plastic clapboards on neo-Williamsburg dwellings from coast to coast. Thus too, the arrival of domestic air-conditioning and TV after World War II encouraged families to move indoors during North America's continental summers, so that verandas have largely disappeared, but even these revolutionary technologies left basic house forms largely unchanged.

In common domestic houses, then, form does not follow function except in a slow and faltering way, and then only under the most extreme pressure of environmental necessity. This view, no doubt, will annoy architectural critics who like to think of vernacular architecture as somehow springing from the fertile earth, or from the soaring Spirit of Humanity. The plain fact remains that most domestic house types, like culture itself, spring from the past, and that is exactly why house types make such reliable cultural spoor.

For if the common architectures of two adjacent regions differ fundamentally, it follows that the cultures of those regions probably differ in important ways. It follows, too, that if a people migrate to a new land, they are likely to carry their ideas about proper house types with them, often as conscious reminders of their homeland, and that one can trace the persistence of their culture through time and space by observing the continuity or discontinuity in the kinds of houses the migrants build. And, above all, it follows that when the vernacular architecture of a nation or region changes in large and fundamental ways—not merely in cosmetics, but in form as well—then it is highly likely that the culture itself is undergoing a wrenching and enduring change. If a people changes its collective mind about its houses, there is a good chance it has changed its mind about many other important things as well.

Nowhere are these propositions more dramatically illustrated than in the United States, where the tracing of some common American house types through space and time provides fascinating if fragmentary insights into the varied and intricate ways by which American cultures have emerged (see especially Kniffen 1965). Regrettably, there are major gaps in the story, largely because of the great sweep of American territory, and of the small (but growing) number of scholars who have sifted the enormous treasure of American domestic architecture. Still, we know enough to sketch in rough outline at least part of the geographic story that American domestic architecture has to tell, and the story is most accurately told in the East, where the culture and architecture of a new American nation first emerged.

ENGLAND'S PERMANENT IMPRINT

A basic article of American faith holds that the United States is a melting pot into which ingredients from various cultures and ethnic stocks were poured in varying quantities and then stirred to form a homogeneous gruel. Biologically, of course, Americans are a mixture, albeit a rather lumpy one. The architectural evidence suggests, however, that the melting pot is largely myth—that from the beginning Americans were an English people, culturally if not biologically. Quite simply, the English were the first to arrive in sufficient numbers and with sufficient resources to call the cultural as well as the political tune. Inevitably, most early American folk houses were really English, or were quickly made to look English, just as American tastes in food, in clothes, and in landscape gardening were English. It is still that way, of course. Tudor houses cling to the hills of Pasadena, and English roses and English lawns perennially wilt under the blistering Kansas sun.

Not everybody came from England, of course. As early as 1700 there were Swedes, Dutch, Welsh, Germans, Scots-Irish, French Huguenots, and even a few Spaniards. Africans came as slaves, and Indians were omnipresent. Some of these groups—notably the Germans—contributed significantly to a growing fund of knowledge about construction methods, and a good many practical structures, like barns and fences and outbuildings, either derived from non-English sources or were invented locally (Jordan and Kaups 1989). But when it came to the really important question of what a house should look like, English standards prevailed from Newfoundland to the frontiers of Spanish Florida.

Exceptions to this generalization merely mocked the futility of those who tried to stem the English tide. In the St. Lawrence Lowland, small in area and poor in resources, the French held sway and still do, so that even today, much of the area from Montréal to the Gaspé is an architectural fossil of seventeenth-century France (as until recently it was a political fossil as well).

So also the lower Hudson, where a handful of Dutch houses in New Paltz and elsewhere stand as cenotaphs of Holland's vain challenge to English dominance. But the Dutch were too few and were engulfed in the English flood. Their houses would probably be gone too, save for the diligence of local preservationists. Even the Pennsylvania and Virginia Germans, who clung, insofar as they could, to old-country patterns of language, diet, and even barn building, gave up or modified their domestic house types and, like all the rest, began sedulously to ape the English. Henry Glassie, who knows more about Pennsylvania German houses than almost anybody, suggests that the interior floor plan of certain Pennsylvania houses is German, although often the facades were self-consciously made to look English. Where the Germans did manage to leave their mark on American domestic architecture, as in central Texas during the mid-nineteenth century, they succeeded very largely because English competition was absent during their first century or so of settlement. The Spanish and Mexicans held cultural and architectural sway over the Southwest for the same reason. Outside their home territories in the United States, however, "German-style" or "Spanish-style" architecture is generally regarded as a bit eccentric by the majority of Americans who were unconsciously reared on English styles.

WHAT THE ENGLISH BROUGHT

The English brought several basic house types to colonial America, partly because colonists came from different parts of England, a land with considerable regional variety in architecture (Meinig 1986, 1993; Fischer 1989). But there were economic constraints too. Few colonial Americans could afford to build their dream-houses—although a good many tried and with considerable success. Given financial freedom, however, upward-striving seventeenth- and eighteenth-century Americans attempted to re-create a fashionable English house, which by early Georgian times—roughly by 1740—had fairly well settled down to one standard form with a number of close relatives (figure 2). Thus, the high-style houses of Boston looked remarkably like those of

FIGURE 2
Domestic Georgian, the American four-over-four, Sharpsburg, Maryland, mid-1960s.

New York, Philadelphia, or Baltimore. (Charleston, then the only Southern town big enough to be worth mentioning, was already an architectural deviant, presaging the political deviations which were to make the city infamous a century hence; see figures 12 and 13.)

The high-style English house of the mid-1700s was simplicity itself, in form if not decoration. Although the house's exterior resembled earlier folk forms, it was basically an academic house, derived from formal architectural designs—not an ancient derivation from folk memory. (Glassie [1975] recounts that portentous change from folk to formal design in the housing of rural Virginia.) The house was rectangular in floor plan and facade, full two stories high, with doors and windows evenly spaced both vertically and horizontally, so that from the front, the house was an exercise in classical bilateral symmetry. In New England during the 1600s the ancestral house commonly had a great central chimney, with fireplaces heading at angles into the corners of the four symmetrically placed rooms. Later on, under the aegis of formal Geor-

gian classicism, chimneys migrated to the gable ends of the house, and the symmetry was completed by a central hallway (figure 2). During the seventeenth century, gambrel roofs (as on a standard midwestern barn) were fashionable, later to be replaced with the hipped roof, beloved in Georgian Britain. But by 1750 in America, vagaries in roof style and chimney placement had disappeared; end chimneys and a gable roof had become standard. In towns, the ridgepole was always parallel to the street, and commonly the house stood immediately on the street or sidewalk with no front yard at all. As in medieval European towns, each house abutted its neighbor with no spacing between. In Baltimore, Philadelphia, Boston, and other style-setting eastern cities, they formed row houses. Windows are impossible on the sides of a row house unless one wants to look at the blank wall of an adjacent house. Significantly, when the standard Eastern row house moved into the fat southeastern Pennsylvania countryside, as it often did, the end windows did not return. Or if they did, they were of erratic size and spacing—mute testimony to the house's urban ancestry. Farmers nowadays explain the windowless gables on environmental grounds—"to keep the wind out"—or some equally plausible environmental explanation. They are wrong. As usual in such matters, the presence or absence of windows is a matter of cultural tradition, not a response to environment. There were rules about where front windows were supposed to go, but no very certain ones for the sides.

Because of its predictable floor plan, students of house types commonly call the house a "four-over-four"—a term which stresses form, as opposed to stylistic cosmetics. Architects usually call it Georgian. Real estate dealers, recognizing that nostalgia is a salable commodity, commonly call it "Colonial," which is not too far off the mark, given the house's dominant position in prenational America. But whatever it is called, the four-over-four is perhaps the most enduring house form in the annals of American domestic architecture. Unlike a host of other house types and styles which have come in and out of favor over the years, the four-over-four has been revived again and again for more than two centuries. Neo-Georgian, or some close relative thereof, is perhaps the single most common house form in middlebrow America.

In the field, the ancestral four-over-four is sometimes hard to recognize, since it frequently sprouts additions or carries embellishments which mask its basic form. Two-story wings to the rear are common, so that the floor plan changes from a rectangle into a *T* or *L*. One- and two-story porches were often built across the front. This seldom occurred in the crowded centers of the older towns, of course, since there was little or no space for a front porch where the front door opened immediately into the street, but porches became increasingly common as four-over-fours were built on the edges of towns or in the country where Americans were gradually learning that they could afford to be prodigal with space (figure 3). Conversely, in the

FIGURE 3
When the four-over-four moved to the country, it often got a porch, and in upstate New York, some Greek Revival detailing as well. Tully, New York. Source: Clayton (1878).

FIGURE 4

The two-over-two is a four-over-four with one side lopped off. When set next to adjacent neighbors, this is the basic row house of East Coast cities like Baltimore and Philadelphia. This one in New Castle, Delaware, is the same thing, but set back and detached from its neighbors. The wing at the right is an architectural afterthought and has nothing to do with the basic house form. Photograph is from the mid-1960s.

crowded town centers, the four-over-fours had one whole side lopped off and became a "two-over-two." With the center hallway shunted off to one side, the two-over-two is the common row house of America's eastern cities (figure 4).

Then, too, uncounted embellishments can mask the basic, rather prim form. The Georgian four-over-four of the late eighteenth century, for example, commonly came equipped with corbie-steps, spindled railings, Palladian windows, and other accoutrements of high-style academic design—a combination which can produce houses of striking grace and beauty (figure 5). And, as with all old American houses, a procession of architectural fads can encrust a house with layer upon layer of cosmetics—multihued asbestos siding; pillars which support nothing, but give

the house "the Mt. Vernon look"; and, of course, gingerbread of all kinds. Someday I expect to find a four-over-four equipped with flying buttresses and gargoyles. But if one learns, in the mind's eye, to strip away the cosmetics, one can recognize the four-over-four and its relatives as some of the most common early house types of the eastern United States, and a continued testament to North America's English beginnings.

Two other common colonial house types deserve mention. Popular among the less affluent was a single-pen (one-room) cabin with exterior end chimney, an obvious design found widely in England and in Europe (figure 6). It is what most Americans think of when they talk of log cabins. Unlike the four-over-four, which derived from academic architectural tradition, the single-pen

FIGURE 5
The four-over-four in full bloom of high-style Georgian elegance—academic architecture with a vengeance. The George Read House, New Castle, Delaware, ca. 1801. Photograph is from the mid-1960s.

FIGURE 6
The elemental southern folk house: a single-pen cabin with exterior chimney. This one was allegedly built of planks from a dismantled Ohio River flatboat. Near Maysville, Kentucky, early 1960s.

FIGURE 7

The dog-trot, one of the commonest folk house types in the traditional upland South, here in one of its numerous variants. Near Orangeburg, South Carolina, early 1960s.

cabin is a genuine folk house, whose form and structure originate from long-standing oral tradition. Because it originates from a nonwritten tradition (very few single-pen cabins have been designed by architects), its roots are poorly known, and because it is so common and takes so many forms, its derivation has been the subject of heated academic debate which will probably never be settled (Kniffen and Glassie 1966; Glassie 1975; Jordan 1978). In the South it was and still is the cheapest house available.

The single-pen cabin was often expanded in predictable ways. One of the most common, especially in the South, was to place two of them side by side, separated by an open space like a breezeway, and furnish them with a common roof. Huck Finn describes such a place next to the lower Mississippi River in the 1840s:

> It was a double house, and the big open place betwixt them was roofed and floored, and sometimes the table was set there in the middle of the

day, and it was a cool, comfortable place. Nothing couldn't be better. (Twain 1885, Chap. 17)

The "big open space" was seldom left open, however—more commonly enclosed to form a central hallway and the result was a dog-trot house—ubiquitous in the traditional rural country of the upland South. In deference to summer temperatures and humidity, the dog-trot was usually equipped with a full-width front porch which was sometimes an addition, but more often an integral part of the house (figure 7). Often unpainted and made of log or slabwood, the dog-trot (along with a congeries of near relatives) became a kind of architectural trademark of the traditional rural upland South. (The house is often portrayed in comics and popular journals as some kind of shack—which may account for the fact that middle-class Northerners would have nothing to do with it.) The house has almost innumerable variants, largely because it was easy to move around, add new cribs, and roof over the intervening space. Contemporary architects, if they could look beyond their prejudices, would admire the modular construction of many such houses, some of which are dignified and handsome (figure 8).

The one-room cabin evolved quite differently in New England, where front porches were unessential, but where interior space was badly needed because of large families and long, hard winters. To meet this need, seventeenth-century New Englanders enlarged the cabin to allow for two or even four rooms with a central fireplace opening into each room (thus, the great central chimney again). They also raised the roof half a story to permit conversion of the attic into living quarters, usually bedrooms. By the eighteenth century, notions of Georgian symmetry had moved the chimney to the end(s) of the house, and sometimes dormers were added to maximize the utility of upstairs space (figure 9). The house was built of wooden clapboard, since the glacial boulders of New England are hard to handle, and brick clay in that glacial country is unreliable. Wood, however, was plentiful, and by the time a century or two had passed, the New England clapboard house had stopped being mere convenience and had become cultural ne-

FIGURE 8
The cabin-and-porch is not necessarily a shack. Goliad, Texas, 1967.

cessity. A proper upcountry New England farmer would as soon have sold his daughter into slavery as he would have built a brick house. Indeed, it is not uncommon in parts of New England to find houses built partly of stone or brick, but decorously covered with wood, as a proper house

FIGURE 9
The New England one-and-a-half, here reincarnated in upstate New York. Source: McIntosh (1877).

FIGURE 10

The I-house of the Middle Atlantic and upper South. The simple exterior conceals complex folk origins. Near Snow Hill on Maryland's Eastern Shore. Photograph is from the mid-1960s.

should be, just as it later became proper to paint the house white. These simple-looking white New England cottages were much beloved of suburban real estate dealers after World War II, who added louvered shutters (green vinyl to retard spoilage), put the house on a concrete slab, and sold it to millions of veterans as "Cape Cod cottages." Others, less reverent, have called it a "Monopoly House"—after the parlor game. Fred Kniffen of Louisiana State University, who first recognized it as an important diagnostic folk house, simply called it a "one-and-a-half." It was wildly popular throughout New England and wherever New Englanders subsequently moved.

A third colonial house type is called an I-house (figure 10; the term is again Kniffen's). It looks very much like the four-over-four, except that it is only one room deep instead of two. Like the four-over-four, its ancestry is English, although its genealogy is considerably less certain than the classic academic four-over-four. Henry

Glassie thinks the house derived from folk sources in sixteenth-century Britain, although I suspect that some may have emerged in America by the juxtaposition of individual log cribs which were subsequently walled in. Either way, it was a genuine folk house and never gained quite the prestige of the four-over-four, perhaps because of its less formidable proportions, and possibly because it was too easy to build of logs and similar unfashionable materials. When the I-house came to town, however, it was often made to look like the more modish four-over-four, an easy task since from the front they look very much alike. Some are quite elegant, especially when built of the red brick so typical of the Middle Atlantic region.

In its early career in America, the I-house found widespread acceptance among well-to-do Middle Atlantic townsfolk and farmers, who took it with them when they migrated into the upper South and lower Midwest. It is still the dominant house type both in rural Delaware and in the middle Ohio Valley, both areas having been settled by people with the same cultural memories. Like the four-over-four and two-over-two, it makes a serviceable row house. And in the muggy climates of the Southeast and Ohio Valley, in the days before air-conditioning, its modest proportions and ease of ventilation have periodically made it a satisfactory prototype for a good deal of mass housing (e.g., figure 11).

Charlestonians, living in a crowded town in a subtropical marsh, found the I-house impossible. With characteristic independence and ingenuity, they adapted it neatly to meet their special needs. They began by putting the house on stilts to avoid floods on the main floor when autumn hurricanes drove tidewater over the seawall and through the city's streets. (They were probably unaware that this has long been standard practice in the tidelands of Southeast Asia and elsewhere.)

To gain ventilation during the steamy South Carolina summer, the house was detached from its neighbors and set perpendicular to the street (heresy in Pennsylvania!). Wide side porches (locally called piazzas) stood along one side of each floor and overlooked a narrow side garden. With the stilted cellar decorously enclosed, the whole house plastered with pastel stucco and dripping jasmine, the result is both picturesque and comfortable (figure 12). In the mainland United States, the "Charleston house" is unique to the immediate Charleston area, although it also occurs in colonial towns of the Bahamas and Lesser Antilles—mute testimony to Charleston's West Indian connections. It is totally absent in the inland towns of South Carolina and Georgia, a fact which strongly suggests that Carolina's queen city had less cultural impact on the antebellum South than many Charlestonians like to imagine. Like the city that adopted it, however, the house

FIGURE 11

Two-family workers' houses in a company town in the coal country of West Virginia—obviously modeled after the ubiquitous I-houses of the neighboring rural territory. The scene reflects a common phenomenon, and not just in America: mass-produced houses, deliberately designed to look like folk houses of ancient provenance.

FIGURE 12

The Charleston house, an I-house turned at right angles to the street and equipped with multistoried side porches (locally called piazzas), 1966. The main floor is elevated, Malay-style, to avoid bugs and floods. This is the charming version.

FIGURE 13

The Charleston house without architectural pretentions. The house form persists (compare figure 12), although the exterior is a bit tattered. Since 1966, when the photograph was taken, this house has been gentrified and made charming again.

is dignified, charming, and more than a little eccentric. As with so many basic house types, it can adopt a variety of architectural guises, even while its basic form remains unchanged (compare figure 13).

TRACING THE SPOOR WESTWARD

It is easy to forget that almost half of America's national history had elapsed before the Revolution, and that during that time Americans had produced fewer than four million people, who had effectively occupied only a tiny fraction of what was to become the United States. Despite small numbers and small territory, the mold of American culture had been set permanently in its English (or neo-English) cast. Nevertheless, great changes were coming, especially after Americans began to pour westward across the Appalachians.

These post-Revolutionary cultural changes are faithfully mirrored in the changing geography of American vernacular housing.

Four major tendencies are particularly conspicuous: (1) increased regional diversity in house types (and presumably culture) between the Revolution and the Civil War; (2) reversal of this divisive trend after the Civil War, and the rapid spread of national, as opposed to regional, house types (this trend was accompanied by the almost total disappearance of folk culture under a wave of mass-produced and machine-built houses); (3) prolonged isolation of the South as a distinctive architectural region, long after other regions had joined the national stream; and (4) an increased tempo of architectural innovation, paradoxically combined with an increased tendency for popular domestic architecture to look backward for historical reassurance.

INCREASED REGIONAL DIVERSITY

As long as Americans huddled close to the Atlantic Coast, they remained in close communion with England and with each other. The relative homogeneity of vernacular colonial house types bears that out, even if other historic records do not. Victory in the Revolution and the eradication of native Indian population, however, opened avenues into isolated places where innovation was prized and ties with the homeland were weak.

Had Americans kept in touch with each other as they went west, the story might have been different, but they did not. As the migrant wave swept across the Appalachians, it was deflected and funneled into three primary channels, each connected with quite a different segment of the Atlantic seaboard, each with its own distinctive architectural personality, and each increasingly unrelated to the other two.

THE THREE STREAMS

The central stream issued from southeastern Pennsylvania, with Philadelphia as its mecca and point of origin (see figure 1). When the stream encountered the mountains, it straightway split again into three parts. One headed due west along the line of the National Road for Wheeling, Zanesville, Columbus, Indianapolis, and St. Louis. A second went southwest from Pittsburgh by way of the Ohio River toward Cincinnati and Louisville, a route which did much to keep Kentucky in the Union domain during the Civil War. A third veered down the Shenandoah Valley to a series of pathways into and through the southern Appalachians. A diverging path led northwest by way of Daniel Boone's Wilderness Road through the Cumberland Gap into the fruitful Bluegrass country of central Kentucky, yet another led from the vicinity of Knoxville via the Tennessee River into the Nashville Basin. The area of Pennsylvania's influence was enormous, fanning out westward in an ever-widening swath which eventually encompassed all the Midwest except for the northernmost fringe.

If the Pennsylvanian cultural domain was extreme in size, there was nothing extreme about its architecture. Indeed, it was an area of marked conservatism. From the turn of the eighteenth century to the eve of World War I, Pennsylvanians and their western relatives south of the National Road continued ceaselessly to build I-houses and four-over-fours. Toward the middle of the nineteenth century, this southern part of the Midwest, as well as the more affluent parts of the upland South, had begun to adopt some of the less daring national forms—this three centuries after Penn had landed on the Delaware shores, and only after other parts of the country had looked upon the new forms and found them good. But Pennsylvania and the area of Pennsylvanian dominance never developed any special regional identity in house types distinct from its eastern progenitor. If architecture is any guide, Middle America is an extension of Pennsylvania, and the people of both areas were not inclined to experiment with new and outrageous things (Baltzell 1979; Elazar 1966). It may be symptomatic that the glutinous white fluff that passes for bread in the United States was probably perfected by Pennsylvanians, and disseminated from Pennsylvanian hearths. Both houses and bread were substantial, if not particularly exciting.

The South was a different matter in architecture as in so many other ways. First of all, there was no single southern stream issuing from a single point of coastal origin. Although the Virginia Tidewater probably contributed more to southern folk architecture than any other single area, lesser tributaries fed the inland current from a number of coastal points in the Carolinas, Georgia, and later on from the Gulf of Mexico. But there was no dominant southern gateway city, no metropolitan Philadelphia or Boston where cultural and architectural tradition was funneled, processed, and formalized. Charleston was an isolated island, and New Orleans was too cosmopolitan and foreign to have much impact on a largely Anglo-Saxon rural hinterland (P. Lewis 1976). Nevertheless, a subtropical climate, combined with a largely rural society, yielded a distinct mélange of house types which reflected the southern social fabric with fair accuracy.

Nowhere outside the South is historic myth further removed from the hard facts of architectural reality. Before the Civil War, the absence of a large middle class produced, on the one hand, a handful of mansions and, on the other, a vast number of folk houses—mostly elaborations of the log pen, either singly or in combination. The number of pillared mansions was vastly inflated by the crinoline mythology of Margaret Mitchell and other southern propagandists, for as Mark Twain and a good many other realists have shown, the average southern planter lived not in classical grandeur, but usually in a somewhat blown-up version of the Appalachian cabin or dog-trot. As late as 1860, serious architectural pretensions were confined mainly to coastal cities like Charleston, Savannah, and New Orleans, river towns like Nashville and Vicksburg, and a handful of inland market towns like Milledgeville and Macon. The poverty of imagination in house types of the antebellum South speaks volumes about the studied suppression of intellectual innovation there—not to mention a persistent yawning chasm between social classes. Most of the South had become Faulkner's Yoknapatawpha County, not Jefferson's Virginia—and certainly not Margaret Mitchell's Tara.

Only in New England, and in New England's mighty extension into the Mohawk Valley and the upper Midwest, can one find evidence of large-scale innovation in vernacular housing. If the architectural record has anything to tell, the tradition of the inventive Yankee is no myth, and if Crèvecoeur's New Man ever existed, he dwelt in upstate New York in the early nineteenth century. Between 1800 and 1850, the strip of territory between Albany and Buffalo sprouted more architectural ideas per capita than any other region of the country, and the innovations took all kinds of forms. No area in the United States, for example, embraced the Classical Revival with such enthusiasm, and the New York State village that had not burst forth by 1840 into Grecian elegance was poor indeed. The average county in east central New York probably had, and some still have, more high Greek Revival domestic architecture than does, say, the entire state of Alabama.

The changes were not merely stylistic, for the basic form of houses was changing too. In contrast with their staid Pennsylvanian neighbors

across the mountain divide to the south, the transplanted New Englanders of New York State invented new house types with enthusiastic abandon and planted them across the land.

The single most characteristic house—and the single most reliable evidence of New Englanders' presence in the trans-Appalachian landscape—is a type which natives of southern Michigan call the "upright-and-wing," pictured in figure 14 in one of its numberless incarnations. More than that, however, the upright-and-wing is a tangible monument to a major shift in the nature of American life and culture—an unparalleled example of house type as cultural spoor.

In its elemental form, the house looks like an unembellished classical temple with a wing attached to it—but that is only partly true. The house is indeed a conjunction of two separate parts, but, counterintuitively, it is a wing, with the temple attached later. The distinction sounds trivial, but it is not.

The idea of hitching buildings together was nothing new in New England, where folk builders had a long-standing habit of connecting farmhouses, outbuildings, and barns, sometimes in sprawling arrays of remarkable extent and complexity (figure 15). The idea of connecting barns to houses was not original with New Englanders, of course; in Europe and China connected assemblages of farm buildings and dwellings can be traced back into antiquity. But in America, the idea took special hold in an area of central and northern New England, where the linkage of buildings allowed farmers to reach outbuildings and livestock without having to wade through snowdrifts. (The story of the New England connecting barn is itself intricate and fascinating. Thomas Hubka [1984] tells the story of how it happened, and what it reveals about the evolving culture that produced it.) When New Englanders emigrated to New York State, they took the idea of the connecting barn with them—and with it a feeling of freedom about hitching buildings to one another as need or fancy dictated.

But here the plot thickens. If a Vermont Yankee moved to New York and built a traditional New England one-and-a-half (as many

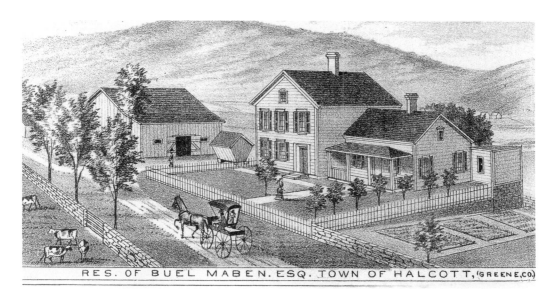

RES. OF BUEL MABEN. ESQ. TOWN OF HALCOTT, (GREENE,CO)

FIGURE 14

The upright-and-wing, the most characteristic architectural fossil left behind by migrating New Englanders. This could be anywhere between central Massachusetts and southern Minnesota but happens to be in Halcott, New York. Source: *History of Greene County, New York* (1884).

FIGURE 15

The hitching together of farmhouses, outbuildings, and barns is a long-standing New England folk practice. This is De Kalb, New York, on the north flanks of the Adirondacks, 100 miles west of Vermont. The house itself, stripped of additions, is a purebred one-and-a-half. Source: Durant and Peirce (1878).

FIGURE 16

Greek house, Yankee carpenter. A modest domestic temple, probably built about 1835. This Classical Revival house came equipped with or without pillars. What makes this house type revolutionary is that its formal face is the gable-end—just like the Parthenon. That was something new in America; heretofore, a house's ridgepole nearly always lay parallel to the road. Compare figures 2–10. Seneca, New York. Source: McIntosh (1876).

did), and then grew affluent selling wheat in the Genesee Country during the early Greek Revival (as many also did), it was common to enlarge the old house but in a totally unprecedented manner by attaching to it a newly fashionable Greek temple (figure 16). The temple, with or without pillars, was naturally placed to the front of and higher than the older, déclassé one-and-a-half. The result is an upright-and-wing, the conjunction of two architectural elements, but—and far more important—the collision and subsequent fusion of two intellectual worlds. The "wing" was a hangover from an ancient folk tradition, while the "upright," by contrast, arrived by way of formal architectural pattern books from the printing presses of Boston and New York and Philadelphia, shipped in by boats on the Erie Canal and then along the newly laid rails of the New York Central Railroad. In short, the upright-and-wing marked the arrival of the mod-

ern world in one of America's richest and fastest-changing regions. That rich, new, aggressive, future-oriented world—with its new wealth and new ideas and new technology—would soon bring ruin to the older folk culture, and the upright-and-wing marks the division between those two worlds.

So, as with most common house types, the upright-and-wing is more than mere shelter marked by a few architectural peculiarities. In its place and time it was another expression of that popular declaration of cultural independence from the strictures of tradition that New Englanders talked about incessantly in political, literary, or religious terms, but also (usually unwittingly) expressed in their domestic architecture. This independence and willingness to experiment often produced some very odd buildings in upstate New York—as it produced a host of religious and social innovations (Cross 1950). New Yorkers, moreover, like most other Americans, have been driven by a special inner demon to tinker constantly with old buildings and "improve" them, with the result that very few uprights-and-wings remain unaltered between eastern Massachusetts and southern Minnesota where the New England spoor finally fades out. But the freshness of viewpoint contrasts sharply both with the complacency of Pennsylvania and with the studied truculence of displaced Tories who settled Upper Canada (Ontario), and continued building English houses as an ostentatious symbol of allegiance to their queen and defiance of the neo-classical Yankees across the border. This difference between New Yorkers and their northern and southern neighbors also produced two of the sharpest architectural divides in North America—one drawn along the Niagara–St. Lawrence frontier, and the other through the wilds of the Appalachian Plateau in north-central Pennsylvania (figure 1; for a rich elaboration of this story, see Gowans [1992]).

But cultural streams are diluted through time, and distance weakens ties with old hearths. Like so many common houses, the upright-and-wing had been invented in response to cultural and demographic pressures, but its origins were gradually forgotten as it spread westward with the New England diaspora. What had begun as a convenient combination of modules somewhere between Boston and the Berkshires became thoroughly institutionalized in central New York, where it flowered in classical glory and—when redesigned by academic architects with proper ideas of bilateral symmetry—was equipped with double wings and a flurry of classical details (figure 17). By the time it reached central New York, people no longer viewed it as a jointure of two house types, but as a single integral unit. In northern Ohio, and across the lower Great Lakes states during the 1830s and 1840s, the upright-and-wing became the house for bankers and other people of position, who draped it with suitable Grecian finery. (Affluent New Yorkers, meantime, had turned to other forms, since, as so often happens, the fashionable house had been enthusiastically embraced by the groundling masses and hence was no longer thought suitable for people of stature [Lynes 1954].) As time passed and the upright-and-wing moved farther and farther toward the margins of settlement, its classic qualities were only dimly remembered, though the form persisted. Thus, when the fertile lands of midstate Michigan and the Willamette Valley of Oregon were opened

to settlement from the 1840s to the 1860s, the upright-and-wing was an instant fixture in most new farming towns—so common that the newly rutted streets were lined with them, and other house types were so rare as to cause comment. But this latter-day upright-and-wing—spare, gaunt, and unembellished save for a poor Gothic furbelow or two—was a distant cry from the patrician magnificence of its Mohawk Valley ancestor. Figure 18 shows one such house in a New York State backwater, built in the late nineteenth century, but there is no material difference between this and its relatives in Michigan or Oregon. New England's architectural spoor was there, but the trail had grown faint indeed.

NATIONAL STYLES AND THE DISAPPEARANCE OF FOLK HOUSES

The Civil War and the technological upheaval that accompanied the war did violence to American architectural regionalism as they did violence to so many social and economic institutions. Regionalism, after all, had fed on isolation—but isolation was dying a quick death at the hands of new telegraph lines, new railroads, and cheaply

FIGURE 17
Bucolic classic upright-and-double-wing, built sometime after 1833. This is academic design, a far cry from folk architecture. Russia, New York, just east of Utica. Source: *History of Herkimer County, New York* (1879).

FIGURE 18
Even for mere tenants, form was not violated. An elemental upright-and-wing in Hector, New York. The only classical element remaining is the name of the town. Houses like this are all over the upper Midwest. Source: Peirce and Hurd (1879).

printed books and magazines which made it possible for everybody to see what everybody else was doing. Carpenters' handbooks (figure 19), showing "the latest fashions in cottages and homes," inundated the mails, and the Era of National Style had begun. Paradoxically, America had once before possessed a "national" house type, the four-over-four, but that was when the nation was a fringe of coastal settlements along the Atlantic, hardly yet a true nation. Now, America's national houses spread almost instantly from coast to coast, across the face of a muscular optimistic nation, now of continental scale.

Traditional folk culture, of course, simply could not stand up under such an onslaught. Folk societies, after all, are dependent on stable communities, and they flourish only in places where ideas are handed down from generation to generation by oral tradition, or where builders learn their trade by long apprenticeships with a respected master. Above all, folk houses (like any folk institution) are built only in societies with reverence for the past—and where the past is the only sure guide for future behavior. That view had never been popular in America, a nation of immigrants who differed in many respects, but were unanimous in agreeing that the future would be better than the present, and regarded the past as something to be gotten rid of as soon as possible. By and large, Americans stopped building folk houses as soon as they had the knowledge and technology to do so.

Knowledge came first, and with it new architectural fads. Typically, the affluent classes were the first to seize upon new national fashions (Lynes 1954), and it was no accident that Georgian architecture first took root among the elite of Virginia and Pennsylvania and New England. And, as we have seen, the Classical Revival had the effect of erasing folk architecture in New England, starting around 1800.

Not until about 1830, however, did national architecture shift into high gear. Increasing numbers of upwardly mobile Americans, bored with classical architecture, happily embraced the new Gothic Revival forms that were coming out of England and were popularized in America by Andrew Jackson Downing and others. The impact of Gothic Revival architecture was fairly limited in geographic extent, but its intellectual impact was profound, for it ushered in the idea that architectural styles were transitory and could be adopted or rejected at moment's notice. No longer was architectural style an eternal verity. Downing, of course, did not call the Gothic Revival a "fad." Instead, Downing and others advanced the argument that Greek and Roman architecture was pagan, and quite unsuited to the United States, a Christian country. And what architectural style could possibly be more Christian than Gothic Revival, with its steeply-pitched dormers topped by finials and lightning rods pointing toward heaven?

But the first truly nationwide architectural fad was the Tuscan or Italianate villa (figure 20), a cubical affair entirely different from the low-slung Greek temples which they had replaced. New Yorkers, typically, adopted the new style with special enthusiasm, as a continuance of that curious Anglo-Yankee fondness for things Mediterranean. The Italianate craze was only the first of many to sweep the country. The paint was scarcely dry on the new Tuscan houses and the iron deer still shiny on their pedestals when new revivals came to supplant the old—now Romanesque, now Second Empire, now Colonial (again), or occasionally even Egyptian or Japanese. Finally, toward the end of the century, appeared the Revival of Revivals, the grandiloquently named "Picturesque Eclectic" (alias Queen Anne)—which simply meant that architects felt free to combine shapes and textures from all sources, stick them all on the same house, the more the merrier (figure 21). Barnegat, New Jersey, and Findlay, Ohio, are full of Queen Anne houses, and so are most other towns in America that prospered during the 1890s and 1900s. So, when San Francisco rose from the ashes of earthquake and fire in 1906, the new city was overwhelmingly built in Queen Anne style, locally called Victorian. Until re-

cently, it was fashionable to think them ugly; more recently they became "camp"; and now they are antiques—which means that more and more of them are safe from the wrecker's ball. Starting about ten years ago, affluent suburbanites discovered that they can get plans for a brand-new Queen Anne house and have it built anywhere in the country. The 1980s and 1990s suburbs of Dallas and Houston are full of them.

But the original Picturesque Eclectic went the way of its predecessors, laid low by the righteous arrows of new troops of architectural critics, who loudly excoriated the sins of previous periods and proclaimed new architectural Zions. Paradise never came, of course, though Americans continued to seek it, simultaneously looking nervously over their collective shoulders to ensure that the New Jerusalem was not too different from the Old, but with enduring faith that the

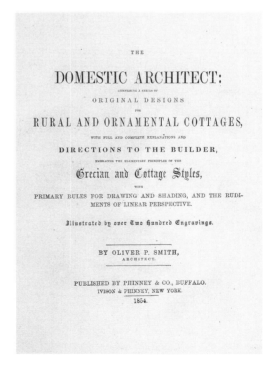

FIGURE 19

Title page from a fairly typical carpenter's handbook of the mid-nineteenth century. Such books were essential to the spread of national house types, as well as all sorts of other ideas. They spelled doom for folk culture.

RESIDENCE of HENRY G. REID, M.D. WESTERNVILLE, ONEIDA C° N.Y.   LITH BY L H EVERTS PHILA

FIGURE 20
The elementary form of the flat-roofed Italianate, alias Tuscan, villa—America's first national house. Westernville, New York, but it could be almost anywhere outside the South. The flat roof may have worked in sunny Italy, but was a disaster in the snowbelt of upstate New York. Source: Durant (1878).

next style would surely be happier and more virtuous than the one before.

THE ALIENATION OF THE SOUTH

The South was the only region that did not immediately join the national architectural mainstream, just as it failed to rejoin the nation in so many other important ways. There were several reasons: poverty, which discouraged the building of high-style houses for several decades after the Civil War; poor communications, which kept the still-rural South ignorant of what the rest of America was doing; and the carefully nourished postbellum resentment which fanned the flames of regional self-consciousness by rejecting anything national and hence Northern. (Northern tastemakers, in turn, dismissed or ignored the South on grounds that it was a cultural backwater—a view still held by a fair number of provincial Yankees.) Whatever the reason, southern do-

mestic architecture continued to differ from the rest of the country's—as late as World War II in cities, and still later in rural areas.

It is quite possible therefore to mark the boundaries of that old southern culture area merely by demarking the geographic limit of two or three characteristic house types. The dog-trot, barely altered since colonial times, is one of them. Another is the shotgun house, a low, narrow one-story affair with gable facing the street (figure 22). The shotgun is a house of simple appearance, and was often built of extremely cheap materials—as workers' houses on sugar plantations or as company houses in upcountry mill towns—commonly for the poorest and most marginalized people, usually black. (A map of shotgun houses in a prototypical southern town is a surrogate for a map of its poor.) The simple appearance of the shotgun, however, is deceptive. Its lineage is ancient—according to Vlach (1976, 47) "at least to the sixteenth century."

Vlach makes a convincing case that the shotgun derived from African sources, brought to New Orleans and the lower Mississippi Valley (where it occurs in greatest density) by freedmen from Haiti, whence it can be traced to Yoruba slave traders in west Africa. To complicate the story still further, the shotgun was adopted in two different forms by mass builders of industrial housing in America. One variant was produced by up-scale New Orleans builders, who endowed the shotgun with Victorian gimcracks and sold it to affluent whites to be built on narrow, expensive city lots. The other became the prototype for cheap mass-produced workers' housing on plantations and upcountry mill towns. (I have seen shotguns as far north as the Ohio Valley of southern Indiana.) Vlach (1976, 49) remarks that the story of the shotgun is "murky and difficult to comprehend," which is simply saying what is true of many common houses. Houses may be cultural spoor, but the spoor is rarely simple or easy to follow.

In the lexicon of southern regional architecture, however, one of the most distinctive features is not strictly a house type at all, but rather a roof style which might be called "Southern py-

FIGURE 21

An early version of the Picturesque Eclectic mode, also known as "Queen Anne." The creator of this Syracuse, New York, house was obviously a bellwether of fashion; by 1890, Queen Anne architecture was all over the country. Source: Clayton (1878).

FIGURE 22

Shotgun house, Baton Rouge, Louisiana, 1970s. The simple exterior conceals very complicated antecedents, perhaps Indian, perhaps African. Endemic in poor parts of the South, especially the lower Mississippi Valley. Photograph courtesy of Sam Hilliard.

ramidal." Almost any kind of Southern house can be made pyramidal, anything from an elemental one-floor box (figure 23) to extreme forms with a veritable haystack of interlocking pyramids, facets, and dormers—enough to dazzle the most sophisticated Yazoo Euclid (figure 24).

Charles Whebell, an Ontario geographer, has described to me similar pyramidal-roofed houses in Australia, and suggests that the form might properly be called a "British Empire" house, rather than simply Southern. Whebell may be right, for much British Colonial architecture, as in the American South, was planted during Georgian times when everybody who was anybody had a house with a hipped or pyramidal roof. Then too, the South often has clung to British ways (whether real or imaginary seems to make little difference), perhaps because its economic links were traditionally so strongly forged to England, perhaps because it received so few immigrants and ideas from outside the British

Isles, or perhaps, as in parts of Canada, merely to declare its independence from Yankee domination (Gowans 1992). But in the United States the pyramidal house is mainly Southern, and especially southeastern. If, as often happens, the house is ringed by ample porches (figure 25), there is no single domestic house type that is more easily recognized or more truly typical of the South.

NEW NATIONAL PATTERNS OF COMMON HOUSES

Outside the South, architectural regionalism was fast disappearing during the last half of the nineteenth century, signaling the rapid decline of American sectionalism after the Civil War. For some students of architectural geography, the rise of National Style was cause for mourning, producing a lamentable loss in regional character. Some have even taken the position that the study of post-1865 vernacular housing is a waste of

FIGURE 23
Southern pyramidal, elemental versions. Coal country near Carbondale, Illinois. Southern Illinois is farther south than many realize.

FIGURE 24
Southern pyramidal elaborated. Dothan, Alabama.

FIGURE 25
Southern pyramidal, comfortable version. Bainbridge, Georgia.

time, arguing that modern America has all of the regional architectural texture of a warm vanilla milk shake.

This view is simply wrong, for the texture was not lost. It merely changed in location and in scale. Architectural variety moved from rural areas into the cities. It was a matter of timing, for just as domestic housing styles had become national, changing modishly from decade to decade, American cities had begun to burst at the seams, so that urban areas were growing just as fast as our architectural fads were changing. It was not a coincidence, of course; both the urban and the architectural explosions were ignited by the same tinder. As a result, America developed a whole new set of architectural regions, no longer drawn in great east-west swaths across the rural countryside, but rather developing as incremental growth rings around America's cities. Each new ring had a different size, shape, and architectural quality than the one before, depending on the time and rate at which the city grew. Sometimes, when a city failed to grow, a

whole ring would be missing—as in a tree that has survived a forest fire. But because nineteenth- and twentieth-century styles can be dated with great precision in most parts of the country, one can walk through the streets of an ordinary American city as one would walk the aisles of a well-ordered and richly endowed museum of cultural history. Even amateurs, if they learn to recognize and date a few elemental architectural forms and then use their eyes intelligently, can make some fairly accurate estimates about when a particular city grew and when it languished, and even speculate about the kind of people who lived there. It is a fascinating and instructive way to look at American cities.

When this essay was first written in the late 1960s, the final paragraph began like this:

The riches of American folk architecture have only been sampled by serious scholars as yet, and the genetic study of America's common architecture is currently in about the state that geology was in the early nineteenth century: 50 percent intelligent guesswork, 40 percent mythology, and the remaining 10 percent split between alchemy and hard facts.

Happily, that state of affairs has changed dramatically. Over the last two decades or so, as historians and geographers have paid more and more attention to ordinary people in ordinary places, there has been an outpouring of books and articles about American folk and vernacular architecture, some of them very good. For the budding student of the subject, the bibliographies in McAlester and McAlester (1984) and Gowans (1992) are good places to begin the search. To make things even better, the ranks of architectural historians—who previously turned up their noses at anything but the most elevated of up-scale architecture—have been swelled by scholars who are paying close attention to vernacular architecture as well. Some of them have joined together in a small but energetic organization, the Vernacular Architecture Forum, which meets annually and publishes its proceedings and newsletter on a regular basis (Vernacular Architecture Forum 1982, 1986, 1989, 1991). Unlike many of the old-fashioned architectural historians, this new breed of architectural historians and geographers is keenly aware of the relationship between the design of dwellings and the social milieu within which that design occurs. It is no longer news, apparently, that common houses are cultural spoor.

Thus, the final sentences of the original paper can stand unchanged:

> For the ardent and curious student who enjoys the prospect of hacking out fresh academic trails, most of a continent awaits exploration. For if you want to know who we are—as W. S. Gilbert put it in another context—one of the best ways is to find out who we were. Looking at common old houses and asking questions about them are good ways to begin.

SOURCE

The first version of this essay appeared under the title "The Geography of Old Houses," which originally appeared in the February 1970 issue of *Earth and Mineral Sciences* 39 (5): 33–37. An enlarged and updated version appeared in 1975 as "Common Houses, Cultural Spoor" in *Landscape* 19 (2): 1–22. The present essay is an updated version of the *Landscape* paper. All illustrations are by the author except where noted.

ACKNOWLEDGMENTS

I have been chasing old American houses for a long time. I have special fondness for the upright-and-wing, which has taught me more than any other material artifact. I first knew it as a child in southern Michigan, where my uncle lived in one. It was in the early 1960s, shortly after coming to Penn State, that I discovered through random traveling that the upright-and-wing was endemic in upstate New York but absent in the Pennsylvania culture region—a fact corroborated by Fred Kniffen's seminal paper on folk houses in 1965. It was Kniffen who taught me that looking at houses was a respectable intellectual enterprise—something that was often hard to know in the mid-1960s, when would-be leaders of academic geography were denigrating fieldwork and urging young geographers to become mathematical scientists. I spent the sabbatical year of 1968–69 crisscrossing the back roads of New England and New York State, mapping the geographical distribution of the upright-and-wing and trying to find its origins. That search brought home to me the powerful truth that houses are more than mere architecture—more than mere shelter—but had the capacity to reveal and illustrate large truths about the evolution of human culture. I also discovered that material objects raise questions that are not likely to be raised by library research and that primary data do not necessarily come from published documents, but from the world itself. That discovery was not original with me, but that scarcely mattered. As I began to untangle the meaning of the upright-and-wing, I felt as if our cultural forebears were speaking to me through the material objects that they had left behind them. The lesson came as a blinding revelation: that landscape mattered, because history mattered. Not surprisingly, I found that others were pursuing similar questions, and in that common search I made the acquaintance of scholars who are among my closest and dearest friends in American geography—Fred Kniffen, Henry Glassie, Sam Hilliard, Jim Parsons, and John Brinckerhoff Jackson. Throughout my wanderings, my colleague Wilbur Zelinsky was an ever-present source of intellectual aid and comfort. And surely one of the happiest accidents of my personal and intellectual life was meeting Donald Meinig, a co-conspirator in trying to decipher the language of the upstate New York landscape, as well as innumerable other matters, both physical and metaphysical. There are many others, of course, and I owe them a debt that I can never repay. But it is my father to whom I owe the most in this wonderful and ceaseless quest. He was a man with a puppy-dog curiosity and effervescent enthusiasm for the ordinary things and ordinary people in the world around him who never failed to stop and look and wonder and talk about what he saw—and then wanted to see more, and think and talk about that, too. He, above all others, by precept and example taught me the joys of looking at the material world around me and trying to make sense of it—in short, to use my eyes and attach them to my brain. As a child, I thought it was a wonderful message—and I still do.

NOTE

1. Just as the form of a house is culturally significant, so is color. Although it is easy to change the color of a house, and thus adapt oneself to the latest fashions, there is still some pleasant variety in the geography of house coloring. In New England, colored paints were available quite early, made from native linseed oil and turpentine, mixed with imported pigments—ocher, white or red lead, and the like. In lean early times, paint was usually omitted altogether, but a Yankee could theoretically paint his house almost any color he liked. In point of fact, New Englanders overwhelmingly liked white. It was the proper color for a proper house. So, also, red brick, painted red, is a hallmark of Middle Atlantic culture. (This is not a matter of perversity; the coat of paint helped preserve the bricks from weathering, a serious hazard when bricks are fired at low and unpredictable temperatures.) Unpainted log and plank was once the chromatic trademark of the South, but that is now almost gone, the result of affluence, national advertising, and color television. Most exuberant of all are the French Canadians, who have their

own domestic version of the tricolor—not *bleu-blanc-rouge,* of course, but turquoise, canary yellow, and flamingo, usually applied to separate houses, but sometimes enthusiastically juxtaposed on the same building. The results are arresting. Unimaginative visitors from Ontario and the United States find the combination takes some getting used to, but it doubtless provides relief during the hard St. Lawrence winter. This is not yet the blandest of all possible worlds.

Since I wrote this, I have discussed the matter of color with Alan Gowans, who has probably looked critically at more houses in the U.S. and Canada than any other serious scholar has. Gowans opines that the two countries had their national tastes imprinted at different times—each in its early stage of national self-definition—and the result is a different palette of acceptable colors for both domestic and public buildings. The United States was imprinted shortly after independence, when the Classical Revival was riding high, and the U.S. taste for gleaming white houses has never disappeared—although it has faltered from time to time. Canada, Gowans avers, was imprinted after confederation in the last third of the nineteenth century, when Victorian polychrome was all the rage. Whether Gowans is right or not, it is an indisputable fact that American and Canadian suburbs do not look the same. The facade of the average American tract house is likely to be painted white, or some other acceptable colonial hue endorsed by the designers of Williamsburg. The facade of a similar middle-class Canadian tract house is much busier, both in color and texture—not a pale American wash, but a rich pastiche of colors and textures. If the reader remains skeptical, I commend a day's excursion to southern Ontario, and a quick tour of a Detroit suburb followed by a tour of an equivalent suburb of Windsor. The differences are very obvious, and should gladden Canadians who worry that their national identity is being lost in a sea of Americanism.

FURTHER READINGS

Edward Digby Baltzell. 1979. *Puritan Boston and Quaker Philadelphia: Two Protestant ethics and the spirit of class authority and leadership.* New York: Free Press.

Baltzell provides a magisterial study of the social and religious roots of cultural differences between the leaders of New England and Pennsylvania. For anyone interested in why New England produced generations of preachers, reformers, and learned literati, while Pennsylvania yielded union-bashing industrialists and James Buchanan, this is must reading.

Daniel J. Elazar. 1966. *American federalism: A view from the states.* New York: Crowell.

Buried in this disorderly book is Elazar's provocative discussion of three American political cultures (traditionalistic, moralistic, individualistic), which, regionally, bear strong resemblance to the architectural patterns described in the present essay (South, New England, Pennsylvania). Elazar, in combination with Baltzell, goes a long way toward explaining the basic differences in the cultural geography of the eastern United States.

David H. Fischer. 1989. *Albion's seed: Four British folkways in America.* New York: Oxford University Press.

This lengthy volume attempts an exhaustive enumeration of the cultural traits that were transferred from British source regions to the major cultural hearths of the eastern United States.

Henry Glassie. 1975. *Folk housing in middle Virginia: A structural analysis of historic artifacts.* Knoxville: University of Tennessee Press.

Glassie is a deeply thoughtful and perceptive student of material culture, how it came to be and what it means. In this brilliant but difficult book, Glassie wrestles with the epistemological question of how a contemporary scholar can get inside the mind of a folk builder who passed from the scene long ago. A good part of the book is a painstaking exercise in historical semiotics, but the last chapter, "A Bit of History," is a clear-eyed evaluation of just how far one can push scientific method in such matters. Most powerful of all, the chapter contains the fearful story of a folk culture being dragged unwillingly into the modern world and smashed, as well as the material evidence that supports the story.

———. 1982. *Passing the time in Ballymenone: Culture and history of an Ulster community.* Philadelphia: University of Pennsylvania Press.

This brilliant and moving portrait of folk life in an Irish border village is a model for the humane study of how culture and material things interact, among many other things.

Alan Gowans. 1986. *The comfortable house: North American suburban architecture, 1890–1930.* Cambridge: MIT Press.

Gowans gives us a careful but lively treatment of a much neglected chapter in the history of ordinary American domestic architecture.

———. 1992. *Styles and types of North American architecture: Social function and cultural expression.* New York: Icon Editions.

This is perhaps the best architectural history of North America. Gowans, a naturalized American born and reared in Canada, understands the subtle and not-so-subtle differences and similarities between the two countries and how architecture reflects them. Unlike most architectural historians, he treats high-style and vernacular forms with an even hand. Gowans, a learned and witty

man, recounts more than just a sequence of architectural events. This is a richly detailed tapestry of North American culture.

Thomas C. Hubka. 1984. *Big house, little house, back house, barn: The connected farm buildings of New England.* Hanover, N.H.: University Press of New England.

An exemplary study of how the New England connecting barn came to be and what an apparently minor architectural element reveals about underlying patterns in the currents of culture.

John C. Hudson. 1988. North American origins of middlewestern frontier populations. *Annals of the Association of American Geographers* 78:395–413.

Hudson has established the migration paths of large numbers of trans-Appalachian settlers, based on scrutiny of innumerable county histories from the mid-nineteenth century. Hudson's maps display migration paths that look like those discovered earlier by Kniffen, Glassie, and others, but are much more detailed. Hudson argues that scholars need not look at old houses to discover historic migration paths, which may or may not be true, but doesn't stress the point that landscape is a clue to all kinds of things. Hudson's distinguished record of painstaking fieldwork is apparent in this outstanding piece of scholarship.

Fred B. Kniffen. 1965. Folk housing: Key to diffusion. *Annals of the Association of American Geographers* 55:549–77.

The word *seminal* applies to this essay with a vengeance. In this presidential address to the Association of American Geographers, the father of American house type studies lays out the basic premises of his research, based on a lifetime of field work and scholarship. This is must reading for anyone seriously interested in the evolution of American material culture.

———. 1990. *Cultural diffusion and landscapes: Selections by Fred B. Kniffen.* Ed. Jesse H. Walker and Randall A. Detro. Geoscience and Man no. 27. Baton Rouge: Louisiana State University, Department of Geography and Anthropology.

This collection of essays provides a good indication of Kniffen's influence on cultural geography, particularly the notions of diffusion of house types and material culture.

Fred B. Kniffen and Henry Glassie. 1966. Building in wood in the eastern United States: A time-place perspective. *Geographical Review* 56:40–66.

This early collaboration between Kniffen and Glassie traces the westward movement of American folk woodworking technology. The line of thought in this essay presages Glassie's later and more elaborate *Folk Housing in middle Virginia* (1975).

Peirce Lewis. 1972. Small town in Pennsylvania. *Annals of the Association of American Geographers* 62:323–51.

The cultural geography of a fairly typical American small town, and how it came to be seen in a national context of geographic change over two centuries. Urban landscape is an important part of the story.

———. 1983. Learning from looking: Geographic and other writing about the American cultural landscape. *American Quarterly* 35:242–61.

This article contains both biographic sketches of the progenitors of landscape study in the United States and a simple model of how common landscapes are made. The bulk of the essay is a broad review of the literature about the American cultural landscape.

Russell Lynes. 1954. *The tastemakers: The shaping of American popular taste.* New York: Harper.

This is the first and still lively account of how high-style taste trickles down through the social hierarchy, leaving behind traceable class differences in architecture and other domestic accoutrements. It is social theory with no fuss and feathers.

Virginia McAlester and Lee McAlester. 1984. *A field guide to American houses.* New York: Knopf.

The McAlesters have given us the best guide to American house types and architectural styles in print, and the essential primer for anyone seriously interested in reading the American architectural landscape. The book is an excellent directory of both high-style forms and common architectural forms and contains a wealth of photos and line drawings to explain and define the architect's often arcane vocabulary. Like most architectural guides, alas, the McAlesters' excellent book pays little attention to systematic geographic differences in architectural form or style.

Vernacular Architecture Forum. 1982, 1986, 1989, 1991. *Perspectives in Vernacular Architecture* 1–4. Columbia: University of Missouri Press.

These volumes are highly eclectic collections of essays on ordinary American buildings. VAF is a prolific, lively assemblage of scholars from diverse disciplines who share an interest in vernacular architecure. VAF regularly publishes extensive and useful bibliographies, as well as regular commentary on new literature. See *Vernacular Architecture News,* Vernacular Architecture Forum: 109 Brandon Road, Baltimore, Md. 21212.

DONALD W. MEINIG **8**

AMERICAN WESTS: PREFACE TO A GEOGRAPHICAL INTERPRETATION

The four cardinal points—north, south, east, and west—are heavily charged with meaning in the American regional consciousness. Such terms do not denote simple grand quarters of the contiguous national territory but rather are used most commonly as pairs—North and South, East and West—referring to vaguely defined "halves" existing in some degree of contrast and tension. At times this set becomes a triad, in which a South and a West are seen as existing in some degree of subservience to a North/East long dominant in political, economic, and social power.

That such regional (or sectional, to use Turner's term) concepts are deeply imprinted in the American mind is attested to by everyday conversation and reporting as well as an enormous literature. That such concepts have received relatively little attention from American geographers, whose field most centrally embraces the intellectual concept of regionalism, may seem rather surprising. Yet this paradox is not really puzzling. For North, South, East, and West, however combined, form only the largest possible set of national regions, the crudest, most vaguely delimited areal frame of reference. It is really not very surprising that those who are especially trained to look intently at areal patterns are more impressed with the complexities lurking beneath such gross terms and therefore have concentrated most of their efforts at quite a different scale of regional investigation. Thus the American West, a world-famous area which has fostered a huge volume of interpretive literature, has been of little concern as a region, as a single unit in a twofold or threefold national set, to American geographers. In the main body of that literature this famous West is generally synonymous with the Frontier and thus is less a place than a process, the realm of a great influential recurring American experience. It is a powerful symbol within the national mythology, but as soon as we attempt to connect symbol with substance, to assess the relationships between the West as a place in the imagination and the West as a piece of the American continent, we are confronted with great variation from place to place. Thus geographers have said little about the West as *a* region, but a good deal about the West as a *set* of regions. The purpose of this paper is to suggest that they could yet say a great deal more, and do so in a way that might involve them much more effectively in the larger, persistent, and important task of national interpretation.

Given the marked variations within the American West, it is rather surprising that in all that interpretive literature there is no well-developed view of the West as a set of dynamic regions. The standard geographies offer several sets of regions, each set offering a consistent comprehensive coverage of the West. But most of these are grounded upon the framework of nature, within which certain patterns of population distribution, land use, and trafficways are apparent. The result is a useful view of the West as a set of regional environments and basic economies but with little historical explication of how these human patterns came to be. On the other hand, the standard histories tend to be strongly Turnerian, recognizing specific regions (though usually but vaguely delimited) but concerned more with national impact than individual character. Thus these treatments are strongly episodic and do not offer anything approaching the continuous developmental history of each region as part of a larger developing West. There are of course more comprehensive histories of individual states and of regions at various scales, but in total these prove a jumble of parts which cannot simply be fitted together to form a whole. Indeed histo-

rians of the West have been discussing extensively among themselves the lack of encompassing theories and the need to find new approaches and schemes in the search for more penetrating interpretations.[1]

It is important at the outset to distinguish between two possible views of the West as a set of dynamic regions. On the one hand is the West as the Frontier, shifting in specific area in conjunction with the sequential expansion of the nation. In this view the inland reaches of the seaboard colonies, Transappalachia, the Mississippi Valley, the Plains and Mountains, the Pacific Slope were each the "West" during a particular phase of American development. In such a usage "West" is a generic term referring to a specific *type* of area within a dynamic national context. On the other hand, there is the concept of the West as a specific "half" of the nation in apposition to the East, a huge area displaying some persisting basis of identity.

This paper is concerned only with this latter view. That means that we are dealing with the area which emerged as the "New West" or the "Far West" in the 1870s and 1880s. Such terms were coined to distinguish it from the older "West," which now increasingly became identified as the "Middle West." It was the area which lay westward of what were then considered the potential limits of contiguous extension of typical American farm settlement, that is, country inaccessible to the direct expansion of Middle Western or Southern agricultures. Broadly, it remains the area which is most generally considered as the West yet today.

SCHEME

Some basic differences between East and West were readily apparent during the emergence of the West as a distinct realm: the marked contrasts in physical environments; the differences in peoples, the West being the country of Indians, Mexicans, Mormons, and of gold rush, cowboy, and other tumultuous frontier societies; and the differences in the overall settlement pattern, Western settlement having a clear insular character, each of the several main areas being isolated by great distances and inhospitable country from its nearest neighbors. These features were very generally perceived and emphasized even if only vaguely or confusedly understood at the time. Such characteristics offer clues for the formulation of a systematic comprehensive view of the West as a set of dynamic regions. Contrary to the popular emphasis of the time and to a later strong tradition in American geography, this proposed view emphasizes the insular pattern of colonizations more than the strong physical contrasts. For a retrospective look at the spatial character of American development does reveal a noticeable contrast in evolving patterns between East and West. Although folk colonization is always selective and uneven in area, in the East the general tide of settlement was relatively comprehensive and local nuclei and salients in the vanguard were soon engulfed and integrated into a generally contiguous pattern. Obviously such a description rests upon a particular scale of observation, but holding to the same scale, the pattern in the West is a marked contrast: several distinct major nuclei so widely separated from one another and so far removed from the advancing front of the East that each expands as a kind of discrete unit for several decades, only gradually becoming linked together and more closely integrated into the main functional systems of the nation. If we then add important dimensions of culture and environment to these nuclei we have the basis for a hypothetical scheme (figure 1), in which each Western area is viewed as passing through four general phases of development as expressed in four general categories: population (numbers and areal distribution), circulation (traffic patterns within and between regions), political areas (basic jurisdictional territories), and culture (selected features characteristic of the local society and its imprint upon the area).[2]

The remainder of this paper is a sketch of the principal specific features in the American West associated with this model of historical geographical change.

MAJOR NUCLEI (STAGES I AND II)

HISPANO NEW MEXICO

The first nucleus of European settlement in the American West was established by the Spanish in the upper Rio Grande Valley at the end of the sixteenth century. The process displayed a number of features common to many imperial movements: conquest of the richest and most densely populated areas, the founding of a new capital city, and the establishment of new towns alongside native settlements; the extraction of wealth from the labor of the native population, and the introduction of new technology and economic systems which greatly altered the resource potential; the emergence of a new "mixed" population, and the concomitant development of a class-structured plural society with chronic ethnic tensions; the abrupt imposition of new culture patterns upon the native population and the subsequent emergence of numerous cultural changes in the whole population arising from the imperial character of the society.

The Spanish superimposed themselves upon the entire Rio Grande Pueblo area of village agriculturists. Santa Fe was founded as a capital pivotal to important populations and security areas, and a number of other formal towns were laid out. The introduction of sheep, cattle, horses, burros, and mules enlarged the resource possibilities of this semiarid region and provided the main basis for settlement expansion carried out by the mestizo population, which emerged as much the largest of the several peoples in the area. These "Hispanos" were a Spanish-speaking, Roman Catholic, peasant, and pastoral people living in close-knit communities structured on strong kinship and patronal relationships. The Pueblo Indians survived the heavy impact of this long imperial experience greatly reduced in numbers and area but basically intact as a general culture and as locally autonomous societies. Some of the peripheral Indian groups were significantly altered. The Navajo were transformed from a minor Apache band into a vigorous pastoral society with a strong sense of identity as a distinct people. Some other Apache bands were invigorated by the greatly enlarged social and economic returns from plundering the imperial frontiers.

For two and a half centuries New Mexico was one of the most isolated regions of European culture. Annual or less frequent caravans to Chihuahua long provided the only link with the civilized

Population

Stage

I — implantation of a nucleus of settlement by migrants attracted by special environmental qualities (resources, refuge, exploitable indigenes).

II — expansion of settlement to the limit of land exploitable with available technology; the completion of the "frontier" phase of "free" land readily available.

III — competition for development from other peoples along bordering zones; influx of new migrants, especially into new industrial and commercial districts.

IV — metropolitanization; population largely urban and suburban; commuting range brings most of the area within close contact of center; high mobility of population, much interregional contact and movement.

fonda

Circulation

Stage

I — isolation; seasonal inflow of people; outflow only of high-valued, low bulk, or self-propelled products; pack trains, wagons, stages; interregional communications infrequent.

II — regional system; emergence of central places linked to regional capital; export of a few primary products; first railroads, improved roads, riverboats, first transcontinental railroad and telegraph connections.

III — interregional network; elaboration of central place system and regional linkages; integral part of nationwide systems; variety of transport and communication systems; railroads, interurban electrics, paved highways, buses, trucks, first airlines, telephones, radio.

IV — inter-metropolitan national network; elaborate metropolitan freeway system; non-stop air service to national and international centers; superhighways, unit trains, products pipelines; television.

fonda

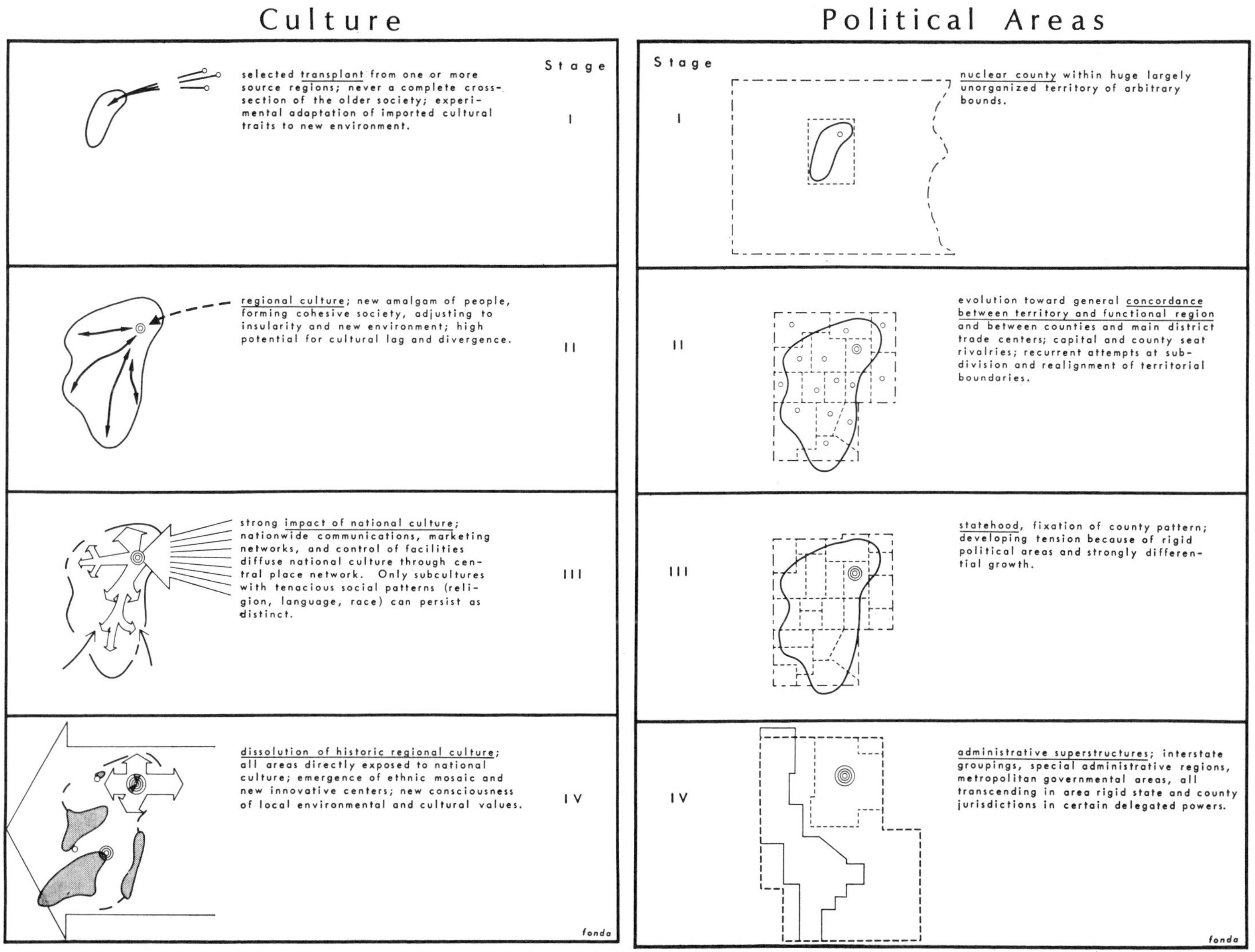

Political Areas

Political Areas

Stage

I — nuclear county within huge largely unorganized territory of arbitrary bounds.

II — evolution toward general concordance between territory and functional region and between counties and main district trade centers; capital and county seat rivalries; recurrent attempts at subdivision and realignment of territorial boundaries.

III — statehood, fixation of county pattern; developing tension because of rigid political areas and strongly differential growth.

IV — administrative superstructure; interstate groupings, special administrative regions, metropolitan governmental areas, all transcending in area rigid state and county jurisdictions in certain delegated powers.

fonda

Culture

Stage

I — selected transplant from one or more source region; never a complete cross-section of the older society; experimental adaptation of imported cultural traits to new environment.

II — regional culture; new amalgam of people, forming cohesive society, adjusting to insularity and new environment; high potential for cultural lag and divergence.

III — strong impact of national culture; nationwide communications, marketing networks, and control of facilities diffuse national culture through central place network. Only subcultures with tenacious social patterns (religion, language, race) can persist as distinct.

IV — dissolution of historic regional culture; all areas directly exposed to national culture; emergence of ethnic mosaic and new innovative centers; new consciousness of local environmental and cultural values.

fonda

FIGURE 1

Regional development within a national context through four stages: circulation, population, culture, and political areas.

world. Under Mexican rule two new routes, the Santa Fe wagon road to Missouri and the droving trail from Los Angeles, somewhat mitigated the isolation but did not alter the insular character of the region. Such isolation over so long a time favored divergence from the mother culture, a feature most notably expressed in religion (i.e., the Penitentes).

American conquest initiated a new imperialism. The "Anglos" superimposed their polity and began to intrude into every important sector. Santa Fe was retained as the capital, but new Anglo facilities and at times whole new towns were established alongside those of the Hispanos. In the 1880s the railroads opened up greater economic possibilities and a considerably elaborated regional commercial system emerged, focused upon Las Vegas, Santa Fe, and Albuquerque and gathering from all but southernmost New Mexico. Wool and minerals were the principal regional exports exchanged for the manufactures ordered through the wholesale houses of Kansas City, St. Louis, and Chicago.

The strong outward extension of the Hispano domain, initiated in late Spanish times, continued to about 1880, when it was halted by competitive expansions of Anglos from surrounding regions. Within that domain the Hispanos were numerically dominant, but were steadily declining in proportion to the number of Anglos. The Pueblo Indians were a relatively stable population, and each town and its immediately adjacent lands were enclosed within federal reserves. The nomadic Indians had been ruthlessly reduced to small remnants and confined to large reserves of unwanted lands on the periphery of the region.

Thus by the late nineteenth century, New Mexico was a functionally coherent provincial system in a complex plural culture area, with only limited commercial and cultural bonds to the national system.

THE MORMON REGION

In 1847 the nucleus of a highly distinctive Western region was implanted in the Wasatch Oasis. The Mormons were a refugee population of unusual cohesion, originally formed by adult conversion to a common faith, unified under charismatic leadership, hardened by persecution,

selected by the harsh experiences of expulsion and migration, sustained by the continuous addition of new converts, and powered by a strong faith in themselves as God's elected people.

Brigham Young, a powerful leader of great practical vision, undertook to create a vast Mormon commonwealth embracing a large part of the Far West. Although unable to sustain the original frame of this Deseret, the Mormons did spread north and south of their Salt Lake Valley nucleus until they had settled most of the habitable valleys from the upper Snake River to the Colorado and far east and west into the deserts and mountains. Most of that colonization was accomplished under some degree of formal direction by the church hierarchy and was in the form of village settlements surrounded by privately owned fields with some communal use of scarce resources. Agriculture was by irrigation, to these people a wholly new, empirical development. The church fostered numerous economic activities aimed at maximizing the self-sufficiency of the Mormon region.

In the 1880s the momentum of that great colonization program waned as along every front Mormons encountered colonists from bordering regions and the church leadership came under severe federal harassment. The Mormons were long a suspect people, widely regarded in America as politically and socially dangerous. In the late 1850s the federal government sent an army to occupy Utah to quell a supposedly recalcitrant people and to protect the interests of the non-Mormon minority ("Gentiles" in Mormon parlance) which had entered Utah in the wake of the early Mormon colonization. The military posts overlooking the valley oases were thus typical landscape symbols of an imperial relationship. Furthermore, the Mormon practice of polygamy was regarded as a shocking departure from accepted American mores and produced wide popular support for its absolute suppression by the national government. The capitulation of the Mormon church on that issue in 1890 after severe persecution by federal authorities was not untypical of the cultural conformity forced upon occupied peoples by imperial powers.

The mineral wealth in the Wasatch region and the strategic location of Salt Lake City and

Ogden with reference to the whole Far West sustained a growing Gentile population, concentrated in these main commercial centers, the mining and smelting districts, and the railroad towns. The rural areas remained almost entirely Mormon. The two peoples were latently antagonistic, ever conscious of their differences, and thus a plural society developed which was peculiar to the region and little understood beyond. Salt Lake City, a focus of unusual power combining political, ecclesiastical, and commercial functions, was the main point of encounter and tension between the region and the nation. Although crossed by the thoroughfare to California, the Mormon-dominated area retained a high degree of isolation and regional integrity, set apart more by its sociocultural peculiarities and the determined efforts of its theocratic leadership to minimize national influences than by its natural girdle of wastelands.

THE OREGON COUNTRY

The Oregon Country, a huge chunk of northwestern America, was under joint claim by Great Britain and the United States for several decades. Momentarily in the early 1840s competitive colonizations were juxtaposed in the lower Columbia district, with the British focus at Fort Vancouver, a major fur trade center with flourishing farms and mills, and American farmer-migrants settling in the lower Willamette Valley. But the British nucleus disintegrated after the compromise division of Oregon along the 49th Parallel and subsequent colonization was by a relatively homogeneous body of American migrants. Local Indian societies had already been virtually destroyed by disease and economic and social disruptions.

The Willamette nucleus was a long-distant transplant from the Missouri–Ohio Valley region with a strong reinfusion of Yankee influences. Migration in the 1840s and 1850s drew about equally from the Free States and from the Slave States of the Border South. The general settlement pattern, architecture, and agricultural system were similar to that broad source region, modified by the failure of corn and tobacco to thrive in the cooler, summer-dry environment. The New England influence was markedly apparent in church, school, and civic organizations, and in commercial and manufacturing activities.

Portland, below the falls on the Willamette and accessible to ocean vessels, became the principal focus with the upsurge of exports to California in the 1850s. In the 1860s it became the regional gateway and supply center for an array of new mining districts deep in the interior, competing for trade as far away as the Kootenay, western Montana, and southern Idaho. Walla Walla, the principal interior trade center, became the nucleus of an expanding ranching and farming region which was settled primarily from the Willamette and served by Portland firms. By the early 1880s Portland was the focus of an extensive system of waterways, roads, and railroads tapping much of the old Oregon Country. Puget Sound, directly accessible by sea with an economy based upon a scattering of large tidewater lumber mills, was in some degree separate. Its incipient geography was obscured by the nervous rivalries among aspiring ports, and its first railroad line led south to the Columbia to tie in with the more substantial Oregon nucleus. This Northwest system as a whole was bound into commercial networks focused on San Francisco. Californian capital was prominent in the lumbering and mining activities of the Northwest, and in the Willamette and especially in the drier Columbia Plain the grain farming system was strongly shaped by Californian innovations.

Thus Portland was the focus of a region which drew originally upon the mainstream of American western migration, but which was increasingly divergent from those antecedents because of environmental and locational differences. Even if it was nevertheless the most typically American of all Far Western regions, that in itself helped differentiate it from its neighbors.

COLORADO

Although nearest to the main body of national population, Colorado was the last of the major Western nuclei to be initiated, and that relative location and timing were important to the character of its beginnings. The discovery of gold along the base of the southern Rockies came a decade after similar electrifying news from California, and the nation responded eagerly to another possibility of such wealth, business opportunity, and adventure. By that time, 1858–59, the edge of the Rockies was by comparison readily accessible. Tens of thousands of people had already crossed the Plains to other Western regions, railroads had almost reached the Missouri River, and settlers were spreading into Kansas and Nebraska. Thus in a matter of months prospectors were swarming over the Front Range, towns were laid out, businesses established, stage and freighting lines put in service, and ample Eastern capital was available to invest in anything that looked promising.

Early mineral discoveries could not sustain the full initial influx, and there was considerable instability in population for many years. The first railroad connections to the East, made in 1870, encouraged more substantial and diversified developments. Eastern and European capital invested heavily in livestock ranching on the Colorado Piedmont. Irrigation agriculture was strongly promoted, and benefited from a few highly publicized and successful colonies (e.g., Greeley and Longmont). Vigorous promotion of the scenic wonders and health-restoring qualities of this "American Switzerland" so conveniently accessible by railway car brought an ever greater number of tourists, summer sojourners, health-seekers, and those attracted by elegant towns of social pretension (i.e., Colorado Springs). Furthermore the mining industry itself underwent steady elaboration from placers to lode mining, and from gold to silver and lead. Location, timing, and special difficulties made Colorado an innovative center of scientific study, tools, and techniques in the American mining industry. Major discoveries, such as in the Leadville district, required far larger machinery, mills, and smelters; coal, available at several points along the Front Range, replaced charcoal. In 1880 a Bessemer iron and steel plant using Colorado coke, ore, and limestone was built at Pueblo to serve the burgeoning demand for structural and railroad iron.

Denver emerged successful from the townsite rivalries at the first ephemeral diggings, was well located to serve the first substantial district (Central City area), and was thereafter never seriously rivaled as the commercial, financial, political, and social center of Colorado. For thirty years its tributary region was rapidly expanded and enriched by significant new mineral discoveries in the Southern Rockies, each the basis for new railroads and ancillary industries and the opening of new ranching, farming, and resort districts.

Denver became the focus of a remarkable railroad network which tapped every important mineral district. Much of it was narrow gauge, a special adaption to the formidable terrain. No train service ran through Denver; it was a true node, the point of interchange between its tributary system and the trunklines across the Plains. Pueblo provided gateway connections between lines from the East and a route across the Rockies, but the actual services were geared to the patterns of the regional traffic focused upon Denver, and Pueblo was not a significant commercial competitor.

Denver's domain was very nearly concordant with the state along three sides. To the north the Union Pacific provided the main axis of Wyoming, the southerly reach of its pull penetrating Colorado only in North Park. On the west, the near-empty wasteland of the Green River country effectively separated Colorado from the main Mormon region. On the south the Colorado line approximated the Hispano-Anglo border zone, with the Colorado railroad system penetrating slightly. On the east, however, Denver served only the narrowing ranching belt and the riverine irrigation strips between the mountains and the advancing edge of dry-farming grain agriculture created by the strong surge out of Kansas and Nebraska in the 1880s.

This Colorado area had much clearer definition as a commercial region than as a culture area. Its population was drawn very largely but very broadly from the Northern states. The development of an industrial labor class with large numbers of foreign-born (and Hispanos from New Mexico) was very like that of the mining and industrial districts of the East but quite unlike most regions in the West. What set Colorado apart was its particular combination of important activities—mining, heavy industry, ranching, irrigation agriculture, commerce, tourism, and recreation—which together formed a rather concentrated, integrated complex sustaining a relatively diverse and cosmopolitan society. The strong focus on Denver and a strong sense of regional identity grounded upon the magnificent mountain setting so boldly and abruptly set apart from all lands to the east further combined to give Colorado recognizable character as a special part of the American West.

NORTHERN CALIFORNIA

On the eve of the Gold Rush Northern California had only a few thousand mestizo and white settlers. There was no clear and substantial nucleus, only a scattering of points and small districts (e.g., Monterey, the Santa Clara, the San Francisco Bay littoral, Sonoma, New Helvetia). However, so great and creative was the power of that event that a major urban focus, a regional axis, and several distinctive production districts were almost instantly apparent.

The general axis connected San Francisco with the north-central Sierras, in detail a water route bifurcating to the valley centers of Sacramento and Stockton from which wagon roads and pack trails fanned into the mountain mineral districts. The political capital of the new state was consciously placed on that axis. Carquinez Strait, the narrow passageway between the bay and the valley, was the preferred location (placed in Vallejo in 1851 and in Benicia in 1853) although because of practical difficulties of accommodations it was soon shifted (by a very narrow vote) to the already-thriving Sacramento (1854). Readily made tributary to that axis was a series of rapidly developing subregions—the Sierra valleys, the Sacramento and San Joaquin, the coastal valleys, and the Redwood and Monterey coasts—tapped by an ever-expanding system of coastal vessels, river boats, railroads, wagon and stage roads.

Beyond this undisputed hinterland, San Francisco was the principal metropolitan center for the rest of California and all of Nevada, and reached out to compete for trade over the entire Pacific Slope from Interior British Columbia to Central Arizona. Indeed a good portion of the people and much of the money to develop this broad realm came from California. A critical feature in Western regionalism is the amount

of locally generated wealth concentrated in San Francisco which made it a financial center of considerable magnitude and independence rather than merely an outpost of Wall Street, as were most other cities in the nation. The building of the first transcontinental railroad, a feat of great practical and symbolic importance, is an effective illustration of this Californian autonomy, for the Central Pacific represented Californian capitalists reaching inland clear to the Great Salt Lake to meet on equal terms the Eastern-financed Union Pacific.

This emerging California was much more than a coherent and aggressive commercial system; it was world famous as a highly distinctive and attractive environment. This region of subtropical summer-dry climate, fertile soils, and beautiful landscapes of mountain, valley, and seacoast was unlike any other in the nation and it became firmly fixed in the national mind as a very special place, an American Eden, a Golden West symbolic of opportunity and dreams fulfilled. From very early in its modern history symbol and substance have been powerfully combined to make California a region of enormous attraction. The special character of its climate and its national location together with its history of sudden influx and continuous rapid growth thereafter has had some special effect upon every kind of economic activity. Speculation was endemic, innovation common, a larger scale and greater efficiency of operations notable.

So, too, there has long been general agreement among Californians and outsiders alike that California society is different, although commentators have not always found it easy to define the nature and basis of that difference. Part of that difficulty is inherent and is itself a feature of significance, for it relates to the dynamic, fluid, open character of a society never stabilized and hardened into fixed patterns. It is generally agreed that the Gold Rush initiated the elements: a great heterogeneous, restless, ambitious horde of relatively young people thrown together in a new kind of country detached from the stable patterns of home. Such people were drawn from all of America, most of Europe, parts of Asia and Latin America. Despite the imposition of caste (with regard to Asians) and some degree of stratification, it remained a relatively open society with widespread social and economic opportunity. Regional development was so dynamic as to make the geography of ethnic groups more a kaleidoscope than a mosaic. In sharp contrast with nearly all Western regions, this Californian population was as variegated and cosmopolitan as that of the East, but differed in specific elements and proportions, and the size and character of development fostered a much more open and broadly integrated society with generally less tension than was apparent among the large ethnic blocs in the urbanized and industrialized East. Most important was the strong self-consciousness of Californians as constituting a dynamic and creative new society, a closer realization of the American dream.

SOUTHERN CALIFORNIA

The country lying south of San Luis Obispo and the Tehachapi Range was so remote from the Mother Lode as to escape the heavy impact of the Gold Rush. Many Anglos passed through the area and some stayed, especially in the Los Angeles Basin, but they had to share the region with the Californios, the Mexican population dominated by the big ranching families. Although the Anglos continually increased in numbers and power, for thirty years Southern California developed in considerable degree as a relatively balanced bicultural society. The extension of irrigation and subtropical crops provided a basis for growth, but the costs of development and difficulties of marketing impeded rapid expansion.

The great "Boom of the 80s" was Southern California's equivalent of the Gold Rush, a sudden transformation which set a new pattern and scale of development. The boom was generated by an enormous speculative real estate promotion campaign which followed hard upon the completion of competitive direct railroad lines to the East. Tens of thousands of people came in, lured by the widely advertised virtues of life in America's subtropical paradise. Ranches were subdivided into thousands of suburban lots and scores of new towns. Although the fervor of the boom inevitably soon waned, the general character of regional development had been established. Southern California's foremost resource

was its overall physical environment, its most persuasive symbol the family-size suburban lot amidst the orange groves between the sea and the mountains in a snowless land of sunshine.

Such a land proved a powerful attraction to persons of moderate capital resources in the Middle West, who could sell farm, home, small business, or professional practice and move to a land of greater comfort and interest. Thus the main body of population was a relatively mature, conservative, property-minded bourgeois, but yet a society loosened by migration, the lack of firm roots, the instability of local communities, and the attractive possibilities for changing styles of life in a new physical and social environment. Since the principal means of expanding wealth was through the sale of land to incoming migrants rather than from the product of the land itself, the dominant figures in the life of the region were not the great industrialists or mercantilists but the developers and promoters and those who provided basic services to an ever-expanding population.

Los Angeles was from the first the main nucleus, but it was the focus of a small region, hedged in by mountains and deserts. Irrigation projects provided an expanding agricultural base, but the main function of Los Angeles was to serve the ever-growing suburban population within its own immediate basin. By 1900 this last of the major Western nuclei to emerge was famous across the nation as a very distinctive place.

SUMMARY

To class these six regions as the major ones apparent toward the end of the nineteenth century is not to suggest that together they encompass the whole of the American West (figure 2). Several cities and districts lay beyond the bounds of clear dominance by any one of these major centers, most notably El Paso and its riverine oases and mining hinterland, Central Arizona focused upon Phoenix, the Black Hills mining and ranching area, the Boise Basin and its extensive but thinly populated surroundings, and the Montana mining and ranching complex around Butte and Helena. Each had some degree of regional autonomy because of distance from large western cities and location on a railroad with di-

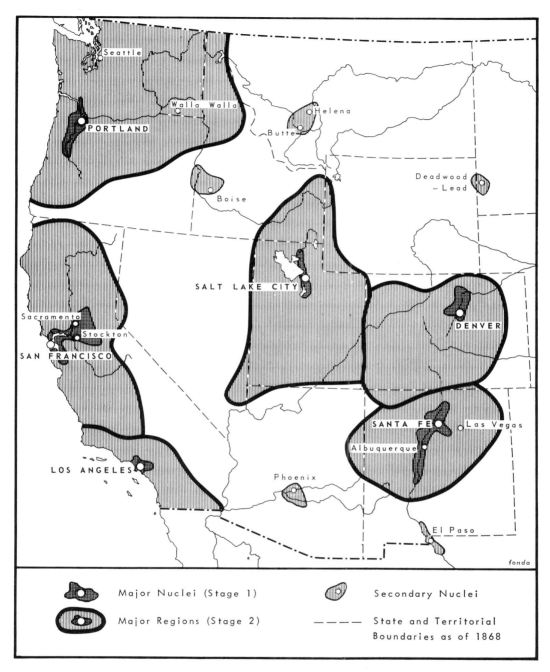

FIGURE 2
Major nuclei and regions of the West in Stages I and II.

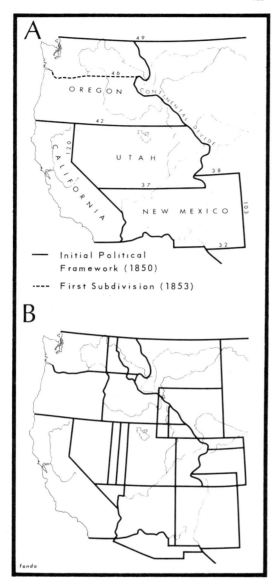

FIGURE 3
(*A*) The initial political framework. (*B*) Composite of boundaries used during evolution through the territorial stage.

to the role shared by Kansas City, Chicago, and Minneapolis–St. Paul for the Rocky Mountain half of the Far West. Denver, Salt Lake City, and Los Angeles were unchallenged regional capitals; Portland also, but within a contracting region, for the quick rise of Seattle near the end of the century firmly detached Puget Sound from any significant Portland influence and also threatened its dominance of the Columbia Interior. New Mexico was the chief variant among the six. Its total population was relatively small and it had no large city, but its special multicultural, "imperial" character made it a very distinctive region wherein the relationships among its peoples had implications for a much broader Southwest. Santa Fe, though small in size and unable to dominate commercially even its own historic region, was nevertheless culturally a focal point of distinctly major significance.

POLITICAL AREAS (STAGES I AND II)

The creation of the state of California (1849) and the territories of Oregon (1848), New Mexico (1850), and Utah (1850) provided the first American political framework for the Far West (figure 3a). The eastern slope of the Rockies was as yet devoid of civilized settlement and remained unorganized Indian Country until the creation of Nebraska and Kansas in 1854. This framework and its subsequent sequential modification to the states of today is illustrative of the general process of territorial evolution in the American political system.

Congress has the power to create political jurisdictions in newly acquired national domain. Normally the first stage was the establishment of a *territory,* governed by officials appointed by the federal government; after further population growth and development a territory may seek admission as a *state,* equal in all legal respects with the other states. Congress has the power to change boundaries between territories. Boundaries between territories and states can only be changed by joint action of Congress and the states involved; boundaries between states may be changed only by agreement between the states with subsequent approval by Congress. Despite these prerogatives of Congress the intent of the

rect service to the East, but each was very considerably smaller in population and commercial significance than the average of the major regions.

Nor does this nomination of six regions as major within the West mean that they were equal in all basic features. San Francisco was at a higher level than any of the other cities, the regional metropolis of the entire Pacific Slope, analogous

system is to respond in large measure to local interests in their quest toward the American ideal of local control over their own affairs.

Because commerce, culture, and politics interact in myriad ways a concordance of their areas is generally desirable, but because commercial and culture areas are inherently diffuse exact concordance is never attainable. Furthermore, although the system contains the legal means to adjust the size and shape of political areas in response to changes in other fundamental patterns, the cumulative complexities and vested interests make such boundary alterations increasingly difficult as the area develops.

The pattern of 1850 was characteristic of the first phase of this geopolitical evolution, each unit containing a settlement nucleus surrounded by a huge expanse of undomesticated country. The boundaries were simply convenient arbitrary lines dividing the total area into four roughly equal parts. Subsequent subdivision was generally in response to the request from new settlement districts in some remote sector of the original territory. Thus Washington (1853) was a reflection of developments on Puget Sound, Colorado (1861) of the Denver–Central City nucleus, Nevada (1861) of the Comstock Lode district, Arizona (1863) of the Anglo settlement along the southern routes to California, Idaho (1863) of Boise and a scattering of mineral districts, Montana (1864) of Helena and nearby mineral districts. Wyoming (1868) was more a residual area, a huge undeveloped block shifted among several jurisdictions, with at the time no more than an incipient coherence from the Union Pacific then under construction.

Most of these territories underwent further revisions after their initial formation, and there have been many fruitless attempts to make additional modifications (figure 3b). In general, the whole process may be seen as an attempt to bring about a greater concordance of political areas with commercial and culture areas, although by the end of this phase (marked in general by statehood) numerous anomalies remained (figure 4a). Among the most important were: (1) the inclusion of two major regions within California, the result of California's direct admission as a state without passing through the more changeable

territorial phase, and of the late development of Southern California; (2) the dominantly Mormon area of southeastern Idaho with much stronger cultural and commercial bonds to Salt Lake City than to Boise; (3) the failure to reshape political geography to the emerging regional co-

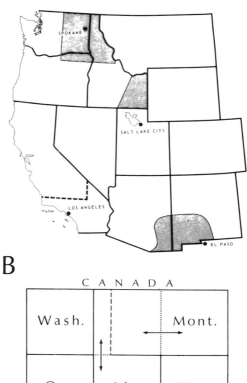

FIGURE 4

(*A*) Major discordances between political and cultural or commercial areas. (*B*) Schematic representation of departures from theoretical symmetrical subdivision.

herence in the Columbia Interior, a pattern increasingly focused on Spokane, perpetuating a discordance which was the source of recurrent proposals for the creation of a new state or for at least the annexation of the Idaho Panhandle to Washington State; (4) the western promontory of Texas, putting El Paso and its main hinterland in separate political areas.

The issues involved in every one of these changes or proposals were complex and controversial, hinging upon a variety of local and national interests, but the resultant pattern in the American West suggests that Congressional decision making in such matters was also influenced by some general sense of scale and symmetry. This is apparent from the very first. The 42d Parallel was an obvious choice for the initial subdivision, for it had long served as an international boundary between imperial claims and was the boundary between the two separate acquisitions of Oregon and the Mexican Cession. But the fact that it was approximately midway between the new national boundaries with British America and Mexico may have influenced the choice of the 37th and 46th parallels for a further halving (in part) of each of the original two segments, giving four latitudinal strips of approximately equal width (figure 3a). Subsequent longitudinal divisions suggest that a general pattern of three north-south strips was in keeping with the same sense of proportion. An utterly arbitrary geometry of the West based solely upon some such sense of form and size would result in twelve units (figure 4b). Fitting the actual eleven states to this arbitrary grid reveals only three major discordances: (1) the Idaho Panhandle, with anomalous elongations of Idaho (north-south) and of Montana (east-west); (2) Nevada as a fourth unit fitted into its tier at the expense (seemingly) of California and (actually) of Utah; (3) California elongated north-south to include two units (the angled eastern boundary of California was designed to be a simple geometric approximation of the trend of the coastline). Although unlike the anomalies cited in the previous paragraph, such departures from a theoretical pattern have no inherent significance, they do help us to visualize in fresh ways the regional character of the West.

CIRCULATION (STAGES I AND II)

Most of the famous Western trails were primarily emigrant roads, serving as a means of getting people across the wilderness to new areas of settlement but by the very nature of the vehicles inadequate for effective communication and profitable commerce spanning such distances. Even the relatively large systems of wagon freighting and scheduled stage and mail service of the late 1850s did not effectively alter the isolation of these Western nuclei. Much of the wagon freighting was in support of military posts and operations, heavily dependent upon government contracts. In the Oregon Country and California, steamboats on the Columbia, Willamette, and Sacramento rivers aided the development of a commercial export agricultural economy, but elsewhere only goods of very high value, such as bullion or highly concentrated ores, or self-propelled, such as mules from New Mexico, could meet the costs of shipment.

The construction of a railroad to the Pacific became a major national issue almost from the moment that the United States acquired its Pacific frontage. The selection of the route for such a line was widely understood to be a momentous geographical decision. Northern California was so much the most important of the several Western nuclei that San Francisco Bay was unquestioned as the Pacific terminus. But there were various possible routes for linking California with the East, and it was generally assumed that the first railroad would become and long remain the principal transcontinental axis, the trunk line of the nation, with enormous consequences for subsequent patterns of development.

Because of the insular character of Western settlement within such a vast area it was also generally accepted that, contrary to the situation in the East, the Pacific railroad would require heavy federal subsidy. The decision as to the route rested with Congress and thus was enmeshed in sectional politics. To appease competing areas the initial feasibility study authorized reconnaissance of five general routes between the Mississippi and the Pacific: one northern, two central, and two southern (figure 5). The War Department agency which carried out these surveys re-

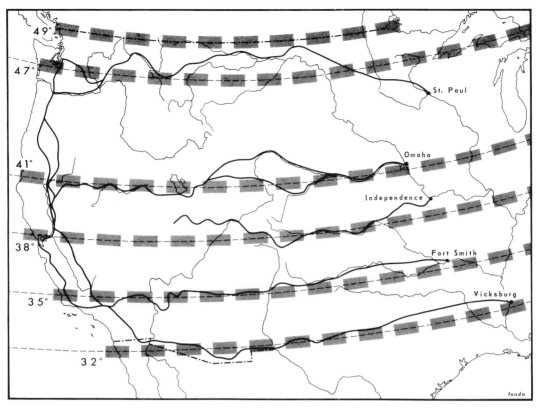

FIGURE 5

United States government explorations for Pacific railroad routes, 1853–58. The routes were designated by reference
to a particular parallel or parallels. The exploration of the 38th Parallel route ended when the leader of the exploration party
was killed by Indians in Utah. All other routes were designated as practicable.

ported four of these routes as possible for a railroad, but recommended the southernmost as the
most advantageous. Sectional rivalries blocked
any decision until after Southern secession, when
Congress selected the central route which had
been advocated by most Northern interests. The
Overland Telegraph, another federally subsidized
service, was opened along the same general route
in late 1861.

The central route was the shortest, extending
directly west from the most aggressive salients of
the vigorously developing railroad system of the
East. It had the added advantage of passing near
Denver and Salt Lake City, thus linking three of
these Western regional systems with the nation.
Land grant subsidies were later allocated to railroads building along all or major parts of the

other five Pacific routes of the initial survey, and
within twenty years after the first golden spike
all of the Western regions were similarly linked
by direct trunk lines to the East. That these several Western areas were more effectively linked
to the East than to one another, except incidentally along transcontinental routes, was characteristic of this stage of development. Indeed the
insular pattern was so marked and regional interdependence so limited among certain areas that
a complete network of direct railroad connections among the six major nuclei was never completed (figure 6).

The railroad was a revolutionary instrument,
but it took a generation or more to work the
revolution. The thirty years following the ceremony at Promontory was the culmination of

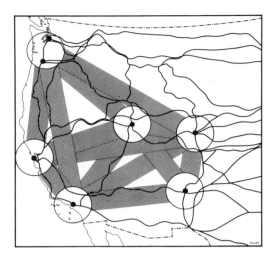

FIGURE 6

Interregional railroad connections compared with a schematic pattern of direct links among all six regions of the West.

Stage II and no more than a prelude to Stage III. During that time the other trunk lines to the East were completed, but the capacity and efficiency of these railroads was still very limited. As links between East and West they were more important in bringing people to the West than in carrying freight out. Meanwhile the regional railroad systems were being very extensively elaborated in support of rapid increases in the density of settlement and intensity of development within these several areas (figure 7).

POPULATION (STAGES III AND IV)

The end of the Turnerian frontier, when no large blocks of land suitable for traditional family farm colonization remained, marked the end of Stage II in the population pattern. Major expansions of agricultural colonization thereafter were dependent upon irrigation, and many of these were in large government projects such as in the Columbia Basin, the Snake River Plain, the San Joaquin, the Imperial Valley, and Central Arizona. Together with new mineral and forestry districts such developments altered Western settlement patterns in numerous details. The growth of a more complex industrial base in the West, something beyond the elemental processing of local primary products, was critically dependent on activities fostered by the federal government,

chiefly during the several wars of the twentieth century: shipyards, aircraft, ordnance, steel, and aluminum plants, as well as military installations. But migrants have also poured into certain areas for other reasons. "Westering" has continued to be a major feature of American life. In depressions as well as booms the image of the West as new country where one might embark upon a new life in more congenial circumstances has persisted as a powerful attraction. To a very considerable degree, industry has followed the population as well as lured it.

The total of such movements over a span of four or five decades did much to alter the shape and insularity of Western regions. Major nuclei persisted, and the largest cities became very much larger, but many lesser centers in outlying districts grew notably (e.g., Bakersfield, Fresno, Klamath Falls, Richland, Yakima, Great Falls, Billings, Roswell), giving a more even incidence of urbanization and blurring the earlier regional border zones. Migration patterns became increasingly complex. Inflows from the East were predominantly channeled to the large urban areas, but affected every district. Two new im-

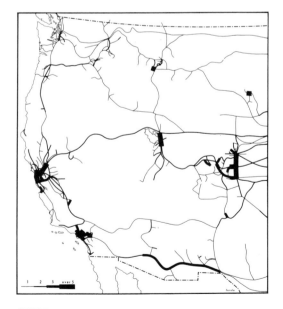

FIGURE 7

Railroad passenger service at least six days per week near the beginning of Stage III. Source: *Official Guide of the Railway and Steam Navigation Lines in the United States, Canada, and Mexico,* September 1897.

migrations of distinct peoples became significant: the northward influx of large numbers of Mexicans, who spread widely though selectively over the West as an industrial and agricultural proletariat; and, more recently, the westward influx of blacks, chiefly from Texas, Arkansas, and Louisiana, especially into urban California. There was also much interregional movement within the West, primarily to California, Portland, and Puget Sound. Most of this migration is obscure, but some of the most important streams are readily identifiable, such as that of New Mexican Hispanos spreading into the industrial and farm-labor districts of Colorado, Mormons colonizing alongside other settlers in the new irrigation districts and moving in large numbers to Pacific Coast urban areas, and the influx early in the century of Japanese and the more recent upsurge in Chinese immigration to California.

In the 1970s the West seems to be entering a fourth stage characterized by the emergence of huge metropolitan clusters of population. The Los Angeles Basin, San Francisco Bay, and the eastern shore of Puget Sound now appear to be truly megalopolitan in character. The older metropolitan centers of Portland, Denver, Salt Lake City, and Spokane have been suddenly joined by San Diego, Phoenix, Tucson, Albuquerque, and Las Vegas, Nevada. The rapid growth of cities is a common feature of the West through several stages, but the scale, character, and impact of recent urbanization is quite unprecedented. The efficiencies of transportation and communication and the relative affluence of a growing number of people combine to spread persons who are an integral part of urban culture far beyond the obvious bounds of continuously built-up urban areas. The seemingly rural countrysides of many Western districts are actually dominated by essentially urban people scattered about in satellite towns, housing tracts, resorts, and homesteads, all in close functional and cultural connection with metropolitan areas by high-speed highways and individual or commuter air services.

CIRCULATION (STAGES III AND IV)

Stage III saw the development of a far more elaborate and efficient combination of transpor-

tation facilities than the early railroad–stage and wagon road–sporadic riverboat combination of Stage II. The electric interurban railroad was a temporary addition; paved highways, local air service, pipelines, and a barge system on the Columbia were successive additions to the earlier railroad network, which was itself completed and greatly increased in efficiency during this period.

There were important similarities in the developmental phases of these spatial networks. Electric railroads began as urban-suburban lines and were later extended to connect neighboring cities. In areas of relatively dense agricultural and urban settlement (such as the Los Angeles Basin, Sacramento Valley, Willamette Valley, and Puget Sound Lowlands) fairly extensive systems were built. The network of paved highways began in similar fashion but went much further: first radiating out from urban centers, then connecting adjacent cities, expanding into regional systems, gradually linking adjacent regions, and ultimately forming a complete interregional network of relatively uniform quality (figure 8). The superior efficiency of such government-financed trafficways soon drove the electric railroads out of business. Similarly, most of the local service

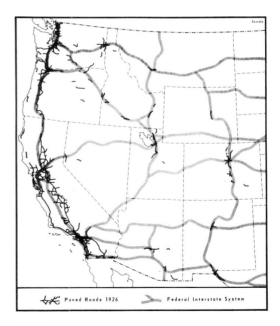

FIGURE 8
Early stage of the highway network, 1926, and federal interstate highway system, 1971.

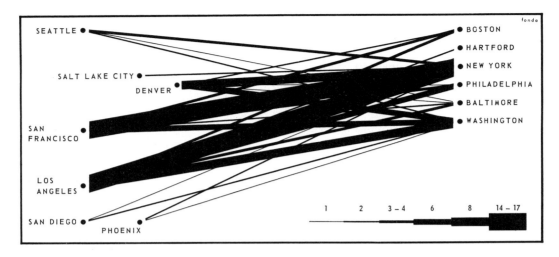

FIGURE 9
Nonstop air service between cities of the West and the Northeastern Seaboard.

airlines began as essentially regional companies connecting smaller cities with the regional metropolis. Next came links between adjacent regions, then the merger of companies to form comprehensive networks radiating from several metropolitan centers. So, too, by the 1930s telephone and radio broadcasting, each begun as local or regional operations, enveloped the nation in vast complexly interlocked networks.

By the 1950s every district was served by some form of modern efficient transportation, every region was served by an elaborate combination of communication services, and all of the Western regional networks were integral parts of a general national network which was itself a complex combination of overlapping regional systems.

The transition to Stage IV is marked most significantly by the initiation of transcontinental nonstop air service, which was rapidly extended during the early jet age of the 1960s. The critical differentiating feature is the very rapid uninterrupted direct connection between major Western urban centers and the national metropolises of New York and Washington and other cities in the national core, overflying intervening regions (figure 9). Such service forms a national and international network of nodal links which obliterates surface regions. This network, like all oth-

ers, has its own peculiar pattern of sequential development: first from the two largest Western metropolises, Los Angeles and San Francisco, to New York, then similar service from Seattle, then such service to other major Eastern cities, then service between lesser Western cities and the largest Eastern cities. Such a sequence could be projected to the point where every major city has direct nonstop air service with every other major city. An analogous sequence is also underway in international service, beginning with scheduled nonstop flights connecting San Francisco and Los Angeles with major European cities.

Meanwhile local feeder airlines continue to amalgamate to form ever-larger systems. Today one company (Air West) dominates the entire Pacific Slope and another (Frontier) the entire Rocky Mountain and High Plains country; the two systems interlock at Tucson, Phoenix, Salt Lake City, and Great Falls.

Complementing these developments are elaborate metropolitan freeway networks and the beginnings of a modern mass-transit system in the most congested megalopolis, and other forms of efficient long-distance transportation, such as pipelines, unit-trains, and the nationwide interstate superhighway system of uniform quality (figure 10). Such developments point toward the emergence of a complex nationwide system of

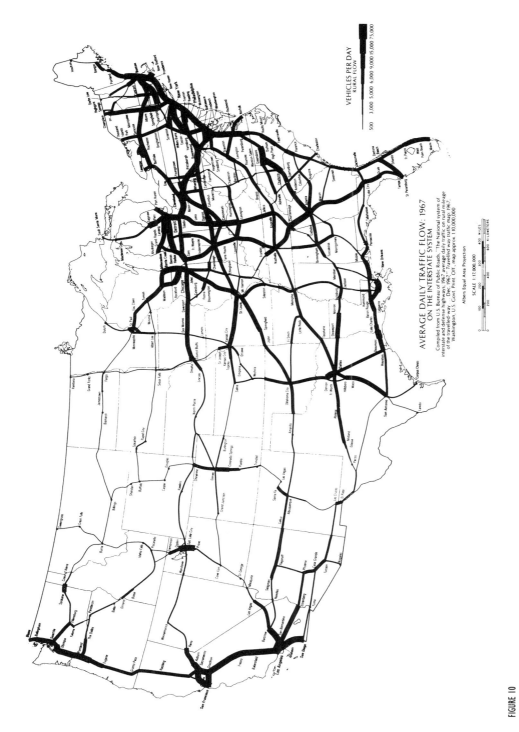

VEHICLES PER DAY
RURAL FLOW

500   3,000 5,000 6,000 9,000 15,000 75,000

AVERAGE DAILY TRAFFIC FLOW: 1967
ON THE INTERSTATE SYSTEM

Compiled from U.S. Bureau of Public Roads "The National system of
interstate and defense highways, 1967, average daily traffic on rural mileage
of the travelled way ... Dec. 1967." Travelled way traffic map: 1967,
Washington, U.S. Govt. Print. Off., map approx 1:10,000,000

Albers Equal Area Projection

SCALE 1:17,000,000

FIGURE 10

Traffic flow on the federal interstate highway system in 1967. A degree of separateness between East and West was still
apparent. Source: U.S. Department of the Interior (1970, 227).

circulation which is fully and efficiently national in operation rather than a combination of interlocking regional systems with attendant inefficiencies of transfer points and separate managements. Direct-dial long-distance telephoning, intercity computer hookups, television, and the prospect for a variety of specialized television networks are other major components.

POLITICAL AREAS (STAGES III AND IV)

The admission of New Mexico and Arizona in 1912 completed the statehood process in the West, an event delayed because of the special cultural character of New Mexico and the relatively small population of both. An effort to combine these two territories to form a single state was defeated largely on the grounds of their sharp cultural differences, a further illustration of the general concern to fit political areas to other basic areal patterns.

The territorial design of the eleven states completed in 1912 has remained unaltered. Discussion of a new state for the Columbia Interior was briefly revived in the 1930s. Much more significant is the growing agitation for the subdivision of California into two states, a chronic movement directly reflecting the existence of two major regions and megalopolitan clusters within a single political unit. Such discordance between state areas and metropolitan areas, putting rival centers within a single state, influences nearly every aspect of political affairs in California and Washington. Oregon, Utah, and Colorado reflect a more singular metropolitan focus; Idaho, Montana, and, until recently, New Mexico, Arizona, and Nevada a more diffuse and nonmetropolitan character.

The county pattern within each state was also completed early in the twentieth century. There has been neither subdivision nor amalgamation of any counties for more than half a century. That pattern is reflective of the settlement and transport conditions of Stage II, but it did not become at all inappropriate in areal scale until the very recent advent of intricate local networks of high-speed highways. Even today, the optimum size for counties is a moot point, de-

pending as much upon philosophies of citizen-government relations as upon efficiencies of transportation.

The most significant geopolitical feature of Stage III was the discordances between a changing population pattern and an unchanging political territorial pattern. As urban areas grew rapidly and most rural areas stabilized there was an ever-widening population differential among the counties of any particular state. To the degree that state governments operated on a basis of equal representation from and equal allocation of resources to counties very serious political tensions were created. Reapportionment of representation became a recurrent problem of major significance.

Because of the cumulative rigidities of autonomous political territories there is likely to be a long lag between generally recognized needs and any actual areal changes. Thus there are as yet no more than glimmers of a shift into a new stage in such geopolitical matters. The definition by the federal government and subsequent widespread use for a variety of public and private planning purposes of "standard metropolitan statistical areas," many of which are contiguous blocks of counties directly functioning as part of a metropolitan system, points up the problem. The creation of special metropolitan political agencies encompassing several incorporated municipalities and transcending county boundaries reflects the need for a new scale of political territory. At the state level, formation of interstate compacts, chiefly with reference to water and river basin development, and the fact that many federal agencies operate on the basis of larger-than-state regions, are further signs of similar needs (figure 11).

However, while further developments of this sort are almost inevitable, they are almost certainly going to be superstructures resting upon the existing county and state territorial grids. Before projecting the inevitable creation of giant metropolitan regions to bring form and function into accord and replace states as the prime units, it is well to remember that the United States is by definition a federal system of states and the significance, tenacity, and, perhaps, de-

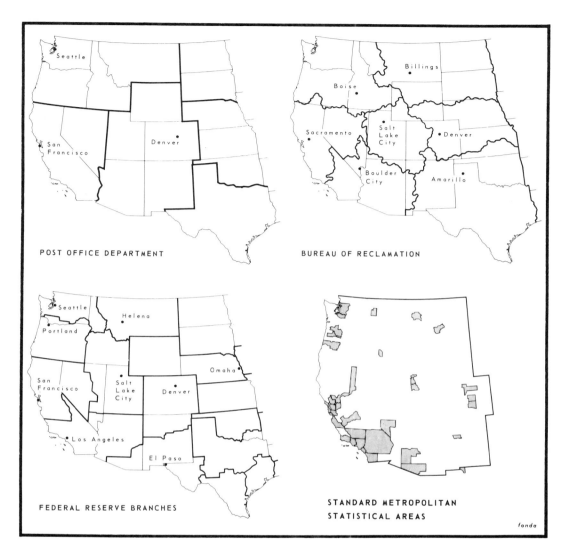

FIGURE 11
Examples of current administrative areas.

CULTURE (STAGES III AND IV)

Stage III marks the end of insularity and a sharp increase in the power of forces working toward national cultural uniformity. Since most Westerners and Easterners have always shared a common basic "American" culture, it is important to define rather carefully the nature of this change.

The West was largely populated by migrants from the East who not only routinely brought their culture with them but sought to stay in touch with and to emulate the East in almost every way. Contrary to some of the more extreme and simple versions of the "frontier thesis," the West was always far more imitative than innova-

sirability of the present state system can hardly be exaggerated.

tive. For example, in such basic social institutions as churches, fraternal organizations, political parties, and educational systems Westerners were mostly part of essentially national networks. Nevertheless, the insular conditions of Stage II allowed the preservation of conscious desired differences, as in the case of the Mormons and Hispanos; fostered divergences based upon isolation and environmental differences, as in diet, dialect, religious schism, and local economic and political issues; and caused a marked lag in the adoption of new features originating in the East because of the inefficiencies of diffusion processes.

Developments during the first half of the twentieth century continuously increased the intensity, rapidity, and comprehensiveness of the impact of national culture upon the regions. Mass-consumption journalism and radio poured out a relentless propaganda in support of standardized products, fashions, behavior, attitudes, and speech. The cinema had in some ways an even more powerful impact, not only as a mass-marketed entertainment that replaced nearly all local forms, but as displaying (at times quite unconsciously) powerfully persuasive examples of modern American life. Indeed, Hollywood put before all the world much the most effective definition of an "American standard of living," a standard which was for the most part not the level most common in America, but one to which most Americans aspired and felt was within possible reach.

The triumph of the national over the regional is perhaps most readily illustrated in commercial activity. In Stage II retailing was dominated by local firms. The rise of the great mail-order houses with the development of a nationwide railroad network provided the first direct link between the Western consumer and the Eastern distributor, but time, cost, and physical separation left it a tenuous relationship of low intensity which did not greatly modify the general insularity of Western regions. The development of national chain-stores and franchised service facilities, branch plants, and the acquisition of regional companies by national firms are the critical changes. Nationwide advertising combined with a nationwide network of distribution centers allowed new items to be introduced simultaneously into every region, and reduced the lag in adoption between center and periphery to relative insignificance.

Furthermore, *center* and *periphery* were no longer obvious characterizations for East and West. The national culture was being markedly influenced by Hollywood and other agencies which displayed a Southern Californian style of life as the most modern and glamorous and thus implicitly worthy of emulation. From the 1920s to the 1960s American patterns of living were profoundly shaped by innovations spreading out from this world-famed Western corner of the nation: the general style of informal, pleasure-centered living; the patio, barbecue, swimming pool, and stylish sports clothes; the architecture of houses and the design of interiors, as attested by the successive diffusion of the California "bungalow," "Spanish" stucco, "ranch-house," and "contemporary" housetypes over all American suburbia. Above all, Southern California set the national style in the use of the automobile and in the design of automobile-centered facilities and environments—carports, freeways, strip-cities, shopping centers, motels, drive-ins of all kinds. Detroit manufactured the cars, but California showed how to live with them, and this critical influential link between the historic core and a burgeoning Western region was a telling indication of a significant stage in national integration.

But the very fact that Southern California could play such a role was itself evidence that regionalism had not been completely eroded in the West. Both Californias, Southern especially, were areas of vigorous growth powered to an important degree by the continual influx of people consciously seeking a "California way of life" as something different and better than that to be found elsewhere in the nation. California's distinctiveness was more than locational and environmental; it was fundamentally cultural, a matter of attitudes and behavior which produce a new style of everyday living.

And despite the massive impact of national culture, other Western regions retained a considerable degree of identity during Stage III. Colorado, never an obvious, self-conscious culture area, continued as a nodal region encompassing a very distinctive physical environment and combination of economic activities. The Pacific Northwest was rather more complex, with its three major urban centers and sharply contrasting environments of coast and interior. Though it had little sense of cultural cohesion, a loose sense of regionalism was based upon economy and environment, location in a far corner, Alaskan and Oriental trade connections, and a feeling of being sharply separate from and very much overshadowed in the national mind by California.

The Mormons illustrate very well the combined national-regional character of Stage III. Although still vigorously nurturing a strong sense of cohesion and identity as a distinct religious society, Mormon leaders worked toward an amicable accommodation with the nation. Indeed one can detect a gradual shift in corporate self-image from a "peculiar people" to "model Americans," the latter not in the sense of typical, but of the ideal godly, familial, puritanical, industrious people prominent in our national mythology. And while a strong sense of Utah as hallowed historic ground remained, the continual influx of Gentiles into the Mormon coreland, and the continual exodus of Mormons into neighboring regions and especially into California metropolitan areas, inevitably modified the strength of such Mormon regionalism. The building of a Mormon temple in Los Angeles in the 1950s was an overt acknowledgment of an important change in regional character and consciousness.

So, too, even though the Hispano culture of New Mexico remained strongly resistant of many facets of national culture, the continual influx of Anglos, reducing the earlier people to a minority in their own homeland, and the dispersal of Hispanos into Colorado and elsewhere tended to blur regional identities.

Thus, while national culture was clearly ascendant, the West continued to display marked variations in regional character based upon a somewhat different combination of factors in each region. It was still an immense land. The transcontinental traveler could hardly avoid being impressed with the differences in land and life from place to place, and the differences in each and all with those in the East.

Transition to the next stage seems clearly underway but far from complete. The characteristics of that stage are as yet more a projection than a reality, but the direction of change seems so boldly evident to so many people and the pace of change so increasingly rapid that the future looms portentously. Briefly, current trends seem to suggest that the West will simply be the western half of a nation of many millions more people, of broadly uniform culture, living some form of urban life within a vast, intimately interconnected, nationwide, multimetropolitan system. Such a population will be fluid, highly mobile in work, impermanent in residence, capable of almost instant dispersal in recreation; the great western mountain and desert landscapes will become mere parks, as accessible and intensely used as city parks of today.

Some of the instruments of this transition are notorious: television, the jet plane, and the all-terrain vehicle; electronic communication and computational systems applied to nationwide management; the economic power of huge corporations and affluent individuals. And the evidence for such trends is readily apparent: the ever-increasing standardization of goods and services and efficiency of nationwide contacts, the continual westward migrations, the relentless expansion of metropolitan areas, the rapid emergence of large urban centers unsupported by the usual tributary areas (Las Vegas, Tucson, San Diego), the ever-expanding swarm of seasonal travelers over Western landscapes; above all, perhaps, the widespread feeling that all areas, no matter how hitherto remote, inaccessible, or undesirable, are wide open to penetration, immigration, investment, development, and control by "outside forces."

Even the common image of these "outside forces" has undergone change indicative of a shift from older patterns. The hold of "Eastern money" upon the West, the essentially "colonial" relationship between the old, rich, powerful, industrial workshop and the new, money-short, vulnerable, raw-material producer was something long recognized and resented in the West. But this necessary dependence upon "Wall Street," which controlled railroads and mines, major industries and financial institutions, was on the surface a scarcely visible link which did not seem to shape directly daily lives and local landscapes (though in fact it did in myriad ways). But in the 1960s the magnitude, comprehensiveness, and mobility of economic speculation and development had so increased and was so different in character as to cause widespread concern. Interestingly, in many parts of the West, the greatest resentment is not directed against "Easterners," but against Californians or Texans. In neither case is this feeling based primarily upon a strong sense of obvious cultural differences (although there is often some tinge of such feeling with regard to Texans); rather it is a fear of an aggressive entrepreneurship backed by great wealth and vigorously growing and restless populations. Residents of neighboring regions see a kind of insidious relentless imperialism, the one spreading over the entire Pacific Slope, the other north and west over Colorado and New Mexico, expressed in a wave of activities: speculators buying farm and ranch lands, choice urban sites, huge suburban tracts, entire recreational districts; financiers investing in retail chains, banks, newspapers, and broadcasting stations; people pouring in as vacationers, hunters, seasonal sojourners, and students. How extensive such movements really are, and the degree to which they can be appropriately identified as Texan or Californian, is not at all clear, but they are common topics of conversation and commonly regarded as threatening whatever remains of local regional autonomy and character.

Despite such developments, the historic regionalism in the West is by no means wholly dissolved, and these common projections are not necessarily immutable. While the West has grown rapidly during the last thirty years it (the eleven westernmost states) still contains only 16 percent of the nation's population in 38 percent of the area of the coterminous forty-eight. Large areas of the West are growing very slowly if at all; Montana and Wyoming were stagnant during the last decade, and Idaho and New Mex-

ico grew by less than 5 percent, as did large sections of several other states. However, much the most remarkable demographic statistic is that net migration into California was only 26,000 in 1970 and may be transformed into a net exodus in 1971. Among the most remarkable recent events was the bold pronouncement by the governor of Oregon that his state had enough people and he would be pleased if no more moved in. Such things reflect something far more profound than temporary economic problems. They express some basic changes in attitude which could have major impact upon the evolving geography of America. For it is now widely appreciated that California is in grave danger of foundering on its own growth. Simple projections of the most obvious trends will define the complete despoliation of the American Eden. If the California dream becomes the California nightmare, and California begins to lose more people than it attracts over a considerable period of time, it would surely mark an important shift in the tide of American affairs. An end to westering would seem at least as important a change as was the end of the Turnerian frontier.

Such a shift can hardly be predicted with confidence at this point. Migrational changes are unlikely to be abrupt or uniform in effect, many other Western areas are still relatively uncrowded and attractive, and the emergence of new attitudes about "growth" and "progress" and "development" will be slow and complex. But the very fact that trends of the recent past do loom in the minds of many Westerners as a threat to their own future may have in itself halted the decline in regional consciousness. A heightened environmental awareness cannot but reinforce in some degree an appreciation of physical and cultural variations from place to place.

These very changes in attitudes have a geography of origin and diffusion, the outlines of which are recognizable in general if inscrutable in detail. Just as Southern California exerted a massive impact upon American society in Stage III, so Northern California seems destined to do so in Stage IV. Here seems to be the most concentrated awareness of many national problems and concern for solutions or alternatives. From here has come the main impetus of the new environmental consciousness, as epitomized by the Sierra Club. Here, certainly, is the major hearth of the "counter-culture" which has mounted a comprehensive critique of American society and markedly influenced national patterns of fashion, behavior, and attitudes. Berkeley, San Francisco, Oakland, and Big Sur have replaced Hollywood in offering images of new ways of life, and although much that is now in vogue will prove as superficial and transient as that of the earlier era, it does appear that vastly deeper philosophical matters are overtly involved. Although national in scope, the impact of such movements is regionally varied, and their prominence and power in Northern California serves to set that region, or at least its diverse metropolitan area, apart from other Western regions, reinforcing earlier cultural distinctions.

Furthermore, some long-standing cultural differences within the West have lately been reinforced and seem certain to become even more prominent. Through all the decades, while national culture was eroding regional differences, a few resistant peaks remained above the broadening plain. A recent series of upheavals makes them loom much larger, and continuing tremors suggest more changes are incipient. American Indians, New Mexican Hispanos, Mexican Americans, and black Americans, never accorded full social integration and long resistant to cultural assimilation, now demand full rights and recognition as Americans even while they accentuate their own distinct culture patterns. Thereby many areas take on a new significance in the social landscape of America: areas such as the Central Valley, the Mexican border country, and the Indian reservations in various states. No one of these constitutes a new region on the scale and with the kind of functional integrity of the old. They are subregions of special distinction, and together with Hutterite colonies on the High Plains, conservative Mormon back valleys, the Hispano stronghold in the mountains, and, perhaps eventually, districts of Basques, Portuguese, Italians, Finnish, and other white groups of heightened ethnic consciousness, they form pieces in a complex American mosaic. That mosaic, which is becoming ever more visible, and which represents another reversal of long-standing projected trends, would seem to be a particularly important pattern for the future.

Thus, while the historic regions have markedly faded as discrete entities, the West is far from even an incipient uniform or united area. And the real test lies beyond academic evidence in what daily life is really like in the actual communities of the West. To any sensitive soul, surely, it does make a difference whether one lives in Provo, Pueblo, Pasadena, Pendleton, or Puyallup; such differences are rooted in historical legacies as well as environmental settings, in what kinds of people came and in what they have created and experienced in particular places.

CONCLUSION

This is a sketch of an approach which would seem to offer good possibilities for breaking new ground in the study of the American West and in the interpretation of the American nation. It combines a number of advantageous qualities.

It is comprehensive as to time and area. Time is divided into periods, and although both the peak of each stage and the transitions between stages are of special interest, the entire course of events (since the entry of Europeans) is a logical and necessary part of the scheme. So too, the area of the West is divided into parts, and although special attention is directed to the cores and peripheries of major regions, full application of the scheme requires that the entire area be examined at every stage. Thus every locality at every point in time has an identifiable place within the scheme.

Secondly, it is developmental. It focuses attention upon a set of interrelated processes which appear to be producing a sequence of recognizable eras, each characterized by a certain general magnitude, intensity, and quality in regional, interregional, and national relationships. In an important sense there is an equal concern for past, present, and future; for although inherently historical in emphasis, this approach offers a perspective which would seem essential for an understanding of the present and for prediction of the future. Indeed, any characterization of Stage IV necessarily is in part a projection of trends and a speculation about new possibilities.

Thirdly, it is synthetic. It requires that a great diversity of elements and processes—environmental, cultural, social, political, economic—be examined in search of structural and historical interrelationships. This will require a great deal of new analysis of detail, but with the aim of contributing toward a richer synthesis, a better knowledge of the parts in order to have a better understanding and appreciation of the whole. It is an approach therefore which invites the attention of anthropologists, sociologists, economists, and political scientists as well as geographers and historians.

Finally, it is a generic scheme. Although shaped specially to fit the general contours of development in the American West, it is a model with wider applications. Clearly it would seem applicable with little adjustment to some other roughly contemporary colonizations in the neo-European world, in Canada, Australia, Argentina, Brazil, and Siberia. Furthermore, it can be fitted logically into a somewhat more comprehensive model of nation building, and it bears some important similarities to models of "modernization" now being worked out for the study of the transformation of the long-settled but "underdeveloped world."

As a new perspective it requires a shift in focus from things long studied to things little known. The unsatisfying exposition of many matters in this paper is not alone due to limitations of space and an incomplete knowledge of that which may have already been done by other students of the West, but also to the undoubted fact that little has been done on many topics which now loom as important. There are many inherent difficulties in this approach: how, for example, to define regional cultures, how to measure interregional linkages, how to identify historical changes, how to trace important diffusions. But we are not complete novices in the study of such things. The application of present skills to such questions could quickly yield important results. In recent American geography, especially, the development of techniques seems to have outstripped the formulation of a significant set of problems worthy of their application. For example, this scheme could provide a pro-

ductive focus for numerous analyses of spatial diffusion, giving a coherence and sense of purpose to an area of interest which currently seems far too fragmentary and eclectic, too much a trying out of techniques rather than an investigation of major topics.

There are of course many inherent limitations as well. No single approach can hope to yield equally significant answers to all possible major questions. Explicitly regional in focus and scale, it is clearly not the most efficient tool for the examination of those features which are narrowly local or broadly national. But it finds a special justification in the fact that it is precisely this intermediate, regional scale which in many ways seems most weakly developed in the literature extant.

An approach which focuses upon the American West can be no more than a partial view of American development, yet this regional scheme has significance for national interpretation in two ways. First, as presented in this paper, in each topic at every stage the West is explicitly linked with the East, and the series of stages describes a cycle of divergence and convergence as between Western regions and the national core and culture. Secondly, if this is indeed a useful generic model for the study of colonization and nation building, the entire scheme could well be applied to the entire nation. For example, the initial European footholds on the American Atlantic shore as clearly fit the characteristics of Stage I as do the nuclear areas of the Far West. Carried forward, it would help define the regional complexities which existed underneath the broad sectional concepts of North, South, and West. With certain modifications the scheme could accommodate the emergence and unique position of a national core to which all other areas have been in some degree subordinate. Although profiting from the rich lode of Turnerian studies, the results would be very different from the old sectional interpretation.

But whether applied to the West or to the nation, such an approach invites American geographers to address themselves directly to a task that they have never seriously undertaken as a field: a really comprehensive look at the full course of their nation's development with the object of contributing to a general assessment of its character. If it is true, as a leading historian has stated, that in the wake of disillusion with a sequence of once widely espoused and now discredited theories, American historians now recognize Alexis de Tocqueville's *Democracy in America* as "the most respected of all interpretations of the United States," it would seem an especially opportune time for the geographers to join in the common quest for significant generalizations (Higham 1965, 221–22).[3] For Tocqueville's interpretation rests upon a view of the United States as an "organic whole" with a recognizable "national character" which encompasses, under great tension, "oppressive conformity" and "kaleidoscopic variety," unmistakable "continuity" and "endless flux," regional diversity held together by multitudinous bonds of heritage and advantage. A penetrating systematic study of the United States as a varying set of regional parts developing through a recognizable sequence of interrelationships would seem to be essential to the explication of such an interpretation or any modern variant therefrom. Thus those American geographers who still see their own field in its historic wholeness, enriched by an equal concern for past and present, regional and topical, the particular and the general, ought to have something fresh and valuable to contribute.

SOURCE

This article appeared originally in the *Annals of the Association of American Geographers* 62 (1972): 159–84.

NOTES

1. See, for example, the report on the free-wheeling discussion at a recent meeting of the Western Historical Association (J. Carroll 1969, 265–99).

2. These four categories are considered to be central to any such analysis, but the scheme could readily be elaborated to bring others into similar focus. Perhaps the most obvious addition would be "economy," giving a more coherent place for topics herein included, if at all, under "circulation" and "culture."

3. All of the words and phrases in quotations in this paragraph are taken directly from Higham.

FURTHER READINGS

William H. Goetzmann and William N. Goetzmann. 1986. *The West of the imagination.* New York: Norton.

This book examines the portrayal of the West as Americans came to terms with the region in the nineteenth and twentieth centuries.

Patricia N. Limerick. 1987. *The legacy of conquest: The unbroken past of the American West.* New York: Norton.

Limerick questions long-standing assumptions implicit in many histories of the American West. She argues that the dominance of the Frontier thesis has had a stultifying effect on our understanding of the region because it forces us to view the places, events, and peoples of the West in terms of stereotypes. Limerick stresses the value of viewing the West as a conquered region that has difficulty facing the consequences of its conquest. By deemphasizing the concept of the West as a unique and now-closed frontier, Limerick is able to conceive of the West as a place worth studying in other terms, for example as a contact zone between widely varied cultures.

Donald W. Meinig. 1982. Geographical analysis of imperial expansion.

In *Period and place: Research methods in historical geography,* ed. Alan R. H. Baker and Mark Billinge, 71–78. Cambridge: Cambridge University Press.

This article provides a succinct statement of Meinig's generic model of imperialism. It is the theoretical foundation of his later work and the mature statement of ideas presented in the article "American Wests."

———. 1986. *The shaping of America: A geographical perspective on 500 years of history.* Vol. 1: *Atlantic America, 1492–1800.* New Haven: Yale University Press.

This is the first number in Meinig's planned three-volume survey of the geographical dynamics underpinning American history.

Thomas R. Vale and Geraldine R. Vale. 1989. *Western images, western landscapes: Travels along U.S. 89.* Tucson: University of Arizona Press.

Using essays and photographs, the Vales compare popular images of the West with reality. The book records a trip from the Canadian to the Mexican border and compares the observed natural environments and cultural symbols with their counterparts in popular culture.

David J. Wishart. 1979. *The fur trade of the American West, 1807–1840: A geographical synthesis.* Lincoln: University of Nebraska Press.

Inspired by Meinig's notions of "strategy" and "ecology," this slim book describes the unstable boundary that di-vided two cultures with radically different modes of pro-duction. The ecological disruption occasioned by the fur trade was disastrous for the local economies of Native Americans, whereas it was only inconvenient for the con-tinental economy of the Anglos.

ROBERT B. RILEY **9**

SPECULATIONS ON THE
NEW AMERICAN LANDSCAPES

Remembrance of a particular form is but regret for a particular moment; and houses, roads, avenues are as fugitive, alas, as the years.

— MARCEL PROUST,
SWANN'S WAY

The American landscape has changed remarkably since World War II. Some of that change has been noted and commented upon, but much seems to have eluded analysis or even recognition. The low-density spread of our cities, for example, has been a major concern of the American media for twenty years, but the concurrent development of a new urban pattern, nonhierarchical and multinoded, and called by Peirce Lewis (1979b) the "galactic city," has been recognized only by a few regional scientists. The impact of the strip and then the shopping center has produced many arguments between developers and the purveyors of taste and ecology, but little understanding. Just as some of our new landscapes have been noted and examined, so have some of the forces that have produced them. The rise of mass affluence, leisure, and mobility derived from the automobile, combined with a merchandising economy exploiting them, have been commonly identified, no doubt correctly, as important contributors to new landscape phenomena.

The changes we have recognized have usually been deplored and viewed as aberrations correctable through better taste and better planning. Our image of the ideal landscape and our relation to it still seems almost capturable by Norman Rockwell, even though the children he pictured skinny-dipping in the creek are probably competing behind the chain-link fence of the local swim club, and their parents fishing in the freeway borrow pit. We see the landscape through filters of custom and taste. We find in it what we seek, for as long as we can. It is not surprising that changes are only reluctantly recognized, nor that changes so obtrusive as to force recognition are condemned and viewed as temporary, insignificant, or correctable. The changes I see might not be those you see; we are even less likely to agree on their importance or their meaning.

What follow are observations on the new landscape: notes on a few of its forms, derivations, uses, and perceptions. These phenomena fit together into no obvious pattern. Perhaps they are not related. Perhaps we are too close to them to perceive their relationship. But the phenomena are widespread and distinctive enough to warrant inquiry and interpretation. And if answers elude us, speculation might at least sharpen our questions.

THE PLURALISTIC LANDSCAPE

Many interpreters of the American scene have sought to characterize *the* American landscape— a whole with a distinct national feel. Variations within that landscape have been seen as large homogeneous regions, differing from one another because of the nature of the land, settlement by groups of distinct traditions, or the technological and legal systems guiding their development. David Lowenthal (1968), J. B. Jackson (1970), and D. W. Meinig (1969a; 1971b) have all written about peculiarly American landscapes or landscape images, regional or national. Leo Marx, in *The Machine in the Garden* (1967), has supplied the best-known and most believable national image, that of the pastoral ideal, a compromise between the equally hostile city and wilderness. Meinig has recently (1979d) furnished a powerful addition, the description of three American landscape symbols of regional origin but eventual diffusion—New England Village, Ohio Valley Main Street, and California Suburbia. The theme of these writers is not only that the American cultural landscape is different from that of other countries but that it or its image (the

disentanglement of image from reality being a tricky business) is understandable as one entity, its values and satisfactions shared by most of its inhabitants. This approach has helped us to look at what goes on around us and aided our understanding.

But a useful way to understand what is happening today might be to think about the current American scene not as one landscape or a few regional ones, but as a pluralistic collection of diverse landscapes created and used by voluntary special-interest groups, each with its own distinctive ways of shaping, using, selling, and perceiving the environment. This may have always been true. The American landscape of the second half of the nineteenth century might be understood as such a collection: the landscapes of the rancher, farmer, railroad, mining town, and so on. Today, however, the role of the landscape as physical resource for specialized interests centered on recreation and merchandising seems to dominate the physical development of the landscape and our attitudes toward it.

This concept of the landscape as a diverse, maybe even centrifugal, collection of independent settings serving special-interest groups has been legitimized and institutionalized through publications and organizations serving its consumers and merchandisers. Proof from the consumer's side is available at any drugstore or supermarket where the magazine racks display *Popular Flyer, Runner's World, Trailer Boats, Treasure Search,* and *Off-Road Travel.* Purveyors can subscribe to *Auto Laundry News, Campground Merchandising, Fast Service* (for managers of drive-ins), *Motel/Motor Inn Journal, Shopping Center Digest,* and *Ski Area Management.* Depending on one's landscape preference and role, one can join the Sierra Club, Winnebago International Travelers, North American Family Camping Association, Hotel-Motel Greeters International, International Carwash Council, Conference of National Park Concessioners, or International Drive-In Association. These publications and organizations not only serve as pressure groups to promote development of landscapes, but define and reinforce specialized attitudes toward the land. Whether this development of specialized landscapes is new or an intensification of an old

but little noted trend is less important than the fact that recognition of it could aid our understanding of the contemporary landscape, how people perceive it, and what can and cannot reasonably be expected of it. This way of looking at our landscape is similar to that advocated by Glazer and Moynihan in *Beyond the Melting Pot* (1970) as a way of understanding our cities.

NEW SUBCULTURAL LANDSCAPES

The term *cultural landscape* has proven a useful designation for both a phenomenon and a field of study. Perhaps the concept of "subcultural landscape" might also help our understanding of the contemporary environment. It might seem pretentious to apply the term *subculture* to surfers or skimobilers, yet its use might offer a new way of looking at our landscapes. If we accept the term, we can immediately distinguish several differences between traditional and contemporary subcultures.

Traditional subcultures were distinguished by at least three features: participation in them was relatively unexamined; membership was nor-

mally long-term, maybe lifelong; and their forms were determined by tradition—regional, ethnic, or both. That some people did examine them and leave them only strengthens the claim for their stability and required commitment, because the pain of such examination and breaking free has been a major theme in our literature. Subcultures often produced their own distinct landscapes, whether the Cajun parishes of Louisiana or the Spanish uplands of northern New Mexico.

Today membership in subcultures is often a conscious selection by the participant, sometimes independent of class or job. Participation no longer need be lifelong; commitment is sometimes associated with a phase of life or personal development and in extreme cases may be only for weekends. Lastly, the forms through which such a subculture expresses itself and confirms its identity seldom stem directly from regional or social traditions; they are likely to be innovations or borrowings from remote times and places.

Whether or not we apply the term *subculture* to contemporary lifestyles, the exercise points up differences between the social associations that formerly shaped our landscape and those that shape it today. Contemporary subcultures, according to Henry Glassie (1968), are popular, or mass, cultures, and their older counterparts are folk cultures. Folk cultures are stable and conservative, with products derived from tradition. Popular cultures are changeable, with forms derived from the media. These distinctions can also be applied to the buildings and landscapes created or used by subcultures.

Our landscape is undergoing what Peterson and DiMaggio (1975) called "massification." This has already happened to our media, popular literature, and ways of building. The landscape—stable, difficult and slow to change—is one of the last parts of society to reflect the dominance of mass culture, but it is finally yielding. The landscape produced is as pluralistic as contemporary mass culture itself. The massification of our landscape has not gone unnoted, but it, too, has been thought an aberration, a commercial connivance to be deplored and if possible stopped. It is, instead, a logical and perhaps inevitable expression of our society. It can be deplored, but short of a drastic change in our society, it is no more likely to be stopped or reversed than the spread of television.

Glassie makes another useful distinction between mass and folk culture in noting that "folk material exhibits major variation over space and minor variation through time, while the products of popular . . . culture exhibit minor variations over space and major variation through time. . . . A search for patterns in folk material yields regions, where a search for patterns in popular material yields periods" (Glassie 1968, 33). This observation reveals two more ways new landscapes differ from traditional ones. The first is more rapid change. Change is not easy to live with, but if accelerated change is an integral part of mass culture we must take it as the rule and not an aberration. The hope that the ordinary landscape, laden with cultural and personal memories, might serve as a stable reference against future shock is forlorn. Attempts at preservation of the cultural landscape, a fashionable topic on the conference circuit, may produce only museum pieces or tourist attractions.

The second difference between old and new

landscapes implied in Glassie's statement lies in their spatial pattern. A mass landscape will not produce large homogeneous regions, distinct one from the other, that characterized folk culture. Just as most new subcultures are, or diffuse to become, national, so do their landscapes. This supposed homogenization of the American landscape disturbs the sophisticated commentators of the mass media. To be sure, we can travel through space but not time. A distant landscape is recapturable, a past landscape is not. Still, we might wonder why temporal change frightens but areal change is admired. This supposed homogenization deserves to be questioned. Given the diversity and fragmentation of current mass culture, the difference between old and new landscapes might lie not in the amount of diversity but in its pattern, specifically in its grain. Writers repeatedly claim that our cities look more and more alike, as in Calvin Trillin's worries over the "Houstonization" of New Orleans. That claim is probably valid. What has not been considered, however, is that New Orleans, Houston, and most of our contemporary cities might contain more diverse landscapes *within* them than ever before. Do our new landscapes really lack diversity, or has their diversity gone unrecognized because it occurs in a finer pattern and at a smaller scale?

A new historic consciousness among designers and the liberal political elite is producing the preservation of fragments of the traditional urban scene and restoring entire neighborhoods. The development of landscapes as diverse as new suburbs, office and apartment complexes lining circumferential freeways, strips and shopping centers, and even, as Grady Clay (1980) has noted, the penetration of the landscape of pornography into suburbia, makes it hard to justify describing our cities as less diverse than those of three decades ago. Diversity is a subjective term. Observers of the landscape apply it mostly to differences traceable to folk traditions of regional or ethnic origin, which are supposedly less self-conscious than those of mass culture. As Glassie has noted, a typology that depends on this distinction is of little use today, when it is impossible for a genuine folk article to be produced in an unreflective manner. Ian Nairn (1965),

an advocate of diversity based on place, said it well: "Making a pattern out of the environment has got to be conscious—the days when it would come naturally are long past." Somehow, though, differences derived from conscious design, whether popular or elite, are assumed to be less real than those of folk tradition, and their diversity continues unnoticed or is dismissed as "plastic."

A good image of the older American landscape might be a quilt made from a few pieces of solid, bright colors, clearly different and demarcated. The image of the newer landscape might be an intricately designed, mass-produced wallpaper, in which elements are repeated all across the country, but exist in propinquity and great variety at a small scale. The diversity of the wallpaper is not less than the diversity of the quilt—only different.

PACKAGED LANDSCAPES

Just as the stability, cultural typology, and spatial pattern of our landscape have changed, so have its forms, uses, and control. These changes

can be seen most clearly by looking at the most popular landscapes, rather than at landscapes traditionally important or landscapes that fit conventional aesthetic or social values. Mass use of a landscape might represent only a choice among inadequate alternatives, not the satisfaction of deep human needs, but knowledge of our needs and satisfaction from the landscape is minimal. The most visible and superficially successful landscapes, as judged on their prevalence and popularity, are a good place to start, because as J. B. Priestley noted in *Journey down a Rainbow* (1955, xiii), "It is not when people are toiling and trading . . . that they best reveal themselves and the character of their society. It is when they are spending the money they have earned, when they are feeling easy and relaxed, when they are most impressionable, that the pattern blazes out."

Many of our most popular, heavily used landscapes and many of the developments distinguishing our landscape from that of thirty years ago are commercial. They can be characterized as landscapes which are openly merchandised, landscapes in which the distinction between public and private is blurred, and landscapes in which management dominates design.

Given the dominant commercial orientation of our society over the last three decades, the extent and visibility of the commercial landscape is not surprising. But as such landscapes have spread they have taken on a new role. They have become competitive merchandising tools and shapers of commercial images—total packages, for sale or hire. The merchandising techniques of Disney World and other theme parks have trickled down to "destination" and "resort" campgrounds where up to 70 percent of gross revenue comes from "profit centers" such as stores, game rooms, and water slides, not from site rentals. Housing developments are promoted as "total environments" with a distinctive image, be it quaint or cosmopolitan—an approach far more comprehensive than the older habit of taking street names from Walter Scott novels. Newer shopping malls offer a similar package to their customers. The space in front of McDonald's restaurants, where parking space has yielded to token tables and chairs, has now evolved into "McDonald Land." John Portman and his imitators have returned to the hotel tradition of monumental space, which had been eliminated in the motels of the 1950s and 1960s. In its most elaborate examples this space approaches a total interior landscape, closer in spirit to the Victorian conservatory than to modern approaches of framing the exterior landscape or dissolving barriers between outside and inside. It rejects the exterior landscape, which is usually devoted to cars, the disarray of the strip, and the decay of the downtown. In its ultimate expressions it makes that rejection, and the abnegation of public responsibility, visually explicit through the use of mirrored glass walls.

As lavish commercial settings evolve into total landscapes, the legal, spatial, and perceptual distinctions between public and private space become more difficult to define. The landscapes of the past were one or the other; the difference between the great estate and the park, courthouse square, or business street were clear. As people entered a store, they clearly moved from one realm to the other. But theme parks, KOAs, and malls seem neither public nor private but proprietary spaces that contain aspects of each, where traditional distinctions mean little.

Perhaps the change began on the strip. There we knew that the highway was public and the interior of the restaurant or liquor store was private (at least in the sense that we were there at the owner's sufferance). But how did we perceive the auto-serving spaces in between? The land was in private title, but the parking lot cruising of the 1950s was as public as any Italian *passeggiata*. The ambitiously landscaped corporate office park abutting the interstate highway is private land, but is meant to be perceived as a public amenity, if only a visual amenity. The enclosed shopping mall transcends purely commercial activity to usurp former functions of public space; the Girl Scout concert and the community art show are held there, and Planned Parenthood competes with Right-to-Life for bakesale dollars. The right to distribute literature in shopping centers, on the grounds that they constitute public space, has been the subject of at least one court case. Sliding shopfronts dissolve the barrier between individual stores and circulation space in the mall; McDonald's lures school groups to its playgrounds; and each weekend thousands of Americans contribute to the growth of proprietary space as they open their garage doors to sell the family's castoffs.

These commercial landscapes seem determined less by principles of design than of management. This distinction is almost as difficult to make as spatial definitions on the strip, but there is still a difference. Perhaps the difference is that design determines and management responds. Perhaps it is that design can convey many values, while management is dominated by only one—efficiency. Certainly a mark of shopping center management is its pragmatism and responsiveness to change, expressed in its decision to rent or refuse space, and its control over the decoration of such space. Dominance of management over design or uncontrolled experience is not limited to commercial landscapes—witness the federal government's concern with "visual management" as a guideline for development of public lands.

Do these packaged landscapes serve people's needs any better or worse than parks and courthouse squares once did? There are no nineteenth-century user-satisfaction studies of parks to compare with those that could be compiled for today's shopping centers. Does the often-noted absence of sleeping winos in suburban shopping malls really mean that those spaces are not successful environments? There might be a difference between what consumers want and what society needs, but who is to define that difference?

Still, we need not be Marxist landscape critics to be uneasy about the fact that our most successful communal spaces are neither created nor controlled by a communal body. Maybe the profit-oriented management of the new landscapes is as attentive to its users' wants as were the builders of the nineteenth-century railroad palaces or the politicians who supported the great turn-of-the-century urban park systems. Maybe the consumer's legendary discretionary dollar is as effective in achieving responsive landscapes as a vote for park commissioner once was. But however cynical and rapacious the political system underlying the City Beautiful movement might have been, it never claimed that all the goals of an Olmsted park system were summed up in a profit and loss statement. In the end, no one is a citizen of Six Flags Over Texas.

A NEW URBANITY?

The strong antiurban bias of American culture has been a persistent theme among observers of our society and our landscape and was most convincingly documented in Page Smith's *As a City upon a Hill* (1966). Yet for three decades the media have assured us that urban revitalization is just around the corner. The centralization of the media in our larger cities (the rare exception is the *Reader's Digest,* which might have invented Pleasantville, New York, if it hadn't discovered it) and its staffing by young people attracted by the urban image may have produced a media message masking the fact that many Americans care no more about the city, except as an unwanted sink for their tax money, than they ever did.

This bias might partially explain the fate of older urban renewal schemes that so often inserted great open spaces into languishing central business districts. The schemes began with skill-ful public relations renderings of big city plazas containing more trees than all the squares of Europe and filtered down through increasingly drab, unimaginative street-to-mall conversions in ever smaller cities. Those spaces almost never fulfilled their promise of attracting new business or public life. Their emptiness is one of the saddest sights of our contemporary landscape.

But something seems different today. The renewed area around Boston's Fanueil Hall draws more visitors in a year than Disney World, a comparative measure of success that seems to surprise no one. Novelty, the long local romance with history, exceptionally sensitive planning and design—any of these might make Boston an unusual case. Still, what is happening there and in other cities is not the indifference that greeted the plazas of the 1960s, nor, so far, the brief popularity and subsequent slide into seediness or squalor of Underground Atlanta, Gaslight Square in St. Louis, or Chicago's Old Town. The spreading rehabilitation of older urban housing also seems to be evidence of a change in attitudes toward the city. If the complex financial role of the federal government disqualifies such redevelopment as pure free-market choice, nevertheless there seems a message of change since the days of renewal by fiat and bulldozer. And if it is primarily the professional and managerial elite and the upwardly ambitious young who are revitalizing the city, well—who led that original movement to the suburbs?

What might be causing this shift in values? One answer is that the suburban dream has faded, that families who might once have moved to suburbia now find it wanting on the same counts on which designers and sociologists have long faulted it—automobile dependence, long commutes, social pressure, and a bland, homogeneous life and setting. A more cynical explanation has been offered in the *Saturday Review* by Karl Meyer (1970), who notes that in 1958 eight of ten most-watched U.S. televisions shows were laid in rural or Old West settings, while in 1975 eight of ten were laid in urban or big city suburban settings—a "long march from hitching post to corner drug store to mean streets." He sees this change, and the boom in urban sports and culture, not as a response to new cultural values, but as the product of a media marketing strategy that packages audiences into metropolitan units.

But there is another possible answer that would mark a deeper change in attitudes. The suburbs were merchandised not only as meeting an American "need" for owning a single-family, detached house on plenty of land, but as the ideal setting for a particular model of family life—a model in which the man was the absent-five-days-each-week income producer and the occasional weekend handyman, and the woman the manager of house, family, and civic activities. How effectively the suburban setting physically supported such activity is an open question, but surely the images of environment and family were linked. Increasing numbers of young middle-class people, particularly women, seem to reject that model of family life, and they might well be a major source of the people refurbishing older parts of our cities. The interest in the city might be less a preference for the traditional urban amenities than for the greater practical facility with which the city supports the life of a family, perhaps childless, in which two adults work outside the home and allot their other roles in accord with individual preferences and needs, not traditional sex roles.

Changes also seem to be occurring in the use of public space and in the image of urbanity. We have learned, finally, that physical design, although it can impede or suppress positive use of a space, seldom generates it. Candid designers point to the role of programmed, well-funded, formal activities as a major generator of such use, and their absence as a serious obstacle. A great deal of the less-structured use of such spaces centers around luxurious, conspicuous consumption—patronage of boutiques, poster, and furnishings shops, and purveying expensive and exotic foods. (Everyone seems to be buying this food or eating it on the spot; who could have foreseen pushcart entrepreneurs selling quiche in that northernmost bastion of southern cooking, Washington, D.C.) Management and merchandising seem as dominant in the new urban street life as in the suburban shopping mall. Successful and active as that street life might be, it is not the same mix of activities associated with the traditional *passeggiata,* or hanging out and promenading. If the support that cities offer to freer family organization raises high hopes for a new urbanism, the dependence of street life on public funding and luxury retailing also raises questions for the future.

Before World War II, the taste maker's image of American urbanity emphasized elegance: tree-filled parks and boulevards, Beaux Arts opera houses, and uniformed doormen beneath cast-iron *porte cochères.* Today the city is increasingly viewed as a place for excitement, not elegance. The essence of urbanity is not seen as an ordered setting for decorous display of wealth and class distinction, but as a chaotic bazaar offering the expense-account society an eclectic and hedonistic assortment of delights ranging from Scandinavian furniture to Szechuan cooking. This is a change from toney to trendy, even to tawdry. If the image is still European, it is that of Montmartre, not the Champs Elysées. It is a change Roger Starr (1966) characterized well in his comparison of *sauce bernaise* to the chicken on the delicatessen rotisserie, a change highlighted in the contemporary advertisement of a Volvo parked in front of a graffiti-covered wall—a safe exposure to delights that border on the dangerous: "a civilized car for an uncivilized world." Like the success of new spaces, the success of this new image is often tied to spending and acquisition.

THE LANDSCAPE OF NOSTALGIA

Nostalgia is not a new element in human appreciation of the landscape. It dates back at least to late Roman times, as David Lowenthal (1975; 1985) has noted. Its omnipresence as a merchandisable commodity, however, is a vivid but discouraging aspect of our contemporary landscape. The landscape of nostalgia is not the use of historic forms or references by elite architects, as in the Renaissance or the revivals of the nineteenth century. It is not the contextualism of today's *avant-garde,* nor the obeisance to *genius loci* of the Townscape school. Neither is it the desire to maintain a visual sense of history and continuity in our urban fabric, nor the desire to conserve building shells of the past for present reuse, whether for visual rationales or energy conservation reasons.

The landscape of nostalgia, although sometimes difficult to separate from such approaches, is an attempt to re-create physically an environment of saccharine comfort associated with a past life thought more simple and reassuring than today's. Fred Davis (1977) defined nostalgia as applying only to events or objects that an individual has experienced personally, limiting the time span to one's own life. This definition seems too narrow—times that we were told about by parents and grandparents, for example, surely can be a part of our emotional life. Lowenthal has even noted a commercial restoration based on this, where everything is continually arranged to appear seventy-five years old. If the goal of nostalgia is successful escape, then its landscape should represent a time and place recapturable in the imagination, but the success of Disney World's Main Street might indicate that clever manipulation can extend that time back further, maybe all the way to Old Sturbridge.

As the element of nostalgia in our relation to the landscape is not new, neither are attempts to design landscapes of nostalgia, such as the rural pastiches at Versailles. But traditionally such designs were limited to creations for the very rich, to special museum settings such as "Yesteryear's Main Street," or more recently, to the landscape of tourism. Today it is a mass phenomenon. We can enter a taxi in almost any large American city and confidently ask to be taken to the local renewed nineteenth-century warehouse district where we find the expected decor of macrame, butcher block, and exposed brick known in the trade as "fern bar" style. Housing magazines advise developers to "cash in on today's wave of nostalgia with early American design. And make the design authentic" (L. Marshall 1979). In Mystic, Connecticut, we can shop in Olde Mistic Village Shopping Center, built from scratch in 1976 to resemble all we imagine of a New England village of 1720. Tolerance and a willingness to suspend value judgments are needed to understand our contemporary landscape, which often violates traditional canons of taste and beauty. But the widespread commercial reconstruction of landscapes that we never knew, but wish we

had, is troubling. It seems to show not only that our relations with the contemporary landscape are unsatisfying, but that we are reluctant to confront that fact. Occasional fantasy, whether Stockbroker Tudor or Disney Main Street, is one thing; the routine substitution of fantasy for reality in the everyday environment, and the willing confusion of which is which, is another matter.

HEDONISM, HIGH TECHNOLOGY, AND ENCAPSULIZATION

The American romance with technology has been a long one. Leo Marx (1967) saw it personified in Benjamin Franklin and illustrated by the locomotives and steamboats in nineteenth-century landscape paintings. But since Thoreau pondered the railroad whistle sounding in the countryside, technology has not only increased the power and speed offered to its user, but has become available to the individual, not just the community, in automobiles, power boats, and recreational and off-road vehicles. As technology has become more personalized, it has become more flexible, more capable of conquering place and terrain, and has come to offer a variety of immediate, personal gratifications. The image of technology and power over nature embodied in the train or steamboat was abstract indeed compared to the feel of a trail bike under our hands and feet.

Sensory delight in speed, motion, and impact, control over our movement and over brute technological power, and mastery over the environment are themes in many contemporary involvements with the landscape. The theme is seen in the new roller-coaster mania, in the musical romanticization of the trucker's landscape (Sulzinger 1979), and even in the use of the power mower, which has so drastically changed the grounds of the farmstead. Some of the newly popular activities—soaring, hang gliding, downhill skiing, surfing, skateboarding, roller-skating, and watersliding—depend on highly sophisticated technology. Even backpacking has developed its own folding-aluminum, high-technology, imported-camping-gear syndrome. High technology has become an object of fascination as important as the experience it serves. The confining upper-class dress and the formalized rhythmic body movement of the eighteenth century—the farthingale and slipper, the polonaise, the thrust and parry of fencing—were seen by Rasmussen in *Experiencing Architecture* (1964) as reflections of the great Baroque systems of channeled, sequential movement and attendant conceptions of space and landscape. Perhaps the eclectically costumed skier or roller-skater, speeding through the landscape wearing radio headphones, could tell us something about the role and image of our contemporary environment, if we only knew what to ask.

The popularity of mobile, miniaturized, encapsulated environments—the trailer, motor home, pick-up camper, and van—is a complementary development. It might be unnecessary to search for deep psychic motivations behind this, because simple convenience explains much of it. Still, it is not difficult to see evidence of territoriality in the physical structuring of a defensible home-territory portable through a strange environment. Nor is it difficult to see evidence of the aedicular complex described by Summerson in *Heavenly Mansions* (1963) and Moore and his coauthors in *The Place of Houses* (C. Moore, Lyndon, and Allen 1974) in the miniaturization of the suburban interior in mobile homes, or the fantasy pleasure palace in Tijuana-Baroque van decor, and of rustic butcher block in the truck houses of the Bay Area. Or maybe the owners of these encapsulated environments are acting out Leo Marx's theme of retreat, exploration, and return, condensed in time and space, with the motor home serving as city and the dirt-bike trail as wilderness.

But whatever human drives might be at work, one aspect of their relationship with the environment has been given little thought. The litter and visual intrusion, the damage and even destruction associated with these mobile dwellings, is thought to show a contemptuous disregard for the environment by the users. But perhaps these people simply have a different concept of their environment than managers and backpackers. To these recreationists, the mobile dwelling might be the essential environment, with the casually visited, interchangeable, exterior physical setting becoming a simple resource of conve-

nience. Care and emotional involvement are encouraged by long exposure through time and enriched by successive discovery. When landscapes become only transient, interchangeable settings, deeper relationships may be missing. The encapsulated environment, not the landscape, receives care and offers emotional meaning, perhaps just as garden and farmstead once did.

Scarcity of gasoline and the rise in its price will undoubtedly affect the use of these motorized, miniaturized environments, but it is not certain that it will significantly reduce their popularity. The 1978 per capita petroleum consumption in California, that supposed source and symbol of nomadic, irresponsible lifestyle, was only 0.3 percent greater than the national average. This indicates that recreational-vehicle use could well survive energy restrictions. Campground owners observed that in the summer of 1979, although use of remote campgrounds dropped severely, those nearer large population centers preserved or even increased their occupancy rates—another measure of the importance and adaptability of this phenomenon. The pollution, land damage, and energy investment involved in this new definition of environment are real. But unless we understand that spontaneity, sensual pleasure, a long-standing fondness for technology, and a flexible concept of environment are not transitory fads or consumer gimmicks, but evolving ways of relating to the landscape, we shall not find effective ways of reducing their impact.

THE WITHERING OF CLASS

Many of our older landscapes were associated with social class distinctions. The elite of nineteenth-century American cities congregated on tree-lined boulevards and park roads, just as the Baroque aristocracy gathered in monumental avenues and plazas. The country clubs surrounding American cities were once landscapes of social class—archetypal settings for the characters of F. Scott Fitzgerald and John O'Hara, just as the streets and pool halls of the city were for the Irish of James T. Farrell. The rituals of the croquet green or tennis court differed from those of the soccer field or baseball diamond in accor-

dance with differences in social status. Today such distinctions still exist, but they are so finely drawn or restricted to so few settings as to offer little help in understanding our landscape. The role of landscape in reinforcing class distinctions, in confirming who or where you were on the social ladder, was perhaps a positive role only for those at the top. Still, the loss of that role eliminates one more source of continuity and one more stable relationship with the landscape.

PROBLEMS AND PORTENTS

The derivation of our landscape forms from the mass media rather than tradition; the loss of homogeneous regional character, and its replacement by variation over time; the role of special-interest groups and voluntary associations; the provision, control, and ownership of landscapes by corporations rather than communities; the loss of public-private demarcation and ties to social class—although these themes fit no simple pattern and their meaning might be unclear, they do allow some general observations on our relationship to the contemporary landscape and

that of the near future. One is that many traditional relationships that gave meaning to the landscape are no longer tenable. Often our relationship with the landscape now is that of visitors to places of which we neither have nor need deep, intimate knowledge. Theme parks, national parks, and urban malls for the weekend visitor are removed in space and time from much of daily life. Even today's farmer might need a more detailed knowledge of equipment, chemicals, and tax strategies than of his land, which becomes, like the desert setting for visiting trail-bikers, another interchangeable resource of convenience. Our settings are provided already packaged by others. We have little involvement and few ties with these settings: no ownership, no control, little legal or emotional responsibility. Our satisfactions derive not from pride of ownership or development, nor from emotional tie to place, nor from tradition. They are, instead, sensory and transient—eating, racing, viewing, buying, and selling—the satisfactions not of builders nor participants, but of quick consumers. Perhaps these relationships are not less satisfying than older ones, only different.

Perhaps they are a first stage in the development of new relationships.

Another discouraging aspect of our new landscapes is that the burden of forging new, meaningful relationships falls on the individual or isolated family, with little help from tradition or other people. If this is a freedom, it is a lonely one. Many activities pursued so fervently in our landscape—the buying and selling of expensive bric-a-brac, the hedonistic quick-fix abetted by technology, the constant movement—could be interpreted as a troubled search for ties, meaning, and involvement. Perhaps they portray a landscape of alienation—the specter hinted at in the ironic humor of Calvin Trillin and sketched with frightening immediacy in recent essays by Herbert Gold (1975), William Kowinski (1978; 1985), and Michael Harrington (1979). We know too little about the role landscapes play in satisfying psychic needs to make easy characterizations. Still, there is a sadness in the spectacle of millions of isolated individuals, Priestley's "nomadmass," making their lonely way across the landscape, seeking vestiges of communal participation through transitory groupings like trailer-club meetings, van-ins, or what Grady Clay (1971) called "swarming," all engaged in a search for pleasure in temporary, almost interchangeable landscapes.

Human adaptability is considerable. If current relationships with landscapes seem superficial compared to those available in the past, that does not mean deeper relationships cannot again be developed. But optimism should not come easily. Adaptation takes time. Given the transient nature of forms derived from mass culture and the even more rapid change associated with the hyped-up commercialism, we might find ourselves always struggling to adapt to yesterday's landscapes. The issue is not whether we can adapt to new environments, but what physiological and psychological costs such adaptation requires. The term *adaptation* carries a connotation of tolerating an environment without incurring excessive stress. Is the best we can expect from our future environment the absence of harmful stress rather than the deeper meanings possible in the past? If adaptation takes more time than we have, what are our chances for developing enduring satisfaction?

If the quickening pace of change raises troubling doubts, so does the fact that our landscapes are increasingly provided, owned, and managed by bureaucracies or corporations such as the Bureau of Land Management and the Marriott Corporation—organizations remote from our daily life and control. Our only power to affect such landscapes is withholding our dollars, which is a negative influence more likely to eliminate unsatisfactory landscapes than to shape fulfilling ones. Our feeling of control over the environment and our sense of competence can be as important as the attributes of the environment itself. That feeling of control is not likely to be significant in a bureaucratically or corporately managed environment.

Finally, the commercial nature of many of our new landscapes raises doubts about their future in an increasingly precarious economy. Equating success with earnings is not confined to commercial landscapes; federal and state campgrounds, for example, are under pressure to raise prices to reduce operating losses in a time of taxpayer discontent and to respond to complaints of unfair competition and hidden subsidies raised by private operators. The high capital and maintenance investment of packaged environments requires those environments to return a profit. If profits fail, will we see a landscape littered with the evidence of unsuccessful competitors, or will HUD money revitalize theme parks and motel pleasure domes? Travel and sophisticated personal technology require affluent consumers; our new landscapes are built not only on leisure, but well-monied leisure. Much of the success of shopping centers and urban malls depends on buying and selling—not merchandising staple goods in bazaars or crossroads grocery stores of the past, but purveying luxury items. We might choose to stroll rather than buy, but unless someone is buying posters, quiche, and pottery, these settings may not survive. The possibility of economic depression, more than energy costs, raises doubts about the long-term viability of many of our new landscapes.

We are faced with forgoing older relationships with our landscape and forging new ones, with little help from tradition or community, in times of faster change and decreasing control. Not all satisfactions sought in the landscape depend on stable, long-enduring relationships, but some do. Those satisfactions may be ever harder to find. The sadness and pain of change are major elements of the human experience; the stability and continuity of the landscape as a counterbalance would be no small gift for troubled lives. But if earth abides forever, packaged landscapes do not. The most troubling environmental problem of the years ahead might not be conserving energy or protecting natural systems, but emotionally coping with a landscape more transitory than we have ever experienced, or than Proust could have ever envisioned.

REPRISE: 1992

My 1981 essay speculated about changes in our landscape. It was meant to be timely. I have made no changes in it except for a few editorial clarifications. A second chance, however, is too rare to pass up, so I will offer a few observations twelve years later. I hope readers will do the same.

The new urbanity continues, as highly developed in galactic nodes as in the original central city. Federal funds for programming open spaces have disappeared, as surmised, but someone must have found the money to replace them. In some of our new nodes, more money and attention seem to go to fostering festivals than fixing up housing.

The hedonistic, hi-tech, quick-fix landscape has become a merchandising art form, with entire catalogs devoted to yuppy adult-child toys for use in the real or artificial landscape: wind surfers, rollerblades, joggers' disc players, and even videotapes of wilderness trails viewed from stationary exercise bicycles. And whatever happened to the landscape changes that we thought would result from higher gasoline prices?

The packaged landscape has become the norm for upscale commercial development. As it is perfected, so it spreads over the globe. I am writing these retrospective comments on the shore of the Aegean in a miniurban complex called "The Village Inn," a blend of late Mediterranean and early Hyatt. Twelve years ago only architects and the odd pop-culture student commented on Walt Disney's "imagineering." Now, laments about Disneyfication pop up in almost every middlebrow publication. West Edmonton

Mall combines residence, theme park, and shopping center in one vast 5,200,000 square foot complex, and a new Las Vegas Mall, with automated, twelve-foot-high Roman orator, complements the fantasy of the casinos and hotels. Confusion between private and public proceeds apace; a recent book on the American built landscape is subtitled *The New American City and the End of Public Space* (Sorkin 1992).

Nostalgia, as I pointed out, has a long history. Its particularly American form, imitating the English gentry, has been reviewed by Wilber Zelinsky (1980). Whole areas of our cities are merchandised as nostalgia. Nostalgia has also spread beyond Anglophiles and urban gentrifiers into most suburban development. Ranch-house, pseudocolonial, and bogus baronial are yielding to postmodern vicarious Victorian, as small lot subdivisions ring our cities with two-story houses overlaid with pseudo-nineteenth-century ornament, lacking both depth and system, applied like giant decals. The four-foot-wide path from carport to front door, now raised and clad in roof and pseudo-Victorian woodwork, has become the ubiquitous nostalgia porch, wide enough only to squeeze by the weathered wreath or swag of dried corn. Seaside, overpriced nostalgia for jetting timesharers spawns its progeny across the countryside.

I wrote that although American cities might be coming to look more and more alike, diversity within them was increasing, even though it was a self-conscious diversity. Diversification continues, but some, in fact, is not self-conscious. Cubans, Haitians, Latin Americans, Hmong, Thai, Vietnamese, and now a second wave of eastern Europeans enrich our cities with their landscapes. Often, of course, the ethnicity goes hand in hand with poverty.

'HOODS AND SUBS

Given the continuing rioting in our cities, my claim about the withering of class now seems quaint, if not downright blind. In fact, there well might be less ostentatious display of traditional class in American cities and suburbs than there was fifty years ago, but after twelve years of "greed is good," we have developed two disparate landscapes: the landscape of cash and comfort and the landscape of decay and despair. In North Dallas, quarter-of-a-million-dollar "middle-class" homes breed like lemmings and race each other toward the Oklahoma border. For miles on the east side of Detroit, a few dilapidated houses are occupied, as many stand gaping, gutted shells, and entire blocks are razed. These contrasts have produced a new landscape of fear, a landscape where the retired huddle in Florida bunkers, where subdivisions are called "gated estates," and security signs, less euphemistically, threaten armed response. The rural counterpart consists of a doberman, chain-link fence, and the sign "these premises protected by Smith and Wesson." The fear mentality has invaded the city centers too, a phenomenon Mike Davis (1990; see also Sorkin 1992) has called "fortress Los Angeles." Some twenty-five years ago, Michael Harrington pointed out that most of us seldom thought about the other America because most Americans never saw it. Most of us are now aware of it because we see it every day, but only in the media. The landscape of fear is a tricky subject, a state of mind as much as physical artifact. Cities have traditionally been perceived as

dangerous, until well into an affluent twentieth century. But as Joan Didion (1992) has observed, the media, in the last decade, have largely recreated that landscape of fear.

THE NEW RURAL LANDSCAPE

Settlement patterns in rural America have changed as drastically as those in urban and suburban America. But, aside from constant lamentations over farmland conversion on the urban edge, rural change has still escaped our notice and our thoughts. Through history, those who lived *on* the land lived *from* the land, whether by farming, timbering, or other extractive industry. People living in villages serviced those living on and from the land. That was the countryside. It has changed radically. Extractive industry uses more machines and fewer men. Agriculture is shrinking in on itself to the better land and leaving the poorer. But the pockets deserted by farming are not deserted by people. Strange sublandscapes remain in the country, landscapes that seldom disturb our image of prosperous grain and animal farming. Such landscapes are as di-

verse as living by wits and welfare in the fiction of Caroline Chute's northern Maine (1985; 1988), as computer publishing around Peterborough, New Hampshire (Louv 1983), as the prosperous *sinsemilla* monoculture that succeeded an extinct timbering monoculture in northern California (Raphael 1985). More than that, a new network of settlement, treating rural land only as a residential amenity, is draped across our continent, an unprecedented phenomenon noted by myself (forthcoming), P. Lewis (1991), Raphael (1986), and Louv (1983), who termed it buckshot urbanization. We have yet even to recognize this new rural landscape, let alone develop a vocabulary or concepts for understanding it.

Finally, any commentary on our new landscapes must note that some old landscapes continue but are ignored. Sociologists, anthropologists, designers, and planners gather in conferences to discuss the dichotomy between urban and suburban settlement patterns, and new designs for combining the best of both of them in "pedestrian-oriented settlements and neighborhoods." It never occurs to these professionals and academicians to think about settlement systems

in terms other than urban or suburban or to consider that "small town" is both a distinct concept and a persistent fact. Small towns have changed. Many of their stores and institutions have closed. People who live in them often work and shop elsewhere. But most small towns in reasonably healthy areas of the United States are now surrounded by new housing. Small-town America has indeed changed, but it has *not* died. It is available for those who, in the jargon, "seek the lifestyle of the neighborhood in a nonurban location." I fear we are sometimes as blind to continuity as we are to change.

SOURCE

This chapter is a revised and expanded version of an article originally published in *Landscape* 24 (3) (1980): 1–9.

FURTHER READINGS

Jean Baudrillard. 1988. *America*. Trans. Chris Turner. London: Verso.

Baudrillard, one of France's philosophers of postmodernism, writes of his travels in the United States. Baudrillard creates a collage of vivid images to characterize what he sees as the "hyperreality" manifest in contemporary American life.

Mike Davis. 1990. *City of quartz: Excavating the future in Los Angeles.* London: Verso.

Davis provides a provocative book that attempts to deconstruct the meaning of Los Angeles. Davis's discussion unravels the conflicts and struggles for power that are expressed in the postmodern landscapes of southern California.

Joan Didion. 1992. Sentimental journeys. In *After Henry,* 253–319. New York: Simon and Schuster.

This long essay speculates on crime, its perception, and its politics in contemporary Manhattan. Didion includes a succinct treatment (276–85) of the perception of safety in the landscape and attitudes toward Central Park and of its social role. She offers insights in the perception of safe landscapes, social class, and the media.

Joel Garreau. 1991. *Edge city: Life on the new frontier.* New York: Doubleday.

Edge City offers a fresh interpretation of the form of the modern American city as thought provoking as Jean Gottmann's *Megalopolis.* Garreau comes to terms with America's disaggregated urban forms by proposing the term "edge city" to characterize the concentrations of social and economic activity that stand apart from the chaos of urban life.

Herbert Gold. 1975. Finding the times in offramp city. *New Republic,* 8 February.

A weary traveler returning from Europe is forced to spend the night in a New York he never knew existed: the ragged surrounds of Idlewild that he calls offramp city. A witty and almost surreal exploration of one of those urban areas that comes up blank in our cognitive maps, but where people live their lives.

William S. Kowinski. 1985. *The malling of America: An inside look at the great consumer paradise.* New York: W. Morrow.

This is the compendium of malldom. Kowinski's attention and speculation range from the smallest tricks of mall merchandising to the blurring of the private, the public, the purchaser, and the purveyor in contemporary American life.

Peirce Lewis. 1991. The urban invasion of the rural Northeast. In *National Rural Studies Committee: A proceedings,* ed. Emery Castle and Barbara Baldwin, 11–21. Corvallis: Oregon State University, Western Rural Development Center.

Like Garreau, Lewis analyzes the landscape of a new city-countryside relationship. He finds not a ragged edge,

however, but a broad and pervasive intrusion of urban living into a changed countryside.

Richard Louv. 1983. *America II.* Boston: Houghton Mifflin.

This book has been unjustly ignored by students of the landscape, perhaps because its author is unabashedly a journalist. Louv was among the first to offer a fresh look at new landscapes in a new America. His observations on the "New Eden," and particularly what he calls "buckshot urbanization," should be read with Lewis and Garreau.

David Lowenthal. 1985. *The past is a foreign country.* Cambridge: Cambridge University Press.

Lowenthal addresses how societies interpret and reinterpret the past. His argument has a bearing on Riley's speculations because, for Lowenthal, even new landscapes represent a reshaping of the past in creative, inventive, but sometimes misleading and self-serving ways.

Karal A. Marling. 1984. *The colossus of roads: Myth and symbol along the American highway.* Minneapolis: University of Minnesota Press.

Marling's book traces her travels through Minnesota during one summer in the early 1980s. Her interest is in the aesthetics of the Midwest and in midwestern stories and symbols. In particular, she focuses on the American penchant for commemorating the past with gigantic roadside statuary. These works are often anonymous, vernacular sculpture, but they are sometimes icons with popular appeal created by well-known artists.

Frank Popper. 1986. There's no place like home, baby. *American Land Forum* 6 (3): 8–10.

Popper takes a short, incisive, and warm look at "saturday afternoon in Highland Pizza." In fewer than three pages he captures the essence of much of urbanized America that eludes our traditional categories of city, town, and suburb.

Ray Raphael. 1985. *Cash crop: An American dream.* Mendocino, Calif.: Ridge Times.

By all accounts the best analysis of the marijuana-growing boom in Humboldt County, California, in the 1970s and 1980s. What distinguishes *Cash Crop* is that the *sinsemilla* story is told in the context of over a century of changing land use in the California backcountry. Raphael places the marijuana culture in the context of comprehensive social change and relates it to changing American attitudes toward land, nature, money, and independence.

Michael Sorkin, ed. 1992. *Variations on a theme park: Scenes from the new American city and the end of public space.* New York: Hill and Wang.

A collection of essays—uneven, occasionally annoying, always provocative—on the new urban landscape and particularly its architecture. Sorkin writes of three major characteristics of the new American city: the loosening of ties to specific places, an obsession with security, and the triumph of simulation. The essays treat these themes, as well as the expansion of corporate space at the expense of public space, in a variety of specific and generic landscapes, from Orange County and Disneyland to Manhattan.

Alexander Wilson. 1992. *The culture of nature: North American landscape from Disney to the Exxon Valdez.* Cambridge, Mass.: Blackwell.

Wilson explores the cultural history of nature in North America over the last half-century. Emphasis is placed on interpreting those environments that contemporary Americans view as natural. Conflicts that result from competing meanings placed on environments are a central concern of Wilson's book.

Sharon Zukin. 1991. *Landscapes of power: From Detroit to Disney World.* Berkeley: University of California Press.

Zukin, a sociologist, sees the transition from modern to postmodern as the shift from production to service and from industrial capital to cultural capital. What makes her work relevant to landscape scholars is that her case is developed in terms of place and landscape, from generalizations about the role of "liminal" places, through generic places like the landscape of nouvelle cuisine, to landscapes as specific as Detroit and Weirton, West Virginia. The result is a difficult, rewarding, and highly integrated interpretation of our contemporary landscape.

10
LOOKING AT A WORLD THAT SPEAKS

In their introduction to "How the World Looks" the editors argue that when cultural geographers observe elements of the world, the objects of their disciplined looking range from the pattern of culture traits associated with small-scale, pre-industrial, rural societies to the diagnostic signatures of contemporary urban (and postmodern) society. In either case the world that cultural geographers see is not the world of the astronomer, a world in which vast distances and great temporal divides separate the object from the viewer. In contrast to asteroids, solar systems, and quasars, the world that cultural geographers study is a world we humans create. Consequently, that world, while most assuredly "out there," is not out there in the same manner that a red giant or a white dwarf is. The difference in the "out thereness" of an Upland South dog-trot remolded by the grandchildren with a parabolic antenna in the front yard and that of a quasar pulsating at the edge of the universe is reflected in the different lookings. The astronomer's looking is made possible through massive instrumentation, whereas the geographer's, although it may be aided by instruments and even sensed remotely, remains considerably more immediate and experiential. Thus, it seems appropriate that this commentary begin by considering the composition of the looking that we cultural geographers (and anthropologists) do and the nature of the world we purport to view. The commentary proceeds to amplify these considerations through addressing the four themes of this section: learning by looking, ordinary landscapes, emblems of authority, and dynamic regions.

LOOKING AS READING

Seeing is the ur-metaphor for scientific investigation. Seeing and knowing are often said to co-occur. "Seeing all there is to see in the universe" extends the limits of our knowledge (Waldrop 1988). Yet seeing, in its brilliance, has a darker side; it objectifies, and in so doing it distances us from a more empathetic interpretation of the subject before us. Its "epistemological austerity" threatens the unity between people and their works and words and may transform culture, artifact and lexicon, into a thing in itself, an overly deterministic, superorganic it (M. Richardson 1981).

Looking, we may remind ourselves, is a mode of behaving. As bipedal primates, as hominids with upright stature, our looking around is located some distance from the solid earth and is propelled forward, or withdrawn in sudden retreat, by the feet. Our looking is sharpened by the inquisitive hand, which reaches ahead, brings back, and tears apart for closer inspection. Looking, in sum, is an adaptive complex of the foot, the hand, the eye, and the brain by which we establish the parameters of our world.

The parameters that we establish first and foremost are those of the everyday world, a world—in Heideggerian terms—that is ready-to-hand. In the everyday world, we look around in such a manner that the screwdriver in the toolbox awaits our grasp, and once grasped, the screwdriver's purpose is the driving of a screw into the porch wall to attach a bracket from which we hang a flowering plant. In our everyday looking around, the world is situated activity in which artifacts—that is, *material culture*— have an in-order-to, for-to quality, and the location of artifacts is in their *place* in the context with which we see the world and implicitly understand it. The book in my hand may be closer than the glasses on my nose. So placed by the implicit understanding of everyday existing within the general boundaries established by our primate inquiry, material culture defines the particular worlds we inhabit socially.

This manner in which we view the world contrasts with a looking that turns artifacts from being ready to fit the hand to simply being there, isolated from their in-order-to and for-to qualities. With this type of inspection, the screwdriver turns into an object with a blade, shaft, and handle. Further inspection reveals that the blade and shaft are of forged steel and the handle, nowadays, is of molded plastic; additional examination, with the appropriate instrumentation, reveals the contrasting molecular structure of the materials. When we look at the world in this manner, individual artifacts become denuded, their in-order-to and for-to qualities stripped away. Indeed, the more we look in this manner, the further we are from the everyday world in which we engage ourselves (Heidegger 1962, 102–07, 136–47).

As human scientists, we are more interested in seeing the in-order-to and for-to qualities of artifacts than in seeing their molecular structure.[1] Responding to the eye's vision, artifacts convened into distinctive patterns on a landscape locate us in our everyday world, and that cartographic knowledge of the where offers us a solution, however tentative, to the existential puzzle of the who we are. Small wonder, then, that looking is so critical to geography. Indeed, looking is so critical to the field that it is tempting to characterize the discipline as not only an earth science, a spatial science, and a social science but also a visual science.

The task is to look at the everyday world, the contextual world in which we have an implicit understanding of what we are up to (that is, the world in which we first and foremost are), without denuding that world of its implicit understanding. We, as human scientists, want to disclose the implicit understanding that we, as different peoples, have constructed. We want to see artifacts in their places, for artifacts in their places, located within their in-order-to and for-to qualities, communicate. To communicate suggests not only visual informing but also a verbal responding. Thus, to learn by looking at the everyday world, we must consider the nature of the world that we humans create.

The world in which we are is a with-world, a social world, an us-world. We are, together. Because they are as much social as technological instruments, if not more so, our mammalian hands, shaped by primate adaptation and caressing with love or pummeling in anger, locate us. Touch, smell, and hearing, the proximate senses, place us in the company of each other. Vision, the distancing sense, nonetheless searches the crowd for the familiar face. Even our brain, the vaunted human computer, may have achieved its size during the course of hominid evolution as a mechanism as much for sorting out, storing, and recalling social information as for processing stomach information (an argument summarized in Lewin 1989, 125–30; see especially Humphrey 1976). Except in cases of acute starvation, and perhaps there as well, our social quest may subordinate the food quest. Consequently, to anticipate subsequent discussion, material culture, although it helps to provide shelter and secure food, is intrinsically social.

For us humans, ever since the Neanderthals, if not before,[2] the world in which we are is also a speech-world. As with artifacts, words are social. To speak is to address someone, even if it is ourselves. In speaking, we constitute the self and its alter, the other. Speaking, however, is not simply transmitting technical information (this is a rock, that is a tree) from one isolated entity to another; rather, speaking is calling forth and constituting the implicit understanding by which we live—or better, in which we are, as in, "Rally around the Virginians, boys, for there stands Jackson like a stone wall," or "Just like a tree that's planted by the water, I shall not be moved."

Everyday talk calls forth and constitutes the ways in which we are; words, along with artifacts, situate our behavior and thereby fill the space about us with understanding of what is going on. As human scientists, we search for a way of talking, a type of discourse, that discloses the taken-for-granted understanding within which people

locate one another without stripping it of its essential existence-supporting context.

As applied to looking at a world that speaks, the looking we seek is a looking that has the same disclosing qualities. Such a looking is reading. Reading is a type of visual discourse that brings us into the world inscribed on the book's pages; it engages us in the book's contextual space. As related to cultural geography, reading is a looking that engages us in the contextual spaces that people have inscribed on landscapes. Perhaps we might say that just as listening is our response to talking, so reading is our response to inscription. Although it engages us, however, reading differs from the face-to-face listening of everyday life. It locates us at some distance from the implicit understanding and thereby permits, if not forces, us to search the understanding for its themes, the images in which it is encapsulated. Reading, consequently, is interpreting.[3]

LEARNING BY LOOKING: THE INSCRIBED HOUSE

The "house is more than mere shelter. It is a personal and social testament. Through their houses . . . human beings etch their culture into the landscape" (P. Lewis, "Common Houses, Cultural Spoor"). In these words Peirce Lewis articulates the Fred B. Kniffen model of cultural geography. Material culture is—and one is tempted to say, always is—more than a technological solution; as a component of human activity, material culture communicates. In producing artifacts, we etch, write, and *inscribe* the communication onto the landscape. To erect a four-over-four is to speak. To speak is to address someone, or better, some *ones*. For us to interpret what the four-over-four says, we must see it both in itself and in its context.

In the Kniffen approach we take the house seriously. We avoid reducing the text of the house to the intentions of the builder or even to the private wishes of the occupants. What the occupants do, their observable (i.e., public) behavior, is, however, critical to our reading. Likewise, we avoid reducing the text to socioeconomic processes. These processes, as important as they are in the determination of the landscape, are nonetheless not what we see when we view the four-over-four speaking.

Lewis uses the term *cultural spoor* to designate what the house communicates. *Spoor* suggests a print of what once was here but now is gone. To see the spoor, Lewis says, we look "in the mind's eye, [and] strip away the cosmetics." We experience the present landscape, but we look at it for signs of the past. Here the eye, far from being the "fabled naked" instrument, has a vision, and the vision is the sweep of Europeans—in English houses—across the continent. In stripping away the cosmetics of the present, Lewis sees the deeper, grammarlike structure of the house. In this reading, he sees a cultural continuity that material culture, because of its enduring composition, so effectively conveys; consequently, he speaks of the conservatism of culture and appropriately concludes that who we are is disclosed in who we were. Given the overwhelming English character of the domestic house as contrasted to the diverse ethnic composition (native Americans, Scots-Irish, Germans, Swedes, plus all the English variants) of those who came to occupy such houses, perhaps it is more accurate to say that who we purport to be is disclosed by who we claimed we were.

Because of their more denuded, grammatical attributes, the instrumental qualities that Lewis sees in houses have more to do with the past in all its continuity and less to do with the present in all its richness. To do justice to the present, which, after all, is the lived-in world of today's implicit understanding, we must appraise the "architectural afterthoughts," the porches, side buildings, and columns that turn a generic structure into the peculiar property of this unique building. Such a shift of perspective highlights the immediacy of the house and brings the structure into the speech of a contemporary text. The family occupants address the street through the uniqueness of the house's facade and thereby long to communicate their social unity to the rest of us, who are willing, at the moment at least, to see an image of "striking grace and beauty."

Some may agree that landscapes have a textlike quality and therefore can be read but argue that common houses, so embedded in the implicit understanding of the occupants, were not meant to be read. Such an argument overlooks the communicative, social function of material culture. As inscribed talk, it speaks both to the observing scientist and to the participating occupant. People read their works and produce their own interpretation; consequently, to Lewis's conclusion that our knowledge of who we are emerges from knowing who we *were*, we may add that we also know who we are by knowing *where* we are.

ORDINARY LANDSCAPES VERSUS EMBLEMS OF AUTHORITY: THE IMPLICIT VERSUS THE EXPLICIT

In a most profound sense, every human landscape is authoritative. Equipped with the capacity to speak, with the capacity to communicate with symbols, we create in nature the world in which we then are. We author our lives. Consequently, the most insipid, bland, carelessly constructed place has the extraordinary, poetic quality that we humans, in contrast to other mammals, inscribe on the earth.

Allowed to speak, places we call ordinary communicate the taken-for-granted understandings of the present. To the reader who looks interpretively, the ordinary discloses the themes of its understanding. J. B. Jackson ("The Westward-moving House") is such a reader. Placed in a present that has passed, the westward-moving house reveals, through his viewing, its alternative images of community, individualism, and mutability. Jackson accomplishes his reading by placing the house not only in the context of its minimal features but also in its relationship with other structures and with the larger settlement patterns—the superfamily of the New England church community, the institutionalism of the Midwest farmstead, and the energetics of the Southwest agricultural enterprise. Importantly, he locates the house not only in its historical continuity but also in the eagerness to leave the past behind, to escape the past's confining traditionalism. He offers us an interpretation of Ray Tinkham's agricultural landscape, for example, not in the easy, comfortable ideology of the family farm but in the compelling ideas of instantaneous well-being. Ray's house has less of a lived-in quality to it because, with the family's constant pursuit of illusive leisure, it is lived in less.

The pursuit of leisure that always awaits the next time "we can get away" suggests a mutability of the self that keeps pace with the consumerism of postmodern capitalism, the economics of which is producing the new American landscapes. Learning how to look at dome stadiums, parking lots, and interstate highways challenges our interpretive stance. The distance of history detaches us from a four-over-four and the magnitude of height separates us from a skyscraper, but a Circle-K pack-and-sack, where "drive offs will be prosecuted," sticks in our face.

Warning us that we may be too close to interpret what they say to us, Robert Riley ("Speculations on the New American Landscapes") suspends his prejudices in a manner uncommon to viewers of the strip and the mall. He reminds us of the pluralistic (or is *fragmentary* a better word?) composition of today's landscape, which articulates the message that participation in the subcultures of today is not a lifelong commitment; rather, one is a surfer today, a biker tomorrow. Landscapes are packaged to create a heightened sense of reality, and the city, with downtown warehouses converted to brightly lit, specialty boutiques, strives to be a place of excitement.

The ordinary landscape of mass culture comes directly from the drafting table with the message, explicit and strident, that it is in no sense ordinary. The packaging wants very badly to persuade us that the place we are entering—the water world, the toyland, the reconstituted Main Street, and certainly Riley's "Olde Mistic Village Shopping Center"—will transform us. We readily suspend our disbelief and enter into a collusion with the message, but even as we do, we know, in the strange knowing of postmodernism, that the implicit understanding is marketing and, consequently, that our attention, our "needs," are up for sale. Who we claim to be is bar coded with an inventory number and a profit margin. We cannot avoid the clash between the packaging and the implicit understanding, and

even as we agree with open-eyed eagerness to the manipulation, we remain deeply suspicious.

Although we would never mistake a skyscraper for an I-house or even for a Walt Disney fairyland, the emblems of authority achieve their extraordinary quality by a further shaping of our implicit understanding of what we are about. The distance between the columns on the facade of the First Baptist Church in Mt. Hope, Louisiana, and those that adorn the World Building in New York City is great; both, however, are artifacts, items of material culture, which always speak. The difference, perhaps, is in the magnitude and explicit nature of the speaking.

The explicit message of the extraordinary place informs the activities within it so as to predispose the viewer-readers to grant those activities certain qualities beyond their instrumental purposes. It is always the hope of the extraordinary place that those qualities transcend the instrumental and become for the viewer-readers the place's primary reality, its *raison d'être*. We might say that a principal characteristic of the extraordinary place is its extraordinary claims. Producing newspapers (and sensational tabloids at that) compares, the World Building proclaimed, with the intellectual exploration of the European Renaissance, and selling insurance, the Metropolitan Tower announced, is on par with sacramental communion. These extraordinary equations, as Mona Domosh makes clear in "The Symbolism of the Skyscraper," ground their acceptance in extraordinary power; they gain our collusion because of the power of their technological expertise, the power of the socioeconomic enterprise, and the power of height.

An extraordinary place states its character by the manner in which it contrasts visually with other places. Visual distinctiveness conveys messages of social uniqueness. Height is one of the primordial ways to achieve the uniqueness for which nineteenth-century capitalism so clearly lusted. Height is what extends our upright stature, our distinctively human posture; height is what we have to look up to. Height, for European and European-derived cultures, equals power; for those cultures, height equals "Envy me!"

Such naked phallocentrism, even in New

York City, cannot stand unabashed. Renaissance eclecticism (which, one suspects, carries certain male overtones) provided cultural legitimization in which to clothe the skyward-thrust assertions. Indeed, a closer look at the aesthetics of last century's skyscrapers will help us read today's much less florid buildings. Then, too, in considering the extraordinary claims of the skyscraper and of any massive testimonial to power, we might recall the boast of Ozymandias:

I met a traveller from an antique land
Who said: Two vast and trunkless legs of stone
Stand in the desert. Near them, on the sand
Half sunk, a shattered visage lies, whose frown
And wrinkled lip, and sneer of cold command
Tell that its sculptor well those passions read
Which yet survive, stamped on these lifeless
    things,
The hand that mocked them and the heart
    that fed:
And on the pedestal these words appear:
"My name is Ozymandias, king of kings:
Look on my works, ye Mighty, and despair!"
Nothing beside remains. Round the decay
Of the colossal wreck, boundless and bare,
The lone and level sands stretch far away.

(SHELLEY 1903, 211)

The extraordinary makes extraordinary claims. It challenges us to leave the everyday understanding and move to another level. In the case of the skyscraper, this extraordinary proclamation rides the soaring thrust of technological and socioeconomic power. Other extraordinary places compel our attention because their avowals draw on the revelatory power of art.

Memorials abound in Washington, D.C., as befits a nation's capital. Across the Potomac, in Arlington, we stand at the feet of bronze giants and look upward to see huge hands of five Marines dressed in the combat gear of World War II planting the American flag atop Mount Suribachi on Iwo Jima, a scene whose sheer size evokes the call to heroism in a battle for sacred causes. Back in the city, on the Mall, we follow a path leading among the trees to a grassy knoll. Presently, we can discern a *V* of black marble extend-

ing into the knoll. At first the wall of the *V* is at our feet, but it rises as we go down toward the apex. At the apex, the wall rises over our heads. We are in the middle of a black mirror of names: Melvin G. Cormier, Walter L. Burroughs, Hector S. Acevedo, Michael L. Poletti, Grady E. McElroy, Mary T. Klinder. Your hand, with a will of its own, reaches out to trace the curve of letters; mine follows. In the black mirror of dark marble we see our hands touching the words, and we see the self and the other, the living and the dead, meet.

As a monument, the Vietnam Veterans Memorial achieves its power through the manner in which it, a controversy itself, encapsulates the greater controversy. In contrast to the Mount Suribachi monument and other war memorials, it is small, hardly visible to the idle glance; it is low, at first, beneath the feet, and the eyes are forced to look down; it is black, unlike the white of tombs; it is reflective, so that when we look at it our eyes look back at us; it is intimate, and we are within it at the apex; it is tactile, the letters engraved in the mirrored surface pulling our fingers into their grooves; and finally, it unites the hand, the mammalian five-fingered hand, with the word, the human existential utterance, within the scope of the contemplating eye, the reflexive eye-self, which ponders the union of the hand-flesh with the word-object and of the self with the now-dead other. The memorial's unique reinsertion of the past into the present permits us now, at long last, to place the past into a perspective that ameliorates our nightmares and eases the burden of our guilt (M. Richardson and Dunton 1989).

DYNAMIC REGIONS: PLACE, LANDSCAPE, AND PROCESS

Inscribed on the landscape, places communicate our implicit understanding of what we are about; they also are the texts that we as observers read to interpret that understanding. How places become inscribed, how the cultural landscape emerges, on the other hand, requires that we look for process. We inscribe places, we author them, even the most "anonymous" vernacular dwelling, but we are also flesh-and-blood creatures, occupying the earth's surface, subject to natural and social forces magnified or generated by that very human sequent occupancy of the planet. Consequently, we authors who inscribe places do so shadowed by the continuing presence of the past and within the swirl of contemporary events. We not infrequently are caught in situations of our own making that paradoxically, we only partially comprehend and over which we have relatively little control. A looking that extends beyond particular places on a distinctive landscape permits us to elucidate the processes, both temporal and regional, that inscribe the landscape.

In "The Mexican American Cultural Capital," Arreola, while centered on San Antonio, expands his view to include the region's historical and demographic factors that have produced the present-day city. Having effectively used these regionwide, impersonal factors to account for the uniqueness of San Antonio, he then shows how food, music, and the relative mix of ethnicity justify the claim that San Antonio is the Mexican American cultural capital. He has not, in this account, turned to the visual landscape to argue the claim (but see, for example, Arreola 1988). The next step is to show us what a Mexican American cultural capital looks like. How does San Antonio visually compare with its rival, Los Angeles? Or is it the case that the city's food and music assume a greater role in defining a presence than landscape does? If this is so, then how has the definition that people place upon the city as the Mexican American cultural capital changed our understanding of the Alamo? How does the Alamo, so often co-opted as the symbol of Anglo superiority, present itself today?

From the Alamo to the California bungalow, from a particular city to half a country, our looking, guided by Meinig's elegant scholarship in "American Wests," moves away from an interpretive reading of place to a synthesis of such seemingly diverse items as railroads, statehood, Hispanic piety, Mormon fervor, and Sierra Club environmentalism; that is, the constituent items of the American Wests. Here is a regional perspective that avoids the homogeneity of an overly generalized area view yet connects variations in a manner that leads us back to particulars with a

renewed sense of their place in both time and space. We can no longer look at Oregon's Willamette Valley without seeing New England, or at Mormon temples without seeing the transforming of a suspect faith into model Americana, or at television frames of burning Los Angeles without seeing the American Dream transforming into a nightmare.

Of the many features of Meinig's perspective relevant to a looking at a landscape that speaks, time and regional consciousness stand out. At least since the spread of the species *erectus* in the Old World and of *sapiens sapiens* in the New, the inscription of places on the landscape always occurs in the context of earlier inscriptions. The later inscriptions incise a landscape already dissected by an earlier human presence, they shape themselves around the conquest of earlier peoples, and they may reach back to earlier occupancies and restore in the light of the present selected aspects of earlier lives. The shaping and reaching back may be driven not only by market forces but also by an emerging regional consciousness. The emergence of the West as a region we consciously endow, at times fallaciously, with certain attributes fills the landscape with meanings, some of which are packaged and offered to us with high-tech virtual reality as the "true" West.

These points about time and regional consciousness find their illustrations with native Americans. Note that Meinig's temporal sequence, for all its sophistication, starts with the first European settlements and thereby commits a particularly Western error of partially overlooking both the groups that occupied the American West at the time of the Europeans and those who came before. Today, we are more ready to admit that the long period of human occupancy of the Western Hemisphere before 1492 has inscribed the landscape in such depth that no amount of haste to get to the "main" events can eradicate these inscriptions. Although often packaged as commodities and ideologically wrapped, museums, battlegrounds, and theme parks nonetheless tell us that the human story of this hemisphere continually poses the species' quest for understanding its own narration, a text whose origin in this side of the world dates back into the Pleistocene.

SUMMARY

Looking at a world that speaks is a hermeneutic endeavor of authors reading their own works. Works on the landscape—material culture in place—inform behavior and communicate to us, that is, you and me, what we are about. In our everyday reading, we scan, even as we act, the material text for the understanding that we take for granted. In our scholarly reading, we place ourselves at some distance from the immediacy of the taken-for-granted and search the text of place for its themes, the images of the reality being constituted.

Reading a world that speaks is not a coldly cerebral act; rather, it requires the hand as much as the eye, the touch as much as the view, and the smell and sound of human concern as much as the logic of types. Reading engages us; through reading we enter the world of the text. The endeavor is more holistic than predictive, more given to addressing the how than the why, more given to pondering words than assigning cause, and less like "an experimental science in search of law [and more like] an interpretive one in search of meaning" (Geertz 1973, 5).

To accomplish this task, we address the world, as Kniffen has taught us, in the firsthand straightforwardness of the material culture of place as it communicates both past and present. Yet we author-readers are caught up in forces partly of our own making and over which we exercise little control. The human record on the landscape speaks both of our finely honed intent and of our careless bumbling. Like any good text, novel or poem, it carries within its house types, skyscrapers, and fast-food drive-thrus, its cities and its regions, the ambiguities of a Shakespearean "tale told by an idiot" and of the quieter, deeper moments of everyday care.

NOTES

1. To be sure, the molecular structure of artifactual material becomes important to the archeologist in establishing prehistoric trade connections (C. Holland and Allen 1975; B. Smith 1991).

2. The argument that hominids at least since the genus *Homo*, if not *Australopithecus*, produced sounds that carried symbolic content—that is, that they spoke—points to the archeological record of worked stone (and also of intentional burials in the case of the Neanderthals). Although many animals exhibit tool use, tool construction among humans is an aspect of the making of material culture and is associated with the objectification of intersubjective experience, the placing of symbolic communication in stone. Therefore, an Upper Paleolithic blade, a Middle Paleolithic flake, and a Lower Paleolithic handax suggest a range of symbolic discourse.

3. The notion of text is central to the notion of reading as interpreting the landscape. Drawn from Ricouer's fundamental discussion (1979), the text metaphor enjoys wide usage in contemporary social science. Later sections in this volume will elaborate its application in geography.

III
HOW THE
WORLD WORKS

INTRODUCTION

This section explores the relationships of individuals and groups, working through organizations and institutions, within natural and social environments. Each article stresses how people make use of the earth and how their cultural modes are woven into social, political, and economic systems. In examining the workings of the world, cultural geographers have until recently preferred premodern, traditional, and especially small-scale societies for their investigations. Certain themes, such as cultural diffusion, human agency in landscape transformation, and the impress of European cultures on non-European peoples, have been central to geographers' attempts to explain how aspects of the world work, especially those dealing with material production and biological reproduction of cultures and societies.

These processes remain central concerns, but they are studied today by geographers whose receptivity to ideas originating from other disciplines is perhaps greater than that of their predecessors. This is not to suggest that previous work in cultural geography has been parochial. By and large, it was not. The best scholarship in the field, which includes much of the collective effort of Carl Sauer and his associates and students of the Berkeley school, demonstrates wide-ranging and expert appreciation of work in anthropology, archaeology, botany, and culture history. Nonetheless, in the past two decades cultural geographers have increased the scope of their interdisciplinary interests. As the articles in this collection attest, cultural geographers are now as apt to seek explanations by analyzing ecological and economic processes as they are to describe geographic patterns of cultural traits. At the same time, this has not weakened cultural geography's strong and traditional ties to anthropology, history, and the natural sciences. Most of these articles suggest a shift away from microscale work to meso- and macroscale analysis and greater attention to theoretical concerns. Together, these articles advance traditional concerns of cultural geography but at the same time situate this research more solidly in the terrain of contemporary social science.

CULTURE AT WORK

Research in these areas stresses a definition of culture as the sum of a society's way of life—its *genre de vie* or mode of production. The articles reprinted here embody the spirit of Wagner's view that "culture has to be seen as carried out in specific, located, purposeful, rule-following, and rule-making groupings of people communicating and interacting with one another" (Wagner 1975, 11). Rendered in terms of the five themes of *Readings in Cultural Geography*, the selections are best viewed as elaborations of culture history and cultural ecology. For the most part, the articles indicate that the appropriate unit of analysis is neither the individual nor the "people" but rather mesoscale organizations and institutions. The writers attempt to show that the workings of the world can be seen, understood, and explained as human activities that affect, and are in turn affected by, ecological and economic processes. In this view, culture has both organic and inorganic referents and is particularly concerned with the conjunction of the two.

Since the publication of *Readings in Cultural Geography*, the work geographers have done within cultural ecology has expanded and changed dramatically. Strikingly, none of Wagner and Mikesell's selections were written by geographers, save for Max Sorre's (1962) "Geography of Diet." Most were written by anthropologists, and except for Harold Conklin's (1954) "Ethnoecological Approach to Shifting Agricul-

ture," the impact of these writings on subsequent work in cultural ecology has been minimal. This is partly because cultural ecology did not become firmly established within anthropology until after the mid-1960s. In geography this took another decade. Today, the problem is not a scarcity of representative studies but rather the opposite.

Ecology is a concept with broad applicability throughout geography and allied disciplines. Rather than being considered as a separate subfield, ecology in general, and cultural ecology in particular, should be viewed as particularly effective and widely used research perspectives (Butzer 1989; 1990a; Carlstein 1982; Carlstein, Parkes, and Thrift 1978; Turner 1989). No longer can cultural ecology be viewed as the unitary theme it was thirty years ago. The literature of cultural ecology must be subdivided if we are to understand contemporary debate. In this respect, all the articles in this section illustrate issues and approaches that ecologically oriented cultural geographers find compelling. But these six articles by no means exhaust the range of issues raised by contemporary cultural ecology. In his recent assessment, Butzer (1989) identifies six key concepts in contemporary cultural ecology that have attracted sustained attention: cultural adaptation, econiche, ecosystems, carrying capacity and agricultural intensification, adaptive strategies, and energetics. A complete exposition of these issues goes beyond the scope of the present survey and is the subject of other more specialized books and articles (Birks et al. 1988; Butzer 1982; Denevan 1983; Ellen 1982; Moran 1990; P. Porter 1978; B. L. Turner et al. 1990).

Culture history is the other theme identified by Wagner and Mikesell that most closely corresponds to the theme of "How the World Works." Since the early 1960s geographers have continued to work and write within the tradition of culture history, but it no longer commands the attention it once did. At microregional scales, cultural ecology is the more popular approach, as illustrated by Zimmerer's paper. At macroregional scales, work that formerly would have been conceptualized in cultural-historical terms is now often construed in terms of economic history or ecological theory. Earle's article illustrates the former departure, whereas Jordan's demonstrates the latter. In addition, the 1970s saw the emergence of critical responses to what were seen as excessively economistic tendencies within the social sciences, especially anthropology (Sahlins 1976) and history (E. Thompson 1978). At higher levels of resolution, this development is evident in the debates among social theorists over structure and agency (Gregory 1978; 1981), or even modernity and its aftermath (Harvey 1989; Soja 1989). Cultural geographers working on topics logically subsumed by this section have been somewhat slow to explore these new directions. Recent work by younger cultural ecologists (Katz 1991; M. Watts 1983b; Zimmerer 1991) suggests, however, that engagement with and exploration of contemporary currents within social theory is becoming more common.

The changes in cultural ecology and culture history over the last three decades necessitate a thematic focus different from that in *Readings in Cultural Geography*. Wagner and Mikesell (1962, 23) argued that work on any one of their original five themes could "properly constitute" cultural geography, but they added that the best work in cultural geography interwove all five. This is just as true of the articles and categories featured here. Five areas of research concentration are identified: (1) Technics and Culture; (2) Agency and Institution; (3) Contact, Conflict, and Change; (4) Innovation and Adaptation; and (5) Reproduction and Resistance. Each article can be placed in a single category, but all touch on broader issues. Together, the articles raise questions about the nature of culture, the character of culture areas, and the formation of cultural landscapes.

TECHNICS AND CULTURE

Some might argue that to explain the workings of the human world, one need focus only on key components, such as culture and technics. Cultural geographers have, however, defined themselves in part through their opposition to reductionism and simplistic determinisms, whether they be environmental, economic, spatial, or technological. Yet cultural geographers following Mumford's (1934) early lead recognize that technology enables all human material production and reproduction, construction, and destruction. For cultural geographers, culture history is

largely the record of the human transformation of the earth's surface. Here, culture and technics go hand in hand. Cultural ecology is concerned with the processes implicit in these transformations, but cultural ecologists accord technics a privileged place in their explications of how humans systematically interact with the natural world.

Cultural geographers have long studied technics such as fire-as-tool; agricultural implements; domesticated plants and animals; infrastructural features such as furrows, fields, and fences; constructions for ceremony and shelter; and so on. Jordan's paper evokes this tradition with its focus on the diffusion of material culture traits from Scandinavia to the Middle Atlantic states and beyond. He also proposes that the ecological concept of preadaptation be used to explain the cultural success of these items on the advancing American frontier. Zimmerer's paper takes the focus on technics even further into the realm of cultural ecology. He shows how the adaptation, if not the independent invention, of small-scale raised-field farming in Andean bogs offers indigenously derived technical solutions to problems confronting these peoples. At the global scale, Crosby (1978; 1986) shows how Europeans consciously and unwittingly used Eurasian pathogens, parasites, commensals, and domesticates as auxiliary forces in conquering the lands they colonized. In this case, Europeans deployed technics of an agricultural nature to spread their culture. The work of cultural geographers who have cast technics in this light is voluminous. It ranges from Parsons's (1970) studies of the "Africanization" of New World tropical grasslands and Butzer's (1988a; 1988b; 1990b) work on the evolution and transfer of Iberian agrotechnologies to New Spain to Galloway's (1989) culture history of the global spread of the Mediterranean-based sugar industry.

AGENCY AND INSTITUTION

By and large, earlier work by cultural geographers had little to say about either individuals or institutions. The question of agency was a major concern, but it was addressed at the level of culture or cultures and dealt primarily with human or cultural agency's role in modifying natural landscapes (Sauer 1925; 1956a). When Wagner and Mikesell (1962, 5) made their famous disclaimer that "the cultural geographer is not concerned with the inner workings of culture or with describing fully patterns of human behavior," they accurately reflected prevailing thought. This statement did not, however, go unchallenged. Harold Brookfield (1964), who was just beginning microregional field work in highland New Guinea, questioned American cultural geographers' reluctance to analyze behavior at either the individual or institutional levels. He also argued that cultural geographers did not need to eschew generalizations guided by explicit theory. Many cultural ecologists accepted and acted on this challenge (Butzer 1976; Denevan 1966a; B. Nietschmann 1973; P. Porter 1965; Waddell 1972). Both Nietschmann's (1979b) and Zimmerer's (1991) selections take seriously the role that individual agency plays in cultural ecological change. Blaut's (1987a) and Earle's (1978) papers are not explicitly grounded in cultural ecological theory, but they have clearly stated theoretical orientations. Jordan and Crosby, each in his own way, propose ecological approaches to the questions they explore.

Today, the concept of agency as used by cultural geographers—and indeed, by social scientists in general—often refers to human agency in relation to social structure as conceptualized in structuration theory (Giddens 1979). Derek Gregory and others began to introduce Giddens's ideas into geography at the end of the 1970s, although Giddens acknowledges his own debt, in particular his concept of time-space distanciation, to Hägerstrand. Since then there has been a shift away from granting primacy to structural explanations of societal workings toward a greater appreciation of the role of individual and collective agency in the construction of culture and society (Billinge 1982).

CONTACT, CONFLICT, AND CHANGE

This triad of concepts encompasses the core concerns of many historical and cultural geographers working at macrogeographical scales. Culture history, as studied by cultural geographers, has always been concerned with cultural contacts. Cultural geographers, because of their links to Ratzel via Sauer, have generally subscribed to the notion that ideas, like epidemic diseases, spread by contagion (Dickson 1988). Blaut points out that such classical diffusionism grants contact great causal power. Simple acceptance, especially involving contact relations between donor cultures (usually European) and receptor cultures (usually non-Western), was viewed as the norm. Questions of conflict in such views of culture change were muted. Since the 1960s a focus on elements of conflict in cultural change, whether involving diffusion or endogenous processes, has become popular. The papers by Blaut, Crosby, Earle, Nietschmann, and Zimmerer illustrate this. Related to the turn from consensus to conflict is the concern to explain change rather than to document continuity or tradition that marked the work of economically and ecologically minded cultural geographers from the mid-1960s through the mid-1980s. Recently there has been renewed interest in cultural contact, but examined through the lens of conflict rather than consensus and interpreted in relation to temporal and spatial disjunctions rather than continuities and contiguities. One example is the renewed interest in ethnic conflict (Mikesell and Murphy 1991; Murphy 1988).

The conflicts and changes resulting from cultural contact have long been an important subtheme in historically oriented cultural geography. The scope of this work has often been projected at macroscales. The second volume of Ratzel's (1891) *Anthropogeographie* surveyed the global history of human migrations. Cultural dislocations and displacements figure prominently in this massive study. Sauer's early work on the aboriginal historical geography of California, Mexico, and, later, the New World as a whole was an elaboration of this theme. Sauer, however, highlighted the European colonists' role in the destruction of indigenous peoples and biota. He declined to analyze the underlying processes much beyond saying they were examples of a *Raubwirtschaft*—literally, a "robber economy"—at work (Sauer 1938b). In the last three decades cultural geographers have become more interested in examining the inner workings of colonialism, imperialism, and other systems of destructive exploitation (Meinig 1969b). Macroscale models and theories derived from historical sociology and political economy, such as Wallerstein's (1974) world-system approach, various neo-Marxist perspectives on underdevelopment and dependency, and related structuralist explanations for cultural and environmental degradation, have been applied, especially in Third World settings (Blaikie and Brookfield 1987; Blaut 1992; Hecht and Cockburn 1989; M. Watts 1983b).

INNOVATION AND ADAPTATION

In general, cultural geographers have studied innovation and adaptation at geographical scales lesser than those at which they studied cultural contact, conflict, and change. In terms of process, innovation and adaptation offer techno-environmental approaches explaining the inner workings of small-scale cultures and societies. In turn, such explanations offer a basis for framing questions about the nature of processes implicit in the larger-scale themes of contact, conflict, and change. Despite significant exceptions, it is perhaps useful to view work on these latter themes as falling more often into the culture history mold, whereas studies of innovation and adaptation follow more closely the precepts of cultural ecology.

All the papers in this section are concerned with innovation, and several address the concept of adaptation. Blaut's critique of diffusion theory challenges orthodox ideas of how cultural innovation occurs. Crosby documents some of the consequences of globally propagated biocultural innovations. Jordan suggests preadaptation as the key to explaining how and why various traits are adopted far beyond their original source region. Earle ties innovation to labor costs in ecologically differentiated settings. Nietschmann shows innovation largely as an externally generated, invasive process that poses a threat to local cultural and biotic survival. At the same time, cultural adaptation is depicted as a response to waves of

political-economic change that break over the region. In Zimmerer's study the emphasis is more on adaptation than on innovation, yet the dynamics of adaptation are cast in terms of regional political ecology rather than the more restricted focus on the inner workings of discrete agro-ecosystems in biophysical detail.

Although many cultural geographers over the past three decades have dealt with topics involving cultural innovations, there is nothing to compare in theoretical ambitiousness with the work of spatial and behavioral geographers such as Hägerstrand (1967) on the diffusion of innovations. Beyond the traditional interest cultural geographers have shown in documenting the movement of new ideas over time and across space, important theoretical work has been done on selected topics involving innovation. Perhaps the single most fruitful area has been agricultural intensification. Geographers such as Brookfield (1968; 1972; 1973), W. Clarke (1966), and Waddell (1972), who studied primitive and traditional agricultural practices in relation to population growth in the western Pacific, have tested and refined Boserup's (1965) influential theories of agricultural intensification (Doolittle 1984). In Boserup's contra-Malthusian theory, agrotechnological innovation is precipitated by population increase. As Mikesell (1978) remarked, highland New Guinea and parts of Melanesia have provided something of a laboratory for cultural ecological testing.

Boserup's theory has served to guide cultural ecological fieldwork in the New World as well. Denevan (1966b; 1970; 1982), Doolittle (1980; 1985; 1988a; 1988b; 1990), Knapp (1991), Mathewson (1984), Parsons (1969), Parsons and Denevan (1967), Siemens (1983; 1989), B. L. Turner (1974; 1983), B. L. Turner and Harrison (1983), and others have discovered and examined evidence of highly labor intensive forms of farming practiced by pre-Columbian populations in a range of New World environments. These systems required vast landscape modifications involving mounding, draining, and terracing fields and constructing irrigation works. Subsequently, archaeologists have followed the lead of these cultural geographers in studying the infrastructural bases of ancient complex societies. Zimmerer's paper in this volume reflects this trend, but it describes a current example of agricultural innovation using raised fields—a local adaptation with ancient roots.

Work by geographers on cultural adaptation has followed the lead of ecologically oriented anthropologists. Again, geographers working in the western Pacific and New Guinea since the early 1960s have produced a richly textured research record. Grossman's (1984) study of peasant subsistence ecology and economic development in highland New Guinea is representative of attempts to analyze modernity's impact on subsistence economies and the resultant changes in adaptive strategies. Theoretical issues concerning the concept of adaptation in cultural geography have been addressed by Denevan (1983), B. Nietschmann (1973), and P. Porter (1965). Knapp's (1991) study of agricultural adaptations in highland Ecuador employed a detailed investigation of current practices for retrodictive analysis and reconstruction of ancient conditions. In Africa, the study of human ecological adaptation has been informed with historical materialist and political-economic perspectives (M. Watts 1983b; Bassett 1988).

REPRODUCTION AND RESISTANCE

One direction that ecological anthropology has taken since the 1960s has been to study the biological ecology of human populations (for a critique of this trend see Sahlins 1976; 1977). Here the emphasis is on biological adaptation and reproduction. Few geographers have pursued these ends. Instead, most cultural ecologists have viewed interactions between nature and society as examples of cultural adaptation, especially those subsistence strategies selected for ecological success.

Although a biologistic view of human reproduction has been largely rejected, the idea of social and cultural reproduction as a central concept in cultural geography has not been widely

accepted either. Some scholars, however, especially those whose writing and research fall within the scope of the critical or "new" cultural geography, have begun to explore the implications of the reproduction of cultural, social, and political systems (Pred 1982) and of gender-based divisions of labor in traditional agricultural communities (Katz 1991; M. Watts 1983b). In these studies the habitual and ritual nature of behavior assumes a key role in defining culture. As yet, there has not been much overlap between this research and the work of cultural ecologists. Several new perspectives, such as political ecology (Blaikie and Brookfield 1987; Hecht and Cockburn 1989) and studies of the "reproduction of everyday life" (Katz 1991), promise potential bridges.

New syntheses may emerge from further exploring processes of cultural resistance. The spate of prefixion that has produced such terms as *postmodern, postprocessual, poststructural,* and *postpositivist* is itself an act of resistance to the various orthodoxies generally identified with academic modernism. Debates on these issues reflect trends in the world at large that demand interpretation and investigation. One curious twist has been the reemergence of traditions as points of reference and nodes of resistance to the globalization of economies, polities, and societies (Warf 1988; M. Watts 1988). Aspects of these tensions are well illustrated in the papers by Nietschmann and Zimmerer.

The majority of cultural geographers have always been comfortable with, and comforted by, study of traditional cultures and their customary ways of doing things. At base, much of the enduring work of scholars in geography and related fields celebrates the persistence of traditional cultures in the face of dominating and homogenizing forces. In this light, cultural resistance in its many forms should provide good ground for cultural geographers, old and new, historical and ecological, to join in the common search for the way the world has worked, is working, will work, and, maybe, should work.

JAMES M. BLAUT   # 12

DIFFUSIONISM: A
UNIFORMITARIAN CRITIQUE

D iffusionism is a way of looking at the world that has long influenced thinking in geography and social thought. Its classical form was described by Malinowksi (1927, 31) as the belief "that culture can be contracted only by contagion and that man is an imitative animal." In other words, culture change does not arise autonomously in most human communities: it comes from without, via diffusion. But diffusion itself must have a source, and classical diffusionism postulated that some places are permanent, natural centers of creativity and invention. Even the opponents of classical diffusionism tended to accept its main proposition that Europe is the world's source of culturally significant innovations.

Classical diffusionism was strongly though not thoroughly criticized. Its most salient form, the "extreme diffusionism" that attributed almost all cultural origins to diffusion and claimed to find a single fountainhead for civilization (see, e.g., G. Smith 1971) was fairly disposed of (see Childe 1951; M. Harris 1968; Kroeber 1937; Leaf 1979; Lowie 1937). A few geographers and anthropologists continued to accept parts of the doctrine, however, such as the claim that New World cultures did not invent agriculture and other civilizing innovations on their own but received them via transoceanic diffusion (Carter 1968; Edmonson 1961). The view that most cultures and most people are uninventive was attacked by Radin (1933) and others (see Leaf 1979, 164–71), and opposing viewpoints gained favor, particularly among those cultural anthropologists and cultural geographers who defended the integrity of folk culture and who understood "tradition" to be dynamic and rational (see, e.g., Kniffen 1965). But Eurocentrism retained its hegemony over most social thought, and the "folk-urban continuum" remained in essence a concept of one-way diffusion.

Diffusionism has become reinvigorated, primarily because it fits with the stance that progress for the Third World consists in accepting the "modernizing" diffusion of multinational capitalism and the material traits, ideas, and sociopolitical behavior associated with it. The ideology of modernization has received considerable scientific criticism, and some writers have associated it with diffusionism (e.g., Blaikie 1978; Blaut 1970; 1977; Brookfield 1975; Chilcote 1984; Frank 1969). But diffusionism in its modern form has not as yet been systematically described and criticized, nor has the full extent of its influence been recognized.

In this paper I describe diffusionism and outline an alternative structure, a way of theorizing about culture change that takes account of spatial diffusion but does not succumb to diffusionism. I also argue that the nondiffusionist alternative has useful implications for a wide range of geographic theories. I suggest some ways to eliminate diffusionism from the part of spatial diffusion theory that relates to agricultural development in the Third World, and I look at a few of the larger problems in historical geography in which an explicitly nondiffusionist approach can be helpful. The project as a whole is best described as a critique of diffusionism, but it is a schematic critique limited by the space available in a journal article. In particular, I do not criticize diffusionist writings except where this cannot be avoided in the context of a theoretical argument, and I say little about the history of diffusionism in geography or in general.

STRUCTURE OF DIFFUSIONISM

Diffusionism is a large and complex doctrine that has influenced many disciplines and count-less arguments for the past 150 years or so. The essential structure of diffusionism is quite simple. From two axiomatic propositions it constructs two interchangeable landscapes, one a two-sector space, the other a space with a continuous gradient between two poles. Finally, it describes the properties of the two sectors and of the two poles (plus gradations between) and the transactions that flow in both directions, with a set of elementary arguments, six of which are crucial and will be discussed here.

Assume a landscape with many communities. (I use the word *community* to designate a discrete social space at any scale, e.g., a settlement or a culture region.) A novel trait appears in one community. Later, the same trait appears in a second community. The second community either invented the trait for itself (a case of what is called independent invention) or acquired it from the first community (a case of diffusion). Thereafter the trait appears in other communities, and each new appearance is explained as a further instance of independent invention or diffusion. So far so good.

But suppose now that we wish to predict where in this landscape some other novel trait will make its initial appearance. Is it reasonable to suppose that the community that invented the first trait will invent all subsequent traits as well? This would be likely only if two additional assumptions obtained: (1) the role of diffusion is more important than is that of independent invention (there is little inventiveness in this landscape); and (2) the community that invented the first trait has a greater capability than do the other communities of inventing traits in general. If both these assumptions hold true, then subsequent trait inventions should come from this one community, which thus becomes the permanent center for invention and innovation for this landscape; thereafter, the appearance of new innovations elsewhere in the landscape would be the result of a diffusion process originating in our single inventive community.

This belief—that changes are produced by diffusion rather than (ordinarily) by independent invention and that certain places are the permanent centers of innovation—is diffusionism. Diffusionism at the world scale usually considers

Europe or the West to be the permanent center of invention and innovation, although this generalization needs to be qualified as to historical epoch. (Classical diffusionists conceived the center, "civilization," to be Europe or northwestern Europe or, for racists, "the Lands of the White Race." Modern diffusionists tend to view the center as the developed capitalist countries, Japan having been recently admitted to the central sector, which is still called "the West" in line with diffusionism's theory of history and culture.) At the regional scale diffusionism considers the part of a region that is most "Europeanized," "Westernized," "modernized," or "cosmopolitan," and perhaps most "progressive," "innovative," or "rational," to be the center of invention and innovation. Innovations then spread by diffusion to the "traditional areas," the "folk societies," the "backward regions," and so forth. Note the implication that the permanent center is always more advanced than the other parts of the region (or of the world) as it is always emitting innovations that are adopted only later elsewhere. Diffusionists often carry this matter of comparative synchronic levels of development one step further: the societies most distant from the center are the most backward and the most ancient; they are sometimes thought of as the "contemporary ancestors" of the societies at the center, as though to travel outward in space is to travel backward in time. Thus diffusionism is in a double sense elitist: the center is at all times more progressive than is the periphery, and it is at all times more advanced, that is to say, more civilized. The classical position was enunciated by Ratzel (1896, 179): "How much more the intercourse between lands and islands has contributed to the enrichment of men's stock of culture than has independent invention. . . . It seems . . . correct to credit the intellect of "natural races" with great sterility in all that does not touch the most immediate objects of life." Here explicitly are the two diffusionist assumptions that invention is rare and that most peoples are uninventive, and here implicitly the double elitism: the "natural races" are backward and they are unprogressive. Today *natural races* would be replaced by *traditional cultures*.

The elementary structure of diffusionism is a two-sector space at any geographical scale and historical depth. Six arguments (possibly more) describe the properties of each sector and the transactions between them. These six arguments are developed from the two basic diffusionist assumptions and are elaborated, in turn, into more complex and specific propositions. In some contexts of discourse diffusionism describes a simple two-sector world with a boundary between the sectors. In other contexts it depicts a space with small gradational changes, such that the six arguments describe small and local differences: e.g., more innovative and less innovative, more traditional and less traditional. A further qualification must be made to distinguish the arguments of the classical and modern forms of diffusionism (about which more will be said shortly). For brevity, the discussion will focus on the world scale, contrasting a "core" sector and a "periphery," and on the classical form of the arguments, as follows:

1. Progressive culture change that takes place in the core sector is autonomous; that is, it reflects inventions occurring within the core, and it owes nothing important to the periphery.

2. The underlying force or cause of inventiveness in the core sector is some psychological or spiritual factor such as rationality (Weber 1958); technological inventiveness (L. White 1962); imaginativeness (as opposed to imitativeness) (Tarde 1903); a logical, theoretical mind (Sack 1980 *fide* Lévy-Bruhl 1966); or "Western economic man" (Chisholm 1982).

3. The periphery is the traditional sector or "traditional world," *tradition* here having two meanings: low level of civilization and low rate of change. Therefore, allowing for exceptions (like the archaic Asian civilizations that rose but then stagnated), progressive culture change in the periphery is not autonomous but is attributable to diffusion from the center. The argument about a "traditional sector" takes a special form when it is applied to settlement of the periphery by people from the core. What is invoked here can be called the "myth of emptiness." The idea of tradition as used in diffusionism is basically an idea of absence-of-qualities. Usually the missing qualities are psychological (e.g., "rationality") or institutional (e.g., "private property,"

"the state"). The myth of emptiness also asserts an actual emptiness of the landscape: there were no indigenous people, or their population was negligibly small (and sparse enough to allow unimpeded settlement by foreigners), or they were "nomads" and thus had no real claim to land, resources, and territorial sovereignty.

4. The predominant form of interaction between core and periphery is the outward diffusion of progressive ideas, intangible intellectual and moral products reflecting the core culture's rationality and inventiveness. In classical diffusionism this is seen as the spread of "civilization" and today as the spread of "modernization." This centrifugal diffusion is not really explained; it is assumed, rather, to reflect the automatic workings of what can be called (with a nod to Malinowski) the principle of ideological contagion: certain ideas diffuse for no reason other than their innate infectiousness and the inherent susceptibility—in this case, the imitativeness—of the recipients. Again there is a variant for settler colonies: the progressive ideas are distributed by their bearers. Classical and modern diffusionism (see the brief historical discussion below) differ in the formulation of this argument. The classical argument tended to emphasize mass migrations (W. Adams, Van Gerven, and Levy 1978) and the transfer of cultures and culture complexes. Modern diffusionism tends to assert that diffusion proceeds "from person to person, rather than from community to community or from culture to culture" (Rouse 1961, 96, commenting on Edmonson 1961), reducing cultural process to the level of individuals, who are thought to be adopting new ideas freely (the myth of "voluntarism") and as a reflection mainly of cognitive processes and interpersonal communication (Blaut 1977).

5. There is a counterdiffusion of material things from periphery to core, things like raw materials, plantation products, art objects, and workers. Classical diffusionism saw this as one side of a grand transaction embodied in colonialism: material wealth in partial repayment—it could never be full repayment—for civilization.

6. There is a second kind of counterdiffusion from periphery to core, consisting of precisely the opposite of civilization. Because the periphery is by definition archaic, it is the locus of ata-

vistic traits that seep back into the core according to the principle of ideological contagion.

Embedded in the foregoing are a number of important contrasts that distinguish core from periphery in classical diffusionist ethnoscience: inventiveness/imitativeness, rationality/irrationality, intellect/emotion (or intellect/instinct), abstract thought/concrete thought, theoretical reasoning/empirical (practical) reasoning, mind/body, discipline/spontaneity, adult/child, sane/insane, and science/sorcery.

FUNCTIONS AND HISTORY OF DIFFUSIONISM

The diffusionist world model became explicit, powerful, and important as the scientific underpinning of colonialism. Its classical form emerged soon after the Napoleonic period and flourished until about the time of World War I.[1] Colonialism itself was of course a diffusion process among other things, but classical diffusionism imposed a theoretical model over the real process to exhibit colonialism and the phenomena related to it (such as the internal characteristics of the colonized societies) in ways that would conform to the interests of the colonizing societies and of the elite groups within them that benefited directly from colonialism. Diffusionism demonstrated, as it were scientifically, that colonialism is normal, natural, inevitable, and moral (that is, a bestowal of civilization).

Classical diffusionism was appropriate to the epoch in which capitalism was expanding mainly by means of colonialism and related processes. This epoch ended after World War I, to be followed by a period characterized by a search for stability, normalcy, and peace, hence equilibrium, and characterized in social thought by models of equilibrium, not of expansive diffusion: Keynesian models in economics, regionalism in geography, functionalism and relativism in anthropology, and the like. Diffusionism was in eclipse during this period, although some diffusionist schools (e.g., the *Kulturkreislehre* of Graebner and Schmidt and the migrationism of Huntington and Taylor) remained active and naive diffusionism still prevailed in children's schoolbooks (see M. Harris 1968; Kroeber 1937; Lowie 1937; Voget 1975).

A new and modern form of diffusionism

gained prominence after World War II, in the period of collapsing colonial empires and an emerging "Third World" of underdeveloped but sovereign countries. These countries were of great economic importance to capitalism in its new era of expansionism and were of equally great political concern to Cold War strategists, who sought (not always successfully) to keep these states from turning to socialism. Both interests required the creation and scientific validation of a modern form of the diffusionist model, a body of ideas that had to persuade the now-sovereign Third World states that economic and social advancement consisted in acquiring so-called modernizing traits from the developed capitalist countries—traits including penetration by multinational corporations; spread of commodity production and consumption; acceptance of and reliance on external capital, military equipment, and personnel; and so on. Advancement also required the suppression of forces that would inhibit diffusion by, for instance, building self-reliant economies, encouraging labor organization, and investing social capital in research institutions rather than in diffusion agencies engaged in propelling foreign traits into the countryside (see Blaikie 1978; Blaut 1973; 1977; Browett 1980; Chilcote 1984; Frank 1969; Yapa 1977; 1980; Yapa and Mayfield 1978).

As with classical diffusionism, modern diffusionism as a world model needs to be distinguished from actual diffusion processes and agencies. Modern diffusionism is a theoretical model in which diffusion from developed countries to Third World countries (along with the phenomena related to it such as the internal characteristics of the Third World societies) are depicted in such a way as to demonstrate, scientifically, that diffusion is the only possible road to development, to "modernization" (the *Modewort* of modern diffusionism). Diffusion, therefore, is still normal, natural, inevitable, and moral. And this is demonstrated with arguments grounded in the two diffusionist assumptions and six basic diffusionist propositions. Modern diffusionism is, if anything, more important in our own time than classical diffusionism was in the last century. This is so because persuasion has now replaced naked force—though not every-

where—and the evident failure of the diffusion process to produce real development thus far means that ever greater emphasis must be placed on theories that prove conclusively that diffusion must lead to development sooner or later.

The foregoing discussion of the structure of diffusionism and its history and changing functions is of course schematic and incomplete. What is perhaps most obviously missing is an explanation of the fact that most social scientists who today put forward diffusionist ideas—all must do so to one extent or another—are unaware of the diffusionism in their (our) thinking. I have addressed this problem elsewhere (Blaut 1979, 2–6).

A THEORETICAL ALTERNATIVE

Let us return now to an abstract landscape and begin to construct a theoretical alternative to diffusionism. In fact there are at least two alternatives, both of which eliminate the diffusionist assumption that one place has more inventiveness than all other places. Instead we assume uniformitarianism—that all communities have equal potential for invention and innovation, regardless of whether for the landscape as a whole the overall propensity to invent is low or high. The original doctrine called "uniformitarianism" was the methodological principle used by nineteenth-century science to counter the claims of theologians and others that physically similar forms across the earth's surface are to be explained as unique interventions of God or the Devil (see M. Harris 1968; Voget 1975). Uniformitarianism asserted, in essence, that a common set of physical laws operates everywhere, and wherever we find similar physical facts we should look for similar physical causes and vice versa. A logically related doctrine, called the principle of the "psychic unity of mankind" (*psychic* here meaning "psychological"), was used some decades later to oppose the diffusionist argument that independent invention cannot be invoked to explain trait adoption by most of the world's peoples because most peoples are not inventive. Underlying the principle of psychic unity was the simple proposition that all human beings share the same basic psychological attributes and capabilities (M. Harris 1968; Koepping 1983; Lowie 1937).

We can take this part of the doctrine, call it "psychological uniformitarianism" or simply "uniformitarianism," and define it for our purpose as follows: in all human communities we should expect to find the same capacity for creation and invention; hence invention and innovation should have an equal probability of occurring in all places. Note that what we are assuming here is not uniformity but equality, and recall that diffusionism assumes inequality.

A uniformitarian landscape can change in either of two ways, depending on whether we choose to retain or discard the diffusionist assumption that diffusion is more important than independent invention because invention is rare. This assumption has tended to be rejected by opponents of diffusionism because it seems to carry with it the assumption that people in general are imitative, not inventive, and that ordinary people are stupid. But in fact, as I outline below, it is not necessary to give an important role to independent invention in order to build a nondiffusionist, uniformitarian schema for diffusion theory. The critique of diffusionism does not have to draw us into the traditional and often futile debates labeled "diffusion vs. independent invention." Let us first assume that independent invention is indeed important and see where this takes us.

In the limiting case, an invention occurs simultaneously in all communities throughout a landscape. If these communities were, say, villages not very distant from one another, it would be extremely unlikely that all communities would acquire a trait simultaneously through independent invention. (I assume that the trait is in some definable sense useful for the population as a whole.) But if the communities were major culture regions, then the scenario of simultaneous independent invention is not necessarily unrealistic. (Think, for instance, of parallel responses to widespread drought, epidemic, or invasion.) At a given time all places would lack the trait; at the end of a defined interval all places would possess the trait. The landscape would thus go through a sequence of stages, each representing the acquisition of one novel trait, and at each stage the landscape would be a uniform region.

It would obviously be more realistic to assume that diffusion occurs along with independent invention. (Nobody has ever questioned the significance of diffusion, merely its claim to hegemony.) In this case, the first novel trait would appear in a number of communities randomly distributed across the landscape, and the trait would spread to the communities surrounding them. The subsequent diffusion process would not necessarily lead to spatial differentiation, and, after a given number of defined intervals, the region would again be uniform, having changed state from trait absence to trait presence. We can complicate the process by assuming that new innovations are appearing while the prior innovations are diffusing. The overall picture would remain one in which diffusion plays a role, yet no part of the landscape acquires characteristics that are not also acquired by all other parts.

Next assume a situation in which independent invention plays only a minor role, a case that may have been overlooked in the classical arguments against diffusionism. Here a trait is invented in one community and subsequently diffuses to other communities. At this point we may pause to consider the properties of what I have been calling "traits." One problem in studies of culture change by anthropologists and cultural geographers has been the difficulty of isolating a single empirical event of the sort called a "culture trait." Every trait is in principle made up of component traits. Sometimes we do reach a definite limiting point below which everything seems to be a part of a trait, particularly when we are dealing with functional items of material culture like bows, houses, and so on. But, in general, the efforts to reduce cultures to "trait lists" proved unworkable, and the concept of "trait" remained imprecise (see M. Harris 1968, 376–77; Leaf 1979, 167; Voget 1975, 372–82). Modern diffusion research tends to ignore this issue and to employ what can be called the "patent office" notion (or the "commodity" notion) of what constitutes a diffusing trait, the notion that it is in some ontological sense whole and different from any existing trait. In the present discussion a *trait* refers to any distinguishable bit or quality of culture, whether or not it is ontologically objectlike, holistic, or systemic. It must, however, be invented, put to use as an innovation, and then diffused to other communities. Defining *trait* in this way has some interesting implications.

The invention and diffusion of definite, whole, recognizable things is much less significant in the real world than is the addition by invention or diffusion of improvements, modifications, or adaptations made to already existing pieces of culture. Though well known, this has surprising implications. Consider again the trait invented in one community and then diffused to others. Let us assume that some other community, after acquiring the trait, modifies it. Generically, this is independent invention, though modest modifications might not be called inventions. The now-modified trait appears in the landscape and begins to diffuse in its own right. Later a new modification is made by one of the communities, and the now twice-modified trait begins to diffuse. Assume that a sizable proportion of the diffusion events in the landscape consist of the emission of traits in a modified form, as compared to the form in which they were originally received and adopted. All of this is going on simultaneously throughout the landscape, in a process that can be called—I will define the term more precisely later—"crisscross diffusion." We continue to assume that the communities that initiate each invention and modification are randomly distributed across the landscape. If there is environmental variation in the landscape, then trait modifications would most likely occur in those environmental contexts where the original trait proves least useful. Hence it might be that the farther one goes from the originating community, the greater is the probability that the trait will be modified. Nonetheless, we are safe if we merely assume randomness in the process of modification. This scenario again produces a uniform region.[2]

This is the base case for uniformitarianism. It denies that some places or people are more inventive than others, and it denies that innovation is rare. It assumes only the level of inventiveness needed to produce modest modifications of existing traits. It gives to diffusion, not to independent invention, the main causal role in culture

change. But this kind of diffusion is very different from the diffusion of diffusionism. It produces spatially uniform or randomly varying changes, not the building up of centers of invention and innovation. It thus draws our attention away from the evolving pattern of a spreading diffusion, what I have described elsewhere as the transitional phase in a diffusion process (Blaut 1977), and toward different kinds of problems.

DIFFUSION PROCESSES

We can now identify seven diffusion processes that become salient in a uniformitarian approach to diffusion theory.

1. *Cellular diffusion.* In a theoretical landscape into which we have not introduced any empirical basis for spatial differentiation (such as hill-valley, town-country, sovereign state–colony, core-periphery) or in which it cannot be assumed *a priori* that such empirical differences will produce spatial variations in the invention and diffusion patterns, the effects of both invention and diffusion will lead to a uniform region. This is because, as we have seen, inventions will occur in randomly distributed communities and diffusion will have no greater tendency to move in one direction than another. Thus in the real world we would have a uniform region changing from the one state to another as a whole. At higher levels of aggregation we would have a pattern of cellular regions, each uniform and separated from all others by a boundary defined by the fact that diffusions do not cross it within a defined epoch. In this situation the problem of major interest would no longer involve the spatial transition from trait absence to trait presence but would relate to why the trait either does or does not diffuse in the region—problems thus of entry conditions and boundary breaching between regions (Blaut 1977, 349). All of this may be called "cellular diffusion."

2. *Ultrarapid diffusion.* Consider three cases: (1) a trait diffuses through a region with great rapidity—almost instantly; (2) a trait diffuses at some moderate, measurable rate; (3) a trait does not diffuse in the region at all. Cases (1) and (3) have received little attention in Third World rural contexts (but see Blaut 1977, 345–47; Yapa

and Mayfield 1978). I think the neglect of both cases reflects, in part, an unperceived influence of diffusionism, specifically its assumption that people are not very innovative (Bowen-Jones 1981, 79–82; Chisholm 1982, 155–63) and that change reflects the arrival of traits diffused from elsewhere (Lentnek 1969; 1971, 163; Hoyle 1974, 5). A large diffusionist mythology has been built up on the basis of "extensionism" in rural sociology (Rogers 1962) and "modernization" theory elsewhere (McClelland 1961; Foster 1962; Hagen 1962) to support the idea that, in essence, Third World people have to be pushed into adopting innovations and tend to do so slowly and reluctantly or uncomprehendingly. An alternative case can be made on empirical evidence that diffusion tends to proceed either remarkably rapidly or not at all. If a trait is information-dependent, if it is patently useful, and if resources to adopt it are present, then it will diffuse nearly at the rate information spreads. This is almost instantaneously in most social systems, unless information is a commodity or is held oligopolistically by power groups and not allowed to diffuse (see Blaikie 1978; Blaut 1977). If human beings are highly inventive and prone to receive and transmit innovations rapidly, trait diffusion not inhibited by extraneous forces (e.g., economic or political) should proceed at rates so rapid perhaps that modeling the transition is either impossible or uninteresting. By the same token, however, inhibiting forces will often—and in most Third World areas typically—prevent the diffusion of useful, development-inducing innovations from taking place at all. As to the intermediate case of moderate, measurable, modelable diffusion, I will argue below that, at least in the Third World, cases of this sort usually reflect processes other than the autonomous diffusion of innovations. Note that this stop-or-go diffusion pattern—ultrarapid diffusion or none at all—is consistent with the cellular model discussed previously.

3. *Crisscross diffusion.* In a uniformitarian landscape, diffusion will proceed rapidly in the absence of inhibiting factors. Traits or trait modifications will be generated, transmitted, and received frequently and will diffuse quickly. At all times novel traits will be crisscrossing the landscape. For large cultural transformations like the Neolithic Revolution and the transition from feudalism to capitalism, the effect of crisscross diffusion would be simultaneous changes throughout a landscape as a whole. Consider a landscape composed of just two communities, 1 and 2. Community 1 invents a trait or modifies an existing trait. The invention reaches community 2 by diffusion. Community 2 adds a modification of its own, which then diffuses to community 1, which may at the same time be transmitting another modification to 2. Both communities are simultaneously inventing, transmitting, and receiving novel traits, which thus are crisscrossing the space between them, and both communities are going through an ordered sequence of changes simultaneously. If the bundle of novelties adds up to a major cultural transformation, a "revolution," we cannot say that the revolution started in one community and diffused to the other: it occurred in both simultaneously. For the same scenario in a landscape with many communities, we would not be able to point to one place as the source or hearth of the revolution and describe other places as recipients-by-diffusion. If we were studying such a transformation empirically, we would assume that the entire landscape participated in the transformation by crisscross diffusion unless we were to uncover empirical evidence to the contrary.

4–6. *Dependent, disguised,* and *phantom diffusion.* Diffusionism, as noted previously, asserts that progressive ideas and their consequences—civilization, modernization, development—flow from the developed capitalist "core" to the more backward and slowly progressing "periphery." Modern diffusionism, for reasons discussed already, strives to show that it is just this spreading of modern knowledge and ways that characterizes the present-day relationship between capitalist metropolis and Third World and strives to argue convincingly that receptivity to flows of all sorts from the metropolis is the only way for peripheral societies to achieve development and "modernity."

Emerging from this is a concrete model in which there is asserted to be a steady flow of information, "modern" social attitudes, and wealth-generating material things like productive farm inputs glissading down from metropolis to periphery. This model has been deployed in one form or another in a number of studies, empirical and theoretical, and claims are made that it has been empirically validated (see e.g., Gould 1969; Rogers and Shoemaker 1971; Pedersen 1970; L. Brown 1981). In fact, it is merely self-validating, because it fails to distinguish traits generating development from traits doing quite different things, such as increasing poverty and landlessness; in effect the model treats all diffusing traits as "modernizing innovations."

The foregoing critique leads us to recognize three specific erroneous argument structures that I will refer to respectively as (4) dependent diffusion, (5) disguised diffusion, and (6) phantom diffusion. In dependent diffusion, assume the diffusion in the same space-time of two traits, x and y; y is dependent on x if the diffusion of x is an autonomous process, explainable in terms of a definite causal model, and if the diffusion of y is wholly explained by the fact that wherever we find x we tend to find y (for whatever reason). Trait y may covary spatially with x, or it may simply be an adventitious attachment to x. In such cases we would be in error if we explained the diffusion of y with a model postulating an autonomous cause of the diffusion. As an example, consider the case of a region in which there is a progressive erosion of farm tenure, with farms tending to slide down what is often called the "tenure ladder," from farm ownership to tenancy to sharecropping to landlessness and sale of labor. As tenure erodes, there may well be a change in crops, productive inputs, and equipment. A novel crop may spread because it provides the same food value on smaller acreage. Another may spread because it can be sold as a commodity to pay rent demanded in cash. Another crop, often a "modern" export crop, may spread because landlords force its growth on share tenants and may spread even more dramatically when farmers have been evicted and the land is cultivated in large plantations. In these two cases (increased sharecropping and conversion to plantation or "kulak" agriculture) we often find an impressive diffusion into the countryside of agricultural machinery and ex-pensive inputs. If we were to claim here that there is an autonomous diffusion of "modernizing" traits—innovative crops, tractors, and the like—we would be mistaken: these are the ys, traits whose diffusion is dependent on the diffusion of x, in this case, landlordism. Yet diffusion researchers often make this mistake in their studies of Third World rural landscapes, falsely characterizing the diffusing ys as innovations that are part of "modernization" and development (e.g., Lentnek 1969; Riddell 1970).

In this case there is a misreading of causality: an explanatory schema is invoked for the diffusion of a trait y, whereas the appropriate explanation would have to account for the diffusion of the independent trait x, with y then being seen as a trait that, so to speak, rides piggyback on x. In the case of disguised diffusion, the independent trait x is simply not observed. This occurs most frequently when the observed trait, y, seems to be an expression of "the diffusion of modernizing innovations," while the x is some economically or socially corrosive process. One further type of disguised (and dependent) diffusion deserves notice. This is the case where the truly significant spatial flow is outward from a region (as in the marketing of farm commodities or the draining of wealth from periphery to core) whereas the spatial flows *into* the region (the diffusion processes normally studied) are nothing more than a preparation of infrastructure: capital investment, road building, and the like. (On the historical importance of diffusion from periphery to core see Lattimore 1980.) Most colonial diffusions consisted of infrastructure of this sort, designed for profit, not development, and leading often to the opposite of development. Yet a number of geographers, e.g., Riddell in his study of Sierra Leone (Riddell 1970, 3–7, 13–14, 40–65, 70–72, 86–93, 95–101, 129–31), treat all such colonial infrastructural diffusions as though they were truly "modernizing," thereby suggesting that colonialism was itself a modernizing process, rather than, as in Sierra Leone, a process of destroying the preexisting social-political, economic, and spatial structure of precolonial development, including roads, schools, and medical institutions.[3]

It can also happen that a diffusion is inferred

to have taken place when none in fact did, a case of what can be called phantom diffusion. This error is easier to make than may seem apparent and is most easily made if the trait is ephemeral (like information) or abstract (like modernization itself); but it happens also with concrete material traits whose actual diffusion was not observed. A classic case is the mythic spread of modern medicine in colonial India.[4] Equally classic is the argument that early Americans did not invent the innovative traits of civilization but received them from some original hearth in the Old World (Carter 1968, 538–63) and the related attempt by Edmonson (1961) to trace the diffusion of pottery to the New World using a form of the principle of ideological contagion and neglecting material evidence.

An important case of phantom diffusion is the inference—based on evidence of known diffusion of certain material traits—that development-inducing information has spread through a region. The spread of such traits in the rural Third World often reflects processes in which information (as that term is used in diffusion research) was either irrelevant or absent: there was no voluntary "decision to adopt" made after the receipt of information; rather, the decision was forced on farmers (e.g., by landlords or creditors), or it took place in a different economic space, such as that of plantations, "kulaks," or merchants (Blaut 1977, 346–47). Thus, inferring that the diffusion of traits like new crops or machinery was based upon the diffusion of information is often unwarranted. This is a crucial point for theory and policy because it cuts the chain of reasoning by which the diffusion of new ideas is judged to be the crucial component of development—that it has some role to play is not at issue—and by which technical assistance and the encouragement of external dependence and control literally take the place of land reform and genuine social change. In this connection we might note that the classic instance of information diffusion in a process of agricultural modernization, the case of extension services to United States agriculture from the 1930s to the 1950s, calls for some reinterpretation. Farmers, acting through the political process (particularly the "farm bloc" in Congress), demanded that they be provided with such services in an environment in which the family farm was gravely threatened by the growth of giant marketing and supply corporations. Hence the critical information diffused *from* the farmers *to* the government, and the reply came back via experiment stations, county extension agents, and the rest.

Another form of phantom diffusion is where the abstract substance, development, is inferred to have diffused into a Third World region when it has not done so. Often this involves a fusing of classical and modern diffusionism in the argument that European colonialism was innately a process of development and modernization and that this process is the only route to development today. Given this model, many colonial traits can be seen as concrete indicators of "modernization." Thus, for instance, Riddell describes a relatively unimportant change in local administration that the British imposed essentially by force on Sierra Leone in the 1930s as a voluntarily adopted, "modernizing" change. He depicts the change, which was imposed mainly over a six-year period by the British in a spatial process accordant with their pattern of administration and control, as a typical case of voluntary diffusion of innovations, with "demonstration effects," "information," a pattern of "acceptance" nicely suited to trend-surface mapping, and the like (see Riddell 1970, 48–55, and supporting comments in Gould 1969, 66, and in L. Brown 1981, 267–69; compare Kup 1975, Chap. 6, and Fyle 1981, 116–17).

A more concrete and interesting case comes from Gould (1969; 1970) and some others (including Riddell) who make the following argument: the colonial powers built roads; roads imply accessibility; and accessibility is an adequate surrogate for development or modernization. This argument is invalidated on three counts. First, accessibility existed in precolonial routes of movement and trade, usually elaborate and often as modern as one can expect for the preautomobile era. Riddell (1970, 3) asserts that precolonial Sierra Leone had only "bush paths and riverine routes," whereas it had two interdigitating transport networks, one leading to the Sudanic economic hearth, the other (Creole) one to Freetown (Riddell 1970, 3, 20; compare Hopkins 1973; A. Howard 1975, 263–64; Kup 1975, 72; Newbury 1969, 69; Fyle 1981, Chap. 15). In the case of Ghana, Gould writes of "total inaccessibility" prior to British road building for an area which also had a complicated network of precolonial (premotor) roads, in fact a well-developed hierarchy of central places (Gould 1969, 64; compare Kea 1982 on road networks and central place systems of precolonial Ghana). Second, colonial road networks are oriented to European economic concerns, mainly of export, and they are not always of much use in transportation planning today; indeed, they reinforce (as they were intended to do) the external economic dependency for which the country may wish to substitute autonomy. Third, road systems do not necessarily provide development. In many colonies and in semicolonies (like China), complex road and railroad systems were developed, but they did not bring development. Today, development does not automatically flow down these networks because of accessibility (Stevens and Lee 1979; Wilbanks 1972). Under certain sociopolitical conditions, they provide accessibility for flows which are antidevelopment.

7. Most diffusions are also *displacements* in that one trait displaces another or one population displaces another. The distinction between displacing and nondisplacing diffusions is not often made, and this leads to theoretical and empirical errors. One source of this problem is the diffusionist argument that I have called the myth of emptiness. Classical colonialism argued that the spread of European populations, cultural facts, and political control was scientifically natural and morally justifiable because (among other things) the landscapes into which these things were inserted were in one sense or another empty. Aboriginal populations were sparse or virtually nonexistent. The people were nomads. They had no state, no property, no commerce. At most they had "traditional society" into which everything modern would flow as if into a vacuum. Modern diffusionism reduces its focus mainly to the case of "traditional societies" and the flow into them of "modernizing innovations."

It would take us far afield to discuss the many ways in which the myth of emptiness still affects geography and social thought, but I shall offer a few examples of this type of thinking. Nostrand underestimates earlier Hispanic population in the Southwest (Nostrand 1975; criticized in Blaut and Ríos-Bustamante 1984). McEvedy has depicted southern Africa as largely empty of Africans other than Bushmen and Hottentots prior to European settlement (McEvedy 1980, 20–112; in a similar vein, see Guelke 1976). Reichman and Hasson (1984, 62) map the Palestinian West Bank circa 1910 as an area of "nomad population." (For an extreme view see G. Rowley 1983, 188). Various theoretical studies employ models that improperly define prediffusion spaces as empty, the most influential example being the depiction by Taaffe, Morrill, and Gould (1963) of transportation development in a hypothetical underdeveloped country (see commentary in L. Brown 1981, 267–69). Such models diffuse into pedagogy, where they supply realistic-seeming models, images, games, and "simulations" of empty-seeming Third World spaces (e.g., French and Stanley 1974; Haggett 1983, 515–21; Haggett and Chorley 1969, 296–98). In the case of diffusions that displace, it seems unlikely that theoretical models (or games) can be of much help unless they take account of conflict, coercion, and political power.

HYPOTHESES

Diffusionism has so pervaded social thought that it seems reasonable to suppose that a nondiffusionist perspective will lead us to rethink some of our larger hypotheses. By way of concluding this paper, I shall discuss five such hypotheses. Four have to do with culture history and the fifth with agricultural development in the present-day world. In each case I put forward a generalization and just enough supporting evidence to render it plausible.[5]

HYPOTHESIS I

The Old World agricultural revolution may have happened everywhere at once. More precisely, we should not look for one or two original and autonomous centers but should expect to find that large portions of Asia, Africa, and Europe were participating simultaneously in the process, however lengthy it may have been. The process may have worked in the following way. First, we make the familiar, though not universally accepted, assumption that a transformation from a preagricultural to an agricultural economy was advantageous for people over most (not all) of the reasonably warm and nonarid portions of the Old World.[6] Second, we assume that human settlement was essentially continuous over most of this area, with discontinuities spanned by land and water routes of movement. Third, we introduce the uniformitarian assumptions that all settlements and cultures were simultaneously inventing, sending, and receiving agricultural innovations. Fourth, the effects of the foregoing were transmitted by crisscross diffusion throughout the entire region at a rapid rate, rapid enough to permit innovations to pass back and forth throughout the region (which stretched at least from West Africa and central Europe to China and New Guinea), and thus gradually to build up an agricultural landscape.

We should take note of recent evidence pointing toward a convergence of dates for earliest agriculture in the neighborhood of 9,000–11,000 B.P. for regions distant from one another and very dissimilar in environment: northern Nigeria and various Saharan sites (c. 9,000 B.P.: Wendorf and Schild 1980), southeastern Europe (c. 8,000 B.P.: Kabaker 1977), Southwest Asia (c. 10,000 B.P.: Kabaker 1977), northeastern India (c. 7,000 B.P.: Vishnu-Mittre 1978), Thailand (9,000 B.P. or earlier: Gorman 1977), highland New Guinea (c. 9,000 B.P.: Golson 1977), and China (c. 7,000 B.P.: Ho 1977). Further research may shift the specific space-time pattern, but no longer will single-center theories be able to assert the hegemony of Middle East antiquity. Various theories of agricultural origins (e.g., M. Cohen 1977; Rindos 1984) are consistent with the hypothesis of a nearly continental-scale agricultural revolution. Some of these theories posit a number of sites that either shared a common environmental character (e.g., maximal biomass-production potential) or were environmentally diverse (e.g., Vavilov's [1951] long list of

domestication hearths), but such sites can be viewed as nodes in a network, and these theories are not inconsistent with our hypothesis.

HYPOTHESIS 2

A number of important theses about agricultural evolution are influenced by assumptions about selective ignorance, noninventiveness, and a primordial directionality of diffusion—assumptions that are sometimes diffusionist and sometimes given momentum because they are conformal to diffusionism. Withdrawing these assumptions should change our thinking in significant ways. I shall suggest two. (1) Why should we believe that irrigation is an evolutionary advance over drained- and dry-field farming systems or that sedentary systems are an advance over shifting systems? When we deal with situations that are not complicated by class pressures for surplus delivery, all of these different farming systems should be capable of providing about the same returns to labor over many different environmental situations. There is nothing about small-scale irrigation that is more esoteric than the way farmers manage moisture supply in drained-field and dry-field farming systems. And we are supposing now that inventiveness and rapid crisscross diffusion are the normal state of affairs. It seems reasonable, therefore, to suggest that drained-field agriculture and shifting agriculture are neither more nor less ancient than irrigated agriculture and that the systems vary for reasons that have nothing to do with selective technological ignorance or cognitive primitivity.[7] And it does not seem reasonable to believe, *a priori*, that an "irrigation revolution" or "hydraulic revolution" occurred separate from the primal agricultural revolution and created centers of social evolution. Large-scale irrigation systems must have been the effect, not the cause, of class processes and the state; the logic of such systems is that they can provide more surplus product per unit of area and facilitate the division of labor. Thus the popular causal model for "hydraulic civilization" is stood on its head, and the notions of "oriental despotism" and an "Asiatic mode of production" are denied their principal means of support. (2) The belief that an autonomous, internally generated agricultural revolution occurred in medieval Europe (see, e.g., L. White 1962) must lose credibility when we withdraw from it the diffusionist assumption that evolutionary change within the European sector is autonomous. Innovations in material culture and social organization of production diffused both into and out of Europe. An agricultural revolution of sorts was indeed taking place but on a hemispheric scale (Blaut 1976), and the changes that took place within Europe cannot be woven into a separate causal theory of progress.

HYPOTHESIS 3

The rise of capitalism occurred in many parts of Asia, Africa, and Europe at the same time. This hypothesis is a simple denial of the thesis that capitalism arose autonomously in Europe and nowhere else and arose because of attributes (e.g., progressiveness, rationality, modernity) unique to Europeans. I defend this hypothesis elsewhere (Blaut 1976; 1987b), but briefly the argument is as follows: First, every attribute of medieval Europe that played a causal role in the subsequent rise of capitalism was also present in a number of other communities across the Old World at the same time, and these communities were not less progressive, more rigid, or more "traditional," nor were Europeans uniquely "inventive" (Weber 1951; 1958; L. White 1962; 1968). Second, emerging protocapitalism was seated mainly in mercantile-maritime urban centers (with small hinterlands), stretching from western Europe to eastern Asia and southern Africa (to Sofala and perhaps southward). These centers were, on the one hand, peripheral to and partially independent of the surrounding feudal states and, on the other, were themselves interlocked in a hemisphere-wide network of trade and communication, a network through which innovations of all sorts were transmitted to all parts of the system by rapid crisscross diffusion with the result that the character of mercantile capitalism, of urban production, and of much else besides was basically common to all nodes in the network. Thus all centers were participating in a common evolution toward a fully capitalist society and policy, an evolution that was taking place at a rapid, perhaps ultrarapid, rate during

the fifteenth century in parts of Europe but also in parts of Africa and Asia. Third, it was the conquest and plunder of the New World—carried out by Europeans because protocapitalist centers of Europe were thousands of miles closer to the New World in 1492 than were any other major protocapitalist centers—that provided the resources enabling European merchant capital to rise toward political power in Europe and to begin the process of destroying competing groups elsewhere. Thus capitalism ceased to rise in Africa and Asia while it was advancing toward a bourgeois and then industrial revolution in Europe alone.

HYPOTHESIS 4

Nationalism did not arise as an innovation in Europe and then appear in other parts of the world as a result of diffusion from Europe. This hypothesis, like the preceding one, I have defended elsewhere (Blaut 1980; 1982; 1987b), so here I will merely summarize the arguments and the issues. The body of theory about nationalism (i.e., national conflicts, the "national question") is dominated by two viewpoints, a mainstream theory that is diffusionist and a form of Marxist theory that is only slightly less so. The mainstream theory derives national processes from a primordial European idea, the "idea of nationalism," which is supposed to have arisen autonomously in northwestern Europe as the idea of, and urge to create, the nation-state. This idea then diffused outward toward the rest of the world, eventually arriving in colonies and sparking national liberation movements. The comparable Marxist theory identifies the nation-state as the most suitable political form for youthful capitalism and thus the goal of political struggle by the bourgeoisie in its rise to power. Capitalism diffused out across the world, and therefore, quite naturally, there emerged everywhere a local class of "rising bourgeoisie" and, in its wake, "bourgeois nationalism." Neither theory gives a real causal role to conditions of exploitation and oppression in the colonies and semicolonies or explains either the kind of nationalism that struggles against colonialism in order to create a socialist state or the kind that struggles to restore a precapitalist state. A nondiffusionist alternative to both theories argues that national struggle is struggle for state power, under conditions where control of the state is in the hands of foreign groups and produces suffering (economic, political, or cultural) for the inhabitants. This can occur in many circumstances and many forms of society. It may reflect colonial oppression, or power struggles in early capitalism, or other circumstances, some set in motion by diffusion processes, others internal to an area, culture, or state.

HYPOTHESIS 5

In present-day rural landscapes of underdeveloped countries, the main variables that determine diffusion rates are not spatial or psychological and are not matters of distance, accessibility, or so-called adopter attributes; the main variables have to do with the political and class environment. Typical diffusion rates for exogenous agricultural innovations that are clearly beneficial to farmers tend to be rapid or ultrarapid where inhibiting political and class conditions are absent. This is the case, for instance, where an egalitarian political environment limits or eliminates the ability of nonfamily-farming groups or classes to prevent family farmers from adopting innovations freely. This is also the case where family farmers, because of farm size and tenure security, have power to make decisions. On the other hand, innovations tend to diffuse slowly or not at all in political environments that favor power groups (e.g., landlords, merchants) that can prevent family farmers from making decisions or in political environments in which farmers are powerless because of poor tenure, small size of farm, and the like.

The influence of social conditions upon diffusion rates is not often disputed. But what this hypothesis asserts is that these conditions play the critical role in matters relating to agricultural change in underdeveloped areas; the factors traditionally emphasized by diffusion theorists (in geography and elsewhere) are of secondary importance in some situations and irrelevant in most others. If the hypothesis is valid, then the effort to explain, predict, and generate agricultural change should proceed in a fundamentally different way. To make this argument I will have

to say a word about the evolution of diffusion theory and the way it became entangled with diffusionism.

When diffusion-of-agricultural-innovations theory began to crystallize, mainly in the 1940s and 1950s, the crux of the theory was the information postulate—the notion that the communication of information about innovations is central to the process of change. There was important confirming evidence from landscapes with strong and stable peasantries; indeed, agricultural extension had much to do with the survival of family farming in North America during and after the Depression. The argument that information flows would be important predictors of change made good sense in that context (see Hägerstrand 1967; Tiedemann and Van Doren 1964). But the context did not extend to politically disfranchised peasantries suffering under landlordism and debt peonage.

In the 1950s geographers, rural sociologists, agricultural economists, and their colleagues began a truly massive effort to apply information-based diffusion theory to this larger and fundamentally different context. The motor force, as discussed earlier in this paper, was the effort to generate economic development in the Third World, but to do so by means of strategies that would not lead to dramatic social and political upheavals like nationalization of foreign holdings, land reform and related attacks on local elites, socialist revolution, and in some areas decolonization. Scholars were enlisted in this campaign in various ways that need not concern us (although it should be noted that all these research workers were convinced that their [our] work was directed against poverty and suffering). What is crucial here is the fact that the diffusionist model was axiomatic for most of the resulting scholarship—empirical, theoretical, and applied. The axiom asserted in essence that development results from the flow of modernizing innovations from the center to the countryside, that development results from not much more than the diffusion of innovations plus a small line of credit. (I am oversimplifying.)

The information postulate itself became diffusionist in this intellectual environment. Information-based diffusion theory assumed a two-sector landscape, one part informed and incrementally developed, the other part uninformed and undeveloped. Information and development spread spatially from one or another kind of center. Distance, accessibility, and the psychological condition of being informed or uninformed are the essential variables. (For examples of this approach see Lentnek 1969; Taaffe, Morrill, and Gould 1963; Wilbanks 1972. A critique is given in Blaut 1977.) But this, overall, was a mild sort of diffusionism, troublesome mostly for its ingenuous disregard of culture (and cultural geography). Rather quickly a more serious form of diffusionism took hold in diffusion research and some other schools of geographic research concerned with rural Third World development, e.g., the "natural hazards" school. Distance and accessibility remained as operant variables. But in place of the information variable there emerged a complex psychological variable, described in diffusion research as "adopter attributes," which postulated that rural Third World people have some fundamental (though curable) psychological disability that limits or inhibits their propensity to develop.

Personality traits do of course vary among human groups, but diffusionism asserts incorrectly that some groups possess crucial traits that permit positive change (development) and other groups lack such traits or possess them in smaller measure. One of these pseudotraits is "achievement motivation" (McClelland 1961; discussed supportively in L. Brown 1981, 235, 252, 254, 274). Another is "locus of control," in essence, the belief that one can control events; this pseudovariable is a part of the explanatory model used by G. White and some of his associates in studies of natural-hazard adaptability by Third World, mainly rural, people (see G. White 1974, 5–10; Baumann and Sims 1974, 28–30; Burton, Kates, and White 1978, 107; Dupree and Roder 1974, 117; for schematic critiques from differing perspectives see Blaut 1984, 150–51; J. Mitchell 1984, 57; Waddell 1977). Still another pseudovariable, already discussed here, is "traditionalism" or "the traditional mind," a notion deployed in diffusion research (see, e.g., L. Brown 1981, 274–75; Riddell 1970, 6) and elsewhere in geography to explain lack of developmental progress in particular landscapes or in general. At the most general level, for instance, Sack (1980) constructs an elaborate theory proposing to explain the evolution and cross-cultural variation of human abilities to conceptualize space, both concrete (political, economic, physiographic) and abstract, grounding the entire theory in the diffusionist dichotomy between the traditional (or "primitive") mind and the modern mind, the former being childlike, ancient, superstitious, subjective, unsophisticated, nonrational, practical (nontheoretical), and characteristic generally of non-Western societies (although peasant societies apparently admix the two forms of mentality) (see Sack 1980, 22–23, 27, 117–38, 142–57, 167–93, 197–200). Sack's construction is close to classical diffusionism in its view of the human mind, but it is also a typical example of a class of contemporary statements in which the traditional-mind–modern-mind dichotomy is used as an explanatory schema for cultural evolution, economic development, and, not incidentally, Third World rural modernization.

Traditionalism in these theories is stubborn tradition, not cherished tradition. The presumption is that some groups resist change when change is beneficial or necessary, while other groups, in other places, are not so stubbornly traditional. It is beyond the scope of this paper to attempt a critique of this view. Five comments must suffice. First, it is not methodologically proper here to argue that individual subjects resist change irrationally until we have established that change is feasible and that change will benefit the subjects; psychological limitations are properly invoked here only when external limitations have been discounted. Second, instruments do not yet exist for confirming the existence of, much less measuring, these postulated mental attributes or pseudoattributes, for getting past those barriers of status, power, cultural distance, and the like, which contaminate all studies (from the outside) about the psychology of rural Third World people. This skeptical view was perhaps the majority view among cultural anthropologists three decades ago, when many culture-and-personality theorists questioned even the seemingly culture-neutral Rorschach protocols as valid cross-cultural instruments (see Bock 1980, 134–37). But the opposing thesis gained popularity because, in my view, it was conformal to modern diffusionism and the belief that, in the rural Third World, poverty is at least partly the fault of the poor. Third, the emerging critique of modernizationism, developmentism, and diffusionism brings with it a new perspective on the role of the individual mind in development (see for instance Freire 1972; Giroux 1981; Pinar 1974; Stea 1980) and the role of technological knowledge in that process (Hansis 1976; K. Johnson 1977; Pearse 1980; Wisner 1977; Yapa 1980). Fourth, to argue that members of different cultures have equal perceptual and cognitive ("intellectual") capabilities is not to deny the fact that personality varies cross-culturally.[8] And fifth, in agreement with K. Marx and F. Engels (1956) and G. H. Mead (1938), I see the self as essentially a social product.

Accessibility is a real variable in some circumstances, and distance may also be significant as a (surrogate) variable. Both, however, are usually functions of political and class forces. L. Brown (1981) tries in essence to add socioeconomic variables to the variables of classic spatial diffusion theory—namely, psychological adopter attributes, information, distance, and accessibility—while accepting certain of the criticisms that have been made about that theory. His discussion of the role of diffusion agencies (public and private) is helpful, but it neglects the difference between theories that predict and those that propose strategies, and it gives little new support to spatial diffusion theory as a predictor. At the same time he pays inadequate attention to the variables of culture (and cultural geography). His perspective is not diffusionist, but the diffusionism of earlier perspectives remains unrecognized and uncriticized. M. Brown (1981) suggests better ways to measure innovation-adoption behavior, but she does not solve the problems discussed in the present paper. In general, diffusion theorists have not succeeded in predicting or generating the diffusion of agricultural innovations in the Third World.

Our hypothesis calls attention to causal forces, and development strategies, that are systemic: mainly matters of class and politics. These forces may vary across the landscape, but spatial (process) diffusion is not usually a central issue. The hypothesis thus speaks of tendencies toward uniform regions in cellular landscapes, regions in which diffusion either covers all possible adopters very quickly or does not penetrate the space at all. There is some empirical evidence in support of the hypothesis: for instance, ultrarapid diffusion has been observed when inhibiting conditions were not present.[9] Much better evidence, though difficult to quantify and uninteresting to map, comes from the innumerable cases in which the inhibiting conditions were present and there was no diffusion and no development.

To explain such cases of nondiffusion in rural spaces we tend, conventionally, to blame the farmers themselves: their inaccessible locations, their traditionalism, their ignorance, their lack of "achievement motivation," and the like. But the farmers will tell us that we are wrong, and they will tell us why if we listen.[10]

CONCLUSION

Why, in the last analysis, should we assume that the natural state of affairs in any region is to have a center from which innovations emanate and a periphery toward which they diffuse? Surely all of us share the belief that all human communities possess the same underlying potential to create, to invent, to innovate. Communities are distributed alongside one another across a landscape, so the premise of human equality is at the same time a premise of spatial equality. Spatial inequality is not something normal, natural, inevitable, and moral. Diffusionism makes it appear to be so. But diffusionism is just a thought-style, and we can put it out of our minds.

SOURCE

This article appeared originally in the *Annals of the Association of American Geographers* 77 (1987): 30–47.

NOTES

1. The ultimate origins of classical Eurocentric diffusionism are to be sought long before the beginning of the nineteenth century. I argue that the world model be-

came explicit, powerful, and important in the post-Napoleonic era because of a confluence of the following historical circumstances, among others: (1) Science was becoming sufficiently free of religious strictures to begin the serious inquiry into origins; e.g., to search for ancient humans and their cultural effects and to consider the earth's history in a uniformitarian methodological framework. (2) The rapid expansion of formal and informal colonial empires meant the systematic gathering, for the first time, of information (no matter how biased) about non-Europeans. (3) The expansion of colonialism, and, beyond that, the great increase in the importance of colonialism to European economies, led to efforts to formulate specific theories about not only the nature and history of non-Europeans but the overall process by which European culture was spreading through and conquering the rest of the world—that is, the theories of classical diffusionism. On the general doctrines of classical diffusionism, see, for example, Césaire (1972); Galeano (1973); Panikkar (1959); Rodney (1972); Said (1978); B. Turner (1978); Venturi (1963). On diffusionism in its specific influence on anthropology, geography, and other emerging disciplines, and on the schools known as "extreme diffusionists" (principally the "British Diffusionists" and the German-Austrian *Kulturkreis* school), see, e.g., Asad (1973); Blaut (1970); Childe (1951); M. Harris (1968); Brian Hudson (1977); Koepping (1983); Kroeber (1937); Lowie (1937); McKay (1943); Radin (1933); Voget (1975, 339–59).

2. This abstract landscape contains no regions that are politically dominant and thus would be able to withhold innovations from diffusion. Although it is theoretically possible that an innovation might give one community such an advantage over others that it would thereby become a permanently dominant center, this would be a realistic possibility only if additional attributes were inserted in the model, one of these being a definition of the individual trait as a truly revolutionary innovation lacking the antecedents that would have already diffused in our model (and in the real world), another being a tooth-and-fang conception of culture in which boundaries are in effect barricades.

3. See Amin (1973, xvi–xvii) for comparison: "[Sierra Leone's] 'creole' bourgeoisie . . . spread along the whole of the western coast in the nineteenth century and filled the role of a *comprador* bourgeoisie for British capital. But this class disappeared at the end of the last century, when the English executed their main creole trading rivals on the pretext that they had taken part in the Temne and Mende revolts. Isolated from the rest of the Empire and relatively abandoned, the colony fell into a doze from which it has not yet emerged." Also see A. Howard (1975); Kup (1975); Osae, Nwabara, and Odunsi (1973); Fyle (1981).

4. On this myth, see Bhatia (1967) and Klein (1973). On the related myth that there was an unchanging "traditional" demographic pattern of high birth rates and high death rates, which diffusing colonial medicine broke open (leading to a fall in death rates and—because of

"traditionalism"—a sustained high birth rate and thereafter overpopulation), see Klein (1973) on death rates and the work of Nag (1980) showing that birth rates increased substantially under colonialism (Collver [1965] argues along similar lines for some Latin American countries, as does Harewood [1966] for Grenada).

5. I do not suggest that methodological and epistemological considerations are in any way a substitute for empirical evidence. At most they direct us toward new evidence and influence the weighting we give evidence in general.

6. It does not matter for our purpose (judging the terrain over which the original Old World agricultural revolution took place) whether the advantages of agriculture over hunting-gathering-fishing-shellfishing resulted from a hemisphere-wide deterioration in living conditions resulting from the environmental changes, whether the period was witness to an epochal advance in an uninterrupted process of cultural evolution, or whether some other causal process was at work, so long as the process affected all of the reasonably warm and moist portions of the hemisphere or its effects were transmitted throughout this zone, e.g., by evening out stresses through human migration. Also embedded in this model is the assumption that the advantages of agriculture were roughly comparable (or became so because of stress-evening population movements) across many ecological zones, from tropical forest to warm-winter midlatitude forest, and from moderately sloping land to swamp edges and natural levees.

7. See Golson (1977) for evidence of 9,000-year-old drained-field farming in New Guinea, and see Denevan (1966b) on the antiquity of raised-field farming in the New World. Today, when suitable land is available, a given farming group usually practices some complex mixture of systems, which may range from extensive shifting agriculture to intensive drained-field or wet-field or natural-levee agriculture.

8. There exists a diffusionist tendency (criticized in Blaut 1984) to apply culturally biased tests to Third World peoples and find them to be inferior to Europeans in terms of perceptual and intellectual traits indicating innovativeness, cognitive development (hence inferentially inventiveness), and the like. That this is normal paradigmatic science can be seen, e.g., from the fact that nearly 10 percent of empirical studies in the *Journal of Cross-Cultural Psychology* are reports by white South Africans and Europeans purporting to show such psychological inferiority in black Africans.

9. The most dramatic cases involve literacy and adult education programs in some Third World countries. Often success reflects the use of an approach in which people come to understand the inhibiting conditions and the need to struggle against them and then literally demand the innovation and struggle to acquire it (see Freire 1972). A case of ultrarapid diffusion of an agricultural innovation in Venezuela is discussed in Blaut (1977).

10. We can listen, for instance, to folksongs like the

widely diffused Populist song "The Farmer Is the Man": "buys on credit 'til the fall / Then they take him by the hand / And they lead him from the land / And the middleman's the man who gets it all."

FURTHER READINGS

Janet L. Abu-Lughod. 1989. *Before European hegemony: The world system A.D. 1250–1350.* New York: Oxford University Press.

This is another important critique of Eurocentric diffusionism. Abu-Lughod argues that Europe was not in advance of Asia in economy and technology in the fourteenth century.

Samir Amin. 1989. *Eurocentrism.* Trans. Russell Moore. New York: Monthly Review Press.

Amin analyzes Eurocentrism as an idea and criticizes Eurocentric concepts about non-European cultures.

Martin Bernal. 1987. *Black Athena: The Afroasiatic roots of classical civilization.* Vol. 1: *The fabrication of ancient Greece, 1785–1985.* Vol. 2: *The archeological and documentary evidence.* London: Free Association Books.

Bernal's thorough and lengthy volumes counter the Eurocentric diffusionist idea that ancient European culture arose *sui generis.* His point is that European culture was greatly influenced by Asian and African cultures.

James M. Blaut. 1987. *The national question: Decolonising the theory of nationalism.* London: ZED Books.

Blaut's central argument is that national struggle is indeed class struggle. His chapter "Diffusionism and the National Question" is a useful reinterpretation of one of Marx's most disputed ideas, his theory of nationalism. Blaut questions the theory that nationalism and the modern state are somehow a diffusion of European ideas and culture to the rest of the world.

———, ed. 1992. *Fourteen ninety-two: The debate on colonialism, Eurocentrism, and history.* Trenton, N.J.: Africa World Press.

This collection contains an essay by Blaut criticizing the diffusionist theory that cultural progress originates, somehow naturally, in the European world and diffuses, again somehow naturally, to the rest of the world. The book includes commentaries on Blaut's critique by Samir Amin, Robert Dodgshon, Andre Gunder Frank, and Ronen Palan that originally appeared as a debate in *Political Geography* 11 (1992): 355–412.

———. 1993. *Diffusionism: Or history inside out.* New York: Guilford Press.

Here Blaut provides a general analysis and history of diffusionism as a world model and further develops the critique of Eurocentric diffusionism in cultural evolution begun in the books listed above.

Andre Gunder Frank and Barry Gills. 1992. The five thousand year world system: An interdisciplinary introduction. *Humboldt Journal of Social Relations* 18 (1): 1–79.

This essay by Frank and Gills argues, broadly, for the coherence of the world's cultures (and for what Blaut calls constant, intensive, crisscross diffusion) over a five-thousand-year span of history.

Peter J. Hugill and D. Bruce Dickson, eds. 1988. *The transfer and transformation of ideas and material culture.* College Station: Texas A&M University Press.

This collection of original essays by anthropologists, historians, and geographers contains empirical and theoretical chapters on diffusion research and diffusion theory. The collection contains several studies critical of diffusionism.

Paul Radin. 1933. *The method and theory of ethnology: An essay in criticism.* New York: McGraw-Hill.
Robert H. Lowie. 1937. *The history of ethnological theory.* New York: Holt, Rinehart and Winston.
Andre Gunder Frank. 1969. The sociology of development and the underdevelopment of sociology. Chap. in *Latin America: Underdevelopment or revolution, essays on the development of underdevelopment and the immediate enemy,* 21–94. New York: Monthly Review Press.
Edward W. Said. 1978. *Orientalism.* New York: Pantheon.
Lakshman Yapa. 1980. Diffusion, development, and ecopolitical economy. In *Innovation research and public policy,* ed. John A. Agnew, 101–41. Syracuse, N.Y.: Syracuse University, Department of Geography.

These five works, listed in chronological order, are important earlier critiques of diffusionism. They set the stage for Blaut's article and for much of the recent work on diffusionism.

ALFRED W. CROSBY **13**

ECOLOGICAL IMPERIALISM: THE OVERSEAS MIGRATION OF WESTERN EUROPEANS AS A BIOLOGICAL PHENOMENON

Europeans in North America, especially those with an interest in gardening and botany, are often stricken with fits of homesickness at the sight of certain plants which, like themselves, have somehow strayed thousands of miles westward across the Atlantic. Vladimir Nabokov, the Russian exile, had such an experience on the mountain slopes of Oregon:

> Do you recognize that clover?
> Dandelions, *l'or du pauvre?*
> (Europe, nonetheless, is over.)

A century earlier the success of European weeds in America inspired Charles Darwin to goad the American botanist Asa Gray: "Does it not hurt your Yankee pride that we thrash you so confoundly? I am sure Mrs. Gray will stick up for your own weeds. Ask her whether they are not more honest, downright good sort of weeds."

The common dandelion, *l'or du pauvre,* despite its ubiquity and its bright yellow flower, is not at all the most visible of the Old World immigrants in North America. Vladimir Nabokov was a prime example of the most visible kind: the *Homo sapiens* of European origin. Europeans and their descendants, who compose the majority of human beings in North America and in a number of other lands outside of Europe, are the most spectacularly successful overseas migrants of all time. How strange it is to find English, Germans, French, Italians, and Spaniards comfortably ensconced in places with names like Wollongong (Australia), Rotorua (New Zealand), and Saskatoon (Canada), where obviously other peoples should dominate, as they must have at one time.

None of the major genetic groupings of humankind is as oddly distributed about the world as European, especially western European, whites. Almost all the peoples we call Mongoloids live in the single contiguous land mass of Asia. Black Africans are divided between three continents—their homeland and North and South America—but most of them are concentrated in their original latitudes, the tropics, facing each other across one ocean. European whites were all recently concentrated in Europe, but in the last few centuries have burst out, as energetically as if from a burning building, and have created vast settlements of their kind in the south temperate zone and north temperate zone (excepting Asia, a continent already thoroughly and irreversibly tenanted). In Canada and the United States together they amount to nearly 90 percent of the population; in Argentina and Uruguay together to over 95 percent; in Australia to 98 percent; and in New Zealand to 90 percent. The only nations in the temperate zones outside of Asia which do not have enormous majorities of European whites are Chile, with a population of two-thirds mixed Spanish and Indian stock, and South Africa, where blacks outnumber whites six to one. How odd that these two, so many thousands of miles from Europe, should be exceptions in *not* being predominantly pure European.

Europeans have conquered Canada, the United States, Argentina, Uruguay, Australia, and New Zealand not just militarily and economically and technologically—as they did India, Nigeria, Mexico, Peru, and other tropical lands, whose native peoples have long since expelled or interbred with and even absorbed the invaders. In the temperate zone lands listed above Europeans conquered and triumphed demographically. These, for the sake of convenience, we will call the Lands of the Demographic Takeover.

There is a long tradition of emphasizing the contrasts between Europeans and Americans—a tradition honored by such names as Henry James and Frederick Jackson Turner—but the vital question is really why Americans are so European. And why the Argentinians, the Uruguayans, the Australians, and the New Zealanders are so European in the obvious genetic sense?

The reasons for the relative failure of the European demographic takeover in the tropics are clear. In tropical Africa, until recently, Europeans died in droves of the fevers; in tropical America they died almost as fast of the same diseases, plus a few native American additions. Furthermore, in neither region did European agricultural techniques, crops, and animals prosper. Europeans did try to found colonies for settlement, rather than merely exploitation, but they failed or achieved only partial success in the hot lands. The Scots left their bones as monument to their short-lived colony at Darien at the turn of the eighteenth century. The English Puritans who skipped Massachusetts Bay Colony to go to Providence Island in the Caribbean Sea did not even achieve a permanent settlement, much less a Commonwealth of God. The Portuguese who went to northeastern Brazil created viable settlements, but only by perching themselves on top of first a population of native Indian laborers and then, when these faded away, a population of laborers imported from Africa. They did achieve a demographic takeover, but only by interbreeding with their servants. The Portuguese in Angola, who helped supply those servants, never had a breath of a chance to achieve a demographic takeover. There was much to repel and little to attract the mass of Europeans to the tropics, and so they stayed home or went to the lands where life was healthier, labor more rewarding, and where white immigrants, by their very number, encouraged more immigration.

In the cooler lands, the colonies of the Demographic Takeover, Europeans achieved very rapid population growth by means of immigration, by increased life span, and by maintaining very high birth rates. Rarely has population expanded more rapidly than it did in the eighteenth and nineteenth centuries in these lands. It is these lands, especially the United States, that enabled

Europeans and their overseas offspring to expand from something like 18 percent of the human species in 1650 to well over 30 percent in 1900. Today 670 million Europeans live in Europe, and 250 million or so other Europeans—genetically as European as any left behind in the Old World—live in the Lands of the Demographic Takeover, an ocean or so from home. What the Europeans have done with unprecedented success in the past few centuries can accurately be described by a term from apiculture: they have swarmed.

They swarmed to lands which were populated at the time of European arrival by peoples as physically capable of rapid increase as the Europeans, and yet who are now small minorities in their homelands and sometimes no more than relict populations. These population explosions among colonial Europeans of the past few centuries coincided with population crashes among the aborigines. If overseas Europeans have historically been less fatalistic and grim than their relatives in Europe, it is because they have viewed the histories of their nations very selectively. Charles Darwin, as a biologist rather than a historian, could not overlook the fated aboriginal population. He wrote, "Wherever the European has trod, death seems to pursue the aboriginal."

Any respectable theory which attempts to explain the Europeans' demographic triumphs has to provide explanations for at least two phenomena. The first is the decimation and demoralization of the aboriginal populations of Canada, the United States, Argentina, and others. The obliterating defeat of these populations was not simply due to European technological superiority. The Europeans who settled in temperate South Africa seemingly had the same advantages as those who settled in Virginia and New South Wales, and yet how different was their fate. The Bantu-speaking peoples, who now overwhelmingly outnumber the whites in South Africa, were superior to their American, Australian, and New Zealand counterparts in that they possessed iron weapons, but how much more inferior to a musket or a rifle is a stone-pointed spear than an iron-pointed spear? The Bantu have prospered demographically not because of their numbers at the time of first contact with whites, which were probably not greater per square mile than those of the Indians east of the Mississippi River. Rather, the Bantu have prospered because they survived military conquest, avoided the conquerors, or became their indispensable servants—and in the long run because they reproduced faster than the whites. In contrast, why did so few of the natives of the Lands of the Demographic Takeover survive?

Second, we must explain the stunning, even awesome success of European agriculture, that is, the European way of manipulating the environment in the Lands of the Demographic Takeover. The difficult progress of the European frontier in the Siberian *taiga* or the Brazilian *sertão* or the South African *veldt* contrasts sharply with its easy, almost fluid advance in North America. Of course, the pioneers of North America would never have characterized their progress as easy: their lives were filled with danger, deprivation, and unremitting labor; but as a group they always succeeded in taming whatever portion of North America they wanted within a few decades and usually a good deal less time. Many individuals among them failed—they were driven mad by blizzards and dust storms, lost their crops to locusts and their flocks to cougars and wolves, or lost their scalps to understandably inhospitable Indians—but as a group they always succeeded—and in terms of human generations, very quickly.

In attempting to explain these two phenomena, let us examine four categories of organisms deeply involved in European expansion: (1) human beings; (2) animals closely associated with human beings—both the desirable animals like horses and cattle and undesirable varmints like rats and mice; (3) pathogens or microorganisms that cause disease in humans; and (4) weeds. Is there a pattern in the histories of these groups which suggests an overall explanation for the phenomenon of the Demographic Takeover or which at least suggests fresh paths of inquiry?

Europe has exported something in excess of sixty million people in the past few hundred years. Great Britain alone exported over twenty million. The great mass of these white emigrants went to the United States, Argentina, Canada, Australia, Uruguay, and New Zealand. (Other areas to absorb comparable quantities of Europeans were Brazil and Russia east of the Urals. These would qualify as Lands of the Demographic Takeover except that very large fractions of their populations are non-European.)

In stark contrast, very few aborigines of the Americas, Australia, or New Zealand ever went to Europe. Those who did often died not long after arrival. The fact that the flow of human migration was almost entirely from Europe to her colonies and not vice versa is not startling—or very enlightening. Europeans controlled overseas migration, and Europe needed to export, not import, labor. But this pattern of one-way migration is significant in that it reappears in other connections.

The vast expanses of forests, savannahs, and steppes in the Lands of the Demographic Takeover were inundated by animals from the Old World, chiefly from Europe. Horses, cattle, sheep, goats, and pigs have for hundreds of years been among the most numerous of the quadrupeds of these lands, which were completely lacking in these species at the time of first contact with the Europeans. By 1600 enormous feral herds of horses and cattle surged over the pampas of the Río de la Plata (today's Argentina and Uruguay) and over the plains of northern Mexico. By the beginning of the seventeenth century packs of Old World dogs gone wild were among the predators of these herds.

In the forested country of British North America population explosions among imported animals were also spectacular, but only by European standards, not by those of Spanish America. In 1700 in Virginia feral hogs, said one witness, "swarm like vermaine upon the Earth," and young gentlemen were entertaining themselves by hunting wild horses of the inland counties. In Carolina the herds of cattle were "incredible, being from one to two thousand head in one Man's Possession." In the eighteenth and early nineteenth centuries the advancing European frontier from New England to the Gulf of Mexico was preceded into Indian territory by an *avant-garde* of semiwild herds of hogs and cattle tended, now and again, by semiwild herdsmen, white and black.

The first English settlers landed in Botany Bay, Australia, in January of 1788 with livestock, most of it from the Cape of Good Hope. The pigs and poultry thrived; the cattle did well enough; the sheep, the future source of the colony's good fortune, died fast. Within a few months two bulls and four cows strayed away. By 1804 the wild herds they founded numbered from three to five thousand head and were in possession of much of the best land between the settlements and the Blue Mountains. If they had ever found their way through the mountains to the grasslands beyond, the history of Australia in the first decades of the nineteenth century might have been one dominated by cattle rather than sheep. As it is, the colonial government wanted the land the wild bulls so ferociously defended, and considered the growing practice of convicts running away to live off the herds as a threat to the whole colony; so the adult cattle were shot and salted down and the calves captured and tamed. The English settlers imported woolly sheep from Europe and sought out the interior pastures for them. The animals multiplied rapidly, and when Darwin made his visit to New South Wales in 1836, there were about a million sheep there for him to see.

The arrival of Old World livestock probably affected New Zealand more radically than any other of the Lands of the Demographic Takeover. Cattle, horses, goats, pigs and—in this land of few or no large predators—even the usually timid sheep went wild. In New Zealand herds of feral farm animals were practicing the ways of their remote ancestors as late as the 1940s and no doubt still run free. Most of the sheep, though, stayed under human control, and within a decade of Great Britain's annexation of New Zealand in 1840, her new acquisition was home to a quarter million sheep. In 1974 New Zealand had over fifty-five million sheep, about twenty times more sheep than people.

In the Lands of the Demographic Takeover the European pioneers were accompanied and often preceded by their domesticated animals, walking sources of food, leather, fiber, power, and wealth, and these animals often adapted more rapidly to the new surroundings and reproduced much more rapidly than their masters. To a certain extent, the success of Europeans as colonists was automatic as soon as they put their tough, fast, fertile, and intelligent animals ashore. The latter were sources of capital that sought out their own sustenance, improvised their own protection against the weather, fought their own battles against predators and, if their masters were smart enough to allow calves, colts, and lambs to accumulate, could and often did show the world the amazing possibilities of compound interest.

The honey bee is the one insect of worldwide importance which human beings have domesticated, if we may use the word in a broad sense. Many species of bees and other insects produce honey, but the one which does so in greatest quantity and which is easiest to control is a native of the Mediterranean area and the Middle East, the honey bee (*Apis mellifera*). The Europeans have probably taken this sweet and short-tempered servant to every colony they ever established, from the Arctic to Antarctic Circle, and the honey bee has always been one of the first immigrants to set off on its own. Sometimes the advance of the bee frontier could be very rapid: the first hive in Tasmania swarmed sixteen times in the summer of 1832.

Thomas Jefferson tells us that the Indians of North America called the honey bees "English flies," and St. John de Crèvecoeur, his contemporary, wrote that "the Indians look upon them with an evil eye, and consider their progress into the interior of the continent as an omen of the white man's approach: thus, as they discover the bees, the news of the event, passing from mouth to mouth, spreads sadness and consternation on all sides."

Domesticated creatures that traveled from the Lands of the Demographic Takeover to Europe are few. Australian aborigines and New Zealand Maoris had a few tame dogs, unimpressive by Old World standards and unwanted by the whites. Europe happily accepted the American Indians' turkeys and guinea pigs, but had no need for their dogs, llamas, and alpacas. Again the explanation is simple: Europeans, who controlled the passage of large animals across the oceans, had no need to reverse the process.

It is interesting and perhaps significant, though, that the exchange was just as one sided

for varmints, the small mammals whose migrations Europeans often tried to stop. None of the American or Australian or New Zealand equivalents of rats have become established in Europe, but Old World varmints, especially rats, have colonized right alongside the Europeans in the temperate zones. Rats of assorted sizes, some of them almost surely European immigrants, were tormenting Spanish Americans by at least the end of the sixteenth century. European rats established a beachhead in Jamestown, Virginia, as early as 1609, when they almost starved out the colonists by eating their food stores. In Buenos Aires the increase in rats kept pace with that of cattle, according to an early nineteenth century witness. European rats proved as aggressive as the Europeans in New Zealand, where they completely replaced the local rats in the North Islands as early as the 1840s. Those poor creatures are probably completely extinct today or exist only in tiny relict populations.

The European rabbits are not usually thought of as varmints, but where there are neither diseases nor predators to hold down their numbers they can become the worst of pests. In 1859 a few members of the species *Orytolagus cuniculus* (the scientific name for the protagonists of all the Peter Rabbits of literature) were released in southeast Australia. Despite massive efforts to stop them, they reproduced—true to their reputation—and spread rapidly all the way across Australia's southern half to the Indian Ocean. In 1950 the rabbit population of Australia was estimated at 500 million, and they were outcompeting the nation's most important domesticated animals, sheep, for the grasses and herbs. They have been brought under control, but only by means of artificially fomenting an epidemic of myxomatosis, a lethal American rabbit disease. The story of rabbits and myxomatosis in New Zealand is similar.

Europe, in return for her varmints, has received muskrats and gray squirrels and little else from America, and nothing at all of significance from Australia or New Zealand, and we might well wonder if muskrats and squirrels really qualify as varmints. As with other classes of organisms, the exchange has been a one-way street.

None of Europe's emigrants were as immediately and colossally successful as its pathogens, the microorganisms that make human beings ill, cripple them, and kill them. Whenever and wherever Europeans crossed the oceans and settled, the pathogens they carried created prodigious epidemics of smallpox, measles, tuberculosis, influenza, and a number of other diseases. It was this factor, more than any other, that Darwin had in mind as he wrote of the Europeans' deadly tread.

The pathogens transmitted by the Europeans, unlike the Europeans themselves or most of their domesticated animals, did at least as well in the tropics as in the temperate Lands of the Demographic Takeover. Epidemics devastated Mexico, Peru, Brazil, Hawaii, and Tahiti soon after the Europeans made the first contact with aboriginal populations. Some of these populations were able to escape demographic defeat because their initial numbers were so large that a small fraction was still sufficient to maintain occupation of, if not title to, the land, and also because the mass of Europeans were never attracted to the tropical lands, not even if they were partially vacated. In the Lands of the Demographic Takeover the aboriginal populations were too sparse to rebound from the onslaught of disease or were inundated by European immigrants before they could recover.

The first strike forces of the white immigrants to the Lands of the Demographic Takeover were epidemics. A few examples from scores of possible examples follow. Smallpox first arrived in the Río de la Plata region in 1558 or 1560 and killed, according to one chronicler possibly more interested in effect than accuracy, "more than a hundred thousand Indians" of the heavy riverine population there. An epidemic of plague or typhus decimated the Indians of the New England coast immediately before the founding of Plymouth. Smallpox or something similar struck the aborigines of Australia's Botany Bay in 1789, killed half, and rolled on into the interior. Some unidentified disease or diseases spread through the Maori tribes of the North Island of New Zealand in the 1790s, killing so many in a number of villages that the survivors were not able to bury the dead. After a series of such lethal and rapidly moving epidemics, then came the slow, unspectacular, but thorough cripplers and killers like

venereal disease and tuberculosis. In conjunction with the large numbers of white settlers these diseases were enough to smother aboriginal chances of recovery. First the blitzkrieg, then the mopping up.

The greatest of the killers in these lands was probably smallpox. The exception is New Zealand, the last of these lands to attract permanent European settlers. They came to New Zealand after the spread of vaccination in Europe, and so were poor carriers. As of the 1850s smallpox still had not come ashore, and by that time two-thirds of the Maori had been vaccinated. The tardy arrival of smallpox in these islands may have much to do with the fact that the Maori today comprise a larger percentage (9 percent) of their country's population than that of any other aboriginal people in any European colony or former European colony in either temperate zone, save only South Africa.

American Indians bore the full brunt of smallpox, and its mark is on their history and folklore. The Kiowa of the southern plains of the United States have a legend in which a Kiowa man meets Smallpox on the plain riding a horse. The man asks, "Where do you come from and what do you do and why are you here?" Smallpox answers, "I am one with the white men—they are my people as the Kiowas are yours. Sometimes I travel ahead of them and sometimes behind. But I am always their companion and you will find me in their camps and their houses." "What can you do?" the Kiowa asks. "I bring death," Smallpox replies. "My breath causes children to wither like young plants in spring snow. I bring destruction. No matter how beautiful a woman is, once she has looked at me she becomes as ugly as death. And to men I bring not death alone, but the destruction of their children and the blighting of their wives. The strongest of warriors go down before me. No people who have looked on me will ever be the same."

In return for the barrage of diseases that Europeans directed overseas, they received little in return. Australia and New Zealand provided no new strains of pathogens to Europe—or none that attracted attention. And of America's native diseases none had any real influence on the Old World—with the likely exception of venereal syphilis, which almost certainly existed in the New World before 1492 and probably did not occur in its present form in the Old World.

Weeds are rarely history makers, for they are not as spectacular in their effects as pathogens. But they, too, influence our lives and migrate over the world despite human wishes. As such, like varmints and germs, they are better indicators of certain realities than human beings or domesticated animals.

The term *weed* in modern botanical usage refers to any type of plant which—because of especially large numbers of seeds produced per plant, or especially effective means of distributing those seeds, or especially tough roots and rhizomes from which new plants can grow, or especially tough seeds that survive the alimentary canals of animals to be planted with their droppings—spread rapidly and outcompete others on disturbed, bare soil. Weeds are plants that tempt the botanist to use such anthropomorphic words as aggressive and opportunistic.

Many of the most successful weeds in the well-watered regions of the Lands of the Demographic Takeover are of European or Eurasian origin. French and Dutch and English farmers brought with them to North America their worst enemies, weeds, "to exhaust the land, hinder and damnify the Crop." By the last third of the seventeenth century at least twenty different types were widespread enough in New England to attract the attention of the English visitor John Josselyn, who identified couch grass, dandelion, nettles, mallowes, knot grass, shepherd's purse, sow thistle, clot burr, and others. One of the most aggressive was plantain, which the Indians called "English-Man's Foot."

European weeds rolled west with the pioneers, in some cases spreading almost explosively. As of 1823 corn chamomile and maywood had spread up to but not across the Muskingum River in Ohio. Eight years later they were over the river. The most prodigiously imperialistic of the weeds in the eastern half of the United States and Canada were probably Kentucky bluegrass and white clover. They spread so fast after the entrance of Europeans into a given area that there is some suspicion that they may have been present in pre-Columbian America, although the earliest European accounts do not mention them. Probably brought to the Appalachian area by the French, these two kinds of weeds preceded the English settlers there and kept up with the movement westward until reaching the plains across the Mississippi.

Old World plants set up business on their own on the Pacific coast of North America just as soon as the Spaniards and Russians did. The climate of coastal southern California is much the same as that of the Mediterranean, and the Spaniards who came to California in the eighteenth century brought their own Mediterranean weeds with them via Mexico: wild oats, fennel, wild radishes. These plants, plus those brought in later by the Forty-niners, muscled their way to dominance in the coastal grasslands. These immigrant weeds followed Old World horses, cattle, and sheep into California's interior prairies and took over there as well.

They did not push so swiftly into the coastal Northwest because the Spanish, their reluctant patrons, were slow to do so, and because those shores are cool and damp. Most of the present-day weeds in that region had to come with the Russians or Anglo-Americans from similar areas on other coasts. The Northwest has a semiarid interior, however, into which some European plants like redstem filaree spread quite early, presumably from the prairies of California.

The region of Argentina and Uruguay was almost as radically altered in its flora as in its fauna by the coming of the Europeans. The ancient Indian practice, taken up immediately by the whites, of burning off the old grass of the pampa every year, as well as the trampling and cropping to the ground of indigenous grasses and forbs by the thousands of imported quadrupeds who also changed the nature of the soil with their droppings, opened the whole countryside to European plants. In the 1780s Félix de Azara observed that the pampa, already radically altered, was changing as he watched. European weeds sprang up around every cabin, grew up along roads, and pressed into the open steppe. Today only a quarter of the plants growing wild in the pampa are native, and in the well-watered eastern portions, the "natural" ground cover consists almost entirely of Old World grasses and clovers.

The invaders were not, of course, always desirable. When Darwin visited Uruguay in 1832, he found large expanses, perhaps as much as hundreds of square miles, monopolized by the immigrant wild artichoke and transformed into a prickly wilderness fit neither for man nor his animals.

The onslaught of foreign and specifically European plants on Australia began abruptly in 1778 because the first expedition that sailed from Britain to Botany Bay carried some livestock and considerable quantities of seed. By May of 1803 over two hundred foreign plants, most of them European, had been purposely introduced and planted in New South Wales, undoubtedly along with a number of weeds. Even today so-called clean seed characteristically contains some weed seeds, and this was much more so two hundred years ago. By and large, Australia's north has been too tropical and its interior too hot and dry for European weeds and grasses, but much of its southern coasts and Tasmania have been hospitable indeed to Europe's willful flora.

Thus, many—often a majority—of the most aggressive plants in the temperate humid regions of North America, South America, Australia, and New Zealand are of European origin. It may be true that in every broad expanse of the world today where there are dense populations, with whites in the majority, there are also dense populations of European weeds. Thirty-five of eighty-nine weeds listed in 1953 as common in the state of New York are European. Approximately 60 percent of Canada's worst weeds are introductions from Europe. Most of New Zealand's weeds are from the same source, as are many, perhaps most, of the weeds of Australia's well-watered coasts. Most of the European plants that Josselyn listed as naturalized in New England in the seventeenth century are growing wild today in Argentina and Uruguay, and are among the most widespread and troublesome of all weeds in those countries.

In return for this largesse of pestiferous plants, the Lands of the Demographic Takeover have provided Europe with only a few equivalents. The Canadian water weed jammed Britain's nineteenth century waterways, and North America's horseweed and burnweed have spread in Europe's empty lots, and South America's flowered galinsoga has thrived in her gardens. But the migratory flow of a whole group of organisms between Europe and the Lands of the Demographic Takeover has been almost entirely in one direction. Englishman's foot still marches in seven-league jackboots across every European colony of settlement, but very few American or Australian or New Zealand invaders stride the waste lands and unkempt backyards of Europe.

European and Old World human beings, domesticated animals, varmints, pathogens, and weeds all accomplished demographic takeovers of their own in the temperate, well-watered regions of North and South America, Australia, and New Zealand. They crossed oceans and Europeanized vast territories, often in informal cooperation with each other—the farmer and his animals destroying native plant cover, making way for imported grasses and forbs, many of which proved more nourishing to domesticated animals than the native equivalents; Old World pathogens, sometimes carried by Old World varmints, wiping out vast numbers of aborigines, opening the way for the advance of the European frontier, exposing more and more native peoples to more and more pathogens. The classic example of symbiosis between European colonists, their animals, and plants comes from New Zealand. Red clover, a good forage for sheep, could not seed itself and did not spread without being annually sown until the Europeans imported the bumblebee. Then the plant and insect spread widely, the first providing the second with food, the second carrying pollen from blossom to blossom for the first, and the sheep eating the clover and compensating the human beings for their effort with mutton and wool.

There have been few such stories of the success in Europe of organisms from the Lands of the Demographic Takeover, despite the obvious fact that for every ship that went from Europe to those lands, another traveled in the opposite direction.

The demographic triumph of Europeans in the temperate colonies is one part of a biological and ecological takeover which could not have been accomplished by human beings alone, gunpowder notwithstanding. We must at least try to analyze the impact and success of all the immigrant organisms together—the European portmanteau of often mutually supportive plants, animals, and microlife which in its entirety can be accurately described as aggressive and opportunistic, an ecosystem simplified by ocean crossings and honed by thousands of years of competition in the unique environment created by the Old World Neolithic Revolution.

The human invaders and their descendants have consulted their egos, rather than ecologists, for explanations of their triumphs. But the human victims, the aborigines of the Lands of the Demographic Takeover, knew better, knew they were only one of many species being displaced and replaced; knew they were victims of something more irresistible and awesome than the spread of capitalism or Christianity. One Maori, at the nadir of the history of his race, knew these things when he said, "As the clover killed off the fern, and the European dog the Maori dog—as the Maori rat was destroyed by the Pakeha [European] rat—so our people, also, will be gradually supplanted and exterminated by the Europeans." The future was not quite so grim as he prophesied, but we must admire his grasp of the complexity and magnitude of the threat looming over his people and over the ecosystem of which they were part.

SOURCE

This article originally appeared in *The Texas Quarterly* 21 (1) (1978): 10–22.

FURTHER READINGS

Noel Butlin. 1983. *Our original aggression.* Sydney: George Allen and Unwin.

This is a careful, though controversial, estimation of the number of Australian Aborigines on the eve of European colonization.

Karl W. Butzer, ed. 1992. *The Americas before and after 1492: Current geographical research.* Special edition of *Annals of the Association of American Geographers* 82 (3).

This entire issue of the *Annals* commemorates the Columbian Quincentennial in essays that explore many of the themes outlined in Crosby's article. See also Karl W. Butzer, "Judgment or Understanding: Reflections on

1492" (*Queen's Quarterly* 99 [Fall 1992]: 581–600) and B. L. Turner II and Karl W. Butzer, "The Columbian Encounter and Land Use Change" (*Environment* 34 [October 1992]: 16–20, 37–44).

Alfred W. Crosby. 1972. *The Columbian exchange: Biological and cultural consequences of 1492.* Westport, Conn.: Greenwood.

———. 1986. *Ecological imperialism: The biological expansion of Europe, 900–1900.* Cambridge: Cambridge University Press.

———. 1991. Infectious disease and the demography of the Atlantic peoples. *Journal of World History* 2:119–33.

These additional works by Crosby develop his ideas in much greater detail. Whereas *The Columbian Exchange* addresses the contacts between Europe and the New World, *Ecological Imperialism* is concerned with the broader worldwide consequences of European colonization.

William M. Denevan, ed. 1992. *The native population of the Americas in 1492.* 2d ed. Madison: University of Wisconsin Press.

This is an excellent and comprehensive assessment of the New World population on the eve of European contact and the resulting demographic collapse.

Andrew Goudie. 1990. *The human impact on the natural environment.* 3d ed. Cambridge: MIT Press.

This textbook addresses humanity's power over nature and comprehensively surveys the major processes and effects.

E. L. Jones. 1974. Creative disruptions in American agriculture, 1620–1820. *Agricultural History* 48:510–28.

This paper documents how early American agriculturalists encountered new biological pests. Jones shows how some of the problems arose from the destabilization of the forest environment, a process begun by the Indians and intensified by European settlers. Jones characterizes the responses to these problems as involving avoidance or creativity on the part of early farmers.

C. G. N. Mascie-Taylor and G. W. Lasker, eds. 1988. *Biological aspects of human migration.* Cambridge: Cambridge University Press.

A slim volume of essays covering the biological impacts that accompany human migration. Of particular interest are the chapters on the impact of disease on the peopling of America and Australia, interisland migration, and rural to urban migration.

Colin McEvedy and Richard Jones. 1978. *Atlas of world population history.* Harmondsworth: Penguin.

This is a dated but still useful summary, in maps and text, of world population history.

Charles D. Rowley. 1972. *The destruction of aboriginal society.* Harmondsworth: Penguin.

Rowley presents a narrative history of the decline in Australia's aboriginal population.

Nicolas Sanchez-Albornoz. 1974. *The population of Latin America: A history.* Trans. W. A. R. Richardson. Berkeley: University of California Press.

This is an excellent overview of the population history of Central and South America.

O. H. K. Spate. 1988. *The Pacific since Magellan.* Vol. 3: *Paradise found and lost.* Minneapolis: University of Minnesota Press.

One of the strengths of Spate's three-volume *magnum opus* is that disease assumes its rightful place as a tool of European expansionism. Spate also stresses the self-destructive urge of Pacific Island peoples for iron tools and weapons to support intertribal warfare, as well as their cynical manipulation of Europeans.

Russell Thornton. 1987. *American Indian holocaust and survival: A population history since 1492.* Norman: University of Oklahoma Press.

This is the latest summary of Native American population history, concentrating on North America north of the Rio Grande.

John W. Verano and Douglas H. Ubelaker, eds. 1992. *Disease and demography in the Americas.* Washington, D.C.: Smithsonian Institution Press.

This is a collection of scholarly essays on various aspects of Native American population history rather than a comprehensive history.

William Woodruff. 1966. *Impact of Western man: A study of Europe's role in the world economy, 1750–1960.* New York: St. Martin's.

This is a useful source for statistics on the expansion of Europe.

CARVILLE EARLE **14**

A STAPLE INTERPRETATION OF SLAVERY AND FREE LABOR

The economic interpretation of labor systems offers a powerful explanation of the geography
of slavery and free labor in antebellum Anglo-
America.[1] Although the past decade has produced a crippling assault on this thesis, I shall
contend that recent critics misapplied the economic model, erroneously concluded that slavery
was the most efficient agrarian labor system in
North America, and incorrectly inferred that the
North rejected slavery for ideological-moral reasons rather than economic ones. When these
critics assumed the comparability of slave–free-
labor efficiencies during a yearly time span, they
unwittingly placed wage labor in an untenable
position. Wage labor was competitive for part of
a year but never on an annual basis. Farmers who
needed labor for a few days, weeks, or months
found the use of hired labor decidedly cheaper
and more efficient economically than slaves. The
decisive factor in the farmer's choice of either
slave or free labor came down to the annual labor
requirements of the staple crop: crops such as
wheat, which required only a few weeks of attention, lent themselves to wage labor; whereas
crops such as tobacco or cotton, which demanded sustained attention during a long growing season, lent themselves to slave labor. The
introduction of these appropriate free-labor costs
into a labor-efficiency model reveals that the ge-

ography of antebellum slavery and free labor conforms rather well to economic theory. Farmers and planters used the economically rational labor supply; and more specifically, northern farmers rejected slavery because it was less efficient than free labor, not because slavery was morally or ideologically repugnant.

The causal link between staple crops and labor supply is revealed most clearly where regions shift from one staple to another. Of special interest are those regions that changed from "few-day" staples to "multiple-day" staples, or vice versa, with the attendant adjustments in labor supply. Accordingly, this paper examines two regions of staple change: the tobacco-to-wheat transition on the eastern shore of Maryland during the eighteenth century, and the wheat-to-corn transition in the antebellum Lower Midwest. In Maryland, tobacco produced by slaves prevailed until the 1720s; but as wheat took hold, hired labor proved more efficient and gradually replaced slaves. Privately manumitted slaves swelled both the free black population and the general wage-labor force. Matters were reversed in the emerging corn belt of southern and central Ohio, Indiana, and Illinois. Wheat was the initial staple, produced by wage labor and by family farm members. But owing to the expansion of corn in the 1840s and 1850s, to the demanding cultivation requirements of corn as compared with wheat, and to rising wage rates, hired labor was steadily pushed into economic competition with slaves. The corn-hog region gave increasingly vocal support to proslavery politics, parties, and legislation and helped force through severely restrictive state laws that curtailed the civil rights of free blacks and led them toward servitude if not enslavement. Slavery was headed for the North in the wake of a corn economy; the only way to halt the laws of economics and preserve northern free labor was to destroy the peculiar institution in a civil war.

The economic interpretation of labor systems is controversial, and the wise course is to proceed cautiously. I begin by briefly reviewing the economic model of labor choice and the critics of an economic interpretation before turning to the refined staple model and the two regions of study.

LABOR: SLAVE OR FREE

Interpretations of slavery and free labor, whether economic or noneconomic, begin at the same place: the calculation of relative labor efficiencies. The rational capitalist farmer, faced with a choice of slavery or free labor, chooses in accordance with Evsey Domar's model of labor profitability (Domar 1970).[2] The farmer compares outputs and costs of slaves and freemen and uses the labor supply that offers the greatest return. Stated more generally, the farmer prefers free labor when $P_f - P_s > W_f - W_s$, where P_f is the net average productivity of free labor, P_s is the net average productivity of slave labor, W_f is the cost of free labor, and W_s is the subsistence and discounted costs of slave labor. The model is simplified when slave and free-labor outputs are shown as equivalent or nearly so, in which case labor choice becomes a matter of least cost, and free labor is used when $W_s > W_f$. Domar, though he did not test his model with data from the United States, speculated that such a test would probably show slavery as the most efficient labor supply for the entire nation; and, therefore, northern rejection of slavery must be interpreted on noneconomic grounds. Yet Domar was ambivalent. As an economist, he knew that if his hunch proved correct, it would seriously undermine economic rationality as a behavioral model.

I know of two tests of Domar's model, albeit crude ones, and each sustains his hunch about the economic superiority of slavery. In 1967, Arthur Zilversmit (1967, 33–53) presented a double-barreled argument on northern labor before 1800 (see also Litwak 1961, 3–29). First, he concluded that slave and free-labor outputs were similar, thus casting doubt on the assumption that the incentive of freedom resulted in greater productivity than slavery. John Hicks (1969, 122–40) independently reached the same conclusion on theoretical grounds. Having set productivities equal, Zilversmit turned to the cost side, compared slave prices with white servant prices and annual free wage rates, and concluded plausibly that slaves, when the costs were discounted over their useful lives, were much less expensive than either wage labor or servant labor. Although more refined economic calculations might increase Zilversmit's slave costs, his conclusions that slavery was the most efficient labor system and that its abolition in the North was rooted in ideology, morality, and ethics remain unshaken.

Domar and Zilversmit weakened the economic interpretation of labor, but the most damaging blow was delivered long ago, in 1795. In that year, William Strickland tried to prove that slavery was a poor economic choice in Virginia, but his evidence showed just the opposite: slaves cost less than free labor not only in Virginia but in all of the United States as well (Strickland 1971, 31–36).

Strickland's method was straightforward. The Englishman believed the Virginia planters' lament that slaves entailed excessive costs and low returns. He set out to verify these complaints by attacking the cost side of Domar's equation, confident that slaves would cost much more than free labor. Using records of construction costs of the James River Canal, Strickland calculated slave costs at £18 a year, which consisted of annual hire rates for adult male slaves of £9 plus maintenance costs of £9. He then computed daily slave cost at 1s. 2d. and compared this figure with Chesapeake free-labor day rates. Much to Strickland's disappointment, slaves cost the planters less than free whites, who hired out at 1s. 6d. a day. In fact, the cost advantage to slavery was even greater. Strickland's estimate of £9 for slave maintenance costs is unusually high, and a more realistic estimate on the order of £3 to £6 a year drives down daily slave costs to 9.4d. or 11.7d., respectively. These figures make the costs of slaves lower than the costs of either free Negroes or free whites. Slavery thus won on the cost side in Virginia and also in the northern states, where free labor received 1s. to 2s. per day, according to Strickland's own estimates.

Strickland nonetheless persisted in pressing his thesis of slavery's economic inferiority. Having lost on the cost side, he launched a vicious attack on slave output—Domar's productivity. Slaves were depicted as inert, recalcitrant, slovenly, and prone to willful destruction and pilfering. Given these traits, Strickland concurred with "the received opinion of the country, that slave-labour is much dearer than any other; and that the price paid for the *time* of a slave, by no means shows the amount of value of his labour; it certainly is much higher than it appears to be; though not knowing the quantity of labour performed by slaves in general in a given time, in a sufficient number of instances, I have not data whereon to calculate the exact value" (Strickland 1971, 33–34). This tactic will not do.

Low slave productivity cannot be inferred from Strickland's exaggerated stereotype of slave behavior. Slaves may have been at times lazy, slovenly, and subversive in the fields, but the evidence we have from colonial America suggests that white servants and freemen behaved in similar ways (Bertelson 1967; Morgan 1975); and furthermore, measures of physical productivity thus far assembled show no appreciable differences in output between white and black, or slave and free. For instance, Chesapeake tobacco growers between 1660 and 1770 consistently produced between 1,500 and 2,200 pounds per year per laborer, and slaveholding planters produced more tobacco than those planters without slaves (Earle 1975, 24–27). Nor is there any compelling reason for believing that free labor produced more corn or wheat than slaves, per unit of labor input.[3] In short, Strickland's invective against the productivity of slaves must be dismissed. The rest of his argument supports the Domar-Zilversmit thesis that northern farmers who hired free labor chose an inefficient labor force.

The economic interpretation of American slavery and free labor, long sustained by tradition and faith, is in disarray as a result of these recent studies. The suggestion that northern farmers used an inefficient labor supply is subtly shifting the attention of economic history and historical geography from South to North and from economic to noneconomic explanations of northern free labor. The issue is not why the South used slaves but why the North did not use them.[4] In the remainder of this essay I address the borderland between North and South, where both slaves and free labor were accessible. Careful consideration of this borderland reveals flaws in the revisionist inefficiency thesis, while refining and clarifying the staple economic basis of labor choice.

A STAPLE ECONOMIC INTERPRETATION OF LABOR SYSTEMS

Domar's labor efficiency model will explain the geography of labor, provided that labor inputs of freemen and slaves are compared fairly. Returning to that model, let us assume that slave and free-labor outputs are equivalent—a point suggested by the evidence cited above. Entrepreneurs select their labor supply by comparing costs and choosing the least expensive, such that they use slaves when $W_s < W_f$ and free labor when $W_f < W_s$. All this is easy enough; the tough problem is assessing the comparable costs. Heretofore, slave-labor and free-labor costs have been assessed as though each group were employed for a whole year. Such a procedure, while appropriate for slaves as permanent fixtures, has the effect of vastly inflating the costs of hired labor, customarily employed by the day or for several weeks or months but rarely by the year. During these short terms hired labor was competitive with slaves, as long as the number of days of hired labor times the daily wage rate was less than the cost of a slave.

It is precisely at this point that staples play a decisive role by regulating the amount of required labor days. During the growing season, staples vary remarkably in their daily demands for labor. The time-honored distinction between plantation crops and small grains reflects these differences in labor requirements. Plantation crops, such as tobacco, cotton, and wet rice, are so called because they are planted separately and command individual attention by labor during the growing season, especially during cultivation (Gray 1958, 1:462–80; R. Baldwin 1956). Their frequent and even demands for labor invariably drove up wage labor costs beyond slave costs. By contrast, broadcast grains such as wheat demand labor in concentrated applications. Wheat labor worked sunup to sunset during fall planting and midsummer harvest, but no labor was required between these periods (Bausman and Munroe 1946; Kalm 1972, 77; Klippart 1860, 475–78).[5]

The economically rational antebellum wheat farmer almost always employed wage labor because the few days of labor required times the daily wage rate usually fell below the cost of slaves.

The plantation–small grain dichotomy, though traditional, confuses the main issue: how many days of attention the staples require during the crop season. Theoretically, the number of days of attention ranges from 1 to 365, and the appropriate dichotomy is thus between few-day and multiple-day crops. For instance, dairy farming, though never regarded as a plantation crop, demands labor during the entire year and is as much a multiple-day staple as plantation cotton or tobacco. Might this fact not explain the otherwise anomalous use of slaves in the dairying zone of colonial Narragansett, Rhode Island (Bidwell and Falconer 1941, 106, 109–10)? To cite another example, corn requires labor days intermediate between the extremes of wheat and cotton or dairying. The extensive labor demands of corn during the three-to-four month period of plowing and tillage made it adaptable to slaves or freemen, depending on wage rates and slave costs (Bausman and Munroe 1946, 181; Russell 1857, 81–82; Bogue 1968, 132–33). Using the "required-days" approach suggested here, we may achieve a more realistic assessment of wage costs that faced the farmer who chose between slaves and freemen.

A caveat is in order. Staple labor days are not to be confused with labor intensity. For example, two crops that use equivalent acreage and require identical labor inputs of three hundred man-hours may have different allocations of labor during the growing season. One crop may be tended in just thirty days, for ten hours a day, while the other requires seventy-five days at four hours a day. Under prevailing wage rates and slave costs in pre-1860 Anglo-America, the former favored freemen; the latter, slaves.[6]

At this point, Domar's model can be refined for free labor by restricting comparison to similar staples. Farmers will choose free labor when $W_r D_t < W_s$, where W_r is the wage rate of free labor and D_t represents the labor days required by the staple.

STAPLES AND LABOR IN THE COLONIAL CHESAPEAKE

Staple change and labor adjustments in the eighteenth-century Chesapeake lend empirical support to this theoretical discussion. Wheat supplemented and then replaced tobacco as the staple of Maryland's upper eastern shore during the period between 1720 and the Revolution. Although the details of regional economic change demand much more elaboration, the outline of changes in staples and labor is fairly clear.[7] The clayey soils of that region produced a poorer quality tobacco which was less valuable than western shore crops. As grain prices rose after 1720, reflecting demands from southern Europe and the West Indies, slave-owning tobacco planters on the upper eastern shore rationally shifted to grains, especially wheat. This new few-day staple also entailed adjustments in the labor supply. Some slaves were hired out for short terms; others functioned as sharecroppers; and still others were emancipated by their owners. Manumission was abetted, of course, by Quaker abolitionists and revolutionary egalitarianism, but the rock-bottom cause was economic. Wheat was produced more efficiently with freemen than with slaves.[8]

An example may clarify the economic pressures on the average planter during the middle of the eighteenth century. On the typical tobacco plantation one laborer produced one thousand pounds of tobacco on about three acres. Total labor input was about 185 person-hours, or 23 person-days. More decisive from the standpoint of labor was the number of days of labor attendance required by tobacco, which amounted to as many as seventy-five days spread over the January-to-November cropping season. The planter who hired free labor at a wage rate of 3s. a day paid out £11 5s.[9] Using slaves effected a considerable savings. A prime male slave field hand cost £5 10s. a year, calculated by using an average slave price of £50 discounted over a useful life of twenty years, or £2 10s. a year, plus annual maintenance costs of £3.[10] Tobacco planters chose slaves for the simple reason that they cost less than half of what free labor cost.

Conversely, assume that wheat became more profitable and that the planter turned to farming. His slave prepared and sowed ten acres in August and September, and harvested one hundred bushels from this land the following July. The labor input of about twenty-five person-days for wheat resembled that for tobacco; but wheat required a mere twenty-five days in attendance, one-third the attendance requirement of tobacco. Slave costs in wheat remained the same as in tobacco, £5 10s., but hired labor costs, at twenty-five days times 3s. per day, fell to £3 15s. For the wheat farmer, wage labor was cheaper than slaves by £1 15s. (Earle and Hoffman 1976, 68–78).

These cost savings resulted in substantial productivity gains for free labor in wheat. A farmer who invested these savings of £1 15s. in additional day labor gained twelve labor days in wheat production. Put differently, the farmer expanded wheat output from 100 bushels to nearly 150 bushels—a gain of 50 percent over slave output. This superior productivity of free labor in wheat resulted, therefore, from cost savings to free labor and from the divisibility of its labor inputs, such that labor could be hired in small daily increments. It had little or nothing to do with the output incentives mythically attached to the condition of freedom.[11]

The unique harvest regimen of wheat conferred another advantage on a divisible labor supply. The maturation of wheat allowed only about ten days in July for harvest. As the grain passed quickly through the dough or harvest stage, the seeds became dead ripe, shattered, and fell to the ground as reaped. Reaping at the maximum rate of an acre a day, a slave was hardpressed to finish ten acres of wheat. Wage labor ensured that the harvest would be completed on time. Instead of hiring one laborer for ten days, the farmer might hire two men for five days, thus minimizing the loss of grain by overripening and shattering (Klippart 1860, 475–78; Rogin 1931, 78).

Slaves and wheat made an unhappy marriage on Maryland's eastern shore. Slaves were more expensive and less productive than wage labor, and pressures for adjustments from slaves to hired labor were inevitable. After 1750, slave owners pursued several alternatives: slaves were hired by the day or week during the harvest bottleneck; share-cropping schemes were suggested to reduce slave costs while keeping available a harvest labor force; and private manumission of slaves increased. Although these adjustments toward free labor are the most important changes, the range of solutions was limited only by the ingenuity of individual planters as they sought to wed staples and labor supply (Berlin 1974, 15–78; K. Carroll 1961, 176–97; Morley 1906, 300; Strickland 1971, 31–36).

The changeover from slaves to free labor on the eastern shore was excruciatingly slow; yet we have no reason to expect instantaneous labor adjustment to the economic model. In the first place, although slaves had become decidedly inefficient, they nonetheless involved a heavy sunk cost not easily recouped. More decisively, wholesale labor change involved the risk that sudden changes in relative labor costs or in the technology of staple production could turn against free labor. For instance, slaves could have produced wheat at less cost than free labor if any of the following conditions obtained: the wheat harvest was extended by rescheduling planting, free wage rates rose, or slave costs fell. Crop scheduling appealed to George Washington, and no doubt eastern shore farmers tried it too. By planting fall wheat at staggered intervals or by sowing several varieties, the fields might mature at different times and spread the harvest over more than ten days. Washington then saw how slaves could be used to advantage: "if Wheat of different kinds are sowed so as to prevent the Harvest coming on at once, it is my opinion that hirelings [wage labor] of all kinds may be dispensed with" (Washington 1925, 1:338; cited in Gray 1958, 1:550). Using our previous calculations, recall that free labor probably handled fourteen to fifteen acres of wheat and slaves ten acres; accordingly, expanding the wheat harvest beyond fifteen days, at one acre harvested a day, would have resulted in a clear-cut advantage for slave labor. Fortunately for northern free labor, Washington's cropping scheme was never successfully implemented, as John H. Klippart (1860, 475–78) observed nearly a century later, and almost two centuries passed before Warren

Thornthwaite worked out the intricacies of crop calendars.

A second condition that favored slave-produced wheat was higher wage rates. In 1769, when Washington toyed with crop scheduling, wheat was in great demand, prices were high, and a bumper crop drove wages up. Day wages for skilled harvesters rose from a norm of 3s. to 5s. a day (Saladino 1960, 45; Bidwell and Falconer 1941, 117–18; U.S. Bureau of the Census 1975, 2:1196). At that rate, ten acres of wheat production cost £6 5s., compared with £5 10s. for a slave. Understandably, slave owners were reluctant to free their slaves until they were assured of a steady, abundant, and low-cost supply of free labor. The year 1769 was atypical, however. Although similar wage peaks hit sporadically through 1860, wage costs generally remained relatively lower than slave costs. When the situation occasionally reversed, farmers supplemented the supply of free labor with marginal lower-cost laborers such as convicts or free Negroes.[12]

Thirdly, wheat farmers would have used slaves if slave costs had fallen; indeed, theory implies such an adjustment and the mechanisms responsible. Assuming a single region in which wheat is produced, the demand curve for slaves shifts downward as slave inefficiencies in wheat production are perceived. While slave prices, and hence discounted costs, are falling, slave masters simultaneously may reduce maintenance costs by cutting expenditures for food, health care, clothing, and shelter (Sutch 1965, 365–66). In practice, however, such cost adjustments by markets and masters seem to have been blunted because of external markets for slaves. Prices for Chesapeake slaves rose rather than fell, suggesting that lower slave demand on the eastern shore was compensated by augmented demand from the expanding tobacco economy of the western shore. The existence of this neighboring slave market thus was decisive in propping up eastern shore slave prices and costs, despite slave inefficiencies in wheat. Put pithily, freedom on the eastern shore depended on the viability of slavery in a nearby region. The market failed to make slaves competitive with free labor, but masters might also have pursued the strategy of lowering maintenance costs. Whether they proceeded ruthlessly by reducing medical care, housing, and clothing of slaves or by affording quasi free-dom via sharecropping and eventual manumis-sion remains an issue of overriding importance.[13]

Slavery lost out in the wheat-producing east-ern shore precisely because none of these three conditions—harvest extension through crop scheduling, rising wage rates, or declining slave costs—seems to have been met. For these rea-sons, a few-day crop such as wheat fostered the development of a labor force that was free, flex-ible, and divisible in its inputs.

STAPLES AND LABOR IN THE ANTEBELLUM MIDWEST

Slavery decayed, albeit slowly, on Maryland's eastern shore with the change from tobacco to wheat. But what of the reverse situation, where few-day wheat gave way to a multiple-day crop? The test case here comes from the antebellum Midwest and deals with the transition from wheat to a corn-hog complex that took place just before the Civil War. This staple change posed a momentous threat to northern wage labor in particular and to society in general. I begin at a more mundane level by comparing the costs of slave labor and free labor under wheat and its successor, Indian corn. Having demonstrated slave efficiency in corn production, I turn to the evidence of proslavery attitudes and legislation in the Midwest.

Antebellum labor costs provide the basic eco-nomic information. Slave costs are from Al-fred H. Conrad and John R. Meyer's estimate of $51 as the annual cost of a slave between 1830 and 1850. They arrive at this figure by first discount-ing the price of a twenty-year-old male slave ($900 to $950) over a useful life of thirty years, or $30, and adding yearly maintenance costs of $21 for a total of $51 (A. Conrad and Meyer 1971, 345–47).[14] Farm-labor wages come from Stanley Lebergott's (1964) wage series for the various states under consideration. Comparison of slave and wage costs from these sources show that wage labor hired by the year was expensive and could not compete with slaves. For example, in 1830 the average monthly wage including board in the United States of $8.85 totaled $106.20 for

twelve months—around double the cost of a slave (Lebergott 1964, 539). These figures cast serious doubt on Clarence H. Danhof's (1969, 73–78) belief that freemen were commonly hired for eight to ten months during the cropping sea-son; eight months of labor in 1830 cost more than $70, still far in excess of slave costs.[15] Long labor contracts of this sort were used selectively, notably during the first years of farm making and sod busting; but otherwise the eight-to-ten-month laborer cost too much. Other students of farm labor lean toward shorter-term hire, rang-ing from a daily basis to several months at a time; and their impressions and evidence conform re-markably well with the hypothesis of labor costs presented here (Bogue 1968, 182–87; Curti 1959, 145–49; Gates 1957, 143–64; Schob 1975, 69, 103–4, 258). Given the prevailing wage rates in midwestern states in 1850, three to five months was the theoretical maximum for wage-labor hire; beyond that time, slaves became cheaper than freemen. Parenthetically, we may note that free labor had improved its economic position vis-à-vis slaves between 1750 and 1850. In the ear-lier year, the annual cost of a slave equaled about thirty-six days of wage labor as compared with sixty-five days of hired labor in 1850 Ohio.

Wheat was the initial staple of the Midwest, and its labor requirements fell easily within the economic range of free labor. The link between day labor and wheat should be clear from the ear-lier discussion of the Maryland case, and repeti-tion for the Midwest is unnecessary. However, subtle changes in nineteenth-century wheat pro-duction gave day labor even greater advantages. The harvest-labor bottleneck of ten days to two weeks persisted into the nineteenth century, but labor demands became even more intense be-cause farmers increased output per acre from the colonial norm of ten bushels to twenty to thirty bushels or more. Accordingly, labor time spent in harvesting and gathering the wheat, despite some efficiencies introduced by the cradle and the flail, increased from 60 percent of total labor time to about 83 percent in the prereaper nine-teenth century. Harvesting and getting in an acre of wheat, according to Leo Rogin (1931, 229–43), required about five days (see also Gates 1960, 156–69; David 1966). That meant that a slave could harvest just two to three acres of wheat, while divisible day labor, hired at the 1850 Ohio wage rate for the time equivalent of a slave's cost and allocating five-sixths of the hired labor to harvest, handled ten or eleven acres of wheat. In other words, a slave harvested and gathered two to three acres for $51.00, or a cost of $17.00 to $25.50 per acre. Day laborers, paid $51.00, harvested and gathered ten to eleven acres, at a cost of $4.64 to $5.10 per acre. Furthermore, day laborers cost less than monthly labor. The hire of two laborers for three months each cost $66.00 at the 1850 Ohio rate; and they harvested and gathered four to six acres, at a cost of $11.00 to $16.50 per acre.[16]

As long as wheat persisted as the midwestern staple, day labor was economically superior to both slaves and monthly hired hands. Nor did this superiority of the day hand diminish with increased scale of operation—a point demonstrated later in the century in the bonanza wheat farms of the Red River Valley, where day laborers at the critical seasons vastly outnumbered laborers hired by the month or season (Shannon 1968, 154–61).

The midwestern staple economy altered between 1800 and 1860, and pressures to adjust the labor supply became evident a decade or two before the Civil War. The wheat staple suffered from disease and humidity, particularly in the south central tier of Ohio, Indiana, and Illinois; and as wheat became less attractive, southern and northeastern demands for hogs and pork encouraged a corn-hog staple economy. Wheat was supplemented and then displaced by these new regional staples.[17] From the standpoint of labor requirements, corn lay intermediate between wheat's few days and the multiple labor days of tobacco and cotton. More precisely, a laborer in corn tended about twenty-five acres and invested perhaps 850 person-hours, compared with wheat's ten acres and 600 person-hours (Shannon 1968, 143). From plowing through the third cultivation, the individually planted and tended corn plant demanded exceptional attention. The corn farmers of Illinois, for example, planted in April or early May and cultivated three times before July 4, when the crop was "laid by." Afterward, labor needs were light un-

til harvest. Although corn harvesting was back-breaking and sweaty work, corn did not create a harvest labor bottleneck as did wheat. The crop was ready for harvest in September, but there was no urgency because the ears could stand in the fields throughout the winter and into early spring. As a result, corn was usually harvested by family members or neighbors during idle moments, rather than by expensive wage labor. Thus for corn it was the plowing and tillage in spring and early summer that established the period of peak labor demand (Russell 1857, 81–82; Bogue 1968, 132–33).

Corn farmers sought labor for the "crop season," the three to four months from April or May through July. Day labor was prohibitively expensive, and corn farmers instead engaged labor on short-term contracts of ten weeks to four months.[18] But this shift upward in labor costs pushed freemen into competition with slaves (it makes no difference that state legislatures and referenda had outlawed slavery in the Midwest in the first quarter of the century). For instance, an Illinois farmer who hired a four-month laborer with board in 1850 spent $12.55 a month and $50.20 for four months, whereas a slave would have cost the farmer $51.00. Wage rates had risen by 1860, when the four-month laborer cost $54.88 (Lebergott 1964, 539).[19] These wage rates, I might add, are conservative figures; David E. Schob (1975, 104) has indicated that the four-month rate may have been $13.00 to $18.00 a month rather than $12.55. By the mid-1850s, slave labor probably cost less than free labor in the production of corn, a multiple-day staple crop.[20] To make matters worse, slaves had long since mastered the techniques of corn production, and they employed these in Kentucky, just across the river from freedom.

The political implications of this analysis are far-reaching. As slavery became more efficient than free labor, we should and do find an acceleration of proslavery advocacy and legislation emanating from the central and lower midwestern corn region during the 1840s and 1850s. Slavery was headed north. The threat was no more nor less than the imminent dissolution of northern society based on free labor. Slavery took on a new urgency, and its enemies, so disarrayed before 1850, molded a unified opposition, focused on the northern margins of the corn belt. Their choice was simple: allow slavery to survive anywhere in the United States and corn farmers eventually would adopt the institution; destroy slavery completely and thus remove this labor supply as a competitor for freemen. The efficiency of slaves in corn culture helps put a new perspective on otherwise confused political behavior in the antebellum Midwest, to which we now turn.

The midwestern states in the first quarter of the nineteenth century prohibited the institution of slavery by referenda. This made economic sense because slavery was already a dead letter for the majority of farmers who produced a wheat staple and used more efficient free labor (Berwanger 1967, 7–29; Pease 1925, 96–113; Dunn 1888). But these referenda posed an ominous threat: if laws and referenda could prohibit slavery, they could also introduce the peculiar institution when it became profitable. That day was not far off, as economic change swept over the lower Midwest and as corn-hog farming supplemented or displaced wheat during the 1830s and 1840s. Slave costs still exceeded those of free labor, but the gap was narrowing. Accordingly, the corn region gave little support to the enemies of slavery; they found more fertile ground for their abolitionist societies, antislavery newspapers, and third-party efforts in the northern wheat counties. The sectional rift was apparent in the elections of 1844, 1848, and 1852, when the northern counties cast increasingly larger votes for antislavery third parties, while the nascent corn-belt counties voted overwhelmingly for the regular parties, particularly the Democrats (T. Smith 1967, 325–31; Paullin 1932, plates 105, 115, 144; Cole 1919, 101–201).

Northern support for third parties intensified when they added a new and powerful argument against slavery—an argument that becomes more reasonable when it is placed in the context of the increasing efficiency of slavery in the lower Midwest. Salmon Chase and the Free-Soil party adopted all of the standard attacks on the immorality of slavery and on its exclusion from the territories, and they went even farther. Northern society, they proclaimed, faced the grave danger of an inexorably expanding slave power or slavocracy. Slavery threatened free labor, which was the underpinning for northern civilization. Chase's argument has been treated unkindly by political historians. Should we accept their verdict that he and his supporters were paranoid, grossly distorting the dangers of slave encroachment in the North, or crassly political, manipulating issues and voters through the use of exaggerated rhetoric and playing on the racial fears of midwesterners?[21] Quite the opposite, if the economic analysis presented here is correct. Chase was on sound ground; if he was guilty of anything, it was of detecting the threat of slavery to the North before more ordinary men and women and of misplacing blame on a conspiracy of expansionist-minded southern slaveowners instead of on a conspiracy of economics favoring the corn staple and pushing up wage rates in the late 1840s and 1850s.[22]

Chase's argument did not win the day immediately. His fear that slavery would expand into the old Northwest was not shared by his natural allies in northern Illinois, Indiana, and Ohio. They faced a more pressing problem—control of an expanding free Negro population. Their anti-Negro attitudes, racism by another name, led them into an uneasy coalition with proslavery advocates in the corn belt. This coalition in the late 1840s and early 1850s voted repeatedly against free Negroes, excluding fugitive slaves and free Negroes from these states and circumscribing the civil and political rights of those who were already there. African colonization for midwestern free Negroes also held broad appeal (Berwanger 1967, 30–59).[23]

The cement of racism began to crack in the mid-1850s. Upstaters who detested Negroes and wanted to get rid of them perceived that downstaters wanted to strip free Negroes of their rights in order to enslave them or else facilitate the introduction of slavery. The subtle schemes of proslavers were laid bare in an 1855 committee report of the Indiana legislature: African colonization, it claimed, originated "in the basest motives and most mercenary considerations. It is one of the offspring of slavery . . . intended to remove the free blacks from the country in order to increase the value and security . . . of slaves"

(Thornbrough 1957, 86). Even more drastic action had been taken by proslavers in Illinois. The legislature of 1853 put through a law that compelled free Negroes new to the state to pay a fine of $50 plus court costs; Negroes unable to pay this exorbitant sum were hired out for six months to the highest bidder. Indiana carried a similar law on the books, and efforts to strengthen its provisions were narrowly defeated in 1851 (N. Harris 1904, 188, 235–36; Cole 1919, 224–29; Thornbrough 1957, 58–59). That these laws favored black servitude, and potentially permanent bondage, did not escape the opponents of slavery. A delegate to Indiana's constitutional convention of 1850 clearly understood the implications of the attack on the free Negro.

> If I am not mistaken the favorite proposition, and it has been already avowed and advocated here, is, that all persons in whose blood negro descent shall be detected, shall be arrested and sold for six months to the highest bidder and the proceeds applied to the operations of the Colonization Society! And what a spectacle will Indiana in that attitude present to the civilized world? We reprobate slavery and the slave trade, denounce the one as inhuman and the other as piracy punishable with death. And yet what is it proposed to do? Nothing less than to erect shambles at every county seat, enjoin it upon officers to sell, not slaves, but those who are confessedly free, into slavery, differing only from the Southern States, as to its duration. (*Report of the Debates and Proceedings* 1850, 1:457–58)

Identical concern surfaced in Illinois, where the law of 1853 permitting court-appointed sale of free Negroes was regarded by some as a harbinger of slavery (N. Harris 1904, 237–38; Koerner 1902, 2:29–32).

Proslavery efforts became more blatant as pressures for a more efficient slave labor supply emanated from the corn belt. Dumas Van Deren succinctly summarized the corn farmers' interests in 1854. He and other Illinoisans were

> prepared to pronounce openly our full and candid preference in favor of slave labor in agricultural business. . . . We have discovered that the novelty of free labor is a mere humbug. . . . We have been endeavoring to learn the sentiments of our people upon this subject, and have been astonished to see with what unanimity they express themselves in favor of the introduction of slave labor. I have conversed with many of our best farmers who were raised in the eastern States, and they will give their hearty cooperation in effecting this object. (cited in Cole 1923, 32–33)

By about mid-decade, the northern counties comprehended that the immediate threat was slavery and not the free Negro. Chase was vindicated and his fear of the slave power carried justifiable weight in the emerging Republican party.

The prospect of slavery in the lower Midwest made the Civil War inevitable and irrepressible; more important, this threat made the issue of the annihilation of slavery a matter of some urgency.[24] For every cent that free wages increased, for every farmer who adopted corn as his staple, the potential for slavery became ever stronger. Yankee morality would not hold the line against slavery because, according to one southern critic, their morality was only superficial: "once persuaded to consider this question [of slave labor] . . . it is not apprehended that moral qualms will hinder their action. It requires the least rudimental knowledge of Yankee nature, and no argument at all to show, that where a real interest, and a question of abstract morality conflict in a Yankee's mind, abstract morality will sustain a grievous overthrow."[25] This jaundiced southerner understood well the moral fragility of the North, but he seriously misunderstood its economic geography—that the real interest of the lower Midwest departed sharply from its northern margins. In the latter areas slavery remained an alien and inefficient labor system that contributed nothing to society except the problem of the free Negro. These northern wheat counties became bastions of free labor, free soil, and antislavery in the late 1850s (Cole 1919, 101–201). Excluding slavery from the territories or confining it to the South did not go far enough. They had to destroy it forever so it would not tempt the "real interest" of corn-growing midwesterners. Such was the unequivocal course of action laid out by Abraham Lincoln on June 16, 1858:

In my opinion, it [slavery agitation] *will* not cease, until a *crisis* shall have been reached, and passed. A house divided against itself cannot stand. I believe this government cannot endure, permanently *half* slave and *half* free. I do not expect the Union to be dissolved—I do not expect the house to *fall*—but I do expect it will cease to be divided. It will become *all* one thing or *all* the other. Either the opponents of slavery, will arrest the further spread of it, and place it where the public mind shall rest in the belief that it is in course of ultimate extinction; or its *advocates* will push it forward, till it shall become alike lawful in *all* the States, old as well as *new*—*North* as well as *South*. (A. Lincoln 1953, 2:461–62)

Corn culture, rising wages, and incipient slavery in the lower Midwest had brought the nation to its greatest impasse.

I have tried to show that moral fiber cannot explain the geography of slavery and free labor and that, conversely, the economics of staple crops and labor costs can. Before 1860, slavery was not good or bad, it was merely efficient or inefficient—and labor decisions were made accordingly. We can no more extol the principles of slave emancipators on Maryland's eastern shore or the Republicans of the upper Midwest who brought the issue of slavery to war than we can denigrate as unprincipled the proslavery advocates in the midwestern corn belt. They all subscribed to and acted on the same set of economic principles. The thesis that moral superiority motivated antislavery northerners must be shown for what it is: a comfortable liberal myth which obviates examination of the basic amorality of the antebellum American economic system.

SOURCE

This article appeared originally in the *Geographical Review* 68 (1978): 51–65.

NOTES

1. Until now, the economic interpretation of slavery and free labor has been sustained on argument more than on substantive evidence of labor efficiency. The best state-ment connecting plantation crops and slavery appears in Gray (1958, 1:462–80). Also, see R. Baldwin (1956) and D. North (1959). A cogent review of the issues is in Engerman (1973).

2. Economic historians have acknowledged Domar's contribution, but they have given too much attention to the land-labor ratio as a determinant of wage rates while disregarding empirical tests of the labor efficiency model. Wage labor can be used in societies with high land-labor ratios, as will be pointed out below.

3. "I have a hard time believing that slaves could not be used in the mixed farming of the North; much food was produced on southern farms as well, most of the slave owners had very few slaves, and many slaves were skilled in crafts" (Domar 1970, 30).

4. Domar urged this refocusing in 1970, but so far the "new" economic historians have disregarded the problem of slave-free labor efficiencies under the same crops and have instead directed their attention to the efficiencies of farms and plantations. These are not the same, as is forcefully pointed out by David and Temin (1976, 202–3).

5. "Our winter crops of wheat, barley, & c. also the oats flax & buckwheat are so disposed of as to require no further care [until harvest] after the seeds are put into the ground" (Bausman and Munroe 1946, 181).

6. Economists have generally regarded labor inputs in terms of intensity (person-hours or person-days); hence systematic data on the more critical labor input of "required days" are lacking. These data are available, however, in sensitive accounts by agricultural historians. See Bogue (1968, 132–33), Gray (1958, 1:462–80), and Gates (1960).

7. This discussion of economic change on the eastern shore derives from many sources, too numerous to be listed here. See especially Earle and Hoffman (1976) and Clemens (1974).

8. On manumission and free blacks on the eastern shore, see the impressive study by Berlin (1974, 15–78). Also, see K. Carroll (1950; 1961). These studies emphasize religion and revolutionary ideology as the chief causes of manumission and the growth of the free black community; yet these interpretations fail to explain the strength of slavery sentiment among tobacco-producing Quakers on Maryland's western shore and the manumission activity that began before the Revolution. In 1790, the proportion of free Negroes to all Negroes was highest in the upper bay counties of Maryland (*Return of the Whole Number of Persons* 1791, 47). On slave hire and hire rates, see Strickland (1971, 31–36) and Morley (1906, 300).

9. These estimates, their sources, and a preliminary, if crude, statement of the argument made here appear in Earle and Hoffman (1976, 36–39, 68–78).

10. Slave prices appear in Clemens (1974, 171), U.S. Bureau of the Census (1975, 2:1174), Kulikoff (1976, 485–88), and Carman (1964, 164). Twenty years as the useful life for discounting the prices of adult male slaves is suggested in Carman (1964, 164) and Clemens (1974, 47–53). However, calculating slave life expectancy is an intrac-

table problem. Among Prince George's County whites in the eighteenth century, expectation of life at age 20 was 27 additional years (Kulikoff 1976, 38–41). Maintenance costs are from Carman (1964, 164).

11. The belief that freedom was a production incentive and resulted in productivity gains over slavery probably rests on free labor's superior output in broadcast grain production—a superiority we have attributed to the few required days of labor and the divisibility of free labor. The incentive of freedom disappeared in tobacco production, where a slave doubled the output of a freeman for a given cost.

12. In the antebellum Midwest, free Negroes were used principally during bumper harvests (Schob 1975, 83–87).

13. On slave prices, see Clemens (1974, 171), U.S. Bureau of the Census (1975, 2:1174), and Kulikoff (1976, 485–88). These prices are not entirely satisfactory, for we need a series specifically for the eastern shore after 1750. However, rather high slave prices are suggested in Morley (1906, 300). Slave clothing allowances, as an indicator of maintenance costs, seem to have remained the same from the 1720s to the Revolution, but the evidence is fragmentary (Clemens 1974, 47–53, 175).

14. The farmer who was considering the adoption of slavery would probably have purchased a prime male field slave rather than an infant or child slave; hence the appropriate costs are given by slave market prices rather than the considerably lower costs of slave reproduction and rearing. For the latter costs, see Yasuba (1961).

15. This criticism should not impugn the remainder of this excellent and essential book.

16. The discussion, of course, concerns prereaper harvest technology. I have used the 1850 Ohio daily hire rate, without board, of $0.78 and the monthly hire rate, with board, of $11.00 (Lebergott 1964, 539; Schob 1975, 259). Somewhat higher daily rates of $1.27 for 1849–53 have been recorded in Illinois, particularly for harvest cradlers (David 1966, 35–37).

17. Midwestern economic change is thoroughly discussed in Spencer and Horvath (1963). See also Bogue (1968, 156–72) and J. Clark (1966, 147–71, 197–211). Regional boundaries were hazy. The lower Midwest continued to produce wheat after corn and hogs were the main staples. But toward the Great Lakes, wheat remained dominant, and the corn-hog complex penetrated more slowly. See the maps of corn and wheat production in Paullin (1932, plate 143).

18. "The general practice in Central Illinois is to hire about the 1st of April for the 'crop (corn) season,' or until after harvest, which includes wheat, oats, hay, & c." (*Merchants' Magazine and Commercial Review* 1859, vol. 71, 760). The small grain harvest was in July, so the author meant that labor was hired from April to the end of July, or for four months. Also, see Russell (1857, 81–82).

19. The labor problem was most severe between 1854 and 1857, when wage rates peaked. David shows that Illinois common laborers received $1.25 a day compared with $0.85 in 1849–53—an increase of 35 percent. Adjusting

our monthly rates according to this percentage increase, we find that monthly wages would have risen from $12.55 in 1850 to $16.94 in 1854–57, making a total wage bill of $67.75. Slave costs fell below this (David 1966, 36).

20. Slave costs rose during the 1850s but at a less rapid rate than free-labor costs. Slave prices moved up to $1,306 between 1856 and 1860. Discounting this price over thirty years and adding $21.00 for maintenance put slave costs at about $64.50—or $3.00 less than the four-month hire rate for free labor, as calculated in note 19. For slave prices, see Yasuba (1961, 60–67). During the 1850s, midwestern real wages generally exceeded all other regions except the east south central states, thus compounding the pressure on free labor in this region (Coelho and Shepherd 1976).

21. See the perceptive examination of Chase in Foner (1970, 73–102). Chase and other antislavery advocates are cast as irresponsible fanatics in Craven (1964). Benson has suggested that Chase and men of his persuasion were guilty of overblown campaign rhetoric and reckless demagogy which got out of hand in the late 1850s. I disagree. See Benson (1972, 225–340).

22. Foner's thesis that northern fears of an aggressive, expanding slave power played a decisive role in the coming of the war is pursued by Gara (1975). A leading advocate of corn culture, the midwestern Yankee Solon Robinson, produced a lengthy apologia for slavery in *DeBow's Review* in 1849. The timing of his conversion, coming as it did when corn culture was expanding into the lower Midwest and labor rates were rising, seems more than coincidental (S. Robinson 1936).

23. For a slightly different view of midwestern racism, see Rozett (1976).

24. A recent quantitative study of the causes of the Civil War concludes that "northern preferences to eliminate slavery were more than twenty times as strong as those to preserve the Union" (Gunderson 1974). This finding is consonant with the argument presented here: if the North had allowed the South to secede peacefully or had they compromised on the issue of slavery in order to preserve the Union, slavery would have persisted and would shortly have expanded into the lower Midwest. The extermination of slavery, either peacefully or forcefully, was the only course open to the upper Midwest and the Republican party.

25. This essay (in *DeBow's Review*) carries the ominous title "African slavery adapted to the North and North-west" (1858).

FURTHER READINGS

Jeremy Atack and Fred Bateman. 1987. *To their own soil: Agriculture in the antebellum North.* Ames: Iowa State University Press.

The authors provide a systematic survey of a large sample of northern farms in the manuscript U.S. census of 1860. These economic historians seek to steer a course between the polar interpretations of rural America as rooted in ethnocultural or capitalist mentalities. See the annotation below to Henretta's essay.

Thomas C. Cochran. 1981. *Frontiers of change: Early industrialism in America.* New York: Oxford University Press.

A concise description, by a historian, of the cultural practices that facilitated American industrial development in the early nineteenth century. Stress is placed on the importance of credit, government assistance, and internal markets, as well as the traditional explanation of American ingenuity.

Bruce Collins. 1986. The Lincoln-Douglas contest of 1858 and the Illinois electorate. *Journal of American Studies* 20: 391–420.

A historian's reassessment of voting in Illinois during the senatorial race between Lincoln and Douglas in 1858. Collins suggests that slavery surpassed other issues (banks, tariffs, and internal improvements) in the campaign and was the critical determinant of voting patterns.

Carville Earle. 1992. *Geographical inquiry and American historical problems.* Stanford, Calif.: Stanford University Press.

A series of essays dealing with important problems in American history between 1600 and the present. Several of the essays extend the political-ecological themes presented here to the American Revolution, the American labor movement in the Gilded Age and Progressive Era, and the Civil Rights movement.

Lou Ferleger, ed. 1990. *Agriculture and national development: Views on the nineteenth century.* Ames: Iowa State University Press.

A useful overview of historical issues arising in various agricultural regions of the United States. In addition to its value as a bibliographic and historiographic source, the volume contains several essays (most notably, Hal Barron's) that point to continuing rural tensions over the market and ethnocultural commitments. The volume also underscores the curious tendency for students of southern agriculture to link their work to the Civil War and for their counterparts in the north to ignore that conflict.

Paul Finkelman. 1986. Slavery and the Northwest Ordinance. *Journal of the Early Republic* 6:743–70.

Finkelman's supple account of the Northwest Ordinance's prohibition of slavery north of the Ohio River serves to remind scholars that this prohibition applied only in the region's territorial phase. Once converted into states, the issue of legalizing slavery reemerged as a point of contention and of ongoing geopolitical fragility.

———. 1987. Slavery, "the more perfect union," and the prairie state. *Illinois Historical Journal* 80:248–69.

A historian's account of the debate over slavery in Illinois during the 1850s. Finkelman accents the importance of the issue of slavery and the fluidity of opinion which ranged from adoption to African colonization to abolition. Illinois, in Finkelman's view, seems not to have been as securely within the antislavery camp as earlier historians have assumed.

Eugene D. Genovese and Leonard Hochberg, eds. 1989. *Geographic perspectives in history.* New York: Basil Blackwell.

These essays, largely authored by historians, address the impact of geography on various episodes of human history. The collection has been described as a harbinger of geohistorical social science.

Steven Hahn and Jonathan Prude, eds. 1985. *The countryside in the age of capitalist transformation: Essays on the social history of rural America.* Chapel Hill: University of North Carolina Press.

A prominent collection of essays, generally espousing the view that capitalism arrived late in the American countryside. As a result, precapitalist notions of communal reciprocity and obligation endured well into the nineteenth century, when they were increasingly besieged by market forces and possessive individualism.

James Henretta. 1978. Families and farms: Mentalité in preindustrial America. *William and Mary Quarterly,* 3d series, 35:3–32. See also reply by James T. Lemon and comment by Henretta in *William and Mary Quarterly,* 3d series, 37 (1980): 699–700.

The Henretta-Lemon exchange joins the debate over the nature of rural Americans, with the former accenting a precapitalist *mentalité* anchored in family, community, and land and the latter emphasizing liberalism and market orientation. The debate has also been cast in terms of ethnocultural versus economic interpretations of the American past.

James T. Lemon. 1972. *The best poor man's country: A geographical study of early southeastern Pennsylvania.* Baltimore: Johns Hopkins University Press.

The classic statement of American liberalism's roots in the individual and the quest for material gains in the market. Lemon's comprehensive geography of southeastern Pennsylvania in the eighteenth century demolishes a series of ethnocultural stereotypes linking, for example, ethnicity to soil preferences, site selection, land use, and self-sufficiency.

Donald W. Meinig. 1986. *The shaping of America: A geographical perspective on 500 years of history.* Vol. 1: *Atlantic America, 1492–1800.* New Haven: Yale University Press.

In this, the first of three volumes, Meinig offers a synthesis of the historical geography of the Atlantic seaboard of

North America between 1492 and 1800. By focusing on the sociogeographic pluralism that emerged along that seaboard, Meinig is able to highlight the development of these diverse regions and to trace their origins in the process of sociocultural innovation and diffusion. In this interpretation, therefore, environment, ecology, and economic geography are accorded modest roles. Volume 2, expected in 1993, carries Meinig's main themes forward to the Civil War. Timely in that regard is his chapter on the Midwest and the coming of war; although Meinig's interpretation does not agree in all particulars with those advanced in Earle's essay, the two are in harmony on the fluidity in the region's politics and the tenuousness of its geopolitical links with northern (that is, free) society during the 1850s.

Robert D. Mitchell. 1977. *Commercialism and frontier: Perspectives on the early Shenandoah Valley.* Charlottesville: University Press of Virginia.

Mitchell's volume documents the swift transformations from self-sufficiency to a market economy on Virginia's eighteenth-century frontier. The author, like Lemon, accents the speed and scope of the market's impact on highly varied ethnic groups in the Shenandoah Valley.

TERRY G. JORDAN **15**

CULTURAL PREADAPTATION AND THE AMERICAN FOREST FRONTIER: THE ROLE OF NEW SWEDEN

Perhaps no traditional American way of life is more intriguing than that of the backwoods pioneers, a group of highly successful forest colonizers who formed the vanguard of European settlement in eastern North America. This colonization culture originated in the middle section of the eastern seaboard of the United States, in the Delaware River valley, rather than in New England, New York, or the plantation South. Moving rapidly westward after about 1720, these forest pioneers caused the American frontier to bulge quite markedly in the middle by the end of that century as they outpaced both Yankees and planters in their expansion to the west (figure 1). The backwoods folk thrived almost outrageously in the forested wilderness, sweeping westward beyond the Mississippi and through the western mountain ranges in a few generations, achieving in the process the most rapid expansion ever known of an agricultural frontier in a wooded habitat.

Living in isolated log cabins; throwing up zigzag log fences around their small ax- and fire-cleared fields of corn; skillfully hunting deer and bears in the woods; gathering berries, herbs, wild fruits, and honey; and herding small semiferal droves of pigs and cattle, these pioneers were ideally suited to the pioneer life (Jordan and Kaups 1989).

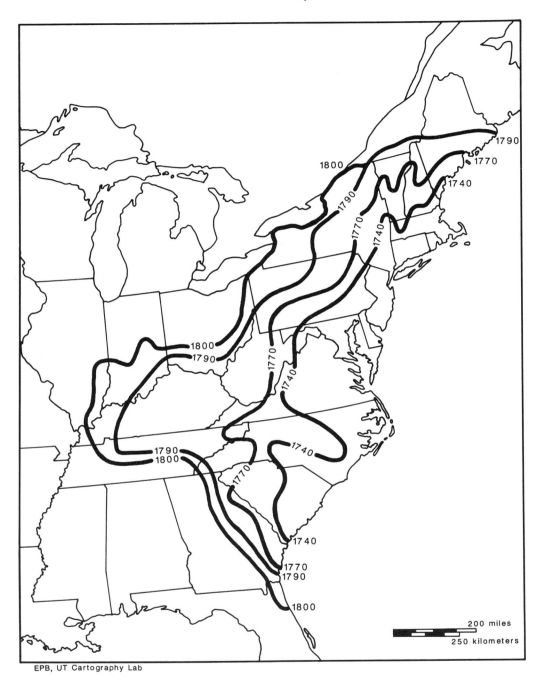

FIGURE 1

Expansion of the American agricultural frontier, to 1800. Note the central bulge. Source: Jordan and Kaups (1989, 13).

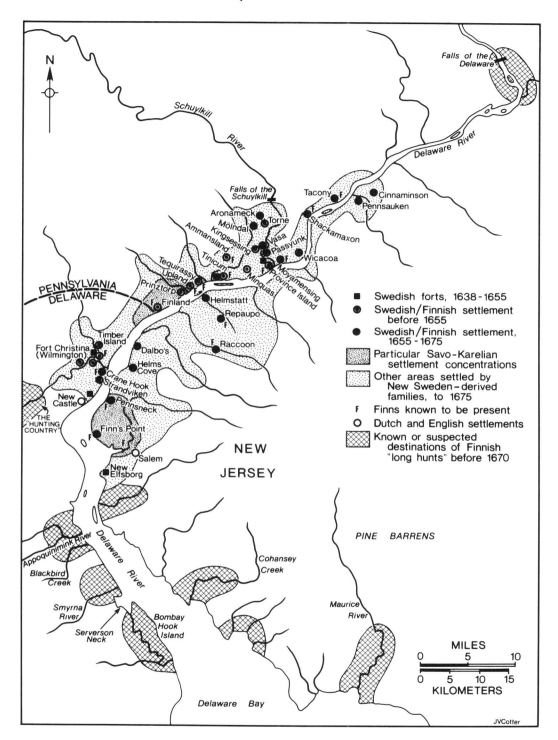

FIGURE 2

New Sweden on the Delaware River, 1638–75. Source: Jordan and Kaups (1989, 54).

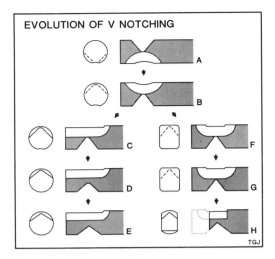

EVOLUTION OF V NOTCHING

FIGURE 3
Key: A = Medieval, archaic Scandinavian form; B, C, F, and G = Scandinavian, numerous field specimens survive; D, E, and H = American. Source: Jordan, Kaups, and Lieffort (1986, 27).

I sought to learn how this wonderfully adapted way of life had come to be, using as my approach the time-honored methods of the Berkeley school of cultural-historical geography. These methods led me to a rather astounding conclusion—that a small, short-lived colony established by the Swedish crown in the lower Delaware Valley of present Pennsylvania, New Jersey, and Delaware was of pivotal importance in shaping the forest colonization culture of the American backwoods. The colony, called New Sweden, existed only from 1638 to 1655, and when it was seized by the Dutch in the latter year, no more than 500 inhabitants, many of them ethnic Finns, resided in the area (figure 2). These Finns, whose ancestry lay in Savo-Karelian districts of eastern and interior Finland, had long practiced a forest colonization culture in northern Europe, and the Swedish crown transported them to America both because of this prowess and because they were poaching game and destroying the royal forests of Sweden at an alarming rate by the early 1600s.

EVIDENCE IN THE CULTURAL LANDSCAPE

Berkeley-inspired cultural geographers often approach a research problem through an analysis of the relict *cultural landscape,* which consists of the greater human artifacts, such as houses, barns, fences, and settlement layout. Learn to "read" that landscape, and you can achieve an understanding of the historical geography of a region. It was exactly this methodology, applied to the artifacts of American pioneers, that led me to the idea that the forest Finns of New Sweden had placed their mark on frontier America. Let me illustrate with some examples.

I will present five specimens of American frontier material culture that constitute diffusionary evidence of northern European influence by way of New Sweden. An appropriate point of departure is notched log carpentry. I present first a type of log corner notching known in the American literature of folk carpentry as "V-notching," so-named because of its inverted V shape (figure 3) (Jordan, Kaups, and Lieffort 1986). This crude type of notch is extremely common and widespread in the United States and has long been considered as evidence of Pennsylvanian or Delaware Valley cultural influence. In seeking its European prototype, I did field research not only in northern Europe, but also throughout the German-speaking lands, for the conventional wisdom used to be that American V-notching was of German origin. I found, to the contrary, that it was a slight modification of a Norwegian type that occurred abundantly as far east as Sweden's Finnskog in Värmland, source of many of the Delaware settlers. A clear and obvious evolutionary path could be documented from the Norwegian to the American type, with the Finns as probable agents of diffusion. The notch was adopted by Finnish settlers after their arrival in Värmland and subsequently transferred by them to New Sweden.

I draw a second material example of northern European influence in frontier America from roof construction. Both backwoods American and Finnish log structures were characterized by a highly distinctive board roof (figure 4). Boards of roughly one meter length were placed loosely on the roof support beams. The lowest tier of these boards butted at the bottom end against a horizontal beam, which was usually notched into logs projecting from the base of the gables. The loose boards were held down by log "weight poles," which were kept from rolling down the roof slope by short wooden spacers, called "knees," resting perpendicularly against the butting board. A second tier of roofboards overlapped the first, in the manner of shingles, and a second row of spacers supported another weight pole. At the roof ridge, boards on the windward side projected by 15 centimeters or more beyond the crest, in the direction of the prevailing wind. Such a roof occurred both in northern Europe and frontier America, and many still survive,

especially in Karelia and Dalarna. So unusual a method is most unlikely to have been independently invented, providing almost irrefutable evidence of the cultural influence of New Sweden on the American frontier.

I draw the next example from folk architecture. American pioneer backwoodsmen applied log construction to a small number of one/two-room floor plans (figure 5). In this frontier folk architecture, houses or barns could easily be enlarged from one log room to two, and an original

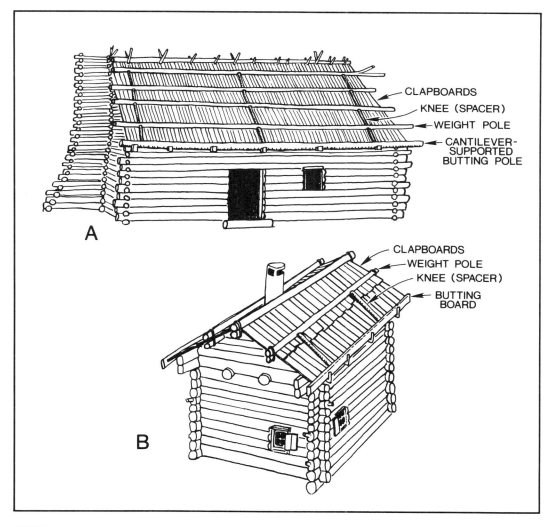

FIGURE 4

Board roofs with butting beams, weight poles, and spacers. Key: A = America; B = Karelian Isthmus. Source: Jordan and Kaups (1989, 168).

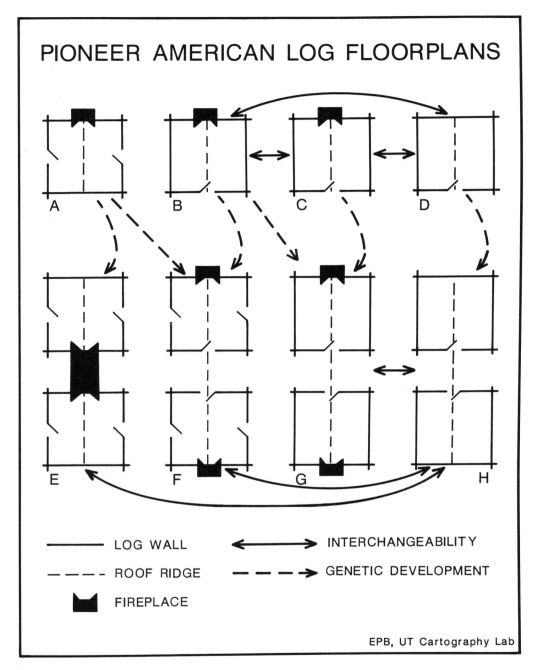

FIGURE 5

Key: A = English-plan cabin; B = Finnish-plan cabin; C = kitchen; D = single-crib barn; E = double-pen "saddlebag" house; F and G = double-pen dog-trot houses; H = double-crib barn. Source: Jordan and Kaups (1987, 64).

house was often demoted to the status of barn, granary, kitchen, or smokehouse. Expansion to double-room size was done in a highly distinctive way, leaving a roofed-over open space about three meters wide between the two log rooms. The double-room dwelling with open central passage is the familiar dog-trot cabin of the American frontier (figure 6) (Jordan and Kaups 1987; M. Wright 1958).

The forest Finns possessed an almost identical assortment of interchangeable single- and double-room log floor plans (figure 7). Duplicating the American pattern, the forest Finns of northern Europe often lived in an open-passage two-room cabin that any American backwoodsman would have recognized. In pioneer America, as among the forest Finns, enlargement to two-room size both was considered a status symbol and provided room for the abundant children of a young, forest-pioneering people. In both cultures, buildings were interchangeable in function and plan. It is significant that the oldest surviving dog-trot house in America, dating to 1696, is located in Pennsylvania, within the territorial bounds of what had earlier been New Sweden.

The builders of this log house, named Mårtensson, are known to have been a Finnish family. Both groups also built a double-crib barn with an open-air runway in the center, duplicating the floor plan of the dog-trot house.

Another specimen of pioneer American folk architecture revealing forest Finnish influence is the hunter's shanty (figure 8). These crude structures consisted of three log walls covered by a single-pitch, lean-to roof. The front, tallest side of the shanty faced the campfire and remained completely open. One backwoods hunter in late eighteenth-century Pennsylvania described how he "cut some small trees and put up three sides of a small cabin, leaving the front open, having our fire on the outside." His shanty measured about three meters square, and most were not over one meter tall at the rear. A more detailed description of the shanty, from the Virginia frontier, mentioned that the rear wall sometimes consisted of a single large log, at a distance of 2.5 to 3 meters from which two pairs of "stakes were set in the ground to receive the ends of the poles for the sides." Above, "the whole slope of the roof was from the front to the back" and made

FIGURE 6

American open-passage dog-trot cabin in Pennsylvania. Note also the Karelian board roof with weight pole and the zigzag rail fence with X-shaped supports. Source: J. Smith (1854, 232).

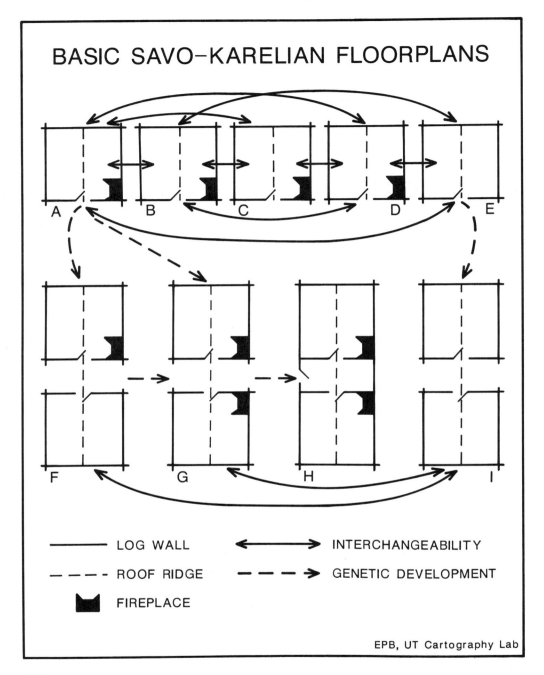

FIGURE 7

Key: A = Finnish one-room cabin; B = sauna; C = kitchen; D = grain-drying shed; E = granary or hay shed;
F and G = two-room house with enclosed hall; I = double-crib hay shed. Source: Jordan and Kaups (1987, 68).

of "skins, or . . . the bark of hickory or ash trees." To complete the shanty, "the cracks between the logs were filled with moss" (Doddridge 1824, 124; Harpster 1938, 223–24). In addition to serving hunters, the frontier log shanty was also used by some pioneers as a first crude dwelling at a new settlement site, a logical development, since the backwoods people often converted their former hunting grounds into farms. The precise prototype of the American hunter's shanty, even to the last detail, occurred among the forest Finns in northern Europe. Indeed, the illustra-

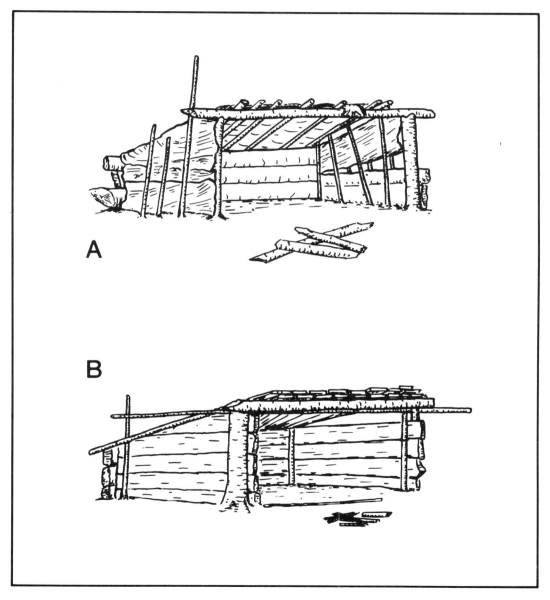

FIGURE 8
The Finnish hunting shanty. Key: A = Russian Karelia; B = northern Finnish Karelia. Source: Sirelius (1909, 19) and Jordan and Kaups (1989, 220).

FIGURE 9
Zigzag, or "worm," fence in the high pastures of the Uinta Mountains in Utah. Photograph by author, 1987.

tions shown here (figure 8), which fit the American pioneer descriptions so perfectly, are in fact both from Karelia.

For the fifth and final example of Finnish-influenced items of pioneer American material culture, I have selected a fence type. Enclosing newly burned clearing was essential to protect the fields from open-range livestock, and fences were built as a normal part of the clearing process in frontier America. Medium-sized trees suitable for fencing material were spared in the burning of the clearing, cut into suitable lengths, and dragged to the edge of the field. There they were usually split into "rails," using wedges and employing the blunt side of the ax as a mallet. Sometimes, unsplit poles from small trees were used for such fencing.

The favored and almost universal style for backwoods American field enclosures made from these rails or poles was the zigzag or "worm" fence, usually about one meter high (figure 9).

No posts were required, since the fence gained its stability from the tripod principle. To add strength, many pioneers placed two diagonal stakes at each joint, set against the ground at an angle, leaning against the top rail of the fence, and crisscrossed in an X shape. Then an additional rail or two were placed atop the crossed stakes to lock the joint. A crude livestock pen was also built by American pioneers using the same basic principle. Instead of zigzagging at each joint, the rails or logs were laid to form an arc, making a polygonal enclosure (figure 10). Such log pens can still be seen today on ranches in different parts of the Rocky Mountains, an area that remains rich in American pioneer material culture.

The earliest reference to zigzag rail fencing in America is from 1680, in a Finnish settlement on the Delaware River called Finns Point. Indeed, all American pioneer fences have precise Finnic prototypes (figure 11). The rail fence, in both zig-

FIGURE 10
American polygonal livestock corrals of the Finnic type in the Rocky Mountains of Montana. Photograph by author, 1987.

zag and polygonal configuration, both with and without the X-shaped supports, exists in northern Europe. A field survey of traditional fence types undertaken by Nordiska museet staff in Sweden earlier in this century yielded a respondent from a Finnish parish in Värmland who recalled that zigzag enclosures were formerly used there in cases where the fence was frequently relocated, as in shifting cultivation and snow baffles. The respondent's sketch leaves no doubt that a zigzag fence was being described. In Dalarna, fences consisting of a zigzag of fallen tree trunks were even called *Finngärds* (Levander 1943, 342). The ultimate origin of the zigzag fence and polygonal pen is apparently to be found among the Lapps or Sami, a people for centuries in frequent contact with the kindred forest Finns. The Lapps used the zigzag log fence to direct game during hunts, and they still today build polygonal corrals for their reindeer. Angled support stakes, on the other hand, appear to be

of Savo-Karelian origin. Put briefly, every type of American pioneer fence is abundantly present in the Finnic tradition of northern Europe.

I have presented five features of material culture as evidence of a northern European contribution, by way of the New Sweden colony, to American frontier life. These five artifacts—the Värmland V-notch; the Karelian weighted board roof; the open-passage dog-trot house plan; the hunter's shanty; and the zigzag fence—may be regarded as diagnostic, since they occur only in northern Europe and on the American frontier. One must, viewing the evidence, either accept the notion of influence by way of New Sweden or else postulate a most unlikely complex of independent inventions.

We did not limit the study to material culture and landscape of the American frontier. Instead, we also considered the entire colonization system—methods of clearing land, burning the field, planting, tilling, and harvesting. I stud-

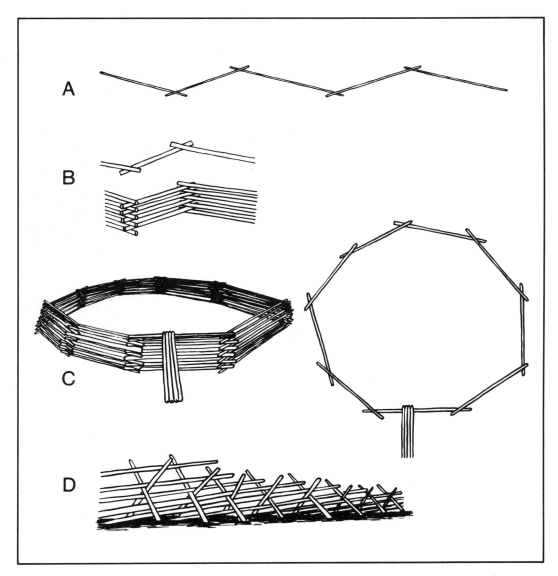

FIGURE 11

Finnic fences in northern Europe. Key: A = Gräsmark area, Finnskogen, Värmland; B = zigzag fence, Sweden; C = Inari area, Finnish Lappland; D = Savolax. All these types appeared on the Anglo-American frontier. Source: Jordan and Kaups (1989, 112) and Nordiska museet archives, Stockholm.

ied livestock herding, rural settlement morphology, hunting, gathering, and fishing (Jordan and Kaups 1989, Chaps. 5, 8). Space restrictions do not permit me to address these here, but all revealed a contribution from the forest Finns of the New Sweden colony, combined with borrowings from the Indians who lived along the Delaware River. By 1670 at the latest, the American frontier colonization culture was already intact in the area of New Sweden, long before the major influx of English, Celtic, and German settlers.

SEEKING EXPLANATION

The weakness of the Berkeley tradition of land-scape and diffusion study is that, while it documents a movement of people, artifacts, and ideas, it remains essentially *nonexplanatory*. Diffusion explains nothing in the causal sense. Even Torsten Hägerstrand's models of diffusion do not deal with cause. We can prove that people and items of culture moved from point A to point B—in this case from interior Sweden to the Delaware in America—but we cannot, using this methodology of landscape and diffusion, explain *why* certain artifacts should have survived the transplanting and been accepted by a pioneer population at large, most of which had British ancestry. Nor can we explain why only *some* items of northern European material culture took root in America while others did not. The traditional Berkeley method permits us to describe a *procession* but not to understand a *process*.

At most, some 500 people lived in the New Sweden colony at the time of the Dutch takeover in 1655. A quite inconsequential amount of land, some 36 hectares, had been cleared of forest and put under cultivation by 1653, only two years before the end of Swedish rule (figure 12). How could a handful of Finns working such a tiny amount of land have possibly exerted any wider influence? The analysis of the cultural landscape study tells us they did, but it fails to explain why.

That missing explanatory power can be found in another methodology belonging in the Berkeley tradition of human geography, namely *cultural ecology*. Practitioners of this methodology view culture as an adaptive system, as the uniquely human method of meeting physical environmental challenges (Denevan 1983). Viewed from this perspective, the European immigrants entering colonial North America introduced adaptive strategies that were immediately tested by the new physical environment. This leads naturally to the concept of *preadaptation,* involving trait complexes possessed in advance of migration which give its bearers a competitive advantage in the new setting (Newton 1974; Jordan 1989b). In other words, some European regional cultures were better suited for colonization in forested

North America than were others. One key to successful preadaptation was a diversified adaptive strategy; that is, cultures which contained a large repertoire of techniques and whose practitioners were individualistic and always open to new ideas. Such cultures usually characterize difficult or marginal environments, such as the Celtic highlands, northern boreal forests, and subhumid zones. Less suitable as pioneers would be practitioners of more stabilized and specialized adaptive strategies, typical of fruitful lands. An example would be Germanic farmers, tied to their rigid three-field system, almost wholly dependent upon farming, and quite conservative when confronted with new ideas. Indeed, mother Europe presented a core/periphery pattern, in which the Germanic core was characterized by stabilizing selection and the multi-ethnic peripheries exhibited diversified adaptive strategies (figure 13).

I might add that cultural ecologists, unlike most students of landscape and diffusion, place great importance upon the individual person. Adaptive strategies, particularly diversified ones, are the products of continual experimentation by innovative individuals. An idea held initially by only one person can spread quickly to a population at large if it offers adaptive advantage. Such spread is most rapid in diversified adaptive systems, where environmental stress is common.

More specifically, preadaptation in this particular case implies that the people in question possessed in Europe prior to migration to America an adaptive strategy suited to the agricultural colonization of heavily wooded country, a strategy that minimized labor, risk, and dependence upon outside contacts and assistance. Again, Germanic peoples such as the English, Dutch, and Germans, whose era of forest colonization lay far in the past, possessed no such strategy, nor did the Ulster Scots or Welsh, whose homelands stood largely denuded of forests in the seventeenth century. In effect, the large majority of immigrants arriving in colonial North America were poorly preadapted for settling the forests. Indeed, many of them perished or depended for decades upon supplies from Europe. They made good secondary settlers but poor pioneers.

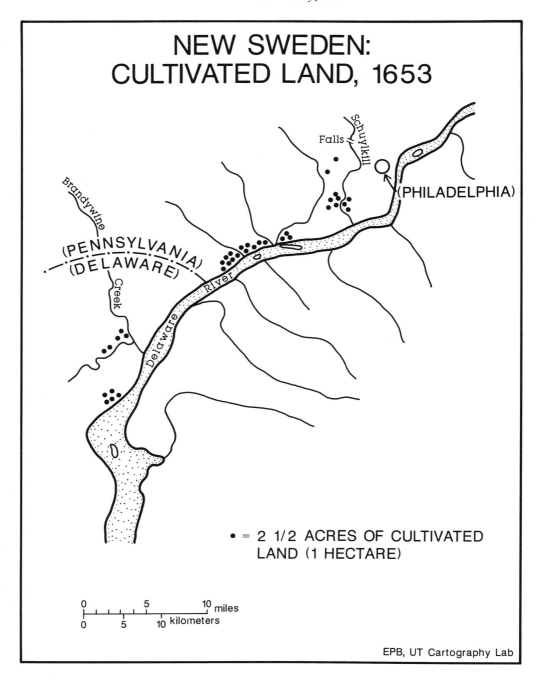

FIGURE 12
Source: Report of Governor Johan Printz, as cited in Jordan and Kaups (1989, 97).

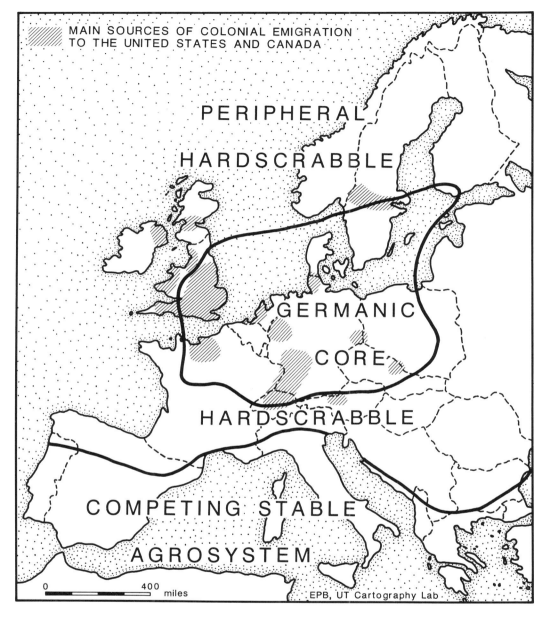

MAIN SOURCES OF COLONIAL EMIGRATION
TO THE UNITED STATES AND CANADA

PERIPHERAL

HARDSCRABBLE

GERMANIC

CORE

HARDSCRABBLE

COMPETING STABLE

AGROSYSTEM

0   400 miles

EPB, UT Cartography Lab

FIGURE 13

Cultural-ecological zones of rural Europe, 1650. The Germanic core, characterized by stabilizing selection and specialized adaptive strategies, stands in contrast to the hardscrabble periphery, where groups such as the Celts, Finns, and Alpine folk practiced highly diversified adaptive strategies. Source: Jordan and Kaups (1989, 34).

In sum, cultural ecology instructs us to look for the origins of the American forest colonization system among peoples possessing diversified adaptive strategies and recent experience in the agricultural settlement of forested lands. It also tells us that such people need not have been numerous. This logic yields only two possible candidates: the forest Finns of New Sweden and their American Indian neighbors.

The Finns had practiced a highly successful system of agricultural forest colonization for several centuries prior to the founding of New Sweden (Montelius 1960; Soininen 1959). Based upon the cultivation of grain in burned clearings, upon the steel ax, crude notched log construction, hunting, fishing, gathering, and mobility, it had permitted their rapid expansion from the Lake Ladoga region through the Finnish provinces of Karelia, Savolax, and Tavastland (figure 14). It had allowed them to vault across the Gulf of Bothnia and take root in the forested morainal interfluves of interior Sweden, where their abundant ethnic traces remain upon the land even today. And, I would add, this same remarkable adaptive system further permitted them to reach the Delaware, where they became the only successful agricultural pioneers of New Sweden and passed their skills first to their Swedish neighbors and ultimately to an entire American frontier population. They arrived as the first agricultural pioneers on the Delaware, and later immigrants copied their methods. Almost immediately upon arrival in New Sweden, the Finns enhanced their adaptive fitness by accepting from the local Delaware Indians certain strategies suited to the mesothermal forests of eastern America. For example, they abandoned their traditional bread grain, a quick-ripening variety of rye, to accept Indian maize. This cultural exchange was facilitated by the fact that the Finns and Indians were very much alike, coming as they did from opposite ends of the same circumpolar belt of boreal forest peoples. Indeed, the Indians recognized this similarity and called the settlers of New Sweden "those men who are like us," while referring to the British and Dutch as "those who are *not* like us." (Acrelius 1874, 55; Holm 1834, 100, 146; Lindeström 1925, 223), Quickly formed, the mixed Fenno-Indian adaptive strategy offered, first, a

method for restructuring the forested environment for agricultural use rapidly and at a minimal expenditure of labor; second, techniques for producing food, shelter, and clothing that were both labor-efficient and, due to their diversity, accompanied by little risk of failure; and third, a self-sufficient socioeconomic structure that could function in the virtual absence of central places. In short, the Fenno-Indian strategy accomplished the goals of forest colonization with the least possible effort, risk, and outside help. New Sweden, for this reason, easily survived a period of some years during which no supply ships came from Europe.

Let me now return briefly to the five artifacts I discussed earlier, in order to illustrate their adaptive advantages. It was precisely these advantages that caused them to survive in America and to diffuse beyond the New Sweden population. First, let us consider the V-notch. This notch is representative of a crude type of notched log construction which uses the most abundant local building material in a minimally processed form. Such carpentry could be accomplished quickly with only an ax and saw, required no hardware, and allowed the pioneer to be free of dependence upon sawmills, brick kilns, and nail factories. The log walls not only provided the weight-bearing frame of the structure, but also formed the outer and inner walls, insulation, and roof support. If only an ax is being used to form the notch, as was normal on the frontier, then the V-notch is the easiest and most labor-efficient type to make. With a minimal number of ax blows, a skilled folk carpenter can form the basic V-notch.

The Karelian board roof, resting upon beams running from gable to gable and held down by weight poles and spacers, offered several adaptive advantages. It was far easier to construct than a Germanic raftered roof and required no nails or pegs to hold the boards in place, as would have been true of shingles; it could be easily repaired, and utilized an abundant raw material in minimally processed form.

The small, simple floor plans of Finnish log structures had the advantage of being interchangeable in function, minimizing the number of buildings that had to be built. The open-

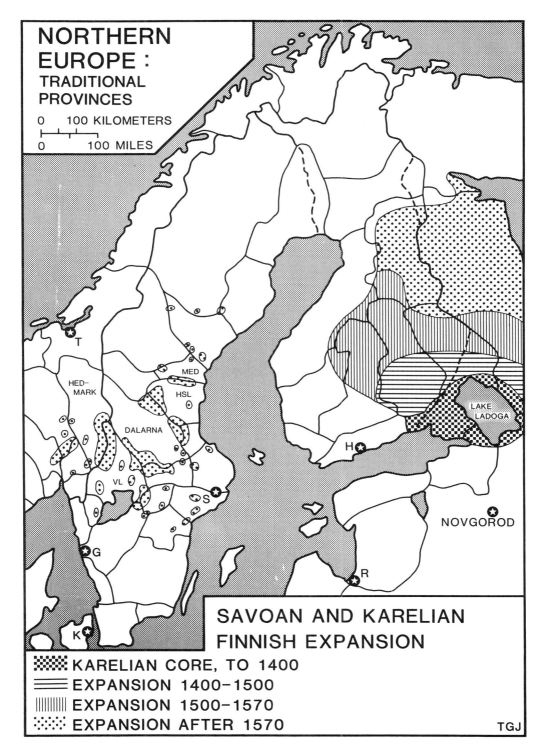

FIGURE 14

The expansion was based upon agricultural colonization of woodlands. Source: Jordan and Kaups (1989, 44).

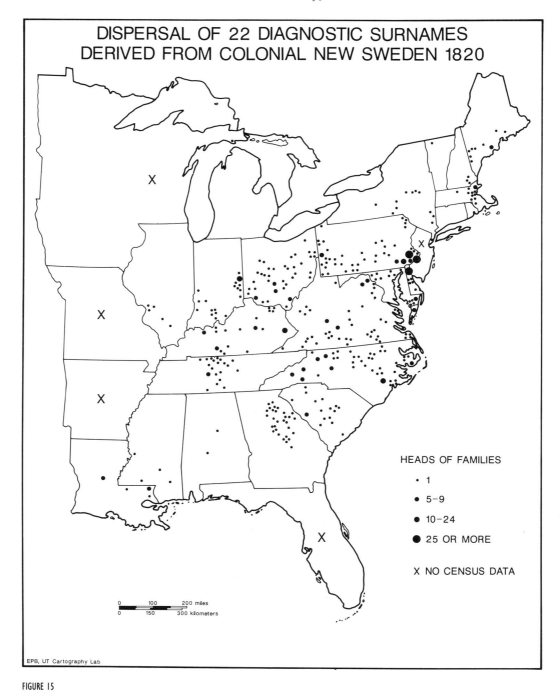

FIGURE 15

Each surname remained unique to the New Sweden descendants at least as late as 1820. The surnames, most corrupted, are Bankston/Pinkston, Bartleson, Clemson, Dalbo, Derrickson, Holston, Justice/Eustace, Longacre, Lykins, Mecum, Mink, Mullica, Oldson, Rambo, Seneker, Stallcup, Steelman, Sturkon, Swanson, Tussey, Vanneman, and Walraven. Source: Jordan and Kaups (1989, 238, 240).

FIGURE 16

These toponyms, such as Lycans Ridge or Justus Gap, usually commemorate an early settler, suggesting the importance of New Sweden descendants as pioneers. The bold dashed lines enclose the Midland culture area, where Pennsylvanian-derived influences are strongest, and the lighter dashed line encloses a concentration of New Sweden–derived toponyms.

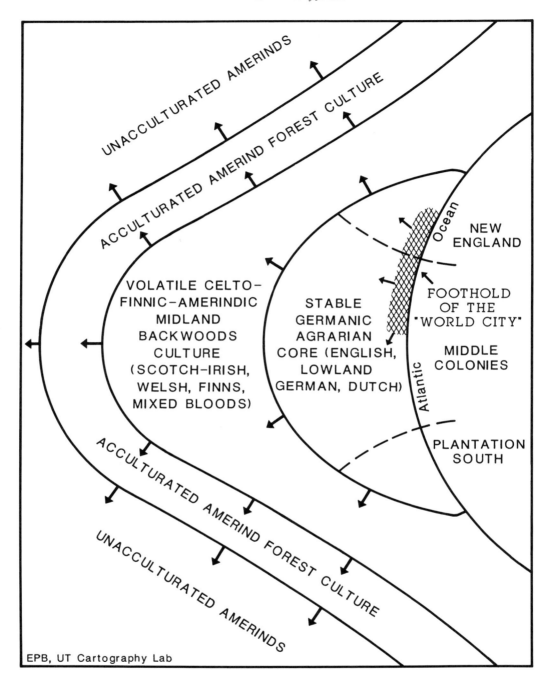

FIGURE 17

A model of the forested American agricultural frontier. Germanic stabilizing selection eventually displaced the Finnish-influenced diversified frontier adaptive strategy. The "World City" represents the greater Thünenian market. Source: Jordan and Kaups (1989, 37).

passage dog-trot house, which could be demoted to the status of a double-crib barn, represented the simplest and most labor-efficient way to enlarge from a one-room size. It made splicing of logs in the walls unnecessary and allowed the use of a crude inclined plane to raise logs into place in the upper wall.

The hunter's shanty introduced by the Finns also enjoyed adaptive advantages in America. It was easily constructed in a matter of hours and, more importantly, benefited from the principle known to physicists as the "heat-reflector oven," in which the campfire's warmth is reflected downward from the underside of the single-pitch roof and trapped, maximizing heat retention. This natural heating efficiency lent it an ecological superiority on the winter hunt.

The adaptive advantages of the zigzag fence, which explained its popularity on the frontier, were several. It was made of an abundant raw material; required no mortising, hardware, or post holes; and could be erected quickly and cheaply with a minimal expenditure of labor in comparison to other fence types. No gates were needed, since the field was entered by pulling down a joint of the fence. The rails could easily be disassembled and taken to a new clearing when a field was abandoned. Following a harvest, the zigzag fence could be thrown down in several places to allow livestock to forage on straw, husks, and weeds.

It is also significant that no aspect of Finnish culture that lacked some adaptive value survived along the Delaware. The Finnish language, the sauna, Lutheranism, and folklore all perished within several generations and made no mark upon the American frontier. In these matters, the culture of the British majority prevailed. New Sweden's shaping role was confined to artifacts and practices that related to survival in the forested wilderness.

I might add that the whole process by which New Sweden's pioneer culture became the American frontier adaptive strategy was assisted by a rapid rate of intermarriage between the northern European settlers and later immigrants. In addition, the descendants of the New Sweden colonists did not remain in an ethnic enclave along the Delaware, but instead scattered with the frontier. I have identified some twenty-two American family names (such as Rambo, Justice, Lykins, and Bankston) that, as late as 1820, were uniquely derived from the New Sweden colony, and by mapping bearers of these surnames over the centuries, one can trace the genetic legacy of the colony (figure 15). They became thoroughly mixed into the American population at large, usually forgetting their northern European ancestry eventually. It is also interesting to plot the distribution of toponyms which include one of these twenty-two diagnostic family names from New Sweden, as for example Swanson Mountain or Mullica River (figure 16).

What, in the final analysis, was the legacy of New Sweden (figure 17)? I say you should seek it in the highly successful forest pioneering culture that permitted the United States to deal in manifest destiny, and to become a transcontinental nation rather than remaining a coastal state clinging to the Atlantic. The historical geographer Ellen Churchill Semple (1903, 74) discerned this true legacy of New Sweden when, commenting upon the achievement of a Mississippi River western boundary by the newly independent United States in 1783, she attributed it to "the presence in these western lands of a vigorous people who had made good their title by ax and plow and rifle, . . . a more solid claim to the debated territory than the yellow parchments of dead monarchs or living potentates." The United States expanded rapidly across the breadth of North America. That is the true geographical legacy of the forest pioneers and their preadapted Finnish teachers.

SOURCE

This article is, in effect, an abstract of Jordan's book, coauthored with Matti Kaups, entitled *The American backwoods frontier: An ethnic and ecological interpretation* (Baltimore: Johns Hopkins University Press, 1989). In a slightly different form, the article was delivered as an invited address before the Swedish National Geographers' Meeting at Linköping in 1989, sponsored by the Royal Swedish Academy of Sciences and first published in *Geografiska Annaler* 71B (1989): 71–83.

FURTHER READINGS

William M. Denevan. 1983. Adaptation, variation, and cultural geography. *Professional Geographer* 35:399–407.

Denevan draws attention to two largely unquestioned concepts in cultural geography—innovation and diffusion—arguing that neither really explains why innovations are adopted. Denevan maintains that the idea of adaptation, or strategy for survival, may have some explanatory power in this context. The mechanisms of adaptation are variation and selection in specific environments, and both can be studied effectively by cultural geographers. Jordan's paper is an attempt to use these ideas about the adaptation process to explain the diffusion of material culture.

Robert F. Ensminger. 1992. *The Pennsylvania barn: Its origins, evolution, and distribution in North America.* Baltimore: Johns Hopkins University Press.

The forebay bank (Pennsylvania) barn is one of the most important agricultural buildings brought to America from Europe. Ensminger provides a comprehensive study of this building type as developed from Swiss prototypes. Ensminger follows the evolution of the design in North America and traces the spread of the design from coast to coast.

Henry Glassie. 1968. *Pattern in the material folk culture of the eastern United States.* Philadelphia: University of Pennsylvania Press.

This frequently cited work examines the broad patterns of folk culture in the East based on the evidence of architecture, tools, cookery, boats, and many other forms of material culture. Glassie effectively integrates the insights of human geography and folklore studies.

R. Cole Harris. 1977. The simplification of Europe overseas. *Annals of the Association of American Geographers* 67: 469–83.

Harris, like Jordan, considers the ways in which emigrants from northwestern Europe sustained their cultural values in overseas territories. Harris makes the point that, in certain circumstances, the settlers gave up much of their cultural inheritance through a process of simplification and generalization of the social, economic, political, and cultural values they had known in Europe.

Stephen C. Jett and Virginia E. Spencer. 1981. *Navajo architecture: Forms, history, distributions.* Tucson: University of Arizona Press.

The authors survey the major types of Navajo architecture, paying particular attention to the description and history of the Navajo dwelling, the hogan. This is perhaps the most systematic and comprehensive survey of Navajo architectural forms and goes far to explain the adaptive significance of these forms through time.

Terry G. Jordan and Matti Kaups. 1989. *The American backwoods frontier: An ethnic and ecological interpretation.* Baltimore: Johns Hopkins University Press.

This book is the fully developed thesis Jordan has abstracted in his article for this volume. Through a comprehensive cultural and ecological analysis, Jordan and Kaups credit the seventeenth-century Delaware Valley Finns, in conjunction with their Indian neighbors, with providing frontier culture the essential know-how needed to foster its rapid colonization of the forested regions of North America. This work is notable for its application of ecological concepts to an important issue in historical geography.

Milton B. Newton. 1974. Cultural preadaptation and the upland South. In *Man and cultural heritage,* ed. H. J. Walker and W. G. Haag, 143–54. Geoscience and Man 5. Baton Rouge: Louisiana State University, Department of Geography and Anthropology.

In this article, Newton presents his thesis that certain traits carried to new environments by migrants—preadaptations—provided certain groups with a competitive advantage in occupying new lands. Furthermore, Newton maintains that the character of American frontier settlement arose to a great extent from assemblages of preadaptive traits common to the syncretic culture of the upland South.

Peter O. Wacker. 1975. *Land and people: A cultural geography of preindustrial New Jersey origins and settlement patterns.* New Brunswick, N.J.: Rutgers University Press.

Wacker's objective is to comprehend how Europeans transformed New Jersey's natural and aboriginal landscapes during the Colonial and post-Colonial periods. Wacker maintains that New Jersey was, before 1800, perhaps the most culturally heterogenous colony. To explain this diversity, Wacker places the transformation of New Jersey's landscapes in the context of the historical cultural geography of both the Atlantic seaboard and the trans-Atlantic diffusion of Old World cultural traits following the voyages of discovery and exploration.

BERNARD NIETSCHMANN

16

ECOLOGICAL CHANGE, INFLATION, AND MIGRATION IN THE FAR WESTERN CARIBBEAN

Along the western edge of the Caribbean, where the sea and land meet, stretches a low mainland shore that was once isolated by tropical forest and savanna and miles of open water (figure 1). Culturally and economically the eastern coast of Central America has long been an integral, yet distinct, part of the Caribbean.[1] In many ways this area is an island, separated culturally and physically from inland Hispanic and Mestizo lifeways. Indigenous coastal peoples had strong adaptations to the sea and to its resources. The years of European contact, trade, and colonization introduced many of the same economic and cultural patterns that earlier had transformed islands to the east. Formerly a back eddy to the economic mainstream that inundated the West Indies, the indigenous peoples of the west Caribbean coast are now firmly caught up in the commercial gulf streams and countercurrents that siphon local resources and labor to produce market items for the north in exchange for manufactured goods and cash. Soaring prices for imported goods, severe declines in local natural resources, endangered species legislation, growing populations, and large-scale migration from villages to distant towns and cities have all worked to mesh once-isolated indigenous peoples with global currents. Distant decisions, economic inflation of market goods, new information and aspirations, and out-migration have overwhelmed culturally insulat-

FIGURE 1
The Western Caribbean. Map by Adrienne Morgan.

ing factors of distance and isolation. Economic dependency and commercialized exchanges have transformed isolation into proximity. All things are near and dear. The indigenous peoples of the far western Caribbean no longer inhabit a cultural island. As Edna St. Vincent Millay once lamented, "There *are* no islands anymore."

In this paper I examine the ecological, economic, and social factors that are influencing the

Miskito Indians—the most numerous and extensive Amerindian group inhabiting the Central American Caribbean lowlands—and their terrestrial and marine environments. My research with these people and in this area has yielded comparable information that spans a long time period, beginning in 1968 and continuing to the present. The bulk of the research was done during sixteen months in 1968–69, with several shorter field trips in 1971, 1972, 1975, and 1976. During the intervening periods, Miskito correspondents provided descriptions of changing economic conditions and the comings and goings of villagers looking for work and sources of income; they also filled out questionnaires that I mailed to them from time to time, giving prices for store goods, local wage labor, and resources, the most recent of which are for March 1978. Material accumulated over this ten-year span allows me to see more distinctly the trends, processes, and relationships that are both cause and consequence of the Miskito's entry into an ecological blind alley: becoming economically dependent on endangered species and declining resources.

One-time village and regional studies allow little perspective on the processes of socioeconomic or ecological change. Without time depth, studies of the "ethnographic present" and "ecologic present" may provide valuable empirical and theoretical information, but they cannot clearly distinguish perturbation from continuing process, nor the course and impact of internal and external pressures for change and resulting adaptations. By concentrating on one point in time, many ahistorical studies describe human adaptation and ecological relationships as if they were static. Yet all societies and environments change reciprocally and mirror each other. The massive impacts of complex urban societies on less-complex traditional societies and their environments have largely transcended the gradual process of human adaptation to local environments (C. Bennett 1968; D. Harris 1965; Parsons 1955; Sauer 1966; J. Westermann 1952; 1953). Cultural and environmental survival are now significantly affected by the nature, speed, and intensity of changes generated by outside systems that influence local systems. To persist and endure, traditional societies must now adapt more to external systems than to local conditions.

Increasing outside pressure on local systems has meant the collapsing of the time intervals necessary for measuring or estimating the transformation of traditional societies and their environments. Even though they may be useful and enlightening, studies done in one area over a long period press hard upon an investigator's time and resources. Understandably, other interests evolve and are followed. Yet to know a place and people intimately requires frequent travels down the same trail. I suppose it's a matter of personal predilection and intellectual return whether to widen trails or to blaze them.

Perhaps this highly condensed presentation of long-term but intermittent research will have more than local significance. Despite differences in cultural and natural histories, the interrelationships between a changing resource base, economic dependency and inflation, and migration are structurally similar to conditions in many other areas of the Caribbean (Davidson 1974; Frucht 1968; Gonzalez 1969; Helms and Loveland 1976; Lowenthal 1957; Lowenthal and Comitas 1962; Parsons 1956; B. Richardson 1975).

ECONOMIC HISTORY: THE COURSE OF EVENTS

Miskito culture and economic history and environment have been described in detail elsewhere, so I present only a sketch here (B. Nietschmann 1973; 1974; 1977; 1979a; see also Helms 1971; T. Floyd 1967). The coastal Miskito of eastern Nicaragua exploited a diverse land-and-water environment composed of many closely spaced microenvironments that provided a reasonably secure and dependable means of subsistence. Tropical rain forest, palm and mangrove swamps, rivers, creeks, lagoons, estuaries, inshore coastal and offshore continental shelf waters were rich in diverse and numerous biota. Miskito subsistence was adapted to maximum returns with minimal ecological disruptions through rotation of fishing and hunting depending on species, site, and season. Swidden agriculture provided a large caloric backstop that allowed the Miskito the leisure to hunt and fish. Pressure on environmental resources was limited by the Miskito's small populations, by intermittent exploitation that ceased when they secured enough to eat, and by seasonal environmental fluctuations that periodically condensed and spread faunal resources. Traditional Miskito livelihood was one of "want not, lack not" abundance. That way of life has passed.

Miskito involvement with foreign markets has gone through a repeated sequence of boom-

and-bust periods, each one leaving a cumulative impact on Miskito society and environment. In the early seventeenth century, English and French buccaneers began trading with the Miskito and often took a Miskito aboard to harpoon turtles, manatees, and fish for the crew during long voyages (Dampier 1968, 15–16). Later, traders came to the Miskito Coast for tropical lumber, dyewoods, spices, medicinal herbs, animal skins, hawksbill shell, and green turtle and manatee meat. In exchange the Miskito received cloth, tools, cooking pots, beads, muskets and gunpowder, and rum. Resources became a means for securing trade goods. The British wanted the resources and the Miskito desired the trade goods, and a long economic relationship developed between the two. In his *History of Jamaica* Edward Long wrote an extensive account of the Miskito Coast and its economic potential and the Miskito's participation in providing valuable resources.

> Nothing then seems more expedient than to give these qualities a direction into walks of industry . . . . The better to attract these Indians to such objects, it is necessary to open a market, where their crops might find a ready price, and yield a quick return. None lies more convenient for them than Jamaica. . . . It is probable, there would be little difficulty in effecting this; for already they aspire to live and cloath [*sic*] themselves in the English manners: and, in order to obtain many things which are necessary to their convenience and comfort, they work at different occupations; some in cutting wood for exportation; others in turtle, fishery, or hunting; and many in land traffic. The plain result of this is, that they perfectly well understand some pains must be taken before they can be supplied with such necessaries as they covet or want. (Long 1774, 318–19)

British trading stations, run mainly by Jamaican agents, were established along the coast. Records from one station show that in 1780 resource exports included three million feet of mahogany, four tons of hawksbill shell, and 120,000 pounds of sarsaparilla root (Stout 1859, 255). By the late eighteenth century the Miskito had come to rely heavily on British trade goods, and their subsistence skills made them expert in securing trade resources from the forest and sea.

Starting in the nineteenth century and continuing off and on into the twentieth century, foreign companies on the Miskito Coast intensified resource exploitation and the Miskito's involvement with the market. Lumbering, rubber collecting, gold mines, and banana plantations attracted Miskito wage laborers, many of whom signed one-year work contracts (figure 2). The *mani uplika,* or one-year men, left the villages in large numbers, creating a labor vacuum in subsistence activities. Women, children, and old people worked the swiddens and fished and collected and waited for the men to return with goods from the company commissaries. Older Miskito today remember the company period as the good times, when there was much work and inexpensive goods were abundant. But the mahogany, cedar, and pine were logged out, gold mines declined in production, and Sigatoka and Panama diseases forced the Standard Fruit and Steamship Company and the United Fruit Company to abandon their plantations. By the late 1930s the economic heyday was over, the big companies were gone, and the Miskito were left with the residue of economic wants and price-tagged labor and resources. Small companies and short-term operations continued into the 1960s, providing little but the dimmed image of what was once a golden era for the Miskito.

During the bust periods and in the wake of the passing economic tides the Miskito were supported by a still-viable subsistence system and by abundant faunal resources (figure 3). They exchanged green turtles for goods and money with Cayman Islanders who made annual voyages to the Miskito Coast from the 1840s until the late 1960s (Carr 1956; Hirst 1910; B. Lewis 1940; Matthiessen 1967). The goods and money dampened the economic droughts.

During the 1960s, small numbers of Miskito, primarily males, temporarily left their villages to seek wage-paying work. Towns were few and distant on the Miskito Coast, as were employment opportunities. Bluefields (present-day population of 18,000) and Puerto Cabezas (7,000) had sawmills and nearby lumber-cutting operations.

FIGURE 2
Miskito and other workers at the entrance of a vein mine shaft, Pis Pis gold mining district (Bonanza), about 1900. Source: Moravian Church, Casa Alemán, postcard series.

FIGURE 3

Green turtles in a canoe shed, Tasbapauni, 1968. Harpooned on nearby ten-fathom-deep seagrass pastures, these turtles were taken by six men in one afternoon. Kept alive until needed with daily dousings of salt water, they provided abundant meat for the village for a week.

Two large shrimp-processing companies—one at El Bluff, the deepwater port facility on the seaward side of Bluefields Lagoon, and another at Schooner Cay, the old United Fruit Company headquarters, just up the Río Escondido from Bluefields—sometimes had available work on boats or in the packing plants. Corn Island (population 2,000), located about forty-five miles east of Bluefields, had a then-emerging lobster fishery and several copra producers. The largest copra plantation was at Cocal, located twenty-five miles north of San Juan del Norte (Greytown). The old mining district of Siuna, Bonanza, and Rosita, situated in the mountains about 100 miles west of Puerto Cabezas, still produced limited quantities of gold and other metals. It was to these areas that some Miskito traveled to look for work. Very few Miskito went to Managua, the nation's capital (population 400,000), because of their low social and economic status among the dominant Spanish-speaking population. For most Miskito, a trip to western Nicaragua ("the interior") was a journey to a foreign country. Rather than face the potential social hazards of venturing to a place and among people they did not know, or having to travel from company to company on the east coast looking for work, the majority of Miskito preferred to remain in their home villages despite the depressed economic conditions. For the time being, a known social world and abundant subsistence resources were more desirable than the speculative economic world that had retreated from their shores.

In 1968, when I first went to the Miskito Coast, it was at the bottom of a long economic depression. Subsistence activities supplied most of the villagers' food, and the sale of coconuts, rice, a few turtles, and animal skins provided most of the cash for market goods. The Miskito felt poor. Subsistence food was plentiful but money was scarce. Traditional patterns of reciprocal food-and-labor exchanges were still followed. The Miskito bought some food from small village stores. Wages were paid to people for the construction of seagoing canoes and to help with cash crops (coconuts and rice).

In 1969 the first of three turtle-processing companies began operations on the coast. The Miskito were the world's best turtle hunters, and the last large green turtle population in the western Caribbean inhabited the nearby shallow waters off eastern Nicaragua. The new companies provided a year-round connective link between local supply and distant demand. The Miskito started to sell large numbers of green turtles to the companies that exported the meat, oil, and calipee[2] to foreign countries. Whereas they were once the central focus of the Miskito's subsistence system, green turtles now became the primary means to secure money to purchase, and the only surviving green turtle refuge came under severe exploitation pressure. From 1969 through 1976, up to 10,000 green turtles were exported every year (figure 4). Already depleted by Cayman Is-

land turtlers on the feeding ground at Miskito Bank and by Costa Ricans on the nesting beach at Tortuguero, the most significant west Caribbean green turtle population was subjected to a sudden and intensive rise in human predation. The resulting reduction of the population soon became evident. The average amount of time it took to capture one turtle went up from two person-days in 1971 to six person-days in 1975. Even though hunting was less efficient, more turtles were taken from the depleted herds because more Miskito were hunting and were doing so almost year-round.[3] Furthermore, tags placed on nesting turtles at Tortuguero to study migration and life cycle patterns began to be returned from Nicaraguan waters in unprecedented numbers, indicating a massive upward change in the scale of exploitation.[4]

The investment philosophy for many foreign-owned companies, such as the turtle factories, is quick return on low investment and overhead and reinvestment elsewhere when the market

FIGURE 4

Green turtles from the Miskito Cays at the "Frescamar" turtle company, Bluefields, 1972. This is part of a 300-turtle shipment received in one day.

or resource fails. The turtle companies, for example, were fully aware that the chelonian population would be decimated through intensive commercial exploitation. No matter, a healthy return would be realized on investment and the resultant ecological "costs" would be borne by others.

The Miskito became locked into a positive feedback system in which further economic intensification created the need for continued intensification: (1) the companies extended credit and supplies to the Miskito so that they could catch turtle year-round rather than seasonally as they had in the past; (2) turtles had to be caught to pay back the credit extended; (3) income had to be secured to purchase food and materials for families in the villages because many subsistence activities could not be maintained when so much of the labor force was engaged in turtling and other cash-yielding activities; (4) as the turtle population declined greater efforts had to be made to capture enough to maintain a cash flow; (5) with so many turtles being sold, less meat was available for reciprocal kin-based exchanges, resulting in social friction; and (6) rather than incur the wrath of villagers by not having enough to exchange or even to sell, many turtlemen decided to sell all turtles to the company to avoid running the social gauntlet at home. The best traditional turtlemen in the world could not get enough turtle to eat.

Whether the resource was green turtles, hawksbill shell, shrimp, lobster, spotted cats, caimans, crocodiles, or river otters, the Miskito entered the same economic and ecological cul-de-sac as had many other peoples in the Caribbean area. Declining faunal resources could not provide enough income to close the gap between subsistence shortfall and purchased needs. Once the subsistence sector becomes monetized, societies lose the stabilizing buffer that permits self-sufficiency and autonomy during downswings in national and international markets. And once local resources become valuable and scarce and goods from the outside become necessities, conflicts between social responsibilities and family needs will surely result. The response is further market intensification rather than subsistence regulation.

Traditional societies do not rush headlong down the monetized road to embrace modernity. But to maintain what is traditional—those things that have social rather than economic value—requires an expenditure in kind, and that expenditure is the piecemeal loss of subsistence flexibility in order to gain economic viability. To remain independent one becomes dependent; to remain economically autonomous one becomes an economic satellite.

THE TRANSITION FROM SUBSISTENCE TO MARKET

In traditional Miskito society, all economic transactions took place within a social context; the society and the economy were one and the same. The only commensurability involved in economic exchanges was social value and status. With the introduction of wage-labor arrangements and resource markets, the Miskito learned a new commensurability, the lowest common denominator of money. An economic involution took place as cash-based exchanges colonized socially based exchanges in the villages. Economic disparity created social disparity (figure 5). Without the circulation of freely exchanged labor and resources, many traditional kinship responsibilities could no longer be maintained. Changes in the rules of production created changes in the means of distribution.

During the years in which I have studied changing conditions in Miskito society and economy and the transition from subsistence to market activities, several general trends and structural relationships have emerged. First, in the shift from production for use to production for sale, diversity and flexibility are initially lost as "rotation subsistence systems" are converted into specialized resource procurement systems. Resources with a market value are diverted from local societies and ecosystems to extraneous human populations, which creates problems of overexploitation, disruption of subsistence timing and variety, and loss of subsistence flexibility. Second, when a society based on generalized reciprocity (free exchange of labor, food, and material between kin) becomes dependent on the sale of labor, food, and materials to external markets, the internal means of production will be colonized by those of the external.

Third, as traditional societies become depen-

FIGURE 5
Traditional (top) and modern (bottom) house types in a Miskito village reflect disproportionate family incomes in what was an egalitarian society. Photographs by Judith Nietschmann.

dent on external markets they lose self-sufficiency and autonomy and become entangled in a long chain of variables over which they have little or no control. Regulation of local systems becomes governed by distant economic and political decisions and conditions. Hypercoherence results with the collapse of buffers as systems are simplified and placed in economic proximity. Changes in any of the remote market variables may send oscillations through the entire chain: "sympathetic" economic vibrations result. Decisions made by the Organization of Petroleum Exporting Countries may determine whether a Miskito can afford to light a lantern.

Fourth, in traditional subsistence, risk of failure is dampened by access to a wide range of plants and animals and by generalized sharing of the yields between kin. Differential procurement is common, but differential receipt is rare. With involvement in market activities, in specialized exploitation of a narrow range of resources, and purchase of foods and materials, economic risk is added to subsistence risk and magnified through the individualization of production efforts. Individual households have to secure resources, income, and food and shoulder the risk of possible shortfall.

Fifth, in an increasingly monetized society, differential returns from resources become more prevalent. Alterations in the focus of production and the individualization of production units create economic differences between individuals and households. The more productive individuals in the society no longer expend as much time and effort to secure a surplus to share with less productive individuals. The intensification of market activities means the diversion of labor and materials that once helped support the less able, the elderly, widows, widowers, the sick, and the injured. Economic change does not affect a village uniformly. Depending on age, sex, status, ability, and kinship distance, differential impacts result.

Finally, with the introduction of new economic rules and valuation, conflicts and distortions occur in social relationships. When labor and materials that once were exchanged between kin are channeled into market sales, social devaluation results. To sell a subsistence resource is a social contradiction. If a family produces food, they are obligated to share; if they purchase food, they are under no such social obligation; if they sell what should be shared, they bring into conflict the opposing rules in the two economic systems.

ECOLOGICAL CHANGE: ANIMAL DOMINOES

A focused surge of exploitation pressure on marine and terrestrial fauna began after the large foreign lumber and banana companies left the Miskito Coast and continued to intensify as wage-earning opportunities diminished. Already affected by increased human utilization and modification of local habitats (logging and expansion of agricultural areas, and more boat traffic on lagoons and rivers),[5] several species became even more threatened by accelerated commercial hunting (table 1). In the early 1970s human pressure on valuable species was high and those faunal populations declined rapidly.

Hunting on such a scale could not be long sustained and the waning of market species was hastened by the market itself. A circular positive feedback relationship developed: greater economic dependence led to increased commercial hunting pressure, which led to reduced faunas and higher prices, which led to increased pressure. By 1974–75, time and economic allocations in commercial hunting were providing less food than could be obtained from subsistence activities. Price inflation of purchased goods, faunal depletion, and new conservation legislation created alterations in economic relationships and strategies in Miskito communities.

The implementation of national and international faunal conservation and protection measures has led to the reduction of human exploitation of some species and an increase in pressure on others. The Endangered Species Conservation Act (1969) and the international agreement on International Trade in Endangered Species of Wild Fauna and Flora (1973) closed many distant markets for animal products from the Miskito Coast. Even though they signed the international agreement, West Germany and Japan continue to import endangered and depleted fauna from Nicaragua, and Nicaragua continues to ex-

TABLE 1
Seriously Depleted and Endangered Market Fauna, Eastern Nicaragua

Common Name	Scientific Name	Market Product
Kinkajou[a]	*Potus flavus*	skin
River otter[b]	*Lutra annectens*	skin
Ocelot[b]	*Felis pardalis*	skin
Margay[b]	*Felis wiedii*	skin
Jaguar[b]	*Panthera onca*	skin
Manatee[b]	*Trichechus manatus*	meat (local sale)
Tapir[b]	*Tapirus bairdii*	meat (local sale)
Caiman[a]	*Caiman crocodilus fuscus*	skin
Crocodile[a]	*Crocodylus acutus*	skin
Green turtle[c]	*Chelonia mydas*	meat, calipee, oil
Hawksbill turtle[b]	*Eretmochelys imbricata*	shell ("tortoise shell")

Sources: "Convention on International Trade in Endangered Species of Wild Fauna and Flora," Special Supplement to *IUCN Bulletin*, Vol. 4, No. 3, March, 1973; *Red Data book* (International Union for the Conservation of Nature, Morges, Switzerland, various editions and supplements); Bernard Nietschmann: Protecting Endangered and Depleted Fauna in Nicaragua (advisory paper written for the Nicaraguan Government, 1975).

[a] Seriously depleted species: not necessarily now threatened with extinction, but the species may become so unless present exploitation levels are reduced or stopped.

[b] Endangered species: presently threatened with extinction.

[c] Still considered a "seriously depleted species" throughout its pantropical range by the International Union for the Conservation of Nature, the green turtle, nevertheless, should be considered "endangered" in many areas of the world. Owing to recent protective legislation in Nicaragua and Costa Rica, the western Caribbean green turtle population may recover from its previously depleted status. Yet the survival outlook for this species is by no means bright. Illegal commercial exploitation still occurs in the waters off Tortuguero; and off the Nicaraguan coast and other shallow-water areas in the western Caribbean, trawlers have begun working new grounds in search of increasingly valuable shrimp. Sea turtles frequently are caught and drowned in their nets.

port them. Nevertheless, local prices for jaguar skins have fallen by 50 percent, and these animals are not hunted as often by the Miskito (part of the reduction in hunting pressure is also due to jaguar scarcity). Caiman and crocodile skins also have declined in value.

The plight of the green turtle in the western Caribbean and the waters off eastern Nicaragua led to two important conservation measures: the establishment in 1975 of a National Park at Tortuguero, Costa Rica, the main nesting beach, with complete protection for nesting turtles and those offshore; and the closing of the turtle companies operating in eastern Nicaragua in early 1977 (the Miskito were permitted to continue subsistence hunting). With the protection of the major nesting beach and the most significant green turtle colony, this species yet may be saved from what looked to be certain decimation.

To save the green turtle meant erasing the major source of income in coastal Miskito communities. Without protective legislation the turtle colony certainly would have declined in a few years to the point where commercial turtling would no longer provide a livelihood for the Miskito. Nevertheless, that their withdrawal from commercial turtle hunting occurred suddenly rather than gradually magnified the economic impact of this governmental decision on Miskito villages and households.

The loss of the green turtle market led to the acceleration of trends that were already developing in the early and mid-1970s. Influenced by resource depletion, protective legislation, and inflation, these trends reflect the adaptive reaction of Miskito communities, families, and individuals to conditions generated by outside forces. The Miskito have responded through increased migration, expansion of small-scale income-earning activities in villages, and a shift in hunting focus to fauna not covered or not fully protected by legislation.

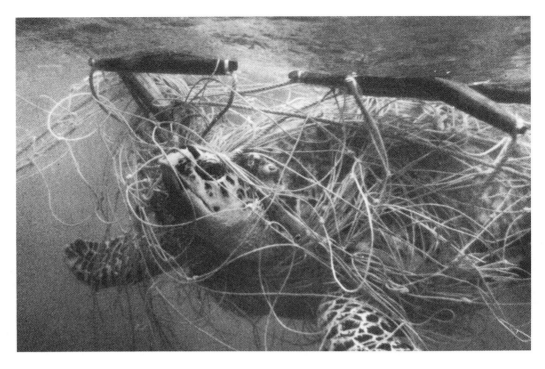

FIGURE 6

A hawksbill turtle caught in a net set over a coral reef, Miskito Cays. This endangered species is sought by the Miskito only for its shell; the meat is not eaten.

The price for hawksbill shell rose 614 percent between 1969 and 1978 to an all-time high of 150 córdobas (US$21.43) a pound.[6] Already considered the world's most endangered reptiles, the hawksbill populations of eastern Nicaragua are being heavily exploited by turtlemen and by lobster divers (figure 6). Lobster no longer can be caught in any numbers with baited pots, so the companies have shifted to using small boats and Miskito and Corn Island divers.[7] This is just one more economic boom that will certainly go bust owing to the extensiveness and thoroughness of removing lobster regardless of size—reef to reef, area to area. Because hawksbill turtles are coral reef dwellers, they are caught as the lobster divers systematically work the reefs.

River otters, kinkajous, caimans, crocodiles, and spotted cats continue to be taken for their skins. Dealers in Puerto Cabezas and Bluefields either export them directly or send them on to larger dealers in Managua (figure 7). Schools of shrimp come into the large coastal lagoons during the dry season and are taken by the Miskito and other peoples (Rama, Creole, Mestizo) with cast nets. Dried or fresh, they are sold to buyers who visit the villages in freezer-equipped boats.

In order to secure income, the Miskito have expanded some activities. Rice and coconuts are grown in larger amounts, copra and coconut oil made, and pigs and chickens raised for market (figure 8). Any income activity that requires more labor than can be supplied by individual families necessitates hiring people to help. Communal labor is still exchanged in subsistence agriculture because portions of the harvest are still exchanged, but market agriculture requires payment in cash. With the migration of productive age Miskito from villages, less labor is available in many families for growing market crops; remittance income is used to hire those who have not left the village, thereby drawing them away from subsistence agricultural tasks. Another pos-

FIGURE 7

Spotted cat (ocelot, margay, jaguar) skins and a stuffed crocodile for sale to tourists in a Managua store. It is illegal to bring any of these items into the United States.

itive feedback cycle results, this one involving the need for income, migration of family labor, the hiring of remaining village labor, reduction in subsistence cropping, and thus the increasing need for income to buy food.

Ecological changes in Miskito environments and communities have been precipitated and intensified by outside economic conditions and by both laissez-faire and protective resource legislation. In the slipstream, Miskito economy and society adjust and adapt.

INFLATION: ECONOMIC ENTANGLEMENT

When a traditional society with only sporadic access to local marketable resources becomes steadily more dependent on outside goods subject to inflationary trends, disequilibrium results. Simply put, the Miskito are faced with a widening gap between family income and increasing costs. Despite their cloistered geographical loca-

tion, they have become citizens of the world, sharing the global problem of making ends meet. Whereas subsistence was once the means to an end, the market now threatens to end the means. As one Miskito told me, "You see what the problem is here, everyone wants to live off money. People follow the money just like ants follow the sugar. The way the place is going, everyone is moving for themselves. Everything that's money gets scarce." Access to income-producing sources is variable in occurrence and amount. Yet the need to purchase is constant and increasing.

Before the 1970s, Miskito livelihood was only partially based on monetary exchanges and purchased foods. However, greater participation in securing protein for export (turtles, shrimp, lobster, fish) in exchange for money to buy imported and increasingly expensive carbohydrates has changed the relationships between production for use and production for sale and purchase. For example, in the coastal village of

FIGURE 8

Squeezing grated coconut to extract oil. To make one gallon of oil (worth US$2.85) requires at least 40 mature nuts and eight to ten hours of work. Women often reinvest money earned from selling the oil in growing rice for market. Week-to-week earnings from women provide much of the financial family support that allows men to seek higher, but more sporadic sources of income.

Tasbapauni (figure 9), which has easy access to varied and species-rich terrestrial, freshwater, and marine environments, average household consumption of purchased foods almost tripled during a ten-year period (table 2).

In 1969, 63 percent of the average household income in Tasbapauni went to purchase food from one of the three small stores in the community. By 1975, despite increased earnings, this expenditure had risen to more than 80 percent.

Between 1969 and 1978, inflationary increases added an average of 100 percent to the price of a purchased diet and livelihood (table 3).

In an effort to generate more income internally, locally grown and obtained subsistence foods once shared freely began to be sold to kin and friends (figure 10). To be sure, reciprocal exchanges are still made by some families to close kin, but "modern ways" necessitate creation of a marketable "surplus." This is done by giving less and selling more, by obtaining more to sell, or by eating less and selling more. The net result has been the penetration of economically regulated external market transactions into the socially regulated subsistence sphere. And with the transformation of traditionally exchanged subsistence foods into purchased commodities has come internal price inflation in the villages. Between 1969 and 1978, food obtained by Tasbapauni Miskito from agriculture, hunting, and fishing, if sold, had risen an average 138 percent in price (table 4). While the average price for imported and local foods has more than doubled since 1969, the market price of externally sold items and the availability of valuable fauna have not kept up with the inflationary pace (table 5).

To offset escalating costs of wage labor (table 6) and imported goods, most families in the village of Tasbapauni began to branch out economically by 1975, involving themselves in several income-producing ventures, each of which had the likelihood of providing some cash. Taken together, the diversity of economic activities imitates the diversity the Miskito once had in their subsistence system, but with three important differences: returns are not shared, the activities are externally controlled rather than internally regulated, and food returns on time invested in market activities are less than for subsistence.

In 1975 many families were engaged simultaneously or sequentially in several activities: subsistence agriculture and gathering, market agriculture (rice and coconuts), copra and coconut oil production, pig and chicken raising, shrimping,

FIGURE 9
The village of Tasbapauni, located on a narrow "haulover" between the sea and a coastal lagoon. A little more than 1,000 people live in 180 households.

TABLE 2

Percentage of the Average Family's Diet Purchased from Stores, Tasbapauni (Population about 1,000)

Year	*Percentage of Purchased Food in Diet (by weight)*
1968	25 (estimated) or less
1969	31 (measured)
1972	65 (measured)
1975	75 (measured)
1976	75 (estimated)
1978	70 (estimated)

and subsistence and market hunting and fishing. Of the 180 households in the village of Tasbapauni, 70 percent were involved in market rice, 72 percent grew coconuts, 68 percent raised pigs for sale, 81 percent raised chickens, and 57 percent took part in the three-month-long lagoon shrimp season (J. Nietschmann 1975, 130–42).

By 1975, average family income had risen about 100 percent from 1969—from 1,575 to 3,255 córdobas (US$255 to US$465)—largely as a result of income received from the sale of rice and coconuts. Yet increased purchasing power was depleted by equivalent or greater increases in the cost of food (table 7).

In 1969 the average Tasbapauni family deficit between money received from the sale of local resources and money spent on food was about 1,250 córdobas (US$179). The difference was made up through prolonged credit from shopkeepers, credit extended from the turtle company, and occasional wage-labor jobs in the village. In 1975 the resources-sold–food-bought deficit was almost 2,400 córdobas (US$343), too much to be extended on credit or to be made up through local wage labor. Most families had similar needs for food and materials but different incomes (larger rice grounds, bigger coconut groves, more workers, more persistent hunters, economic ability to purchase expensive shotgun shells, and twine and line for making turtle nets). Nevertheless, there was only so much money to circulate and it was always less than the day-to-day need of village households. Credit, broken promises, waiting for payment on jobs done, and social friction were the by-products of a purchase system that was extended beyond its financial carrying capacity. In 1968 everyone was sharing abundant subsistence resources; by 1975 some families were only sharing promises.

Caught up in an inflationary spiral and deepening involvement with a market economy, it became more and more impossible for Miskito families to close the widening gap between resource income and maintenance expenditures.

TABLE 3

Price of Commonly Purchased Store Items, Tasbapauni, 1969–78

Item (per pound unless noted)	1969[a]	1975[a]	1978[a]	% Change
Rice	.80	1.80	1.50	88
Beans	1.00	1.60	3.00	200
Flour	.80	1.80	1.80	125
Sugar	.90	1.20	1.50	67
Coffee	4.00	5.00	8.00	100
Salt	.60	.60	.60	0
Kerosene (1 pint)	.50	.75	1.00	100
Shotgun shell (1)	2.00	5.50	6.00	200
.22 cartridge (3)	1.00	2.25	2.25	125
Nails	2.50	7.50	7.00	180
Macaroni (½ pound)	1.50	2.25	3.00	100
Baking powder (1 tin)	4.00	7.50	5.00	25
⅜-inch nylon rope (harpoon line)	17.00	25.00	36.00	111

[a]Values in córdobas; 1 córdoba = US$0.14.

FIGURE 10

Villagers crowd for the chance to buy a small portion of turtle meat from the small quantity available. Decisions on whom to sell to are determined by closeness of kinship relationship, ability to pay rather than promise to pay, and whether the person received meat from a previous butchering.

TABLE 4

Cost of Locally Produced and Obtained Food, Tasbapauni, 1969–78

Item (per pound unless noted)	1969[a]	1975[a]	1978[a]	% Change
Green turtle	.50	.75	1.00	100
White-lipped peccary	.75	1.50	2.00	167
Whitetail deer	.75	1.50	2.00	167
Manatee	.80	1.50	2.00	150
Tapir	.75	1.00	2.00	167
Beef	1.50	2.50	3.50	133
Chicken (1 live)	4.00	12.00	10.00	150
Freshwater turtle (1 medium-size, 8–12 pounds)	3.00	6.00	7.00	133
Coconuts (2)	.25	.60	.60	140
Manioc	.20	.25	.50	150
Bananas				
(1 hand)	—	.50	1.25	150
(1 bunch)	—	8.00	12.00	50

[a]Values in córdobas; 1 córdoba = US$0.14.

TABLE 5
Prices of Items Sold to Buyers in Bluefields, 1969–78

Item	1969[a]	1975[a]	1978[a]	% Change
Green turtle (live) [b]	60	80	150	150
Green turtle calipee (dried, per pound)	7	7	8	14
Hawksbill shell (per pound)	21	40	150	614
Jaguar skin	750–900	600	300	−.67
Ocelot skin	500–600	400	500	0
Margay skin	30	40	60	100
River otter skin	20	30	60	200
Caiman skin (per foot)	30	20	16	−.53
Crocodile skin (per foot)	15	10	5	−.67
Dried shrimp (per pound)	2	5	5	150
Coconut oil (per gallon)	9	10	20	122
Hulled rice (100 pounds)	60	130	120	100
Pig (live)	300	250	200	−33

[a] Values in córdobas; 1 córdoba = US$0.14.
[b] Sold to turtle companies until 1977; now a few are sold to merchants in Bluefields.

In order to secure additional income for their families many individuals began to leave the villages to seek wage-paying jobs elsewhere.

MIGRATION: LEAVING IN ORDER TO STAY

As a response to changing ecological and economic conditions, many Miskito are migrating from villages to towns, cities, or other countries.

The pattern is one of circular migration: individuals temporarily leave villages to look for employment, send remittances home, and most return after varying periods away.

Wage-seeking migration is a stabilizing mechanism that relieves local population pressure on scarce economic resources and provides income for economically pressed village families. Migration is one of the most common of the many

TABLE 6
Village Labor Rates, Tasbapauni, 1969–78

Item	1969[a]	1975[a]	1978[a]	% Change
Market Agriculture (day rate)				
Ax work	7	8	15	114
Machete work	5	7	10	100
Planting	3	3	5	67
Replanting rice	5	5	5	0
Weeding (including food)	3	5	5	67
Harvesting rice (per 100 pounds)	5	7	10	100
Carpentry (day rate)				
General work (house building, boat repair)	12–20	25	35	118
Construction of canoe (not including cost of materials)	300–500	500	700	75
Passenger transport				
Trip to Bluefields (per person, one way)	10	15	20	100

[a] Values in córdobas; 1 córdoba = US$0.14.

economic options used by Miskito families to adapt to internal and external conditions.

Historically, temporary migration of Miskito males has been a persistent adaptation: they accompanied buccaneers on long-distance voyages; they made trips in their canoes along all of eastern Central America to secure resources to exchange for desired goods from the early European traders; and they served as lumber scouts, loggers, rubber tappers, boat pilots, and banana-plantation workers on contract agreements. They returned to the villages after these absences with goods, and later with money, which added a measure of status to life in the villages. In the intervening economic bust periods between the labor-siphoning booms, the Miskito stayed home, tended their swiddens, and hunted and fished. And when they were away on contract labor jobs, subsistence activities were done by women and the remaining men. In adapting to the outside world that had come to their shores, the Miskito had for many years maintained the security of subsistence and gained access to foreign goods and materials they saw as useful and attractive.

Even though similar in many ways to previous migrations, the present one is different in some respects. Migration is now a response to the decline of security of livelihood within the villages rather than an adaptation to maximize external opportunities. Moreover, it is now more extensive and intensive, in that it involves males and females and larger numbers of people who leave for longer periods and go farther—some only returning to their home villages for short visits. Also, prolonged absences tend to amplify the stimulus for others to migrate by creating a labor vacuum in the villages.

With growing inflation and declining resources, many Miskito started to migrate between 1971 and 1973. Some found jobs in the shrimp-packing companies in Bluefields and Corn Island; some worked on shrimp boats, others in the Siuna-Bonanza-Rosita gold mines. Some went to Managua, where they found jobs in hotels and restaurants owing to their ability to speak English, and some left Nicaragua for other Caribbean countries.

Between 1972 and 1975, 256 people left the

TABLE 7

Average Family's Daily Purchases, Tasbapauni, 1969 and 1975

| Item | Amount | Cost[a] | |
		1969	*1975*
Flour	2 pounds	1.60	3.60
Sugar	1 pound	.90	1.20
Rice	1 pound	.80	1.80
Beans	1 pound	1.00	1.75
Coffee	2 ounces	.50	.75
Coconut oil	1 pint	1.00	2.00
Baking powder	2 teaspoons	.30	.50
Kerosene	½ pint	.50	.75
Cigarettes	3	.25	.40
Turtle meat	2 pounds	1.00	1.50
Total		7.85	14.25

Source: J. Nietschmann (1975, 162).

[a] Values in córdobas; 1 córdoba = US$0.14.

village of Tasbapauni; most were single, but a few entire families departed. The majority of the migrants (53.5 percent) went to Bluefields, Corn Island, or Puerto Cabezas; 12 percent went to Managua and Corinto (a Pacific coast port and the most important in the country); and 16 percent left Nicaragua (table 8). The migrants made up a quarter of the entire village population. Before this exodus, the village population was increasing at 3.3 percent a year; 51 percent of the population was under 15 years of age, 45 percent was between 16 and 69, and 4 percent was more than 70. Almost all of the migrants were between 16 and 69 years of age—the age group that makes up the major economic production units in the village. Within this age group, 47.5 percent of the women and 57.1 percent of the men left Tasbapauni, or about half of the potential labor supply. The population pyramid for Tasbapauni became a population hourglass, constricted in the middle with a wide, young base. To be sure, all 256 people were not gone over the entire three-year period. Some came back after several months or a year away, but many remained for longer periods (J. Nietschmann 1975, 167–76).

The migration has had a strong impact on the community. Village demographic patterns have changed to households filled with old and young

TABLE 8
Destination and Numbers of Migrants from Tasbapauni, 1972–75

Destination	Female			Male			Total	
	Number	*% total female migrants*	*% of all migrants*	*Number*	*% total male migrants*	*% of all migrants*	*Number*	*%*
Bluefields	34	29.6	13.3	37	26.2	14.5	71	27.8
Corn Island	16	14.0	6.3	23	16.3	9.0	39	15.3
Managua	10	8.7	3.9	18	12.8	7.0	28	10.9
Puerto Cabezas	13	11.3	5.1	13	9.2	5.1	26	10.2
United States	2	1.7	.8	18	12.8	7.0	20	7.8
Costa Rica	7	6.0	2.7	6	4.3	2.3	13	5.0
El Bluff	6	5.2	2.3	2	1.4	.8	8	3.1
Set Net	6	5.2	2.3	1	.7	.4	7	2.7
Bonanza-Siuna-Rosita (mines)	0	0.0	0.0	6	4.3	2.3	6	2.3
Pearl Lagoon	5	4.3	1.9	1	.7	.4	6	2.3
Panama	2	1.7	.8	2	1.4	.8	4	1.6
Prinsapolka	4	3.5	1.6	0	0.0	0.0	4	1.6
Rio Grande Bar	2	1.7	.8	2	1.4	.8	4	1.6
Corinto	0	0.0	0.0	3	2.1	1.1	3	1.1
Jamaica	0	0.0	0.0	2	1.4	.8	2	.8
San Andrés	0	0.0	0.0	2	1.4	.8	2	.8
Other	8	7.0	3.1	5	3.5	2.0	13	5.1
Total	115	99.9	44.9	141	99.9	55.1	256	100.0

Source: J. Nietschmann (1975, 172).

people, marriage pools have dried up, remittances have helped even out economic problems, and a village labor vacuum was created which has led to decreases in subsistence provisioning and has stimulated further migration. Probably the most significant effects of migration have been a reduction of pressure on local fauna, a release of population pressure on the village's economic carrying capacity, and the remittance income received by families in the village.

Analysis of Miskito migration cannot be broken down into simple "push-pull" factors, causes and effects, or the move from village lanterns to attractive city lights. The Miskito migrate as Miskito, not as moths or as players in a tug-of-war game. Migration is both a traditional process and a new activity; it is a way of maintaining the family by leaving the family; and it is also a means of going away without leaving. No matter how far one goes or how long one is gone, a Mis-

kito never really leaves his home village. In many ways, Miskito leave the villages in order to stay. The decision to leave maintains others at home, yet encourages more departures.

THE VIEW FROM THE FAR EDGE OF THE CARIBBEAN

Research and information on Miskito communities collected over a ten-year period have led me to reconsider many of the earlier assumptions and conclusions that stemmed from my first study. Miskito society and culture are much more resistant to deep erosion from outside economic waves than I believed at first. The Miskito system has made recurrent adaptations to cyclical economic boom-and-bust periods over more than 350 years of contact. During the years that I have observed the Miskito they have experienced another economic boom, one that led to the commercialization of subsistence turtle hunting, and an economic bust, the closing of the turtle companies and increasing inflation that brought the poverty of economic dependency to their shores. Through the cyclical economic swings Miskito economy was at first simplified and then again became diversified. The long history of trade, market relationships, and resource extraction has had the cumulative effect of creating both the influences to change Miskito society and the collective cultural experience to adapt to change. To be sure, Miskito culture and society have gone through major transformations and adjustments and are no longer "traditional." But tradition is often more an image of the observer than of the observed. To survive culturally within the context of a highly articulated and hypercoherent modern world a society must change to remain unchanged. Change usually does not occur to take advantage of new, untried opportunities but to maintain old ways by adapting and absorbing rather than by blindly adopting and conforming. The Miskito have kept a flexible capacity for continued change and adaptation even though they are now economically dependent on a system beyond their control.

The Miskito are caught up in several positive feedback relationships that are leading them into closer integration with what they call "the outside world." Resource depletion, inflation, and migration are all part of interrelated cause-and-effect processes that are creating the need for adjustment to scarcity rather than their former accommodation to abundance. From an outsider's point of view and from the perspective of the older Miskito, these trends are unsettling and give cause for great concern. For the younger Miskito, however, they are part of an everyday world, one in which they participate. The visiting academic sees an abstract culture, and the elderly of the society see a memory culture; we both interpret the present in terms of the past. The younger Miskito, however, must relate to the coming of modern times to once sequestered shores in terms of both previous and new experiences.

A few weeks ago while I was at work in my office at home in Berkeley, looking over a list of prices for store goods sent to me by a Miskito in Tasbapauni, I received a telephone call from a young Miskito from the radio room of the *Sun Viking,* a cruise ship on its way from Miami to Kingston, Jamaica. The ship-to-shore call was from the son of a Miskito hunter, a man with whom I had lived for many months and with whom I had traveled deep into the rain forest and far out to sea. His son had taken a job on the ship and called to let us know he was well and to pass on the latest information he had received from his family at home. He had already made several voyages around the Caribbean and told us about the places he had seen—where Columbus had gone, the old pirate bases, the early European settlements. He was seeing things that he heard his father and me talk about, the events that were part of the cultural history of his people, and he called to say that these things were worth knowing about. The work on board was hard but the pay was good. He had run into other Miskito here and there in his travels and that made being away from home more tolerable. He said he had a vacation coming up when the ship got back to Miami and I asked him to come visit us. Many thanks, he replied, but he was feeling homesick and his family needed his help and he was planning to take the first LANICA flight out of Miami to go home to Nicaragua.

SOURCE AND ACKNOWLEDGMENTS

This article appeared originally in the *Geographical Review* 69 (1979): 1–24. The article was presented as a paper at the 74th Annual Meeting of the Association of American Geographers, New Orleans, April, 1978. The author wishes to thank his Miskito informants, friends, and correspondents, and especially Baldwin Garth, Flannery Knight, Pungi Perez, and Cromwell Forbes, for their continued assistance and interest in this research effort. The author also wishes to thank the foundations and institutions that supported the research among the Miskito in eastern Nicaragua: the Foreign Area Fellowship Program, the Social Science Research Council, the National Geographic Society, and the John Simon Guggenheim Memorial Foundation. Many ideas and materials were first presented by Judith Nietschmann, who took part in all the field projects between 1968 and 1976.

NOTES

1. That the Caribbean region is a distinct culture area is perhaps best argued by Lowenthal (1972) and Mintz (1974). That the Central American coastal lowlands should be considered part of the Caribbean culture area was put forth by Augelli (1962), but see also Segal (1968). For a discussion of the cultural complexity of the Central American rimland, see D. Jones (1970).

2. Calipee is the cartilaginous, amber-colored material obtained from inside the bottom (plastron) and top (carapace) shells of the green turtle. Calipee imparts a delicate flavor and unique gelatinlike consistency to green turtle soup (see Parsons 1962, 7–8, 15–22).

3. During a twelve-month period (1972–73) 913 turtles were caught by 108 men and teenagers from the village of Little Sandy Bay. Despite their high labor input, 72 percent of these individuals caught less than 10 turtles owing to their inexperience, to decline of the turtle population, and to attempts at turtling during unfavorable weather conditions. The top ten experienced turtlemen accounted for 414 of the year's catch. Of the turtles taken, 743 were sold to the companies; only 170 were consumed within the village (Weiss 1974, 174).

4. Zoologist Archie Carr (1984) and his students have been tagging nesting turtles at Tortuguero, Costa Rica, since 1955 to study the migration, life history, and ecology of *Chelonia mydas.* Each metal tag is imprinted with an individual number, an offer of a reward, and a mailing address. To date, more than 12,000 turtles have been tagged and 1,110 tags returned. Carr estimates that perhaps two-thirds of the turtles nesting at Tortuguero are from Nicaraguan waters, yet a disproportionate 82.6 percent of all tags recovered are from Nicaragua. "Obviously, the abundance of the Miskito Bank returns does indeed reflect concentrated exploitation there, because the tags come back to us only when turtles are caught. However, this exploitation is heavy because the feeding colony there is big and stable. It is by far the largest in the entire Atlantic system" (Carr, Carr, and Meylan 1978).

5. Habitat alteration and disturbance are major influences behind the local disappearance or decline of some faunal species and the increase and concentration of others. Large-scale deforestation and modification of primary tropical forests are resulting from the accelerating wave of pioneer agriculturalists moving from the mountainous interior onto the Caribbean lowlands, and from the several logging operations that still continue in various parts of the coast. Aquatic habitats too have been increasingly disturbed. Lobster divers, shrimp trawlers, and Jamaican fishermen increased their exploitation of coastal marine habitats, reducing the abundance of several species and affecting the presence of many others through noise and dumped wastes. Increased boat traffic along the newly completed inland canal from Bluefields to the Río Grande, and seasonal prevalence of cast net shrimping have led to the further decline of manatee in Pearl Lagoon because they shy away from noise and human activity.

6. In 1975, Nicaragua exported more than 2,200 pounds of hawksbill shell to Japan, the world's largest importer.

7. Encouraged by the presence of a new freezer plant and a dependable overseas market, many Corn Island inhabitants began to exploit local lobster (*Panulirus argus*) grounds beginning in the mid-1960s. High monetary returns led the islanders to invest heavily in boats, motors, and lobster pots, to greatly reduce or give up subsistence provisioning, and to pay inflated wages and prices for available labor and imported goods. By the early 1970s the local lobster grounds were fished out, leaving the Corn Islanders with debts, overgrown agricultural fields, and an inflated economy.

FURTHER READINGS

Mac Chapin, ed. 1992. The co-existence of indigenous peoples in the natural environments of Central America. *Research and Exploration* 8 (2): Map supplement.

This wall map helps to show that the surviving natural environments are found mainly within the territories of indigenous peoples. The Miskitos have the largest territory of any indigenous people in Central America and the largest expanses of still healthy natural environments.

William V. Davidson. 1984. The Garifuna in Central America: Ethno-historical and geographical foundations. In *Black Caribs: A case study in biocultural adaptations,* ed. M. Crawford, 13–35. New York: Plenum.

Davidson examines the historical diffusions and current distributions of the Garifuna or Black Caribs of the western Caribbean littoral. Their processes of ethnogenesis under colonial conditions and ecological adaptations to coastal environments invite comparison with the Miskitos' experiences.

Clarissa T. Kimber. 1988. *Martinique revisited: The changing plant geographies of a West Indian island.* College Station: Texas A&M University Press.

Kimber's is a major study of the cultural plant geography of an eastern Caribbean island. She demonstrates the importance cultural geographers attach to understanding both the human and the biophysical bases of environmental change in the Caribbean.

Peter Matthiessen. 1975. *Far Tortuga.* New York: Random House.

This is a widely acclaimed novel set in the Cayman Islands and the keys and reefs of the Miskito Coast. The author, a master naturalist and writer, evokes seascapes and subsistence practices with an expert ear for local dialects.

John A. Murray, ed. 1991. *The islands and the sea: Five centuries of nature writing from the Caribbean.* New York: Oxford University Press.

This is a collection of five centuries of writings on nature and natural history in the Caribbean Rim and islands. The book includes articles written on the wildlife and environments of the Miskito Coast.

Bernard Nietschmann. 1979. *The Caribbean edge: The coming of modern times to isolated people and wildlife.* Indianapolis: Bobbs-Merrill.

This is a collection of stories and accounts of fieldwork on the Miskito Coast of Nicaragua. Nietschmann succeeds memorably in bringing to life both the quotidian trials and cosmic rewards of working on the edge of the Caribbean Sea. Many of these pieces first appeared as articles in *Natural History.*

————. 1989. *The unknown war: The Miskito nation, Nicaragua, and the United States.* New York: Freedom House.
————. 1990. Conservation by conflict. *Natural History,* November, 42–49.
————. 1991. The Miskito nation and the politics of self-determination. *Journal of Political Science* 19:18–40.

In 1979, the Miskitos' major problems changed from cash market dependency and wildlife depletion to attempts by the new Sandinista government to annex and dismantle Miskito territory, society, government, and economy. As a result, the Miskito went to war—their eleventh against an invader since the 1500s—raised the only Indian army in the Americas, and fought Central America's largest army to a standstill. These three sources are about the war, its environmental consequences, and the Miskitos' political strategy. "Conservation by Conflict" makes the point that, because of war, environmental destruction caused by logging, mining, fishing, and ranching was halted. As a result, wildlife and environments rebounded, especially on the Miskito Coast.

Arthur Ray. 1974. *Indians and the fur trade: Their role as trappers, hunters and middlemen in the lands southwest of Hudson Bay.* Toronto: University of Toronto Press.

This is a study of changing relationships to the environment in a zone of cultural contact. Focusing on the adaptive responses of the Assiniboine and the Western Cree to the fur trade and the ecological changes it engendered, this book is a particularly rich ethnographic study.

Bonham C. Richardson. 1983. *Caribbean migrants: Environment and human survival on St. Kitts and Nevis.* Knoxville: University of Tennessee Press.

This book focuses on the mobility of Caribbean peoples from the perspective of the eastern islands. Using St. Kitts and Nevis as examples, aspects of Caribbean migration processes are placed in historical context.

————. 1992. *The Caribbean in the wider world, 1492–1992: A regional geography.* Cambridge: Cambridge University Press.

This is a creative regional synthesis of Caribbean economic and environmental history since European contact. Richardson achieves an effective balance between the world-system perspective and the cultural-historical geographer's traditional concern for local detail and knowledge.

Carl O. Sauer. 1966. *The early Spanish Main: The land, nature, and people Columbus encountered in the Americas.* Berkeley: University of California Press.

This is Sauer's classic account of the early impact of Europeans on the Caribbean islands and littorals.

Ian G. Simmons. 1989. *Changing the face of the earth: Culture, environment, history.* New York: Blackwell.

This volume attempts to provide a comprehensive history of human impact on the environment. It is organized around the concepts of ecosystems and energy flows.

David Watts. 1987. *The West Indies: Patterns of development, culture, and environmental change since 1492.* Cambridge: Cambridge University Press.

Watts presents a regional historical geography from cultural and biogeographic perspectives. This is a good example of the emergent work on tropical environmental history by cultural and physical geographers.

Robert C. West and John P. Augelli. 1989. *Middle America: Its lands and peoples.* 3d ed. Englewood Cliffs, N.J.: Prentice-Hall.

This is perhaps the best general text in any language on Mexico, Central America, and the Caribbean. The book employs Augelli's Middle America mainland-rimland construct as the main heuristic device. A strength of the book is the authors' intimate and authoritative knowledge of the biophysical, historical, and cultural landscapes of this diverse, complex, and contested realm.

KARL S. ZIMMERER **17**

WETLAND PRODUCTION AND SMALLHOLDER PERSISTENCE: AGRICULTURAL CHANGE IN A HIGHLAND PERUVIAN REGION

R oughly twenty years ago, peasant cultivators in the Colquepata District of southern Peru began to convert montane bogs into agricultural fields. At that time, geographers and those interested in the organization of farming systems would have been likely to debate whether this change resulted from population growth, market demand, new technology, or alterations in the sectoral articulation of agriculture (reviewed in B. L. Turner and Brush 1987). Yet, rather than a single cause, all four conditions figured into the development and persistence of wetland agriculture in Colquepata District. Attempting to integrate the ecological and socioeconomic relations girding agriculture and other land use, growing numbers of geographers and other social scientists have situated empirical studies in models of "political ecology" (Bassett 1988; Blaikie and Brookfield 1987; Hecht 1982; M. Lewis 1992; Schmink and Wood 1987; Sheridan 1988; Wolf 1972; see also Grossman 1984 and the review by Emel and Peet 1989). The present study further elaborates political ecology concepts to provide both an integrative account of the emergence and persistence of montane-bog agriculture and a cross-historical comparison of wetland production.[1]

Political ecology seeks to merge two major theoretical fields in contemporary geography, ecology and political economy. Defining its widest reach, Blaikie and Brookfield (1987, 17) state that "'political ecology' combines the concerns of ecology and a broadly defined political economy." Others such as Bassett (1988) likewise describe an expansive conceptual terrain traversing the microscale (behavioralist) approaches of human and cultural ecology (e.g., Brookfield 1972; 1984; Nietschmann 1973; Denevan 1983) and a macroscale (structuralist) political economy (e.g., Blaikie 1985; Peet and Thrift 1989; M. Watts 1983b). Although these political-ecological models have encompassed a range of perspectives, they have not sought to settle the contradiction between the primacy attributed to the individual in human and cultural ecology and the structuralist framework of political economy. This gap is perhaps most evident in political ecology's view of socioeconomic structures solely as constraints or a prefigured "context" for those making decisions about land use. Rather than only bounding the opportunities of decision-makers, such structures are formed by the interaction of diverse social collectives and individuals, including the persons that choose and carry out land-use strategies. Formative social practices contributing to the context of local land use do not occur on a neutral ground but instead take place through strategies of domination, accommodation, and resistance. While the cultivators of Colquepata District inarguably converted montane bogs into agricultural fields in response to structural incentives, the entire forming of such structures was not externally imposed, but instead resulted partly from the social practices of these peasant smallholders. The mutual dependence of structure and agency is expressed by the concept of "structuration," which holds that "the structural properties of social systems are both the medium and the outcome of practices that constitute these systems" (Giddens 1979, 69; see also Bourdieu 1977; Pred 1984). By incorporating a structuration concept into political ecology, the present study attempts to link the social practices of land users to the structural conditions of peasant agriculture.

The structuration concept aids also in providing political ecology with a means of analyzing the spatial form of agricultural change and environmental degradation. The importance of this dimension is not overlooked by Blaikie and Brookfield (1987, 17), who state that

> the adjective "regional" is important because it is necessary to take account of environmental variability and the spatial variations in resilience and sensitivity of the land, as different demands are put on the land through time. The word "regional" also implies the incorporation of environmental considerations into theories of regional growth and decline.

Due to the constant attention that cultural ecologists focus on the geographical variation of environmental conditions, *regional* in the first sense clarifies rather than extends the political ecology perspective while in the second it refers to a wide-ranging regional political economy. The framework developed below takes a step in the direction of "regionalizing" political ecology by examining how the spatially structured interaction of indigenous peasants and local elites constituted a "politics of place" (*sensu* Agnew 1987a) and, more specifically, shaped a "region of resistance" where rural Quechua resisted domination by estate owners and villagers. Drawing on historically structured practices and ideology, peasant cultivators in the study region later were able to pressure the Peruvian state for subsidies that underwrote the transformation of montane wetlands. Examined through the framework of structuration, the geography of social power and political-economic structures can bring into view spatial patterns of resource allocation and thereby advance a regional concept in political ecology.

Physical and biological conditions of production form the ecological basis of regional political ecology. The present study details how cultivators in Colquepata District modify otherwise limiting agro-ecological features of montane bogs.[2] Despite the extensive examination of prehistoric wetland agriculture (reviewed in B. L. Turner and Denevan 1985), little research has been concerned with the biological ecology of the growing environment. Yet the prevalence of disease pathogens and insect pests so seriously threatens wetland production that careful monitoring and flexible labor inputs are found necessary to ensure its viability. In fact, the ecological requirements of wetland cultivation supplied a key cost advantage to peasant agriculturalists and thus contributed to the competitiveness of these producers in the course of widening commercialization. Persistence of smallholding peasants runs counter to the scenario posited by both neoclassical and (classical) Marxist theories of economic development (Schultz 1964; Lenin 1976).

Finally, the importance of production ecology and spatial scale in the wetland agriculture of peasant smallholders in Colquepata District engages an ongoing debate about prehistoric economic organization. Among Andeanist scholars, Kolata (1986) most recently has articulated the assumption that wetland production was necessarily organized by centralized political authorities due to the need for coordinated water control. Kolata's assumption of centralized political-economic organization, analogous to Wittfogel's (1957) claim of large-scale irrigated "hydraulic agriculture" in the basins of major river valleys, predicates the use of medium or large production units in wetland sites. Yet several counterexamples to Wittfogel's hydraulic agriculture thesis have been enumerated by researchers working on irrigated agriculture in both the prehistoric Old World (Butzer 1976) and the present Peruvian Andes (W. Mitchell 1976). Contemporary cultivation in Colquepata District likewise reveals the "large-scale" assumption as flawed. Rather than requiring large-scale economic and political organization, present-day wetland agriculture depends on the provisioning of labor by individual peasant households able to monitor production closely and provide labor in varying amounts and on short notice.

This paper opens by reviewing the geographical study of field systems in Andean agriculture. Next, it assesses the ecology of current wetland production in Colquepata District. Cultivation techniques and rationales, ecological constraints, labor scheduling, and geographical scale anchor this discussion to the analysis of agricultural change. The third section examines the conditions leading to the initiation, location, and persistence of wetland agriculture in Colquepata District. In the fourth section, the wetland production system of Colquepata is fitted into pro-

posed land-use classification schema. Finally, application of the regional political ecology perspective in the case study is used to draw conclusions concerning agricultural change, wetland production, and peasant smallholder persistence.

ANDEAN AGRICULTURE: BACKGROUND

Agriculture in the montane bogs of Colquepata District resembles two Andean production types of much greater areal extent: prehistoric wetland agriculture and contemporary dry farming. Each counterpart of contemporary bog agriculture encompasses a different set of production structures comprising agricultural environments, technologies, field landforms, cultivation practices, and the social organization of labor. Prior to European conquest, these two agricultural systems were foundations in the production of food for as many as twenty-five million people (reviewed in Denevan 1976, 2–4). Today only dry farming supplies a substantial portion of subsistence for the large peasantry that inhabits the Andes from southern Bolivia to central Colombia (Wolf 1966; de Janvry, Sadoulet, and Young 1989). In recently converting montane bogs into fields, cultivators in Colquepata District developed an agricultural strategy based on contemporary technologies and forms of social organization, many derived from dry farming, while confronting biophysical conditions analogous to those characterizing prehistoric wetland production.

During the centuries prior to conquest by Spaniards and Portuguese, elevated planting surfaces ("raised fields") covered more than 170,000 hectares in the pre-European New World (Denevan 1970, 648). In South America, geographical research has located the majority of prehistoric raised fields in two environments: riverine floodplains, especially in the lowlands, and the lacustrine plains as well as other poorly drained areas of the Andean highlands (Parsons and Denevan 1967).[3] Denevan (1980, 226) has estimated that raised fields extended over at least 92,000 hectares of highland habitats. As remains of relict raised fields surfaced during the 1960s and 1970s, geographers designed taxonomic classifications based on the shapes and patterns of field landforms (Denevan and B. L. Turner 1974; Mathewson 1985). The vast majority of planting surfaces were found to resemble "platforms" that measured between one and twenty or more meters in width. An "open checkerboard" of planting beds marked most fields, although other configurations such as "riverine," "irregular embanked," "ladder," and "linear" also were widespread (Denevan 1970; Knapp 1988; C. Smith, Denevan, and Hamilton 1968). Under massive social and political upheavals prior to the Spanish Conquest and throughout the sixteenth century, most if not all platform-field agriculture in the Andes was terminated. Despite the lack of written accounts, a group of geographers, archaeologists, and cultural historians has begun to interpret the social organization of prehistoric wetland production using material artifacts.

The development of wetland cultivation in the Andes has been studied most thoroughly in the high-elevation basin that surrounds Lake Titicaca (e.g., Smith et al. 1968; Erickson 1985; Kolata 1986). Investigating raised fields south of the lake, Kolata (1986, 760) has concluded that "the construction, maintenance, and production of these [raised] fields were managed by a centralized political authority [the Tiwanaku state (A.D. 100–1000)]." While he cites artifactual evidence that centralized political power and raised fields coincided geographically, Kolata concedes that the contemporaneity of raised-field construction and state rule is not demonstrated. Although his interpretation might be proven correct, Kolata's assumption of centralized sociopolitical authority in wetland agriculture is disputable on empirical grounds. Erickson's (1985) combined archaeological and ethnographic field research elsewhere in the Lake Titicaca Basin, for example, argues that prehistoric raised fields could have been cultivated under small-scale forms of social and economic control. Brief mention of a small area of historic platform-field cultivation near Bogotá (Colombia) by Eidt (1959, 386) similarly suggests that cultivation was carried out by peasant smallholders.

Today, most agricultural production in the Andes is organized by households of peasant smallholders. Although based on the nuclear family, households in the Andes frequently include nonkin. Less than one-half of Andean peasants belong to communities, a suprahouse-hold level of social organization whose direct involvement in production generally does not extend beyond relatively small areas of communal plots and the coordination of certain land-use types such as open-field systems (Orlove and Custred 1980). The task of marshaling capital and labor for most production therefore falls on the individual household. Persisting in a "refuge sector" symptomatic of the stagnant national economies of the Andean countries, peasant households produce crops for both the market and subsistence (de Janvry et al. 1989). Through lowering consumption costs, subsistence production permits peasant farmers to continue provisioning markets even when profit margins reach nominal or even negative levels (de Janvry 1981; Reinhardt 1988). While smallholder households in the Andes increasingly articulate with extra-household economies through temporary labor migration as well as commercial farming, their agricultural production retains the high labor and low capital attributes of the peasant economy.

To cultivate upland sites, most present-day Andean agriculturalists utilize a form of raised field that diverges substantially from the platforms constructed by prehistoric wetland cultivators. Classified as a ridged field (Denevan and B. L. Turner 1974, 25), it is comprised of narrow, cambered beds.[4] Frequently designated *lazy beds,* a term originally applied to the planting surfaces of abandoned fields in Celtic portions of the British Isles (Evans 1973; Robert West 1959, 282), the elevated portions of contemporary ridged parcels are labeled most precisely by the Quechua term *wachu* (Gade 1975; Knapp 1988). Cultivated by the majority of Andean peasant farmers, *wachu* fields yield crops of potatoes as well as the secondary Andean tubers (*añu, oca, olluco;* see Sauer 1950) that are either consumed by producer households or marketed.

WETLAND AGRICULTURAL PRODUCTION

On midslopes at intermediate elevations (3,500–3,900 meters) in Colquepata District (see figure 1), the ridged-field (*wachu*) agriculture that predominates in surrounding regions is replaced with a wetland field type containing a complex drainage network. Highly distinct drained-*wachu* fields are found in an approximately

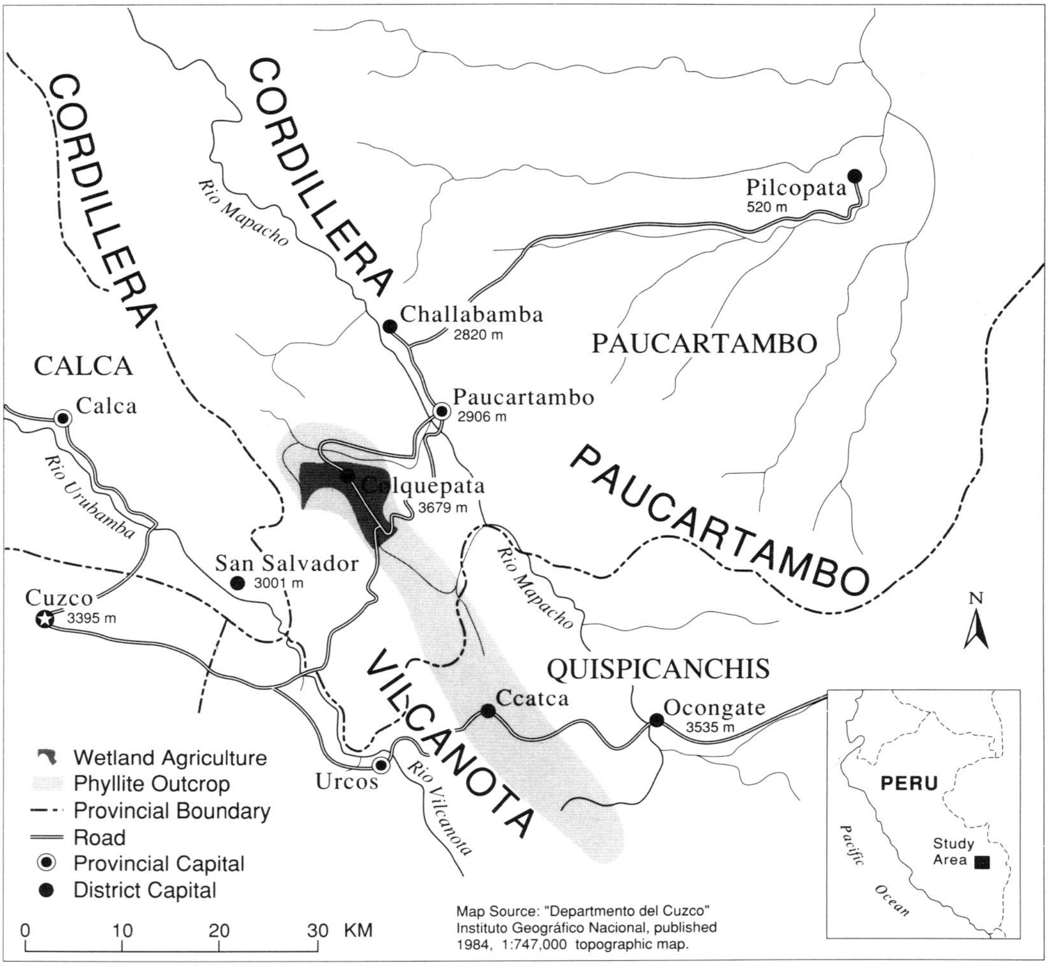

FIGURE 1

Wetland agriculture in the Colquepata District of the southern Peruvian highlands.

eighty-five-square-kilometer area centered on the village of Colquepata (1981 population 425). In more than a dozen nearby communities inhabited by roughly 3,000 Quechua-speaking peasants, drained-*wachu* agriculture is a major economic activity uniting distinct biophysical environments and the production structures organized by peasant households. Local ecological and social resources, including agricultural knowledge, complement external forces in favoring drained-*wachu* agriculture.

The layout of drained-*wachu* fields (see figures 2 and 3) resembles neither its prehistoric nor contemporary counterparts. Intended to meet the opposing objectives of both subirrigation and drainage, fields contain an elaborate network of canals absent from the standard ridged-field design that abounds in adjacent upland areas. While standard ridged fields facilitate drainage by orienting beds and alleys parallel to the slope (Robert West 1959, 281; Parsons and Denevan 1967, 98), the highly engineered drained-*wachu* fields of Colquepata District connect primary, secondary, and even tertiary drainage canals into a modified herringbone pattern. The distinct pattern of canals and the narrowness of planting

FIGURE 2
Drained-*wachu* field occupying a wetland swale at 3,780 meters in Colquepata District.

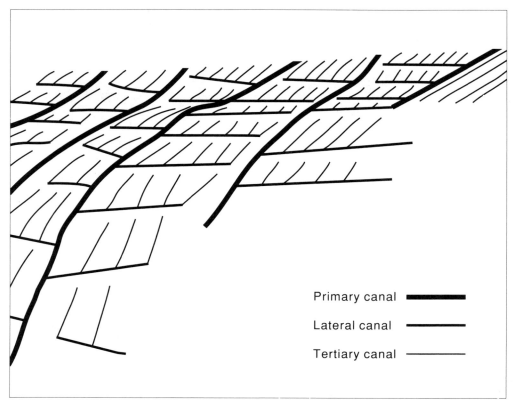

Primary canal ━━━━

Lateral canal ━━━

Tertiary canal ──────

FIGURE 3
The design of canals draining the field shown in figure 2.

beds (0.3–0.5 meter) not only differ from prehistoric platform fields but also reflect contrasting physical conditions of the wetland environment supporting each agricultural system.

Rather than occupying lakeshore plains or broad basins, drained-*wachu* fields occur in the northern portion of a rolling badlands landscape that stretches at least eighty kilometers south of Colquepata. Underlain by phyllite (mudstone similar to slate), intermediate-elevation slopes in the area contain low-lying depressions, or swales, interspersed with concave rock surfaces and sometimes inclined as steeply as fifteen degrees. Although swales rarely cover more than 500 square meters, they usually contain soil deposits of one or more meters. The accumulation of run-off from surrounding slopes saturates swale sites, which, if left uncultivated, support a montane bog vegetation of mat-forming herbs.[5] Thus, although the size and topography of swales

differ significantly from that of lacustrine plains where prehistoric Andean cultivators practiced raised-field agriculture, the two habitat types share the key commonality of waterlogged soils. Like the platform design of prehistoric fields, the distinctive layout of drained-*wachu* fields is well suited to the hydrologic conditions shaped by regional topography.

Peasant agriculturalists cultivating drained-*wachu* fields channel considerable labor through a large number of tasks to produce potatoes, the main wetland crop. In addition to the ten field tasks typical of standard ridged fields, drained-*wachu* production requires a minimum of four extra field tasks (including supplementary weeding, pulverizing, agrochemical applications, and the construction, scooping, and grading of canals) and approximately 20–35 percent more labor overall.[6] Contrast in the need for labor arises principally from mounding, which in a drained-

wachu field claims nearly twice the work time of an equal-size ridged plot (149 person-days per hectare versus 78 person-days per hectare).[7] The importance to drained-*wachu* producers of major labor inputs at several stages during the growing season is equaled by the need to schedule these and other less-demanding agricultural tasks in response to highly variable ecological conditions.

Ecologically, drained-*wachu* fields are marked by the unpredictable occurrence of potentially damaging field conditions. Saturated soils, for example, require not only the excavation of the herringbone canal network, but also the subsequent modification of drainage surfaces at periodic intervals. To initiate the canal system, cultivators first dig shallow secondary (lateral) canals, later connecting them to primary canals that run parallel to the slope (figures 2 and 3). They then plow additional secondary canals in portions of the field that require further drainage. In preparation for planting potatoes, the Andean "foot-plow" (a foot-driven hoe) is used to construct

elevated beds that typically stand 0.4 to 0.8 meter above the uncultivated surface, although they sometimes reach a height of 1.0 meter and thus tower 2.0 meters or more above the bottom of the excavated canal (C. Allen 1988, 39). Nearly three weeks after planting, cultivators complete a major grading and scooping of canal surfaces (see figure 4), tasks that are repeated at a reduced scale later in the growing season.

Several biophysical hazards in addition to excess soil moisture also endanger drained-*wachu* plantings. Weed growth plagues cultivation throughout the growing season and requires the intermittent allocation of household labor. Insects and pathogens, which abound due to the year-round humid conditions in drained-*wachu* sites, also infirm the wetland crop.[8] The magnitude of these problems is exacerbated by the production calendar of most drained-*wachu* fields. Planted during the middle (July–August) of the approximately six-month dry season, drained-*wachu* fields are not harvested until either January or February. Heavy rains late in the growing

FIGURE 4
Cultivator scooping soil to aid in grading the canals of a wetland field. By covering emergent seedlings, this task also reduces the risk of frost and hail damage.

season add to field humidity and stimulate pest and pathogen outbreaks, which, if untreated, cause considerable crop damage during the crucial period shortly before harvest.

Much work in monitoring and alleviating potential threats to production, such as weed competition and insect predation, is carried out by the women and the older children of smallholder households. To limit crop losses during the end of the growing season, for example, the close scrutiny of field conditions and the flexible allocation of household labor are frequently used to advance harvest by several days or even a few weeks. Regular monitoring also is necessary for the effective utilization of numerous agrochemicals in drained-*wachu* production. Cultivators apply an array of insecticides, fungicides, and fertilizer in response to short-term plant stress, disease, and infestation. Exclusive reliance on scientifically bred ("improved") varieties of potatoes, which possess poor below-ground storage capacity and are susceptible to harvest-period loss from pests and pathogens, further magnifies labor demands and their temporal uncertainty in drained-*wachu* fields.

In summary, peasant smallholders in Colquepata District produce potatoes in wetland sites at intermediate elevations by using a well-defined combination of production structures (agricultural environments, technologies, field landforms, cultivation practices, and the social organization of labor). The environmental hazards of wetland sites—poor drainage, weeds, disease, and pests—exhibit extreme spatial and temporal variation. Unless modified, biophysical threats jeopardize drained-*wachu* production. Successful production therefore depends on the vigilant monitoring of field sites and the capacity of agricultural households to allocate labor for ameliorating field conditions and reducing risk on short notice. Tasks such as subirrigating, draining, mounding, weeding, and applying pesticides and fungicides are undertaken primarily by household members, including women and older children. Smallholder management of the close links among production structures in drained-*wachu* agriculture did not arise *in vacuo* but rather developed historically within a specific context of environment and regional society.

REGIONAL AGRICULTURAL CHANGE

As late as 1965, the intermediate-elevation montane bogs of Colquepata District remained uncultivated. Diverse crops and small herds accounted for the subsistence production of households in the district while, since the opening in 1931 of a roadway from Cuzco (the departmental capital) to the provincial capital of Paucartambo, agriculturalists also had sold increasing amounts of potatoes to buyers who furnished Cuzco's urban market (Villasante Ortiz 1975, 52). Peasant households also marketed sheep, camelids (llamas and alpacas), and cattle, which, like potatoes, were mostly bought by either wholesalers in Cuzco or itinerant merchants in Colquepata. Despite a moderate level of commercialization, the pre-1965 economy of Colquepata District did not presage the more dynamic commerce that would emerge with wetland agriculture.

The location of drained-*wachu* production in Colquepata District during the late 1960s and 1970s depended on the response of local agriculturalists to a fusion of favorable conditions. Intermediate-elevation bog habitats, the existing constellation of household economic activities, transportation costs, demographic growth, and population density favored the development of drained-*wachu* agriculture. Examining the spatial patterning of such factors, however, reveals that they occurred in nearby regions as well as the drained-*wachu* area of Colquepata District:

(1) The distribution of intermediate-elevation bogs, coterminous with the zone of phyllite outcrop, extends well beyond the core of wetland production (figure 1; also Institute for Applied Geosciences 1984). (2) The local agropastoral economy was similar to that of peasant households and communities throughout the zone of phyllite outcrop. (3) Roads to Cuzco providing transportation access and shaping shipping costs pass through areas between Urcos and Ocongate (Ccatca District) that also contain intermediate-elevation bogs, but where wetland production is minimal or nonexistent (figure 1). (4) Population growth rates (1961–81) in Colquepata District (1.3 percent per year) were lower and hence less favorable for agricultural intensification and the

development of wetland production than those in nearby areas, such as Ccatca District (1.7 percent per year), where the agricultural conversion of wetlands did not occur (Dirección Nacional de Estadística y Censos 1966; Instituto Nacional de Estadística 1983). (5) The density of population and mean holdings of land per person in Colquepata District (33.9 persons per square kilometer and 2.94 hectares per person) were less conducive for agricultural change than conditions in nearby areas, such as Ccatca District (41.0 persons per square kilometer and 2.44 hectares per person), where wetlands were not converted (Dirección Nacional de Estadística y Censos, 1966).

Thus, the above elements, prominent in environmental and demographic models of agricultural change (reviewed in Brush 1987), served as necessary but not sufficient inducers of development. The key differentiator to which the peasant smallholders of Colquepata District responded in developing wetland cultivation was a pair of regional economic structures providing demand and production incentives. Rather than being imposed on peasant households by an externally determined political economy, the local constitution of these structural stimuli was shaped critically by the ethnic struggles waged by the past and present inhabitants of Colquepata District.

COLQUEPATA: A REGION OF RESISTANCE

In 1565, a tax record listed the *colquepata* among the tribute payers in the province of "Los Andes" (Paucartambo's sixteenth-century apellation). Analogous to dozens of diverse Andean cultural groups, *colquepata* people of the early colonial period shared a readily recognizable ethnic identity and cohesive territory. Under the late sixteenth-century reforms of Spanish Viceroy Toledo, the regional population was forced to resettle in the newly founded village of Colquepata. In Colquepata, as well as other mandated settlements in the highlands of southern Peru, forced relocation magnified the crises of declining food production and population collapse (C. Allen 1988; Gade and Escobar 1982). Although most nucleated settlements later attracted non-

indigenous villagers (*mistis* or *mestizos*), many of whom became local elites, few if any of this group populated the village of Colquepata.[9] The combination of badlands topography and inhabitants' land claims based on descent from prestigious Inca clans deterred outside ownership and commenced the social construction of the Colquepata countryside as a "region of refuge" where Andean natives (*runa*) resisted control by landowners.[10] The conspicuous free communities (*ayllus*) and mostly indigenous population, along with the near-absence of nonindigenous elites, demarcated a division of social and economic power in Colquepata that differed notably from neighboring regions dominated by manorial estates (*haciendas*).

Land and labor conflicts between free communities and surrounding estates multiplied in certain regions of highland Peru following the transfer of communal property rights to individual Indians under the postindependence laws ratified by Simón Bolívar in 1825. In Cuzco and Peru's southern highlands, however, the weakening of trade ties to the mines of Bolivia initiated a decline in the regional economy, thus limiting outside pressures on the resources of indigenous communities. Most communities in Colquepata successfully resisted territorial usurpation so that, two decades after the Bolívar decree, native communities still outnumbered estates by two to one in the region (then a *repartimiento*), whereas estates predominated by factors of 6.5 and 5.0 in nearby Paucartambo and Challambamba, respectively. Following the national government's establishment of the District of Colquepata in 1857, native communities maintained their de facto territorial independence until, in 1926, the government of Peru conceded to powerful urban liberals and began recognizing official "Indigenous Communities" (*Comunidades Indígenas*). Most communities in Colquepata District, including those in the core of contemporary wetland agriculture, received land titles within two years. Legal titling by the Peruvian state permitted members of Indigenous Communities to control territory through a usufruct arrangement forbidding the negotiation of land as private property.

Despite the official recognition of Indigenous

Communities, peasant inhabitants of Colquepata District were forced to resist external social and economic domination in order to maintain local control of land and labor. Due to the state's contradictory objectives and its general weakness in Andean regions such as Colquepata District, the entitling of communities did little to protect indigenous land and labor from local elites, while concurrently, the desirability of these resources was enhanced by completion of the Cuzco-Paucartambo road and the ensuing economic growth of provincial estates. In defense, rural inhabitants drew on a wide range of tactics to block, deflect, and defuse the efforts of estate owners and villagers. Although violent conflicts periodically erupted, peasants in Colquepata District primarily drew on "everyday forms of resistance" (J. C. Scott 1985; M. Watts 1988), such as feigned obsequiousness and evasion. In addition, they persistently pursued official means of protest, filing a web of judicial charges that eventually enmeshed most of the village elite, privately held estates, and nearly all Indigenous Communities (see figure 5). When Peru's newly installed "Revolutionary Government of the Armed Forces" appropriated highland estates in 1969, land tenure in Colquepata District was scarcely altered. Local forms of new state policies, however, presented cultivators with incipient conditions that, when combined with changes in agricultural market structures and the advent of Green Revolution–type potato technology during the 1960s, stimulated the agricultural conversion of montane bogs.

AGRICULTURAL MARKETS

Export-led growth and import-substitution industrialization during the 1940s and 1950s fueled the expansion of Peru's internal markets and exerted a forceful "pull" on peasants in the economically stagnant highlands. More than a million rural highlanders had migrated to urban centers by 1960 (Thorp and Bertram 1978). During the following decade, overvalued national currency and international borrowing entrained yet greater urban growth, leading to further deepening of internal markets, including those for staple foods. Although most migrants were destined to coastal urban centers, highland cities

also swelled. The departmental capital of Cuzco, a city of 80,000 in 1961, surpassed 200,000 by 1981 (Censo Nacional 1961, 1981). The elevation of food prices, along with the stabilization of production costs, reversed a steady twenty-year decline in the terms of trade for the agricultural sector starting in 1969 (Thorp and Bertram 1978, 278). During the first half of the 1970s, wholesale food prices continued to accelerate more rapidly than production costs.

The generally favorable climate of staple food markets was accentuated intra-annually by the discordance of seasonal supply and uniform demand. Resulting price variation was especially pronounced in perishable crops such as potatoes. Moreover, the magnitude of fluctuation was greater in potato markets of the highlands than those of the lowlands.[11] In the late 1960s, the seasonal fluctuation of retail potato prices exceeded 100 percent. And as late as 1984, after more than a decade of gains in off-season production, prices still varied by roughly 70 percent (see table 1). Wholesale prices, which tracked the seasonal swings of retail costs, offered potato growers a strong incentive to devise off-season systems of potato agriculture.

In the early 1960s, seasonal price fluctuations in the burgeoning food market of urban Cuzco motivated agriculturalists outside of Calca in the Urubamba Valley to enlarge off-season potato production (Ortega Dueñas 1987). Located less than 30 kilometers from the departmental capital and connected by a major road, the temperate and well-watered bottomlands of the Urubamba depression provided irrigated fields well suited to dry-season (or "early-planting") production (Gade 1975, 212). Prior to this commercialization, Urubamba agriculturalists had cultivated two crops of dry-season potatoes, both of which supplied subsistence needs during the several-month period before harvest of the main rainfed planting. The first producers of the commercial dry-season planting adopted techniques and technologies that had formerly met the needs of household consumption. Fast-maturing native cultivars of the species *Solanum phureja* (one of the eight cultivated Andean potato species) were a key component of the earliest dry-season production for commercial purposes. Responding

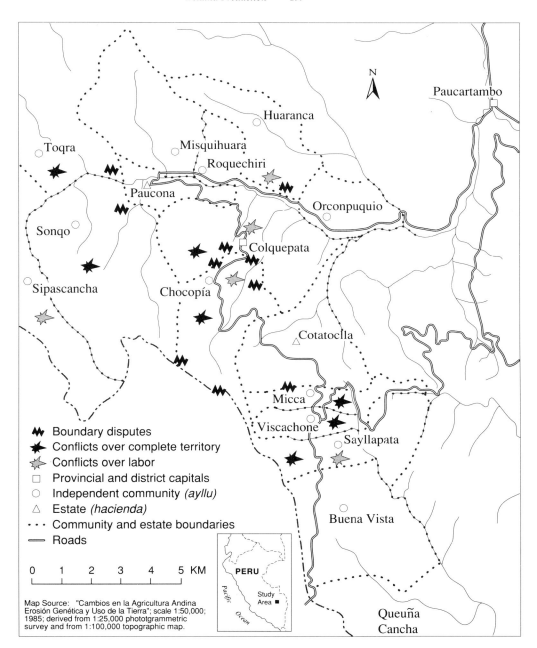

Paucartambo

N

Huaranca

Misquihuara

Toqra

Roquechiri

Paucona

Orconpuquio

Sonqo

Colquepata

Sipascancha

Chocopía

Cotatoclla

Micca

Viscachone

Sayllapata

Buena Vista

Queuña
Cancha

♦ Boundary disputes
★ Conflicts over complete territory
☆ Conflicts over labor
☐ Provincial and district capitals
○ Independent community *(ayllu)*
△ Estate *(hacienda)*
••• Community and estate boundaries
══ Roads

0   1   2   3   4   5 KM

PERU

Pacific Ocean

Study
Area ■

Map Source: "Cambios en la Agricultura Andina
Erosión Genética y Uso de la Tierra"; scale 1:50,000;
1985; derived from 1:25,000 phototgrammetric
survey and from 1:100,000 topographic map.

FIGURE 5
Conflicts between estates, villagers, and communities in Colquepata District (1920–69).

TABLE 1
Seasonal Variation of Retail Potato Prices in Cuzco

	J	*F*	*M*	*A*	*M*	*J*	*J*	*A*	*S*	*O*	*N*	*D*
Price[a]	1.8	1.7	1.6	1.4	1.2	1.0	1.1	1.2	1.2	1.3	1.4	1.5

Source: Agrarian Reform Archive, 1985.
[a] Monthly per kilogram price; 1.0 = 396 soles (January 1984) = US$0.20.

only slightly to fertilizer amendments, the moderate yield of native cultivars constrained the capacity of commercial growers to compete in the Cuzco market.

To further increase dry-season production, cultivators in the Urubamba Valley adopted several Green Revolution–type technologies for potato cultivation. Developed by Peru's national potato program, the country's leading agricultural university, and the International Potato Center in Lima, the introduced technologies included fertilizer, pesticides, and insecticides. The core components were high-yielding varieties that responded to applications of chemical fertilizers with greater yield increases than native potatoes.[12] Although slower to mature than some native cultivars, scientifically bred varieties nonetheless yielded a crop rapidly (five to six months at 3,500 meters). Both fast maturation and genetic resistance strengthened the capacity of improved varieties to weather disease infestations, a critical asset in the irrigated environments necessary for dry-season cultivation. (By 1970, native *S. phureja* potatoes had become rare in the Urubamba Valley.) Despite the availability of similar technological elements in nearby Colquepata District, the majority of cultivators there did not initiate early-planting production until nearly a decade later than their Urubamba Valley counterparts. The inception of wetland agriculture required more than the introduction of technological innovations.

AGRICULTURAL CHANGE

Drained-*wachu* production in the intermediate-elevation bogs of Colquepata District was spurred by the stimulus transmitted through both market conditions and state subsidies. The regional convergence of structural incentives contravenes depictions of government policy and market structures as having so completely disadvantaged development that agricultural change was thwarted in highland Peru during the late 1960s and the 1970s (e.g., Thorp and Bertram 1978). Based on considerations of spatially aggregated economic indicators and distance-related costs such as transportation, macroscale analyses admittedly signal differences in the economic structures of large areas. The rise of wetland production in Colquepata District, however, illustrates a mesolevel of spatial complexity in the economic organization of agriculture. To account for agricultural change at a local scale, the regional political ecology perspective formulated earlier is used to reveal how the historically structured social practices of indigenous peasants in an Andean region of resistance shaped the spatially uneven realization of state policy and markets.

Notwithstanding rampant rhetorical support for the country's peasant smallholders, the Revolutionary Government of the Armed Forces (1968–75) under General Juan Velasco Alvarado maintained the strongly skewed "urban bias" of previous development policies in Peru. Within the disadvantaged agricultural sector, export-oriented enterprises in coastal valleys received a disproportionate share of benefits (Thorp and Bertram 1978). Nevertheless, beginning in 1969, government institutions enlarged some programs —such as technical advice, state-sponsored distribution and subsidies of inputs, and agricultural credit—aimed at peasant smallholders. But these programs reached only a small percentage of cultivators. Their insufficient benefits were neither distributed evenly (socially or geographically) nor dictated solely by urban-bound bureaucrats as has been assumed (Thorp and Bertram 1978, 307). Far from acting as passive recipients of structural biases, the inhabitants of

Colquepata District directly and indirectly pressured local and regional authorities in order to garner a share of meager state resources. In particular, the leaders of SINAMOS (National System for Social Mobilization), an agency instituted by the Revolutionary Government of the Armed Forces to foster pro-state ideology among peasants and the urban poor, held views of rural society in concordance with the anti-estate political beliefs and social practices of Colquepata inhabitants.

Despite the small size of Colquepata relative to other Paucartambo villages, SINAMOS officials installed their largest post in the "peasant town," as elites in nearby villages referred to it. SINAMOS representatives, comprised mainly of personnel relocated from urban centers outside the province, were notoriously ineffective, corrupt, and frequently abusive. Nevertheless, agriculturalists in Colquepata District applied their skills in managing social relations with non-Quechua to deal effectively with the newly arrived government bureaucrats. Moreover, they formed a peasant federation (*La Liga Agraria Miguel Quispe,* named after a prominent Colquepata leader of the early twentieth century) and elected officials to represent the interests of the predominantly rural populace. From 1968–74, SINAMOS officials guaranteed loans from the national agricultural bank for peasant smallholders, thus obtaining credit for local cultivators who otherwise would not qualify. Together with peasant leaders, they persuaded government officials to locate a distributorship of the state-owned fertilizer industry (ENCI, National Company for the Commercialization of Inputs) in the village of Colquepata. In effect, the peasant cultivators of Colquepata District managed to capture scarce production subsidies. Although awash in neither credit nor fertilizer, they managed to channel their new-found inputs into reclaiming montane bogs whose primary usefulness—pasturing livestock during the dry season—was deteriorating in any case due to infestation by a zooparasite (see note 8).

During the late 1960s, dozens of peasant households in Colquepata District drained bog sites and mounded the fertile muck into ridges for agricultural use. To establish a wetland production system, they adopted familiar techniques and hand tools while also introducing manufactured technologies. At first, cultivators dug a design of parallel beds and alleys similar to the standard ridged-field system common in upland areas of the district. Fields cultivated in this pattern were overwhelmed by disease infection and pest predation due to poor drainage. Cultivators soon transplanted techniques and layouts from isolated drained-*wachu* fields found in nearby portions of the Cordillera Vilcanota to the bog-containing swales in the zone of phyllite outcrop.[13] By borrowing a field design from high-elevation sites and infusing it with sufficient labor and capital inputs, households cultivating the new agricultural system could count on substantial yields ready for harvest near the height of cyclical price fluctuation.

Within a few years of initiating cultivation, households had commercialized wetland fields to a greater extent than their other agricultural systems, and income from drained-*wachu* parcels formed a substantial flow in the small but growing monetary circuits of household economies. Pushed by a growing demand for consumer goods (radios, bicycles), continued population growth, and the decline of production in other field systems, the reliance of households on commercialized wetland production increased rapidly. To intensify production, cultivators simplified rotation schedules and reduced fallow periods. Continued cropping depleted soil fertility and triggered a build-up of agricultural pest and disease loads. In response, the currently widespread four-year rotation of potatoes-potatoes-oats-fallow was adopted by most cultivators. Nonetheless, drained-*wachu* production soon demanded even greater inputs of pesticides, insecticides, and fertilizer. Furthermore, fungal and bacterial blights made harvested tubers unsuitable for seed and forced cultivators without separate seed-producing plots to exchange for or purchase seed tubers. The amassing need for chemical amendments and potato seed barely braked the momentum of wetland agriculture. Provisioned with sufficient and inexpensive labor by its members, along with subsidized credit and agricultural inputs supplied by government institutions, most households were able to initiate and continue drained-*wachu* production.

While households in Colquepata District expanded commercial production of dry-season potatoes during the 1970s, so too did producers in neighboring regions of Paucartambo Province. Rather than rely on intermediate-elevation bogs, other cultivators of the dry-season crop utilized irrigated fields, floodplain sites, and cloud-forest habitats that collected substantial fog drip (see figure 6). The continued viability of commercialization in each region depended on economic advantages vis-à-vis other producers. The competitiveness of dry-season production in Colquepata District benefited from both social and spatial-scale factors. Socially, a crucial advantage originated in the minor extent of clientage relations both among rural agriculturalists and between these cultivators and villagers, a feature distinguishing Colquepata District from nearby regions due to the former's history of free communities and Quechua peasant resistance. As a result, Colquepata commerce was relatively unencumbered by socially powerful and economically restrictive nonindigenous elites (Fonseca Martel and Mayer 1988).[14] Moreover, following the ouster of the Revolutionary Government of the Armed Forces in 1975, enterprising cultivators in Colquepata District continued to gain disproportionately from subsidies provided by the state (most recently, bank loans under President Alan García's *Trapecio Andino* program [1983–86]) and international aid agencies. Three of the latter (Canada, the Netherlands, the European Economic Community), attracted at least in part by the lesser extent of socioeconomically oppressive clientage, were operating in Colquepata District by the mid-1980s, while equally needy districts to the east did not benefit from a single comparable program.

The small size of drained-*wachu* fields favored cultivators in Colquepata District due to the agro-ecological and related labor requirements of wetland agriculture. Following Brewster's (1950) argument for "technical cost advantages" accruing from temporal and spatial constraints on increased capitalization and farm size in agriculture, three properties of dry-season production differentially aided the competitiveness of Colquepata agriculturalists. First, the near-equality and small extent of land holdings in Colquepata District helped assure drained-*wachu* producers a ready supply of labor for tasks

demanding several workers (mounding, planting, harvest). In contrast, land-rich producers such as those in the lower (northern) Mapacho Valley (figure 6) struggled to recruit labor following the 1969 Agrarian Reform and often paid a higher daily wage than in Colquepata District. Secondly, the small area of drained-*wachu* fields (50–300 square meters) permitted individual households to monitor crops effectively and modify the growing environment with little difficulty. Finally, drained-*wachu* producers in Colquepata District were also favored differentially by the high risk of crop failure in dry-season production resulting from physical (frost, drought, and hail) and biological (pests, disease) hazards. Combining several income sources, the diversified household-economic strategies of Colquepata smallholders retained a greater flexibility in production strategies and more capacity for risk taking than those of specialized dry-season producers in other regions.[15] In summary, prominent ecological attributes of wetland agriculture complement the smallholder form of social organization and thereby contribute to the continued economic viability of dry-season farming in Colquepata District. Ecological and social features underlying changes in the agriculture of Colquepata District can also be viewed in light of geographical schemata for classifying the modification of land use in peasant societies.

LAND-USE CHANGE

Doolittle (1984, 124–25) has proposed a typology of land-use change in nonmechanized agriculture that distinguishes between systematic and incremental modifications. Systematic alterations entail the "periodic addition of [newly constructed] individual fields and associated features such as terraces and canals," whereas incremental changes involve "new fields and associated features [that] are not swiftly changed to a final form but are transformed while in use." Although Doolittle emphasizes the areal importance of incremental land-use change, other reviews highlight the prevalence of systematic modifications in the agriculture of peasant and indigenous farmers (e.g., Denevan 1983, 404). The drained-*wachu* field system of Colquepata District evinces systematic land-use modifica-

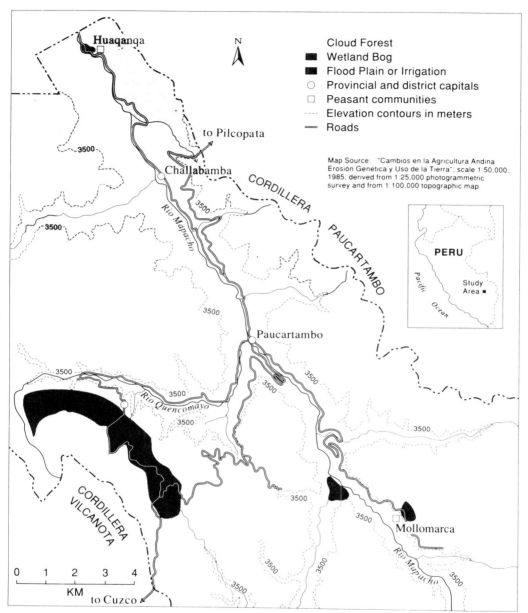

FIGURE 6

Environments of dry-season potato production in Colquepata District and neighboring regions.

tion. It also demonstrates that the scheduling and amount of labor contrasts systematic change (immediate alterations/high labor requirements) with incremental modification (gradual change/ low labor inputs). Furthermore, the wetland agriculture of Colquepata, which would qualify as small-scale by most metrics, highlights the salience of field size. To consider only the temporal and spatial dimensions of land-use change, however, would be remiss in not addressing the social organization of such modifications.

Land-use change in nonmechanized agriculture needs to assess the sociospatial structures of power through which cultivators organize production and modify environments. This feature defies simple description. In establishing the drained-*wachu* fields of Colquepata District, smallholder households stand out as the primary units responsible for marshaling labor, land, and other resources. Yet households only account for proximate social organization, that is, the social group most directly managing land use. The agricultural conversion of montane bogs linked several spatial scales of social and economic power, extending from the international political economy through the state and its institutions to power relations within households. Claims that smallholder households in Colquepata District were able to make on the local representatives of international and state institutions, as well as the labor of their members, were crucial for developing drained-*wachu* production and, to a large extent, prefigure its future.

Finally, examination of the recent emergence and production of drained-*wachu* fields demonstrates that spatial patterns of agricultural change interconnect to other elements in the production strategies of smallholder households via the demand for labor, land, and capital. In most peasant agricultural systems, these links lead the changes in single fields to rebound through the multiple parcels cultivated by a household (Mayer 1985). Although peasant smallholders in Colquepata District did not cease cultivating several dispersed fields belonging to various production systems as they undertook the agricultural "colonization" of wetland sites, they were forced to adjust household economic strategies and production practices. Maize cultivation, for instance, was abandoned at this time by many smallholders because of the conflict between the scheduling of its labor requirements and those of drained-*wachu* fields. In this case, land-use change located far from wetland parcels resulted from amplifying the already constraining seasonal shortage of labor within households.

CONCLUSION

Regional political ecology attempts to integrate the multiple social and ecological relations em-

bodied in the organization of agriculture and land use. Applied to the recent conversion and continued cultivation of montane-bog habitats in the Colquepata District of Peru's southern highlands, this approach indicates that wetland production developed when smallholder households of Quechua peasants responded to a convergence of favorable production and demand conditions during the late 1960s and 1970s. Counted among coincident changes were the decreased opportunity costs of alternative land use (capacity for livestock production), expanded market demand (potato prices, seasonal price fluctuation), and increased production stimuli (agricultural credit, fertilizer). Rather than viewing these structural modifications as mere contexts within which actors arrived at decisions, a reformulated and more integrated regional political-ecology perspective has been used to examine how altered conditions of production relate to the social practices of local cultivators and land users.

Modeling a regional political ecology perspective on the interplay of social practices (agency) and political-economic conditions (structure), the analysis of agricultural change in Colquepata District demonstrates that the struggles of indigenous peasants shaped not only a "politics of place," but also the temporal and spatial contours of drained-*wachu* development. Following centuries of refuge from and resistance against dominant landlords and villagers, rural inhabitants in the region commercialized agriculture little fettered by feudalistic clientage with village elites. At the same time, land-centered and place-specific peasant ideology led to the region's disproportionate capture of scarce propeasant agricultural subsidies under Peru's Revolutionary Government of the Armed Forces. Spurred by the combination of historically and regionally contingent incentives, Colquepata inhabitants drew on stocks of local agricultural and environmental knowledge to carve out a highly distinct form of wetland agriculture.

The development and persistence of drained-*wachu* cultivation by peasant smallholders in Colquepata District attest to close ties woven among wetland field environments, spatial scale, and the social organization of agricultural production. Prominent agro-ecological traits (water-logging, weed infestation, plant pathogens, insect pests) favor the flexible scheduling of field tasks and therefore provide a technical cost advantage to smallholder households. The ecological and spatial rationales favoring smallholders challenge the assumption that direct state-level intervention is necessary for food production in wetland habitats (*pace* Kolata 1986). Moreover, the expansion rather than the disappearance of smallholder production that accompanied the economic growth of wetland agriculture in Colquepata District contravenes expectations that, through agricultural change, the majority of smallholders will be converted to capitalist farmers (Schultz 1964) or proletarians (Lenin 1976). Rather than representing a unique configuration, the combination of technical cost advantages, peasant claims on state institutions and international agencies, and the exploitation of household labor below the level of market wages complements national economic stagnation in contributing to the persistence of peasant smallholders in Latin America and other Third World regions (de Janvry et al. 1989; Reinhardt 1988).

Reformulated concepts in regional political ecology contribute to a multifaceted debate concerning the design and implementation of rural development policy in economically underdeveloped countries. Rather than emerging exclusively from a topdown process dictated by government officials or aid agencies, development planning is increasingly recognized to necessitate the involvement of local inhabitants (Friedmann 1987). The diverse groups of Colquepata inhabitants (e.g., households, small informal groups, the peasant federation) that collectively sought to obtain state resources for development comprised one of a growing number of "social movements" in Latin America and other world regions, both economically developed and underdeveloped (e.g., Slater 1985). Consisting of social aggregations that seek to change the relations of power in areas such as production, science, and ethics, such movements are often characterized by democratic and local-scale forms of organization. Several of the potential advantages afforded by the incorporation of social movements into rural development planning are illustrated by both the "regional" and "political-ecological" emphases of the present study.

Participation of rural social movements (or "grass-roots" groups) can strengthen the democratic planning of regional development, thereby making more effective use of local resources (Slater 1985). As demonstrated in the present study, most Colquepata inhabitants were able to develop wetland agriculture by marshaling the triad of land, labor, and capital while also mastering the skills and knowledge necessary for successful production. Aid agencies and government planners in financially strapped underdeveloped economies such as Peru would have been hard pressed to identify the window of economic opportunity presented by drained-*wachu* agriculture. In effect, rural social movements can expand the level of both spatial (and ecological) disaggregation and democratic decision making employed in the formation of development strategies. Notwithstanding the advantages afforded to regional economic planning by the participation of local inhabitants, their social and economic betterment will continue to depend also on the political-economy base of regional political ecology (M. Watts 1988).

The window of economic opportunity opened by wetland agriculture in Colquepata District is propped up precariously as a result of political-economic disadvantages afflicting agriculture in highland Peru. Short-term success and the local accumulation of wealth are threatened most directly by the likely decrease of off-season potato prices as well as the possible reduction of production subsidies. Emanating from political and economic crises of the Peruvian state, dissolution of the primary stimuli that induced wetland agriculture would probably prompt its demise. The constraints on development in Colquepata District echo conditions besetting rural regions in many crisis-ridden and economically underdeveloped countries (e.g., M. Watts 1983b). Successful development based on regionally specific land-use strategies, whether planned or unplanned, will not only depend on the involvement of rural social movements at the local level but also on their effectiveness in promoting a favorable alignment of national markets and government policies.

SOURCE AND ACKNOWLEDGMENTS

This article appeared originally in the *Annals of the Association of American Geographers* 81 (1991): 443–63. Fieldwork for this study was undertaken with the support of the Fulbright Foundation, the National Science Foundation, and the Joint Committee on Latin American Studies of the Social Science Research Council and American Council of Learned Societies with funds provided by the Andrew W. Mellon Foundation. The initial research (March–June 1986) was undertaken while the author was employed as field supervisor for the "Changes in Andean Agriculture" project of Stephen B. Brush and Enrique Mayer. The author gratefully acknowledges the cooperation of project members, especially Leonidas Concha and the preceding field supervisor, César Fonseca Martel. In addition, he thanks Enrique Mayer for pointing out the importance of seasonal price fluctuations in stimulating changes in highland potato agriculture. This paper originated as a presentation to the "Historical Approaches in Cultural Ecology" Symposium at the 1989 AAG Meetings. W. M. Denevan, M. W. Lewis, K. Mathewson, M. S. Meade, B. L. Turner II, and two anonymous reviewers provided helpful comments and suggestions.

NOTES

1. Research for the present study was undertaken while the author resided in the province of Paucartambo, which includes Colquepata District, from March 1986 until August 1987. Interviews and oral histories involving sixty cultivators and villagers complemented participant-observer ethnography. Ecological methodologies included the mapping of seventy-five fields, random sampling of twenty field sites for soils analysis, and the collection of tubers. Identifications of insects, bacteria, fungi, and disease were made at the Center for the Investigation of Andean Crops (CICA, Centro para la Investigación de Cultivos Andinos) in Cuzco and the International Potato Center (CIP, Centro Internacional de la Papa) in Lima. Ing. Ramiro Ortega Dueñas and Dr. María Mayer de Scurrah were especially helpful in making identifications. Archival materials were consulted in Cuzco's Agrarian Reform Archives (Archivo de la Reforma Agraria), the Cuzco Departmental Archive (Archivo Departamental del Cuzco), and the archive of the Archbishop of Cuzco (Archivo del Archobispado del Cuzco).

2. Bogs are usually considered to be a type of wetland. Cowardin, Carter, Golet, and LaRoe (1979, 3), for instance, define wetlands as "lands where saturation with water is the dominant factor determining the nature of soil development and the types of plant and animal communities living in the soil and on its surface" (see also Martin, Hotchkiss, Uhler, and Bourn 1953). Geographers writing on the agricultural use of wetlands (or wet land) also have used the term in reference to those areas characterized by waterlogged soils (including bogs) (Denevan 1970; Knapp and Denevan 1985; B. L. Turner and Denevan 1985). It should be noted that the definition of wetlands held by some biological ecologists does not include bogs (e.g., R. Lincoln, Boxshall, and Clark 1982).

3. In addition to riverine floodplains such as the San Jorge of Colombia (Parsons and Bowen 1966) and Ecuador's Río Guayas Valley (Parsons 1969), raised-field cultivation in lowland South America covered extensive areas of interior savannas, including Bolivia's Llanos de Mojos (Denevan 1966b) and the Llanos de Orinoco of Venezuela (Denevan and Zucchi 1978).

4. Extant ridged fields in the Andes consist of narrow (0.3–0.5 meter), parallel ridges separated by slightly wider intervening alleys (0.4–0.6 meter). Their "wave length," or distance from ridge-top to ridge-top, ranges from 0.8 to 1.0 meter. The height, or "amplitude," of ridges varies between 0.3 and 0.6 meter (Denevan 1970, 651).

5. The texture and fertility of swale soils is well suited to agriculture. Although upper layers of the soil contain a high content of organic matter (7–10 percent), this level decreases rapidly once plowing and cultivation are initiated. The significant acidity (pH 3.5–4.8) of swale sites does not impair acidophilous plant species such as cultivated potatoes.

6. The major tasks used to cultivate standard ridged fields include the following: plowing, leveling and pulverization of planting beds, planting, first mounding, second mounding, fertilization, application of insecticide, application of fungicide, weeding, and harvest.

7. The figure for ridged fields is from Erickson (1985). The mounding of prehistoric platform fields presumably required considerably more labor than the drained-*wachu* parcels of Colquepata District (Erickson 1985). Platforms, however, probably were not mounded anew each year, suggesting that the average annual demand for tillage (and perhaps other tasks) in these fields might have been similar to drained-*wachu* production.

8. The causes of crop loss in drained-*wachu* fields include fungal (e.g., Potato Late Blight, *Phytophtera infestans, Q. soqra, Sp. la rancha*), bacterial (e.g., Potato Soft Rot, *Esclerotinia sp., Q. saliasqa, Sp. pudedumbre*), insect (e.g., Potato Flea Beetle, *Premnotrypes sp., Q. papa quru*), and other invertebrate (e.g., Liver Fluke, *Fasciola hepatica, Q. kayutaka, Sp. alicuya*) agents.

9. A 1690 report catalogued all of its population as "natives" (*naturales*) as opposed to "Spaniards," who were common in nearby villages (Urteaga Villanueva 1982).

10. My use of the concept "region of resistance" benefits from the concept of the "region of refuge" formulated and described by Aguirre Beltrán (1979) while differing significantly in both its social and spatial content. I use the term to indicate how the social and territorial dimensions of a region arose through ethnic conflict and particularly indigenous resistance. Aguirre Beltran, on the other hand, emphasizes a biological interpretation of territoriality and the domination of indigenous peoples. Secondly, he uses the concept to refer to larger areas than Colquepata District, sometimes a state or department but more frequently a province.

11. Potato prices varied more in highland markets than coastal ones for at least two reasons. First, highland regions differed from their coastal counterparts in not receiving much year-round production from valleys on the coast. Secondly, the demand curve of highland consumers, with less purchasing power than those on the coast, was correspondingly less elastic (G. Scott 1986).

12. The most important improved varieties at that time (known as *mantaro* and *renacimiento*) belonged to *S. tuberosum* subsp. *tuberosum,* the one potato taxon that includes all "improved," or scientifically bred, lines. The Green Revolution package for potato production was rapidly incorporated into Andean production—albeit at an uneven rate socially and geographically.

13. From the Papa Llacta portion of the Cordillera Vilcanota, J. Sánchez Farfan (1983) describes a field layout similar to the drained-*wachu* pattern of Colquepata District. Other ethnographic accounts of small areas of extant wetland cultivation in the Andes indicate field designs that differ significantly from the drained-*wachu* one (e.g., Flores Ochoa and Paz Flores, 1983).

14. Neighboring districts such as Paucartambo, Challabamba, and San Salvador, on the other hand, contained numerous non-Quechua village elites who controlled commercially restrictive webs of clientage (Fonseca Martel and Mayer 1988). Recognizing the prominence of Quechua inhabitants who maintain dual residences in and outside of the village of Colquepata, residents of other Paucartambo villages describe it as a "peasant town" (*pueblo campesino*).

15. By locating subsistence production in environments less risky than those used for commercial production, the household-economic strategies of drained-*wachu* producers in Colquepata District resemble those of most peasant smallholders (Brush 1987, 33).

FURTHER READINGS

Gonzalo Aguirre Beltrán. 1979. *Regions of refuge.* Washington, D.C.: Society for Applied Anthropology.

This is an early work examining how social and environmental conditions distinguish underdeveloped and spatially distinct "regions of refuge" in highland Latin America.

Piers Blaikie and Harold Brookfield. 1987. *Land degradation and society.* London: Methuen.

Blaikie and Brookfield expound a framework of regional political ecology that focuses attention on the decision making of individual land users within the context of their various opportunities and constraints.

Stephen B. Brush. 1987. The nature of farming systems and views of their change. In *Comparative farming systems,* ed. B. L. Turner II and Stephen B. Brush, 11–48. New York: Guilford.

The authors furnish a comprehensive review of explanations dealing with agricultural change, especially among peasant peoples. They argue for consideration of structural (economic) features and individual behavior.

William M. Denevan. 1970. Aboriginal drained-field cultivation in the Americas. *Science* 169:647–54.

Denevan provides a review and classification of pre-European wetland agriculture emphasizing the location, environment, and morphology of these field systems.

William E. Doolittle. 1984. Agricultural change as an incremental process. *Annals of the Association of American Geographers* 74:124–37.

This is a detailed study of field modifications among Mexican (Sonoran) agriculturalists that demonstrates the role played in agricultural change by spatial scale of the productive unit.

Daniel W. Gade. 1975. *Plants, man and the land in the Vilcanota Valley of Peru.* Biogeographica No. 6. The Hague: W. Junk B.V.

This major work on cultural-historical geography in a prominent central Andean valley demonstrates convincingly that peasant farm technologies and knowledge have undergone significant historical changes and do not represent timeless cultural adaptations.

Anthony Giddens. 1979. *Central problems in social theory: Action, structure, and contradiction in social analysis.* Berkeley: University of California Press.

Giddens's book is one of several major works in social theory that formulate the concept of structuration, or the "mutual dependence of structure and agency."

Gregory W. Knapp. 1991. *Andean ecology: Adaptive dynamics in Ecuador.* Boulder, Colo.: Westview.

Knapp's study of pre-European wetland agriculture in Ecuador highlights the adaptive environmental and economic features of these farming systems. Environmental change, population growth, and socioeconomic pressures are considered as forces that lead inhabitants to develop wetland agriculture.

Kent Mathewson. 1985. Taxonomy of raised and drained fields: A morphogenetic approach. In *Prehistoric intensive agriculture in the tropics,* ed. I. S. Farrington, 835–45. Oxford: British Archaeological Reports, International Series 232.

The author's recent review and classification of wetland agricultural systems delineates a taxonomic scheme based primarily on field form and biophysical environment.

Enrique Mayer. 1985. Production zones. In *Andean ecology and civilization: An interdisciplinary perspective on Andean ecological complementarity,* ed. Shozo Masuda, Izumi Shimada, and Craig Morris, 45–84. Tokyo: University of Tokyo Press.

This article describes how the morphology of central Andean land use is created and modified through sociospatial organization. The article is a crucial addition to the extensive literature that depicts landscape form in the Andes.

Steve J. Stern. 1987. *Resistance, rebellion, and consciousness in the Andean peasant world, 18th to 20th centuries.* Madison: University of Wisconsin Press.

This collection of twelve contributions, introduced by historian Stern, advances considerably the understanding of the cultural and historical dimension of agrarian conflict involving Andean peasants. Like Stern's earlier work, it shows how Andean peasants have often sought to engage their political and economic worlds through strategies of resistance and accommodation.

Michael J. Watts. 1988. Struggles over land, struggles over meaning: Some thoughts on naming, peasant resistance, and politics of place. In *A ground for common search,* ed. Reginald G. Golledge, Helen Couclelis, and Peter Gould, 31–50. Goleta, Calif.: Santa Barbara Geographical Press.

This wide-ranging essay brings together various concepts concerning peasant politics, production, and places. Land resources are shown frequently to occupy a common ground where meet the material struggles and ideological conflicts of peasant producers as they face social domination, state manipulation, and muted commercial opportunities.

JAMES J. PARSONS **18**

CULTURAL GEOGRAPHY AT WORK

T his volume seeks to place in context past work in the field, especially as represented by the tradition so largely attributed to Carl Sauer (1889–1975), and then complement and enrich it with new developments and currents of thought. The dizzying array of introspective texts, mostly originating with an academic elite of Commonwealth background, on what might constitute a reformulated or "modern" human geography has challenged cultural geographers to rethink their goals and their place within the larger scholarly arena. The extreme form of the new critical discourse, which demands merging modern social theory and geography and often emphasizes the subjective meaning of space (a kind of "deep geography"), proposes a conceptual shift so dramatic as to make the field all but unrecognizable to more orthodox practitioners and, one presumes, to most of the general public.

The much heralded "debate" within cultural geography in which this new paradigm is being discussed and defined seems at times less a debate than either a discordant claim to priority accommodation within, or "reinvention" of, an established and respected subfield of the discipline (M. Price and M. Lewis 1993). In North America, cultural geography, with its historical-ecological-landscape emphasis, has generally stood firm and apart from the plethora of "revolutions" experienced by much of the rest of the field. It traces its origins back to nineteenth-century Germany and France. A distinguished British geographer and planner could recently refer to "the cultural geographical revolution in the U.S.A. with its throwback to the grand old man of American geography Carl Sauer" as "a strange development for British geographers" (P. Hall 1980).

Some will see the present volume as a step toward the development of a more formal conceptual and theoretical framework for cultural geography, broadening and clarifying its position within the larger field, as well as bringing the subdiscipline more in line with critical currents within contemporary social science. This revisionist approach would give primacy to theoretical concerns, particularly those related to political economy and social justice or alternatively extending its scope beyond empirical reality to include the entire range of subjectivity.

I have chosen to focus here on some of the distinguishing features of a more traditional cultural geography, reaffirming past achievements and the potential for further elaborating and extending familiar ecological and human-environment themes in their regional and historical contexts. The identification of the common ground between these two quite divergent points of view is a problematic endeavor, yet it is one worthy of our best efforts.

I start from the assumption that geography is, as its name says it is, the description and study of *geo*, the earth, and that its "cultural" subset is responsible for that part of the subject concerned with the human occupancy of the land, now and in the past, by different peoples with differing cultures. Further, I assume that one of its central concerns, at varying scales, is with recognizably distinct places, regions, or culture areas and how they "tick"—in other words, how they work. We may tarry along the way, according to our temperaments and purposes, to consider the inner workings of culture, causation in human behavior, or distribution patterns of items of material culture, language, religion, or attributes that help define how and where people live or have lived and how they differ and why. But we inevitably come back to the primacy of place, geography's original defining *raison d'être* and the context within which the themes we address are most commonly embedded (Hart 1982). This

is the geography a supporting public recognizes and readily accepts.

Geography's contribution to the social sciences is especially its connection with the physical world; at the same time, it may give new and broadened meaning to the component facts of natural science. Thus it may be seen as a peculiarly liberating pursuit that links the scattered sciences together and gives to each a context and meaning of which they may be barren when standing alone. The biologist F. Raymond Fosberg (1976:120) has even suggested that "geography, which makes possible a view of the earth or any large part of it or major aspect of it as a whole, is increasingly justified as a *sine qua non* for the continued tenure of the human race, at least as we know it, on earth." I review here a few arbitrarily selected culture-related aspects of how the world works that have seemed to me underrepresented in the literature of geography.

ENVIRONMENTAL HISTORY

Environmental history is a neglected theme in this volume. It deserves better. It has become a recognized subfield of history, where it has its own society and journals. Environmental history has much in common with geography. Both use data from the past to explain the dynamics of human and natural systems. In taking the long view, environmental history seeks to discover patterns in the ways human beings use and modify the landscapes and ecosystems around them. Demanding a certain familiarity with affiliated fields of study, especially the earth and atmospheric sciences, cultural anthropology, and archeology, as well as history, it is well accommodated by the concept of geography as cultural ecology (B. L. Turner 1989).

The roots of such concerns within geography lie deep in the past (Glacken 1967). We can trace them through George Perkins Marsh's *Man and Nature* (1864), the Princeton symposium entitled "Man's Role in Changing the Face of the Earth" (Thomas 1956), and the recent Clark University conference entitled "The Earth as Transformed by Human Action" (B. L. Turner et al. 1990). Yet apart from their contributions to the Princeton and Clark gatherings, geographers have not assumed the roles that might have been expected of them on the larger stage of environmental debate (but see Hammond, Macinko, and Fairchild 1978). When the environmental movement came of age—at a time when we should have been most concerned—geography as a profession was looking the other way, caught in the alluring glare of the social science paradigm.

The history and consequences of environmental degradation had been central to Sauer's geography (Speth 1977). Sauer had played a major role during the Depression in establishing the U.S. Soil Conservation Service and working on the policy-oriented President's Science Advisory Board. Two of his papers, "Destructive Exploitation in Modern Colonial Expansion" and "The Theme of Plant and Animal Destruction in Economic History," both published in 1938, were eloquent harbingers of looming environmental crises. The latter was described by the editor of the avant-garde *CoEvolution Quarterly,* in reprinting it forty years later, as a paper that "could be given next year and be the best thing said all year" (Brand 1976b). Sauer was, the editor noted, "so routinely correct about matters so fundamental that a popular following never caught up with him" (Brand 1976a). Yet few of our colleagues followed Sauer's example. As a matter of sad fact, the silence of a later generation of geographers on environmental issues and global change until recently has been deafening.

NATURAL HAZARDS AND VEGETATION CHANGE

As the global crisis deepens, deforestation, soil erosion, air and water pollution, floral and faunal extinctions, and the effects of toxic materials are among the environmental issues crying out for the geographer's attention (Kates 1987). All, including the relentless growth of human populations and the never-ending demands on the earth's resources by the improvident and wasteful ways of consumption-based Western societies, are deeply rooted in human attitudes and expectations—that is, in human cultures—as are our perceptions and responses to the seemingly increasing numbers of floods, droughts, hurricanes, killing frosts, wildfires, earthquakes, volcanic eruptions, destructive landslides, and pest invasions that collectively impose such tremendous and unpredictable costs on humankind every year (Burton, Kates, and White 1978; Kates and Burton 1986; M. Watts 1983a).

The "new ecology" that recognizes disequilibria, chaotic fluctuations, and the randomness of ecologic disturbances in nonhuman environments is beginning to recognize the intrinsic interdependence of humans and environment. Given this interdependence, chaos theory—now held in respect by theoretically inclined social and physical scientists alike—might well provide useful concepts leading to new ways of looking at geographical problems. Natural hazards research, with its dictum that society must work more with nature and less against it, has been a bright star in the firmament of geography. Although the principal investigators involved might not see themselves as cultural geographers, there is no question that culturally based perceptions of risk and reactions to it lie at the foundation of their studies. Landscape ecology, agro-ecology, and political ecology embrace similar concerns. Flood plains do not have to be occupied, and cities need not be built on earthquake-prone terrain. People do so of their own free will, despite the dangers, and will probably continue to do so.

The renaissance of biogeography (Veblen 1989), and particularly its subset of cultural biogeography, has sensitized us to human-induced changes in flora and fauna worldwide. A strong case can be made for vegetation cover as *the* overriding geographic factor, the most obvious and visible element in landscapes, whether forest, grassland, desert scrub, or farmland. It is often a proxy for the condition or health of an ecosystem. Street trees, gardens, and lawns, too, give special character to urban places. Human manipulation of the plant cover, especially through agricultural clearing and fire but also through afforestation and cultivation, is the most evident of all human relationships with the physical earth and is thus central to cultural geography (read "cultural ecology").

DEVELOPMENT AND POPULATION

The ominous environmental changes occurring on the planet are chiefly the result of two linked processes—the out-of-control growth of human population and the phenomenon we call development. Westerners have seen it as a moral imperative that peoples all over the world should come to live according to European dictates. Today they are no longer justified in terms of Christianity and civilization but rather in terms of development (Maybury-Lewis 1992). Yet if the rest of the world lived the same way that we do in this country (the richest, most comfortable population ever known), the planet could not take it. If it duplicated our automobile-based lifestyle it would choke to death. Nevertheless, how many of us have come out of the closet to challenge the precept that growth equates with progress, that the Elysian fields lie ahead for all when "development" matches the dreams of the futurists (Zelinsky 1970a; Luten 1980; 1991; Wallach 1991)?

Global change, whether the consequence of human activity (e.g., desertification, air pollution) or natural forces (e.g., rising sea level, El Niño), now requires behavioral adaptations that may soon confront all humankind (Mather 1991). Adaptation to changing environments, broadly conceived, has been suggested as a peculiarly appropriate concern for a modern cultural geography (Butzer 1990b; Denevan 1983). "Modernization," of course, has been taking a tremendous toll and will inevitably continue to do so, but there are other ways of facing the future. An example of the positive contributions of cultural geography in this regard is the considerable research on indigenous technologies and their conservative values, especially as related to tropical land use (Altieri and Hecht 1989; W. Clarke 1990; Klee 1980; Knapp 1991; Wilken 1987). The quincentennial of the arrival of Europeans in America has notably stimulated such work, as reflected so well in the special issue of the *Annals of the Association of American Geographers* edited by Karl Butzer (1992a) and entitled "The Americas before and after 1492," with perceptive contributions by several leading cultural geographers (see also B. L. Turner and Butzer [1992] on land-use change in the New World since 1492).

UNREPRESENTED "NATIONS"

The persistence of cultural grouping based on ethnicity, language, religion, territory, and a common history and way of life is emerging as a powerful new political reality as the twentieth cen-

tury draws to a close. A wide variety of the world's peoples are speaking up for their national or tribal rights and self-determination. Indigenous groups, their cultures long subordinated to the authority of powerful central states, are awakening, organizing, and fighting back, demanding recognition and some measure of autonomy. These territorially based minorities are political orphans, hidden within the arbitrary boundaries of some 170 recognized states. They constitute a Fourth World of close to five hundred "nations" of distinct peoples with an emergent sense of "belonging" (Kohr 1986).

From Tibet to the Albanian enclave of Kosovo inside Serbian Yugoslavia and from nationalist strongholds in the former Soviet Union to the islands of the Indonesian archipelago and the Indian tribes of North America, such groups are banding together to seek solutions to their perceived common problems. The Unrepresented Nations and Peoples Organization, based in The Hague, represents many such groups. They are engaged in the "little wars" against what to them are oppressive central states (Nietschmann 1987). These newly aroused nations or folk are striving in different ways to attain various levels of self-determination, often including control over the mineral resources underlying their lands. As exemplified by the newly independent Baltic republics and others of the Russian borderlands, by the Miskito in Nicaragua, the Cuna in Panama, and the Slovenians and Slovaks of central Europe, they are winning and in the process beginning to redraw the world map (Mikesell and Murphy 1991). Structures of traditional nation states appear less meaningful and so less durable than older loyalties marked by cultural distinctiveness and a sense of connectedness with the premodern past. A different way of packaging the world, with boundaries defined more by culture than by either state power or historical accident, may lie ahead. Cultural and political geographers will be called on to monitor and report on such developments, which are of potentially great significance to the future world.

AGRICULTURAL THEMES

Agriculture not only provides most of the foodstuffs that are the first imperative of our existence. It also represents the most widespread and conspicuous mark of the human occupancy of the earth. It is remarkable that American geographers have given it so little attention (but see Hart 1991), the more so in view of their frequent claim of representing a "spatial science."

By their nature, domesticated crop plants have been an especially attractive topic of study for diffusionists, of which geography has many (e.g., Kniffen 1990). The principles of botany and plant genetics essentially rule out the independent invention of these plants (a point passed over by the stimulating essay by Blaut in this section). A number of culturally oriented scholars, following Sauer's (1952) lead in *Agricultural Origins and Dispersals,* have looked at the domestication process (e.g., Blumler and Byrne 1991; D. Harris and Hillman 1989; D. Harris 1990; Johannessen 1970). Animal domestication has also attracted significant attention, though less of it (J. Baldwin 1987). Increasingly, such studies, although geographically focused, employ the advanced techniques of modern archeology and genetics.

Farming systems, except for tropical slash-and-burn agriculture, have been little examined. However, following in the steps of Boserup (1965) and Geertz (1963), geographers have shown substantial interest in agricultural intensification (Brookfield 1972; Doolittle 1984; Knapp 1991; M. Lewis 1992; B. L. Turner, Hanham, and Portararo 1977). On other aspects of agriculture representative contributions include those on irrigation (Doolittle 1990), terracing (Denevan, Mathewson, and Knapp 1987; Donkin 1979; L. Williams 1990), relict raised fields (Denevan 1970), wetland reclamation (M. Williams 1991; Zimmerer 1991) and intercropping (Innis 1983). Most describe tropical or Third World situations.

The dispersal of economic plants, as well as hunting techniques, from their presumed centers of origin both before and after 1492 has attracted interest (Carter 1977; Crosby 1972; 1978; Jett 1991; Johannessen and Parker 1988; Parsons 1972). Also considered have been pre-Columbian navigation systems that would have been necessary for postulated early exchanges between the Old World and the New World (e.g., Doran 1971; Edwards 1965; C. Riley et al. 1971).

A HUMANISTIC DISCIPLINE

When Sauer said "we are moralists," he seemed to be speaking for cultural geographers in general. He was deeply concerned with the progressive using up of the earth's capital by modern society and its obsession with consumption. It was a matter that continued to involve him throughout his long career. He became counsel to several of the leaders of the new conservation movement, always insisting that the transfer of Western technology to the less developed world, as in Latin America, had the potential for vast cultural and environmental mischief and that there was much to be learned from simple country folk. He was particularly distressed by the patronizing assumptions foundation-funded "experts" made in showing Mexican peasants how to grow corn and carry out their other farming activities (A. Wright 1984; Jennings 1988).

Despite their users' good intentions, methods of natural resource management derived from the social and climatic conditions of the North have proven to be poorly suited to conditions in many of the regions to which they have been introduced. A Social Science Research Council study group on environmentalism and the poor is currently looking at the little-understood linkages between socioeconomic and political inequities on the one hand and environmental sustainability on the other (Martinez-Alier 1992). But no geographers are represented on the panel. Ecologically inspired popular movements such as those of the Chipko "tree-huggers" of India or the rubber tappers of Brazil, or mobilizations against large dams by potentially displaced peoples, are examples of survival imperatives for the poor whose existence is not being ensured by either the market economy or the welfare state (Hecht and Cockburn 1989).

The need for wild land and open space, an appreciation of what is lost when living landscapes vanish, and the importance of the natural world to the health of the human spirit so basic to the land ethic of most indigenous American groups have gained new sympathy and attention with the Columbian quincentennial observances. Humans are increasingly seen as part of the global ecology, not separate from and above it. One reflection of this may be the grass-roots "bioregional" movement (Parsons 1985; Sale 1985), in which responsibility for the maintenance of a sustainable relationship between people and their environment is specifically allocated to local communities in microscale and mesoscale settings.

Cultural geographers have been especially attracted to diversity—unique cultures, unique culture elements, unique places, and how they have come to be. In other words, using a term more popular in the past, "culture history." Diversity, yes, and also survivals and their utility along with the importance of particulars—e.g., endangered species and habitats, threatened cultures, customs, landscapes, and production systems that have worked in the past.

PLACE, AREA, REGION, LOCALITY

Places, areas, or regions (*localities* is the currently fashionable term) must be a significant concern of geography, if only because the public expects geographers to provide information about them (Abler 1987). The mounting evidence of persistent localist attachments and influences, even in highly industrialized societies (Murphy 1991), has awakened a new interest in the notion of place and how to deal with it, even among those cultural geographers responding most enthusiastically to the charisma of contemporary social thought and theory (A. Gilbert 1988; Pudup 1988; Thrift 1990; 1991). The ultimate goal has been described by one as representing "the whole way of life of a region in a fully theorized way" (Thrift 1990, 276). In such a context, unfortunately, the region or area tends to be of less interest in itself than as a receptacle and background for "social structures and processes," the "medium for social interaction," and the "local response to capitalist forces." Its significance thus derives from the social processes that have produced it and are being created by it. Thus, the so-called locality debate in the more critical literature involves a quite new way of thinking about the uniqueness of place, with ends very different from those of the more orthodox geography.

The contributions of Nietschmann and Zimmerer in this section provide appropriate examples of the best that the newer cultural geog-

raphy has to offer in the realm of locally focused analysis. They inform the reader on the basis of their direct observations without obtrusive theoretical posturing or theorizing. They call to mind Loren Eiseley's comment that it is better for emissaries returning from the wilderness to record their marvel than to define its meaning, that substance or specificity of place beats definitions.

THE ROLE OF FIELDWORK

For cultural geographers of the more traditional cut, fieldwork and the primary data derived from it have been crucial to their identity. The attractions that field study offered brought many of us into the discipline in the first place and continue to provide a wide range of challenges and opportunities. The provision of trained field-workers, sensitive to both culture and environment and willing to get their boots muddy, may be one of geography's most important contributions to scholarship. It is one source of our subject's special status in academia. Since the mid-1970s, however, human geographers have produced less field-based research than ever before in this century (Rundstrom and Kenzer 1989). Remotely sensed imagery, the availability of detailed maps, and especially the computer data bases with their unprecedented masses of census and other statistical data have made "armchair" geography an increasing reality, as has the priority given to "meaning," of how to think about geography as opposed to the gathering and presentation of evidence. As the anthropologist Kent Flannery (1982, 271) has remarked of his own discipline, "every year there'll be fewer people down on the field and more up in the booth"; pretty soon, that is where all the noise will come from.

The decline of foreign area study, for which cultural geography has had a special affinity, undoubtedly reflects in part a disciplinary shift in focus to the new terra incognita of the imagination and the more abstract and systematizing goals of spatial science. A perceived shrinkage in the stock of "undiscovered places" may also be involved, but that would be more than counterbalanced by the increased facility of overseas travel. In an era of rapid technological change, such disengagement from field contact and the shift away from research, writing, and teaching about the more remote parts of the world (i.e., remote from Europe and North America) means that large areas of the earth are much less familiar than they once were or ought to be, given their intrinsic importance (Cleary and Lian 1991). The abandonment of foreign language requirements in graduate training undoubtedly contributes to this regrettable state of affairs.

Fortunately, the opportunities for exploration and discovery (and their consequent pleasures for the investigator) are far from over, given the woefully deficient knowledge of many parts of the world (Stoddart 1986). Funding may increasingly be an obstacle, but foreign fieldwork remains the icing on the cake for many. At Berkeley, at least, fieldwork reaffirmed the spirit of geographical adventure and, as often as not, proved critical for the validation of intuitive judgments or as Sauer termed them, hunches. It lifted us decisively out of the quagmire of defining our subject and methodology. There, in the out-of-doors, in direct engagement with reality, we had no doubts about what geography was or why we were geographers.

COMMUNICATION

As geographers our business is communicating. This demands good writing, much as might be expected from the more talented essayist or news reporter (see P. Lewis 1985; Meinig 1971a). There is no better place for literary virtuosity to express itself than in responding to the common curiosity about the world and how it works. Sauer—and we keep coming back to him—set the pattern, as attested by the reverence accorded him by some of our most innovative contemporary writers and poets. The late Charles Olson, enigmatic but renowned author of *Call Me Ishmael* and leading figure in the Black Mountain poetry group, termed Sauer's prose "too much for novelists to match" (Butterick 1980). Others described it as "spare, direct and pragmatic . . . his best essays having the rhythm and lucidity of a long symphonic poem" (Parsons forthcoming). Sauer's "Personality of Mexico" (1941b) and *The Early Spanish Main* (1966), as well as his unpublished correspondence, have been cited as ex-

amples of his mastery of measured prose. Happily, there are still cultural geographers in our midst with such a gift. The names of Donald Meinig, W. George Lovell, and Bret Wallach come to mind, but everyone has his or her own list. Their inspiration almost invariably stems from an intimate association with a particular landscape, whether local, regional, or national. A flair for evocative yet precisely detailed expression combined with insight on social-environmental relations also characterizes a notable number of semipopular writers who are "geographers at heart" (e.g., John McPhee, Joel Garreau, James Michener, Barry Lopez, Peter Matthiessen, Bill McKibben). Cultural geographers embrace them with special warmth.

In the end, of course, we must have something concrete to write about, with or without the encumbrance of method and theory. This means new information, new facts, artfully arranged either to describe an area or place or to address a geographical problem. As in all science, facts are indispensable. They do not mystify; indeed, we cannot get anywhere without them (Feynman 1988). The whole aim of research is to extend the facts and reduce the area of speculation, although the latter may direct us toward the kind of facts we require. "Details are the stuff of humanistic perspective" observes a *New Yorker* editorial:

> Unambiguous and unpredictable, details undermine ideology. They are connective. They hook our interest in a way ideas never can. If you let in the details of some aspect of life [the reference is to the disintegration of the Soviet Union] you almost have to allow that aspect to be what it really is rather than what you want it to be. Readiness to be interested in details of lives unlike our own is a profound measure of trust. Resisting details is usually an expression of xenophobia, of insecurity, or shyness, of a need to keep safely to one's self. ("Talk of the Town" 1989).

Lacking details, we lapse into abstractions about a place, a people, a relationship; with them, a map of the former USSR, for example, once an unarticulated landmass to most of us, is broken down into numerous subdivisions as republics and groups hitherto submerged within it have leaped out with singular, often discordant, identities.

ATTRACTIONS AND REWARDS

For most of our community geography is not just another academic discipline. We have chosen it because it has special meaning to us, an important premise that does not apply to all professionals. "Where else," asks Fred Kniffen (1976, 6), reflecting on a long life in the field, "can one study how humans live and have lived in any part of the physical world?" The joys of exploration and discovery have been some of the wellsprings of our subject's strength since antiquity.

The idiosyncratic qualities of traditional American cultural geography—its bias toward small-scale, non-Western cultures, its generally antitheoretical spirit, the arbitrary nature of the cluster of themes on which it has concentrated, and the resolute nonconformist character of some of its principal figures—have been commented on by Gade (1976; 1989), as well as by several contributors to this volume. A catholic curiosity, a shared concern for the substance of both our own surroundings and those of the wider world, hardly lends itself to clearly defined disciplinary boundaries. The cultural branch of our discipline uniquely responds to a naive curiosity about how the world functions, as well as what it looks like and what it means, and it does this from a distinctive geographical point of view. Its potential contribution to public policy making and to aesthetics ("landscape appreciation") provides us with other sources of satisfaction.

To the extent that cultural geography becomes divorced from the realities of place, the environment, and cultural patterns relating to the human occupance of the earth, now and in the past, it loses touch with the wonder and richness of the real world that has been the underlying basis of its appeal for many of us. For others, social welfare, the problems associated with race, class, and gender in the modern urban context, or conceptual issues regarding the subject's position in the larger theoretical field are where the rewards lie. The continuing philosophical and intellectual debate over the nature of geography would seem to call out for validation by empirical, content-oriented scholarship. A geography studying itself has no future. When the tail begins to wag the dog it is time to watch out. Where humans and their habitat are or have been involved, and distributions are uneven in space (i.e., mappable), our field literally has no bounds. Land use, settlement forms, housing, communication, field patterns, production systems, sacred places, tourism, place names—along with virtually every element of popular culture (Rooney, Zelinsky, and Lowder 1982)—are all fair game. The invisible elements of culture, such as language, religion, attitudes, and perceptions, have been the basis of some of the best recent work, as have food and food habits (Hilliard 1972; Simoons 1960; 1991) and medical geography (e.g., Simoons 1981), including the introduction of lethal Old World pathogens to the Americas following 1492 and the nature and extent of native population collapse and subsequent revival (Denevan 1992a; Lovell and Cook 1992).

If our work entails mapping, reconstructing, and explaining origins, dispersals, spatial patterns and processes, behavioral responses, elements of material and nonmaterial culture, routes, linkages—the entirety, really, of human-land relationships—what, it may be asked, is left out? Not much. But is not this very inclusiveness, with its integrative promise, the attraction and justification of our field? The late Archie Carr, philosopher-biologist and the world authority on turtles and tortoises, may have said it best: "A geographer is a man to envy. Being by definition a student of the earth, he is free to go anywhere he can get a ticket to tell of almost anything he can understand. . . . He can report on anything he wants to. One function of geography is to account for man as a feature of the landscape—and what is not grist for such a mill as that?" (Carr 1962).

IV
WHAT THE
WORLD MEANS

KENNETH E. FOOTE **19**

INTRODUCTION

Humans search for order and meaning in the worlds in which they live, and they shape these worlds of nature and society to meet their needs and expectations. This section addresses the ways in which humans perceive and ascribe meaning to environments, develop emotive attachments to their surroundings, and interpret the world through artistic media. Stress is placed on the moral, ethical, and ideological values that guide human interaction with environment. In this realm of research, culture is most often defined as *the set of shared values and collective beliefs* that shape individual and group action within a community but are themselves reshaped little from one generation to the next. These values and beliefs may be said to be expressed or represented in individual and social behavior, but such behavior holds little power to influence or transform the underlying moral strictures except over long periods of time.

In this sense, examples of culture are to be found in systems of religious beliefs, language, and patterns of kinship. Geographers are still interested in these examples, but they are likely of late to be concerned with belief systems that pertain directly to human interaction with environment, such as cultural attitudes toward nature, environmental ethics, landscape tastes, and the ways in which cultural values condition human perceptions of environmental risks and natural hazards. One of the greatest difficulties in this line of research lies in inferring beliefs from consistencies of human social and environmental behavior. A distinction between cultural and social geography is sometimes easier to assert abstractly than to demonstrate empirically. This area of research has become one of the most contentious in the whole of human geography owing to disagreements concerning appropriate explanations of patterns of cultural values. Research in this area has been instrumental in reawakening interest in cultural geography while simultaneously cultivating issues and methods that are not easily reconciled.

A DIVERSITY OF RICHES

The definition of culture as a system of collective beliefs and values has a long pedigree in cultural geography, as was noted in this book's general introduction. The idea of turning to literature and the visual arts for insight into these values has also attracted interest over a long period. The important point is that, although these topics gained attention before the 1970s, they were never dominant. *Readings in Cultural Geography* is largely silent on these issues. The writings of J. K. Wright and Sauer can be credited with foreshadowing recent developments, but they do not account for the rapid rise in popularity of these departures in the last three decades. Lowenthal (1961; 1967; 1968; Lowenthal and Prince 1965) was among the first to act on these ideas, and Tuan advanced the cause with a series of influential articles and books (Tuan 1974a; 1974b; 1975; 1977). Such writings motivated research into environmental meaning that has continued to the present. Eventually these investigations became a point of convergence for a number of research initiatives: the study of environmental perception, fresh departures in American historical geography and British social geography, and the rise of humanistic geography.

These initiatives have expanded the definition of cultural geography, provided new models of investigation based on alternative philosophies and methods, and extended the range of material falling within the subdiscipline's purview. From the standpoint of the articles in this section, the last benefit is particularly important. Here, in one place, are articles that look for evidence of cultural attitudes in sources as varied as filmmaking, novels, Christian theology, the architecture of contemporary America, the history of Niagara Falls, and interviews with Indians of the distant North. This is hardly an exhaustive list. One of the hallmarks of contemporary cultural geography is its willingness to explore novel materials in pursuit of insights into human attachment to and interaction with environment. Any tangible modification of the earth's surface—any landscape, however small or transitory—is fair game for study, as are human endeavors to express or interpret such attachments, whether in feats of artistic creativity or the ordinary prose of everyday people.

The articles of this section give a clear indication of how the bounds of cultural geography have expanded over the past thirty years. None of the articles could have been placed easily in *Readings in Cultural Geography,* yet all are of the mainstream today. The literature that has emerged in the last two decades is so rich that its diversity can hardly be captured in the six short articles presented here. Nonetheless, each represents a good example of a key research theme evident in contemporary cultural geography. Each benefits from being read in the context of closely related books and articles that pursue the themes in more detail and from other points of view. The discussion is organized around five themes: (1) The Environment Perceived; (2) Privileged Views and Visions; (3) Sense of Place and Identity; (4) Ethical Senses of Nature; and (5) The Iconography of Landscape.

THE ENVIRONMENT PERCEIVED

Perceptual issues have a long history in cultural geography and remain at the center of much contemporary research, often crosscutting one or more of the other thirteen themes outlined in this book. The premise of these departures is that cultural values are interwoven with the cognitive processes through which humans experience, perceive, organize, and act on information about the environment. Thus, although cultural geographers are interested in belief systems that transcend the individual, they gain much from studying the ways in which cultural values are expressed in individual behavior. This line of investigation was presaged in the writings of Sauer, William Kirk, J. K. Wright, and Gilbert White. The earliest seminal statement is that of Kirk (1952), published somewhat obscurely in the *Indian Geographical Journal* and not well known until reprinted later. As a result, real development of behavioral themes in geography dates to the late 1960s and the 1970s, when cultural geographers sought alternatives to the quantitative revolution. Work in environmental perception and behavioral geography was so influential by the 1970s that it became widely accepted throughout the discipline, much as the concept of ecology came to be applied to a wide range of topics far beyond its field of origin. Several recent reviews make clear the progress achieved in environmental perception and behavioral geography over the last thirty years (Aitken et al. 1989; Boal and Livingstone 1989; K. Craik 1986; Saarinen, Seamon, and Sell 1984).

Cultural geography and environmental perception studies overlap, but not on every research frontier. Cultural geography's interest in behavior has been in the behavior of groups. Researchers have studied the values and beliefs of such groups as they are reflected in religion, language, economic systems, and the like. Environmental perception takes as its starting point consistencies of perception, cognition, and behavior at the individual level, however much these may be filtered through the lens of culture. Research in environmental perception thus relies heavily on first-person surveys, interviews, and experimental methods that can be applied to some— but not all—questions raised by cultural geographers, particularly when they address historical processes, human institutions, and complex social organizations. This means that, in some cases, cultural geographers turn to other sources of information to assess how perceptions and cognitive images change through time and how these perceptions come to be held in common by large numbers of individuals within particular social and cultural groups.

The work of McManis (1972), Doughty (1987), Jakle (1977; 1982), and Lowenthal (1985) provides examples of the ways in which the insights of perception research can be applied to such topics. A fruitful interaction has also emerged between ecological studies and perception research in investigations of resource use in small-scale subsistence societies. In these situations, decision making regarding agricultural and other economic production can be traced to well-developed principles of resource use held by individual agriculturalists and based on extensive culturally transmitted knowledge of the environment. Sonnenfeld's (1991) article in this section provides a good example of the ties between environmental perception research and cultural geography.

Research on environmental perception has had the added benefit of promoting alternative methodological and philosophical departures. In trying to better understand human cognitive processes, researchers have turned to source materials such as fiction and the visual arts. These sources may not assess perception and cognition as directly as surveys and questionnaires, but they offer substantial indirect evidence of human attitudes and beliefs about environment and landscape. Furthermore, durable artifacts like books, diaries, and art are among the few sources of information from which researchers can make inferences about perceptions and beliefs held by humans in times past. Research using these sources is the particular concern of the section on privileged views and visions.

Environmental perception research can also be credited for inspiring investigations based on well-developed humanistic and structural philosophies, phenomenology being the most important. Despite the claims of some geographers, the principles of phenomenology can be applied only with great difficulty to most geographical problems (Pickles 1985). The phenomenological method is, however, well suited to answering questions concerning human perceptions of the environment. As used by geographers, the method stresses the inward, subjective nature of human environmental experience as expressed in the words and actions of ordinary people (Buttimer and Seamon 1980; Relph 1981; Seamon 1979; Seamon and Mugerauer 1985; Tuan 1974a; 1975; 1977). Through the use of in-depth interviews, researchers employing phenomeno-logical methods have generated valuable insights into the worldviews of particular social and cultural groups, such as the elderly and the sightless (Hill 1985; Rowles 1978). Recent writings in psychogeography by a number of psychologists and psychoanalysts hint at further provocative connections between inner psychological life and cultural preconceptions about the natural and social worlds (Stein 1987; Stein and Neiderland 1989).

PRIVILEGED VIEWS AND VISIONS

Certainly some of the most exciting departures in cultural geography have involved assessing how environments of affect and meaning are portrayed in a variety of artistic media. It should be noted, however, that this research continues an important theme of Alexander von Humboldt's *Cosmos* (1849) (Bunkse 1981). Pocock's (1981b) article in this section is one of many important contributions to the study of landscape in literature (Aiken 1977; 1979; Barrell 1982; Mallory and Simpson-Housley 1987; Porteous 1990; Salter 1978; Short 1991, 159–77; Squire 1988). Broader surveys of landscape in literature are often grouped by nation, as is Drabble's work on Britain (1979) and Kazin's (1988) and F. Turner's (1980, 1989) studies of the American literary imagination. Landscape painting has been investigated through the examination of the work of individual artists, such as John Ruskin (Cosgrove 1979) and J. M. W. Turner (Daniels 1987), and through broader studies of entire schools and genres of painting (Cosgrove and Daniels 1988; Rees 1975; 1976; 1978; Short 1991, 197–222). Howard's recent work on the history of British landscape painting is one of the most complete studies to date (P. Howard 1991).

Although photography has gained some limited attention (Foote 1987; Justim and Linquist-Cook 1985), cinema and television have been far more attractive foci of research because of the important part that they play in modern and popular culture. Even though these studies began to appear relatively recently, major surveys have now been assembled (Zonn 1990; Burgess and J. Gold 1985), and detailed studies are available (Aitken 1991; Short 1991, 178–96). Burgess's (1982) article in this section is exceptional in this context, not only because it considers the extent to which regional identity can be captured cinematically, but also because Burgess directly participated in the film-production process, an unusual role for a geographer. Studies of other art forms, such as the design of landscape gardens (Cosgrove 1984), are fewer in number but suggest the great potential for further research in these areas.

SENSE OF PLACE AND IDENTITY

The concept of place has gained much attention in recent years as a means of characterizing human emotive attachments to particular environments, whether of regions, cities, neighborhoods, or homes (Tuan 1974a; 1975; Buttimer and Seamon 1980). In most cases, research has dwelt on the positive bonds of comfort, safety, and well-being, but affective attachments are not always strong or always positive. Relph (1976) coined the term *placelessness* to characterize the weakened bonds of attachment to community and home common in some modern contexts, and Tuan (1979a) has gone so far as to consider "landscapes of fear." Study of place has helped to focus recent work in cultural geography because it offers a means of synthesizing the insights of so many varied research departures (J. Gold and Burgess 1982; Seamon and Mugerauer 1985). Because the study of place weaves together the varied concerns of cultural value, symbolism, individual behavior, and social action, the concept is sometimes viewed as a point of intradisciplinary unity within today's pluralistic geography (Agnew and Duncan 1989).

A good deal of research has been concerned with how emotional bonds of place arise. This involves considering how people shape the environment to reflect their social identities and tastes symbolically in the built environment of cities and suburbs and the landscape design of garden and countryside. Lowenthal and Prince (1965) were instrumental in calling attention to the symbols of identity in their examination of English landscape tastes. Recent works by Arreola (1984; 1988), Cosgrove (1984), Duncan (1973), Duncan and Duncan (1984), Hugill (1986), Lewandowski (1984), Ley (1987), Rowntree and Conkey (1980), and Shields (1991) have considered the symbolism of identity and place in different contexts. In his most recent articles, Tuan (1990; 1991) considers place making from the perspectives of language and fantasy.

Three of the articles in this section address the issues of place and identity from very different perspectives. Burgess's (1982) interpretation of regional character blends concern for sense of place with sensitivity to landscape identity to characterize the distinctiveness of England's Fens. Pocock (1981b) addresses the ways in which sense of attachment to place is developed in fiction writing. Indirectly, McGreevy's (1987) argument shows how a sense of place can be said to develop for Niagara Falls as a natural wonder and community on the basis of generations of public debate and action.

THE ICONOGRAPHY OF LANDSCAPE

The concept of landscape is as important to this section as it is to "How the World Looks." Cultural geographers are fascinated by the ways in which humans modify the natural world to create distinctive landscapes in rural, suburban, and urban settings around the world (P. Lewis 1983). More than at any time in the past, these landscape studies have focused on urban settings, what is termed the *urban built environment* (Domosh 1987; 1989; Krampen 1979; Relph 1981; 1987; Schuyler 1986). The interpretation of these landscapes in terms of fundamental cultural values and beliefs has stimulated tremendous methodological debate within cultural geography. Indications of this ferment can be found in the varying approaches assumed in several important collections of essays such as *The Interpretation of Ordinary Landscapes* (Meinig 1979b), *Landscape Meanings and Values* (Penning-Rowsell and Lowenthal 1986), and *The Iconography of Landscape* (Cosgrove and Daniels 1988).

One of the great difficulties in assimilating this varied research lies in disagreement over the appropriate methods for exploring symbolism and meaning. P. Lewis's axioms for reading the landscape (1979a) are a concise empirical short-

hand, whereas Lowenthal's (1985) concern for the rich historical allusions manifest in landscape indicates the complexities of symbolic interpretation. Experimentation with new methods is a hallmark of this research, including attempts to reframe landscape interpretation in terms of textual analysis (Duncan and Duncan 1988; Duncan 1990), iconographic theory (Cosgrove and Daniels 1988), nonverbal communication (Hugill 1975; Rapoport 1982), and semiotic theory (Foote 1985; 1988).

Attempts by geographers to address the complexities of modern urban society compound the problems of establishing agreement on goals and methods of research. Much has appeared of late concerning the geographical interpretation of modern and postmodern society, including key works by Entrikin (1991), Harvey (1989; 1990), Porteous (1990), Relph (1987), and Soja (1989). Although these works may provide some indication of the direction of future debate, their arguments have yet to produce a broad consensus among cultural geographers. Still, some of the rich possibilities of research in the domain of landscape meaning and value are indicated by the articles by Barbara Rubin Hudson (1979) and Patrick McGreevy (1987) in this section. Both are concerned with fundamental aspects of modern urban landscapes, American commercial architecture on one hand and urban development and promotion on the other. Both search for pattern in process—the gradual development of canons of aesthetic and commercial appeal over several generations. Like Harvey (1979) as he carefully reads the construction history of Paris's Sacré-Coeur, Barbara Hudson and McGreevy attend to historical detail in their attempts to find meaning in contemporary landscapes. Close contacts between cultural and historical geography are likely to remain a key feature of further investigations of cultural landscapes.

ETHICAL SENSES OF NATURE

Geographers and nongeographers alike have long been interested in the extent to which long-held moral and ethical precepts guide the human use of the earth. J. K. Wright's essays (1966a), Glacken's monumental *Traces on the Rhodian Shore*

(1967), and L. White's (1967) influential statement on the historical roots of the environmental crisis are three of the many works that set the stage for debate through the 1970s and 1980s (Sitwell 1990a). Doughty's (1981) article in this section provides an account of how ethics of land use and conservation in Western society derive from theological principles and the ideological imperatives of contemporary thought.

These ideas have been taken up on a number of fronts in recent decades in geography and neighboring disciplines (Lowenthal and Bowden 1976; Bunkse 1978). Scholars such as Cronon (1983), J. B. Jackson (1970; 1972a; 1984), Oelschlaeger (1991), and Wilson (1992) address how American conceptions of wilderness and nature evolved from first settlement onward. The deep ecology movement is presently the focus of tremendous debate (Devall and Sessions 1985; Naess 1988; Kohak 1984; Parsons 1985; Tobias 1985). Utopian and dystopian visions of society have also been studied by geographers to explain modern environmental ethics. In this context, interest in sacred spaces and spirituality expressed in landscape, pilgrimage, and tourism has added energy to current debate and suggested that geographers are begining to turn again to study of systems of religious belief as a means of understanding human interaction with environment (Jakle 1985; Lane 1988; Nolan 1983; M. Richardson 1989).

Dystopian views are an appropriate theme for us to end on. Sauer was one of the few true conservatives in modern academia, where there is a general belief that the human condition is perfectible. Sauer debunked such claims for any improvements in the human condition that depend on the heavy use of nonrenewable resources, and he was only slightly more positive about agrarian societies, far too many of which fail to renew the fertility of their soil. Current thinking in cultural geography has rather lost this perspective, for Smithian liberals and Marxists agree on the goal of perfected societies, disagreeing only on the means to achieve them. McGreevy's invocation of H. G. Wells's underregarded *War in the Air* comes nearest to putting forward a dystopian view in this collection, but the sense that decline was possible pervaded the Berkeley school. Hägerstrand (1988) has argued persuasively that we should be as concerned with denovation as innovation. In good times such a concern is ignored, but bad times have characterized human societies almost as often as good ones, and cultural geographers have been unusually willing to write about them. Such skills should not be abandoned.

JACQUELIN BURGESS **20**

FILMING THE FENS:
A VISUAL INTERPRETATION
OF REGIONAL CHARACTER

In 1977 I was given the opportunity to participate, as consultant and coresearcher, in making a television documentary about regional character. Entitled *A Sense of Place: The Fens,* it was intended as a pilot program for a series of regional films to be shown by BBC Television at peak evening viewing. It represented a departure from the traditional format of regional documentaries that were made for television during the 1970s. Such films as *The Making of the English Landscape, A Bird's Eye View,* and *A Writer's Notebook: The Pennines* had depended on an expert commentator, either literary or academic, to make the necessary interpretations about the landscape and to give credence to the subject matter.[1] The poet laureate, Sir John Betjeman, eulogized from the cockpit of a helicopter, while W. G. Hoskins extemporized from Lake District mountainside or Norfolk marsh. By contrast, our film was made without any reliance on an expert reading a commentary or appearing in front of the camera, the intention being to explore and elucidate by means of film those values that the inhabitants of a region themselves attribute to their landscape, and to capture the particular, special, and significant features of the place as local people experience them. "Reading the landscape is a humane art, unrestricted to any profession, unbounded by any field, unlimited in its challenges and pleasures" (Meinig 1979c, 236). In this essay I want to describe some of the challenges and pleasures, as well as the difficulties, that were encountered in capturing the sense of place.

FINDING THE STORY

A good documentary film has been described as one "which earns the shock of recognition from a mass audience" and may take one of two approaches to its subject matter (A. Smith 1973, 6). It may seek to provide an objective and impartial account of things, people, or activities, or, alternatively, it may be a personal film which deliberately embodies the perceptions, emotions, interests, and biases of the director. Personal documentaries are often more "concerned with people rather than things, with the 'why' of life rather than the 'how' of it" (Swallow 1965, 176). John Schlesinger, the film director who made a number of personal documentaries for British television in the early 1960s, describes them as "catching spontaneously the essence of what we had seen" (Swallow 1965, 180). This comment highlights the most significant point about the content and style of these films. Their subject matter is that of everyday life: "the drama on the doorstep, the drama of the ordinary," and the style is that of *cinéma vérité* (J. Grierson quoted in Sussex 1975, 206). Ordinary people going about their normal lives provide the content for the film, with no predetermined scripts, actors, or shooting schedules. *Cinéma vérité* asks nothing of people beyond a willingness to be filmed, and the camera is used to compile visual notes which are later edited to produce the story of the film. Devices such as music or intermittent commentary have given way in recent years to a reliance on "wildtrack sound," in which recorded interviews with people are used almost as a counterpoint to the visual images of places or of activities. This "wildtrack" is often much more effective than synchronized sound, in which individuals are filmed giving an interview, not least because people become self-conscious in front of the camera. The lack of congruence between visual image and spoken comment is more subtle and effective than a literal correspondence between the two. The power of personal documentaries is recognized by Denis Mitchell, whose

films *Night in the City* and *Morning in the Streets* remain as great artistic achievements and profound social comments about urban deprivation. He writes:

> I believe it is possible to express the essence of the human situation in our own time more effectively, because more truthfully, through the documentary than, say, through a fictitious drama . . . [what the producer manages to say] is in my opinion much more significant than what is said in a current affairs program with a spoken, pseudo-objective comment. (quoted in Swallow 1965, 177–78)

Why make a film about the Fens, a seemingly placid and peaceful agricultural region without any pressing social or environmental problems to catch attention? Our choice of region was determined by several considerations. We were anxious to move away from the familiar "TV regions"—the Lake District and the Pennines—where audience interpretations would be colored by their expectations about content. We needed a visually distinctive area, since the film itself would establish the location, and additionally a landscape sufficiently coherent so as not to confuse people with many changes in physical appearance. By no means insignificant was the fact that I grew up in the Fens and always had a strong intuitive "feel" for the area, while the director, who did not know the region, found it a strange, exciting, and compelling place. His commitment was crucial, and on the basis of his fascination, we began to explore the Fenland.

The initial preparation for the film involved extensive fieldwork by the director, Geoffrey Haydon, and myself. Norman Swallow, who directed several personal documentaries during the 1960s, commends intensive fieldwork to his contemporaries. Making *A Wedding on Saturday* took almost three months in the coal mining villages of South Yorkshire, for "the producer/director, if he is to express the essential character and feelings of those whom he has chosen, must live among them for at least several weeks . . . to discover their true characters and their genuine (though often superficially concealed) attitudes" (Swallow 1965, 185). The academic might blanche at the bold presumption that "several weeks" is quite sufficient. In our case, the film (which took nearly three years to make) required many months of research, fieldwork, preparation, and filming. The length of time reflected a desire to structure the film around seasonal changes in activity, as well as a number of unexpected technical difficulties. The landscape proved inordinately difficult to photograph with the vast gray skies so characteristic of Fen country ending up as blank, white, featureless spaces on the film. Finding the right locations which capture the essential feel of the landscape on film was also problematic. Editing large quantities of filmed material to produce a coherent whole took the director and film editor many months more. Filming landscapes and activities was not carried out to any script or predetermined schedule; rather, it was dictated by events. The chance discovery that a small farm was to be auctioned the next day meant bringing a lighting crew, camera operators, and sound recordists from London at short notice. Similarly, great flexibility was needed to capture a spectacular skyscape or random event on film.

The Fens cover some 1,300 square miles, stretching from just south of Lincoln to the edges of Cambridge, from Peterborough in the west to Lakenheath on the Suffolk borders. Within this large area, it is possible to distinguish the silt fen of Lincolnshire from the peaty area of the Black Fen (figure 1). We decided to concentrate on the Black Fen, formed from drained swampy marshes and meres. Falling broadly within a triangle bounded by Peterborough, Wisbech, and Cambridge, the Black Fen is the heart of the old Isle of Ely administrative division. Even narrowing the focus to this area (some 730 square miles), we were aware of distinctive differences not so much in the landscape as in the culture of the inhabitants. The people of Lotting Fen around Ramsey do not consider that they have much in common with the populations of Burwell or Feltwell Fens around Ely. The Fenlanders who look toward Cambridge have aspirations and expectations that are different from those who turn to Peterborough.

For several months we were involved in intensive accidental fieldwork—a most exhilarat-

ing experience. A small number of initial contacts in the area led us to farmers, National Farmers' Union representatives, drainage board officials, publicans, retired Members of Parliament, Women's Institute members, auctioneers, poachers, roadmen, tenant farmers, factory hands, land workers, mystics, eccentrics, and thieves. We met people who had never lived out of the Fens and people who had moved in from elsewhere, people who had a great affinity for the place and people who wanted nothing so much as to leave. We talked to stoics, agronomists, conservationists, the apathetic and the involved, the hopeless and despairing, the angry and alarmed. We visited fish and chip shops, local museums, factories, young farmers' meetings, pumping stations, farms, fields, dikes, droves, barn dances and discos, probation offices and gypsy encampments, strip clubs and gymnasiums, schools, churches, chapels, and pubs. Almost without exception we were welcomed: people showed us their personal treasures and memorabilia, lent us books, photographs, and homemade movies, allowed us to participate in family and farming life, and agreed to be filmed going about their lives. Secondary sources of information lent support to much that we were told and substantiated many of our own impressions and interpretations. The meaning of the ordinary is indeed rarely obvious. The sources used included published recollections of life in the Fens; travelogues by locals and visitors at various dates; collections of folktales and local myths; portraits of the Fens in literature; and academic works, notably those of H. C. Darby.

The sensory experiences which together combine to create a sense of place are usually lost in verbal accounts of character. The felicitous phrase or poetic insight may capture something of the feel of an area, but generally writings are unable to do justice to the quality of experience. Film allows one to re-create a living landscape through combinations of sights and sounds. "A good documentary should tell not only what a place, or a thing, or a person looks like but it must also tell the audience what it would feel like to be an actual witness to the scene" (R. Stryker, quoted in W. Stott 1973, 29). Through the use of the camera and tape recorder, it is possible to

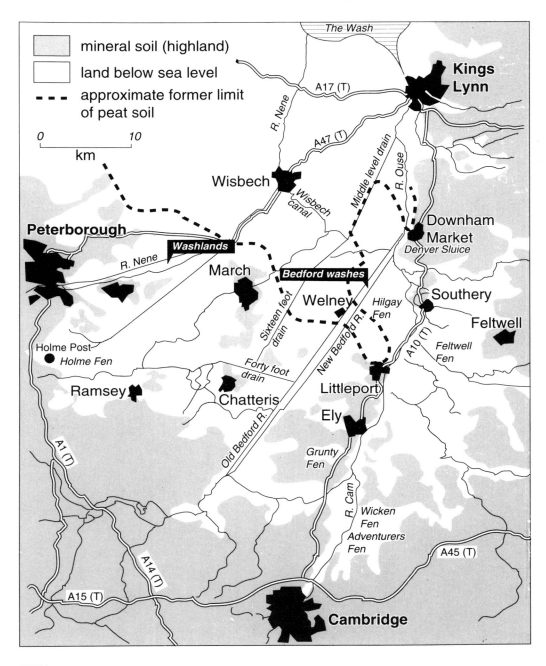

FIGURE 1
The Black Fens.

take the audience with you through the landscape. A number of sequences in the Fen film were shot at water height moving along in a boat: reeds brushing the camera lens touch the shoulders of the audience; the startled call of a moorhen scurrying out from under the prow startles the viewer as well. The sense of immediacy and directness is retained in the transformation of these experiences.

A number of themes began to emerge from

our experiences with the Fens which seemed to encapsulate the sense of place felt by the inhabitants and visitors. Despite very many excursions up blind alleys, for example, filming Perkins's diesel factory, speedway racing, bell ringing, and the back streets of Wisbech, three remained constant—*leitmotifs* for the region. Of greatest significance, the Fens are a man-made landscape and the inhabitants are acutely conscious of their continuing struggle against the natural environment, particularly the permanent threat of inundation by flood waters. Secondly, the people who have made the place have a deep-rooted "peasant" mentality which is reflected in their overwhelming desire to own land, their exploitation of their natural resources, their aggression and cruelty. These characteristics are embodied in the myth of the "Fen Tiger" (see below). Finally, the strong feeling of isolation is an important key to the sense of place. The flat land separates rather than connects families, communities, and villages. Traditionally, the area was cut off from the rest of England, and this geographical isolation continues in the suspicious, hostile reception given to "foreigners," that is, people not raised in the Fens. These three themes were eventually to structure the film in the sense that the landscapes, activities, and events were used as symbols for these interpretations of character.

A MAN-MADE LANDSCAPE

More than any other landscape in England, that of the Fens represents the struggles and achievements of countless individuals against the elements. Their names have been lost, but the landscape stands as their epitaph: "Millions of faceless and nameless peasants and townsfolk the world over have through the centuries molded, designed and designated their environments . . . having disappeared into the landscape much as their corporeal selves have turned into dust in some forgotten stretch of the Great Wall or ancient Fendyke" (Samuels 1979, 81). As so many Fen people said (not without pride), "this is a man-made landscape, we have won our lands from the waters." The present-day landscape is largely treeless, with vast open fields stretching away in all directions under an immense sky—"a similar land, repeating itself for ever" (Belloc

1906, 95). To stand on one of the small hills on the edge of the Fens in August is to look over a sea of wheat and sugar beet. It is a dramatic landscape with great scudding clouds, stunning sunsets, and bitter winds. "*There is a saying round here that it's a lazy wind, it don't bother to go round you, it goes straight through.*" The distinctive sounds of the place include the wind, burning stubble, machinery working in the fields, and skylarks. Most evocative of the sensory experience are the Fenland smells—burning stubble and bog oaks, reedy dikes and water.

Villages perch on small slit islands which stood out from the marshes; buildings lean at crazy angles due to the uncertain and shrinking peat. The villages and small towns like Chatteris and March are plain, functional, and unadorned, refuges from the often bitter struggles down on the Fen. "Whatever opinions we might hold of the unlovely clustered drabness of a Fen village, there comes easily to mind a sudden reaction on leaving it with a journey ahead in the gathering darkness of a winter night, as one enters the almost empty space of the Fens themselves. It is rather a feeling of going over the edge of beyond" (Bloom 1953, 29). Even the smallest change in height is crucial, since it provides safety from the flood waters know to local people as "drownings," with the last great drowning occurring as recently as 1947 (figures 2 and 3). An obsession with altitude is reflected in conversation, for people always talk of life "down in the Fen" even though their own dwellings may only be five feet above sea level.

FLATNESS

Contemporary visitors to the area are struck most forcibly by the flatness in the same way that travelers in earlier centuries were appalled by the marshes and swamps. Flat land is not often considered beautiful; it is not valued by most people with preferences for hills, valleys, and mountains. "It is generally accepted that hilly, broken country from its very nature is beautiful and it is perhaps too little realized that there is a beauty of the plain alone. . . . Light succeeds light in exquisite gradation, in endless perspective. The Sun's rays glinting in the middle distance stretch further than the eye can reach to the dim

FIGURE 2
The bank breaks during the 1947 flood, Southery.

FIGURE 3
Contemporary photograph of 1947 flood, Southery.

horizon, where far and misty, the plain ends" (Wedgewood 1936, ix–x; see also Shoard 1982). Vaughan Cornish, a geographer much concerned with the beauty of landscape, suggested that people find the Fens a stimulating scene and "yet one which nobody would expect, least of all those brought up among the hills." He described an encounter on a train to Ely with a Scottish gamekeeper who "was as much thrilled by the sense of space as a newcomer is thrilled by the sense of height. 'Whichever way I look' he said, 'there is nothing to interfere with the view'" (Cornish 1943, 48). In his memoirs of forty years' research in the Fens, the paleoecologist Sir Harry Godwin describes the "outstanding and, to some, entrancing quality of the Fenland landscape, an interminable flatness . . . [which] conveys feeling of vastness and remoteness." Godwin believes that the flatness itself is the key to the affection for the area among its inhabitants and quotes a local who said that "any fool can appreciate mountain scenery but it takes a man of discernment to appreciate the Fens" (Godwin 1978, 1).

We found that local people were less effusive in their praise of the flatness, for the majority take it for granted and are not able to articulate what, if anything, they like about it or find beautiful. "*To be honest, I've never thought about it*" was a typical reaction. Some people spoke of disliking other areas, frequently describing a feeling of being "shut in" in hilly areas, others mentioned a sense of freedom in the Fens, and a few put forward the belief that local people have better eyesight because they can look further than anyone else! One lady said she could not stand hills—"*they block the view and you never know what funny people might come running down to carry you off*," while another woman, whose windows look out over an expansive fen, said speculatively about the view, "*well, perhaps I wouldn't mind a small hill to look at. Nothing too big though.*" If the issue is pursued, many people will say that what they do like about the area is the peace, quiet, and tranquility of the Fens. The comments from one Fenman perhaps catch the key to the beauty for local people: "*The beauty comes from open, well-drained, well-cultivated land. There is a desire for straightness and accuracy,*

rows of plants. People feel in their bones that this is how it ought to be."

Such insight gains support from Alan Bloom in his account of his struggle to bring the wilderness of Adventurer's Fen back into cultivation during World War II. He describes the intense satisfaction that he and his workers gained in burning, clearing, and draining the fen "as men who were to be instrumental in changing the face and purpose of this locality, which had long been annoying and useless" (Bloom 1944, 96). He captures the beauty of Fenland farmed and goes some way to articulating the feeling of Fen farmers which others described as "a land passion, a Fenland fixation."

> I had prided myself on being used to the Fens, on having been born and bred where I could smell the tang the floods left on the grass . . . but I loved also the associations of fenland farmed; the green of winter wheat, the smell of black earth freshly turned, of twitch fires and the far-away smell of muck being carted from a dungle; the musical clattering of a mower, the rhythmic clickswish of a binder leaving the smell of wild mint behind; the sight of a long straight dyke and trimmed willow trees; and the wide horizons. All these things appealed, and were to be found in those fens where men had not ceased to struggle and to strive. (Bloom 1944, 19)

A FENLAND FIXATION

The desire for straightness and geometric precision in planting and tending crops is associated with intense cultivation. Every piece of available land is cultivated, trees and hedges have been grubbed out. "*Fenmen hate trees. They have to chop them down*"—ostensibly because they overshadow the crops, but in reality because they are a waste of space. Gardens are small and most often given over to vegetables, with perhaps a few token flowers. Deserted farmhouses and buildings down on the Fen are ruthlessly demolished to make way for more crops. People living on the edges of the Fenland interpret this desire to cultivate as indicative of the hard, greedy attitude of the Fenman, which often repays itself: "*It's such valuable land, they cultivate it right up to the edges of the dykes. They are always falling off their tractors into the dykes and drowning themselves.*" The straight lines and lack of adornment are repellent for many outsiders. The somewhat jaundiced view of one Norfolk man reflects the opinion of many: "*I don't like its dykes; I don't like its straight roads. It's such dreary country especially in winter, it's such miserable countryside. You go out for a walk and what can you do, walk along the dykes—a mile out, a mile back, two miles out, two miles back? As far as you can go.*" He caught a similar feeling to that expressed by a London family who moved into a remote part of Hockwold Fen on the strength of cheap housing and a mistaken belief about the country life. They bemoaned the lack of footpaths and places to walk in pleasant surroundings: "*There is no landscape here. Only land.*"

Fen people will tell you that the lack of "prettiness" is indicative of the hard lives they are forced to lead. Farming takes up every available moment of the day, leaving no time to enjoy a country stroll. Their time is given over to the much more important task of growing food. As Sybil Marshall has said, in sanctimonious tones, "The wild beauty may be gone, but it is replaced by a new beauty more useful to the overpopulated world" (S. Marshall 1977, 46). However, the neglected appearances also reflect what, for want of a better word, could be described as a "peasant" mentality. Time and again we met ragged, scruffy-looking farmers who gave a realistic appearance of having no means of financial support, only to be told later "*Oh him, he's worth thousands*"—and most of it would be kept under the mattress. The wife of one farmer describes her life: "*Well, he comes home. Sleeps. Eats supper. Sleeps. We've never had a holiday because he can't be bothered and, like all farmers, he's mean.*"

One visitor to the area attributes the general lack of concern with appearances to the struggles of past generations: "an inhospitable land where man snatched a difficult livelihood is an unlikely object for his beautifying care. Those who owned it did not live on it and those who acquired it did so with covetous hearts; . . . Untamed, it was unloved; and those who tamed it forgot to love it" (Wedgewood 1936, 45). The significant point

about the feelings for land in the Fens is that it is not loved in the sense of creating pretty views or pleasant woodland glades or ornamental gardens; the land is valued for its usefulness, its productivity, and its monetary value. The desire to own land is paramount in the minds of most contemporary Fenmen. We met many inhabitants who felt angry that people could no longer acquire smallholdings: "*You can't buy five acres any more, so you've got nowhere to start.*" As a farmer who owned 120 acres told us: "*There is a high proportion of agricultural workers who would dearly love to have a farm of their own. Don't stand a chance though. Farms are getting bigger and smallholdings are not available.*" The almost rapacious desire to own land creates a hostility between neighbors which is often barely disguised. Illness on the next farm is viewed with pleasure. It was said that "*People round here don't ask how you are, they ask about your potatoes and hope they aren't doing very well.*" Many people now work in occupations removed from agriculture. The factory hands at the Perkins diesel factory in Peterborough, for example, represent the first generation of Fenmen not to be tied to the land. Many are unhappy with factory life and keep smallholdings, others help out with the harvest and planting, not least because "*I like to get my hands dirty. Keep in touch with the soil.*" The wife of a farmer who was forced to sell up because he was unable to find or afford labor to carry on was worried. "*He is too young to stop working,*" she said, "*and I don't know how he'll cope without the farm. It's in his blood.*" Her husband talked about his feeling about losing his land: "*It's my own land at the moment. When I look out of that window I own what I see. After Christmas I shall be trespassing on what was mine. I don't like it.*"

WATER

The deep-seated fear among Fen farmers is the threat of flooding. The waters are kept at bay by an intricate system of drainage channels, dikes, and sluices constructed over the past three hundred years at great cost in terms of both lives and money. Much of the Fenland is several feet below sea level, so water has to be pumped out to the

Wash. Roads often run below the level of the water in the dikes, creating a peculiar sense of anxiety: "You stand above the landscape by five or six feet but so—you feel—does the impatient sea" (R. North 1977, 47). The appreciation of the drainage network is acute among Fen people, for as one farmer announced, "*These drains are our lifelines, all would be lost without them.*" Hilaire Belloc, however, viewed them in a less favorable manner: "These dykes of the Fens are accursed things: they are the separation of friends and lovers . . . there comes another man from another part armed with public power, and digs between them a trench too wide to leap and too soft to ford. The Fens are full of such tragedies" (Belloc 1906, 45).

Predrainage, the Fens were a wild, watery, and inhospitable place, with inhabitants living in mud and reed hovels on small islands and feeding themselves from the fish and wild fowl. The only surviving remnant of Fen landscape is in Wicken Fen, owned by the National Trust and kept as a nature reserve. This small area was the only way for the film to recapture the original appearance of the region. Historic accounts catch something of the desolate nature of the Fens and help to create a disparaging and hostile attitude among outsiders which lasted beyond the period of drainage. "There is in many parts of our country, a vague idea that the Fens are really gloomy, unhealthy and swampy even at the present day [1878]. . . . It is natural to infer that the description of a country abounding in muddy lands and black stagnant waters would convey the impression of insalubrity" (Miller and Skertchly 1878, 413–14).

It is difficult to appreciate just how much the landscape has been changed. St. Guthlac in the ninth century wrote of "a fen of immense size . . . [with] now a black pool of water, now foul running streams and also many islands and reeds, and hillocks, and thickets," which was populated by devils with fiery breath and tusks, conjured up from too much fasting. Daniel Defoe, coming to the Fens from Cambridge, wrote:

As we descended Westward, we saw the *Fenn* Country on our Right, almost all cover'd with Water like a Sea, the *Michaelmas* Rains having been very great that Year, they had sent down great Floods of Water from the Upland Countries, and those Fenns being, as may be very properly said, the Sink of no less than thirteen Counties. . . . In a Word, all the Water of the middle Part of *England* which does not run into the *Thames* or the *Trent*, comes down into these Fenns. (Defoe 1724, 119–20)

The burden of being the sink of thirteen counties is not lost on contemporary farmers, who feel and express great resentment at having to pay for drainage works, clearing out the dikes, and maintaining the pumps for "highland water." "*The highland man pays no drainage rate and his water comes tumbling down onto the Fens and we pump it out for him into the sea, and the Fenman has to stand the cost of all this.*"

The history of the draining of the Fens is one of tremendous hardship for the local people who were dispossessed of their common land and rights. Sir William Dugdale, in his petition to King Charles II for more reclamation, recognized the injustice but made light of it:

As for the decay of Fish and Fowl, which hath been no small objection against this publick work, there is not much likelyhood thereof . . . so many great Meeres and Lakes still continuing. (Dugdale 1662, vii)

The Adventurers who engaged in early reclamation, using the engineering skills of the Dutchman Vermuyden, were rewarded with pieces of land while the inhabitants were forced to leave. The drainage commenced in 1630 with the cut of the Old Bedford River from Earith to Denver and continued throughout the seventeenth century with the construction of the Twenty Foot, Sixteen Foot, and Forty Foot drains. The biggest task was the creation of the Hundred Foot, or New Bedford River, running parallel to the old, which created a washland of some five thousand acres to act as a reservoir in times of flood. The Middle Level drain was completed in 1848 and the last great mere at Whittlesey was drained in 1851. The history of the drainage of the Fens is that of improved technology, with windmills giving way to steam pumps and eventually to electric equipment (Hills 1967). The achievement was recognized in the piece of doggerel which rests on the Hundred Foot Engine:

> These FENS have oft times been by WATER drown'd,
> SCIENCE a remedy in WATER found.
> The power of STEAM she said shall be employ'd
> And the DESTROYER by itself destroy'd.

Or, in more constructed phrase, Darby quotes a chronicler writing in 1685:

> I sing Floods muzled, and the Ocean tam'd,
> Luxurious Rivers govern'd, and reclaim'd.
> Waters with Banks confin'd, as in a Gaol,
> Till kinder Sluces let them go on Bail;
> Streams curb'd with Dammes like Bridles, taught t'obey,
> And run as strait, as if they saw their way.
> (Darby 1956)

Most Fen people are aware that control of the waters is tenuous. The last great Fenland flood in 1947 caused extensive damage. The breach in the bank at Southery was remembered as "*the sound of an explosion and then the water rushed in, just like a steam engine.*" This flood could be considered "an Act of God," but in earlier times the Fen would have been flooded intentionally by landowners concerned to protect their own lands. Many of the folktales in the Fen record faithfully the condition of life and preoccupations with floodwaters. Chaser Legge, in his stories of the 1861 flood, tells how Fen people would mount bank watches to prevent the gentry from blowing up the banks and flooding the peasants in their hovels down on the Fens. As he says, "ever since the Fens were drained, whenever the Little Ouse topped up, someone would come down and blow the banks. They reckoned this was a poor old fen anyway and if it got flooded then the ones higher up would be safe. My grandfather used to say 'don't trust anyone when the river is full'" (Barrett 1963; Porter 1969). Such distrust is deep in the folk memory of Fen people and still comes out in conversation, for floods are an ever-present threat. A smallholder who gave up farming said, "*If I had my time again I would have done it different. You didn't buy land then because there wasn't any money and you were frightened of debt and you got into debt because you were flooded virtually every year. I had £400 once and said, right we'll put that on one side but the wife said put it into potatoes. But I shouldn't have listened to her, it was a wet year, we got flooded. So that was gone. As if we had never had it.*"

The supreme irony of the Fens is that the peat land, won at such cost and effort, is disappearing. Drainage has resulted in the fall of the water table and as the peat dries it both shrinks and blows away. A particularly distressing phenomenon of springtime is the peat "blow," when great dust storms sweep across the Fens. "*It's like black pepper. It just seems to seep under closed doors and windows and covers everything.*" The blows also damage young crops and remove seed. Peat shrinkage is held up as an indication of the rapaciousness of the farmers by nonagricultural people in the area, and the Post in Holme Fen, which now stands some thirteen feet above ground level, is a symbol of their greed. For farmers anxious to hand on their land to their children, the thought of watching their lifeblood blow away and shrink is too horrifying to contemplate. "*It frightens us to think about it sometimes.*" Yet there is little attempt at soil conservation, partly because of a belief that it is beyond their power. "*Shrinkage,*" we were told with great authority, "*happens because it's all to do with bacteria eating the peat.*" Peat is a difficult substance to handle, being friable and readily combustible. "*I'd not had much experience with peat farming; I lit the straw and by a cruel trick of fate really, the wind changed and it swept across the whole farm and before long there was sixty acres of turf burning.*" This farmer's neighbor told us the same tale with much amusement at his misfortune. Farmers are often reminded of the antecedents of their land by bog oaks—great trunks of trees, often 100 feet long, which lie buried in the peat. Machinery is broken and much time wasted while these remnants from a former age have to be dug out, carted away, and burned. The stoical attitude toward environmental hazards is interpreted by outsiders as apathy. "*These locals see themselves as victims. Because of the seasons, they have to stand back and let it happen."*

THE FEN TIGER?

A strong notion of environmental determinism is evident in interpretations of Fen character. Both local inhabitants and outsiders attribute many of the past and present characteristics of the people to their environmental conditions. "Fen folk can be coarse, dour, close, clannish and untrusting, having little respect for persons or niceties, lacking in appreciation for art and beauty. Many are materialistic to a degree. But they are also realists" (Bloom 1953, 148). It is often suggested that these characteristics are inherited through the struggles between locals, and between people and the forces of nature. The conditions of life horrified many visitors in the times before drainage and well into the twentieth century. Many people still describe the old Fenmen in terms of the environmental hardships they had to bear. "*Look at your typical Fenman, he was a poor little bent old man, full of rheumatism. The damp, it must have affected him.*" W. H. Barrett was anxious to place on record the stories of men who were the last of the real old Fenmen, to give outsiders some idea of what life was really like in the desolate Fenland a century ago. The lack of culture is evident still, as we found virtually no interest in music or art; indeed Fenmen rarely express themselves in song except when filled with tavern ale or religious fervor. The heritage of present day Fen people seems close to those of their ancestors, who were "a savage race by the end of the seventeenth century, living in isolation and harassed by disease and floods" (Barrett 1963, ix–xiii).

Fen people were isolated from the rest of the country by the dreadful physical conditions. Dugdale perhaps overstates the hardships experienced by people, for he was anxious to press his petition for drainage:

> In the Winter time . . . the Inhabitants upon the hards and banks within the Fenns, can have no help of food, nor comfort for body or soul; no woman aid in her travail, no means to baptize a Child, or partake of the Communion. . . . And

what expectations of health can there be to the bodies of men, where there is no element good? the Air being for the most part cloudy, gross, and full of rotten harrs; the Water putrid and muddy, yea full of loathsome vermin; the Earth spungy and boggy; and the Fire noysome by the stink of smoaky Hassocks. (Dugdale 1662, vi–vii)

Daniel Defoe also felt great concern for the Fenland inhabitants and was not a little surprised at their stamina:

> One could hardly see from the Hills and not pity the many thousands of Families that were bound to or confin'd in those Foggs, and had no other Breath to draw than what be mix'd with those Vapours and that Steam which so universally overspread the Country . . . [yet] those that are used to it, live unconcern'd, and as Healthy as other Folks except now and then an Ague. (Defoe 1724, 121)

Ague was indeed the blight of Fen people, resembling a form of arthritis or rheumatism, in which they were taken with fits of shaking which, it was commonly believed, could be cured by a strong dose of gin or brandy. Charles Kingsley was appalled at the intemperate habits: "The foul exhalations of autumn called up fever and ague, crippling and enervating, and tempting, almost compelling, to that wild and desperate drinking." He extolled the benefits of drainage: "at least we shall have wheat and mutton instead, and no more typhus and ague; and it is to be hoped, no more brandy-drinking and opium-eating" (quoted in Miller and Skertchly 1878, 421). Opium, the consolation of the poor well into the 1920s, was considered to be a vice peculiar to the Fens. In the present day, newcomers express surprise at the amount of underage drinking and general drunkenness they see around them: "*But it's oblivion and that's why the kids start drinking at fifteen.*" Many feel that people seek oblivion to get away from the drudgery of life: "*You see kids of twelve driving tractors. They are forced onto the land. Every waking hour they're working.*"

The boredom of youth and lack of opportunities in the area are characteristic of many isolated rural areas. Fashions are behind the times, trends are missing. One group of lads who formed a pop group played in Cambridge to a constant barracking from the students: *"They treat us as if we are a bunch of yokels."* Young people want to get away. Crime is a major concern for local people, as is the drug problem in Wisbech. Often exaggerated in newspaper reports, the problems are put into perspective by a March probation officer: *"Well, there is hard organized crime in Wisbech. March has a few inexperienced crooks that everyone knows. And Chatteris has just twelve hooligans."* Many people, however, speculate about the possible causes: *"Well I think it's all to do with the depressing countryside. They get bored."* The lack of employment opportunities in the area also disturbs people. March refused to allow the Metal Box Company to build a factory in the town, and Wisbech has not encouraged light industries, which now go to Kings Lynn or Peterborough in preference. *"I think they have been incredibly stupid, they have lost out on jobs and now they are losing their young people."* Certainly the bright children leave the area. Those who remain can choose seasonal land work, but the farmers prefer women. It is arduous and backbreaking work, often on hands and knees. Work is available in prepacking and food-processing plants where vegetables are graded, but it is dirty, unrewarding work which is poorly paid and which offers no future. Many times, we met an apathetic air of resignation from those left behind.

There is considerable social distance between inhabitants and newcomers. Some people are prejudiced against "foreigners" (see above): *"I don't mind outsiders, but not too many of them."* The general response to outsiders is to ignore them. *"These outsiders, people from London, think local people are stupid country bumpkins. So local people tend to play up to them and get better deals. In the main, they might just as well not be here."* This comment supports exactly the experience of a Californian living on the edges of Wisbech who said that as an outsider, he might just as well be invisible. Newcomers find the Fen people unfriendly and antisocial. *"Life here is bleeding terrible,"* confessed one Londoner who bitterly regretted his decision to retire to March. *"They are*

antisocial. They never go anywhere. Think if they go to Kings Lynn they'll fall off the edge of the world." The common experience is one of suspicious and shifty locals who will "do you" if they can. Fen people are described as hard, greedy, and lacking in sentiment, like the farmer who, when his gun dog failed to retrieve a bird, shot the dog then and there.

Fen people will acknowledge that there is a streak of cruelty and a lack of compassion in their nature, but a semiretired poacher justified it thus: *"We had to eat anything then—birds, eels, bream, pike, moorhen, sparrows, anything that was alive. We had to eat them or starve because there weren't no money about. We were cruel, it's no good saying we weren't. Ain't got no sympathy for nothing in them days, not even for ourselves."* He was talking about life in the early decades of this century, but the Fen people's reputation for cruelty and savagery has a long tradition which is encapsulated in the myth of "Fen Tiger." *"The old Fenmen, what we call the old Fen Tigers, I mean, they were a tough breed. They were isolated communities, at war with each other, always fighting."* We failed to find anybody who claimed to be a Fen Tiger, and most people seemed to be embarrassed to be asked. Well, what were they like? "I don't know why the old Fenmen were allus called Tigers, unless it were because they used to act so wild and shy, not being used to seeing many folks or whether strangers thought they looked a bit fierce. There is a saying you can use about any man who got a good crop 'air (specially if it's on his chest) and a good set o' teeth. You can say ''E's all 'air and teeth like a Ramsey man'" (S. Marshall 1967, 8–9).

At least part of the myth stems from the fierce reactions of Fen people to the activities of the reclaimers and those in the pay of the landowning aristocracy and the church. The peasants living down on the Fens would cheerfully attack the representatives of the authorities. "Big farmers daren't live there; they put foremen in to run the farms and the farmers only came into the fen in daylight and they rode back to the towns, where they lived, before dark, and ganged up for the ride home with others like themselves. . . . The parsons were as bad, if they weren't worse. They wanted to keep in with the gentry so they used to tell the people to put up with their miseries and not grumble, then, when they got up top, they'd be ever so happy listening to the sound of harps (Barrett 1963, 87–88). The established Church of England had little compassion or concern for the poor. As a result of the Littleport riot in 1816, five Fenmen were hung. Their bodies lie in St Mary's Church in Ely under the plaque: "May their awful fate be a warning to others." It seems such a short time ago: in 1979 a legal battle was fought in Ely between two descendants of the main protagonists over an attempt to get the gravestone moved back to Littleport.

Feelings about the Established Church run just below the surface, and Ely Cathedral is for many a symbol of exploitation. The Methodist chapels were the source of the true religion in the Fens, a fact acknowledged by one vicar we spoke to who agreed wholeheartedly with one of his forebears: "*A minister condemned to live in such a place must be a man of iron nerve or unrefined taste.*" A wave of religious fervor swept the Fens in 1900, when many people were baptized in the rivers. "The converts were led into the water till it was up to their waists, then ducked under and they scrambled out as the believers sang hymns and the unbelievers expressed their opinion on those being ducked, stating it was the first good wash they'd had for months" (Barrett 1965; Randell 1969). There is a contemporary revival of Baptist fervor in the Fens near Cambridge. The preacher would like to reinstate the habit of ducking in the river but is unable to, because the water authority keeps the level of the sluice too low! How far the revival is a resurgence of old beliefs and how far a response by the young to the charisma of the preacher is difficult to judge.

ISOLATION

Fen people may indeed prefer a personal God, but they also feel isolated from the Established Church and its services. Indeed, the isolation is a major experience of life in the Fens, and it is no small irony that the flat land separates rather than connects communities. Many of the houses and recent buildings which straggle along the high roads reflect an unwillingness among the women to put up with life down on the Fens (Chamber-

lain 1975). Typically, the farmhouses were connected with the main road by a soft, peaty drive which became impassable in winter. Women and children would be marooned in the Fen, sometimes for many months. One teacher spoke of the "*special isolation of women and children. Most of the children down on the fen are semiliterate because they never hear any conversation.*" Many people acknowledge that they left school unable to read and write because they missed so much schooling. One described the children as having "*a quiet reticence.*" The isolation has led to a recognizable and sizeable problem of mental illness in the Fens. Many people will quite happily admit to being on ten or fifteen milligrams of Valium a day "for depression"—and drugs seem to have replaced a reliance on opium and poppyhead tea.

The traditional isolation of farmsteads in the Fens encouraged incest. Generations of inbreeding have promoted the growth of various genetic diseases such as Huntingdon's Chorea: sufferers tend to be somewhat retarded. A hostel for twenty-five mentally subnormal people was established in the town of March in the late 1970s. In previous generations, these people would have been given menial tasks on the land and cared for within the family. The mechanization of farming has greatly reduced the demand for unskilled labor and brought to light this previously hidden problem. However, people have long been aware of the apparent simple-mindedness of Fen people, "slow in speech, they were often thought by strangers to be dull witted," and one Fenland physician attributed the subnormality to poppyhead tea: "In frequent use and taken as a remedy for the ague . . . to children during the teething period poppyhead tea was often given and I do think this was the cause of the feeble-minded and idiotic people frequently met with in the Fens" (Lucas 1930). Apart from genetic retardation, there is a recognizable psychological illness within the Fenland community which many people believe is caused by the isolation experienced down on the Fen and the flatness: people just give up. A Cambridge psychiatrist describes the symptoms: "We call it cultural retardation. People out there are often retarded, but it's not so much an illness as a way of life; you only find out about it when they are struggling with our city ways in Cambridge. Then the pressures and expectations of the urban existence are too much for the fenman and he breaks down. In his own context he can operate quite successfully. . . . The 'fen syndrome' is a way of coping with the isolation" (Garvey 1977, 429). A recent migrant to the Fens captured well the sense of isolation and desolation experienced by many in the area when he said, " *There is so much sky. It has an effect on the psyche. You are all the time waiting for something to happen.* "

THE SENSE OF PLACE

Looking back at the experience of researching for the film, I realize that we nearly came to grief in the Fens. The involvement with so many people, combined with the sheer volume of information we gathered and the increasing complexity as we became more deeply involved with the social undercurrents of the area, threatened to overwhelm the film. It was essential that the story be crisp, clear, and relatively straightforward, for there would be no narrator to point the way; the film was only to be fifty minutes long, and perhaps most important, it was to entertain people as well as telling them about life in the Fens. Many aspects of the economic and social conditions which would be essential to any sound geographical interpretation would complicate the story and confuse the audience. My involvement with the film ended with the identification of those themes which provided the key to the character of the Fens. It was the task of the director and film editor to take all the information on film and tape-recorded interviews and re-create the sense of place. "It is not enough to show bits of truth on the screen; separate frames of truth. These frames must be thematically organized so that the whole is also a truth" (D. Vertov, quoted in Barnouw 1974, 57).

As befits the title, the film is primarily a sensual experience. The atmosphere of the Fenland is caught in beautifully photographed landscapes and the commentary is constructed from the sounds of the Fens—birds, reeds, the wind, stubble burning, pumps working, plainsong in the cathedral, and the sounds of machinery—

interspersed with occasional reflective comments from Fen people themselves. Two threads running through the film provide the basic structure of the narrative. The first is the experience of the physical environment, its visual qualities and characteristic sounds. There are no villages or towns in the film, for the essential Fen remains the landscape. The second thread is the agricultural life of the area, and seasonal changes, starting in late summer and ending in late spring, provide the main story. Crops are harvested and processed, land is ploughed and sown, dikes are cleaned, and plants and animals tended. Within this framework, scenes are used as symbols to express the interpretations of character by the inhabitants and the beliefs of the director. Geoffrey Haydon experienced a strong feeling of empathy for the young and the poor in the Fens, who, he felt, were trapped by the sheer drudgery of agricultural life and who were unable to break away. The heart of the film, at the end of the winter sequence, shows a youth shoveling carrots in the mud under a dripping conveyor belt. The scene has the sound of a factory running beneath it; it changes to the interior of a canning factory with sheets of tin flowing like water through the cogs of machinery and then, finally, cuts to a churchyard with a fallen cross and gravestone.

Objects and events are used as symbols of Fen character—the teeth of a combine, the spikes of an eel glave, tearing flesh from a rabbit and spraying water lilies in the dikes, dead moles hanging on barbed wire, and eels trapped in a box convey ideas of cruelty, utility, and exploitation. Impoverished-looking farmers pick through the detritus of a farm sale, stubble burns, and bog oaks are hauled from the ground and fired. All these activities happened in the remote landscape. The flat lands and enormous skies are photographed with telegraph poles marching into the distance. Endless dikes flow through the picture; men working in fields are engulfed by the sky, and deserted houses lean at peculiar angles in vast, empty fields. The Fenland obsession with water grows through the film. The camera moves along dikes and drains, records a baptism with the total immersion of the convert; observes men clearing and cleaning the drainage channels, and watches sluices emptying, pumps being primed, and washlands flooding. Archive film recaptures the horror of the 1947 flood and the film ends, as it begins, with the indistinct boundary between the land and sea in the Wash.

It has been argued recently that the familiarity of television and its significance in the development of popular culture "makes it so important, so fascinating and so difficult to analyse" (Fiske and Hartley 1978, 6). In this essay, I have commented on my experiences in the Fens; the final question must be to what extent these interpretations reflect the experiences of the inhabitants. A number of films made for television have deeply offended the inhabitants of the places depicted in them. Denis Mitchell's film about Chicago, for example, was banned in that city for six years because it was considered dishonest, distorted, and disgusting by local representatives. *A Wedding on Saturday,* mentioned earlier, led to complaints from local councillors because it neglected to show "such splendid amenities as parks, swimming pools, maternity hospitals and the like" (Swallow 1965, 185). A drama documentary, *The Land of Green Ginger,* which was about the life of fishermen in Hull, created such intense anger among local people that a public meeting was organized to take Alan Plater to task for having written it. In all three cases, the films failed to emphasize the environmental qualities and amenities valued by the inhabitants. The television companies are blamed for first creating and then perpetuating a bad or unfavorable image of the place.

People create images of places, forming impressions about the beauty of landscapes, making assumptions about the ways of life of the inhabitants by drawing on a rich variety of popular cultural texts. Television documentaries are particularly influential in this process precisely because they appear to be showing people and places "as they really are." In fact, the processes I have been describing in this chapter reveal the extent to which *all* media texts are the result of a complex series of professional, technical, and social negotiations between the production team and different people within local communities. Our field research was both extensive and intensive, providing a strong ethnographic base for the meanings of the Fenland that were finally encoded in the film. *A Sense of Place* can be criticized for being too selective in that it did not include any material about life in the towns and villages. It may also be criticized for having insufficient commentary and not making its exposition more clear. I suspect that some viewers may have found it boring, but I do believe that it is a faithful reflection of the interpretations of regional character and values that the inhabitants themselves have of the Fens.

SOURCE

This article appeared originally as a chapter in *Valued Environments,* ed. John Gold and Jacquelin Burgess, 35–54 (London: Allen & Unwin, 1982).

NOTE

1. *A Sense of Place: The Fens,* directed by Geoffrey Haydon, produced by David Collison, BBC 1980. Other regional films made by the BBC include three films with John Betjeman, entitled *Scotland—The Lion's Share; Wales—More than a Rugby Team; A Prospect of England, 1977. The Making of the English Landscape* comprised twelve films: Series I: *Ancient Dorset; Conquest of the Mountains; Marsh and Sea; Landscape of Peace and War; The Deserted Midlands; The Black Country.* Series II: *Behind the Scenery; The Fox and the Covert; No Stone Unturned; Brecklands and Broads; The Frontier; Haunts of Ancient Devon, 1978.* From Independent Television came *A Writer's Notebook: The Pennines,* a series of four films with Ray Gosling (1979).

FURTHER READINGS

Paul C. Adams. 1992. Television as gathering place. *Annals of the Association of American Geographers* 82:117–35.

This article examines the role of television in contemporary society. Adams argues that television is a center of meaning that helps society define "us" and "them" and thereby confer value on persons and objects. By providing a context for sensory communion and social congregation, television allows people to develop a sense of "place without location."

Stuart C. Aitken. 1991. A transactional geography of the image-event: The films of the Scottish film director, Bill Forsyth. *Transactions of the Institute of British Geographers* n.s. 15:105–18.

Aitken explores the way filmmakers use the "image-event" to draw viewers into their narratives but also to violate certain filmmaking conventions and thus challenge viewers to question everyday expectations and myths. Forsyth's films are used to examine the dynamic qualities of the image-event. Aitken argues that Forsyth uses his films to challenge certain pervasive myths and stereotypes about everyday Scottish life and culture.

Jacquelin Burgess. 1990. The production and consumption of environmental meanings in the mass media: A research agenda for the 1990s. *Transactions of the Institute of British Geographers*, n.s. 15:139–61.

This article might be considered an inventory and prospect of contemporary media research in geography. Burgess identifies key issues and draws attention to some of the interdisciplinary investigations likely to gain increasing attention in the next few years.

Jacquelin Burgess and John R. Gold, eds. 1985. *Geography, the media, and popular culture*. London: Croom Helm.

An excellent collection of essays that articulate the major issues in this developing field of study. The contributions by the editors are of particular value.

Jacquelin Burgess, Carolyn M. Harrison, and Paul Maiteny. 1991. Contested meanings: The consumption of news about nature conservation. *Media, Culture and Society* 13:499–519.

This article uses a case study to explore the role that print and broadcast communications play in mediating between the public and private domains of social life. At issue in the case study was the proposed development of an environmentally sensitive site on the eastern edge of London. The findings suggest that the scientific and political arguments surrounding nature conservation are not clearly understood by the public. Their presentation in the media is still perceived by the general public as a distant debate—as discourse carried on by a scientific and political elite rather than as a debate about pressing local concerns.

Peter B. Hales. 1984. *Silver cities: The photography of American urbanization, 1839–1915*. Philadelphia: Temple University Press.

Hales demonstrates how photography was used both to communicate and to shape attitudes toward the American city from the time of photography's invention through the end of the first major period of American urbanization and industrialization.

Peter Howard. 1991. *Landscapes: The artist's vision*. London: Routledge.

Howard considers landscape painting, rather than film, in this encompassing survey. Although the mode of expression is different, Howard identifies many of the same sorts of themes in the visual arts that characterize the portrayal of landscape in other media.

Joshua Meyrowitz. 1985. *No sense of place: The impact of electronic media on social behavior*. New York: Oxford University Press.

Meyrowitz writes of the roles people play and witness in everyday life and how these are increasingly played before new audiences that are not physically present and on stages that exist outside time and space. The situational analysis he offers attempts to come to terms with how electronic media affect social behavior. He suggests that the media influence the public not through the power of their messages but by reorganizing the social settings in which people interact and by weakening the relationship between physical place and social place.

Vera Norwood and Janice Monk, eds. 1987. *The desert is no lady: Southwestern landscapes in women's writing and art*. New Haven: Yale University Press.

A book of eleven essays that consider the impressions of the southwestern landscape that women artists and writers have formed and recorded in their art. Difference in perception is primarily attributed to gender, although the book also takes ethnicity into account.

John R. Short. 1991. *Imagined country: Environment, culture and society*. New York: Routledge, Chapman, and Hall.

The book contains three chapters examining the expression of landscape meaning in varied media. The discussions touch on the portrayal of meaning in the English novel, "Western" movies, and Australian landscape painting.

James R. Shortridge. 1989. *The Middle West: Its meaning in American culture*. Lawrence: University Press of Kansas.

This book represents an attempt to uncover the subjective sense of place that is embodied in changing concepts of the Middle West.

Leo Zonn, ed. 1990. *Place images in the media: Portrayal, experience, and meaning*. Savage, Md.: Rowman and Littlefield.

Zonn's collection is a sampler, with essays by a wide range of geographers examining place images in widely varied media. Literature and the visual arts are well represented.

ROBIN W. DOUGHTY **21**

ENVIRONMENTAL THEOLOGY: TRENDS IN CHRISTIAN THOUGHT

Twenty-five years ago, historian Lynn White (1967) expounded what many people came to regard as the conventional wisdom about religion as the basis of environmental problems in the West. Couched in historical and doctrinal terms, his message, in a sense, excused modern society for its ecological sins, because people were dutifully fulfilling a Christian imperative, namely, to "increase and multiply," to "subdue and have dominion" (Genesis 1:27–28). This aspect of the creation story in the Old Testament encapsulated for White a profound disjunction between humans and nature. It also explained arrogance and hostility toward an environment degraded in modern times by population growth and a burgeoning technology.

This declaration in the well-respected publication *Science* sparked a lively and enduring debate. In geography, it contributed to a dialogue about the linkage of belief to behavior (Tuan 1970; Kay 1985; W. Norton 1989) and the role of institutions in influencing environmental activity and perception, including landscape values and the conservation and management of resources (Black 1970; O'Riordan 1976; Penning-Rowsell and Lowenthal 1986).

This essay examines philosophical arguments related to White's premise that Christianity bears a huge burden of guilt for current ecological disruption. (White claims that Saint Francis of

Assisi, characterized as a radical and heretic, provides unique illumination because of his compassion for animals.) It concludes with a discussion about a theology of nature based on process thinking and set in the context of postmodernism.

Responses to White's position range through a spectrum of opinions. Some authors agree substantially with White's accusations, others express new possibilities in contemporary theology for instilling ecological values within the Christian church. Eugene Hargrove (1986), editor of *Environmental Ethics* (a quarterly journal founded in 1979 to address expanding interest in philosophy, religion, and ecology), wished that the debate about White's statements had never occurred. The role of religion in solving environmental issues has gone nowhere, he said, due to the stridency and entrenchment that the historian himself had catalyzed. "Constructive borrowing" from different points of view was necessary, asserted Hargrove (1986, xvii). This essay embraces the impulse for a new theology of nature in the spirit of an open debate.

RESPONSES: FAITHS AND DENOMINATIONS

White's original depiction of Western Christianity is both generalized and partisan. Several authors have sought to differentiate trends. Kay (1988) singles out the appeal of the Millennium expressed by the Hebrew Bible as upholding and fostering a mutual respect between humans and other animals. Ehrenfeld and Bentley (1985) and Helfand (1986) maintain that ancient Jewish texts and traditions are sympathetic, not hostile, toward the environment. J. Baker emphasizes how Hebrew Scriptures subordinate humankind to God, making people respect "the all-controlling rights and power of God" (J. Baker 1990, 19). John Passmore (1974) claims that Stoic and Neoplatonic thought colored attitudes toward the natural world in early Christian beliefs. It is useful, therefore, to make distinctions between Hebrew texts and so-called classical Christian doctrines of humanity's domination of nature.

One argument is that reformist movements in Western Christianity bear responsibility for the hostility about which White speaks. Certainly, famous commentaries by Weber (1958) and Tawney (1936) depict Puritan doctrines as reconciling material and worldly success with supernatural election. Tawney's Puritan mourning for a "lost Paradise and a creation sunk in sin" (Tawney 1936, 228–29) sees grace to be won on the battlefield, in the counting house, and in the marketplace. Landscape transformation could be as much a blessing as business acumen—a sign of God's selection.

There is, however, another rendition. H. Paul Santmire, an expert on Reformation textuality, regards Luther's theology of creation (rather than Calvin's) as ecologically quite sensitive. He admits, however, that until recently Protestant thought has been largely indifferent to environmental concerns; spiritual communion between humankind and God, not ecological rapport, has guided most theological inquiry (Santmire 1975). In the past decade, this Lutheran pastor has challenged the proposition that Western theology is ecologically bankrupt, although he admits that ambiguity and tension complicate a theology of nature. In *The Travail of Nature* (the title declares this ambiguity), Santmire (1985) describes how three root metaphors—ascent, fecundity, and migration—have shaped belief and thinking in the West. Reformation teachings tended to emphasize the image of fecundity from which the elect were instructed to draw in order to build the new kingdom. Human activity and migration assisted in bringing about this objective. Speaking of Calvin's ethics, Santmire claimed that because the door for ascent to God was closed, divine election had "the effect of calling the believers at the practical level, horizontally as it were, to rise above nature (and history) to transform its [bounteousness] for the sake of the greater glory of God" (Santmire 1985, 127).

Biblical scholars have likewise challenged White's rendering of biblical texts. A number of these scholars consider humanity to be a life tenant or caretaker rather than a freeholder on earth. In this exegetical framework, stewardship with responsibilities, not merely rights, tempers dominion, while charity softens dualism between humanity and nature (Moule 1967; Dubos 1969; DeCelles 1974; Bratton 1984).

Glacken (1967) bolstered this line of thought. He referred to a Patristic tradition, exemplified by Basil and Ambrose, as turning toward the world, not away from it. Writings of such churchmen drew lessons from the animal kingdom that exemplified virtuous and praiseworthy activities. These affirmations refer to biblical texts ignored by Lynn White. They include the Psalms, Book of Job, and St. Paul's Epistle to the Romans (1: 20), which together with similar revealed texts celebrate the goodness, fecundity, and beauty in the "Book of Nature" described by clerics and philosophers down through the centuries.

Rather than accepting religion as directly influencing environmental behavior, some authors have drawn attention to the role of institutions in guiding secular activities with ecological significance. Moncrief (1970), an early respondent to White, interposed other "lenses," namely, democracy, capitalism, urban growth, individual wealth, and the private ownership of property, between organized religion and environmental decay. Such secular and modern social forces are connected with traditional Christian teaching less directly.

Initial debate, therefore, about White's 1967 article drew on a large body of textual interpretation, biblical commentary, and orthodox theology, mostly deductive and universalist in content. Several authorities have noted the profoundly anthropocentric, even androcentric, aspects of the creation allegory in the Bible. In agreement with White, they argue that the trajectory of Western thought, certainly since the Enlightenment, has privileged an instrumental view of nature portrayed in Genesis that regards the world as something to be used exclusively for human ends. Reason has been employed to manipulate and manage a mechanical universe in order to supply immediate, material needs. Faith is thereby reduced to an afterthought, a private act of worship, and has become increasingly divorced from day-to-day life and livelihood.

FOUNDATIONS FOR A THEOLOGY OF NATURE

"Theology fell from grace in the modern world," declares theologian David R. Griffin (1989, 1). He advances several reasons why this came about.

First, conservative and fundamentalist doctrines are grounded on the Word of a transcendent, omnipotent, and single Creator. In medieval times, such a nonhistorical set of truths about the nature of God held universal sway in a church that acted as a bulwark or rock against alien or secular ideologies. These views are out of kilter in contemporary society. They are more appropriate to universalist theologies promulgated by hierarchical authorities who claim a special relationship with God (J. Holland 1989).

DIVERGENT TRADITIONS

Appeals for a more personal interpretation of the Scriptures challenged the hegemony of authoritarian sacrality. Some reformists tended to replace one set of directives with another, while others called for literalist interpretations of the Holy Word in the quest of personal faith. Whatever their structure, the forces of established "Christendom" ignored trends in worldly science and technology as they allied themselves with the rich and politically powerful.

In this worldview, a theology of nature is difficult to sustain; it must be based on the more implicit or underemphasized statements in the Bible and Christian tradition (Joranson and Butigan 1984). Stewardship as discussed in the White argument is one of them. Susan Bratton (1986) refers to Old Testament scholars Walter Eichrodt (1967), Gerhard von Rad (1962; 1964; 1980), and Claus Westermann (1974; 1982) to propose the concept of God's continuous care for a good and very special creation. Humanity's rationality and special place in the world must be employed carefully, she argues, to respect both the intrinsic values of creatures and the mystery of God, whose providential concern is manifested in the diversity and splendor of the earth (see also J. Baker 1990).

Using the idea of a covenant between God and humanity, Granberg-Michaelson extends care to all things. "Creation is God's loved possession and gift" (Granberg-Michaelson 1990, 29), and both the power of the Gospels and the message of a new life in Christ are keys to human salvation and ecological restitution. A commitment to evolution as a root metaphor to renew a covenant with God, according to another author, will enable the Church to "update its principles with a monistic and communal understanding of human existence" (Rue 1989, 186). Evolution, replacing the image of God as a person, will empower "this generation to a commitment to serving the conditions of human existence" (Rue 1989, 189).

"Sacramental theology," or the appeal to the saving action of God in Christ, is another way to elevate material reality through human cooperation with the divine plan. People undertake the priestly function of dedicating or offering creation back to its Creator. We must accept nature as God's special gift, cherish it as such, and reconsecrate the earth to its founder (Habgood 1990).

Lynn White's characterization of St. Francis as a heretic who was never punished for his heresy supports the idea of a supposed trend in Christian thought that makes peace between man and nature. But historians who examined the man from Assisi challenge this characterization. Sorrell's (1988) statement about St. Francis of Assisi emphasizes his novelty as a troubadour for God but affirms his theological orthodoxy, his zeal to save souls and reform the Church rather than to preach the democracy about nature that White mistakenly ascribes to him.

A LAND ETHIC

One way of dampening traditional dualism between people and the earth is to expand horizons of reach and concern to include the biosphere and web of relationships that sustain us through a "land ethic." Such an environmental ethic is a way of guiding human behavior. Attributed to the biologist and philosopher of the environment Aldo Leopold (1887–1948), this popular concept is both an evolutionary possibility and ecological necessity for the late twentieth century. Basing his land ethic in Mosaic law, Leopold suggested an eleventh commandment "dealing with man's relation to the land and to the animals and plants which grow upon it" (Leopold 1966, 238). The idea is that each one of us is a member of a community of living things. Such recognition impels us to both deepen and broaden our concern and values so that "a thing is right when it tends to preserve the integrity, stability, and beauty of the biotic community." It is wrong when it does not (Leopold 1966,

262). This biologist and philosopher insisted that people become plain citizens of the land community rather than conquerors of it.

Religious experts and nature writers have drawn inspiration from Leopold's admonition. Vincent Rossi, for example, leader of the Eleventh Commandment Fellowship, calls for a new Christian imperative: "The Earth is the Lord's and the Fullness thereof: Thou Shall not Despoil the Earth, nor Destroy the Life thereon" (Devall and Sessions 1985, 34).

Some theologians also have turned to the land ethic because it contributes to "creation consciousness" whereby we accept restraints and responsibilities for dealings with both the living and nonliving world. Plants and animals are not merely instruments for our own exclusive use, valuable because we make them so; rather, they are "carriers of values" (McDaniel 1988).

Nature writers demonstrate that watchful attention and modesty before wild nature about which Leopold spoke. The land ethic has gained broad acceptance and popularity as the public is fascinated by media tales that unravel the mysteries of animal behavior and describe the special biophysical needs of various species in different regions (W. Berry 1985; Lopez 1986; Harrigan 1992).

MODERNISM AND ENVIRONMENTAL THEOLOGY

Like traditional thought, liberal modern theology loses its appeal due to its willingness to subordinate dogma to science, according to Griffin, as well as in its failure to address ecological needs. In this picture, theology is a "gloss over secularism's nihilistic picture" (Griffin 1989, 1). Moreover, contemporary society has substituted material satisfaction as a path to salvation. Economic competition becomes a special form of divine providence, and science and technology reduce God to the role of watchmaker in a mechanical universe. Piety and ecological thinking are difficult to sustain, although some have articulated what they term a "theology of radical secularity" (Dean 1975).

One way that neo-orthodox Protestant beliefs reconciled themselves with science was to refer to religion as posing different sets of questions and using a different language. Theological commentary is based on divine revelation, set in an eschatological framework in which faith is an expression of a personal relationship with God and separated from the mechanical and disinterested world of science (Barbour 1990).

In a theology based on the premise that God made the world and fashioned humankind as a special creation, nature becomes merely the stage on which the drama between God and humanity, the *imago dei,* is enacted. The natural world supports human activity and is incorporated into salvation history through Christ's birth and death. Christ provides an important outlet for this inner-directed, personal, and more mystical trend in modern theology. One of its chief architects, Rudolf Bultmann, discovered in Christ the answer to personal salvation and self-understanding. For Bultmann, it is Christ's special love and grace that shine as a path for individual hope and community integrity (Bultmann 1984).

Redemption signifies holism, not history. The Man-Christ has so sanctified the world that in relating to creatures humankind expresses truly what theologian Joseph Sittler (1970) termed a "beholding," that is, standing among things with reverence (Meland 1974). By understanding the event of Christ's coming not as in opposition to the world but as restoring the proper relationship of humankind to God and creation, the tension between humans and nature is dissolved. Christ's force has sanctified all things so that ecology and theology conjoin. Grace from this redemption illuminates and guides human activities, so that we "behold" the diversity and fecundity of nature as an expression of God's love for His entire creation: a love for which He gave his Son (Sittler 1970; N. Scott 1974; Carmody 1980).

Religious existentialist Martin Buber addressed this separation of religion from science and steered toward ecological rapprochement rather than domination in his small poetic book *I and Thou* (1937). Buber based I-Thou relationships on mutual respect, that is, those linkages we reserve for other people—family, friends, and colleagues. I-It relationships exist between humans and the natural world and form the appropriate realm of science. They engender little reciprocity or egality.

Architect and planner E. A. Gutkind (1956) drew from Buber's ideas to explore geographically how traditional and preindustrial societies lose a sense of I-Thou connections under pressures for economic development and modernization. The result is alienation and homelessness. Others are not as pessimistic. Technological optimists such as Buckminster Fuller (1970) celebrated what he saw as a new era of habitation through cumulative advances in living standards.

Although Buber was prepared to consider some relationships with nature as I-Thou, H. Paul Santmire (1968) attempted to extend Buber's commentary toward an environmental ethic. He sought to overcome the problem of insufficient mutualism with natural things by posing an intermediate linkage between humans and the world that Buber had never used. For Santmire, this I-Ens (Being) captures those relationships that cannot in Buber's framework be properly mutualistic (speech, for example, is essential for an I-Thou type format). Santmire regards I-Ens as going beyond the usual functional and utilitarian linkages portrayed by I-It relationships. I-Ens, he says, is a "subjective pole and an objective pole bound together in an intimate community," and it shifts from detached, impersonal inspection to a "givenness" that takes place, for example, when the person is struck by the beauty of tree blossoms. An I-Ens relationship discovers symphonic unity in diversity, the unity that John Muir, for example, encountered in his sojourn in Yosemite Valley, California. In sum, Santmire states that "encountering the Ens, I am captivated by the Ens's openness to the Infinite, by its openness to a dimension which lies behind and permeates its givenness, its mysterious activity, and its beauty" (Santmire 1968, 273; also P. Reed 1989).

BORROWING FROM OTHER TRADITIONS

If the ultimate power in the world was a personal one for medieval thinkers, the ultimate power in the modern world was thoroughly impersonal. Evolutionary chance and mechanical necessity, shriven of consciousness or value, ruled, indifferent to human conduct or status. Therefore, Paul Tillich's *The Courage To Be* (1952) affirmed life in this world bereft of meaning. Existentialist thinkers sought value in an absurd universe by employing the sense of self in opposition to determinism. Friedrich Nietzsche's nihilism, however, reduced the human self to illusion, so that criticism of the modern lifeworld pointed to an antiworld, "therapy to prevent seduction by any and every worldview" (Griffin 1989, 20).

One response has been to pursue fundamental and perennial issues by turning to Oriental religions and practices. This premodern stance initiated a dialogue about hermeneutics and universalist beliefs in comparative religions. Most concern has focused on Eastern traditions that are life-centered (they include also non-Western beliefs, native American cosmologies, and feminist theologies) and committed to the search for personal enlightenment. Both endeavors include the repositioning of ethical regard for nonhumans (McDaniel 1990). Such belief systems undermine categorical distinctions between self and others and point to universal messages that include ecological awareness.

In such thought, the boundary of community expands beyond the human realm. Sacred power is manifest in the world both in the possibilities that interactions between things suggest and in the cycles and processes embedded in time and space. Self-revelation and abnegation shine out in Buddhist beliefs especially. Such traditions celebrate individual striving for improvement and acknowledge responsibility for both self and others, including the land (Geffre and Dhavamony 1979; Eckel 1987; Halifax 1990).

Some religious experts warn against a "cocktail" of religious beliefs and values mixed from various doctrines of Eastern and Western thought. In their view, apologetics tend to point out lacunae in one system and suggest another religious tradition that can fill a need. While guarding against dual or even poly-citizenship, the recognition of fundamental principles common to major religions propels one to reflection and self-criticism. This need for more tolerance and sharing leads to greater openness to the cultural practices and ethical values of non-Christian peoples (Kung and Ching 1989).

Closer to home, as it were, cultural historian and priest Thomas Berry celebrates the "numinous qualities of the earth" (T. Berry 1990, 154). He calls us to return to basic issues: What is it to be human? What should we do in the world, es-

pecially when conscious of our freedom? We are indeed the *hsin* of heaven and earth, that is, the veritable "consciousness of the world," he exclaims (T. Berry 1990, 155). Berry joins appeals to mystery and regards the world almost as God's body. He seeks to unify the historic and cosmic into one process as "we discover ourselves in the universe and the universe discovers itself in us" (T. Berry 1990, 155).

In a similar vein John Haught (1990) regards the universe as "an adventure into mystery, and our religions are simply ways of explicating this inherent character of the universe at the human level of emergence" (Haught 1990, 178). He opposes the trend to make nature the victim of a "theory of homelessness." Rather, he celebrates the adventure of luring the cosmos into novelty and new experiences. The power of the Holy Spirit is a positive force in this regard. This mysterious indwelling in nature (Bump 1974) calls for both human solicitude and creative involvement (R. Moore 1990).

T. Berry, Haught, and similar contemporary thinkers draw on ideas of evolution and religion popularized by the French Jesuit priest and scientist Pierre Teilhard de Chardin (1881–1955). Teilhard recognizes two critical stages in earth history: first, a point of "vitalization" when life appears at some threshold of complexity and matter; and second, a period of "hominization," that is, reflexive consciousness manifested in the emergence of hominids. This "epoch of man" is a higher level of awareness; it includes self-consciousness manifested by humans and institutions that exemplify novelty, or the "noosphere." The noosphere is an envelope of thought that crowns the layer of life or biosphere, itself covering the lithosphere of basic matter. This layer of reflexive thought makes possible civilization, and the preservation and transmission of cultural traits that mark increases in social processes and levels of cooperation. The upper limits of such socialization are collective reflection, perfect individuality, and self-fulfillment at some final and transcendent "Point Omega." This final stage in cosmogenesis knits together nature with supernature, thereby realizing the Christian concept of beatific vision (Mooney 1966; Klauder 1971; Grau 1976).

Placing stress on the attributes of God-in-the-World, exemplified by the trajectory of evolution toward complexity and love, and bolstered by faith in Christ's life and redemption, Teilhard and others have formulated ontological arguments for a divine immanence in nature. In this way a theology of nature alters the concept of God as absolute, transcendent, and omnipotent to proportions analogous to the natural order of things.

PROCESS THEOLOGY AND AN IMMANENT GOD

Postmodern theology reconstructs and liberates the role of people in the world. Combining memory and creative imagination with a dialectical view of history, the future challenges the past. The basic concept is that of community, consisting of ecological relationships in space and time. Community splinters the hegemony of Newtonian atomism and opposes the reductionist vision of modern science. Joe Holland puts it a similar way, saying that "the root metaphor of the postmodern period becomes artistic (the work of art), expressed in the creative ecological communion of nature and history, across time and space flowing from the religious Mystery" (J. Holland 1989, 21). A theology of nature in this perspective includes process thought based on the works of Henri Bergson, Teilhard de Chardin, Alfred N. Whitehead, Charles Hartshorne, and others.

Process philosophy offers an invaluable synthesis of religious faith, modern science, and environmental ethics. Its chief exponent, Alfred North Whitehead (1861–1947), and a number of followers, notably Griffin (1989) and Barbour (1990), from whom I draw, offer a philosophy of nature that makes no absolute distinction between human and nonhuman life (Whitehead 1920; 1925; 1927; Hartshorne 1948; 1967; Leclerc 1958; Sherburne 1966).

Drawing from twentieth-century physics (relativity and quantum theory), Whitehead's starting point is becoming, not being. Interrelated events, not unchanging particles or isolated atoms, make up reality. Reality is a process of activity and transition among interlinked events. The word *event* emphasizes the temporal aspects

of these moments of experience, and the word *entity* emphasizes integration and interrelatedness of events within experience. Entities differ in their abilities to combine qualities of richness and degrees of intensity in various experiences. Like interwoven fields of energy throughout space, the world exists as a web of connectivity that shifts and changes constantly.

Like an organism, reality is a highly integrated, dynamic system of entities that vary in their levels of organization based on capacities for different experiences. For example, Whitehead calls a rock a democracy—a collection of quite stable, unified patterns of events. Cells, on the other hand, act more as units; plants are centers for connected, usually repetitive events. Vertebrates unify their experiences in memory and learning. Humans integrate all these lower events yet raise them to new levels through the unique intensity and richness that show in their consciousness. There exists, then, a hierarchy of values in a world regarded as a community of events. All entities have intrinsic value, but humans have the greatest due to the intensity with which they live their lives.

In sum, the world is a network of individual moments of experience (events and entities). Every entity responds to others but retains its individuality or freedom to receive and express relationships in its own way. Causality refers to the influence of entities on each other. There is also self-causation or novelty through which an entity may contribute something new by appropriating the past and drawing on various possibilities for the future. This selectivity is not deterministic but possibilistic. And it is to God as the ground of potential novelty that Whitehead and theologians turn. God lures the world into new things without determining their outcome. There is no sharp distinction between God and nature, humans and nonhumans, and living and nonliving things.

Theologians have expanded process philosophy. Describing the position of God as "panentheism," Charles Hartshorne characterized the world as "in God," a view that steers a course between identifying God with the world (pantheism) and separating God from the world (theism) (Sia 1985; Barbour 1990). He describes God as "the wholeness of the world correlative to the wholeness of every sound individual dealing with the world" (Hartshorne 1971, 105). A theology of nature, therefore, seeks out and respects an immanent deity as the "ground of novelty." God is the deepest creative power, who beckons each one of us to new experiences and richer adventures in the celebration of life (Griffin 1989, 81; Zimmerman 1988).

Ethically, process theology speaks for the liberation of all life, human and nonhuman. It demands a shift from manipulation and management and the objectification of the environment to a "respect for life in its fullness" (Birch and Cobb 1981, 2). In this sense, liberation is emancipatory. In their excellent synopsis of biology and religion Birch and Cobb (1981) note that "to trust life is to be responsibly open and sensitive to its call" (Birch and Cobb 1981, 3). The ecological model they construct notes how humankind is continuous with the rest of nature; people have greater intrinsic value only because of the type and intensity of experience open to them. All life has value (but not equal value), therefore, the world is impoverished by environmental decay and the loss of diversity.

This postmodern worldview which confronts both dualism and mechanical materialism presents humans in a panergistic world in which all things are energy rather than matter. Energy is creativity existing in living things, and all things are experiences having importance in themselves, deserving respect. God's role is to call or lure into order the energistic events that make up objects in the universe. God inspires creativity, making life important in the beauty, goodness, and truth that result (Griffin 1989).

Process thinking coincides with deep ecology and liberation theology, both of which have gained international recognition in recent decades. North American practitioners of deep ecology, such as Devall and Sessions (1985), reject resourcism that regards ecosystems as machines to be engineered as too modernist and embrace a biocentric position whereby community and ecological relationships form the basis for all organic existence. Both are geared to earth wisdom, the promotion of the richness and diversity of life. This long-range exploration of nature and

self in regard to nature expunges anthropocentrism in order to return to biological and psychological roots wherein humankind is an element within nature (Naess 1984).

Deep ecology has its critics (Sale 1988). Max Oelschlaeger regards it as "partly defined in opposition to the status quo" (Oelschlaeger 1991, 302). Its explicitly ecocentric orientation is too absolute and implicitly arrogant. Oelschlaeger asserts that deep ecology refuses to acknowledge contingency and context—the root of postmodern challenges to science and thought.

Spokespersons for deep ecology such as Naess, Devall, and Sessions have railed at anthropocentrism and instrumental values in conservation since the term *deep ecology* was coined by Naess in 1973. However, they do not limit themselves to protests but suggest alternative ways of living in the world. They regard "humans as beings who are an expression of a nature deeper, more mysterious, and creative than any of our abstract theories appreciate" (Drengson 1988, 83).

Self-realization as humans is the key to deep ecology, as well as to process thought. And maturity goes beyond the anger, greed, and power that inform so many cultural practices and contemporary institutions. As a liberation movement, deep ecology, like liberation theology on the ecclesiastical and social level (Sigmund 1990), promotes personal growth and understanding through establishing open and creative connections with the environment as home. Drengson (1988) notes "one's ego self may be small and insecure, but one's full ecological self can embrace the whole of nature with a liberating love that enables a diversity of forms of dwelling in states of mutual, intrinsic value" (Drengson 1988, 84).

Deep-ecological positions and process theology coincide in terms of their ecological and evolutionary understanding of nature as a dynamic, open system of activity and experience. As a theology of nature, process thinking avoids traditional dualisms between the world and a distant deity, between body and mind, humanity and animality. We can, therefore, with Barbour, "tell an overarching story that includes within it the story of the creation of the cosmos, from elementary particles to the evolution of life and human beings" (Barbour 1990, 269–

70). It is a story that respects other stories (see Dryzek 1987).

GEOGRAPHY AND THEOLOGY

Geography must embrace theology, especially as theology shifts from universal and absolute approaches to local theologies mindful of actual cultural settings (Lakeland 1990). In this postmodern situation a theology of nature shucks off stentorian claims from the musty cloisters of authority and recognizes the indecency of the modernist stranglehold that shouts "*homo mensura est.*" Today, and into the next century, theology and geography must ground themselves in stories that are historically and spatially satisfying and fulfilling. Currently, theology involves a panoply of knowledge, including a geosophy, in creative contact with historical consciousness yet capable of reflecting on modern experience in the service of true, total emancipation. Like deep ecology the query about how to be in the world as dwellers and home builders opens a debate among geographers and experts on religion alike about the nature of self. This dialogue must go beyond pure selfhood, or contingency, and therefore the object only of language, to a sense of the self as committed to life in its fullest novelty and plurality. It is a dialogue about our growth in "cosmic consciousness" in the deepest sense, about giving loving attention to objects in their own places and homes and on their own terms. It is a story about participating in the cosmic synergism (Oelschlaeger 1991) of constant unfolding. And it is our privilege to make that commitment and show off the true richness of our nature in helping expand the universe by being citizens and companions.

SOURCE

This essay is a revised version of the article appearing under the same title in *Progress in Human Geography* 5 (1981): 234–48.

FURTHER READINGS

Ian G. Barbour. 1990. *Religion in an age of science.* San Francisco: Harper & Row.

Barbour presents a splendid synthesis of process theology in the postmodern world.

Irene Diamond and Gloria F. Orenstein, eds. 1990. *Reweaving the world: The emergence of ecofeminism.* San Francisco: Sierra Club.

This is a collection of twenty-six essays, with a selected bibliography, that takes an ecofeminist perspective on the earth and environmental humility.

Clarence Glacken. 1967. *Traces on the Rhodian shore: Nature and culture in Western thought from ancient times to the end of the eighteenth century.* Berkeley: University of California Press.

Glacken's massive survey of Western views of nature remains unchallenged in scope and detail.

Thomas Keith. 1983. *Man and the natural world: A history of the modern sensibility.* New York: Pantheon.

An important history of the emergence, between 1500 and 1800, of the modern attitude of concern for the natural environment. Written by a historian, this book is of interest to the geographer because of its discussion of new sensibilities felt toward animals, plants, and landscapes and of how and where these sensibilities developed.

Erazim V. Kohak. 1984. *The embers and the stars: A philosophical inquiry into the moral sense of nature.* Chicago: University of Chicago Press.

Kohak presents a provocative essay about the philosophy of personalism and the place of the individual in nature.

Lily Kong. 1990. Geography and religion: Trends and prospects. *Progress in Human Geography* 14:355–71.

A recent review of an area of cultural geography that has received scant attention in recent years. Kong calls attention to the many paths that research might follow in the near future.

Belden C. Lane. 1988. *Landscapes of the sacred: Geography and narrative in American spirituality.* New York: Paulist.

Lane explores the ways in which particular groups of Americans have found spiritual nourishment in the places they inhabit. Lane also suggests principles for recognizing and understanding sacred places in the American landscape.

Carolyn Merchant. 1992. *Radical ecology: The search for a livable world.* London: Routledge.

This is an excellent compilation of the problems, thought, and movements connected with self, society, and environment.

Richard K. Nelson. 1983. *Make prayers to the raven: A Koyukon view of the northern forest.* Chicago: University of Chicago Press.

Nelson's book is a careful discussion of the environmental values and relationships to nature found among indigenous peoples.

Oelschlaeger, Max. 1991. *The idea of wilderness: From prehistory to the age of ecology*. New Haven: Yale University Press.
————, ed. 1992. *The wilderness condition: Essays on environment and civilization*. San Francisco: Sierra Club.

These books provide masterful and comprehensive surveys of the idea of wilderness as it defines and is defined by civilization.

Jamie Scott and Paul Simpson-Housley, eds. 1991. *Sacred places and profane spaces: Essays in the geographics of Judaism, Christianity, and Islam*. New York: Greenwood.

This balanced volume looks at the role of sacred sites, regions, and geographical phenomena in each religion; the symbolic roles these sacred phenomena play; and the role of the geographic imagination in developing religious self-knowledge.

David E. Sopher. 1967. *The geography of religions*. Englewood Cliffs, N.J.: Prentice-Hall.

Although dated, this classic work is still an excellent statement on religion as a spatiocultural system. Philip Wagner notes in his brief introduction that Sopher's primary concern is "the ambiguous and fascinating interplay of symbolic values with environment" (Sopher 1967, viii).

22
AESTHETIC IDEOLOGY
AND URBAN DESIGN

In the early 1970s, the Atlantic Richfield Oil Company (ARCO) sponsored a series of advertisements which appeared in popular magazines in the United States. Entitled "The Real . . . The Ideal," the series featured full-color, full-page institutional ads intended to draw attention not to ARCO and its products, but to the American social malaise and especially to its urban manifestations. In one typical ad, "The Real" was depicted as an urban commercial street described generically as "Main Street garish . . . neon nightmares . . . graceless buildings . . . billboards [that] block out the sun" (figure 1). By contrast, ARCO's "The Ideal" was represented not by a commercial environment, but by Frank Lloyd Wright's famous "Falling Water," a residence built for a wealthy client in rural Bear Run, Pennsylvania. ARCO's description of "The Ideal" called for "structures designed for beauty and long life as well as for practicality. Man's greatest architectural achievements are those that blend in perfectly with the natural environment, or somehow create an environment of their own. They become as permanent as their natural surroundings."

Implicit in ARCO's juxtaposition of these images of a national "real" and a national "ideal" is the assertion that urban commercial environments are inevitably ugly and probably immoral,

The real

A new American art form is emerging:
Main Street Garish.
Some of our cities have become neon nightmares.
Billboards block out the sun.
Graceless buildings flank artless avenues.
Man is separated from nature.

In our haste to build and sell, we have constructed
a nation of impermanence. There is a feeling of built-in
obsolescence in our cities and homes.

FIGURE I

"The Real" as seen by the Atlantic Richfield Oil Company in its advertising campaign of the early 1970s. Source: *Time Magazine,* 3 September 1973, 26.

and, by contrast, that rural or suburban environments are wholesome and beautiful. Implied also through the medium of advertisement is the notion that we all share a uniform and homogeneous perception of environmental wholesomeness and beauty, and that we are in agreement that "Falling Water" might be an attainable reality for everyone if only we clean up the garish neon nightmares which have become our cities.

An even less sympathetic view of the urban environment was promulgated in advertisements published by Volvo, the Swedish auto maker. In promoting the reliability of its product, Volvo presented its auto as a mobile fortress—"A Civilized Car Built for an Uncivilized World." The "uncivilized world," to Volvo, is the contemporary city symbolically represented in its ad as a wall dense with graffiti (figure 2). Graffiti, as we well know, have come to be associated with juvenile gangs, urban poverty, alienation, lawlessness, and racial minorities—the stereotypic components of the "uncivilized world" as viewed by the predominantly white, upper-middle-class American to whom Volvo markets its cars.

The diversity of an urban population, or the cosmopolitan range of goods and services exchanged, is rarely taken as an index of urban success by students of urban culture. Instead, urban success is found in a catalogue of a city's noncom-

mercial, nonindustrial institutions: a philharmonic orchestra, art museums, parks, religious and historical shrines, theaters, fine arts architecture, and unified, monumentalizing plans.

This dichotomy between urban function and urban "culture" reflects a deeper polarization in Western civilization, wherein sensitivity to art, music, poetry, and other "exalted manifestations of the human spirit" are appreciated essentially and ostensibly for their own intrinsic formal qualities. By placing a primary value upon aesthetic behaviors associated with transcendental aspirations, students of culture have been unable to come to terms with the city—the modern city—as a symbolic manifestation of values mediated by forms. As a result, we have not yet been provided with demystified and pragmatic characterizations of urban form and urban function and the ideological relationships between the two. Instead, the modern city is persuasively characterized as an environment of "endless string commercial strips," "thickets of billboards," "unsightly mixed usages," "cheap, tawdry honkytonk store fronts," "a gross commercial carnival," "a Barnum and Bailey world." These are aesthetic responses to urban function which reflect unspoken but deep antipathies toward a society "committed to the maintenance of efficiency and preservation of individual liberties through free enterprise" (B. Berry 1963, 2).

WHO DESIGNS THE CITIES?

In the history of urbanization in the United States, the few master plans which transcended functional prerequisites can be exemplified by George Washington's late-eighteenth-century commission to Pierre L'Enfant to design the nation's new capital city. In contrast to the planned design of Washington, D.C., most cities in the United States evolved as pragmatic mosaics of individual functions within a geomorphological framework. By 1890, almost 30 percent of the entire U.S. population was living in cities as a result of unprecedented urban growth during the nineteenth century (Handlin and Handlin 1975, 143).

In the shift from a rural culture to an increasingly urban one, the centers of social and economic power in the United States also shifted. In the nineteenth century, the inventor-entrepreneur was chiefly responsible not only for the growth of cities already in existence, but also for the new towns and cities which developed around his workshop or factory (Meier 1963, 76). As an "old money" agrarian aristocracy shifted its base of operation from the rural estate to the city, it confronted a "new money" entrepreneur indigenous to the metropolitan environment. This confrontation engendered conflict. In coming to the city, the agrarian aristocracy

> wished more than indulgence in a lavish style of life . . . it also wished general acquiescence in its position. . . . The aristocracy—genuine and putative—wished to bring with them the commodious features of their landed estates. They expected the city to provide them with the elegant squares to set off their homes, with picturesque monuments, and with parks and boulevards . . . for the gentleman on horseback and for the lady in her carriage. (Handlin and Handlin 1975, 21–22)

FIGURE 2
The Uncivilized World according to Volvo: the company's 1973 multimedia promotional theme for radio, television, and the press. Source: *Time Magazine,* 21 November 1973, 42.

FIGURE 3
An example of commercial competition for skyline dominance: the Bromo-Seltzer Tower Building in Baltimore, Maryland.

City-building entrepreneurs were neither to the manor born nor yet socialized by the responsibilities and protocols of economic power. The urbanizing agrarian aristocracy, unable to compete in numbers or in economic strength with the urban entrepreneur, nonetheless asserted its birthright claim to preeminence. Seizing upon the transcendental symbols of high culture, the agrarian elite

> transformed the theater, the opera and the museums into institutions, to display its dominance . . . [It] turned music into classics, art into old masters, literature into rare books, possessions symbolic of its status. (Handlin and Handlin 1975, 21–22)

Following suit, the inventor-entrepreneur similarly staged himself according to his own standards and priorities for measuring success and accomplishment. He built his corporate and commercial buildings as monuments to, and advertisements of, himself. While the culture elite were competing for Old Master paintings, the emergent titans of industry were competing for preeminence on the urban horizon (figure 3). A city's capacity to support museums, operas, theaters, and art galleries was limited by civil interest and collective financing; a city's capacity for monuments to commerce and industry was constrained only by the limitations of space.

Predictably, the culture elite could find little comfort in their control of "enculturating" institutions. By the latter part of the nineteenth century, they had moved their theater of operation to aesthetic criticism of the urban environment. Because they controlled the institutions of "official culture," their aesthetic campaigns carried weight and credibility. They found urban commercial streets to be "bizarre, blatant, and distracting." Although they understood well the competitive nature of "free enterprise" with its base in individual liberty, they objected to the use of the city as a backdrop for "hideous advertisements . . . [buildings with] striking colors . . . great height [and] sudden littleness in a wilderness of skyscrapers" (C. Robinson 1901, 132).

The inventor-entrepreneur, on the other hand, despite his anarchic and individualistic approach to economic competition as manifested in his use of urban space in the late nineteenth century, entertained "cultural" aspirations commensurate with his wealth (Lynes 1954, 167). These aspirations became a source of vulnerability. Employing the tyranny of high-culture aesthetics—*terra incognita* to the entrepreneur—the culture elite soon joined forces with architects, designers, planners, and social reformers, a highly cosmopolitan corps of professional tastemakers. By this alliance, they attempted to codify and disseminate standards of "good taste" in the latter half of the nineteenth century.[1] The "good taste" industry was relatively new, however, and no hierarchical ranking of "schools of good taste" or "morally correct" style was available. Merchant kings and entrepreneurs, industrialists and inventors, employed architects or designers whom they believed respectable, only to find photographs of their new corporate headquarters illustrating "Architectural Aberrations," a regular feature in the professional journal *The Architectural Record* (figure 4). Under these circumstances, confusion prevailed.

CONFUSION RESOLVED

The promulgation of legislated aesthetics would not occur until the middle of the twentieth century.[2] In the late nineteenth century, persuasion by example alone was to suffice, and a very effective program it became. The medium which was to carry the message was already in place.

A series of international expositions and world's fairs had been held in England, Germany, France, Austria, and the United States (New York and Philadelphia) during the second half of the nineteenth century. These events were arenas in which nations vied with each other to display cultural and economic superiority; they were showcases in which technological innovation could be disseminated worldwide (Pickett 1877). An implicit dimension of all these fairs became, eventually, quite explicit: the forms of architectural packaging came to be as important as the didactic displays they contained. The occasion of the 400th anniversary celebration of Columbus's discovery of the New World provided the opportunity for the culture elite, in alliance with professional tastemakers, to create the first world's fair explicitly intended to set a standard for architectural and urban design. The fair was held in Chicago in 1893. According to Daniel Burnham, its supervising architect, the overall plan of the exposition and its individual buildings was intended

> to inspire a reversion toward the pure ideal of the ancients. . . . The intellectual reflex of the Exposition will be shown in a demand for better architecture, and designers will be obliged to abandon their incoherent originalities and study the ancient masters of building. There is shown so much of fine architecture here that people have . . . the

vision before them here, and words cannot efface it. (quoted in M. Schuyler 1894, 292)

In other words, the prevailing aesthetic confusion of the late nineteenth century called for the imprinting, by example, of appropriate architectural design. A precedent, of a sort, existed. In France, L'Ecole des Beaux Arts increasingly had sought to train architects whose designs would blend artfully with the earlier buildings which crowded most of the major cities of Europe (Hamlin 1953, 605–9).[3] The Beaux Arts style received its first major American showing at the Chicago Fair of 1893. For the United States, the imported historicism of Beaux Arts design

FIGURE 4
An "Architectural Aberration:" The Record Building in Philadelphia. Source: *Architectural Record* 1 (3) (1892): 263.

FIGURE 5

At the Chicago Exposition of 1893, Daniel Chester French's *Statue of the Republic* rises from the waters of the Grand Basin in front of the arched peristyle crowned with quadriga. Source: *Shepp's World's Fair Photographed* (Chicago: Globe Bible Publishing Co., 1893), 25.

had not to reconcile new urban construction with sanctified architectural relics; American cities were too new to be so demanding of architects' sensitivity and erudition. Instead, the importation of this eclectic classic/renaissance/baroque idiom was intended to codify, by virtue of its "high culture" associations with Europe and antiquity, the hierarchical framework by means of which "good taste" in America could be distinguished from "bad taste."

THE ECONOMICS OF THE IDEAL

The Columbian Exposition at Chicago, or "White City," as it was popularly called, had a phenomenal impact. Its courts, palaces, arches, colonnades, domes, towers, curving walkways,

wooded island, ponds, and botanical displays elicited ecstatic responses from visitors to whom the White City was little short of a fairyland. Its monumental sculptures and gondola-studded watercourses and lagoons (created expressly for the exposition) were tangible references to the "jewel of Italy"—Venice (figure 5). And its ground plan, complex and curvilinear, was the antithesis of the nineteenth-century urban grid pattern characteristic of most American cities.

The fair as a three-dimensional architectural pattern book opened—and closed—to mixed reviews. Some found in its historic references to European architecture evidence of America's economic and cultural maturity; to others it was a blatant and calculated exploitation of architectural style as social and cultural propaganda, masking "the monstrous evils and injustices of *fin-de-siècle* America" (Fitch 1948, 127; see also Coles and Reed 1961, 137–211). Arguments over the implications of the fair's imported Beaux Arts style masked a more portentous feature, to wit: that its grand-planning design and monumental architecture derived from a single, unified, imposed aesthetic program, and was possible only under circumstances of centralized, authoritarian control. In addition, the realization of so grand a scheme was possible only through decentralized funding, and most of the funding was derived from the public. Public guarantee of debenture bonds purchased by banks and railroads and other corporations, public subscription through stock purchases (unbacked and unguaranteed, and subsequently unredeemed), and public admission fees to the fair itself made construction of the exposition possible (*Review of Reviews* 1893, 522–23). The exposition represented no financial burden to the elite tastemakers, their lobbyists, theoreticians, and technicians, or to the city builders and commercial-industrial magnates for whom it was intended as an object lesson in design. Such were the economics of "The Ideal."

THE ECONOMICS OF THE REAL

It was intended that the Chicago Exposition of 1893 create an image of an urban ideal which would be "widely understood and approved" (Cawelti 1968, 319). To accomplish that end, individual liberties and competitive enterprise were suspended for the higher good of unified planning and aesthetic qualities. These ideals, as exemplified by the White City, seemed to require no visible means of economic support. Nonetheless, the success of the exposition was definitely measured in economic terms—increased railroad revenues and an estimated $105 million left in Chicago by the three million visitors to the fair (*Review of Reviews* 1893, 522–23).

By the late nineteenth century, the demographics peculiar to international expositions had given rise to a class of petty entrepreneurs who specialized in exploiting the commercial opportunities the fairs made possible. At the Phila-

delphia Centennial Exposition of 1876, for example, "shrewd outsiders" developed a "play area" beyond the sacrosanct precincts of the city-owned exposition grounds, in a section which became known as Shantyville (McCullough 1966, 31–34). By 1893, the offerings of these business people were for the first time acknowledged as a formal component of an exposition (McCullough 1966, 31–34). But because the emerging ideology of urban aesthetics could not admit commerce, and since by definition commerce could not be aesthetic, a separate quarter within the walled precincts of the Chicago Exposition was set aside for these commercial activities—a quarter which became known as the Midway Plaisance or amusement zone.

The Midway Plaisance was a separate strip, arranged in a rigid grid pattern, set perpendicular to the grounds of the exposition proper. In stark contrast to the sinuous arrangement of parks, ponds, and palaces in the White City, the Midway was a street one mile long by one city block wide, with a central axis upon which commercial attractions lined up neatly along each side. In its straightforward presentation of commercial functions and in its morphology, the Midway Plaisance anticipated the twentieth-century string commercial strip or linear shopping center.

Originally, the Midway had been conceived as "Department Q of the Ethnological Division," established for the purpose of gathering "the peculiar and unknown peoples of the world" for display (Barry 1901, 8). Because a living museum of humankind did not conform to the aesthetic program of the fair, Department Q was assigned quarters adjacent to, rather than integrated with, the exposition city, and was left to its own devices for funding. By virtue of the necessity of turning a profit simply to exist, the "living museum" and its attendant support activities (curio stands, food stands, amusement rides and entertainments) quickly became a "hilarious amusement zone . . . synonymous for masked folly" (Barry 1901, 8).

Environments, more or less authentic, were constructed to display their exotic inhabitants: Dahomean, Dutch, Turkish, and American In-

ephemeral environment in which structures were built merely of stucco applied over lath (attached to framing). The stucco had been ingeniously worked to create the impression of permanent materials: brick, marble, travertine, granite, and other materials and techniques of construction which suggested a material and structural integrity. Almost all the buildings on both the Midway Plaisance and in the White City were dismantled and discarded at the conclusion of the exposition. It was only the White City, however, which was intended "to leave a residue in the minds of men and in printer's ink" (Bancroft 1893, 4).

The exposition's spiritual residue was made manifest in tangible programs and artifacts which appeared outside the walled city. The Chicago fair was credited with stimulating the "City Beautiful" movement which spread nationwide through the organization of local municipal arts societies (C. Robinson 1899, 780; 1901, 275; Kriehn 1899, 597; Blashfield 1899). It was a movement concerned solely and exclusively with urban aesthetics and not with the economic realities of urban function or the social realities of poverty and class stratification which made the city "ugly."

Civic beautification programs developed the exposition's baroque and neoclassical architectural vocabulary and planning syntax in new banks, city halls, schools, skyscrapers, fire stations, and urban squares throughout the United States (figure 7). Urban furniture, such as Dewey Arch in New York City,

> stirred local pride and national interest, and for a mile up Fifth Avenue to the top of Murray Hill its features are most prominent in the view of that thronged thoroughfare. For the whole distance, in a blaze of color by day and a glare of electric flashlights, by night, the sculpture and the lines of the Arch . . . stand out. (Warner 1900, 276)

Dewey Arch was not alone in commanding this spectacular vista; set against it

> in the daytime, [is] a thirty foot cucumber, in bright green on an orange background above a field of scarlet, lettered in white. . . . In the evening the dancing flash-light of the "57 varieties"

FIGURE 6

"The Streets of Cairo," a popular exotic environment of the Midway Plaisance, World's Columbian Exposition, 1893. Source: *Shepp's World's Fair Photographed* (Chicago: Globe Bible Publishing Co., 1893), 507.

dian villages, a Moorish Palace, a Chinese Pagoda, and a street in Cairo (figure 6). Cultural merchandising proved effective. The raucous, colorful, competitive commerce of the Midway developed as the antithesis of the noneconomic aesthetic ideal of the Beaux Arts White City. Although the Midway may have sacrificed some veracity in environmental design in favor of sensational impact, visitors judged its impact to be

> far better than any dead collection of antiquities. To see the people themselves, alive, moving, acting in their costumes, manners, building, businesses, is far more instructive than to look at their remains in art, or their empty armor, or their skeletons. (Snider 1895, 360–61)

The Midway Plaisance and the White City alike were architectural illusions. Each was an

of beans, pickles, etc. [is] thrown in the faces of all who throng Madison Square. (Warner 1900, 276)

The sacred "ideal" of the White City as well as the profane "real" of the Midway had escaped the controlled precincts of the exposition, but in the urban milieu the boundaries separating the "real" from the "ideal" blurred. No form was sacrosanct, and no medium was immune to exploitation (figure 5). Even the sculptural centerpiece of the Chicago Exposition—Daniel Chester French's monumental *Statue of Columbia*—ultimately found its way into billboard advertising, and is, in reproduction, an awesome presence in Hollywood's commercial necropolis, Forest Lawn (figure 8).[4]

Overwhelming the aesthetic program so clearly delineated by the Chicago Exposition, the "advertising curse" proliferated across urban

FIGURE 8

One-third the size of the original *Statue of the Republic,* Forest Lawn's *Republic* stands opposite a monumental statue of George Washington in the cemetery's Court of Freedom. Also an original, this *Republic* was one of two produced by French after the Chicago Exposition. Its height was 18 feet 2 inches, with head and arms of Carrara marble and the remainder cast in bronze with draperies overlaid with gold.

FIGURE 7

An urban "Ideal" confronts an urban "Real": Dewey Arch vs. Heinz Pickles in Madison Square, New York. Source: *Municipal Affairs* 4 (1900): 275.

landscapes of America. Its progress was viewed by tastemakers as "a measure at once of progress of civilization and lack of culture" (Warner 1900, 269). Fundamentally different from the outset, "The Real," unlike "The Ideal," had to pay its own way.

MIGRATIONS OF THE PROPAGANDA MACHINE

Despite the massive initial impact of the White City, the exposition's aesthetic propaganda almost immediately began to dissipate over space and time. To capitalize on the energy and momentum begun by the Chicago Exposition, a series of similar fairs throughout the United States quickly followed: in 1897, Nashville; in 1898, Omaha; in 1901, Buffalo; in 1904, St. Louis; in 1905, Portland. At each, the separation of commerce and culture was maintained essentially as

FIGURE 9

In the Beaux Arts tradition, a White City constructed for the Louisiana Purchase Exposition, St. Louis, 1904: Festival Hall and the Grand Basin. Source: *The Universal Exposition* (St. Louis: Official Publication, 1904).

had been the case at Chicago. Beaux Arts White Cities, with minor variations and in a different scale, were reproduced at each new site to reinforce the ideals of architectural and urban design (figure 9). Whereas the aesthetic ideal for urban design remained more or less static, the competitive ethic of commerce fueled the continued evolution of midway merchandising.

Midway concessionaires migrated with the expositions. In continuously adjusting and adapting their entertainments and attractions, they sought the optimum synthesis of art and commerce. It was a dual concern which made the midway zone a dynamic environment for architectural merchandising (figure 10). No environment was too exotic and no experience too alien to escape commercial exploitation on the midway. At the Buffalo Pan-American Exposition of 1901, where midway visitors were offered a trip to the moon, an enervated critic lamented:

The prodigal modern Midway is fairly using up the earth. A few more Expositions and we shall have nothing left that is wonderfully wonderful, nothing superlatively strange; and the delicious word "foreign" will have dropped out of the language. Where shall we go to get us a new sensation? Not to the heart of the Dark Continent; Darkest Africa is at the Pan American. Not to the frozen North; we have met the merry little fur-swathed, slant-eyed Eskimos behind their papier-mache glacier at Buffalo. Not to the far islands of the Pacific; Hawaiians, and little brown Filipinos are old friends on the new Midway. Not to Japan; tea-garden geisha girls, and trotting, mushroom capped jin-riksha men have rubbed the bloom off that experience. Not Mexico, not Hindoostan, not Ceylon, not the Arabian Desert, can afford us a thrill of thorough-going surprise. . . . The airship Luna leaves in three minutes for a Trip to the Moon . . . not satisfied with exhausting the earth, they have already begun upon the universe. Behold, the world is a sucked orange. (Hartt 1901, 1097)

The exposition impulse had migrated to California by 1915. On the occasion of the opening of the Panama Canal, California was host to not one, but two, international expositions. Grand design for expositions had not been substantially altered in the westward migration of world's fairs. At the San Francisco Exposition of 1915, the Beaux Arts architectural environment was a polychrome version of Chicago's White City. At the San Diego Exposition, held simultaneously with San Francisco's, the same building technology (stucco applied to lath attached to framing) was used to create a Hispanic-colonial "mission-style" architecture which would ultimately make its own distinctive contribution to the architectural history of California (Barbara Hudson 1977).

As an object lesson for urban designers, the San Francisco Beaux Arts landscape was anachronistic even before it opened; it represented the last grand florescence of what had begun with the Chicago Exposition of 1893. The entertainment zone at San Francisco, however, was to be of some consequence in its impact upon urban design.

The midway at the San Francisco Exposition was host, for the most part, to attractions and concessions of proven commercial viability. For the first time at an exposition, the fair's administrators and designers turned their attention to midway design. Not only were the professional services of exposition designers offered to midway concessionaires, but the exposition management announced the requirement that all concessions were to be self-identifying without the aid of billboards or signs (Todd 1921, 155).

As a result of the sanction against signing, the midway at the San Francisco Exposition became a zone of out-of-scale "signature architecture." Each attraction became an advertisement of itself either in its three-dimensional form or by means of visual cues—"facade architecture"—attached to the front of the structure. A gigantic Golden Buddha announced the presence of a

Japanese concession (figure 11). "Tin soldiers," approximately ninety feet tall, housed merchandise booths in their feet (figure 12). The Atchison, Topeka and Santa Fe Railway constructed a scale model of the Grand Canyon of Arizona; the Union Pacific Railway reproduced Yellowstone Park (with Old Faithful and the Inn); a large and realistic pueblo was occupied by real Indians; and a scale model of the Panama Canal had an actual working canal with an ocean at each end. Other exhibits included the Blarney Castle, a Samoan village, and a troupe of Maori tribesmen who also camped on the zone (Todd 1921, 147–58). Amusements and displays, as advertisements of themselves, depended on their architectural merchandising for continued commercial success.

On the opening day of the exposition, all but twenty-six feet of the entire midway footage of

FIGURE 10

An extraordinary facade on the Zone: the entrance to Dreamland, "A Midway Mystery at the Pan-American Exposition," Buffalo, 1901. The "mystery" was how to exit after entering. "Dreamland" was a maze. Source: *The World's Work Magazine* 1901, August.

FIGURE 11

The golden Buddha claiming attention for the "Japan Beautiful" exhibit on the Zone at the Pan-Pacific Exposition in San Francisco, 1915. Source: Special Collections, University Research Library, University of California, Los Angeles.

six thousand feet had been sold to concession-aires. Along these empty twenty-six feet, the concessions manager ordered that false fronts be erected and painted to make the vacant footage appear to belong to adjacent occupied booths and theaters (Todd 1921, 158). In an aesthetic peculiar to any commerce, any sign of activity— however illusory—was preferable to a void. Emptiness disrupted economic symmetry and signaled dysfunction and blight.

LEAVING THE WALLED CITY

Midway design was acknowledged to be of "a necessary garishness," whereas the exposition proper had been designed for another sort of impact: "to refine and uplift and dignify the emotions" (Todd 1921, 155, 173). Both were architecturally didactic. It is hardly surprising, however, that American entrepreneurs chose to exploit the idiom of the amusement zone for

the architecture of commerce: the midway mode was the end result of two decades of intensive experimentation and refinement of commercial forms in the hothouse environment of midway competition.

In California, and especially in southern California, the transition from midway to urban commercial street was relatively simple. The stucco construction methods employed to produce ephemeral structures for the expositions were particularly suited to southern California's mild climate. The addition of cement to the stucco mixture—a technological breakthrough which occurred in time for the San Diego and San Francisco expositions and which enabled the stucco to carry pigment—was the essential ingredient for stabilizing this previously unreliable building material.[5]

This new genre of commercial architecture was most apparent in Los Angeles, where the streets seemed choked with windmill bakery

FIGURE 12

Ninety feet tall, these monumental toy Tin Soldiers housed stores in their feet on the Zone at the Pan-Pacific exposition in San Francisco, 1915. Source: Postcard, Special Collections, University Research Library, University of California, Los Angeles.

shops, giant tamales, Sphinx heads, outdoor pianos, owls, and landlocked ships (figure 13) (M. Mayo 1933; "Low Camp" 1965; Jencks 1973; Fine 1977). The ultimate origin of these structures was confirmed by a visitor to Los Angeles in the 1920s who noted that here was a city where "one must even buy one's daily bread under the illusion of visiting the Midway Plaisance" (Comstock 1928). The unreality of this dispersed midway landscape was heightened by the presence of the film industry in Hollywood. A Swiss visitor to Los Angeles in 1929 wondered:

Why do they build special Hollywood towns? One hardly knows where the real city stops and the fantasy city begins. Did I not see a church yesterday and believe it belonged to a studio—only to find out it was a real church? What is real here and what is unreal? Do people live in Los Angeles or are they only playing at life? (Moeschlin 1931, 98)

The convergence of urban commercial realities and Hollywood commercial fantasies, in addition to the profusion of midway-style structures in southern California, began to earn for the region its reputation as the home of the hard sell—a region in which "culture" did not vitiate commercial densities, but where commerce became instead the predominant form of culture. Nonetheless, midway-style architecture was not unique to southern California. A poultry store on Long Island established itself in The Big Duck; a dairy stand in Boston could be found in a gigantic milk bottle; a Cincinnati snack shop was built into a giant sandwich flanked by monumental salt and pepper shakers; a Texas gas station was built in the shape of an oil derrick, and one in North Carolina was built as a sea shell; in Iowa, a giant coffeepot housed a diner, and in New Orleans a nightclub named Crash Landing was partially constructed from the front end of a Lockheed Constellation (complete with wings).[6]

FIGURE 13

Clockwise, from top left: A windmill bakery in Los Angeles in the 1920s (Source: Los Angeles Public Library); a tamale food stand in Los Angeles in the 1930s (Source: Los Angeles Public Library); an evangelical ship of good hope: The Haven of Rest Radio Studio; constructed in the mid-1930s, and still in use in North Hollywood; the Hoot Owl Ice Cream Shop in Los Angeles in the 1920s (Source: Special Collections, University Research Library, University of California, Los Angeles); the Big Red Piano Store, built in Los Angeles in the 1930s and a survivor until the mid-1970s, when preservationists attempted to transplant it (Source: Seymour Rosen, SPACES, Inc.); and a real estate office in the head of a Sphinx, Los Angeles (undated) (Source: John Pastier).

These, and countless examples which have escaped documentation, bore witness to the nationwide exploitation of midway signature architecture in which form often quite literally followed function.

Architectural idiosyncracy in the midway genre quickly established itself as a successful medium for merchandising. By the late 1920s, suburban business districts (which followed suburban residential subdivision and development) had their share of signature structures and facade architecture. The encroachment of commerce upon the suburban residential fringes became synonymous, to critics, with social pathology. Displeasing architectural design seemed to represent an environmental threat equivalent to garbage dumps:

> In American cities of any considerable size our new outlying business centers frequently are becoming the ugliest, most unsightly and disorderly parts of the entire city. . . . Buildings of every color, size, shape and design are being huddled and mixed together in a most unpresentable manner. A mixture of glowing billboards, unsightly rubbish dumps, hideous rears, unkempt alleys, dirty loading docks, unrelated, uncongenial mixtures of shops of every type and use, with no relation to one another; shacks and shanties mixed up with good buildings: perfectly square, unadorned buildings of poor design, are bringing about disorder, unsightliness and unattractiveness that threaten to mar the beauty and good appearance of the residential regions of American cities.
> (Glaab and Brown 1967, 294–95 quoting real estate developer Jesse C. Nichol's 1926 observations)

But the spatial organization of a society ideologically committed to the maintenance of efficiency and preservation of individual liberties through free enterprise permitted and even required the areal repetition of commercial centers and the competitive and economical design of the structures which comprised them.

FRANCHISE ARCHITECTURE

By the middle of the twentieth century, the rhetoric of economic competition, fundamental to midway philosophy and morphology, had become formula. Signature architecture ultimately served as the cornerstone upon which a massive franchise industry developed in the United States after World War II.

Franchising in the United States has been a method of marketing and distribution of goods and services based upon a clear delineation of territory. The geographic foundations for American franchising can be traced to the system of merchandising devised by the Singer Sewing Machine Company at the end of the Civil War. Later, the auto industry developed a similar system of franchised dealers for achieving a national distribution of cars, and with the proliferation of auto franchises, a national network of franchised service stations was also established. Similarly, at the turn of the century, Coca-Cola and Pepsi Cola launched their soft drink empires based solidly upon the use of franchised distributors. By the 1920s, the well-known names of Howard Johnson and A&W Root Beer had entered the American franchise scene. This franchise method of distribution, however, did not inspire widespread emulation until the 1950s (*Franchised Distribution* 1972, 1–2).

Often mistaken for a giant corporate monolith intent upon smothering the nation with its corporate presence, each unit within a franchise is actually a locally owned business operated by independent entrepreneurs. Owners typically buy the right or privilege to do business in a franchisor's prescribed manner, in a specific geographic region, and for a specific period of time. The purchase of a franchise generally involves the use of the parent company's methods, symbols, trademarks, architectural style, and network of wholesale suppliers (Vaughn 1974, 2). The effort to produce a "package appearance" and to maintain a "chain identity" despite independent ownership has made modern franchising successful within the context of multiple competitors for the same market (Rosenberg 1969, 44).

The franchise system was almost a century old when it suddenly became a widespread phenomenon in the United States. At the end of World War II, a growing pool of economically alienated Americans, especially returning veterans and displaced farmers, dreamed the dream of

FIGURE 14

Original McDonald's architecture of the 1950s. (Advertising postcard offering one free hamburger for redemption of card.)

financial and personal independence conferred through private ownership of a business (Vaughn 1974). So successful were some franchise operations that the United States seemed, in the 1950s and 1960s, to be overrun by franchised hamburgers, ice cream, donuts, fried chicken, motels, and rental cars, all engaged in mortal combat for national, regional, and local markets. In almost every case, a franchise was closely identified with its signature architecture. One of the most successful franchises—McDonald's hamburgers—underwent in twenty years an architectural evolution indicative of the manner in which values are mediated by forms.

McDonald's became a franchise operation in 1955. The original McDonald's stand was built in San Bernardino, California, by the brothers McDonald, who owned and operated a drive-in, fast-food stand under their name. The transformation of this single stand into an international franchise network was made by Ray Kroc, a traveling salesman impressed by the volume of business generated by this single store.[7] Integral to the transformation was the McDonald's name and the signature structure which was to become synonymous with the product in its initial phase

of expansion: a building with red and white stripes, touches of yellow, oversized windows, and a distinctive set of arches which went up through the roof. These "golden arches," when viewed from the proper angle, described the letter *M* (figure 14). A generation of Americans has proved that such highly abstract signature architecture can effectively come to signify standardized hamburgers, milkshakes, and french-fried potatoes.

As the franchise system began to expand, however, the original McDonald's signature structure was found to be inappropriate in temperate climates. The building had been designed for San Bernardino's semidesert location; it had a wide roof overhang, huge windows, no basement, and required only an evaporative cooler on its roof, with no space provided for a heating plant (Kroc 1977, 70). Acknowledging the importance of signature architecture to franchise success, the corporation designed a series of adaptations for different climatic conditions which would result in no discernible displacement of signature elements. By the mid-1960s, McDonald's golden arches blanketed the nation, each stand keeping score of the number of hamburgers (by then in the billions) which had been sold by McDonald's. At the same time, evidence began to accumulate from California—the hearth region which had generated the original form—that golden-arched hamburger sales were in decline (Kroc 1977, 70). Because Los Angeles had been the cradle of drive-in restaurants, the parent company sent an investigator to the city. He conducted his field research in front of "an invitingly clean" McDonald's which was doing no business, and observed:

> the flow of people in bizarre looking cars and the pedestrians walking brightly ribboned dogs, typical Angelinos in their habitat. [He concluded]: "The reason we can't pull people in here is because these golden arches blend right into the landscape. People don't even see them. We have to do something different to get their attention." (Kroc 1977, 127)

The Los Angeles experience highlighted a major limitation of the extreme forms of signature architecture: in a hypercompetitive commercial environment, by some Alice-in-Wonderland inversion, the extraordinary becomes normal and thus invisible; the restrained and understated stand out.

In the mid-1960s, McDonald's initiated a new architectural style for its franchised structures. Agreeing now with critics who had long decried the original flat-roofed, candy-striped, golden-arched design as a major contributor to visual blight in America, McDonald's "new" architectural recipe drew upon "elite," conventional forms, materials, and behavioral modes: brick-surfaced buildings with mansard roofs, pseudo-antique furnishings and fixtures, and interior eating areas (Kroc 1977, 161).[8] Because the franchise logo was heavily invested in the "golden arch" motif, that element, in an abbreviated, scaled-down, detached, two-dimensional version, was preserved as the signature feature, completely independent of the structure itself (figure 15). The separation of the signature element from the structure made good economic sense because it

FIGURE 15

The McDonald's "new look" of the late 1960s: brick walls, mansard roof, and interior dining spaces. Constructed in Santa Monica in the 1960s.

FIGURE 16
Jack in the Box: a rectangular building with changeable facade and freestanding sign, in Los Angeles.

eased the transition in recycling a building to other commercial uses.

Following the McDonald's example, many franchises in the 1960s eschewed signature architecture in favor of portable statements of franchise identities placed adjacent to the relatively conventional buildings they occupied (figures 16–17). Others, however, elected to accept the risk of investing identity and success in a continuation of midway merchandising (figure 18). Moreover, the earlier stages of franchise architecture seem to have stimulated a renaissance in architectural design based more closely on midway principles. Entrepreneurs operating businesses unassociated with franchise networks began, in the late 1960s, once again to exploit unusual forms and architectural assemblages intended to arrest, amaze, and delight. Gigantism as exploited in the 1915 San Francisco Exposition, and subsequently in the 1920s and 1930s in regions sustaining urbanization and suburbanization, began to reappear (fig-

ure 19). Unlike the early stucco structures, these latter twentieth-century architectural whimsies represent substantial economic investments: a bulldozer office building for a heavy equipment company; Victoria Station (from whose initial success was cloned a chain and numerous independent imitators) as a restaurant in an assemblage of freight cars and cabooses; and Best Products Company has claimed national attention with its "indeterminate facade" buildings— among others, a showroom in Sacramento which appears to have had a bite taken out of one corner (actually its entryway) (Kinchen 1977).

Under these circumstances of heightened architectural merchandising, it was inevitable that the architecture of modern urban commerce would be drawn ever more closely to its source. "Theme" shopping centers and malls of the 1970s now provide the illusion of other times and other places. Like the Midway Plaisance they emulate, they represent walled enclaves wherein are merchandised an international panoply of products, services, and exotic experiences (figure 20). The ultimate architectural statement in this regard is, of course, Disneyland, itself a synthesis of the great American world's fairs of the nineteenth and twentieth centuries.[9] There is, in fact, less and less to distinguish between the conventional forms of retail merchandising and the Disney version of wonderland: an architectural review of the opening of a new regional shopping center in Los Angeles was entitled "A New Kind of Amusement Park" (Seidenbaum 1976).

THE COMPELLING AESTHETIC

As the styles and forms of the architecture of urban commerce evolved in the United States, so

FIGURE 17
Colonel Sanders' Kentucky Fried Chicken, with brick detailing, mansard roof, and freestanding sign, in Santa Monica.

FIGURE 18
The first successful Taco Bell made its appearance in Los Angeles in 1963 and became a franchise in 1965. By the mid-1970s, 325 franchises had been sold, with the largest concentration of Taco Bells in the Middle West, California, and Texas. This one, photographed in Santa Monica, was constructed in 1966. See "A Promising Mañana," *Forbes,* 1 August 1977, 120.

FIGURE 19

Office building in a two-story tractor, built by the United Equipment Company near Fresno, California; architect-designed structure was completed in 1977.

too did the actors competing for dominance of the social and economic life of the city. The main features of urban morphologies had been, for the most part, delineated and established by industrialists and entrepreneurs during the late nineteenth and early twentieth centuries. The latter part of the twentieth century might be characterized as a period of the filling-in of the urban interstices. Key economic functions—industrial, commercial, and governmental—continue to occupy central places and satellite nodes, and within them, express increasing densities through vertical expansion. Less costly horizontal expanses of the city are still claimed by the petty entrepreneur, however.

The problems of gaining control of urban space—and ultimately of urban life—which engaged the rural agrarian elite in contending for the nineteenth-century city are the same problems which confront the corporate elite today. Not surprisingly, members of the contemporary elite exploit the same institutions through which their predecessors had sought to accomplish the same objective. Centers of culture and their taste-making, trend-setting, culture-validating functions have come to be controlled on a national scale by political, corporate, and elite-family dynasties. Business and genealogy play the same role on regional and local scales. Higher education, in particular, has been acknowledged as probably "the single most powerful factor" in

the standardization of taste, and indeed, in the standardization of culture (Burck 1959).[10] Thus it is also not surprising to find in the latter half of the twentieth century that the corps of professional tastemakers has expanded to include educators whose role it is to disseminate "official culture" as defined by those who increasingly control their institutions. Just as the nineteenth-century agrarian elite sought to neutralize and divert the growing economic power of the corporate entrepreneur, the corporate elite, now dominant, seeks to control and manipulate mass culture and the petty entrepreneur.

The exploitation of the American ideology of urban aesthetics is difficult to refute. Its objectives are appealing, and it seems not to conflict with that other American ideology which postulates a society committed to the preservation of individual liberties through free enterprise. In the nineteenth century, the culture elite and professional tastemakers excoriated the corporate monoliths which had begun to dominate the urban skyline. Their twentieth-century counterparts devote their critical faculties to condemnation of the myriad small businesses which have filled in the urban interstices and occupy now-valuable urban space. The contemporary urban boulevard is characterized as "a gross carnival of signs and billboards . . . with no style or unity, little architecture and few aesthetics" (Faris 1974). Urban commerce is described as a "relentless, oppressive attack on the senses . . . the beat of the sell is nearly constant, like living under a tin roof in a monsoon" (Chapman 1977). The small businessman is accused of

> crude architectural huckstering which never helped the economy of a town. It helped kill it. It destroyed not only the integrity of old buildings but also the town's integrity—the image of innocence, wholesomeness and honesty. (Von Eckardt 1977)

The canons of these critics would thus exclude from the marketplace of the city those who are usually the most lively and the most vulnerable—the small businesspeople and entrepreneurs whose capital is so limited and whose footholds so tenuous that their survival depends upon maximally effective, portable icons: neon signs, billboards, and fiberglass totems (figure 21). Not surprisingly, aesthetic campaigns gain momentum when urban commercial space appreciates in value.

Where "crude architectural huckstering" metamorphoses into massive corporate success, however, the contempt of tastemakers is supplanted by respect. When it became evident that the McDonald's formula was working, its architectural aspect soon became

> the object of much serious discussion in architectural classes. James Volney Righter, who teaches architecture at Yale, says he believes the [new] style "holds great potential in that it links the energy of the lively American 'pop' forms with functional utility and quality construction." (Kroc 1977, 161)

Ada Louise Huxtable (1978), architecture critic for the *New York Times,* began to find "aesthetic merit and cultural meaning" in these urban vernacular commercial forms. And with transparent cynicism, Charles Jencks, writer and teacher of architectural history, has suggested that

> since you can't escape Bad Taste any more, . . . the only thing you can do is apply standards to it and discover when it is really subversive and enjoyable. Today, most man-made things are horribly mediocre, but happily, a few of them are really awful. We have to cultivate principles of banality not just to survive but to keep the lovably ridiculous from slipping into the merely no-account. (Jencks 1973, 601)

Professional tastemakers are doing precisely that. In 1976, the Society for Commercial Archaeology was founded "to promote the un-

FIGURE 20
Old Town Mall, an enclosed shopping center constructed in the early 1970s in Torrance, California, was designed with Disneyland's Main Street as its architectural model.

FIGURE 21
Lowe's Tire Man, an attention-getter on Lincoln Boulevard,
a commercial route in Los Angeles.

the 20s and 30s as the home of architectural anarchy. . . . In retrospect, the worst of the kookie structures seems less abortive than ill-timed. With the advent of pop art and "camp" movements, they might have found homes in art galleries rather than on street corners. ("Low Camp" 1965)

In the ideology of American aesthetics, it is understood that those who make taste make money, and those who make money make taste. In the twentieth century, this logic manifests itself primarily in an urban context: it is pivotal in the battle for urban territory and urban markets. No one worries the farmer for his unaesthetic barns. All ideologies have their time and their space.

THIS IS NOT A CONCLUSION

A fundamental contradiction is evident in examinations of the forms and structures of contemporary American commerce in its urban context. Investigations of function and morphology have revealed the operation of coherent, efficient systems. The inherent instability of the urban economic environment is accepted as a corollary of the free enterprise system. Nevertheless, urban economic networks have been abstracted and analyzed quantitatively and cartographically, revealing evidence of logic and order accepted by most scholars and policymakers. In contrast, the material culture of urban commerce, the framework within which networks of distribution and consumption are operationalized, has been portrayed in diametrically opposite terms. Few students of culture would claim that the architectural forms and the syntax of commercial competition conform to discernible patterns deriving from a coherent system of belief and behavior, parallel to the free enterprise logic which provides a rational basis for the analysis of economic behavior. The three-dimensional space occupied by urban commerce—the heritage of world's fair amusement zones—is invariably characterized as dysfunctional, even pathological. How is this conceptual disjunction, originating in different aspects of one and the same urban space, and within a single framework of objectives, to be explained?

derstanding, documentation and preservation of significant structures and symbols of the commercial built environment" (Liebs 1978, 35). Earlier, Yale architect Robert Venturi paid tribute to a spectacular efflorescence of gambling architecture in his book *Learning from Las Vegas* (R. Venturi, Brown, and Izenour 1972). In the process of manufacturing academic and professional capital, tastemakers have begun to invest the remnants of an earlier age of architectural refugees from world's fair midways with the aura of transcendental meaning. Los Angeles's few surviving hot dogs, donuts, and derbies are now being apotheosized as significant Urban Art:

> Of all the landmarks threatened with eventual extinction by bulldozer and high rise, none will be mourned with such mixed feelings as the[se] grandly eccentric monuments. . . . Holdovers from a more rococo era, they gave Southern California a colorful and often unwelcome stamp in

One explanation resides in the fact that the "aesthetic impulse" which filters perception of three-dimensional space has little to do with the formal appreciation of shapes, colors, or combinations thereof. As chronicled in this paper, the merchandising of "good taste" in urbanizing America long ago coalesced as an aesthetic ideology which has permeated public policy and public programs. Urban "ugliness" and urban "blight," variously defined, have been employed as rhetorical gambits in propaganda campaigns to control the use of appreciating urban space. Typically, the costs of aesthetic programs, beginning with the White City of 1893, have been borne most heavily by those who benefit from them the least. Yet aesthetic ideology continues to mold attitudes toward environmental design and urban development because it is reinforced by academics and policymakers who operate as powerful allies of "official culture." Aesthetic ideology remains a potent vehicle for the perpetuation of urban, economic, and social inequalities, and serves as reinforcement for another oppressive ideology: that our economy is based upon the maintenance of efficiencies through free enterprise.

It is only a matter of time before academics and policymakers will be forced to confront the inconsistencies and disjunctions arising from the evidence of their own research. Ultimately they will have to go beyond the quantifiers' and cartographers' two-dimensional discussions of the mechanics of urban economics and the impressionistic value judgments of critics and historians of architecture. To begin, they will have to examine the manipulations and special pleadings which have operated to distort and impede their understanding of the symbolic, syncretic, and integrated nature of that dauntingly complex nexus which is the modern American city. In that vast no-man's-land separating "The Real" from "The Ideal" lie many opportunities for enlightenment.

SOURCES

This article appeared originally in the *Annals of the Association of American Geographers* 69 (1979): 339–61.

NOTES

1. Periodicals such as *Cassel's, Harper's New Monthly, Lippincott's, Atlantic Monthly, Scribner's,* and others regularly featured treatises on appropriate and inappropriate development or embellishment of urban space, and appropriate lifestyles for urban culture.

2. In 1949, Congress passed the Federal Housing Act, making available a number of federal aids to local redevelopment agencies for the rehabilitation of substandard housing. The Housing Act required that displaced families be found housing, but it was not necessary to return them to the original site. As a result, virtually any urban site could be declared blighted by a local authority, and then reclaimed for shopping centers, luxury housing, or other high-yielding projects developed by private companies benefitting from public subsidies. By 1954, urban redevelopment was no longer viewed with alarm as a form of social engineering; rather, its programs were increasingly interpreted as the federal sanctioning of the use of police power to achieve aesthetic ends by seizing urban properties through condemnation in areas judged (by developers, planners, and politicians) to be "blighted," and to rebuild these areas in conformity with imposed "master plans" (M. Scott 1969, 491).

3. Many aspiring American architects received their training at L'Ecole des Beaux Arts in the nineteenth century and returned to the United States to promote a revival of its particular form of architectural historicism. The principal designer of the Chicago Exposition of 1893, Daniel Burnham, had not been trained at L'Ecole, but clearly subscribed to its principles.

4. An illustration of a cut-out *Statue of Columbia* gracing a billboard in Newark Meadows can be found in Warner (1900, 274). For an analysis of the development of Forest Lawn Cemetery, see Barbara Rubin Hudson (1976).

5. The Chicago Exposition of 1893 had been called The White City because technicians were unable to introduce pigment successfully into the stucco. The fair's promoters thus made a virtue out of a limitation in bestowing upon the colorless landscape the title "White City" ("The great International Pan-Pacific Exposition" 1915; "The Color Scheme at the Panama-Pacific International Exposition " 1914; Denievelle 1915).

6. Long Island's Big Duck is illustrated in Blake (1964, 101) and discussed in R. Venturi and Brown (1971) and Wines (1972). The Sankey Milk Bottle and seashell service station are illustrated in *Historic Preservation* 30 (1): 30.

7. Two books chronicle Ray Kroc's machinations in transforming a San Bernardino drive-in hamburger stand into an international franchise: Kroc (1977) and Boas and Chain (1977).

8. More recent McDonald's construction has superseded the mansard style, with emphasis on conforming to regional architectural flavor. A McDonald's constructed in 1977 in Santa Monica features a red-tiled roof and

stucco walls in keeping with southern California's largely fabricated Spanish colonial tradition. In San Francisco, near City Hall, a McDonald's completed in August 1978 exhibits a formal modernism consistent with the most up-to-date construction in civic buildings and avant-garde residential construction: greenhouse windows, large expanses of concrete wall meeting at unusual angles, and ornamental graphics.

9. Evidence for the origins of Disneyland are discussed in Barbara Rubin Hudson (1975, 445–62).

10. The role of education and its impact upon the "American way of life" is cogently discussed in O'Toole (1977). Objections to the use of public cultural institutions and public monies for the dissemination and validation of "official culture" were outlined in "an anti-catalog" produced by a group calling itself the Committee of Artists Meeting for Cultural Change in New York in 1977.

FURTHER READINGS

Reyner Banham. 1971. *Los Angeles: The architecture of four ecologies.* Harmondsworth: Penguin Books.

Banham's book is a classic, pioneering study of the architecture of Los Angeles. In contrast to conventional architectural histories, Banham's sets Los Angeles's architects and buildings in a broader social, historical, and topographical context. He considers the distinctive features of each architectural niche of the Los Angeles Basin—its beaches, plains, foothills, and roadways—and then discusses each of these "ecologies" with respect to the designers, architects, and social groups that have shaped them through time.

Denis E. Cosgrove. 1984. *Social formation and symbolic landscape.* London: Croom Helm.

This book considers the idea of landscape as it has developed in Western society since the Renaissance. Cosgrove argues that the landscape idea represents a way of seeing the world and representing social relationships that has changed in certain novel ways over the last several hundred years. He develops his argument around case studies drawn from different periods and regions, including Renaissance Italy, sixteenth-century Venice, and eighteenth- and nineteenth-century Britain and America.

Denis E. Cosgrove and Stephen Daniels, eds. 1988. *The iconography of landscape: Essays on the symbolic representation, design, and use of past environments.* Cambridge: Cambridge University Press.

This collection of essays interprets the symbolism and aesthetics of landscapes in terms of their historical and social contexts.

James B. Gilbert. 1991. *Perfect cities: Chicago's utopias of 1893.* Chicago: University of Chicago Press.

Gilbert presents an account of several competing visions of the city that emerged in late-nineteenth-century Chicago and set the context for the White City examined by Hudson.

David Harvey. 1989. *The condition of postmodernity: An enquiry into the origins of cultural change.* Oxford: Basil Blackwell.

Among the topics addressed by Harvey is competition for meaning in the urban environment in the context of conflicts and contests over power and political dominance.

David Ley. 1987. Styles of the times: Liberal and neoconservative landscapes in inner Vancouver, 1968–1986. *Journal of Historical Geography* 13:40–56.

Using the examples of the liberal reform landscape of False Creek, and the neoconservative landscape of British Columbia Place, Ley argues for the intermittent appearance of the rational (or instrumental) and romantic (or expressive) ideologies in Western culture (after Bernice Martin). This position characterizes modern planning as rational and postmodern planning as romantic. The first is seen as a response to the need for social order in a mass society; the second, a solution to the problems of placelessness, anomie, and the need for community.

Edward Relph. 1987. *The modern urban landscape.* Baltimore: Johns Hopkins University Press.

Relph addresses many of the same issues raised by Hudson: the interrelated changes in architectural and aesthetic conventions which have shaped the twentieth-century city. Relph ties these changes to new planning traditions and to social and economic conditions.

Lester Rowntree and Margaret Conkey. 1980. Symbolism and the cultural landscape. *Annals of the Association of American Geographers* 70:459–74.

Concern for the preservation and protection of traditional symbolic landscapes increases in times of stress, since they bolster the shaken sense of identity. Rowntree and Conkey argue that a concern for preservation expresses a condition of uncertainty and anxiety.

Edward Soja. 1989. *Postmodern geographies: The reassertion of space in critical social theory.* London: Verso.

The last two chapters of this book examine the postmodern landscape of Los Angeles, provocatively analyzing the struggle for control over the social production of space.

Gwendolyn Wright. 1991. *The politics of urban design in French colonial urbanism.* Chicago: University of Chicago Press.

The author, an architectural historian, explains why many early-twentieth-century French architects worked in the colonies and how they legitimized French rule with a combination of serviceable design and symbolic manipulation.

PATRICK MCGREEVY **23**

IMAGINING THE FUTURE
AT NIAGARA FALLS

From the beginning of the nineteenth century until the Civil War, Niagara Falls was the primary goal of North American travelers who sought sublime natural scenery. As the setting of the falls became more and more humanized, many visitors found that they could no longer feel that peculiar combination of rapture and terror they associated with the sublime. But, near the end of the nineteenth century, Niagara began to stir the imaginations of many North Americans and Europeans in a new way. They attached a special meaning to Niagara Falls: it was to be the focus of the future. We find this idea expressed by poets and novelists, but also by entrepreneurs, inventors, engineers, and scientists. They each imagined a future world in which Niagara was to play a central role. In this paper I investigate these visions of the future, most of which appeared between 1890 and 1910, in order to learn how people of this period viewed Niagara Falls and also how they viewed the future. In addition, I explore the relation between the Niagara people imagined and the Niagara they created. Many twentieth-century visitors have found the landscape at Niagara Falls surprising. They have come expecting a natural spectacle but have discovered instead an urban, industrialized place. This industrial development is partly the product of Niagara's relative location and the timing of particular technological innovations. But for many visitors the fact that Niagara could be so idealized as a natural object yet so thoroughly exploited for human purposes has seemed puzzling. I suggest here that the industrial development and the idealization are intimately connected. Examining turn-of-the-century visions of the future at Niagara will help to make that connection clear.

GEOSOPHY

Cultural and historical geographers have had a long-standing interest in the meanings people attach to places. More than fifty years ago Ralph H. Brown (1943) compiled a variety of firsthand geographical descriptions to show how the Eastern Seaboard of the United States might have appeared to a Philadelphia geographer in 1810. The term *geosophy* was proposed by John Kirtland Wright (1947) as the study of the world as people conceive of and imagine it. William Kirk (1952) suggested that the world people actually inhabit is the world they perceive; he called it the behavioral environment. Yet these early examples of interest in images of places inspired little geographical research during the 1950s.

More recent attention to geosophy can be traced to a seminal article by David Lowenthal (1961). Acknowledging his debt to Wright's formulation of geosophy, Lowenthal set out to investigate all the factors that can influence an individual's perception of the world. He concluded: "Every image and idea about the world is compounded, then, of personal experience, learning, imagination, and memory" (Lowenthal 1961, 260). It was only in the late 1960s and early 1970s, with the rise of what has been called humanistic geography, that a significant number of geographers finally took up the work that Lowenthal had started. This new humanistic geography had roots apart from the tradition of geosophy; most notable among these influences was the Sauer tradition of cultural geography. Indeed, much of the literature of humanistic geography consists of attempts to synthesize the several strands of the humanistic tradition within some philosophical system such as phenomenology (Relph 1970; Tuan 1971) or idealism (Guelke 1974).

There has been considerable agreement on one serious shortcoming of humanistic geography. Entrikin (1976, 627) observed that "since most of the humanistic literature is prescriptive, only a few examples are available of humanistic studies of place." R. C. Harris (1978, 134) noted this same lack and attributed it to the fact that "those who call themselves 'humanistic geographers' are inclined to philosophical reading and methodological writing." According to R. J. Johnston, this situation still obtains; because humanistic writings have been mostly "programmatic," there is still "little to review to illustrate the nature of humanistic work" (Johnston 1983, 74).

This paper is offered as one detailed study of a place from a humanistic perspective. It will examine the facets of a particular idea of Niagara Falls and assess the importance of that idea to understanding the place itself. In the process, this paper will help to illustrate the nature and some of the possibilities of humanistic geography.

THE REMOTE WATERFALL

Although images of the future became numerous at Niagara Falls only in the late nineteenth century, these images had roots in earlier perceptions of the place. When word of Niagara Falls first reached Europe in the late seventeenth century, the falls almost immediately took on the proportion of myth. This was a time of great cultural change in Europe. The fascination that for centuries had been directed vertically toward heaven and hell was now being trained upon the distant horizon. Lewis Mumford (1944, 232) has summed up this new European perspective: "By degrees, Western man lost his respect for boundaries: the unknown, the untried, the unbounded began to tempt his imagination." Niagara's supreme isolation allowed Europeans to imagine it as a place that had no parallel in their own world, as a fabulous, overwhelming place (McGreevy 1985a). Niagara remained inaccessible even to North American centers of population until the opening of the Erie Canal in 1825. But even with the beginning of tourism on a large scale, the image of a fabulous remote waterfall did not entirely perish: people simply found new ways of imagining it as if it were remote. One of these ways, often expressed in travelers' accounts and poetry, was to see Niagara as a symbol of death. In part, this reflected a widespread fascination with death that characterized the Age of Romanticism (Ariès 1974; Levin 1970; Rowell 1974; G. Thompson 1974). The brink of the falls symbolized the moment of death. One nineteenth-century poet, for instance, described Niagara's brink as "that mysterious line / That separates eternity from time" (Liston 1843, 36). Like a world beyond the ocean, the world beyond the doors of death is remote. It cannot be known directly; one can only imagine what it is like. During the nineteenth century there appeared at Niagara Falls a whole series of visions of the afterlife, speculative descriptions of heaven and hell (McGreevy 1984, 115–33). This was one way that the old European image of Niagara was transformed in the nineteenth century.

A second way nineteenth-century visitors kept Niagara remote was by imagining the falls as an embodiment of primeval nature. Niagara seemed a survivor and hence a representative of the distant past where nature reigned, undisturbed by human will. There are numerous descriptions of this primordial world in the poetry and travel literature of Niagara. Some visitors imagined it as Eden, but others saw it as a world of dark chaos. In one poem, for instance, Niagara Falls was the "Sole relic of that awful day / When all in wild confusion lay" (Lord 1869). But nature does not have to be ancient to be remote. By definition nature is outside the human world; as Northrup Frye (1976, 60) puts it, nature has a quality of "otherness, the sense of something not ourselves." The concept of the sublime provided nineteenth-century travelers with the means to grasp and appreciate Niagara's "otherness." The sublime was an attempt to account for the attraction, indeed the rapture, people felt in the presence of overwhelming and terrifying natural objects. As refined near the end of the eighteenth century by Kant, the sublime response resulted from the realization by the viewer that there was a capacity within the human psyche capable of expanding to appreciate the vast natural spectacle (S. Monk 1935; Hipple 1957; Wood 1972; McKinsey 1985). The concept of the sublime provided both a justification for visitors' reactions to Niagara and also a vocabulary in which to express them. The bulk of nineteenth-century written and graphic descriptions of the falls interpret the "otherness" of Niagara in the vocabulary of the natural sublime.

A third way that people continued to see Niagara as remote was to imagine it in the future. Throughout the nineteenth century some visitors had spoken of the Niagara River as the "stream of time." The falls, to these visitors, represented a radical break in the stream of time—a break that separated the present from the future. One 1849 visitor, for example, described the abyss below the falls as a "frightful gulf, scooped out as if to embrace the descending flood, and conduct it to some new destiny;—as the present receives the past in its passage onward, and impels it by a new impulse, together with all it bears on its tide, to the mysterious future" (Dixon 1849). The future is another realm whose nature is, to a large extent, a matter of imagination.

Although this image of the future as remote and mysterious appeared early in the nineteenth century, it was not until the beginning of hydroelectric power development in the 1890s that the idea of the future really became bound up with Niagara Falls. It was then that people began to speculate about what lay beyond the break in time that Niagara's brink represented. They began to imagine various futures in which Niagara was to play a central role. At first these visions of the future were almost uniformly optimistic. Usually proposed by scientists, entrepreneurs, and engineers, they took the form of massive utopian development schemes for Niagara Falls. After the turn of the century, negative visions of the future began to appear at Niagara; these usually took the form of poems and novels. The optimistic view clearly dominated, particularly among those people who played major roles in shaping Niagara's landscape. Although, as we have seen, several important images of Niagara Falls emerged in the nineteenth century, the discussion here will focus on this neglected connection of Niagara with the future.

THE BRINK OF A NEW WORLD

Before examining specific visions of Niagara's future it is important to consider briefly the historical milieu in which they developed. The earlier perceptions of Niagara provided a fertile soil for the growth of these images of the future, but there were other reasons why they appeared when they did. As the nineteenth century drew to a close, people in all parts of the industrialized world were becoming obsessed with the future. One indication of this was the blossoming of a literature of the future. The enormous success of Jules Verne's *Five Weeks in a Balloon* (1863) touched off a steady stream of tales of the future. By the 1890s the stream had become a flood. Technical forecasts and serious utopian proposals also formed part of this literature of the future, which continued to grow until World War I (I. Clarke 1979). The writings on the future at Niagara were part of this burgeoning literature.

Historian J. B. Bury (1955) attributed this obsession with the future to the quickening pace of material progress. He also noted that many expected moral and social progress to accompany the material progress of the future world. The sense of expectation was particularly strong in the United States, where an unprecedented outpouring of futuristic utopias followed the publication of Edward Bellamy's *Looking Backward: 2000–1887* (1888). Kenneth Roemer, who has recently examined this literature, suggests that many Americans of this era expected a kind of "final transition," a complete rupture from the past (Roemer 1976, 19). The conquest of nature seemed nearly complete: industrial civilization had changed the material face of the world; it had spread itself over vast new continents. Now the ends of continents were being reached; the frontier was disappearing. But the impending limits to growth appeared to many people of this time as a threshold. Beyond the "final transition" they imagined a future world in which human control would be absolute.

The hydroelectric development of Niagara Falls in the 1890s seemed to many as a sort of capstone on humanity's victory over nature. The process that had been increasing human control over nature throughout the century was finally being turned on this last stronghold of natural power. The development of Niagara came to represent, for some observers, the ushering in of a new, totally human order. As one poet put it, "With power unrivaled thy proud flood shall speed / The New World's progress toward Time's perfect day" (Copeland 1904, 11–12). Ironically

these forward-looking people clung to a view of nature that had been popular throughout the nineteenth century, particularly at Niagara. This was the idea that nature was unfathomable and exhaustless, a notion integral to the concept of the sublime. Developers felt that if they could harness the power of Niagara, there was absolutely no limit to what they could do.

The images I shall examine here are part of this new fascination with the future. Although some have argued that the future was anticipated with particular enthusiasm in the United States (Roemer 1976, 19; P. Conrad 1980, 130–58), this anticipation was neither originally nor exclusively American. Niagara Falls straddles the border between Canada and the United States; certainly there are important contrasts to be drawn at this border (Miele 1979; McGreevy 1985b), but the fascination with Niagara's future was something late nineteenth-century Canadians and Americans shared. Indeed many Europeans also shared it. I shall consider visions of the future that originated on both sides of the Niagara River and both sides of the Atlantic Ocean. The assumption throughout is that the fascination with Niagara's future, in its most important aspects, was a transnational phenomenon.

In the sections that follow I first deal with visions of a fabulous future at Niagara Falls from the pre–World War I era. The second section examines pessimistic images of the future from the same period, and a final section focuses on ideas of the future at Niagara from the post–World War I period.

INDUSTRIAL UTOPIA

The small group of settlers who founded the village on the American side of Niagara Falls in 1805 were excited about the industrial possibilities of tapping Niagara's power. They named the place after the greatest industrial center they knew: Manchester. Although the village's name later was changed to Niagara Falls, the dream of an industrial metropolis remained because people continued to imagine that Niagara's power was unlimited. Schemes to create this metropolis were proposed in nearly every decade of the nineteenth century, but an unprecedented num-

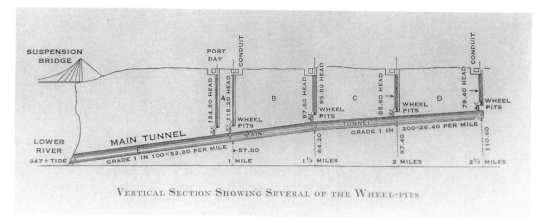

VERTICAL SECTION SHOWING SEVERAL OF THE WHEEL-PITS

FIGURE 1
Power tunnel, cross-sectional view. Source: E. Adams (1927, 2:114).

ber appeared in the 1890s. Four development proposals from this decade will be examined in detail. Each presented a fabulous picture of Niagara's future as well as a prescription for attaining that future. Some of these plans were implemented or partially implemented, while others inspired no action at all. The line between practical proposals and those that appear today as wild utopian schemes can only be drawn in retrospect. All were tinted with an image of Niagara Falls as an inexhaustible, almost magical source of power. All were informed by a belief that the future would be both more fantastic and more humane than the present as a result of humanity's increasing ability to subdue nature and to transform its energy for human purposes. The natural sublimity of the falls lived on in the ingenious schemes designed to capture Niagara's fire.

THE POWER TUNNEL

In 1890 construction commenced on one of the most daring and ultimately one of the most successful of Niagara's power projects (E. Adams 1927; Special International Niagara Board 1931). Headed by New York financier Edward Dean Adams, the Niagara Falls Power Company was digging a deep tunnel beginning at the foot of the falls and extending 2.5 miles beneath the Village of Niagara Falls to a point on the upper river where water could be diverted through a series of

vertical shafts into the tunnel (figures 1 and 2). Each shaft was to be capped with a turbine. A power canal had been supplying mechanical power to various mills since 1875, but this was the first large-scale attempt to generate electricity at Niagara Falls.

Adams and his associates considered the power tunnel a futuristic scheme. Past methods and experience, they felt, could shed little light on an engineering enterprise this new and this massive. They began by consulting and permanently retaining a series of experts including Thomas Edison. They also established the International Niagara Commission, a think tank headquartered in London. Lord Kelvin, the chairman of the commission, was charged with researching methods of power generation and transmission. In 1895 George Westinghouse received the contract to install and operate the electrical equipment. Westinghouse, who had been persuaded by Nikola Tesla to adopt the alternating current system, successfully completed the world's first long-distance electrical transmission in 1896.

The leaders of the Niagara Falls Power Company had more in mind than generating electricity. They secured vast tracts of land for both industrial and residential development and soon completed a large electrochemical complex and an electric railway to service it. For the workers, a model residential town was built. They called it Echota, which in Cherokee means "town of

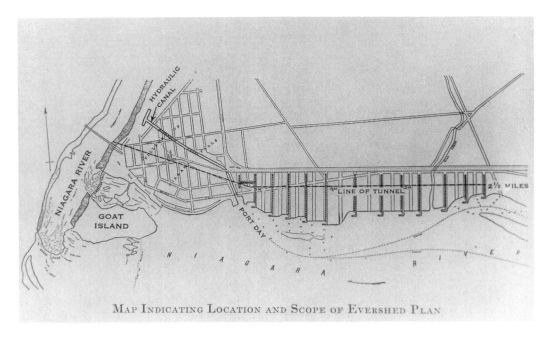

MAP INDICATING LOCATION AND SCOPE OF EVERSHED PLAN

FIGURE 2
Map indicating location of power tunnel. Source: E. Adams (1927, 2:114).

refuge." Echota featured a New York Central passenger station and workers' houses designed by architect Stanford White. White also created a color scheme for painting all the houses in the town (E. Adams 1927, 1:321–22). This metropolis was meant to be a model not only of industrial progress but also of social and even aesthetic progress.

The power tunnel project created a great deal of excitement at Niagara Falls. Many believed that it would usher in a new era. Nikola Tesla, who designed the transmission system used on the project, predicted that electricity generated at Niagara would soon power the streetcars of London and the streetlights of Paris. "Humanity will be like an ant heap stirred up with a stick," the passionate Tesla exclaimed, "see the excitement coming!" (Goldman 1971). By the turn of the century, the power tunnel was known as the "new Niagara" (Fawcett 1902). Many who were involved in the creation of this "new Niagara" clearly hoped that it would retain the magic of the old Niagara.

Perhaps the most striking illustration of how the people behind the power project viewed the harnessing of Niagara was a mural placed in the Schoellkopf Station by the Niagara Falls Power Company (figure 3). Edward Dean Adams, the president of the company, described the mural in these words: "This allegorical painting tells in vivid and powerful tone, but with eerie lightness, the romantic birth story of humanity's modern servant—electrical power. Torrents of energy tumble into the eddying pool of human waves from which emerge the two poles imparting the spark of life to the giant genie—POWER" (E. Adams 1927, 1:i). Why a genie? By harnessing Niagara, the leaders of the power company felt they had acquired a power that, like Aladdin's, was almost magical. With it, they could transform the world. This gain in power signaled a break with the past; now the future seemed entirely in human hands. The genie was the "new Niagara." The hydroelectric development of the old Niagara transmuted the chaotic power of the falling water into a controlled and focused

FIGURE 3
Willy Pogany's mural, *The Birth of Power*. Source: E. Adams (1927, 1: frontispiece).

force. Using the very power of nature, humanity was able to rise above it. The same sense of expectation that surrounded the power tunnel project found expression in several less successful schemes, examined next.

MODEL CITY

In 1893 a flamboyant entrepreneur, William T. Love, released an investment prospectus with the title "The Model City—Niagara Power Doubled." Love had purchased a huge tract of land extending from the Niagara Escarpment to Lake Ontario and comprising almost ninety square miles (figure 4). His plan was to build a

navigable power channel from the upper Niagara River to the Model City site, thus utilizing the drop of the upper and lower rapids as well as the drop of the falls itself.

Love was a skillful promoter. He constantly appealed to his contemporaries' image of Niagara. Model City was "destined to become one of the greatest manufacturing cities in the United States," he wrote, because it would tap "the great water power of Niagara Falls" (Love 1895, 1). To manufacturers he offered "unlimited water-power" with the "risk of loss entirely eliminated" (Love 1895). Love also appealed to his contemporaries' sense of expectation about the immediate future. Model City was to experience "'rapid development' such as no other city in the world has ever experienced" (Love 1895, 1). Love be-

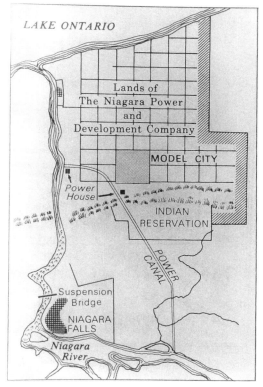

FIGURE 4
Map of Model City. Source: Adapted from Love's original (1895, 12).

FIGURE 5
Map of Metropolis. Source: Gillette (1894, opposite p. 89).

lieved its population would reach at least one million. But Model City was to illustrate more than material progress. It was to be a carefully planned community, a model city, "designed to be the most perfect city in existence" (Love 1895).

The success of Love's pitch was remarkable. He persuaded the leaders of New York State to allow him the privilege of addressing a joint session of the legislature in 1893. After listening to his proposal, the state's leaders granted him the right to condemn and appropriate whatever property was necessary and to divert as much water as he wanted (Michael Brown 1979). Construction commenced immediately at both ends of the canal. A factory, several homes, and about one mile of the canal were completed when the depression of the mid-1890s forced investors to withdraw their money. Love's company became bankrupt. Ironically, Model City survives today as a tiny hamlet.

METROPOLIS

Perhaps the most elaborate of all visions of Niagara's future came from the inventive mind of the famous razor blade magnate King Camp Gillette. He presented the plan in his book *The Human Drift* (1894), published several years before his razor blade made him wealthy. Observing the growing concentration both of capital and of industrial production, Gillette concluded that eventually there could be only one corporation and one city in North America—perhaps even in the world. The site of this city, which he called Metropolis, would be Niagara Falls, because here was a power source that Gillette considered almost infinite. A map he included in *The Human Drift* (figure 5) illustrates the colossal scale of Metropolis: the city's boundaries form a rectangle 45 miles by 135 miles. Gillette estimated that Metropolis would eventually contain at least 60 million people.

Like many of his contemporaries, Gillette felt he was living in an unprecedented era of change. On the title page of his book an epigram proclaims: "the very air we breathe is pregnant with life that foretells the birth of a wonderful change." Gillette believed that his proposal would initiate that change. He issued this call for action on the book's final page: "Let us start the ball rolling with such a boom and enthusiasm that it will draw the wealth and sinew of the nation into its vortex—the great future city 'Metropolis' . . . and let a new era of civilization and progress shed its light of hope on the future of mankind" (Gillette 1894, 131).

The key to attaining the perfect future world was the application of human intelligence to all matters, whether material or moral. "The world is a diamond in the rough," reads an epigram on the front cover of *The Human Drift,* "and intellect, the only progressive entity, must cut the facets to discover its beauty and power." Gillette believed that humans should trust the power of intellect. This meant that "the whole aspect of nature must assume new meanings and ends" (Gillette 1894, 84). Nature must be transformed as clay is transformed by a sculptor. The economic and industrial system also lacked rational order, but it too could be transformed by intellect. Metropolis was to be the ultimate embodiment of intellect. It would replace chaos with order in two ways.

First, Metropolis would replace the chaotic system of production and distribution with a perfectly logical and orderly one. The new system would realize the ultimate economies of scale by consolidating all industry under a single corporation at a single industrial site. There would be only one steel mill, one flour mill, and one shoe factory in the whole of North America. Moreover, nearly all of the workers and consumers would live at the same site. Like so many before him, Gillette imagined Niagara Falls to be a great deal more than it was. "Here is a power," he wrote, "which, if brought under control, is capable of keeping in continuous operation every manufacturing industry for centuries to come, and, in addition, supply all the lighting facilities, run all the elevators, and furnish the power necessary for the transportation system of the great

central city" (Gillette 1894, 87). Like Love, Gillette hoped Niagara's reputation would help sell his project; hence, he included a photograph of the falls as the frontispiece in *The Human Drift.*

Rationalizing the production system, Gillette argued, would create great excess wealth, which would provide the basis for social progress by opening opportunities for all: "for civilization, under these conditions of equal opportunity, would be as full of life as a boiling cauldron, and all its dirt and filth would gradually rise to the top and disappear" (Gillette 1894, 130). Gillette proposed other social changes for his utopia. Women were to have full equality in all matters. Since automation would reduce the need for physical labor, all the citizens of Metropolis would have the right to choose their occupation freely. Social harmony, in short, would follow as a by-product of economic and industrial orderliness.

The second way that Metropolis would replace chaos with order was more concrete. The rapids and the falls made Niagara's landscape particularly chaotic; in Gillette's eyes, this was a waste of power. He planned to put all of the falling water to work and thus eliminate Niagara Falls itself. He intended to transform this natural landscape further by imposing a rational urban pattern. To begin with, the shape of Metropolis was to be a perfect rectangle (figure 5). On Gillette's map, the smaller rectangle (indicated by dotted lines) represents the residential section of Metropolis. Like ideal cities of earlier ages, the futuristic utopian cities of late-nineteenth-century fiction often had symmetrical shapes (Roemer 1976, 85).

The most dramatic expression of Gillette's intention to impose order on the chaotic natural landscape of Niagara Falls was his plan to build a 100-foot platform covering the entire surface of Metropolis, even extending over the Niagara River. The platform was to be divided into three levels: one for water lines and other infrastructure, one for transportation, and one for recreation. On top of this featureless surface, Gillette planned a hexagonal street pattern. His depiction of this pattern (figure 6) shows six apartment buildings, each twenty-five stories, surrounding each educational building (marked

FIGURE 6
Residential plan of Metropolis. Source: Gillette (1894, 94: plate 1).

FIGURE 7
"Man Corporate." Source: Gillette (1910, opposite p. 94).

A), each amusement building (B), and each provisions building (C). This arrangement would provide each apartment building with maximum accessibility to each of the special buildings.

After eliminating the natural landscape, Gillette planned to reintroduce nature with a scattering of lush gardens. Allowing human intelligence full reign over the material world would produce a civilization that was not only efficient, but also beautiful. In the gardens of Metropolis, Gillette wrote, "would be found a panorama of beauty that would throw into shadow the fables of wonderful palaces and cities told of in the 'Arabian Nights'; yet the genie of all this would be naught but the intelligence of man working in unison" (Gillette 1894, 93). As a symbol of united intelligence, Gillette offered a genie, which he named "Man Corporate" (figure 7). Gillette's genie holds the earth as if it were a baseball. The

symbolism is clear: Man Corporate can take the world in the palm of his hand and make anything of it he wishes. "We have found Aladdin's lamp," Gillette proclaimed, "let us profit by its possession" (Gillette 1894, 75).

Gillette's vision of the future apparently inspired few. Nevertheless, he continued to promote it throughout his life, at least in his writings (Gillette 1910; 1924). Gillette even offered Teddy Roosevelt a million dollars to become president of his so-called World Corporation, but this too met rejection.

THE GREAT DYNAMIC PALACE AND INTERNATIONAL HALL

In 1896 Leonard Henkle, another inventor and entrepreneur, released an imaginative proposal to develop Niagara Falls. He envisioned a lavish palace of gigantic proportions stretching across the entire width of Niagara River just above the crest of the falls. Henkle's intention was "to combine the most imposing grandeur of art with the natural beauty of Niagara Falls" ("Aladdin quite outdone" 1896, 9). The building was to be a half-mile in length and nowhere less than forty-six stories. He called it "The Great Dynamic Palace and International Hall."

Henkle planned to utilize all the water flowing beneath this structure for generating electricity. He believed there would be enough power to supply all the needs of every city in North America. With the receipts from the sale of this power, Henkle intended to finance two additional undertakings. First, he planned to construct a large fleet of steamships to sail out of the St. Lawrence to every port in the world. Second, he proposed to build two four-track transcontinental railroads: one from British Columbia to the St. Lawrence, and the other from California to Maine. These two railroads were to cross at Niagara—in fact, they were to cross right inside the Dynamic Palace; the section above the turbines was designed to be a massive railway tunnel.

The floors above this tunnel would house manufacturing and commercial establishments. Henkle reserved the forty-sixth floor for an enormous "International Hall" with room for seventy thousand people. He envisioned this hall as a sort of United Nations headquarters. Each nation was to have a representative and a special place in the hall. Here Henkle hoped that the nations of the world would realize their essential unity and work together to eliminate war and poverty. Like Gillette's Metropolis, Henkle's Great Dynamic Palace and International Hall was planned to be the embodiment of moral as well as material progress.

After the turn of the century, visions of a colossal industrial city at Niagara Falls continued to surface (Van Cleve 1903; Agassiz 1912; T. Norton 1916). By World War I, it had become obvious that Niagara's power, to the surprise of many, was indeed limited. Moreover, its power was transmissible. Meanwhile, the actual exploitation of this power continued at a rapid pace—inspired, at least in part, by the same images of Niagara and of the future that had motivated Love, Gillette, and Henkle.

NIAGARA AND THE DARK FUTURE

Before World War I, most who spoke of the future in connection with Niagara Falls accepted that the human race was progressing and would continue to progress in almost every way. The harnessing of Niagara seemed itself to be excellent evidence of this progress. To a few, however, the increasing human power over nature portended disaster. This is illustrated here in two stories of the future written in the first decade of the twentieth century; in each, Niagara becomes the focus of a future world in which human progress has gotten out of hand.

Unlike the utopian visions of Niagara's future, these pessimistic stories had little precedent at Niagara Falls. A few visitors had described Niagara as a herald of the Apocalypse; while gazing at the falling water, their thoughts had turned to the terrifying future events predicted in Revelation (Howell 1867; Tudor 1834; H.M.D. 1842; Lord 1869). There was one nineteenth-century work that used Niagara as a symbol of impending disaster. Thomas Carlyle, in his book *Shooting Niagara: And After?* (1867), prophesied that the mechanization of modern society would lead to chaos. Carlyle intended the book as a response to attempts to extend suffrage in Great Britain. He associated democracy with the mechanical culture he was the first to name as "industrialism." Complete democracy, he feared, could only release the debasing force of individualism by which all English people would be free "to follow each his own nose" (Carlyle 1867, 2). Niagara's brink offered the perfect metaphor for the coming catastrophe. Extending suffrage to the masses, Carlyle wrote, "accelerates notably what I have long looked upon as inevitable;—pushes us at once into the Niagara Rapids: irresistibly propelled, with ever-increasing velocity, we shall now arrive; who knows how soon!" (Carlyle 1867, 11).

THE MASTER OF THE WORLD

Niagara Falls provides the setting for the climax of Jules Verne's last book, *The Master of the World* (1905). Verne had perhaps done more than any of his contemporaries to make the future seem exciting, but, as his life neared its end,

FIGURE 8
"The Escape from Niagara." Source: Verne (1905, opposite p. 224).

hour. After terrorizing pedestrians and motorists throughout the United States for several weeks, Robur demonstrates that his vehicle is also a boat that can travel at similar speeds on the surface of the Atlantic. Finally, the vehicle appears once again, but this time as a submarine in a small lake in Kansas. When the governments of the world offer to buy the invention, Robur refuses. "With it," he answers, "I hold control of the entire world" (Verne 1905, 201).

As the story reaches it climax, Robur's luck finally seems to be running out. U.S. gunboats pursue his ship in Lake Erie. When he attempts to dive, the submarine apparatus malfunctions. The gunboats force him into the Niagara River toward the falls. But just as the ship reaches the brink, mechanical wings unfold from its sides and it rises into the air (figure 8). This is Robur's moment of triumph. He has transcended a limitation that nature had imposed upon our species; he has defied nature and proven himself "mightier than the elements" (Verne 1905, 252). If Niagara's brink represents a break in the stream of time, he has passed through to that future world where nature is entirely subdued. But this was a future that Verne was not eager to enter. Robur's new power over nature was arrogant and dangerous. The book ends a few pages later when Robur flies his ship into the eye of a hurricane. He howls to the storm, like Ahab to the white whale: "I, Robur! Robur!—The Master of the World!" (Verne 1905, 258). A flash of lightning sends him crashing to his death.

THE WAR IN THE AIR

H. G. Wells used Niagara Falls as the setting for a world cataclysm in his novel *The War in the Air* (1908), a story that projects a future of rapid technological advances. The most important development is the airship. It frees humans from an immemorial natural limitation, a liberty they are ill-equipped to handle. The nations of the world proceed to build colossal air fleets. The German fleet crosses the Atlantic, levels New York City, and proceeds to Niagara to establish a fortress and take advantage of the "enormous power works" (Wells 1908, 251). The Germans then bomb away every structure within ten miles of the falls to discourage a ground attack.

At the climax of the book, a huge Asiatic air

he apparently was having some apprehensions about the future. The story centers on a scientist named Robur who had also appeared in one of Verne's earlier works (Verne 1886). In the earlier book, Robur had been a brilliant scientist and inventor who had wisely chosen to withhold "the secret of his invention" for fear that it would "greatly change the social and political conditions of the world" (Verne 1886, 143). At the conclusion of this first book, Verne had described his protagonist with these words: "Robur is the science of the future. Perhaps the science of tomorrow! Certainly the science that will come" (1886, 143). The man of science in this story was a man with a balanced view, a wise man.

In *The Master of the World*, Robur returns as a mad scientist with a powerful new invention—a vehicle capable of speeds over 150 miles per

fleet crosses the Pacific and advances on Niagara. When the two fleets clash in the sky over Niagara Falls, the German flagship is shot down into the river and swept over the falls (figure 9). The conflict quickly spreads to the entire Great Lakes region, then across most of the continent, but still it is called the "Battle of Niagara" (Wells 1908, 250). Like a vortex, the battle continues to widen until it has engulfed the entire world. The final result of the battle is the total destruction of civilization. The people of both the New World and the Old revert to a savage, primitive existence. Wells summed up the story with these comments: "For a time it had seemed that by virtue of machines and scientific civilization, Europe was to be lifted out of the perpetual round of animal drudgery, and that America was to evade it very largely from the outset. And with the smash of the high and dangerous and splendid edifice of mechanical civilization that had arisen so marvelously, back to the land came the common man, back to the manure" (1908, 272). Today it is possible to imagine a future that is worse than this; it is even possible to imagine no future at all. But in 1908 this was a gloomy picture indeed.

Niagara provided Wells with a fitting setting for *The War in the Air* because the story turns ironically on the theme of the human struggle for mastery over nature. Wells and many of his contemporaries saw in the landscape of Niagara a prime example of this struggle. To most, the struggle seemed nearly over; humans had won. Wells was one of the few at this time who could imagine a different outcome: more and more technological power, instead of bringing release from the struggle against nature, might in the end force humans to accept the "hard struggle against nature for food" as "the chief interest of their lives" (Wells 1908, 371). In Wells's story, nature's ironic victory first becomes clear in the striking image of the German flagship being crushed by Niagara Falls.

NIAGARA AFTER THE WAR

World War I profoundly affected the way people on both sides of the Atlantic viewed the future. Centuries of progress had culminated in an unparalleled display of brutality. Although indus-

FIGURE 9

"The airship staggered to the crest of the Fall—and vanished in a desperate leap." Source: Wells (1908, opposite p. 272).

trialists and technical forecasters continued to predict a grand expansive future, the writers of futuristic fiction were totally disillusioned (I. Clarke 1979, 227). These authors described horrible future wars and disasters that would destroy civilization or humanity itself. At Niagara Falls, however, an optimistic view both of the future and of technological progress continued to dominate. Before examining the ways this optimism was expressed, there is one work of futuristic fiction that must be discussed.

NIAGARA IN THE TWENTY-FIFTH CENTURY

The original story of *Buck Rogers in the Twenty-Fifth Century* first appeared as a comic strip in 1929 (Dille 1962). The story demonstrates that even fiction of the most popular sort could no longer sanguinely present progress as inevitable. Perhaps it also shows that the audience for this fiction was not yet willing to give up hope in the possibility of progress. The story begins when Buck Rogers inhales some strange gas in a cave near Pittsburgh and falls into a five-hundred-year sleep. He awakens to find that North America has been invaded by "mongols," a technologically superior race armed with devastating airships and disintegrator rays. The original Americans have been reduced to a single stronghold: Niagara City. Here, the water power of the falls provides a shield of fire making Niagara "the one spot in all North America safe from mongol air raids" (Dille 1962, 23).

The story presents an ambivalent view of the worth of technological progress, of human power over nature. In the hands of the mongols, advanced technology is a destructive force. Furthermore, machines have made the mongols soft and effete. The Americans, in contrast, continue to work eight hours a day instead of letting machines lighten their load "because people must work or civilization would decay" (Dille 1962, 23). On the other hand, nature is entirely dominated in Niagara City. There are no lawns or trees. It is a landscape entirely of human design, almost as extreme as Gillette's Metropolis. Moreover, it is the Americans' technological ingenuity in tapping the power of Niagara that preserves their freedom. Indeed, as the story unfolds, the Americans are able to strike back from their impenetrable fortress and eventually win back the continent. The story of Buck Rogers begins as a tale of future disaster but ends by affirming that progress will ultimately continue.

CONTINUING VISIONS OF PROGRESS

After World War I, many people continued to express confidence that Niagara's future would be a story of great progress. The future would be better, they believed, because of increasing control over nature and over the forces of social and political chaos. From 1925 until 1930 a "Festival of Lights" was held each June at Niagara Falls (Mizer 1981, 100; Coombs 1930, 88–89). The festival was a celebration of industrial and technological achievements. It featured parades, fireworks, and the crowning of "Queen Electra."

The festival also celebrated international cooperation and peace along the Niagara frontier. In 1925, for instance, government officials from both nations held a peace ceremony on the international bridge below the falls. Although these festivals were enormously successful, in some years drawing over two hundred thousand visitors, the worsening depression brought the tradition to an abrupt halt in 1931.

Just after World War II, the peaceful border at Niagara Falls helped to inspire another expression of optimism about the future. The war and the bomb had so changed the international order that some saw a chance for a new beginning. The old hope for the unity of humankind was revived. The most concrete result of this was the establishment of the United Nations. At Niagara, local leaders on both sides of the river argued that Navy Island, which sits in Canadian waters just above the falls, would be a perfect site for the new United Nations headquarters (International Committee to Promote Navy Island as Permanent Headquarters of the United Nations 1945). The promoters who submitted the Navy Island proposal were apparently unaware that both Gillette and Henkle had imagined Niagara as the focal point of a united humanity fifty years before them. When the United Nations decided to locate their headquarters in the United States, local promoters offered a site on Grand Island, just upstream from Navy Island, and Grand Island became one of the final four sites considered (Pringle and Pringle 1948).

Perhaps the clearest expression of continuing belief in progress at Niagara has been the eagerness to push on with the work envisioned by men like Love and Gillette and started by such firms as the Niagara Falls Power Company. There has been a will to develop ever greater amounts of power at Niagara, a will to take nature's power into hand with the confidence that a better future can be created by doing so than by leaving nature to expend that power in its mindless, if impressive, way. This trend has met little organized resistance. An international treaty in 1909 had limited total diversion by the power plants to about one-quarter of Niagara's average flow. In 1950 a new treaty simply specified minimum flows to be reserved for the falls itself (International Joint Commission 1953, 18). Under the requirements of this treaty, the power plants were allowed to divert approximately two-thirds of the normal yearly flow. Withdrawing these volumes would have thinned the flank areas of the Horseshoe Falls to a trickle and left the American Falls virtually dry. To prevent this, the flank areas were sculpted out to provide an even flow and a large control structure was installed to divert water toward the American Falls (International Joint Commission 1953, 39). In the early 1960s, massive new hydroelectric plants were completed on both sides of the river. Together they have the capacity to use almost 85 percent of Niagara's average flow (Forrester 1976, 134).

After World War I, industry also expanded greatly at Niagara Falls. By 1940, the area had become the largest producer of electrochemicals in the world (MacMullin, Koethen, and Richardson 1940, 308). The electrochemical industry had been created virtually out of nothing. Nonexistent before 1900, this industry produced insecticides, medicines, and hundreds of other products merely by shooting electrical currents through brine and other solutions. During the 1940s and 1950s, the publications of the chemical companies, and even the professional journals of chemical engineering, described the industry as magically expansive. A pamphlet issued by the Union Carbide and Carbon Corporation, for instance, described the industry this way: "The chemical genie is creating new products faster than the historian can record them" (Union Carbide and Carbon Corporation 1954, 9). By the mid-1960s, however, Niagara Falls was running out of hydroelectricity to feed the "chemical genie." To remedy this situation, a planning report by the Hudson Institute suggested that a nuclear power plant be built at Niagara Falls to attract more industry. The authors of the report argued that such a plant would be "right in the tradition of the area" (Panero, Candela, and McGuigan 1968).

CONCLUSIONS

Why did so many people, particularly between 1890 and 1910, imagine Niagara Falls as an important focus of the future? One reason was that the novelty of the future was almost universally associated with technological progress, with humanity's struggle for dominance over nature. This was true for those who considered the new technological power good as well as for those who thought it evil. As Niagara had long been seen as a symbol of nature, and as there had been continuous attempts to harness its water power in the late nineteenth century, the struggle to overcome nature—and therefore to usher in the future—seemed both symbolic and literal at Niagara Falls.

There was a second reason why people's imaginations turned to the future at Niagara Falls. During the long period before Niagara became accessible, an image of a stupendous waterfall had developed from afar. Then, in the nineteenth century many people began to associate Niagara with the distant past of primeval nature and the mysterious world of the afterlife. Each of these was a remote realm whose nature, like that of a distant waterfall, could only be imagined. Those who imagined the future at Niagara near the turn of the century were extending this old image of Niagara Falls in a new direction.

Does the future Niagara that these people imagined bear any relation to the Niagara one finds today? Niagara Falls is not North America's greatest metropolis, but neither is it a national park. The falls definitely sits at the center of a landscape that has been vigorously developed. Development, of course, was only possible because of Niagara's location and the timing of certain technological innovations, but the evidence presented here suggests an additional factor. The image of Niagara's future presented in the utopian schemes of the 1890s has not been realized. Yet that image made development sufficiently alluring to give momentum to greater and greater exploitation of Niagara's power. As those who suggested a nuclear power plant for Niagara commented, development has been "right in the tradition of the area." It was the old image of a stupendous, immeasurable waterfall that lured Gillette, Love, Henkle, and the leaders of the Niagara Falls Power Company. Niagara was vigorously developed not because developers thought so little of the falls' natural splendor, but rather because they thought so much of it.

Those who imagined a disastrous future for Niagara Falls were, on the whole, wrong. There has been no catastrophic battle here; neither have people reverted to savagery. Yet there is some irony in the fact that Love's canal, instead of leading to the perfect future city, has become a place that, as far as human habitation is concerned, has no future at all. The Love Canal disaster is an example of how human mastery over nature—human technological power—can get out of hand and become a destructive force.

SOURCE

This article appeared orginally in the *Annals of the Association of American Geographers* 77 (1987): 48–62.

FURTHER READINGS

Trevor J. Barnes and James S. Duncan, eds. 1992. *Writing worlds: Discourse, text and metaphor in the representation of landscape.* London: Routledge.

This collection includes another fine essay on Niagara Falls by McGreevy. It also contains essays, both empirical and theoretical, that consider the various ways in which geographical reality emerges from the practices and metaphors of written discourse.

Joseph C. Corn, ed. 1986. *Imagining tomorrow: History, technology and the American future.* Cambridge: MIT Press.

A collection of essays, written from the vantage of American studies, that examines the futuristic fantasies of the early decades of the twentieth century. The chapters on utopian planning and technological optimism should be of particular interest to geographers.

Robert Fishman. 1977. *Urban utopias in the twentieth century: Ebenezer Howard, Frank Lloyd Wright, and Le Corbusier.* New York: Basic Books.

Fishman considers the work of three visionary planner-architects who sought perfect design in an imperfect world. All were captured by a vision of an ideal city, one that combined the beauty and power of modern technology with enlightened ideals of social justice.

Dolores Hayden. 1976. *Seven American utopias: The architecture of communitarian socialism, 1790–1975.* Cambridge: MIT Press.

Hayden's work documents the histories of several important American utopian communities, both secular and sacred. These communities provide some measure of the strength of American attachment to "ideal" environments and serve as a frame of reference for the discussion of utopian ideologies in American life more generally.

Krishan Kumar. 1987. *Utopia and anti-utopia in modern times.* Oxford: Basil Blackwell.

Kumar's synthesis of utopian literatures is particularly strong in addressing the dystopian trends of thought that have arisen since the 1880s. Kumar is effective in showing how promising utopian visions are often countered by dystopian warnings about the dangers of modern life.

Rob Shields. 1991. Niagara Falls: Honeymoon capital of the world. Chap. in *Places on the margin: Alternative geographies of modernity,* 117–61. London: Routledge.

An examination of another way in which Niagara Falls has come to be characterized in the modern mind. Here, Niagara Falls is viewed as an important site for the honeymoon, as the setting for a rite of passage that combines religion, ritual, commerce, wilderness, spectacle, and tourism.

DOUGLAS C. D. POCOCK **24**

PLACE AND THE NOVELIST

Within the field of imaginative literature the writings of the novelist are of particular interest to a geographer exploring the critical concept of place. It is an interest which goes deeper than acknowledging the writer's ability to capture the full flavor of the environment, a quality recently emphasized by Meinig (1971a, 4), for, when the novel replaced the epic and drama as the main literary form in the early eighteenth century, its chief novelty was to add to the ancient portrayal of "life by values" that of "life in time," to use Forster's terms (Forster 1976, 40–53). Medieval stories had traditionally accounted unchanging moral truths in timeless settings, the plots themselves being freely borrowed between different countries and cultures; now, the novel was time-specific and, thus, by implication, *place-specific* also.

In English literature, to which this review will largely be confined, place specificity took over a century to emerge. It was initially presented in a generalized sense, the main dichotomy being between town and country, with seasons being largely social ones. Sense of the particular, as opposed to the generalized, needed the detailed eye of the romantics, who approached the general by concentrating on the particular. The generalized worlds of Fielding or Richardson thus yielded to the detailed, historical eye of Scott and the subtle etchings of a few southern localities by

Jane Austen. During the second quarter of the nineteenth century the novelist's pen began more fully to depict particular localities, thereby giving rise to the genre of the English regional novel (Bentley 1941; Tillotson 1954). The amount and nature of environmental description, literal or symbolic, together with the nature of the relationship to character, has been the basis for recognizing distinctive subsequent phases in the regional novel—picturesque, sentimental, interpretive, modern (Leclaire 1954). It is not proposed here to concentrate on the regional novel per se, for not only are there difficulties in defining and allocating works to this particular genre, but the term implies a particular spatial scale too restrictive for the present theme.

Place may refer to a variety of scales, in each of which, in experiential terms, there is a characteristic bounding with internal structure and identity, such that insideness is distinguished from outsideness. At its most obvious and familiar, it is wherever we feel "at home," where things "fall into place," beyond which we feel "out of place," intruders in someone else's domain. We therefore inhabit a hierarchy of places, bringing into play the appropriate level of resolution according to the particular context in which we find ourselves. Each level or state is born of experience of the mutual interaction between person and environment. The aim of this paper is to illuminate aspects of this topic through the perceptive record of imaginative literature, the ultimate aim being to enrich our own experience and understanding of the human condition.

AUTHOR AND PLACE

Following years of foreign travel D. H. Lawrence expressed the view that "different places on the face of the earth have different vital effluence, different vibration, different chemical exhalation, different polarity with different stars: call it what you like. But spirit of place is a great reality" (Lawrence 1923, 8–9). Such response to place is an obvious entrée for the geographer into the literary field, where he may lament that in terms of traditional literary criticism the contribution of place vis-à-vis characterization and plot has gen-

erally been undervalued as a criterion in the assessment of worth among novels. A higher evaluation, however, may be held by the novelists themselves. Hardy, for instance, classified one group of his Wessex writings as "novels of character and environment," referring to the "inevitableness" of both in "working out destiny" (Hardy 1888, 64). Lawrence Durrell is quite emphatic:

> What makes "big" books is surely as much to do with their site as their characters and incidents. . . . When they are well and truly anchored in nature they usually become classics. . . . They are tuned into the sense of place. You could not transplant them without totally damaging their ambience and mood. (Durrell 1969, 163)

Recognition of the importance of place to novelists is also seen in the reticence they often express toward the portrayal of foreign scenes and characters. Examples abound. Our most regionally conscious author, Hardy, felt obliged to reply to criticism over the authenticity of Farfrae amid Casterbridge society in terms that he "be allowed to pass, if not as a Scotchman to Scotchmen, as a Scotchman to Southerners" (Hardy 1912, 19). More recently Somerset Maugham has expressed similar apprehension at creating any foreign character, remarking that "observation is not enough . . . you can only know them if you *are* them" (Maugham 1944, 3). Forster also reflected in later life that his acclaimed depictions of Italian settings and characters had been drawn in youthful ignorance of the "grave" limitations of being an outsider (Forster 1975b, viii). Most recently, Graham Greene has written in similar vein, "Perhaps no one can write in depth about a foreign country—he can only write about the effect of that country on his own fellow countrymen. . . . He can only 'touch in' the background of the foreign land" (Greene 1978, vi).

The problem notwithstanding, novelists *have* written of foreign places. Ignoring those where place is relatively unimportant, a mere exotic backcloth (e.g., Haggard, Wallace, Waugh), it is evident that some are acknowledged as having captured the spirit of place of their nonnative homelands in works now considered to be classics. Even here, however, it is interesting to note that the authenticity accorded by English critics may not be shared by authors and critics native to the areas depicted—in India (Greenberger 1969) or Africa (Obiechina 1975), for instance. In a recent survey of the West African novel, a Nigerian writer has shown how European novelists, even after long residence in the country, still portray "Africa of the European imagination," misunderstanding the roles of nature, music and art, and space and time. Even Joyce Cary's *Mister Johnson,* which we might acclaim as his supremely authentic depiction, fails to impress the indigenous critic who summarizes it as "largely created out of the fabric of Cary's own imagination" (Obiechina 1975, 25).

The difficulty in setting a novel in a foreign context illustrates the bias imparted by one's native place. The resultant ethnocentric evaluations just mentioned, however, are but part of the universal problem of the relationship between the author and the world as he or she observes and depicts it. As such, the problem relates not only to place, but also to time, society, and class. Peasants and children, for instance, do not normally write books, yet numerous works portray their worlds. The authenticity of their characterization is adjudged by the literate and literary society producing the works and not by those whose world is being depicted. The appearance in imaginative literature of novels depicting the world as perceived by animals highlights this aspect in an unusual manner (R. Adams 1974; 1978). It is a problem general to literature, as stated. In poetry, for instance, Wordsworth, despite his claim to describe "low and rustic life" in a "selection of language really used by men," is a middle-class observer of rural scenes (Wordsworth and Coleridge 1968, 21).

EARLY PLACE AND SUBSEQUENT PLACE

The hesitancy of some authors over the depiction of foreign parts springs from the indelible bond established with the place of earliest activities and relationships. Except for the recluse, however, this initial bond is complemented and authenticated by contact with subsequent or foreign places. In this process a duality emerges, for place has within it an ambiguity arising from the dialectical nature which underlies human experience in general. Some of the properties are well illustrated in the world of the novel.

Although a hierarchy of places emerges as our engagement with the world enlarges beyond our earliest activities, a crucial and indelible bond is established with early place, or "home," as we most commonly use the term. It remains the center of our egocentrically ordered cosmos, containing our own unique, unrepeatable beginning. We may move, but we cannot begin again a second time. The displaced family in *The Grapes of Wrath* muse thus in contemplating their journey to California, "But you can't start. Only a baby can start. You and me—why we're all that's been. . . . We can't start again" (Steinbeck 1951, 81).

Our birthplace leaves a mark in determining the way we perceive the world. Thus, an American Midwesterner such as Nick Carraway is aware of the different "vibration" in the East, yet experiences it as "a quality of distortion . . . beyond my eyes' power of correction," making him "subtly unadaptable to Eastern life" even after years of experience of Long Island (Fitzgerald 1954, 183). In a sense we are rooted and grounded in place, by place. Divinely ordered or not, according to Sillitoe, "We are all born into the world with a sense of place, simply because a certain part of our senses are rooted forever in the locality in which . . . we first saw light" (Sillitoe 1975, 59). George Eliot, another soul bred in the English Midlands, would agree. "The gamut of joy" in people's native landscape, she wrote, grew from "the things they toddled among, or perhaps learnt by heart standing between their father's knees while he drove leisurely" (Eliot 1982, 102). Early place and the importance of roots is a recurring theme in her novels (Auster 1970, 135–74).

Place, then, contains our roots, our unique point of reference. We may not be able to begin again, but it is a point to which we can return. It is exactly this bond of which Bragg was aware:

> When my first wife died I found that one of the courses of action I eventually took was to bring our daughter back to the place where I was born. For better or worse I wanted to root her into a

part of the world and a family of relationships I knew. My present wife and I found a place which looked north to the sea and south to the hills. And the three of us dug in. (Bragg 1977, 1)

It is the same bond that E. M. Forster acknowledges when visiting his Hertfordshire house of "Rooksnest" after an absence of half a century. "The house is my childhood and safety—the three attics preserve me" (Forster 1975a, 8; note the tense of the verb). This house is known to the world of literature as Howard's End, and there is no better example in the English novel of the family home being at the very core of an egocentrically structured world. (Abroad, the Buddenbrookhaus and the Königsbrücker Strasse are of similar significance to Mann and Kästner, respectively, and give rise to comparable themes in German literature.)

Being a point of return, home place is a point of stability during the changes and chances of this fleeting world. In the same way that a child seeks the safety of his mother, or a penitent the church, home place is itself a symbol of assurance and reassurance. (Both home—whether earth, land, city, or dwelling—and church have traditionally been viewed as mother.) Continuing with the church analogy, Dickens likened entering a church to looking down the throat of time; our own family house or home place offers a similar experience. It transfixes time; in so doing it offers not only a symbol of past stability but also future assurance. This is the conclusion of Margaret Schlegel on the family house of Howard's End: "I feel that our house is the future as well as the past" (Forster 1975a, 329). Collectively we may note that "sense of permanence" is Kenneth Clark's summary definition of civilization (K. Clark 1969, 14).

Stability during the early, "formative" years—note the phrase—with its spatial restriction and temporal repetition ingrains particularity, the identity of both place and us. Norberg-Schulz argues that an intimate acquaintance with a particular place is the foundation of human identity; indeed, that human identity *presupposes* the identity of place. Following Heidegger, he presents linguistic evidence to show that *dwelling* means "to be at peace in a protected place," and that the Old English and High German for

"building" (*buan*) meant "to dwell" and is intimately related to the verb *to be*. (*Ich bin, du bist* thus mean "I dwell," "you dwell" [Norberg-Schultz 1976, 8–9]). Our *abide/abode* provides evidence in similar vein.

The role or influence of home place, however, is not unidimensional; it has within it an ambiguity and tension which underlie human experience in general. It is on the one hand home, the place of security, stability, belonging. It has at the same time, however, the potential of boredom, drudgery, entrapment, for which subsequent or foreign place offers excitement, release, freedom. Hence our age-long fascination with travel and the importance of subsequent place. The modern novelist H. E. Bates clearly expresses this in his autobiography, *The Vanished World,* where the Midland earth of the Nene valley is acknowledged to be "a paradise that remains to this day utterly unblemished, a joy forever"; nevertheless, the early long rambles with his father or occasional visits to the sea are referred to as "blessed escape from imprisonment" (Bates 1969, 1:18, 71). (The reversible image of imprisonment is widespread in literature, offering as it does both victimizing confinement and freedom for artistic creativity or religious meditation.)

In the English novel it has been argued that the balance or tension between home and distant place came to a peak in the first two decades of the present century (Alcorn 1977). At this time spirit of distant place came to the fore as authors wrestled with this basic insight into human experience. The novel during this period became an antiphony of place, with characters seeking liberation, both geographical and spiritual, through change of place. Thus, after Hardy, whose stories concerned one location which represents entrapment, a succession of authors chose two locations to represent the two states of mind. Leading examples were Kipling, Forster, James, Lawrence, Joyce, Douglas. The geographical dialectic was often international, between England and Italy or India, between East and West, or between Europe and North America. (On the continent Gide and Mann were leading authors, exploiting the dialectic between North Europe and lands to the south of the Alps.) Within England a contrast in worlds between north and south is a theme which has persisted through this century, the escape being made from northern industrial cities to London and the south by both novelists and the characters they create (Pocock 1978).

A fuller appreciation of place is achieved through the mere threat of departure or separation, the sentence of severance, like that of death, wonderfully concentrating the mind. Thus Margaret Schlegel's "eyes were not opened" to the meaning of Wickham Place until the lease expired (Forster 1975a, 116). Even Jane Austen's Miss Dashwood, on her last evening before quitting Sussex for Devon, shed many tears for "a place so much loved," including "well-known trees" (Austen 1948, 22).

"In every parting there is an image of death"— George Eliot's (1907, 100) comment on the fate of Amos Barton—is an experience we may all share; on the other hand, separation may well crystallize previously unconscious, inarticulate affection for place. In this sense, after separation absence may well "make the heart grow fonder." Whatever the degree of emotional involvement, it is travel which provides the comparative basis for a fuller appreciation of place: "What should they know of England who only England know," in Kipling's well-known line (Kipling 1933, 218). And here it may be noted that many authors who may be classed as regional or acutely sensitive to place have undergone separation from their native place before re-creating it in the printed word. Hardy spent several years in London— and underwent architectural training—before returning to Dorset to produce his Wessex novels. George Eliot had left the West Midlands forever before re-creating the setting in her novels. The regional works of Bennett, Lawrence, and Joyce all strongly reflect the contemplation of their native heaths from afar. Joyce is perhaps the extreme example. Forced to leave his native Dublin, he increasingly concentrated on re-creating the city of his youth while exiled in Trieste, Zurich, and Paris, none of which places appeared in his works. (In the realm of poetry, it may be noted that even Wordsworth "needed" the experience of the continent and the ferment of the French Revolution before out-pouring the ballads of his "dear native regions.")

Travel, then, provides the basis for comparative assessment; in this process, however, subsequent place is inevitably evaluated in relation to home place. This accounts for Nick Carraway finding the East "distorted beyond [his] eyes' power of correction" (Fitzgerald 1954, 183), or the reaction of Lee's village children on their first outing where "everything began to appear strange and comic," so much so that they "began to look round fondly at [their] familiar selves, drawn close by this alien country" (Lee 1962, 193). Kipling's comment therefore needs to be interpreted carefully. Chesterton, for instance, would remind us that travel narrows the mind. Certainly the nature of seeing foreign places is different. Dickens, an avid traveler himself, was aware of this and muses extensively on the theme in *Little Dorrit.* Throughout their travels in Italy the Dorrits find the encounters with attractive new places less real than the Marshalsea, the London prison which had been their home. *All* tourists, muses Little Dorrit, take their *mental prison* with them. In Rome in their party:

> Everybody was walking about St. Peter's and the Vatican on somebody else's cork legs, and straining every visible object through somebody else's sieve. . . . The whole body of travellers seemed to be a collection of voluntary human sacrifices, bound hand and foot, and delivered over to Mr. Eustace and his attendants, to have the entrails of their intellects arranged according to the taste of that sacred priesthood. . . . Nobody had an opinion . . . not a flaw of courage or honest free speech in it. (Dickens 1895, 486–87)

One of Jane Austen's characters attacks any who "pretend to see and to feel" toward any landscape according to convention, such appreciation being deemed "mere jargon" (Austen 1948, 82). Awareness of cultural or place-bound filters is healthy, although to imagine that we can achieve some acultural, pristine perception is naive.

PLACE AS PEOPLE AND PEOPLE AS PLACE

The relationship between place and people is a reciprocal one. Descriptions by modern writers of people being "impregnated" with landscape (Sillitoe 1975, 117), "functions" or "children" of landscape (Durrell 1969, 156; 1957, 41), "not only themselves . . . also the region in which they were born" (Maugham 1944, 3), emphasize differing positions along the continuum of a place-person symbiosis. In this relationship people may be considered as place. Thus Steinbeck's tenants, undergoing displacement from their Oklahoman homes through mechanization, reflect that "this land, this red land is us . . . and when the tractor hits the house, that's us until we're dead," while those with property can only ponder that "if a man own a little property, that property is him, it's part of him, and it's like him" (Steinbeck 1951, 81, 34).

The family home, leased or owned, is a key element in the concept of place as the embodiment of the essence of self and self-identity. (In Freudian symbolism, house signifies the human body.) The home, as we have seen, is inseparable from self—it not only preserves one, it *is* one. A clear example from Hardy is his description of Tess returning home to see her sick mother:

> As soon as she could discern the outline of the house—newly thatched with her money—it had all its old effect upon Tess's imagination. Part of her body and life it ever seemed to be; the slope of the dormers, the finish of its gables, the broken courses of brick which topped the chimney, all had something in common with her personal character. (Hardy 1975, 369)

Such identity of house and occupants is evident in many of the works of Dickens. Dombey, Gradgrind, Dedlock, and Mrs. Clennam, for example, are diverse illustrations from four separate novels, each of which contains numerous examples of affinity between dwelling and dweller (Schwarzbach 1979, 151–71). Place-person symbiosis is particularly evident in the Russian novel: Goncharov's apathetic Oblomov and the featureless steppe is but one example from a vast literary quarry.

People then are place, but place is also people. Places have long been recognized as possessing personality. Personalities, however, are as complex and as changeable as the percipient. And here there is an evident contrast between the percipient as visitor, who *observes*—and at the most superficial is sightseeing—and those who are "at home" and who thus *experience* place. In Orwell's words "nobody involved in the landscape actually sees the landscape" (Orwell 1946, 38); such people are too much part of place for it to be viewed without prejudice: when happy we admire, when miserable we may detest it. The difference between what in existential terms are called insiders and outsiders is commitment or attachment; without this bond, initial excitement can rapidly turn to boredom. Such a sequence is well illustrated by Cary's Celia Rudbeck, wife of a District Officer in Nigeria, who initially found the country marvellous, the people charming, but whose superficial engagement subsequently resulted in a careless, absent-minded, complaining attitude to a land about which she soon "knew" everything (Cary 1981, 110–12).

Places may also be considered people through their associative quality, by which they come to represent particular persons, actions, or events. In this so-called contextual environment it is the accretion of meaning which is paramount, with activation of memories overriding the physical form in which memories are anchored. The philosopher may find "sermons in stones," the poet an "impulse from a vernal wood," but Forster's Lilia Herriton put it more prosaically. She was "determined to have the man and the place together" (Forster 1975b, 31), by which she meant that her young husband was to buy her the big rambling house opposite the Volterra gate in Monteriano, for it was here that she had first seen and been captivated by him. (Interestingly, back in England, Mrs. Herriton, refusing to believe that Lilia can have possibly married an Italian, could not be more wrong in concluding that "the place has nothing to do with it at all" [Forster 1975b, 13]. The author's comment is that "more than personalities were engaged . . . the struggle was national" [Forster 1975b, 50]).

We *all* share the associative experience of place. Anyone, for instance, who has had to spend some time in his or her empty family house will readily appreciate the dimensional difference between house and home. Body and spirit are the terms applied to describe the twofold nature of Forster's Wickham Place. Spirit, or personality, arises from habitual or memorable experiences. Lack of such experiences precludes any recognition. Thus, Lawrence's Gudrun Brangwen, waiting to leave the empty Beldover house, denies that the experience is ghostly, for the building had no personality: "only a place with personality could have a ghost" (Lawrence 1960, 423). At the other extreme, where an old house has accommodated generations of families, the spirit of the past may be overpowering. Hardy's Sue Phillotson, for instance, complains of feeling "crushed into the earth" by the previous lives spent in Old Grove Place, preferring instead a newer place where there was "only your own life to support" (Hardy 1974, 223). In such expressions we may directly transpose "felt place" for Henry James' phrase, "felt life."

There is, then, a bond between place and person which fashions our identity. It is this which induces Sillitoe—a person of entirely *urban* background—to write that "real love begins with one's feeling for earth, and that if you do not have this love then you cannot really begin to love people" (Sillitoe 1975, 73). Or Hardy to describe the relationship of the hills and dales of Blackmoor to Tess thus: "they seemed a part of her own story. Rather they became a part of it" (Hardy 1975, 114). It is a bond which prevents Bentley's young David Oldroyd from leaving Marthwaite with his family after they had been brought near to bankruptcy in the interwar depression after generations as successful West Riding weavers: he leaps from the train as it is about to enter a tunnel to take them out of Yorkshire to make his own way in his "own bit of the world" (Bentley 1932, 590). It is a bond which Storey's Saville painfully insists is entirely made by man. For him, tension of place was overwhelming. Footloose after being educated and socialized out of his community, he found that the "shell had cracked," and he felt the need to leave although he knew not where. His place-bound but perceptive girlfriend retorts:

> Shakespeare never travelled farther than London; Michelangelo never went farther from Florence than Rome; Rembrandt stayed virtually where he was. It's an illusion to think you've to break the mould. The mould may be the most precious thing you have. (Storey 1976, 503)

Forster, with his comments on middle-class nomadism, the "civilization of luggage . . . accret-ing possessions without taking root in the earth" (Forster 1975a, 154), would have agreed with these sentiments. Further afield, the rootlessness of the English middle class living in India in the 1940s is explored in the novels of Paul Scott, while Doris Lessing, born abroad of English parents, knew the experience from the other side. Having lived in England since leaving Rhodesia when thirty, and having been declared a prohibited immigrant after her last return visit, she records in her autobiographical *Going Home,* "The fact is I don't live anywhere; I never have since I first left home on the kopje" (Lessing 1968, 37). Her rider, "I suspect more people are in this predicament than they know," suggests that we may all have this latent urge for "going home." Pilgrimages have been the visible sign of this urge from time immemorial, as people have felt compelled to pay homage to a particular place enshrining the familial or wider cultural-religious origins. We acknowledge geopiety, to use Tuan's (1976a) phrase. Literary examples abound. In the modern novel an extraordinary pilgrimage is undertaken by Shute's heroine in *Requiem for a Wren* (Shute 1955). After her Australian fiancé dies on a wartime mission to Normandy, she is drawn halfway round the globe to immerse herself in the roots of her lost one, even to the extent of becoming—incognito—housemaid in the family home where she might have been mistress. Most recently it has underlain the conception, and reception, of Haley's (1976) popular work *Roots.*

PLACE AND TIME

Finally some comments on place and time; not that the time element can be isolated as if it is some distilled or crystallized deposit. It has already been mentioned that place transfixes time by providing points of stability which continue to recall people and events to the percipient or percipients concerned. On the other hand, the dynamic quality of time can occasion points of instability or at least surprise, for, while the percipient sees time transfixed, he is in fact being borne inexorably along. The inevitable result is a mismatch between the imagined and the re-experienced, the isomorphism being related to the length of intervening time interval. "You remember it in great detail, and you remember it all wrong," is Orwell's (1948, 178) description of the common experience of the surprise, disillusionment, or pain that may accompany our journeys into the past. Dickens, living for forty years on a myth founded on four early years of formative experience, found his eventual return "home" to Chatham profoundly unsettling. Speaking with a childhood friend was like "speaking of our old selves as though we were dead and gone" (Schwarzbach 1979, 182). More recently, Lee on a return visit to San Antonio openly acknowledges the fault to lie within himself:

> I went forth into the town and tried to reacquaint myself with the pattern of it. But of course it was not the same at all. My memory, over the years, had torn the old town down, rebuilt it, laid out the streets in quite different order and obliterated some of their most dominating landmarks. In that time I also had been torn down, rebuilt and had many landmarks obliterated. The town, after all, remained the truth, and I the shifting fable. (Lee 1956, 12–13)

Past and distant places are kept alive and "real" by memory, which, if not a goddess as deemed by the ancients, seems nevertheless under the influence of nostalgia. We may assume hindsight with its 20:20 vision; it would be more appropriate to think in terms of "mindsight," with its critical initial vision and subsequent refining and embellishment. Hilton's schoolmaster Mr. Chips was aware of the crucial importance of the present moment in the manner in which he would remember the boys during his retirement: "I *do* remember you—as you are *now*. That's the point. In my mind you never grow up at all. Never" (Hilton 1935, 89).

Of major authors, Hardy was particularly conscious, in both prose and later poetic writings, of the importance of what he called a "permanent impression." In *A Pair of Blue Eyes* he writes:

> Every woman who makes a permanent impression on a man is usually recalled to his mind's eye as

she appeared in one particular scene, which seems ordained to be her special form of manifestation throughout the pages of his memory. (Hardy 1976b, 48)

The passage prefaces the description of Stephen Smith's image of Miss Elfride. Being a semiautobiographical work, this novel also clearly evokes the author's image or after-image of Emma, his first wife. Among other recalls of this particular lady is the one in "After a Journey," where after a journey of forty years he revisits the spot to "see" his young love. He is an old man, Emma is now dead, but the place retains their presence as it was "at the then fair hour in the then fair weather" (Hardy 1978, 381).

"Permanent impressions," then, incorporate place as well as people. Gino *and* the house by the Volterra Gate were important to Lilia. "Emotions will attach themselves to scenes that are simultaneous," is Hardy's explanation for Cytherea recalling slanting shafts of sunlight in any mental agony, these having been first associated with the regaining of consciousness following her fainting at witnessing the agony of her father's death-fall from a church spire (Hardy 1976a, 44). Joyce in particular is held to be the clearest exponent of "epiphanies"—the actual fusing of place and person in a visionary image transcending ordinary experience (Paulin 1975, 29–31).

Time does bring change to the physical attributes of place, of course, and thereby contributes to the surprise encountered on revisiting, especially if that which is imagined dates from childhood origin. Moreover, its contribution has increased as the rate and scale of change have altered its character, from gradual evolution and natural aging to machine development and artificial environments. The accompanying historical residue of invested meaning is inevitably diminished or destroyed with equal rapidity or, as regards new environments, not present in the first instance. The absence of past time in new environments may well produce an air of unreality. Witness, for example, Lawrence's description of the newly intruded colliery village of Wiggiston:

The whole place was just unreal, just unreal. Even now, when he had been there for two years, Tom Brangwen did not believe in the actuality of the place. It was like some gruesome dream, some ugly, dead, amorphous mood become concrete. (Lawrence 1949, 346)

While the colliery manager held disbelief, the miners and their families experienced alienation from the rootless place, resigned that they must "alter themselves to fit the pits and the place" (Lawrence 1949, 347) rather than feel part of any evolving symbiosis. We may have intimations of this unreality as travelers if unexpectedly halted or disembarked before our destination. In the world of the novel perhaps the clearest such example is at the beginning of *Doctor Zhivago,* where the suddenly interrupted rail travelers view the locality outside the carriage as "brought into being by the halt," with even the sun seeming "a stage prop" (Pasternak 1961, 25).

A well-known and early example in literature of the effect of landscape change is the mental agony and eventual insanity suffered by John Clare as a result of enclosure of the open fields of Helpston and consequent loss of detailed orientation and intimacy. At the beginning of *The Rainbow* Lawrence makes the simple statement of the Brangwens being made "strangers in their own place" by the building of a canal across farmland which had been in the family for generations (Lawrence 1949, 12). The canal with its coal barges, however, represents the evil force of industrialization extending at the expense of nature, a process which Lawrence decried and which has been a major theme for many artists, no less than for historians or scientists, over the last century and a half (Clayre 1977).

General change occurring in place, with the accompanying passing of communities—their economies, social networks, and customs—appears to have been a stimulus, a creative element for several writers. Some outpourings, therefore, are almost in the nature of a "literary dig," rescuing what was obscure or about to pass into obscurity. Such an interpretation may be given to many of Scott's works, rich in Scottish history and folklore. (Wordsworth's poetic treatment of Lakeland life may be similarly interpreted.) Hardy's depiction of the Wessex peasantry is one of a world rapidly disappearing after centuries of stability, exact temporal authenticity being achieved by setting the novels two or three generations back in time. The outburst of modern "northern" novels, with their stereotype depictions of industrial towns and working-class society, may be similarly interpreted, for the world described is that up to the early 1960s, with none of the subsequent societal and environmental transformation.

CONCLUSION

The novelist has the gift of articulating our own inarticulations, offering, among other attributes, an insight into place. Imaginative literature thus offers the geographer a valuable storehouse in which to explore his central theme of human-environment relationship. In particular, it is a source of wide interest to current humanistic approaches where experience has been conceptualized in terms of insideness-outsideness (Relph 1976), lived reciprocity (Buttimer 1980), or as a dialectic between rest and movement (Seamon 1979).

The very size of the literary field in which to search will always present the geographer with a peculiar sampling problem, such that any "use" of this source will reflect to a degree that researcher's own bibliographical history. Acquaintance with literature is no less personal than experience of place. At the same time it may be noted that it is of the essence of literature to reveal the universal while apparently concerned with the particular. To a degree, therefore, the test of this, or any similar, engagement is whether the results "ring true" with the reader.

SOURCE AND ACKNOWLEDGMENTS

This article originally appeared in *Transactions of the Institute of British Geographers,* n.s. 6 (1981): 337–47. The author thanks David Seamon and J. Richard Watson for comments on a draft of the original article.

FURTHER READINGS

Charles S. Aiken. 1979. Faulkner's Yoknapatawpha County: A place in the American South. *Geographical Review* 69:331–48.

A geographer's attempt to answer the question of whether Faulkner's fictional county was a microcosm of the South or, rather, a fictional place situated in the geographical and historical context of the South.

Margaret Drabble. 1979. *A writer's Britain: Landscape in literature.* London: Thames and Hudson.

A readable survey of the ways in which British writers have addressed the landscape and its many elements. Drabble provides an overview that allows the reader to set particular writers and themes in a very broad context.

Geoffrey Grigson, ed. 1980. *The Faber book of poems and places.* Boston: Faber and Faber.

A collection of poetry from the fifteenth to twentieth centuries that demonstrates the power of poetry to re-create place. The major sources of poetic imagery are the places and landscapes of England, Wales, Scotland, Ireland, and the Channel Islands, although some poems deal with France and Italy.

D. N. Jeans. 1979. Some literary examples of humanistic descriptions of places. *Australian Geographer* 14:207–14.

This article makes a useful distinction between "visual" description, technical description, and humanistic description, the last of which attempts to communicate subjective responses and meanings.

Alfred Kazin. 1988. *A writer's America: Landscape in literature.* New York: Alfred A. Knopf.

This is a study of the pervasive influence of the American landscape on poets, essayists, and novelists. Kazin considers several of the competing images of America that have emerged as central themes in American letters over the last two centuries.

Leonard Lutwack. 1984. *The role of place in literature.* Syracuse, N.Y.: Syracuse University Press.

Lutwack, a literary historian, examines the use of metaphors and images of place in literature and demonstrates how writers have imbued landscapes and places with psychological meaning.

William E. Mallory and Paul Simpson-Housley. 1987. *Geography and literature: A meeting of disciplines.* Syracuse, N.Y.: Syracuse University Press.

In this volume, writers, literary critics, and geographers consider the role of language in literature. Perhaps the greatest strength of this collection is that two of its articles

reach outside the English-speaking world to Latin America and Russia. Other than that, some of the usual suspects are present: Bennett, Cather, and Hardy. The articles on Arthurian Britain and Nebraska are noteworthy. Of the twelve essays, only four are by geographers, so that literary criticism sometimes takes precedence over sensitivity to place.

Douglas C. D. Pocock, ed. 1981. *Humanistic geography and literature: Essays on experience of place.* Totowa, N.J.: Barnes and Noble.

The first collection of essays by geographers to explore the distinctive contributions that their discipline has made to the study of imaginative literature and the way literature, as a form of environmental information, complements and enriches more conventional sources. The book includes essays on Ruskin, Lawrence, Lessing, Eliot, and Steinbeck, as well as several topical essays.

———. 1988. Geography and literature. *Progress in Human Geography* 12:87–102.

In this article, Pocock provides a progress report on recent research into geography and literature. He maintains that literature can be viewed as both a source and a tool for geographic research. For some geographers, literary texts offer primary sources of information useful for global studies of culture and social reproduction. For geographers interested in humanistic studies, literature is a tool that helps articulate qualities of lifeworld and place that might otherwise remain obscure. Pocock organizes his discussion around the themes of person, plot, and place.

J. Douglas Porteous. 1990. *Landscapes of the mind: Worlds of sense and metaphor.* Toronto: University of Toronto Press.

Landscape in literature is one of several important themes pursued in this volume. The fiction of Graham Greene and Malcolm Lowry is the focus of several chapters.

Christopher L. Salter and William J. Lloyd. 1977. *Landscape and literature.* Washington, D.C.: Association of American Geographers, Resources Papers for College Geography No. 76–3.

This short volume remains useful for its suggestions on the incorporation of literature into the classroom.

Paul Simpson-Housley and G. Norcliffe, eds. 1992. *A few acres of snow: Literary and artistic images of Canada.* Toronto: Dundurn.

This collection of essays on Canada contains noteworthy articles by geographers, including "Ways of Seeing, Ways of Being: Literature, Place, and Tourism in W. L. Montgomery's Prince Edward Island" by Shelagh Squire and "Deriving Geographical Information from the Novels of Frederick Philip Grove" by O. F. G. Sitwell.

Frederick Turner. 1989. *Spirit of place: The making of an American literary landscape.* San Francisco: Sierra Club.

In this volume, Turner continues the pursuit of the themes he first addressed in his earlier work, *Beyond geography: The western spirit against the wilderness* (1980). Turner considers how American writers have come to terms with place, landscape, and environment.

Raymond Williams. 1973. *The country and the city.* London: Chatto and Windus.

Williams examines the contrasting portrayal of the country and the city in English literature and the social context of this literature. This book, and Williams's other writings, have been very influential in the "cultural studies" school of British cultural geography.

JOSEPH SONNENFELD

25

WAY-KEEPING, WAY-FINDING, WAY-LOSING: DISORIENTATION IN A COMPLEX ENVIRONMENT

PROLOGUE

Geographers who work in the area of environmental perception and behavior differ sufficiently, one from the other, to require explication of personal professional orientation (see Sonnenfeld 1984a). The role of environment in behavior is an important part of my concern, but my concept of environment differs from the more positivist perspective on environment as contributor to behavior (compare Sonnenfeld 1972 and Wohlwill 1973). I assume the existence of an environment as I see and feel and understand it, and I assume that others may see and feel and understand it differently. However, I also acknowledge that there is a separate, independent reality by which we test the efficacy of our perceptions and the behaviors to which they contribute; for if there were not such a reality test for perceptions, our survival as a species would be seriously at risk.

Given this dependence on individual sensing and perception of environment, it is easy to understand why we are so variable in the behaviors we direct to the environment. The source of such variability is in all the things that influence the way we see and think and act in the environment, including the sensitivities and abilities we are born with and also what we have come to learn from our circumstances: being born into a place, culture, and "class," subsequently to develop the skills, fears, and faith that are the product of social and geographic conditioning.

This paper deals with certain issues of behavior in the spatial environment, which is one dimension of the geographic environment. There is much to engage us in this environment relating to the contribution of age, sex, and personality to variability in spatial behaviors. In addition, there is the cultural infrastructure of spatial behavior to consider, specifically, those things that culture contributes to the character of the spatial environment (as perceived), as well as to the development of spatial skills of the sort that make the environment accessible and safe for us, thanks to the rules cultures "devise" to protect those who are important for the well-being of the community at large.

I have found it useful, as a means of distinguishing between universal and group dimensions of spatial competence, to consider the issue of spatial incompetence: what it is that we fall short of in the performance we (and others) expect of ourselves in dealing with the demands of travel in the spatial environment. As with competence, incompetence can also be expected to vary, meaning that there are cultural as well as ability and experiential dimensions to the incompetence we and others sense in how we deal with environmental complexity. And, not surprisingly, there are equivalent sources of variability in how we react to such incompetence, including how we recover from disorienting experiences. Such reaction involves not only those of us who become disoriented, but, again, also the communities to which we belong and which assume responsibility for our safety.

The paper that follows treats some of this behavioral complexity in southeast Alaska. It involves both native and nonnative populations in a particularly complex spatial environment. I am currently working on field data from a similar study in northern Alaska of Inupiat (Eskimo) travel behaviors. Both studies seem to emphasize not only how different populations deal with ambiguity in the travel environment but also how those with a consistent cultural tradition vary among themselves in the ways in which they relate to travel space and in the risks that they

assume as a consequence. This is a variability especially characteristic of populations in the process of culture change. The point is that while the reality—the geographical environment within which travel occurs—is the same for all, it can be perceived and dealt with quite differently, in ways that can impact seriously on the experience of risk.

The lesson of this is that we are treating of other than a universal sensing and perception of environment. Not only do we perceive differently what exists in the environment that we are required to contend with, but we have a different sense of what constitutes an appropriate response, a "rational" response to the ambiguity we are attempting to resolve. Even the use of the irrational, such as imposing certain fearsome spirits onto the persona of places that are dangerous in order to make them more memorable, can be viewed positively in terms of the rational contribution that such imposition of meaning on the landscape makes to safe travel. This is an example of people as more than spatial information processors, implying a culturally and personally creative dimension to travel behavior that cognitive spatial science too often ignores (see Bruner 1990).

One final comment I wish to make is that the models used as illustrations in this paper are descriptive models; they help me organize my understanding of the behavioral issues under examination. These constitute a synthesis of data and concept that seems to help me—by the spatiovisual perspective it provides—to "see" and consider additional variables in those segments of the model that seem to demand more balance; and these, in turn, stimulate the search for equivalents in the environmental behaviors I am trying to understand. My descriptive models combine the visual and the verbal in an effort not only to obtain conceptual clarity and balance but, subsequently, also to disrupt or disturb this balance, as if there is reason to suspect the conceptual symmetries that result. I can only hope that if the models do this for me, they may function similarly for readers who bring their own logic and experiences to bear on the problem of understanding variability in environmental behavior. This kind of modeling constitutes a kind of creative and affirming process, one consistent with the way our brains seem to work. But, if this desire for symmetry also produces uneasiness in regard to models that seem too balanced to mirror complex realities accurately, then we must open ourselves again to the content of reality to gain a truer sense of its nature.

INTRODUCTION

Geographic disorientation tends to be a negative experience. It implies spatial confusion or misdirection. It is common in complexly structured spatial environments, but it can also result from a lapse in attention to location or some malfunction of the neurosensory or spatial memory systems. In this paper, *geographic disorientation* will refer to experiences that include, at the one extreme, the sense of being "lost" that one associates with brain-damaged victims who are no longer able to remember where they are (De Renzi, Faglioni, and Villa 1977), and, at the other, with inattentive travelers who are disoriented because they are unconcerned with where they are going. Depending on person and setting, disorientation can be either normal or abnormal. It is the product of a confusing environment or of behavior that confuses or distracts one's sense of location and direction in the environment. It includes the nonconscious drift away from the intended path and the more purposeful following of inappropriate cues that lead the traveler away from his or her intended destination.

This paper describes a study carried out in southeast Alaska, involving a community of wayfinders who proved more sensitive than most to problems of orientation and way-finding. Such are the hazards to travel in this environment that survival skills as well as orientation skills are critical for travel away from home. It is appropriate, therefore, to begin with an account of a disorientation experience that involved some rather considerable risk.

DISORIENTATION IN A WILDERNESS SETTING

In the early winter of 1979, a member of a small Tlingit community near the center of southeast Alaska's panhandle became lost while out hunting for deer. He was in his mid-thirties, and was originally from British Columbia. He had lived there on a reservation, some three hundred miles from the coast; this was an area that had been logged, so that when he went out hunting he was never very far from roads that he could follow to find his way home. In his early adult years, he left the reservation for a logging job in southeast Alaska, married a local Tlingit woman, and now called her village home.

He had been living and working in the central part of southeast Alaska for several years at the time that the incident he reported had occurred. It was early in the winter, and he and a friend had decided to go deer hunting. Because deer were scarce on their home island, they traveled by boat to a small island some thirty-five kilometers from their village. They arrived at the island rather late in the day, about 3 P.M.; at this season it gets dark early and quickly by midlatitude standards. The two hunters soon found deer tracks and decided that each should go his own way. The subject of this account followed a set of deer tracks up the mountain slope, but it started getting dark, which meant that it was time to return to the beach where the hunters had left their boat. Unhappily, he was not sure of the direction that he had to travel to get there. This was the first time he had been on that particular island.

He decided to keep walking, hoping to find his way out of the woods and to the coast where it would be easier to locate his boat. He walked into the night, which one does not normally do in the woods in this area. There was snow on the ground, and in places it was waist deep. As he walked, he dropped things on the trail—bits of toilet paper at first, and then clothing articles, so that if someone was looking for him they would be able to follow his trail. At night, he said, things all look the same, and the large trees that are common in this area seemed even bigger. Despite the snow cover, it was so dark that he could not see even his own tracks. He said that he walked until about 1 A.M. and then decided to build a fire. He was able to get a small fire going, but the wind soon blew it out; his cigarette lighter broke, and he had no matches to start another. He tried sleeping, and succeeded for about fifteen minutes, but the snow melted and ran down his back. He was getting very stiff; now he had to fight to stay awake. He exercised to keep warm and awake, trying also to keep from sweating.

At dawn, he began moving again. He covered a lot of ground. He discovered that he had traveled completely around the mountain the night before. He had traveled in a circle and had come back to his own trail, though initially he did not even recognize his own tracks when he saw them in the morning—he had not looked at his boots to see the kind of tracks he was making. He subsequently headed for open spots on the mountain. He traveled what he described as a zig-zag course, from open spot to open spot. Occasionally he would stop to wring out his socks, which were soaking wet. That morning a helicopter flew above him at tree-top level, and when he saw it overhead he waved, but they apparently did not see him. He had his rifle but could not fire it, because water from melting snow had seeped in during the night and frozen the firing mechanism. At one point that morning he climbed a tree hoping for a better view of the surrounding area and some features that he might recognize; but he couldn't even see water, which was when he knew he was really lost.

The hunter remarked that when he realized he was lost that first night, he tried to keep from panicking, but knowing that he was lost he still had a sense of panic. "The first question you ask," he said, "is what are you going to do? You feel the panic, although you know that you need to keep your 'cool.'"

The hunter continued walking. He was getting very thirsty; he did not have any water and started to eat snow, but was weakened by it. The sun only occasionally came through the cloud cover, and it was cold. To make a long story shorter, he was found later that day by a search party from his village. When located, he was moving onto higher ground; he had climbed about three quarters up the side of the mountain. Search crews from his home village had been organized into shifts to find him. The second of these finally located him; the third crew had been ready to take over. They were strung out in a line, prepared to cover the whole island, if necessary. The hunter for whom they were searching said that when he first heard a voice calling, he did not believe it; he was afraid he was hallucinating. But he heard it again, called back, and received an answer; and then he started running to where the voice was coming from, falling and tumbling along the way. He thought at first that this was the friend from whom he had been separated the previous night, and only after he had jumped onto the man and hugged him did he realize that a search crew had been out looking for him.

It took about three hours to get back down to the beach where the hunters had originally come ashore, and which was almost straight down from where the lost hunter had been found. On the way back he had to stop every now and then because his leg muscles were cramping so badly. That he had lasted as long as he had he attributed to his good physical condition; he had always done a lot of running, and this undoubtedly had helped him through the walking of the first night and much of the second day. The night after the search crews had found him it was even colder than the previous night had been. He was sure he would not have survived another night out, and the others agreed with him.

Subsequently he has not had any urge to go hunting. He said that he had some bad dreams for awhile. He burned his boots and the clothes and other things that he had with him on the mountain. A pile of ashes outside his house was all that was left; he said something about trying to save some of the ashes as a reminder. Others who were asked about the island where he had been lost indicated that it was one of the worst places for getting lost; there were a lot of hills on it.

A COMMUNITY OF WAY-FINDERS

The discussion which follows is based upon data derived from a study of geographic orientation in a community located approximately in the center of the southeast Alaska panhandle. Those interviewed were a rather heterogeneous group of fifty men and women who were mostly nonnatives; however, approximately 10 percent were

Tlingits from the same community and from a neighboring native village. The study community is a rather distinctive one, in the sense that it is largely non-native, which is atypical for towns of its size in southeastern Alaska. But if few members of this community are native in a racial sense, equally few are native by residence; most come from places outside of Alaska.

While this study included testing for spatial abilities, using a variety of more or less conventional paper-and-pencil tests, more time was spent in both formal and informal interviews, and it was here that most of the information on disorientation was obtained. I might only mention, as a commentary on the test portion of the study, that there was relatively little relationship between "natural" spatial abilities, as measured by performance on the paper-and-pencil tests, and those "real-world" spatial skills that could be inferred from success in activities obviously demanding of such skills (Sonnenfeld 1985; 1988). More in the context of this paper, it was also found that most of those who get lost in the area (since corroborated in some other areas as well) are not the newcomers, who, while they do suffer at least temporary disorientation, are also the more likely to be sufficiently forewarned and intimidated by the surrounding environment not to make the kind of trips that puts them at risk. Rather, those who get lost tend to be the longer-term residents and, in fact, as often as not, also native Tlingits, suggesting that the orienting skills one expects to be able to protect the native are not always enough to ensure success in way-finding.

Among reasons for getting lost, two appear to be critical in my study area: an inappropriate orientation style and a difficult travel environment. The nonnatives are especially susceptible to orientation-style problems, because many of the skills that they bring with them were developed in other environments and thus are variably appropriate for way-finding in southeast Alaska. But this is difficult to generalize since individuals differ both in the kinds of skills they develop and in the degree to which these skills are developed. Generally, those with a more diverse travel experience have an easier time than do the less traveled in adapting to what way-finding in wil-derness settings of southeast Alaska requires of them. The reason for this, quite simply, is in the development by the well-traveled of a sensitivity and flexibility not dependent on place-specific cues, which is what the less-traveled tend to require, given their more limited environmental experience. The less-traveled know their own travel spaces well enough not to have to worry about developing way-finding skills, but this is also why they are likely to have greater difficulties in finding their way in unfamiliar settings.

But the complexities of the physical environment are at least as critical as orientation style in causing difficulty in way-finding, and this is particularly the case in southeast Alaska.

THE WILDERNESS AS WAY-FINDING ENVIRONMENT

Southeastern Alaska is a fjord coast environment in which tidal waters, land surfaces, and weather conditions are all liable to rapid change. The orientation environment is considered complex because of a variety of both short-term and long-term features. For boat pilots, fog and darkness are only short-term impediments to travel: after night comes day, and in time the fog lifts. However, when visibility is reduced, tidal velocities (from five- to over ten-meter tides) and rock- and shoal-infested channels in the region's "inland sea" interact to make boat control (and way-finding) difficult and hazardous even for professional pilots, notwithstanding the availability of radar. Fog and nighttime loss of visibility are equally disorienting on land, and given the confusion of local topography and ground cover, either fog or darkness is sufficient reason for waiting for visibility to improve, even if stressful weather conditions would seem to demand otherwise.

For land travelers, the persistent problem is that of way-finding more than way-keeping, given the generally roadless character of most of southeast Alaska. This is an area of islands; of thick forests and swampy bogs; and of hills and mountains, none of which is easy to travel on or through. Seasonal rain and snow can exceed 250 centimeters of precipitation per year. Cloud cover and local fog are such that one does not always have visual access to distant peaks, or even to shorelines for orientation. In addition, the sky is normally cloudy enough for the sun, moon, and stars to be almost useless for navigation; and even when these are visible, high-latitude solar and lunar positions are difficult to decipher. Even compasses might prove minimally useful, unless a record of bearings and back-headings is kept, but this is made more difficult by magnetic anomalies in certain areas, as well as a normal magnetic declination of almost thirty degrees, and this in terrain that does not often permit one the luxury of taking shortcuts. Similarly, coastal streams might not always be helpful in directing the traveler, given the large tidal range and reverse river flows (at high tide) common in the low-lying area. Nor, given the intricate island-studded coastline, can one count on consistently structured coastal features to orient by, as is common in many of the less complex environments which non-natives call home.

Simply put, southeast Alaska is largely undeveloped country, with few settlements, most of which are oriented to the coast, and with access to these primarily by boat or by air. The waterways are complexly articulated, with patterns of topography and vegetation on islands and the mainland coast sufficiently random to make it difficult to maintain orientation even under the best of weather conditions. Given the potential for stressful weather at any time of the year, in addition to the difficulty of visual search by aircraft over surfaces as cluttered as those in this rainforest environment, one rather easily comes to understand why disorientation is such a problem for native as well as non-native travelers.

POPULATION ADAPTATIONS

The ways in which the natives and non-natives in this area adapt to the potential for disorientation are interesting and differ in some important respects. As one might expect, natives seem better conditioned to local settings and weather conditions, although, as with acclimatization, this is not generally at a level beyond the capacity of non-natives to achieve. For those Tlingit who are fortunate enough to have been trained in traditional hunting and fishing techniques, the travel skills they have also learned tend to be

sufficient for local way-finding or for survival when weather conditions interfere with normal travel; unfortunately, the traditions currently being transmitted are often incomplete, which is at least part of the reason why the Tlingit seem to get lost as commonly as non-natives. During my visits to this area, over a period of three years, search parties twice had to be sent out to locate lost hunters, and in both cases local Tlingits were involved, neither of whom was especially prepared for way-finding in the environments that disoriented them.

Yet, under normal circumstances, this is the exception, as it was traditionally. The Tlingit were expected to know the land in terms of the visual specifics of place; this is a talent which comes with the extension of the "domicentric" orientation style (Sonnenfeld 1982, 70), similar to that which most of us develop in our own home spaces, to include also intimate knowledge of the surrounding subsistence area. In addition, they could also orient "geocentrically," by wind and water patterns and related vegetation features, which, if not infallible as cues to direction, were still useful in the absence of more conventional indicators of place. It was also implicit that natives would develop a sensitivity to time: to the schedule of tides, to the time required to cover a certain distance by boat or on foot, and to the length of time remaining till darkness, meaning, also, an ability to accommodate seasonal variations in sunlight and the condition of water and land routes. To keep travel at nightfall to a minimum, a mythology emerged, and remains among some Tlingit, of sea and land creatures who ensnare and enslave people. The stories are occasionally reinforced by individuals who are lost and never heard from again, and even by those not lost who encounter reputed "land otters" or other creatures. The strength of the myth is such that these encounters get reported not only by those who are caught out alone but even by those for whom the mythic encounter is a group experience. If there is reason to question the existence of the creatures described, there is less question that the myth of their existence acts effectively to instill, from early childhood, the discipline necessary to get wayfarers back home before dark.

One is tempted to explain the persistence of the myth behind the fear as a recognition of limits to the application of skill in an environment not completely known or predictable, or an effort at making sense of the disappearance of an individual that is not otherwise explainable; but, in Tlingit terms, the fear behind the myth had a different, more culture-specific logic. According to Frederica de Laguna (1960, 28), such fear was based on the belief that "those who were never found . . . could not enjoy the warm afterworld reserved for those whose bodies were cremated [the ashes subsequently being placed "inside the sacred totem poles" (Oberg 1973, 52)], but were doomed to wander in the guise of land otters, lurking to kidnap the shipwrecked or children lost in the woods whom they transformed into creatures like themselves."[1]

In sum, the more traditionally trained Tlingits seem to be fairly secure in their relationship with a travel environment that they make use of both for subsistence and recreation. If they should become lost or not return home, the community has "search and rescue" capabilities that include access to other individuals likely to be knowledgeable about local travel environments. Equally important is the motivation of kinship or other social obligation that gets the community to persist in the search for one of its own.

The situation for non-natives is a bit different. Generally, boat pilots are more likely than their equivalent among the Tlingit to have access to coastal charts and radar and sonar, while hunters and other land travelers are more likely to use topographic maps and aerial photographs in addition to the compass. Still, non-natives also become disoriented, and they occasionally get lost. As already suggested, they tend to have orienting skills nurtured in and more suited to other than local environments. They do not always use compasses when they should, or they mistrust compasses when they should trust them, or they trust them in places where geomagnetic anomalies make such trust unwarranted.

Problems also result from the inadequacies of maps and charts of the area, and occasionally a traveler imposes inappropriate meaning—or imagery—onto the landscape by misinterpreting visible surface and coastal features for those on maps and aerial photographs of the region. Too often, even long-term residents of the area do not know the country they travel in well enough, or they think they know it and themselves better than they do. They do not keep a record of compass headings; they do not look back to see what the profile of the landscape they passed through appears like in reverse; or they attempt shortcuts based on the logic of geometry rather than on knowledge of the terrain to be covered. Commonly, they misjudge the weather, the time remaining to darkness, or the distance they have come and the length of time it will take to return to boat or to camp. Too often they go out alone,[2] run into confusing and disorienting terrain, and run out of time.

When non-native travelers become aware that they are disoriented, it may be difficult for them to deal with this rationally. Some become frightened at the prospect of being lost; they start walking faster or running to get out. If they could just go faster, they think (when they think), they are bound to come to some place they recognize. As they heat up because of the stress and exertion, they start stripping away some of their clothing; when fatigue sets in and they have to rest, they suffer additionally from the cold; and, depending on the season, they may not survive the exposure. The only consolation is that such shed clothing may be found by search parties and used for tracking those reported missing. The more sensible travelers, when they get delayed by the weather or by nightfall, or when they become disoriented for other reasons, stop for the night. If confused by a fog, they wait for it to lift. They keep a small fire going for warmth or for drying clothes. They burrow into a protecting snow bank when they need rest and lack other shelter. And, in time, they generally find their way out or are found by a search party sent out by a community alerted to the fact that they are overdue.

Ultimately, survival for those who get lost may depend on the community response. The resources available to the non-native community are considerable, but they are also at times less dependable than those available to the Tlingit community. Not too many years ago, the search and rescue group in the study community was a formal organization. Individuals placed in charge of specific search parties were those who were known to be especially knowledgeable about the areas to be searched. But in time the organization faltered. In part, this was because of lapses in leadership; and, as might have been expected in a non-native community, there was also a change in interest as individuals moved into the community who had few kinship or other ties of the sort that get people to commit themselves to what search and rescue operations require. While search and rescue groups would still go out when requested to do so, the study community was a less consistent community-of-the-concerned than that represented by the nearby native community. In effect, the non-native community contains individuals less acquainted with the places they travel in and with fewer survival skills, who are only variably able to depend on compass and map to guide them or on the community to search them out should it become known that they are missing.

WILDERNESS RISKS AND THE SUPERNATURAL

An obvious question to ask is why individuals are not more anxious about traveling in this largely uninhabited environment, or at least better prepared for it. For those who seek out a wilderness experience, there is no doubt the positive anticipation of being immersed in a distinctive natural setting. One does not always consider issues of safety, and, as is common in national parks, one checks in with local authorities to report expected times of departure and return. In addition, being disoriented is not always considered to be a negative experience. Some perceive it as being a challenge. Indeed, one of my respondents, a young woman who reported that she easily and regularly becomes disoriented in cities, rationalizes her affliction as an opportunity to meet people and visit places she otherwise would not have been exposed to. Those sensitive to the risk of being lost in a wilderness setting may have similar feelings. But for hunters there may also be an opposite kind of concern; they are aware of

a balance of forces in nature, which the wilderness epitomizes, and they have a sense of being fair game when they are no longer in control.

Interestingly, getting through an experience of being lost does not seem to lessen the anxiety of those with wilderness fears. Nor does having lost control once seem to make it easier either to ignore or to accept the possibility that one may also lose control in the future. Yet there was an exception to this. At least two of those I interviewed—one of whom is a professional hunting guide and the other a helicopter pilot— described situations in which they were obviously disoriented and at serious risk because of this. Yet somehow they got out of their situations in ways that they—as practicing Christians—interpreted as divine intervention. For example, when one of them was caught out in a heavy fog while en route to a seldom visited port city, the fog lifted long enough at a critical point for someone in their boat to get the compass bearing that was able to direct them to safety. Both respondents reported that they continue to get anxious in such situations, but they feel, at least in retrospect, that they are being protected. There appears to be little of the postepisode trauma that affected the native whose experience was recounted earlier in this paper.

None of those Tlingits interviewed who expressed a concern about supernatural creatures indicated that being saved from potential disaster produces any lessened sense of beings to be feared "out there." They continue to attribute reality to the supernatural and continue to feel vulnerable; their only recourse is to make sure that they know the location of the more dangerous places so that they can avoid these and that they develop the travel skills, including awareness and discipline, needed to keep them on course and on schedule (de Laguna 1960, 28).[3]

WAY-FINDING MODELS

Data from my southeast Alaska study indicate that the way-finding styles in use among members of a specific community can differ considerably when residential histories—implying prior environmental conditioning—also differ. This

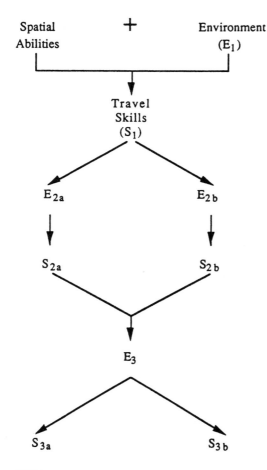

FIGURE I
Adaptation model of travel behavior.

has suggested the evolutionary-developmental model of way-finding depicted in figure 1. This "adaptation model" is intended to account for variability in the development of travel skills by members of most contemporary societies. It involves (*a*) spatial abilities, A; (*b*) travel skills, S_n; and (*c*) the travel environment, E_n. For any given population in a given setting, the major variables influencing the development of travel skills are spatial abilities, largely the product of genetic inheritance (McGee 1979; Gardner 1983), and age and sex. Travel experience increases with age, but aging also influences visual sensitivities and memory; at the extremes, the young lack experience,

while the aged tend to suffer from sensory and memory deficits (D. Cohen, Schaie, and Gribbin 1977; F. Craik 1977; Kirasic 1988). Sex differences do not necessarily imply differences in spatial or travel skills, but rather differences in the development of these among adults, based, in turn, on differences in the opportunity to develop such skills (Gillmartin and Patton 1984; L. Harris 1978; Munroe and Munroe 1971; Nerlove et al. 1974).

Among a subsistence-oriented population, the spatial skills that develop as the population expands into a new territory are assumed to be appropriate to the demands of subsistence in the new travel environment. The travel environment is defined not only by subsistence needs but also by transportation technology and travel skills. If a fishing people have access to boats, then the open sea can be included as part of their travel environment, the dimensions of which are further determined by their navigational skills.

According to this model, as a population increases in size or extends its activities into environments that differ from that originally occupied, travel skills change, from S_1, to S_{2a}, S_{2b}, and so on, according to the new sensitivities and talents that are appropriate for travel in the new environments. S_2 builds on and derives from S_1 as new environmental constraints require and as opportunities allow; this may include losses of particular skills that are no longer relevant in E_{2a} or E_{2b} and the addition of new skills that appear better suited for travel in these new settings.

Subsequently, should individuals from these different communities migrate to a common new environment, E_3, they will develop travel strategies appropriate to the new setting based on what they are differently prepared to learn by virtue of their previous—and differing—travel experiences. In other words, they will accommodate their travel skills to the characteristics of the new travel setting, but they may do so quite differently, one from the other (S_{3a} versus S_{3b}).

What this model indicates is that travel behavior is always adapted to a specific setting but that the form this adaptation takes will be affected by prior environmental conditioning; this is why orienting styles were so variable in my study community. However, prior environmental conditioning not only produced differences in orienting styles, it also contributed to at least some forms of disorientation (Sonnenfeld 1984b; 1985). For example, many of my non-native respondents had lived earlier in Oregon and Washington, as well as in other parts of Alaska. The physical characteristics of these other—conditioning—environments were often sufficiently similar to those in the study area to permit the use of orienting styles that had been learned in these other settings, generally with minimal modification. But there were instances in which even the minor differences between the conditioning and immediate travel environments were excessive. When way-finding decisions had to be made quickly, as with rapidly deteriorating weather conditions, the decisions proved inappropriate to setting and potentially serious disorientation occurred.

Other models have been constructed in order to identify the more specific elements of the disorientation experience. These are intended to apply to the natives as well as non-natives in the study area, notwithstanding the preconditioning that may predispose the latter to a distinctively non-native form of disorientation; and they are general enough to apply, as well, to other populations of travelers in other environmental settings. The series begins with the way-finding system suggested by Downs and Stea (1977, 124–35), who identify the essentials of way-finding in terms of a rather easily diagramed process model (figure 2). This is expanded to include the determinants of disorientation, and the "involuntary way-finding" that ensues, as shown in figure 3. The possible outcomes of the disorientation experience are shown in figure 4, which adds the role of personality and community to the way-finding equation. It is implicit (in the dashed line emanating from the search and rescue quarter) that "irrational acts" may cause one to become irreparably lost, but even rational behaviors do not ensure recovery.

Additional variables could have been added to these models, but enough is included to indicate the complexity of the disorientation experience. This is an aspect of way-finding that is generally

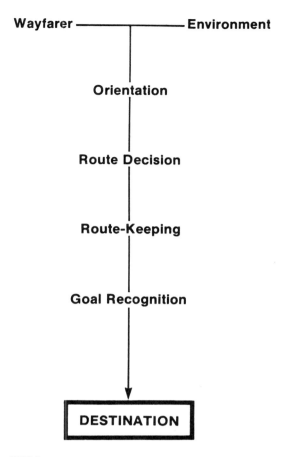

FIGURE 2
Wayfarer process model. Source: adapted from Downs and Stea (1977).

lacking in the literature on spatial behavior, most of which seems to focus on urban and small-scale or laboratory settings, and, in these, rarely do the issues of population diversity, community, and personality receive adequate attention.

CONCLUDING REMARKS

Disorientation in any environment can be unnerving. When it occurs in the wilderness, it is either accepted as part of the challenge of a wilderness experience or as more fearsome for the isolation and dangers implicit in the term *wilderness*. In southeastern Alaska, both natives and

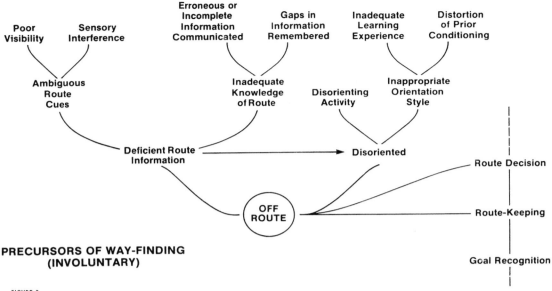

FIGURE 3

Precursors of way-finding (involuntary).

non-natives may have difficulty in keeping track of space, time, and place, but they appear to respond differently to such uncertainty. For the native, mental maps of place are more complete, survival skills are more developed, and the local community is likely to be more aware of and more responsive to those who are missing. The non-native is a more variable quantity, as well as more vulnerable. At worst, non-natives have less adequate knowledge of the travel space; they are less fitted for survival under local conditions; and they come into the wilderness from a community that may be minimally sensitive to their absence, if only because it may be minimally dependent on their presence. The native Tlingit is motivated to take precautions designed to keep from getting lost, and even from being out alone in the wild after dark, based at least in part on fears that appear relatively undiminished by experience. Fears among non-natives appear to relate more to the loss of confidence in one's ability to remain in control, as well as an uneasy dependence on unknown others for survival.

Much of southeast Alaska is a virtual wilderness. In such a setting, it would seem obvious that training and discipline are necessary for one to become an effective way-finder. Yet these do not always appear—for either native or non-native—to ensure survival in the absence of a caring community, or faith in other-than-self, which seems to suggest that the wilderness—in this respect, at least—is not too different from many of the environments for which "wilderness" is increasingly intended to be an escape.

SOURCE

This is a revised and expanded version of the original published in the *National Geographical Journal of India* 37 (March–June 1991): 147–60.

NOTES

1. Oberg, who worked with the Tlingit some fifteen years before de Laguna, relates the fear of being lost to the belief that "the spirit of a person so lost does not go to join the ancestors, but becomes a *Kustaxa* and wanders about forever, haunting the living with his doleful cries" (Oberg 1973, 52). He identifies Kustaxa as a shaman "changed into an evil spirit who takes the otter form. He robs the souls of people who are lost at sea or who die alone in the woods. He then changes the man's soul into another Kustaxa spirit" (Oberg 1973, 18).

2. A long-term director of the local search and rescue unit in the study community indicated that, as he remembered it, those lost individuals they were called on to help find were always out alone.

3. According to de Laguna (1960, 28), "in the old days the use of a respectful formula for addressing the water" also helped to make dangerous places safer. Interestingly, not all mythic beings known to the Tlingit were to be feared. De Laguna (1960, 60) was told of an area described as "the home of little dwarfs . . . who were helpful to men although they would never show their faces." One wonders if these are related to what Suedfeld and Mocellin (1987, 33) describe as the "occasional experience of another entity appearing to provide help or advice, even when no such entity was in fact present." They relate a number of accounts of such a "sensed presence," differently manifest, who offers advice, direction, and encour-

agement to obviously distressed solo voyagers (Suedfeld and Mocellin 1987, 38).

FURTHER READINGS

Stuart C. Aitken, Susan L. Cutter, Kenneth E. Foote, and James L. Sell. 1989. Environmental perception and behavioral geography. In *Geography in America,* ed. Gary L. Gaile and Cort J. Willmott, 218–38. Columbus, Ohio: Merrill.

This article reviews the major themes of contemporary environmental perception and behavioral geography. It identifies four areas of concentration: (1) analytical behavioral geography stressing patterns of spatial cognition and human behavior; (2) ecological dimensions of person-environment relationships; (3) landscape perception and

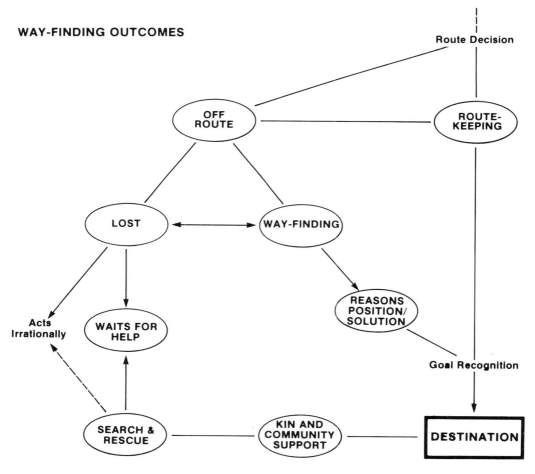

FIGURE 4
Way-finding outcomes.

experience; and (4) comparative research among varied social and cultural groups. The article includes a lengthy bibliography, an additional resource worth exploring.

Frederick W. Boal and David N. Livingstone, eds. 1989. *The behavioural environment: Essays in reflection, application, and re-evaluation.* London: Routledge.

This collection is in memory of William Kirk, whose landmark article of 1952 is reprinted therein. The contributors approach Kirk's ideas from a variety of philosophical viewpoints but within the framework of a reconstituted human geography. Spate's all too brief introduction is refreshingly candid.

Piet H. L. Bovy and Eliahu Stern. 1990. *Route choice: Wayfinding in transportation networks.* Dordrecht: Kluwer.

This book investigates route choice and way-finding skills in modern, urban societies. It also provides a good introduction to recent theories of way-finding.

Reginald G. Golledge and Robert J. Stimson. 1987. *Analytical behavioral geography.* London: Croom Helm.

This book is a comprehensive synthesis of work in behavioral geography carried out over the last two decades. Although the research presented relates only tangentially to cultural geography proper, the book demonstrates the sophisticated range of tools available to geographers interested in drawing on both subdisciplines.

Thomas F. Saarinen, David Seamon, and James L. Sell, eds. 1984. *Environmental perception and behavior: An inventory and prospect.* Chicago: University of Chicago, Department of Geography, Research Paper No. 209.

This anthology contains papers intended to take stock of the field of environmental perception research at the start of the 1980s. The book is a collection of relatively short position papers by a number of the then leading figures in environmental perception research.

Howard F. Stein. 1987. *Developmental time, cultural space: Studies in psychogeography.* Norman: University of Oklahoma Press.

The author, a psychoanalytic anthropologist, presents a study of the psychoanalytic sources of spatial representations in an unconventional and thought-provoking study. Stein provides one of the best statements of how humans project their mental worlds outward onto landscape and environment and so develop a sense of place.

Daniel Stokols and Irwin Altman, eds. 1987. *Handbook of environmental psychology.* New York: Wiley.

Like the Golledge and Stimson volume cited above, this book is a useful inventory of the wide range of techniques and sources available to cultural geographers interested in environmental perception research.

26

WORLDS OF MEANING: CULTURAL GEOGRAPHY AND THE IMAGINATION

I n *Metamorphoses* the Roman poet Ovid brings together an array of myths and stories, giving them poetic unity with the theme of metamorphosis or transformation: literally, a change of *form* within which character or personality remains unaltered. Ovid's metamorphoses take place between gods, humans, and the natural world: Narcissus becomes a spring flower, Atlas is changed into a mountain chain, the teeth of the serpent slain by Cadmus become warriors, and Jupiter takes the form of a bull to carry away Europa and found the Minoan dynasty. Poetically, Ovid refuses to draw a stable distinction between humankind and the natural world; he acknowledges that transformation is an essential feature of life and directs his poetic imagination to the generation of meaning in natural, supernatural, and human worlds.

Cultural geography sets itself a similar task. For all the divergence of theory, method, and material apparent among its texts, including the six essays collected in this section, cultural geographers share the common aim of describing and understanding the relations between collective human life and the natural world, the transformations wrought by our existence in the world of nature, and above all, the meanings that cultures ascribe to their existence and to their relations with the natural world. Unlike Ovid, cultural geographers do not rest easily with a unitary existence in which the same vital forces permeate all aspects of creation, allowing for physical change in form between human, natural, and supernatural life. This may be because the critical modern mind questions the relations between myth and truth, characteristically bracketing the existence of the gods. I will return to this aspect of modern cultures in due course; for now, it is sufficient that we recognize the considerable theoretical difficulties faced by cultural geographers in bringing together what in modern thought are the distinct realms of culture and nature. These difficulties are manifest in those debates between idealism and materialism or voluntarism and determinism that regularly recur among cultural geographers.[1] We recognize that humans are part of nature, formed of the same materials and responsive to the same rhythms and processes as the nonhuman world, and in direct communion with nature through our corporeal existence, our senses and our passions. We recognize, too, that our intellect and reason allow conceptual separation and distinction between the human world and the world of nature. In satisfying both these aspects of our human nature we intervene in the natural world and alter it, transforming ourselves in the process. For us humans there is no such thing as a natural world existing for itself, or at least if there is, our apprehension of it is mediated through consciousness and thus makes it a product of culture. By the same token, there is no such thing as a natural man or woman, for we are all the bearers of culture. Our most intense debates about what the world means therefore revolve around the relative significance we give to material existence in shaping and containing culture (environmentalism, materialism) or to consciousness and culture in shaping and transforming the natural world (voluntarism, idealism).

Ovid's metamorphoses are imaginative and poetic. They should serve to remind us that the primary mode of transformation as the condition of human existence in nature is through the imagination. Imagination is what gives the world meaning. Imagination is neither purely of the senses, which align us to nature, nor purely of the intellect, which separates us from nature. The work of the imagination is neither purely *reproductive* (that is, determined by sense data from the external world on which it depends) nor purely *productive* (that is, an image-making negation of that external world). Rather, imagination plays a symbolizing role, seizing on sense data without reproducing them as mimetic images and "metamorphosing" them through its metaphorical capacity to generate new meaning (Kearney 1991, 137 ff.). Transformations of the world in the imagination may lead to material transformations in nature: draining wetlands, conserving species, or finding a route through the wilderness. Recognizing the centrality of the imagination in the construction of meaning releases us from the antagonism of free will and necessity, idealism, and materialism. In Paul Ricoeur's words, "we have thought too much in terms of a will which submits and not enough of an imagination which opens up" (quoted in Kearney 1991, 139).

By highlighting imagination as central to the work of cultural geography, I intend to reference more than those features of human relations with the natural world that we commonly think of as imaginative. Douglas Pocock's "Place and the Novelist," for example, deals with "imaginative literature," at first sight constructing a cultural geography very different from that described by Burgess, who cites the mundane and often brutal physical practices of Fenlanders: "spraying water lilies in the dikes, dead moles hanging on barbed wire, and eels trapped in a box." But Burgess's landscape is no less imaginative than the most dreamlike landscapes of Pocock's novelists. We may identify at least three levels of imaginative meaning in her representation of the Fens: the elements of water, earth, sky, and fire—seemingly as old as the mythic imagination itself—which appear unmediated in the treeless natural environment and whose raw directness seems to run through the personality of Fenlanders; the geometry of drainage channels and roads—works of an engineering imagination that has greatly transformed nature in this region and that also seems to speak through the voices of local people; and the imaginative processes of representing the Fenlanders' sense of place in film and text that occupy so much of Burgess's discussion. Furthermore, the visceral bond between people and land on which Burgess insists, although differently articulated, is a recurrent theme in Pocock's survey: "different places on the face of the earth have different vital effluence, different vibration, different chemical exhalation, different polarity with different stars; call it what you like. But the spirit of place is a great reality," states D. H. Lawrence. It is the imagination that metamorphoses human community and natural environment into the meaningful unity of place.

Recognizing the centrality of imagination in generating meaning for the world may help us escape some of the persistent theoretical dualisms of cultural geography, but it does not resolve all the theoretical problems posed for a study that seeks to disclose what the world means. Four of these emerge with varying clarity from the papers collected in this section. They are: (1) the relationship between individual and collective imaginations and their geographical implications; (2) the ways that the imagination seeks to bring together the conflicting time horizons of human existence and the natural world; (3) the related issue of past and future in the cultural imagination; and (4) the critical character of the modern imagination, whose awareness of the significance of ideology subverts apparently innocent mythological syntheses of human life and the natural world such as we may identify in Ovid's *Metamorphoses*.

INDIVIDUAL AND COLLECTIVE IMAGINATION

We commonly think of imagination as the gift of individuals, yet by definition cultural geography deals with human groups, their relations with other groups, and their collective transformations of nature. Communication is the foundation of intersubjectivity: the shared values and beliefs that constitute the collective imagination and define nonmaterial culture. Language is the primary mode of human communication, constituting the very individuality of the individuals who use it. For this reason cultural geographers concerned with the question of what the world means have given increasing attention to the symbolizing role of language in our relations with the natural world, some to the point of regarding all cultural landscapes as texts constructed accord-

ing to linguistic rules.[2] Each of the essays in this section works largely from linguistic sources, either direct interviews or texts, rather than from material forms in the landscape. In his discussion of the symbolic imagination Paul Ricoeur identifies three categories of symbol that bear directly on the concerns of the cultural geographer: the cosmic, the oneiric, and the poetic.

Cosmic symbols emerge from the characteristically human imaginative act of reading the natural world simultaneously as thing and as sign of meaning beyond itself. Naming earth, air, and water, or land, sun, and stars, for example, attributes to them a dual signification. They are at once material and meaningful: the earth is fecund mother; air is freedom and spirit. Such meaning varies between cultures, although there are some remarkable consistencies.[3] This cosmic symbolism lies at the root of the issues discussed by Robin Doughty. The debate over Christianity's responsibility for contemporary environmental problems through its postulation of a deity outside nature and uninvolved in the life of creation and through its belief in a mobile rather than place-specific epiphany (the portable host rather than the sacred grove or mountain [Muir and Weissman 1989]), turns on the cultural power of cosmic symbols. Even in modern Christian cultures, however, God seems able to intervene directly in the world, as Sonnenfeld's survivors frequently claim, while common language still preserves composite meanings for the natural world and its elements, as the sublimity attributed to Niagara Falls testifies.

Oneiric symbols are the symbols conjured in dreams, allowing us to link the individual imagination to the collective, the local to the global, for not only can dreams be told, thus entering language, but as we know from twentieth-century psychology, individual dreams draw on the same symbolic repertoire from the natural world of cosmos, earth, and human body as cosmic symbols: "cosmos and psyche are two poles of the same 'expressivity': I express myself in expressing the world" (Kearney 1991, 144). It is this unity of psyche and cosmos that gives such imaginative power to terms like *wetlands, deserts, forests, poles, seas,* and ultimately, *the whole earth:* "real love begins with one's feeling for earth and . . . if you do not have this love then you cannot truly love people" (Sillitoe 1975, 73; quoted in Pocock 1981b, 343, and this volume). It is foundational also for the sense of dwelling, with all its ambiguities, that Pocock finds recurring in the novel, that Burgess elicits among those who live in the Fens even if they loathe the landscape and dream of escape, and for which Doughty pleads.

Poetic symbols reveal the human imagination at its most creative, drawing on the meanings generated in cosmic and oneiric symbols but, through the metaphorical power of language, discovering and creating new, perhaps unexpected meanings. The poetic is the most strictly cultural form of the imagination, entering the intersubjective world of discourse in the images and metaphors of representation. McGreevy's description of Niagara Falls' changing symbolism provides a wonderful example of the poetic imagination at work. For European culture the discovery of a vast waterfall in the depths of a new world directly addressed symbolic phenomena (water, air, rainbow, isolation, descent) tapping deeply into the cosmic and oneiric imaginations. The poetic imagination, as McGreevy demonstrates, not only continued to find new ways of sustaining Niagara's remoteness long after it was physically accessible but, in speaking new meanings for the falls, promoted the material transformation of the physical landscape of Niagara into one of the most managed cultural environments in North America.

It is the poetic imagination that is of most interest to cultural geographers. In generating new meaning, poetic creativity is what produces and differentiates cultures. The "mysterious East," "darkest Africa," the "icy poles," and "paradise islands of the South Seas" constituted an imperial geography of the world for Europeans in the early twentieth century. The exotic environments constructed at the Chicago Exhibition and later world's fairs that Barbara Rubin Hudson describes responded to and addressed the imperial imagination, and today cultural geographers direct much attention to the significance of these geographies, not only as stimuli to human action in transforming nature to accord with our poetic constructions of it, but also as

significant moments in the constitution of ourselves and our own cultural identity. European culture has characteristically constructed itself as male, active, moral, powerful, and progressive in large measure through defining "other" places and peoples as female, passive, immoral, weak, and undeveloped.[4] In the light of this recognition, Pocock's (1981b, 338, and this volume), claim that in Rider Haggard's novels place is "relatively unimportant, a mere exotic backdrop" and his comments on the theme of home and overseas in English writing from the early 1900s should perhaps be reassessed (R. Stott 1989; M. Pratt 1992). Such self-definition through construction of different "others" is common to all cultures, as is indicated by Sonnenfeld's finding that obligations to help perhaps fatally lost "others" is considerably lessened among the Tlingit of the Alaskan peninsula.

TIME HORIZONS AND THE IMAGINATION

Experientially, the natural world lacks history. In modern Western culture it has acquired a history only in the past two centuries, the result of geological and biological science. Intuitively, however, the natural world remains in indefinite time, a constant repetition of cycles without beginning or end: of the heavenly bodies, of seasons, of organic life. Collective human life, too, is a continuum that we join at birth and leave at death. Awareness of the cyclical patterns of day and night and of seasonality is so deeply etched into our consciousness and our conduct that their difference in a "foreign" place is among the most significant features of disorientation. It can even be life threatening: Sonnenfeld's study of way-finding reveals that one of the most common reasons for outsiders becoming lost in the northern latitude he studied is their inability to predict nightfall accurately. Cosmic symbols tend to reflect this cyclical time, and cultures characteristically align their practical and ceremonial activities directly to the cycles of nature. This is more than merely a functional response—by agriculturalists to the annual seasons, or fishermen to the daily tides, for example—it is also an expression in most cultures of that ecological consciousness for which Doughty pleads in a revised form of Christianity. Even in the most urbanized, secular cultures, much of the meaning of the world is still articulated in symbols of cyclical time—in events like Christmas and Thanksgiving and their appropriate foods and kinship imperatives (McGreevy 1990).

But precisely because, unlike life in the natural world, our human lives are defined by the discreet origin and termination points of birth and death, "we insist that beginnings and endings must be much more deeply built into the reality of things than the universe around us suggests, and we shape our myths accordingly" (Frye 1982, 108).[5] All human cultures have origin myths (Ovid's *Metamorphoses* begins with the ordering of chaos into cosmic regularity, whereas our largest scientific budgets today go to subatomic particle research into the origins of matter), and most cultures also have myths of Armageddon. The human need to impose the teleology of our own lived experience onto nature produces linear time and directional space. Not surprisingly, oneiric symbols are as frequently linear as they are cyclical. There is a tension between the forms of cultural imagining and symbolizing appropriate to circular (natural) and linear (human) time and space. The former underwrites meanings of stasis and security, of *being;* the latter, meanings of change and risk, of *becoming.* We see in Doughty's paper an emphasis on the former in his discussion of cultural relations with the natural world, whereas Hudson's concern with meanings in architecture deploys the language of past and future, direction and change. In its creation of meaning in the world, the poetic imagination constantly attributes significance to these two modes of apprehending the world, mapping them onto other discourses such as gender, age, or different parts of the body. For example, the idea of fate (nature) and containment within a circle are frequently associated with female gender. To break out of the cycle of fate is an imaginative act, it goes "against nature," and this is frequently gendered male (Frye 1982, 107). Cultures struggle to reconcile the circularity of natural time with the linearity of human time, expressing this geographically in the most universal of all spatial symbols—the mandala of circle and cross.[6]

Among the most recognizable cultural transformations of nature is the imposition of linear form on the landscape. Geometry is the product of the human intellect, a discourse of imaginary forms not given primarily in sense data. *Traces on the Rhodian Shore,* Clarence Glacken's (1967) study of relations between Western culture and nature, takes its title from the story of the shipwrecked Aristippus coming ashore on the island of Rhodes and spying geometrical figures in the sand. "Be of good heart," he tells his companions, "here are the signs of men." But even here the poetic imagination seeks to incorporate the cosmic symbols of nature: geometry is frequently cited as the language of God, the secret discourse of creation, a logic veiled behind the formal appearance of the natural world. In imposing geometry on the natural world, humans thus take on the role of the demiurge. Sonnenfeld's wayfinders constantly attempt to impose a geometrical logic on the trackless wilderness, and the Fenlanders' greatest pride lies in the geometry of dikes and roads: "there is a desire for straightness and accuracy"; "I loved . . . the sight of a long straight dyke and trimmed willow trees; and the wide horizons."[7] Geometry signifies human order, control over the natural world. Each of the maps and diagrams that McGreevy reproduces in his discussion of schemes for the transformation of Niagara Falls is an exercise in the geometry of straight lines and angles, except for Gillette's utopian plan of "Metropolis," which, appropriately for a perfect future world in which the "rough diamond" of nature is crafted by human hands to reveal its true beauty and power, combines linear and circular geometry in a repetitive mandala pattern. Geometry is thus the form through which the *telos* (becoming) of cultural time seeks to metamorphose the *kuklos* (being) of natural time.

PAST AND FUTURE IN THE CULTURAL IMAGINATION

The linearity of human time implies past and future as the necessary coordinates for fixing the present. Both past and future are spaces of the imagination; neither exists directly as sense data. In giving meaning to the world of the present, the imagination constructs narratives that bring past and future into some form of synthesis. Such a synthesis involves both symbolically confirming the past, which Ricoeur calls the *ideological* function of the imagination, and symbolically opening up the future, its *utopian* function (quoted in Kearney 1991, 152). Both these aspects of the poetic imagination are well exemplified in Barbara Rubin Hudson's cultural analysis of contemporary urban design in the United States. She contrasts two forms of urban design in the architectural discourse of the early twentieth century: a Beaux Arts style that drew on the classical and Renaissance architectural vocabulary of the European past, its choice justified in terms of education, taste, tradition, and authority; and a pastiche, playful, irreverent, and commercial style that owed its origins to urban merchandising and the fantasies of popular culture. Both were illusory in that they sought to deflect attention away from the present in time and space, and their constructional materials were equally ephemeral. Hudson addresses the ideological aspects of both these design types, but in Ricoeur's rather more narrowly defined terms it is the former that is ideological. It tended toward *integration*. The Beaux Arts style consciously appealed to the past, seeking to preserve and promote a sense of shared meaning, identity, and stability. Hudson quotes one of its promoters: "Man's greatest architectural achievements are those that blend in perfectly with the natural environment, or somehow create an environment of their own," a statement that exemplifies the ideological tendency to "naturalize" tradition (significantly, the ground plan for this style adopted the curving line as its articulating geometry). In Ricoeur's terms, the architectural forms of the Midway Plaisance, whose reference was to other places and times, were utopian; that is, they worked in the direction of *rupture* rather than tradition. Here was an aesthetic of novelty, difference, and discontinuity anticipating the future (unlike the "natural" curves of the Beaux Arts style, its plan favored linear and rectangular forms).

For Ricoeur ideology and utopia are necessary and complementary elements of the social imaginary in any culture. Ideology offers foundational myths and symbols that ground institutions and collective actions through ritual. The official culture of the United States expresses its historical foundation in the memory of the 1776 Declaration of Independence, celebrated in the annual rituals of the Fourth of July. It expresses its geographical foundation in the stars on "Old Glory." The federal structure and constitution are laid out in the street plan and street names of Washington, D.C., while the architecture of the capital city refers to historically deeper traditions in Western culture: those of Periclean Athens and republican Rome (Cosgrove 1984, 181–83). Not only nations but all cultural groups use the "'social imaginary' as an ideological recollection of sacred foundational acts . . . to integrate and legitimate a social order" (Kearney 1991, 158). The geographical expression of such acts are of obvious concern to cultural geographers.

Utopia is that part of the social imagination directed to the future, challenging tradition and seeking a break from the present. In constructing stories and images of possible futures, utopias provide the motive for action and change. Utopian landscapes have long been of interest to cultural geographers, whether they remain on paper or have achieved some sort of realization. Again, the United States offers innumerable examples: in the Jeffersonian utopian vision of American democracy founded on the independent yeoman family farm that produced the landscape of township and range in the Midwest or in the modernist visions surrounding the development of Niagara Falls documented by McGreevy.

Whereas utopia is a common theme in cultural geography, its dialectical unity with ideology, which Ricoeur sees as critical to the maintenance of a culture, has perhaps been insufficiently emphasized. Without the conservative force of ideology, utopias can become brutally destructive agents of change, to the point of wiping out whole cultures and their landscapes. Failure to recognize, let alone respect, native American ideology allowed the utopian visions of the young American republic to engage in a systematic destruction of these other cultures; the utopias promoted by Stalin and Pol Pot in the twentieth century have had equally dramatic consequences for cultures seen as standing in the way of their respective futurist visions. On the other hand, the conservative force of ideology can become equally repressive unless tempered by the disruptive radicalism of utopian visions, as the story of fascist Germany and countless examples of religious zealotry testify. The example of Germany serves to remind us that perhaps one of the most significant geographical manifestations of ideology's conservative power is the sense of organic attachment to land and place, often strong in peasant cultures and identified on the Fens by Burgess. That the sense of blood and soil *(Blut und Boden)* remains a particularly potent element in conservative nationalisms is evidenced by the brutal ethnic and cultural struggles that have followed the collapse of communism's utopian vision, which formerly controlled much of the territory of central Asia and eastern Europe.

CULTURE, MODERNITY, AND MULTIPLE MEANINGS

Cultural geography, like anthropology, has a long tradition of interest in rural, folk, and peasant cultures, frequently with cultures outside the European and North American world. Such societies have been represented as traditional, that is, relatively closed to the influences of modernity and rapid change, which have so affected the cultural realms of which most cultural geographers are a part. With the possible exception of Sonnenfeld's paper, all the pieces collected under "What the World Means" are concerned with "modern" cultures, that is, cultures that have experienced urbanization, industrialism, capitalist social relations, political democracy, and the cultural dominance of formal science, its links with technology, and its secularizing tendencies. As this list implies, such societies are characterized by many features differentiating them from the premodern cultures that have long held the primary attention of cultural geographers. Among the distinguishing features of modernity we may highlight two that bear immediately on the cultural geographer's project of establishing what the world means; these are cultural self-awareness and criticism and the recognition of cultural pluralism. The concept of culture as the shared beliefs and values of a human group emerges only

with an awareness of systems of belief and values alternative to those of one's own culture and with a spirit of "disinterested" study of them. In modern societies this has led to increasing recognition of the relativity of cultural truths. Concomitant with such relativism has emerged a willingness to subject modern cultures themselves to critical attention and a recognition of the degree to which they are composed of a plurality of voices differently constructing meaning for the world. The rapidity with which meanings are transformed and reconstituted seems to increase radically as modernity proceeds. Undoubtedly, modern cultures place a premium on utopia rather than ideology, on change and disjuncture rather than tradition, on the future rather than the past, on linear rather than cyclical time (Harvey 1989; Cosgrove 1990).

Modern societies thus display a marked bias toward disjuncture and rupture in their cultural expression. The implications of this in their visible landscapes, traditionally one of the main objects of cultural study within geography, are evident in Hudson's paper. She demonstrates how the architectural forms initially developed on the midway have become the dominant vocabulary of the American urban scene and are increasingly apparent across the globe. Many of the observations made by early observers of this kind of landscape accurately anticipate contemporary commentators on the cultural geography of the postmodern landscape: [8]

> The prodigal modern Midway is fairly using up the earth. A few more Expositions and we shall have nothing left that is wonderfully wonderful, nothing superlatively strange; and the delicious word "foreign" will have dropped out of the language . . . not satisfied with exhausting the earth, they have already begun on the universe. Behold, the world is a sucked orange. (Hartt 1901, 1097, quoted in Barbara Hudson 1979, 348, and this volume)

This conscious elaboration and juxtaposition of meaning in architecture and landscape is now a significant feature of both urban and rural landscapes in large parts of the world. It affects newly constructed places, past environments conserved and interpreted as heritage, and the nonmaterial landscapes and places of film, painting, and writing. It accords well with the critical turn of modern thought that promotes the constant deconstruction of stable meanings. It appears that for increasing numbers of people, what the world means is a matter of personal choice, communicated through self-representation in such matters as housing, clothing, and taste in cuisine, music, or even sexuality. Ironically, as communication media that allow the individual to participate in the reproduction of culture become more sophisticated, instantaneous, and global in their reach, cultural meanings in modern societies become ever more fragmented and volatile.

Increasing attention to contemporary cultures and their expressions within modern societies has expanded the perspective of cultural geography, challenged many of its traditional concepts and methods, and opened up questions of direct social relevance. We have already referred to the linguistic turn in contemporary cultural research. This has forced us to recognize the degree to which the poetic imagination, when aligned with social power, can mask as well as disclose meanings, subordinating certain interpretations of the world in favor of others (P. Jackson 1989). If meaning is the creation of imagination, it is difficult to attribute to it foundational authority: the meaning of the world is indeed open to endless elaboration, challenge, and re-presentation. Such polyvocalism is increasingly apparent in modern societies, especially in metropolitan places composed of highly mobile populations, diverse in ethnicity, language, religion, lifestyle, and other conventional indicators of culture. Voices that in the past have been defined as culturally "other" to the universalizing discourse of Euro-American, white, male, middle-class culture, which these voices claim long dominated the texts of cultural geography, now demand an audience for their own imaginative constructions of what the world means.

Such localism, even if not contained within a traditional spatial matrix, accords well with cultural geographers' long-standing, if ethnocentric, recognition of the richness and diversity of the world's lands and peoples. It sits less comfortably with their equally deep commitment to understanding the relations between people and the brute materiality of the natural world, with their sense of the importance of tradition. For a field whose object of study has often been encapsulated in the phrase "land and life," the consequences for the natural world of becoming "a sucked orange" must be of vital concern. Doughty expresses this concern, and his conclusion that "comprehension of an ontological relationship between God, man, and the natural order in post-Newtonian cosmology discovers a creative purpose in reality" is a teleological statement addressing the need recognized by Ricoeur to keep ideology in balance with utopia. It also brings us full circle, for it is just such a comprehension (although decidedly *pre*-Newtonian in the case of Ovid) that is expressed in the *Metamorphoses*. In classical myth, however, unlike in Christianity, the creative purpose is never revealed (the Fates never show their hand), which may be one reason for the continued and even renewed fascination with myth within our contemporary fragmented culture. The creative power of the poetic imagination to transform the meaning of the world both mythically and materially remains undimmed, so that perhaps metamorphosis is the only constant in the fluctuating equations of cultural geography.

NOTES

1. I first commented on these difficulties in my paper "Place, Landscape and the Dialectics of Cultural Geography" (Cosgrove 1978) and elaborated some of the arguments in "Towards a Radical Cultural Geography: Problems of Theory" (Cosgrove 1983). In the period since these papers appeared there has been a marked revival of theoretical debate within cultural geography. Something of this debate is summarized by P. Jackson (1989) and Duncan (1990). The editors' introduction to this volume further summarizes and contextualizes this debate.

2. Philip L. Wagner (1972) was among the first to call attention to the centrality of communication in cultural geography; Duncan's *The City as Text* (1990) adopts an explicitly linguistic explanatory model.

3. Yi-Fu Tuan has given considerable attention to cross-cultural similarities and differences in the signification of nature and environment in numerous texts (Tuan 1974b; 1977; 1979a; 1984; 1986).

4. Edward Said's (1978) "orientalist" thesis has been enormously influential in what has come to be called the

postcolonial debate, which now extends to the interpretation of European response to non-European cultures generally, not merely those of the "mysterious East." See, for example, Driver (1992).

5. The discussion in this section draws heavily on Frye's (1982, 108) interpretation.

6. The mandala is the earliest and most consistently cross-cultural symbol of both city and cosmos (Tuan 1974b, 17–18). On the mandala as archetype see Jung (1968).

7. For an extended study of the relationships between geometry and landscape see Cosgrove (1992).

8. On the contemporary urban landscape see Baudrillard (1988) and Harvey (1989, 66–98).

V
FUTURE WORLDS OF CULTURAL GEOGRAPHY

KENNETH E. FOOTE **27**

INTRODUCTION

The previous sections of this book have explored cultural geography in terms of component themes and key issues. They have, in a sense, deconstructed the subdiscipline and traced the genealogy of its formative concepts and ideas. Now is the time to reconstruct the subdiscipline, to consider cultural geography again as a whole. Such reassessment is particularly important because cultural geography is clearly more than the sum of its parts: it thrives on the interplay of many and varied ideas. In their commentaries, Miles Richardson, James Parsons, and Denis Cosgrove all alluded to the excitement of being free to range across disciplinary and interdisciplinary boundaries in pursuit of new ideas and fresh insights. These last essays make this point explicit: cultural geography is a subdiscipline of synthesis, one capable of addressing the central issues of contemporary geography in innovative ways.

In the essays that follow, James Duncan, Karl Butzer, Kit Salter, and Marvin Mikesell reflect on this point in different ways. The essays move, so to speak, from the inside out—from the internal coherence of the subdiscipline, to the position of cultural geography within the discipline, and finally to assessments of its position in the intellectual world at large. Duncan begins by arguing that cultural geography can no longer be viewed as a subdiscipline in the strict sense of the term. For Duncan, cultural geography—like many other contemporary disciplines—is characterized less by a common, unifying intellectual project than by the juxtaposition of disparate and occasionally conflicting programs of research. Duncan applies Foucault's term *heterotopia* to this situation, to cultural geography as an intellectual arena distinguished less by similarity than by difference. Yet in Duncan's view, even if cultural geography has become more akin to a loose federation of intellectual homelands, the differences that divide are also the differences that bind; they deserve to be celebrated accordingly.

Butzer calls attention to the fact that, if cultural geographers really attend to the implications of their own research, then they must rethink their curricula. The pressing issues of today's world are not well addressed within academia. They are forced to fit disciplinary boundaries that were defined in the late nineteenth century and have changed little since. Forcing students to define themselves and their research in terms of these out-dated categories does nothing to cultivate the talents that will be needed of tomorrow's geographers, cultural or otherwise. These scholars must have a facility in many methodologies and a ready familiarity with issues that crosscut all the social sciences and branch into the natural sciences and humanities as well. Butzer proposes one possible outline of the curriculum he envisions, one based on examples that demonstrate precisely why new departures are needed. Although Butzer's syllabus is of necessity only a first approximation rooted in his own interests and experiences, it must be considered as a challenge to all geographers to profess in the classroom what they practice in the field.

Salter, too, is concerned with education, but from a far different perspective. His point is that geography should look outward from the discipline to the world. Geographers have at their disposal fundamental pedagogical tools that help

students, and a broader public audience, to discover, explore, and comprehend the world. Salter develops his ideas around the five fundamental themes of geography promulgated by the Association of American Geographers and the National Geographic Society, showing how each of these—location, place, human-environment interaction, movement, and regions—can be used to call attention to important dynamic processes affecting all peoples in all environments. Salter draws some of his insights and inspiration from literature—both fiction and nonfiction—and he uses quotations from these sources liberally in the article to show how geographers can reach out to a public larger than the one they are accustomed to addressing.

Finally, Mikesell uses his essay to range across the subdiscipline, touching on issues that relate to its internal coherence and to its position within geography and the intellectual world at large. Since the publication of *Readings in Cultural Geography* in 1962, Mikesell, perhaps better than any geographer, has kept abreast of the burgeoning literature of cultural geography. From his perspective, it is possible to discern continuity of interest in the changes that the subdiscipline has undergone in the past decade. Paradoxically, however, this continuity is expressed as much in persisting problems and unresolved issues as it is in unalloyed intellectual progress. For example, Mikesell notes that despite the proclivity of cultural geographers to pursue fieldwork all around the globe, the subdiscipline itself retains (or even cultivates) an air of monolingual provincialism. Also at issue are the important research topics identified years ago and still current today that have yet to attract concerted research efforts. Nonetheless, one cannot help but wonder whether cultural geography has always set off to do too much. Perhaps that is its strength and its attraction, now and for the next generation.

28

AFTER THE CIVIL WAR: RECONSTRUCTING CULTURAL GEOGRAPHY AS HETEROTOPIA

Anyone reading the literature would have to be unobservant not to have noticed that a civil war has been going on in cultural geography since the early 1980s. This struggle has largely, although not exclusively, had an intergenerational character, younger cultural geographers trained in the late 1970s and 1980s assailing the positions of an older generation trained in the 1950s and 1960s. Throughout this battle the older generation has been content to remain in their well-entrenched positions within the academy as the younger generation fired the occasional salvo at them to little apparent effect. The younger generation launched its attacks using an arsenal of theory-seeking weapons provided by suppliers in the humanities and social sciences. Some direct hits were scored on the lightly camouflaged theories of the older generation, but such hits proved indecisive in the war for a number of reasons. Many of the older generation were unaware that they had any theories in their camp; others insisted that these were relic theories long since abandoned. Still others claimed that the theoretical targets had in fact been surreptitiously inserted into their camp by the younger generation to discredit them. At any rate, they argued that no meaningful losses had been sustained.

Whereas the older generation is overwhelmingly North American, the younger generation, although still predominantly North American, has been joined over the past few years by British social geographers who have, under the influence of British cultural studies, taken the "cultural turn" that is increasingly common in the social sciences (Philo 1991). To many of these new British recruits to cultural geography, unfamiliar as they are with traditional American cultural geography and having no cultural geographic tradition of their own, the intergenerational disputes that began the civil war in the 1980s appear as debates at "the farther reaches of human time." Consequently, they have focused their theoretical, methodological, and empirical attention on debates with other members of the younger generation, some of whom are seen as the old guard of the avant-garde.

It is perhaps ironic that a paper (M. Price and M. Lewis 1993) representing relief for the position of the older generation of traditional cultural geographers should arrive at a time when the seige of that position has been essentially lifted. It was lifted not out of a sense of victory or defeat but rather out of *ennui* and a realization of the debate's unprofitability. The intellectual patrimony of the new cultural geographies has become so diffuse that many younger geographers see rebelling against a particular patriarch as increasingly obsessive and irrelevant.

But I get ahead of myself; at least, I get ahead of what I believe to be the intent of this volume. For this book does not so much address the debates within the new cultural geography as it attempts to resolve the civil war between the generations and thus restore unity to the subfield. It argues for unity on the basis of a common genealogy.[1] The first strand of this genealogy is the existence of this volume, which is quite self-consciously the successor to Wagner and Mikesell's (1962) *Readings in Cultural Geography,* that superb summary of the first forty years of cultural geography in the United States and tribute to the influence of Carl Sauer on the eve of his retirement. The second strand argues for a unity on the basis of the continuity of certain themes transcending the intergenerational divisions that have rent the subfield over the past decade.

The editors of this volume have charged me with reflecting on the internal coherence of the subdiscipline and considering how unity may be achieved. But how is one to talk about unity in a field that has, in the editors' own words, exploded beyond its traditional boundaries? How does one speak of unity when cultural geography is no longer an exclusively American project? Can one fruitfully speak of unity when young British cultural geographers do not share the American genealogy that the editors of this volume outline? I, for one, cannot. Further, I believe unity to be a highly problematic modernist goal that might profitably be put aside. I say this not because I wish to revive old disputes but rather because I believe that the best way to deal with them is to admit that there exist real differences within the field that appeals to unity cannot mask. Furthermore, although the appeals for unity stem from a desire to end conflict, the whole idea of imposing unity in the face of diversity reflects the modernist will to order and discipline, to be governed under a master narrative. Perhaps what is necessary today is not simply the reluctant admission or even the willing acceptance of difference but its celebration. What I am suggesting is that we conceive of cultural geography not as a single contested space of power/knowledge but as a kind of epistemological heterotopia that, according to Foucault (1986, 25), "is capable of juxtaposing in a single real place several spaces, several sites that are in themselves incompatible."

This is not to suggest, as the anthropologist Robin Fox once did, that disciplines are held together by little other than sentiment and dynastic interest, although cultural geography has displayed both in good measure. Rather, it is to argue that contemporary cultural geography, like so many disciplines at present, is no longer as much an intellectual site in the sense of sharing a common intellectual project as it is an institutional site containing significant epistemological differences. Such a rationale, however, moves us away from the Enlightenment project and one of its institutional mainstays: the "disciplinary" structure of the modern university. Although most cultural geographers still embrace the modernist project of unity, the subject matter of the field resists, fragments, breaks away into plurality and difference, with multiple futures shaped by multiple pasts. The "blurred genres" about which Geertz (1983, 19–35) wrote so eloquently over a decade ago are perhaps nowhere more in evidence than in cultural geography today. As a cultural geographer I applaud this richness and in the spirit of a fledgling postmodernism suggest that we celebrate it rather than attempt to discipline it.

DISCIPLINING CULTURAL GEOGRAPHY: TAXONOMIC SHIFTS

Many of the disputes that occurred in cultural geography during the 1980s are associated with the broader taxonomic shifts that have been underway within human geography since the 1970s.[2] During the 1980s these shifts posed a series of challenges to the subfield's dominant structure. This taxonomic structure is most cogently laid out by Wagner and Mikesell in their introduction to *Readings*. The mandate of the subfield, they argue (1962, 1), is to describe and classify typical complexes of environmental features that coincide with cultural communities, to explore the histories of these complexes, and to study cultural ecology, the process by which humans manipulate their environments. They identify five key themes that structure the subfield: culture, culture area, cultural landscape, culture history, and cultural ecology.

The concept of culture is used primarily as a classificatory schema to divide people into well-defined groups and also to classify space into culture areas (1962, 2). Culture, then, is used in a descriptive fashion rather than as an analytical concept or object of study. Wagner and Mikesell (1962, 5) are quite clear about how the geographer should approach culture:

> The cultural geographer is not concerned with explaining the inner workings of culture or with describing fully patterns of human behavior, even when they affect the land, but rather with assessing the technical potential of human communities for using and modifying their habitats. In order to achieve such an assessment, cultural geography studies the distribution in time and space of cultures and elements of cultures.

Cultural geographers are encouraged to show only limited interest in cultural or social processes, even when these directly affect the land. Instead, they should concentrate primarily on patterns on the land—the study of cultural distributions in time and space. By investigating the past and present distribution of culture traits either singly or as complexes, geographers can then go on to identify and delimit culture areas "characterized by relative internal homogeneity in regard to certain criteria" (1962, 9). Because of the geographer's orientation to the land, the culture area "is always also a 'cultural landscape'" (1962, 9). The cultural landscape serves to indicate the impact of culture on the face of the earth. The methods used to study the effects of culture on landscape are as follows: "the plotting of single and joint distributions and densities of given features; the delimitation and comparison of regions by various criteria; the mapping of spatial arrangement and organization of complexes of related or connected features; the charting of movements; the identification of physical and biotic zonation" (1962, 12). What these methods all point to is the study of pattern rather than process. According to Wagner and Mikesell, cultural geography studies the distribution of objects on the face of the earth. They claim, however, that this distribution of objects into culture areas must be understood historically, as cultural landscapes are built up over time. The geographer must then adopt a culture history perspective in order to discover "the origin in time and place of given cultural features; the routes, times, and manner of their dissemination; the distribution of former culture areas; and the character of former cultural landscapes" (1962, 15).

The editors further claim that the study of the history of cultural landscapes requires a close cooperation between cultural and physical geography (1962, 17), which brings us to their final theme, cultural ecology. Wagner and Mikesell distinguish between cultural history and cultural ecology as follows: the former deals with the sequence of events that leads to the creation of a cultural landscape, whereas the latter "concerns the process implied in a sequence of events" (1962, 19). Examples of processes to be studied are the links between farming practices and soil degradation and those between "technologically simple cultures" and their environments (1962, 20).

Wagner and Mikesell conclude by arguing that the cultural ecology perspective cannot be effectively applied to "Western commercial cultures" (1962, 22). Presumably, since the whole emphasis of the cultural ecology perspective (at least as they have outlined it) is on modes of livelihood such as farming or hunting and gathering, it has little to say about societies where most of the inhabitants have other occupations. In fact, the authors go further still when they argue that, "because of the difficulty of applying the cultural concept to the study of such complex communities—so far, at any rate—geographers have had to deal with them in a different manner and have had to develop economic and technological, rather than cultural, concepts as research tools" (1962, 22–23). The message appears to be that if cultural geographers have any interest in process, then (*a*) those processes lie at the interface of cultural and physical geography, (*b*) the processes should be applied to livelihood systems, and (*c*) they must be studied in the rural sectors of Third World societies.

This taxonomic structure outlined by Wagner and Mikesell defined the discipline of cultural geography for its practitioners. But what of a new generation of cultural geographers who wished to write a different cultural geography? Could they operate within the taxonomy? Was their research to be disciplined by this same structure? It is to this question that I wish now to turn.

I have stressed the importance of taxonomic structure because I believe that it was this hegemonic epistemic order that forced the rupture of cultural geography in the 1980s. I say hegemonic because within America, cultural geography was exclusively associated with this structure. By this I mean that anyone who claimed to be a cultural geographer was simply assumed to do *this* particular kind of work. In the face of this hegemonic structure a number of young cultural geographers sought to create space for alternative cultural geographies associated with intellectual currents such as humanism, Marxism, and various other forms of critical theory running through geography at the time. This was attempted by engaging in theoretical critique of the reigning practice while offering theoretical,

methodological, and taxonomic alternatives to that practice.

To begin to understand the shifts in cultural geography in the 1980s we have to move both beyond the subdiscipline and back in time. The 1950s and 1960s were a time of major change within geography. The spatial analytical movement, which traced its intellectual roots to an early twentieth-century analytical philosophy of science, challenged descriptive regional, and to a lesser extent cultural, geography, which was based on a nineteenth-century natural history model of science. Cultural geography withstood this challenge better than regional geography did, in large part because of the strength of the intellectual project championed by Carl Sauer and codified by Wagner and Mikesell.

However, although spatial analysis posed a genuine challenge to both functionalist regional geography and genetic cultural geography, it shared with them a prioritization of the visual and a commitment to the spatial—an overarching concern with mappable patterns of concrete phenomena.

It is for this reason that the 1970s marked another epistemological shift, in some respects even more fundamental than those of the 1950s and 1960s. Perhaps David Harvey's disavowal in the early 1970s of his book *Explanation in Geography* (1969), and by extension of the whole spatial analytical project, stands as a synecdoche for this new challenge. During the 1970s spatial analysis was under attack by Marxists on the one hand and by humanistic geographers on the other. Even behavioral geographers entered the fray in a kind of autocritique of positivism. The spatial analysts were criticized primarily because they viewed the field as a spatial science rather than as a social science. These critics saw the focus on spatial patterning and the "black-boxing" of both the individual and the sociocultural and political-economic contexts as highly problematic. The mystique of spatial theory was replaced for these critics by the allure of social theory, whether it be Marxism, phenomenology, or behavioralism. These critiques, although not specifically directed at cultural geography, were nevertheless felt to apply to the subfield, for it, too, was heavily engaged in pattern analysis and had quite explicitly chosen to disavow interest in process except as it directly related to cultural ecology.

The 1970s were also a time when many young geographers sought to steer the field in the direction of "social relevance," which within the context of North American geography primarily meant a focus on contemporary social problems in urban North America. This again put many young cultural geographers at odds with the discursive structure of a cultural geography that explicitly confessed a paucity of analytical tools for studying contemporary urban Western societies (see Wagner and Mikesell 1962, 22–23).

In retrospect, the problem with this attempt by young cultural geographers to create a space for difference within the old taxonomic structure of cultural geography lay not so much in the substance of what was said, for there was much merit in their critiques, but in the fact that it never questioned the idea of the unity of the field. By working within the same discourse of unity as did traditional cultural geographers, the new cultural geographers[3] were forced to try to substitute a hegemony of the new for that of the old; for unity, as I stated earlier, tries to discipline difference, to smooth over incompatibilities in the name of a hegemonic order.[4] The goal of unity necessarily implies domination. I will not, therefore, offer a new and better set of taxonomic constraints or causal variables for the new cultural geography, as Wagner and Mikesell did for the old; rather, I will suggest strong lines of difference within cultural geography now so prominent that they can be used to define it. These differences, which stem on the one hand from the rapid expansion of cultural geographic inquiry into the other social sciences and humanities and on the other from the incorporation of a large British contingent with a different intellectual genealogy,[5] have, whether we recognize it or not, transformed the subfield into a heterotopia (a site of incompatible discourses). The following are some categories around which such difference is structured. These categories crosscut each other in complex ways, and the work of various researchers may intersect in different ways with them, but the result is the production of incommensurable discourses.

EMPIRICISM AND THEORY

This remains one of the most divisive issues in cultural geography today, not only because of the old association of theory with the attacks of the spatial analysts in the 1950s and 1960s on empiricism but also because a critique of theoretical weakness was used as a basis for dismissing traditional cultural geography in the 1980s. In fact, I believe that valuable work can be produced both by empirically minded cultural geographers who make no attempt to theorize their research explicitly and by theoretically minded ones who have little interest in conducting their own empirical research.[6] Furthermore, even among the theoretically minded there is no consensus on what constitutes appropriate theory and whether it should be developed with reference to the social sciences or the humanities. To complicate matters further, there is little agreement at present on what subject matter should be theorized.

Cultural geography has been divided not only because its practitioners cannot agree on whether they should ever let the theoretical base of empirical work go unarticulated but also because they have wandered into other fields, returning with alternative research questions and new objects of study, new methodologies, and new vocabularies. The new objects of study include the philosophical, political, and rhetorical aspects of the very act of representing the world and the cultural, class, or gendered positionality of the researcher.

The introduction of new vocabularies that are unfamiliar to traditional cultural geographers is one of the surest signs that the subfield has become a heterotopia. Differences in language, far from being an attempt to say the same old thing in different words, represent the construction of entirely different objects of study. This is particularly difficult for traditional cultural geographers to grasp because of their continuing attachment to the idea of theory-neutral, value-free, "given" objects out there in the world. The new vocabulary is sometimes dismissed as simply constituting the private, idiosyncratic language of a small group of geographers. Although such an interpretation may be politically useful in marginalizing subgroups and disciplining difference, it

*self styled radical
yet entirely polar. around
issue of nature/culture?*

fails to capture the import of language shifts. Far from being private languages, these are widely shared languages uniting a group of geographers to specialists in other fields (for example, deconstructive literary theorists or practitioners of neo-Marxist cultural studies) who share a common set of research questions, methods, language, and objects of study. Problems of incompatible language also arise from the traditional geographers' attachment to binary oppositions such as *objective/subjective* or *concrete/abstract,* whereas the taxonomic structure of new cultural geography effectively rejects such distinctions. There exist in cultural geography today different vocabularies because the field is heterotopic and connections are, therefore, often much stronger between fields than within them.

CULTURAL PATTERN AND CULTURAL PROCESS

There are divisions here over the extent to which cultural geographers should be concerned with process. Whereas for Wagner and Mikesell the study of process was largely the concern of cultural ecologists, this is no longer the case. At present, although some researchers continue to be concerned primarily with mapping patterns of culture alone, others feel that cultural geographers should be concerned with cultural process, but only as long as those processes explicitly affect or are affected by landscape, place, or space. There are still others, many of them British (see Philo 1991), who believe that cultural geographers should study cultural process irrespective of whether it is directly concerned with landscape, place, or space. We have, in other words, at present within the subfield a range of inquiry stretching from those who study patterns of objects in space without reference to cultural process to those who study cultural process without reference to space, place, or landscape. The links between these are at best tenuous.

THE ''NATURAL'' AND THE CULTURAL ENVIRONMENT

Here again we must admit a bifurcation between those cultural geographers for whom the "natural" environment is important and those for whom it is not. If one is studying farming systems in Mexico, then it is clear that a knowledge

of physical geography is required. If, however, one is studying carnival in London or postmodern architecture in Vancouver, then a knowledge of physical geography is clearly irrelevant. This is not to suggest that farming systems in Mexico and carnivals in London are in any way opposed to each other or more or less important as objects of study; they are simply and irremediably different in the sense that they are unrelated. This split between a cultural geography that is centrally concerned with the "natural" environment and one that is not has become institutionalized within the Association of American Geographers by the creation of separate specialty groups for cultural ecology and cultural geography.[7]

WAYS OF LIFE AND LIFESTYLES

Much of traditional cultural geography is concerned with studying the ways of life of agricultural communities in the Third World, which produce relatively little material surplus. As such they focus on patterns of work (the economic) and the infrastructure (housing, etc.) necessary to reproduce the community. The new cultural geographers, in spite of periodic self-admonitions for not paying more attention to economic production, tend to be more concerned with lifestyle issues in First World cities. Predominant concerns are with consumption styles, on the one hand, and class, ethnic, and gender relations, on the other. Again, what is striking is the incommensurability of the projects.

THE THIRD WORLD AND THE FIRST WORLD

Although I have already alluded to this difference, it bears repeating, for it marks one of the major shifts in contemporary cultural geography. The traditional focus of cultural geography on subsistence economies in the rural Third World has been replaced in the new cultural geography by the study of consumption-based identities in First World cities and suburbs. When new cultural geographers do turn their attention to Third World peoples, it is usually in one of two ways: first, by engaging in theoretical debates over the relationship between the Euro-American "self" and the "other" in colonial or postcolonial societies rather than actually doing research in Third World societies; and second, by studying the peoples of other cultural backgrounds living in First World cities. My point is that there is an important difference between the approaches of traditional and new cultural geographers to non-Western cultures. Traditional cultural geographers have been genuinely fascinated by the "otherness" of other cultures, for example, by the manner in which individuals in other cultures earn their livelihood and the materials they use to construct their dwellings. Although one might judge this interest to be a kind of nostalgic romanticism about the rural Third World, a "world we have lost" in the industrialized West, it nevertheless represents an interest in foreign cultures themselves. On the other hand, one cannot help but feel that many of the new cultural geographers are fascinated not with other cultures per se but with their own culture and its problematic relationship with the cultures over which it has had representational power. One could even argue that their interest is not driven by a nostalgic romanticism but by a desire to salve the conscience of Western intellectuals for their predecessors' imperialism.

CELEBRATING DIFFERENCE

In conclusion, like the editors of this volume, I applaud the end of the civil war that has caused such ill will in cultural geography over the past decade. I do so, however, not because we have much in common but because the projects that characterize contemporary cultural geography are so disparate that there is very little over which to quarrel.

This volume can be seen as a draft of a peace treaty between the warring factions in the subfield. The editors have suggested one set of terms for the peace, and I another. For them, the commonality of interest and perspective that remains among cultural geographers is sufficient to reconstruct the divided nation of cultural geography as a coherent whole. I, on the other hand, suggest a set of terms that recognize that cultural geography has become much more akin to a state than to a nation; furthermore, it is a state composed of semiautonomous provinces for which the center is little more than an administrative structure for the distribution of academic resources. Let me sum up why I believe this to be

the case. The taxonomic structure of the subdiscipline that Wagner and Mikesell confidently outlined thirty years ago depended on a shared intellectual genealogy. Following the changes that took place in cultural geography during the 1980s, such a shared genealogy no longer exists. Rather than figuring this lack of unity as loss, I suggest we see it as an intellectual gain, for the cultural geography that Wagner and Mikesell codified still thrives in the United States and has been supplemented by a new cultural geography that has a very different contribution to make.

It might appear to the unwary that I am advocating a position of uncritical relativism in this essay. This would be a serious misunderstanding of my position. My point is that cultural geography is best conceived of as an epistemological heterotopia and that we must come to terms with the implications of this increasingly common condition within academia. An important part of this coming to terms is to realize that the norm of a "master" discourse, able to establish an intellectual unity, is illusory. We cannot posit one method or taxonomic structure against which all cultural geography can be measured; rather, what we have are "sites of difference," each with its own discourse linked to similar sites in other fields in the humanities and social sciences. Those cultural geographers and others within the interlinked network of sites must critically reflect on their own and others' intellectual practices. However, none of those who occupy the "incompatible sites" within the subfield should be excluded. I argue this on the grounds that there is a world of difference between being incompatible and being wrong.

ACKNOWLEDGMENTS

The author wishes to thank Nancy Duncan, Joanne Sharp, Jonathan Smith, and Judy Walton for their critical reading of earlier drafts of this paper.

NOTES

1. I use *genealogy* here simply in the sense of ancestry rather than in a Foucauldian or Nietzschean sense, although I certainly concur with Foucault that systems of ideas are inextricably bound up with sets of power relations.

2. I use the term *taxonomy* here to refer to that which is seen to be the proper subject matter (objects of study, analytical categories) of a field of study.

3. I do not intend in this essay to reify the categories "old" and "new" cultural geography. I recognize that the new cultural geography is quite heterogeneous and very much in a state of flux and critical self-examination. Although it is possible to state what some of the newly constituted and reconstituted objects of investigation are, it is not possible to say what might be excluded as potential objects of study or potential ways of theoretically delineating shifting categories. This may be in part because of a refusal by some to be constrained by disciplinary boundaries, however constituted.

4. One of the practical reasons why different groups struggle over the possession of subdisciplinary labels is that academia allocates social and economic rewards to those who have proven themselves to have a "legitimate" claim to the disciplinary structures. It is, therefore, much simpler to create space for a new cultural geography by displacing a portion of the old than by attempting to create a new subdiscipline and convincing the profession to allocate resources to it.

5. See Philo (1991) for a statement of the intellectual antecedents of the British cultural geographers. Most of them look to Raymond Williams, John Berger, the Birmingham school of cultural studies, and social geography for their sources of inspiration. The American tradition of cultural geography that Wagner and Mikesell outline, although known to the British geographers, is seen as of little relevance to their interests. A few British cultural geographers, such as Denis Cosgrove and Stephen Daniels, however, are of a more mid-Atlantic mindset, being influenced both by British cultural studies and by the landscape tradition in American cultural geography.

6. I should of course still caution those who do not articulate their theoretical position that there are various dangers in remaining silent.

7. There are some exceptions to the general trend among new cultural geographers away from studies of the natural environment (for example, see Cosgrove and Daniels 1988; Philo 1991, 25; Katz 1991; Katz and Kirby 1991). However, in the cases where relations between the natural environment and human beings are the focus of attention, the natural environment is usually seen as culturally constructed.

KARL W. BUTZER **29**

TOWARD A CULTURAL
CURRICULUM FOR THE FUTURE:
A FIRST APPROXIMATION

DO WE NEED A NEW CURRICULUM?

Geography, like the other social sciences, is in a state of flux. A remarkably open spirit of inquiry prevails as geographers explore nondogmatic and flexible blends of ideas and methodologies in their research. Our meetings provide a forum for increasingly diverse sessions and papers, and our journals present ever more articles of a less inhibited, interdisciplinary bent. Although fewer geographers feel comfortable with subdisciplinary labels, most continue to find common ground within a discipline that has become, for them, more versatile and interesting.

The fashionable interpretation of this situation is to posit a paradigmatic shift, in which the prevailing atmosphere of "postmodernism" represents a backlash to the excesses of an earlier uncompromising social-science positivism ("modernism"). But such labels, drawn originally from architectural history, provide imperfect analogs for the social sciences. Also, many casual users of terms such as *modern* and *postmodern* are not really aware of how complex (and loaded) those concepts are. Another reservation is that Kuhn's (1962) paradigm shifts involved change over far longer time intervals and were intended to describe far more fundamental change—such as the Copernican Revolution. Such shifts are uncharacteristic of the social sciences, which seem incapable of achieving paradigmatic consensus and which have responded to governmental or economic opportunities as often as they have been shaped by intellectual imperatives.

An alternative interpretation is to explain the ferment in the social sciences as a reaction to anachronistic disciplinary agendas. The current pervasive dissatisfaction with these agendas seems rooted in the fact that the social sciences diverged into separate disciplines during the late 1800s, and the boundaries that emerged then were fortuitous, to some degree arbitrary, and most certainly far removed from today's concerns. The division of intellectual labor represented a compromise between (*a*) the centrifugal or centripetal role of key personalities; (*b*) the cumulative impact of countless major and minor decisions by administrators in leading institutions; and (*c*) the interests of a literate public that strongly influenced government, university, and private-donor decisions to support specific research or academic appointments in new fields.

In the case of geography, despite the influence of exemplars such as Ritter and Humboldt, the creation of the discipline was primarily a matter of expediency, a response to public interest in colonial exploration, settlement expansion, and geopolitical goals. Like all the other new disciplines taking shape between 1885 and 1910, geography thrived on this diet. The Great Depression led, perhaps, to a modest retraction, but since the 1940s geography has responded continually, and all too willingly, to the exigencies of polity and economy. From military service in the 1940s, Cold War intelligence gathering in the 1950s, and economic development and market analysis in the 1960s and 1970s, geography has consistently turned to where the money is.

With hindsight, it seems almost ironic that *Man's Role in Changing the Face of the Earth* (Thomas 1956) found its way into print. This landmark volume, inspired by Carl O. Sauer, was so much ahead of its time that it assumed, at best, an uncomfortable place in the geography curriculum of the period. Its message ran counter to the illusion of inexorable progress, fed by steady economic growth and technological prowess, that by then formed the core of geography's research agenda. Given the uneasy welcome accorded *Man's Role in Changing the Face of the Earth,* it was of little surprise that Earth Day of 1970 caught the discipline totally unprepared— and unable—to train young professionals with the biophysical competence to deal with environmental issues. But the first Earth Day represented more than geography's loss of a unique opportunity to lead in matters of the human use of the earth resources; it signaled the start of a period of increasing economic stringency.

A change in United States tax laws sapped private-sector research funding, and the first oil embargo ended an economic boom. As geology and biology introduced innovative environmental courses, geography's general science enrollments were eroded. Universities stabilized their social science faculties, and most geography departments, unable to increase their enrollments, had to face retrenchment. Government funding of social science research barely matched the rate of inflation, and opportunities for foreign field study began to decline.

Geography was, of course, not alone in this predicament, but the resulting flux was much more than the reversal of the intellectual pendulum implied by postmodernism. It is better diagnosed as a crisis of self-confidence, a questioning of disciplinary purpose and goals. After decades of opportunistic distortion of academic ideals, the social sciences have begun to accept the realities of no-growth and to reevaluate their curricula and research priorities. Geography, perhaps better than most of its interrelated fields, has recognized the cost of insularity and turned outward, displaying a new appetite for an eclectic menu of long-neglected themes.

More than at any other time in its history, geography now appears disposed to listen to what the increasingly diverse culture-interested professionals have to say. Consequently, this volume has an unusual opportunity not to proselytize but to inform students about cultural themes and issues, many of which have been glossed over in the traditional curriculum. Ideally, it will open a fruitful discourse that will help to bring geography back into the intellectual mainstream. To achieve that, I believe we must begin to grapple vigorously with major contemporary issues on a broad front, irregardless of how they are conventionally partitioned among the social sciences, irrespective of how they are studied by other social scientists. The well-trained geographer must be free and able to pursue research across any intellectual frontier and beyond the entrenched positions of today's social sciences without being challenged at every disciplinary guardpost. And our curriculum must equip students with the skills and confidence needed to reconnoiter this terrain.

DEVISING A CULTURAL CURRICULUM

How does one develop a curriculum for the future when research is cheerfully diverging along new trajectories with little consensus? Ideally, one convenes a so-called Renaissance Weekend, with a few days for several dozen people to talk it out. That would not—and should not—lead to a unified master plan of some sort. More productive and more realistic would be a variety of different agendas that would serve to provoke creativity and innovation. Such alternative visions should emphasize conceptual questions and major issues rather than lists of nuts-and-bolts methods.

Any statement should also be constructive, explaining the nature of shared premises and drawing attention to potential intersections with related methodologies. We would, of course, express our personal convictions, but in a manner that does not belittle the intelligence or motivation of others who espouse different perspectives or arrange their priorities differently. Geography has far too long been inhibited by its old orthodoxies; it cannot now afford to proscribe new ones. The next generations of students should be able to choose from an attractive menu of options, both in regard to the range of cultural themes and with respect to particular research methodologies.

An essay such as this can only offer an example of how one such curriculum proposal might be developed. Of necessity, it must be a personal statement, reflecting the experience, interests, and views of one individual. To begin, however, I want to call attention to a number of the most pressing problems of the next ten to thirty years: (*a*) the consequences of exponential demographic growth; (*b*) finite global resources and an endangered environment; (*c*) unequal allocation of resources, both between world regions and within most societies; (*d*) ethnic strife and political instability; and (*e*) replacement of culturally homogeneous societies by ones with increasing cultural, ethnic, or racial diversity. There probably is widespread agreement about the gravity of these problems, however they are formulated, but there will be substantial differences of opinion about whether or how to approach them professionally. The general assumption is that culture-interested geographers, like many other social scientists, have contributions to make in dealing with these general problems through analysis and formulation, understanding and education, or policy making and implementation.

The next step is to use these concerns to illustrate a methodology. My choice, for reasons of interest and experience, must be cultural ecology, but to illustrate my points effectively, I must first make clear the domain and substance of this methodology. The nuances of cultural ecology are too easily and too often misconstrued; they deserve a brief exposition in this context.

CULTURAL ECOLOGY: ONE POSSIBLE METHODOLOGY

Cultural ecology identifies an interdisciplinary arena of research that has rapidly attracted interest during the last few years (Butzer 1989). Although individual interests and methods vary widely, geographers and anthropologists, as well as a few sociologists and historians, have found cultural ecology to offer substantial common ground. Its practitioners as often as not consider it to be a perspective or a methodology rather than a subfield in its own right. There even is disagreement about the name itself, some preferring *human ecology, political ecology,* or *ecological anthropology.* But regardless of the labels, there is a fairly coherent methodology here when the different approaches are brought together and given a more humanistic cast. Its primary purpose and value in the present context are heuristic. As a didactic device it will serve students and outsiders well.

Cultural ecology focuses on four themes—

subsistence, work, reproduction, and resources—and the interrelationships between them, as embedded in the rules and values of a particular society (Butzer 1990b). The final qualifier is critical because it raises the relationship into human terms, emphasizing that people are mentalistic beings, although with animal needs. Cultural ecology must at some level include the reconciliation between mind and body. It is in this sense that there is dichotomy between people and nature—they are one, but they also are apart or different.

Cultural ecologists today deal with their subject matter at several levels, of which the most basic is the *functional*. Here the emphasis is positivist, with both systemic and processual perspectives (Knapp 1991). The first emphasizes cultural strategies as they are interlinked via feedback and influenced by a measure of economic rationalization. The second emphasizes cultural processes that affect continuity or change, such as routine or larger-scale adaptations, innovations, information diffusion, or migration. The functionalist approach initially focuses on food production, demography, and resource sustainability, taking a systemic view of the interconnections between society and nature. Typical themes include dietary, technological, settlement, reproductive, and maintenance strategies; energy and information flows, including feedback loops; and decision making and alternative options and outcomes. Empirical detail is essential to allow plausible links between conclusions and a data base. Given the prominent role of resources and resource management in this approach, functionalist cultural ecology requires considerable expertise in biophysical geography and offers an important integrative opportunity for physical and cultural expertise or, in prehistoric contexts, for geoarchaeology and anthropological archaeology. Functionalist cultural ecologists do not attempt to predict outcomes, although they may offer probability estimates; they explicitly recognize a multiplicity of social, economic, and environmental factors in understanding decision making and problem solving, and they view cultural adaptation as a reflection of human creativity.

The *behavioral* approach of cultural ecology represents a higher level of analysis that is postprocessual and nonnormative in spirit, although it builds on normative appreciation. The premise is that decision making and the selection of alternative strategies or solutions are based on community choices anchored in traditional values as much as they are on economic rationalization (Butzer 1990b). People spend as much mental energy focussing on interpersonal relationships as they do worrying about their livelihood—which is part of the constant tension between personal needs and social responsibilities. Behaviorist cultural ecologists incorporate (*a*) the dialectic of the individual and the community; (*b*) the interplay of individual and collective decisions in management, crisis mitigation, or fundamental change; and (*c*) the encoding of past experience in communal institutions and values as transmitted through several levels of social solidarity, such as family, community, society, ethnicity, or nation.

Individual initiative, actions, goal conflicts, and unpredictability constitute potential agents for change, especially as they are informed and screened through institutions or ideologies and resisted or implemented through community behavior. At this level the role of culture can be compared with a social contract. Food acquires symbolic meaning while significant actions are ideally taken in the context of the past ("who we are"), the present ("what we need"), and the future ("what we preserve for our grandchildren"). This form of cultural ecology requires more intensive person-on-person field research than its functionalist counterpoint; it is dependent on a degree of "insider" understanding of perceptions, attitudes, beliefs, and mental processes.

The *structuralist* perspective shifts from the community to the socioeconomic or sociopolitical context in which individuals or communities make decisions. The scale of study is augmented and the focus is no longer inward, on how the community thinks and acts in an idealized microcosm, but outward, on how the community's decisions are constrained by the structures of the real world (Hecht and Cockburn 1989; M. Watts 1983b). In the traditional rural world, tenant farmers and day laborers have limited access to land, credit, or markets, just as migrant labor in the world of agribusiness has limited access to education, health care, and social services. In cities past and present, the urban poor or ethnic minorities are similarly limited in their access to jobs, amenities, or social advancement. In Third World countries, rural communities, if they are to have access to markets and services, are pressured to produce export crops rather than staples at the recurrent risk of subsistence stress, and landless farmers may be obliged to move to the frontiers of "development," clearing virgin forests or working as peons on large estates. Alternatively, ethnic or religious refugees are confined to rural slums after they have fled from the arbitrary use of force, chronic insecurity, or brutal expulsion. These are examples of marginalized communities that do not have the luxury of making informed decisions in conformity with deeper-seated values; typically, they have little or no choice and opt for short-term survival. This vision of a less benign world not governed by traditional cultural values is the realm of "political ecology." It emphasizes different dialectics between technology and development, productive sector and multinationals, and who gains and who loses.

These three forms of cultural ecology embrace distinctive questions, subjects, methodologies, and insights. They are complementary to one another, presenting different windows on the same subject matter. A good comprehension of one facilitates the study of another, and functionalist perspectives now are commonly combined with either a behaviorist or structuralist investigation. Different skills and predilections serve to steer students into particular directions, but despite the differences of personalities and philosophies, all continue to profit from exchange in the periodic markets of ideas.

The methodology outlined here emphasizes microstudy. However, the aggregate experience provided by productive case studies (within and without cultural ecology) can and should be directed to more deductive examinations of macroproblems.

I have now laid the groundwork for drafting a curriculum. The five broad themes outlined below are not predicated on cultural ecology, although that methodology would be useful in several instances. The selection and formulation of these themes reflect my professional experience and personal convictions. The first theme presents a fine-grained focus on institutions, values, and change with reference to traditional societies or to institutional "blockage" and reform in contemporary society. The second uses the time-honored polemic concerning the interrelationships between cultural, economic, and political change to argue for instruction in how to conduct theory-informed research in a pragmatic spirit. The third is directed to the problems of ethnicity, dominance, socioeconomic stratification, and strife that threaten to tear apart whole societies. The fourth concerns managed environments, sustainability, and conservation. Finally, the fifth looks at long-wave population and political-economic cycles and how demographic growth, deteriorating resources, and anarchy have begun to bring pieces of our world system to the brink of devolution. These five examples will allow me to demonstrate ways of weaving the insights of geography around pressing contemporary concerns.

ADAPTIVE PROCESSES AND CHANGE

New ideas are conceived and implemented by individuals, but they must be screened and approved by the community through the media of institutions and values.

Institutions are more than churches, courthouses, and bureaucracies. They run through all components of society, from family, schools, and social networks to professional sodalities, government, and religious groups. They include practices, relationships, and organizations that define and channel overlapping spheres of sociocultural, economic, political, and ideological behavior. Institutions serve as mechanisms to store, transmit, and translate cultural information into behavioral and material form. They also reflect values, the body of shared beliefs that express and prescribe individual and group behavior as well as responsibilities. Values serve to legitimize and interpret institutions, but they are difficult to define unambiguously, so that perceptions of values vary from person to person; they are also liable to change over time.

Some changes do not interfere with established ways of doing things, but those that appear to contradict values and institutional structures depend on a gradual building of consensus. They may require mobilization in a broad social context, perhaps in the face of crisis, and remain difficult to implement without the initiative, sanction, and ritual assurance of leaders or religious institutions. Racial integration, voting rights for women, or a declaration of war provide examples. Although institutions and values constrain the range of acceptable behavior, they remain human constructs, subject to changing interpretations.

Cultural adaptation is a processual concept applied to such changes. It is useful to characterize adjustments in established practices as a response to new information, structural problems, or external crises. As people cope with social stresses and constraints or external challenges and opportunities, their adaptive strategies ideally would be adjusted to maintain a balance among population, resources, and productivity. To elaborate an earlier point, adaptive decisions are consciously made by individuals in the context of community institutions and values. Most such decisions are small-scale and continuing, a matter of equilibrium maintenance, but they may be painful in personal terms, such as choosing methods to limit reproduction. Others are episodic, such as short-term responses to natural disasters, wars, or epidemics. Some are more fundamental, however, involving technological and behavioral accommodations, with possible adoption or loss of new cultural traits, in response to changing markets, urbanization, or industrialization (Butzer 1982, 286–94; 1990b).

The formulation of adaptation used here avoids its inherited biological connotations, such as measures of adaptive "success" or its supposed role for homeostasis—as opposed to facilitating a dynamic equilibrium. In a cultural context, adaptation must incorporate a strong humanistic component. For example, when land runs out in an overpopulated rural village, young adults may be obliged to migrate to a distant city to find employment. At the aggregate level this may be an anomalous process or just a statistic; at the personal level it commonly is a traumatic experience. Emigration implies a loss of close relationships, of a place rooted with personal memories, and of a landscape rich in symbolic meaning. That emotional loss may translate into permanent scars, a lack of anchoring in traditional values, and a sense of placelessness in the tenements of an industrial city. Alternatively, expatriates in a distant urban center may band together as a substitute support network, wherein myths of an idealized rural background are shared, sustained by the hope that their own children may be able to spend a future vacation back on the old farm, now deserted or converted into a tourist home. How much more painful transatlantic migration must have been for poor immigrants to a foreign land, scrabbling their way through several generations to regain some self-respect, clinging pitifully to small vestiges of their ethnic heritage. Painful, too, is migration translated to a contemporary idiom: mobile Mexican farm families moving from one trailer camp to another. Change commonly has profound human dimensions, and these too should be studied and chronicled.

Small wonder that traditional societies are wary of any change impinging on institutions and values that encode a legacy of experience derived from trial and error. Continuity with the past not only fills a deep emotional need but also cautions against taking risk. Change is a crapshoot, and players may win or lose. The conservative solution is to avoid the risks, even if stasis implies continuing high infant mortality rates, malnutrition, and disease; indeed, the cumulative costs of conservatism may prove to be higher than those deemed possible with change. More progressive societies may opt for the improvements promised by change, regardless of the potential hidden costs. Consequently, in the case of diffusion studies, the most interesting questions are the reasons why people may reject change or, if they accept it, why and how they accommodate it.

Such an explicitly cultural and humanistic approach to adaptive change would add important dimensions to the study of process. It would cast the community dialectics of continuity and change as an intriguing challenge to be understood rather than as an unwelcome "black box" to be glossed over or ignored. Such tensions yield insights into the relationships between perceptions, attitudes, and behavior, as well as on the potential role of communities in the contemporary world. Attention to the dialectic between the individual and the community can be equally productive. Individualism can be a positive force for innovation or for resistance in adversity; it can also disrupt community cohesion or lead to the squandering of resources needed by future generations. That has profound implications for ideals and realities in ecological behavior. Last but not least there is the dialectic of specific gender roles and the question of the cultural, ecological, and biological roots of gender roles that has aroused considerable interest in a period of social change.

Such a fine-grained method of analytical disassembly is applicable to the institutional blockage (J. Bennett and Dahlberg 1990) that paralyzes so many governments today. Here the problems are of two kinds, individual and structural. First, elected representatives, as well as executives in government agencies, weigh their mandate to promote the common good against their own self-interest, especially as it is affected by the prospects of financial rewards and political pressure from vested interests capable of influencing their reelection. Bureaucracies, on the other hand, may be more interested in perpetuating themselves than in implementing directives for change. In the United States, some states have a history of demanding accountability, whereas others are equally notorious for corruption; the number of felony indictments among the appointees of successive federal administrations also varies sharply. Ethical standards in government tend to mirror the values of local societies or particular constituencies—a true challenge for reform. Second, the major structural problems impeding government responsiveness relate to scale. As the size of political systems expands, federal government tends to co-opt the functions of local and state administrations, which also are most likely to be controlled by entrenched interest groups. Concentration of power at the top tends to prescribe generic solutions for problems that are better dealt with in a particularistic context; at the same time, powers are subdivided horizontally as well as hierarchically, with functional specialization of agencies, resulting in competitive jurisdictions and institutional response that is divided rather than holistic (J. Bennett and Dahlberg 1990). As a result, overly centralized ("verticalized") governments consume too much energy while neutralizing information pathways; crises are seldom anticipated (reaction rather than action), and response to grass-roots initiative tends to remain nominal (Butzer 1980).

This simplified outline illustrates the vast differences of scale between community and government in regard to the challenges of adaptive change. The community remains the best referent of cooperative human behavior, whereas the insights and recommendations of research must ultimately be communicated and possibly implemented at the level of government.

It is precisely to bridge this gap that nongovernmental organizations (NGOs) have sprung up in many countries and continue to coalesce and grow, providing an intermediate level of informal institutionalization. These include progressive corporations (on the Japanese model) that promote genuine worker participation, provide welfare, and undertake environmental initiatives; volunteer organizations (such as the Sierra Club) that have graduated from watchdog groups to constructive forces for change; and Third World NGOs that comprise a mix of grass-roots and professional participants (both indigenous and foreign) who strive to advise and work with government as well as international organizations. In a wide variety of ways, the NGOs are taking on both governmental and societal functions; their expanding role in the future justifies guarded optimism that today's institutional blockage can be remedied, both through bottom-up participation and through institutional reform.

The NGOs provide a range of suitable opportunities for effective engagement by future generations of scholars. Academicians will also need to expend more energy in directly mobilizing the many communities embedded within modern society, especially through their educational mission; at the same time, consultants used by government must act with greater responsibility, and academicians within government should be actively used to channel information and policy initiatives; finally, all academicians must strive for institutional reform and provide better role models in the matter of values. In short, our future curriculum must include participation in our own system.

SOCIOPOLITICAL COMPLEXITY AND ECONOMIC BEHAVIOR

The yawning gulf between small communities and megastates is connected on the yardstick of human history by millennia of directional change known as cultural evolution (Newson 1976). The idea is that increasing social and political complexity will eventually culminate in urbanized, bureaucratic states with socioeconomic stratification. Anthropologists have long used this conceptual device to arrange their case studies of various ethnographic groups around the globe according to different criteria of social complexity; they then invoke archaeological evidence of increasing technological and economic sophistication to argue that their own (synchronic) record of graduated complexity is a palimpsest of directional (diachronic) change across the last ten millennia (A. Johnson and T. Earle 1987). That argument is flawed for several reasons: (*a*) social organization observed on some Pacific islands during the 1920s cannot be applied as a valid model for social organization in northwestern Europe in, say, 800 B.C.; (*b*) archaeological inferences of social hierarchies before the threshold of the historical era tend to be no more than interpretations; and (*c*) the model simply assumes that socioeconomic functions are linear and hierarchical and that social and cultural phenomena are tightly correlated (Butzer 1990a).

In rejecting the historicity and implied explanatory value of such evolutionary stages, it becomes apparent that the processes of long-term cultural, economic, and political change remain largely inferential. According to one body of views ("integration theories"), stratified state societies arose in response to stress: (*a*) in dealing with warfare, (*b*) in accommodating more and increasingly complex information, (*c*) in mobilizing labor forces for public works or the utilization of critical resources, and (*d*) in integrating

a diversified resource region or guaranteeing access to critical imports (Tainter 1988, 34). The state and its developing institutions thus served broad social needs by centralizing and coordinating disparate social, economic, and spatial components. Although the state provided distinct advantages for almost all segments of a society, it also concentrated power in the hands of a few, thus increasing inequality and social stratification. Another body of opinion ("conflict theories") claims that economic stratification created internal conflicts, so that state institutions were devised as coercive mechanisms to safeguard the power and privilege of the elite at the expense of the masses (Tainter 1988, 33).

Explicating competing views in this fashion has heuristic value, but we are not in the business of canvassing opinions. Unfortunately, empirical testing is limited to the archaeological evidence, since the earliest states—in Mesopotamia and Egypt—came into existence a few centuries before the documentary record begins. Egyptian cemeteries reveal a rapid differentiation of wealth just before formalization of the first state structures. That argues for intermeshed processes but does not clarify whether stratification led to political integration or vice versa. Another such chicken-and-egg question is whether technological changes that required increased labor investment in food production ("intensification") stimulated new sociopolitical accommodations or were themselves the result of sociopolitical changes. Here we have the advantage of comparative, historical, or cross-cultural data sets. These do not show a correlation between increasing institutional complexity and greater socioeconomic stratification; intensification takes place in contexts both with and without social inequalities.

The root problem of deductive inference can be illustrated by the case of Egypt, where large-scale irrigation was in place by 3000 B.C. Wittfogel (1957) claimed that this system was imposed by central authority, controlled by a bureaucracy, and used as a tool of empowerment to dominate a dependent peasantry. In fact, irrigation was subdivided into autonomous natural units (flood basins) that were not interlinked until the 1860s of our era. These independent canal networks were locally operated and maintained, and there is no record of officials assigned to administer them; instead, the communities within any one basin assumed such responsibilities under the village headmen, with individuals taking turns in attending to particular tasks (Butzer 1976). Big estates utilized sharecroppers or wage laborers, but the bulk of the peasantry held permanent leaseholds, with obligations equivalent to the paying of income tax—namely, a percentage of the produce. Decisions were made to meet subsistence needs and market demands, not the dictates of great absentee landlords. Open questions remain, however, about the changing proportion and status of sharecroppers versus tenant farmers over time. In Mesopotamia, another irrigation society, the context differed in that all water came from a centralized system of radial canals that could indeed be controlled and manipulated; but we know little about the system of land tenure and its implications for free decision making.

In the Egyptian example, neither the integrationists nor the conflict theorists were asking the right questions, let alone providing the correct answers. The very complexity of the empirical data should tell us that traditional causality models, whether unicausal or multicausal, work poorly, if at all. Factors that appear to be intermeshed need not be directly interlinked. Here the systemic analog becomes useful, because it posits multiple feedback loops; theoretically, there can be several parallel outcomes of "change," some of which are only distantly interlinked. R. N. Adams (1988) has therefore offered a very different theoretical framework for cultural evolution, one based on energy processes. He views societal change as a natural selection of self-organizing energy forms and its inherent triggering processes. Whether this systemic view can be operationalized is less important than that such natural selection calls for less simplistic questions and places a premium on a good and complex data base.

The old model of cultural evolution is only one example of how a body of assumptions can be foisted on a legitimate question so as to generate spurious inferences. It is well known that ancient empires controlled external commerce and internal revenue flows and that twentieth-century governments have imposed downward-extending economic systems affecting basic decisions at the grass-roots level. But can we assume that all "directed" economies will create a "dependent" rural sector? Was political power necessary to induce or compel a rural society to increase productivity and, indirectly, elite wealth? Does the commercialization of agriculture require state pressures, or does the state merely provide institutions that facilitate commercialization? Does feudalism imply a dependent class, if not a servile one, practicing agriculture according to the will of an empowered elite? Such questions have profound implications for functionalist and behaviorist case studies in "traditional peasant societies," because an over-hasty structural generalization can color the questions asked and impede collection of a more complex, pragmatic data base.

The directed economies found in parts of the Third World today are historically anomalous. Global interdependency is a new phenomenon, and the necessary degree of government intervention in rural affairs is possible only with modern communication. Historical investigations that attempt to impose such a model on their data confuse institutional complexity with economic disempowerment. By analogy, future historians could claim that the imposition of an income tax undermined American individualism. Much of the confusion stems from imperfect cultural and linguistic translation of obligations, either in the past or in another culture. Americans pay property, school, utility, sales, social security, Medicare, and income taxes; they believe they own their property, but in fact local government does, because if property taxes are not paid, confiscation results; if they sell or inherit property, they are subject to other taxes. This is not substantially different from medieval (feudal) permanent leaseholds, except that the duke or squire has been replaced by county or city government.

To take a concrete example, country people in eastern and northern Spain lived under a semi-feudal seigniorial system until the 1830s (Butzer 1990b). The lord who owned the land was entitled to a sixth or a tenth of the agricultural produce, equivalent to an income tax in lieu of property taxes; he received fees from the use of gristmills, the village bread ovens, the butchery, the olive press, etc., equivalent to utility district taxes; and his charges for hunting, trapping, or collecting dead branches for fuel were akin to hunting and fishing licenses. The Catholic Church took a cut of the first fruits, crops, or young animals of the season and a tithe proportional to the crop yield; in turn it provided most of the services expected of modern county governments, as well as charity and, in larger towns, hospital facilities. The total tax equivalent was as low as 30 percent of actual income, more typically close to a third, not counting selective sales taxes—similar to the tax liabilities of a middle-income American today and lower than those of European counterparts. When the aristocracy was "bought out" during the 1830s, the local community began charging similar fees for use of facilities or the resources of the commons, but the safeguards on sales of lands were lifted, with the result that richer people began to buy up the lands of poorer people. Both before and after 1830, however, commercial crops were expanded or shifted in response to market demand, but this pattern was not universal. In pre-Revolutionary France peasants were liable for up to two-thirds of their produce, an unusually stiff demand. In southern Spain a substantial percentage of the rural population had—and still has—no access to land, not even as sharecroppers; common people lived in large villages and hired out as day-laborers on large estates.

Like the Egyptian and Mesopotamian examples, this case and the exceptions noted show that few generalizations hold up to critical scrutiny—except perhaps the generalization that misconceptions are deeply ingrained. It is unacceptable simply to assume that hegemonic forces of one kind or other restricted or controlled decision making in traditional societies. Whether they pertain to ancient societies or the contemporary Third World, questions must be examined empirically and without preconceptions. Institutionalized inequalities of wealth or power do not necessarily imply economic dependency or imposed economic behavior in either the rural or urban world. Systemic interrelationships are not that simple. Choice from a restricted set of options can confront broad segments of society in the industrialized world just as well as in the Third World—yet researchers tend to ask different questions abroad than at home, and they incline to interpret their data with different biases.

Theoretically informed research is highly desirable, but it is equally important that theory be used as a means, not as an end. Understanding is the end. Elevating theory to the status of an ideology can lead to reification of models even though they are contradicted by counterexamples. Deductive formulation of research hypotheses is important for generating fresh questions, but if the hypotheses are not periodically subjected to critical reappraisal, they can also become blinders, skewing the questions and slanting the inferences. As the caveats raised above show, deductivist approaches to structural issues can have unfortunate consequences. In a new curriculum, theoretically informed research should also be pragmatic in spirit. This pragmatism will require seminars that critically consider alternative theories and models so that students can acquire a sound grasp of the advantages and limitations of each.

ETHNIC STRATIFICATION AND CONFLICT

Because general evolutionary theories do not yet allow a satisfactory understanding of structural constraints and inequality, it is preferable to look for alternative but more particularistic approaches to the realities of socioeconomic stratification. One such opening is suggested by the Columbian quincentenary, which should remind us that conquest societies were established in the New World after 1492 (Butzer 1992a; 1992c).

In Mexico and Peru, where large indigenous populations with complex social organization survived the Spanish Conquest, the native peoples lost much of their land as their numbers dwindled through epidemic disease and settlements were consolidated or relocated. By 1810, rural Indians were mainly reduced to sharecroppers on large estates, with barely enough land for subsistence, while those living in cities or peri-urban barrios supplied labor for textile factories, construction, and other menial jobs. Various mixed-race categories continued to expand demographically, until the aggregate of mestizos formed the majority of the population; such "new peoples" occupied intermediate positions within a complex socioeconomic and racial hierarchy. The nominally white Creole elite began to intermarry with mestizos by 1810, but even after independence, socioeconomic stratification remained unchanged until at least 1917, despite an advanced degree of ethnic and racial homogenization. There was greater social mobility, of course, through military service or client-patron relationships that facilitated "marrying up," and families could also sink in the hierarchy through bankruptcy or political disgrace. Nonetheless, the conquest had created entrenched inequalities reified through family networking, type of occupation, or place of residence and perpetuated through differential access to property, credit, and education. This class order, less formal or rigid than that of the colonial period, continues to have a life of its own.

In British North America—and its American, Canadian, and Caribbean successors—indigenous peoples were progressively expelled from their lands, the survivors marginalized as government wards on reservations. In the Caribbean and American South, African slave labor was imported to work on sugar or cotton plantations. After emancipation, this institutionalized stratification persisted informally. In Canada the conquered French population was reduced to an underprivileged class, even after constitutional reform in the nineteenth century, and remains locked in cultural and economic confrontation with the national majority.

In the northern United States the flood of ethnic immigrants between 1820 and 1914 normally went to the bottom of the socioeconomic ladder. Those who were physically indistinguishable (Europeans) could begin to improve their socioeconomic lot after a generation or two, particularly in the Midwest or West. But in the East they long remained excluded from the best schools and positions by local family networks (those appearing in the *Social Register*) dating back to the country's independence. For Mexican and Asian immigrants, upward mobility was and remains much more difficult. These examples represent immigration by infiltration (immigrant-subordinate) rather than conquest (immigrant-dominant), but like a conquered people, recent immigrants typically have access only to the least desirable economic niches, receive inferior educations and health care, and are treated harshly under the law. With circumscribed options, the mass of ethnic immigrants remains undereducated and poor across many generations, particularly if new waves of different ethnic immigrants continue to reinforce the structures of inequality by entering the system from the bottom. Even internal migration, such as the country-to-city movements of the Industrial Revolution, can serve to disfranchise the descendants of unskilled newcomers, creating a class system (as in Britain) that perpetuates unequal access to resources and opportunities.

The last five hundred years provide countless documented examples of how colonization, international migration, or internal migration have created inequality and social stratification on a vast scale. Such phenomena are not new, as various ancient and medieval warrior castes or colonial aristocracies show. They may well be the most common, tangible, and universal processes that create, sustain, or accentuate social stratification. Allowing for differences of scale, neocolonialism—with its transnational control of captive economies—suggests another such category of institutionalized inequality that limits the opportunities of immense numbers of people. Ultimately, this too is a matter of ethnicity.

Ethnicity promises to be the most pressing social, cultural, and political problem of the foreseeable future. Increasing friction and sociopolitical mobilization based on old ethnic differences (significant or not, depending on the perspective) threaten to tear apart the state fabrics created during the last two centuries (Mikesell and Murphy 1991), as political organizations once held together by dynastic loyalties are displaced by states based on national loyalties. Flemings and Walloons in Belgium now function as autonomous states within a state. Czechoslovakia has broken up into two parts, and Yugoslavia is dissolving in a bloodbath among southern Slavs. The former Soviet Union has embarked on a course of subdivision and realignment, the outcome of which is anybody's guess. India is threatened by violent three-way religious-ethnic differences, and Canada is almost paralyzed by the dissonance between French and English speakers.

The concept of *Blut und Boden*—ethnicity and territory—articulated by Bismarck (in an ambiguous phrase that literally means "blood and soil") derives from the French Revolution, which created the first state consciously based on nationalism. The ensuing nineteenth-century world order of national states that incorporated the aspirations of only the dominant national group appears destined for major revision, if not fundamental transformation. As the constraints imposed by superpower confederacies disintegrate, ethnic minorities are freer to express their growing lack of confidence that national states serve the interests of all their peoples. Much as human thought is acted out in the guise of animal behavior, new ethnic aspirations are projected onto a tangible landscape, embedded with a mix of old and new symbolic meaning. The number of atomistic states in the United Nations is rapidly approaching three hundred, and there is no end in sight. With strife or fragmentation well underway, venturesome social scientists are in active pursuit, judging by the flood of new books (Balibar and Wallerstein 1991; Hobsbawm 1992; Nash 1989; R. Walker 1988). The curriculum, as usual, is bogged down in committee, plagued by uncertainties about how to reconcile past patterns of investigation with new needs. Culturally oriented geographers of all kinds have much to contribute to a comprehension of both the particularistic and the common problems. It is to be hoped that they will help to chart new ways to understand the nesting of ethnic identity, territorial aspirations, and political-economic organizations.

In a way parallel to the sundering of national fabrics through the new militancy of old ethnicities, once homogeneous societies in Europe and North America are confronted with a new multicultural diversity as they continue to absorb streams of foreign workers and immigrants that are more culturally or racially distinct than ever before. Pakistanis and Antillians in Britain, Algerians in France, Turks in Germany, and Hispanics and Asians in the United States have created tenacious new realities that cannot be accommodated by traditional goals of homogenization; yet the dominant national groups resist contemplating a multicultural solution. As ethnic friction and mobilization reinforce social stratification, older social cleavages remaining from the Industrial Revolution or the Slave Era are reinvigorated or compounded.

Very close to home, several generations of future cultural geographers have an open mandate to study immigrant communities so as to educate the dominant group, influence policy makers, and ultimately help build transethnic bridges. The scale of crisis in failed integration continues to build, with superficial acculturation more than offset by a disintegration of traditional values among immigrant populations. The resulting social problems and insecurity exacerbate ethnic friction, setting in train feedback patterns (all too familiar from the faltering accommodation of African-Americans into the mainstream) that tacitly institutionalize stratification. The challenge is to find ways to enable such communities to hold on to their own cultural values, to reinforce their informal institutions, and to allow them to retain their self-esteem as they seek acceptance rather than rejection by the dominant group. Once a minority has been totally deculturated—and before it can properly embrace the value system of the dominant group—the social problems become almost intractable. If nothing else, the very scale of finding a new multicultural accommodation with old and new minorities, which will make up almost half of the American population within thirty or forty years, is a compelling reason for dealing constructively with the issues today rather than paying the incalculable costs of failure tomorrow.

MANAGED ENVIRONMENTS AND SUSTAINED PRODUCTIVITY

In line with bringing a new curriculum for cultural geography to bear on contemporary "cultural" problems, another obvious arena for application is the dilemma of how to feed exploding world populations in a time of deteriorating environmental quality. These are broad questions that lend themselves particularly well to a cultural ecological approach.

Most world environments have long been transformed into human ecosystems. They are dominated by open landscapes planted with a small selection of cultivars or supporting herds of domesticated livestock. Human settlements of many sizes, interlinked by roads, interrupt in the form of built environments. There also are vestiges of spontaneous vegetation, their biota composed of indigenous species or a mix of introduced and indigenous forms. Even large stands of forest may be little more than tree farms.

Landscape painters have been attracted to such humanized landscapes, interpreting them as symbols of human husbandry redolent of beauty and an age-old harmony between humankind and nature. More recent generations of ecoenvironmentalists have read these same landscapes as a record of human despoliation through which countless biota have been removed or irretrievably extirpated, to be replaced by alien plants and animals. Amid patterned fields they search for evidence of eroded soils or point to the impact of now-aggressive floods along stream channels. Both views may well be valid, to one degree or other; they exemplify two competing perspectives on the environment, as well as a more universal ambivalence as to how to reconcile the basic needs of human survival with higher needs for scenic beauty and recreation.

Cultural ecologists are primarily concerned with the second of these tensions. Despite their nominal emphasis of survival strategies, the heart of the matter is how to manage natural resources so that productivity can be sustained indefinitely (Brookfield 1988; W. Clarke 1990). Cultural ecologists also recognize that a wise long-term strategy for sustained use involves much more than economic considerations, with aesthetic and symbolic perceptions significantly shaping attitudes and attachment to the environment. Indeed, the presumption of cultural ecologists is that traditional societies will, whenever possible, seek "satisficer" rather than "maximization" solutions— that is, solutions that reduce risk, provide reasonable returns, and are consonant with their own cultural values. It is further assumed that traditional dietary and management strategies incorporate the cumulative experience of trial and error over long spans of time, and that substantial parts

of that experience are incorporated into long-term cultural attitudes and behavior through ritual and symbolic expression (Ellen 1982).

Environmental degradation is not universal but specific to particular places, times, or technologies (Worster 1988). Is there a linear correlation between population growth and increasing degradation? Do some peoples tend their environment with greater care than others, and if so, is that a result of different experience or attitudes? Does a similar technology consistently have a similar ecological impact? In a broad way, of course, the Industrial Revolution has spawned technologies that have damaged large areas across the globe and at exponentially growing rates (Headrick 1988), but to deal with a particular case we need to understand the full range of variables that affect strategies of environmental management.

The long-term picture suggests that past environmental behavior was complex and difficult to predict (Butzer 1982, 123–56, 181; 1990a). The earliest Neolithic agricultural peoples in Europe had a massive impact on vegetation in some areas; the destruction of woodland was out of all proportion to the small number of groups, probably numbering only several score people. This probably reflected the use of fire to open forests for grazing or short-term cultivation. One might describe this as exploitative management, probably due to little cumulative experience; such land use may even have been unviable in the long run, that is, without a decline in productivity or an involuntary increase in mobility. From Bronze Age to Roman times, populations and settlement density increased substantially, to several orders of magnitude greater than in Neolithic times, but in many regions the evidence for environmental degradation increased arithmetically rather than exponentially. In other areas, rapid population growth coincided with episodes of striking soil erosion; in yet other cases, massive soil erosion ensued after widespread depopulation and land abandonment.

Two inferences are suggested by this seemingly confused picture. First, Bronze Age and later environments were overwhelmingly managed rather than pristine. In northeastern Scotland land remained largely open, even when small populations used the environment for extensive grazing. In eastern Spain woodlands were extensively reduced to secondary scrub but recovered during periods of unrest and population decline; there was some loss of topsoil, but nothing catastrophic until the medieval period. This supports the notion of environments managed with the benefit of considerable experience, maintaining their productivity for many centuries at a time. Even growing populations and shifts to new technologies and labor strategies left this equilibrium in place as often as not, which implies that a conservationist bias is adaptive and that it should be the rule rather than the exception. Second, those periods and regions affected by disequilibrium suggest additional, complicating variables. Conservationist safeguards normally used to minimize risk for the environment appear to have been abandoned by some populations at certain times. Perhaps this was in response to insecurity in regard to long-term occupancy or to extreme subsistence stress or unanticipated population growth. Information may also have been misread; for example, when people move into new environments, they may introduce practices based on experience derived elsewhere and unsuitable in the new setting. Finally, a shift to a new technology may have had its hidden costs.

There are, then, salient factors affecting resource management other than population density and technology. Equal emphasis should be given to long-term regional experience, short-term subsistence stress, long-term demographic crises, and insecurity that would place the value of long-term strategies in doubt. It seems counterintuitive not to include differences of environmental attitudes or land ethics here, but in traditional societies land use is conservative, and communities are probably aware that maximization strategies are maladaptive. "Wise use" or "working with nature" is not included in the European religious or philosophic heritage, unlike China's, but such an attitude was an explicit part of the secular and pragmatic sphere, as Greek and Roman agronomic works inform us.

The problem is that emigrants transplanted to a new environment can lose their traditional attitudes in regard to transgenerational stewardship of a piece of land. Equally so, liberalization of land sales or short-term leasing can totally undermine the ethic of long-term conservation. Finally, the loss of traditional bearings in the modern world, additionally disrupted by increasing mobility, can spell disaster for strategies that once committed farmers to preserve their land and its productivity for future generations. In other words, environmental attitudes and land ethics are contextual. They can be assumed in stable, traditional societies. Today they have become the overriding problem, almost on a worldwide scale, and must now literally be taught and inculcated in the hope that new generations in consumer societies will reassume their responsibilities in the social contract that binds people and generations.

Managed environments differ from natural ecosystems in four fundamental ways: (*a*) they partially or almost completely substitute cultivars, livestock, and associated weeds for indigenous biotic components; (*b*) they introduce differences in systemic energy flow, that is, the productivity of food plants and meat-on-the-hoof versus primary productivity and animal biomass; (*c*) they entail structural changes, in that the nature and diversity of biota are culturally controlled, so that productivity can be maintained only by the investment of technology and labor (the managed ecosystem is patently artificial); and (*d*) they require equilibrium conditions different from those of a natural ecosystem, because a managed environment is commonly not allowed to undergo successional change (except in the case of shifting agriculture), whereas the related substitutions and structural changes short-circuit normal feedback loops, creating a metastable system liable to degradation or even catastrophic simplification. The inherent problems of managed environments vary greatly between the agribusiness approach, which is predicated on massive capital investment, and the ethnoagriculture perspective, which emphasizes traditional methods of maintaining fertility and the advantages of intercropping and polyculture, not least as a natural means to control pests and pathogens (Soule and Piper 1992).

Critical questions for cultural ecology concern the long-term balance of inputs and outputs; for example, would productivity decline without increasing technological or labor investment? Sustainability of a managed ecosystem could thus be defined as an indefinite maintenance of productivity without an increase of either technology or labor. Equally pertinent is whether a managed environment has the resilience to recover—with the help of remedial measures—after an episode of declining productivity resulting from degradation. Can stream baseflow be resuscitated, peak discharges reduced, and topsoils revitalized through improvement of ground cover and soil amelioration? That is the question as it would be framed by a cultural ecologist concerned with long-term productivity. An ecoenvironmentalist would probably frame the question very differently: if an environment is protected and allowed to revert to wilderness, what is the potential for reconstitution of its biota, hydrology, and soils over several centuries? The focus would be on components (biota) and structure (pathways) rather than on energy flows (productivity) and equilibrium state.

The question of biotic reconstitution demonstrates why ecoenvironmentalists and cultural ecologists must recover their common ground and natural complementarity. Reconstitution of what? A landscape of eight thousand years ago, not affected by agriculture, as reconstructed from paleoecological evidence? An implausible datum, because post-Pleistocene species migration and forest succession was still incomplete at that time. The picture gets murkier, because Holocene vegetation and human land use coevolved in the Mediterranean basin and Europe (Birks et al. 1988), so that even the rank order of characteristic species cannot be predicted for a hypothetical "natural ecosystem." In the New World, there is a proclivity to consider biotic patterns described by the earliest travelers as pristine. This is incorrect, because seemingly primeval woodlands of 1750 were the open and ecologically simplified landscapes of 1500, prior to indigenous population collapse (Denevan 1992b; B. L. Turner and Butzer 1992). The Peten rainforest had been totally cleared before A.D. 1000, suggesting that primeval forests seen here by the first Spaniards can indeed be reconstituted within centuries, perhaps even on degraded soils; that in turn raises doubts about some popular assumptions in regard to biodiversity. Natural fires, storm catastrophes, and the selective effect of plant diseases have demonstrably altered the rank order of dominant and subdominant forest species over the millennia, whereas human "protection" favors forest composition and structures different from any of those recorded paleoecologically (Schoonmaker and Foster 1991).

Prevailing concepts of wilderness are simplistic, even as applied to prehistoric times. More cautious designations such as "old-growth forest" avoid a great deal of conceptual confusion and offer more practicable norms for current conservation efforts. The unromantic fact is that almost all world environments have been humanized or even managed for millennia. Functionalist concerns about inputs, productivity, sustainable utilization, and stability are no less important than humanistic ones about images, symbolic roles, or psychological needs. A new curriculum must develop a more balanced agenda for conservationist land use, environmental preservation, and the mitigation of ecological damage. Such an agenda should serve to reverse environmental deterioration and provide long-term incentives for business and industry, while not alienating a public increasingly alarmed by radical environmentalists. Finally, it will require substantially greater collaboration between academia and NGOs. Without a holistic, unified, and realistic approach, the diverse academic clusters and advocacy groups are liable to be discredited, their efforts ignored.

GROWTH, DECLINE, AND THE PROSPECTS OF DEVOLUTION

Managed environments have thresholds beyond which they begin to unravel, but problems of metastable equilibrium also plague the human ecosystem as a whole. Historians and archaeologists have long been aware that empires both rise and fall (Cowgill 1988; Tainter 1988), and historical demographers note that, over the long term, populations grow and then decline in "millennial long-waves" of variable wavelength and amplitude (Whitmore et al. 1990). At a smaller scale, since about 1600, there also have been cycles of economic growth coupled with technological innovation followed by deep recession and social crises; these have a periodicity of roughly fifty years ("Kondratieff cycles") (B. Berry 1991; Earle 1992). Such periodic or aperiodic cycles of political, demographic, or economic growth and decline highlight significant internal processes (rather than "extraterrestrial intervention"!), such as the interplay of positive and negative feedback loops. The role of the inherent dynamics resulting from feedbacks are widely recognized by environmental scientists, for example, in anticipating hidden costs. Analogous processes in the economic arena—or in more complex systems that also incorporate institutions, resources, and demography—are less widely recognized, even though they have drawn increasing attention by an interdisciplinary spectrum of social scientists.

Since 1500, the population of the Old World has been increasing exponentially, following the demographic disaster of the Black Death (after 1347). At a macroscale, this process was coupled with growing economic and political integration. It began during the late 1400s, as strong rulers put an end to chronic political instability and banking institutions facilitated rapid commercial growth in western Europe. The economic upswing was initially fueled by the influx of New World bullion, then by the profits of the slave trade and plantation sugar, and later by cotton. Asia was added to this increasingly global economic network, exploited indirectly for raw materials and as a captive market for finished goods. The profits of this international trading system, which was controlled by British naval power, financed the Industrial Revolution, even after the slave trade ebbed and plantation agriculture fell away. By compensating for scarce home resources, industrialization created employment just as the English population struggled through its demographic transition. Surplus farm labor flowed to the burgeoning industrial cities that formed the manufacturing hub of a world empire. Other nations, one by one, were drawn into the demographic transition. Countries with lagging or limited industrialization found a safety valve in massive emigration to Argentina, Canada, and especially the United States, which became a major economic and political competitor of Britain.

This is a five-hundred-year scenario of economic centralization, accelerating energy flows, and systemic growth, by which a core of capitalist states grew at the expense of a vast periphery of dependent nations. It is the focus of the world-system concept (Wallerstein 1974; Braudel 1984; Gilpin 1987), a geopolitical model at a scale so vast that the successive changes in power structure during the twentieth century are little more than details. Population growth becomes part of a feedback loop integral to economic integration and systemic expansion. Prior to the unique modern world system there had been earlier imperial systems ("world empires") and interconnected mega-economies ("world economies") at a continental scale (Wallerstein 1974; Abu-Lughod 1989). The world-system model provides another interpretation of growth and decline, although the latter is given little attention.

Models, at least until they become reified, have heuristic value in that they draw attention to apparent regularities and stimulate research on new questions, until fresh problems are recognized that in turn generate further models. The world system is the ultimate structural model, illuminating the political economy of an interdependent world effectively controlled by the industrialized nations. Alternative models emphasize different perspectives, usually at different scales, serving to focus research on the interplay of other sets of variables.

At the longest scale, the prehistoric record verifies long-wave population cycles long before the advent of capitalism or geopolitical structures (Butzer 1990a). Archaeological surveys in the Near East and Europe show that prehistoric populations repeatedly increased, then leveled off before declining or even disappearing. Whereas settlement histories vary from one district to another, declines or discontinuities of several centuries' duration tended to affect larger regions, and at least two such breaks seem to have affected most of Europe. Possible explanations include (a) new epidemic diseases of zoonotic origin—the prehistoric Old World precursors of the pandemics that swept away 85 percent of the New World populations after 1500; (b) declining productivity of mismanaged, primitive agrosystems—which would affect only smaller areas; and (c) warfare with ethnic displacement—but only in later prehistoric times.

The rise and fall of empires, from Mexico to the Indus Valley to China, provide more specific insights at an intermediate scale. The most intriguing case is ancient Egypt, where four cycles of political centralization, economic expansion, and demographic growth—each followed by decentralization, economic dissipation, and population decline—can be identified between 3200 B.C. and A.D. 600 (Butzer 1976; 1980; 1984). During the first two cycles of growth, Egypt was self-contained, with very limited external commerce; during the third there was external expansion, whereas during the fourth, Egypt was a dependent part of a much larger regional system. Superimposed on a long-term trend of population growth, these cycles show notable regularities. Economic and demographic growth coincided with times of strong government and institutional change, suggesting an effective channeling of centripetal forces that favored systemic integration to stimulate higher productivity and sustain larger populations. Decline coincided with weak and unstable government, allowing centrifugal forces to undermine political institutions and socioeconomic structures to the point where productivity and population dropped alarmingly.

Feedbacks between growth and political-economic integration, in one form or other, are quite generally invoked to explain imperial expansion, but decline is much more difficult to rationalize (Cowgill 1988; Abu-Lughod 1989). Predicating his claim primarily on the exemplary case of the Roman Empire, Tainter (1988) proposes a general interpretation based on changing marginal product, that is, returns per increased unit of investment. Expansion initially provides a high rate of return, but the logistics of transport and communication eventually impose a limit on further conquest. At that point there are no more accumulated surpluses to appropriate from the conquered nations, and the costs of administration and occupation rise. As the subject populations gain rights and benefits, the marginal returns of empire continue to fall, leading to counterproductive increases of taxation until the

real output begins to decline. Although true capitalist economies can achieve higher returns through commercial hegemony, it is tempting to view British colonial devolution in the 1950s as a response to accelerating marginal costs. However appealing, this model overemphasizes strictly economic factors and must be stretched to accommodate the integration and disintegration of nonexpansive, self-contained societies.

Both economic and geopolitical models overemphasize energy flows at the expense of information pathways; they also ignore the implications of population growth, facilitated or stimulated by economic expansion, which creates fundamental problems for the system once expansion gives way to retraction. An alternative possibility is to stress the latent instability of political-economic systems made vulnerable to a number of possible triggering mechanisms by political inefficiency and severe economic constraints. Ecological simplification suggests a useful analog, to examine political devolution as a product of inherent thresholds and multiple feedbacks (Butzer 1980). From such a perspective, economic fragmentation may be only a dependent variable.

Effective government can facilitate the dissemination of new information and technology. It provides the necessary security for commercial networks and long-term investment in agricultural growth. It can minimize risk through institutions that provide direct safeguards (e.g., storage) or indirect mitigation of shortfalls by forging interregional links. Ideally, government will provide the leadership through which crises can be anticipated and, if they occur, accommodated by short-term remedial measures or long-term institutional adaptation. Just as readily, government can also be the cause of decline, through inadequate institutional organization and response, inaction or the cumulative impact of poor or uninformed decisions, and the placement of the selfish interests of an elite above those of the common good, that is, dissipating energy into nonsustaining activities. Finally, the roles of managerial and bureaucratic castes tend to change over time: initially they serve to improve efficiency by channeling information; with time they tend to grow like organisms, feeding on energy, impeding information flow, and reducing efficiency. Whatever the factors reducing government efficiency, greater fiscal demands are the result.

Periods of sustained demographic growth eventually bring rural populations close to "carrying capacity," at a particular level of technology and socioeconomic organization. This makes common people vulnerable to shortfalls, malnutrition, and disease; harvest failures or virulent epidemics can lead to heavy mortality (Rotberg and Raab 1985; Newman 1990). In England almost two centuries of population growth came to an abrupt halt with the harvest disaster of 1315–16; recurrent bouts of Black Death after 1348 then reduced the population by half, with demographic stagnation continuing until 1520 (Grigg 1980, 51–82). A convincing case of population overshoot can be seen in Spain, where the population doubled between 1510 and 1590, leading to painful "corrections" in the wake of economic stagnation. Rural births declined 25 percent between 1580 and 1620, and at least 500,000 people were swept away by two major epidemics; together with military losses and emigration, the overall population declined by 15 percent between 1600 and 1660 (Butzer 1990b). These examples highlight the impact of malnutrition and susceptibility to disease as a result of overpopulation. When, in addition to population pressure, economic recession leads to increasing fiscal demands, the resulting rural flight, disintensification, and depopulation can reduce net productivity, thus deepening recession. Whether long-term economic recession, population pressures, and declining productivity lead to substantial population decline and political devolution depends in substantial part on government effectiveness. The point is not to explain some case of political collapse in the historical past but to recognize and alert ourselves to the feedbacks typical of "decline." The context for such concerns is that during the last three hundred years, world population has increased from 500 million to 5 billion. Although demographic growth seems to be leveling off, there are premonitions that economic growth has also reached a plateau. Such a high world population may prove difficult to sustain with declining marginal returns, and such

"stabilization" would imply adapting to nongrowth of per capita income in the developed world. For the Third World the picture is even more worrisome.

In point of fact, we have been witnessing government failure and spreading anarchy, coupled with overpopulation and famine, in the Horn of Africa. Ethiopia devolved after 1973 in the midst of deepening famine, the cronies of the old order standing idly by and unable even to distribute incoming food shipments. A year later the senile emperor was shunted aside, and inexperienced military men began a fifteen-year experiment in using famine as a tool in civil war, resettling starving minorities in drastically different environments and thus reducing the once-exploding population of Ethiopia by perhaps a third. Now a victorious coalition of two minority groups is trying to put the pieces back together. In Sudan a military government has continued to wage a brutal ethnic and religious vendetta against its minority tribes for a dozen years, both sides using hunger as a weapon and refusing outside food aid, leaving vast regions in southern Sudan almost devoid of people. Somalia, equally plagued by overpopulation and a chain of drought years, had devolved into a random, internecine struggle until United Nations troops intervened to distribute food and impose a semblance of order.

In each instance incompetent governments, unable or unwilling to cope with exploding populations and inadequate resources, succumbed to civil war, the countries slipping into national or regional anarchy. As examples of devolution they are qualified only by the fact that they are embedded within an otherwise operational world system. They illustrate how an entire region of Africa has been able to deteriorate into chaos, with drastic population decline, under our very eyes. Seduced by the world-system model, we try to explain away the significance of what is going on as a result of past superpower rivalries, when instead we should perhaps be looking to precolonial sociopolitical models. The pattern in the Horn of Africa is not unique; other countries, such as Afghanistan and the new nations of the Caucasus, also threaten to disintegrate. This is not a time for simple interpretations but for pragmatic investigation of dysfunctional systems.

Exactly what are the various ecological and structural problems, and how are they interconnected? What are the possible options for containment or resolution through the efforts of NGOs? When is international intervention justified, or should overarching international structures be devised to contain internal anarchy?

Thus far, disintegration has been restricted to component parts of the world system, and during the Sahel drought of the 1970s or the Horn anarchy since 1990, its potential spread has been artificially contained with the advantage of unprecedented communications. But containment of anarchy can be implemented only selectively, as the unraveling of Cambodia, Liberia, and Bosnia show. Other nations seem unwilling to lead, so that the United States, severely constrained by declining marginal returns, is left with the responsibility of intervention. Sooner or later it will no longer be possible to check disintegration, the potential devolution of the former Soviet Union suggesting one such possibility. Only our blind faith in the efficacy of modern communications and international cooperation has made future devolution unthinkable.

Large parts of the world can now be regarded as metastable, as once-competitive world alliances come apart and allow mismanagement, population pressures, and a pervasive declining productivity to create widespread subsistence stress (Newman 1990). The issues are far more complex than simply the ethical dimensions of military intervention; international efforts to contain and mitigate economic and subsistence disasters will depend on popular goodwill, fiscal realities, and a fragile equation in regard to truly collaborative participation by all affluent countries. The promised new world order looks more like a new time of troubles, compounding the steadily mounting problems of global environmental deterioration.

TOWARD A BROADER CONSENSUS

These are examples of macroscale problems, historically flavored but also contemporary and immediate. They transcend the scope of any one discipline, which is appropriate if geography is to broaden its specifically cultural horizons and engage in a wider discourse of issues. The problems to be confronted today cannot and should not be carved up into niches, and future research must bring people together if it is to be effective. That will require accepting diversity, rejecting exclusivity, and emphasizing complementarity—both within and outside geography.

Other professionals no doubt will prefer to revise, rearrange, rewrite, or replace much of what I have written, depending on their vision of what is most important. Still, I suspect that many would agree in principle with at least a few of the premises on which my position is based. First, several cultural perspectives on contemporary problems require professional expertise in aspects of biology or the earth sciences, whereas some do not. Others call for expertise in anthropology, economics, or another social science. Genuine competence in a pertinent cognate field is highly recommended, both as a practical skill and as a passport to productive interdisciplinary exchange.

Second, many geographers are genuinely interested in people. Dealing directly with people gives not only real insights into how things are done but also a glimpse of why they are done in a particular way, perhaps how people think about things, and what their attitudes and inhibitions are. Direct conversation and informally structured interviews are not the preserve of any one discipline, but anthropologists are particularly well informed about the advantages and shortcomings of direct engagement, and geography students can learn a great deal from those experiences. A profound understanding of the many faces of culture can best be gained from hands-on experience, even though reflection on other authors' thoughts about culture, cultural behavior, and cultural processes remains indispensable.

Third, dealing with people, human actions, and a host of other variables is a tremendous challenge to conceptual organization. Subjective and objective views of actions or events are both important. At greater distance such dichotomies tend to fade as the problem shifts to sorting out multiple variables, for which systemic models may be of heuristic help, if only to appreciate the complexity of causality and explanation. Structural models serve equally well to put things in another kind of perspective. Regardless of the particular subject matter, it is very helpful to have a firm grounding in several alternative philosophical and theoretical positions. They can be of great assistance both in the field and in subsequent discourse and publication. Many professionals use different stances in alternation, consciously or not, sometimes explicitly but more often as unobtrusively as possible.

Fourth, in-depth fieldwork or small-scale community studies are a fundamental part of culturally oriented research (B. L. Turner 1989), providing the closest approximation of laboratory conditions in which cognitive decisions and economic actions can be analyzed to explain how people evaluate different strategies and choose among available options. Not everyone needs to engage in such work, but all must understand its purpose and significance. Small communities are the threads, dysfunctional or healthy, that constitute the fabric of urban or rural societies. Whether in a Third World village, a Texas barrio, or a New Hampshire town, the small community is where the social scientist can acquire hands-on experience in understanding how real people act out their lives with respect to community, institutions, accepted cultural behavior, and ideologies. It can be the microcosm in which to observe the role of group cooperation, reproductive strategies, attitudes to the environment, social inequities, and intolerance of the other. Experience gained in working with small communities with simplified parameters can contribute to formulating informal policy or to understanding the interrelationships of larger communities within much more complex societies.

Fifth, there are significant advantages to shifting the scale of study from micro to macro and back again. Such a shift switches attention from detailed processes to large-scale patterns, from the behavioral and partly subjective realm to the systemic or structural arena, and from personalized resource needs to actual management of resources. Each perspective informs the other and stimulates the formulation of fresh hypotheses.

Fortunately, shifting of scale is a habitual skill for many geographers.

Sixth, and finally, historical perspectives are a standard component of most culture-related research. Quite apart from culture-historical problems of intrinsic interest, culture itself is cumulative, representing learned behavior that is transmitted from generation to generation. It cannot be divorced from a diachronic perspective. Historical examples provide important comparative evidence as precedents for contemporary phenomena. Time depth commonly adds a welcome dimension to a fuzzy synchronic picture. In general, historical investigation serves to analyze and monitor processes, to explain contemporary configurations, and to draw attention to trends that may have future implications.

I suspect that most geographers interested in cultural themes would agree in principle with four or five of these premises. If so, that would be a good start. But finding some common ground is far more important than achieving consensus. A curriculum is, after all, but a pathway of studies. Each one of us must write his or her own agenda, identifying either current issues or processes that link historical experience with contemporary problems. These should form the core of our experimental seminars, with students subsequently encouraged to move on and focus on themes of particular interest. In this way, our seminars would, ideally, attract a broad spectrum of students, including those best qualified in public policy or international relations. Above all, a new curriculum would encourage competence, conscience, and commitment rather than expedience.

ACKNOWLEDGMENTS

The author wishes to thank Jane Ferson and Christine Drennon for encouragement and feedback in exploring these curriculum ideas and Ken Foote for discussion of preliminary drafts of this chapter. Greg Knapp provided valuable suggestions in regard to the issues of ethnicity and institutional change.

CHRISTOPHER L. SALTER **30**

CULTURAL GEOGRAPHY AS DISCOVERY

Walking was my project before reading. The text I read was the town; the book I made up was a map. First I had walked across one of our side yards to the blackened alley with its buried dime. Now I walked to piano lessons, four long blocks north of school and three zigzag blocks into an Irish neighborhood near Thomas Boulevard.

I pushed at my map's edges. Alone at night I added newly memorized streets and blocks to old streets and blocks, and imagined connecting them on foot. From my parents' earliest injunctions I felt that my life depended on keeping it all straight— remembering where on earth I lived, that is, in relation to where I had walked. It was dead reckoning. On darkened evenings I came home exultant, secretive, often from some exotic leafy curb a mile beyond what I had known at lunch, where I had peered up at the street sign, hugging the cold pole, and fixed the intersection in my mind. What joy, what relief, eased me as I pushed open the heavy front door!—joy and relief because, from the very trackless waste, I had located home, family, and the dinner table once again. (Dillard 1987, 44)

As curious as it sounds, let me set the stage for this essay by exhorting you to put aside your books. If you are truly to gain some sense of the power of landscape, and consequently the power of cultural geography, get yourself away from the printed page. Turn, rather, to a more effective teacher. Turn to the most omnipotent primary document at your command—the cultural landscape.

In the evocative description that Annie Dillard gives us above in *An American Childhood* (1987), she shows us the power in exploring geographic space, observing landscape, and developing one's own personal map of the world. Whether the world being charted is composed simply of the neighborhood blocks surrounding a child's home or it is the broader universe to which later literary excerpts will introduce us, this lesson of learning from the landscape is intrinsic to the vigor of cultural geography, particularly when studied through the medium of the cultural landscape.

If one thinks about the importance of literacy—that is, the capacity to read the record of earlier peoples in their efforts to make sense of the world—then learning to read the most primary document of all must be a serious consideration in attaining such literacy.

The cultural landscape is the document society has created through the often discordant use of systems of technology, aesthetics, economics, and sometimes even whimsy. These landscapes that we continually create and re-create are honest and ubiquitous reflections—albeit approximate ones—of what our varied cultures value. Understanding such valuations, such landscape icons, must top our list of educational goals if we are to play a useful and intelligent role in the management of the earth, its fragile cover, and its vital resources.

Discovery in cultural geography relates closely to one's ability to read the landscapes that surround us and have surrounded us since the first cave entrance was modified for warmth or the first stream was ponded to provide a more reliable water source. Our capacity to touch the landscape, to begin to shape it in our own images of desire and need, is the beginning of real understanding of the landscape's power and significance.

Charting the composition and meaning of the cultural landscape can be done in a thousand ways. Every time you guide your car into a parking slot at a convenience store, you are assessing and reacting to the cultural landscape. When you ponder the new facade on a remodeled store, you are evaluating landscape. When you attempt to decide where to beach your canoe as you travel on an unknown stream, you are seeking meaningful landscape markers. Common sense, experience, and the nature of the specific demand you are making on this specific place together compel you to read landscape.

However, since you are reading pages now—even though I asked you to put books aside at the opening of this essay—let me provide a structure for reading the cultural landscape that can take you through any landscape and help to provide meaning for you along the way. Let us build our assessment and analysis out of current geographic themes that are increasingly important in the renaissance of our discipline in the American educational system. These are the Five Fundamental Themes of Geography (Association of American Geographers 1984).

The five themes came out of a creative effort by the profession to provide organizing concepts for geographic phenomena that would be useful to teachers and others who knew geography was important but were often without any formal training in the subject. The themes—location, place, human-environment interaction, movement, and region—furnished an intellectual framework that could be adorned with details and observations. Every observer of the cultural or unmodified natural landscape could begin to make order of the scene being considered.

However, adding one other dimension of analysis to the five-themes structure facilitates the discovery that studying the cultural landscape should furnish any student of the earth. This is a quartet of geographic tools that I package in the following mnemonic device: O, SAE, Can You See? The *O* stands for the most basic tool in landscape study, observation. The first *S* is for speculation. The *A* is for analysis that needs to be researched in sources that lie outside the landscape being studied. And the *E* is evaluation. All landscape study ought to lead to a thoughtful evaluation of the landscape's appropriateness in terms of resource utilization, social equity, or economic and cultural utility.

This quartet of demands provides the observer with a guideline for more thoughtful landscape study: what do you see there (observation); why do you suppose the scene has that look, or how is that landscape being used (speculation); what additional sources, people, maps, and references do you need to verify or augment your speculations (analysis); and finally, how appropriate a landscape design is this (evaluation)? Let us combine these themes and tools of exploration with evocative literary passages to guide us in this process of discovery in the cultural landscape.

LOCATION

> A map in the hands of a pilot is a testimony of a man's faith in other men; it is a symbol of confidence and trust. It is not like a printed page that bears mere words, ambiguous and artful, and whose most believing reader—even whose author, perhaps—must allow in his mind a recess for doubt.
>
> A map says to you, "Read me carefully, follow me closely, doubt me not." It says, "I am the earth in the palm of your hand. Without me, you are alone and lost."
>
> And indeed you are. Were all the maps in this world destroyed and vanished under the direction of some malevolent hand, each man would be blind again, each city be made a stranger to the next, each landmark become a meaningless signpost pointing to nothing. (Markham 1983, 245)

Location begins any process of geographic discovery because of the power of context. Television news brings us words like *Somalia, the Black Sea, South Central L.A.,* or *Hilton Head,* and immediately our minds turn to the mental maps of the world we all carry around in our heads, trying to attach that word to some specific space and place. This effort, if successful, provides a sense of climate, cultural pattern, or political setting—or possibly all of those dimensions.

Maps are our charts of locations, and as Markham says above, they bring order to the world. As such, they are basic to this first theme in geography. The search for geographic meaning in a given landscape is gained in part by answering questions of location. Why is the restaurant found at this intersection? Why is the automatic teller machine inside the bank and not on the

building's outer wall, where it could be reached at all hours? With four dead gas stations at this intersection, why has this particular one been resurrected and turned into a convenience store and self-service gas station? The series of questions about location is endless, yet every one requires some exercise in making sense of what you see before you. Discovery in geography rides on that vehicle of observation and speculation, and understanding the theme of location is one of the goals in that transit.

PLACE

> The physical landscape is baffling in its ability to transcend whatever we would make of it. It is as subtle in its expression as turns of the mind, and larger than our grasp; and yet it is still knowable. The mind, full of curiosity and analysis, disassembles a landscape and then reassembles the pieces—the nod of a flower, the color of the night sky, the murmur of an animal—trying to fathom its geography. At the same time the mind is trying to find its place within the land, to discover a way to dispel its own sense of estrangement. (Lopez 1986, xxii–xxiii)

Place, the second of the five themes, describes the two realms that comprise all landscapes you will ever see: the physical landscape, unmodified by human activity and depicted so powerfully by Barry Lopez, and the human (cultural) landscape that has been transformed one or many times by human effort.

Discovery in geography is often derived from the experience of looking at a scene that you have seen many times before and suddenly seeing it differently. Elements of color, texture, and composition that have undoubtedly been there before emerge surprisingly and become apparent and important. The demands you make through careful observation—an essential element in cultural geography and in any analysis of the cultural landscape—and by asking questions about the meaning of a scene will lead you to the fuller discovery of place.

Cultural geographers are inclined to talk about the number of words Eskimo peoples have for snow, or Bedouins for light, or the Japanese for spirits in nature. These linguistic nuances not only help to identify a people and their understanding of place but also serve to remind the geographer that the physical landscape has a dramatic role in a culture's sense of identity with place.

If the student of a given scene wants to understand the evolution of a place better, he or she must make an effort to strip away the years of cultural transformation that are evident in the landscape and get back to the original setting and environment found by the earliest settlers. The whole nature of the vegetation, the availability of water, and the potential threat and resource that local fauna represented all change the contemporary equation of landscape evaluation. This second of the five themes requires that we learn to read the physical as well as the human nature of the setting under consideration.

HUMAN-ENVIRONMENT INTERACTION

> Grandpa worked the leading edge of the suburban advance, speculating in the land that suburbanization was steadily translating from farm into tract house and shopping center. He grasped the powerful impulses that drove New Yorkers farther and farther out east because he shared them. There was the fear and contempt for city ways—the usual gloss on the suburban outlook—but there was also a nobler motive: to build the middle-class utopia, impelled by a Jeffersonian hunger for independence and a drive to create an ideal world for one's children. The suburbs, where you could keep one foot on the land and the other in the city, was without a doubt the best way to live, and Grandpa possessed an almost evangelical faith that we would all live this way eventually. (Pollan 1991, 14)

The third theme, human-environment interaction, leads us into another realm in the structure of the five themes. The first two themes, location and place, are concerned primarily with observation. In the study and pursuit of those perspectives, we observe and make note of the elements of the landscape before us. In the final three themes, we look more closely at the dynamics of landscape change. It is this realm that supports geographic analysis (Salter 1987).

In the re-reading of cultural geography, and in the associated concern for discovery and understanding of the cultural landscape, this concern for human-environment interaction is absolutely axial. Why have we made the changes that we have in the natural landscape? Is it simply for improvement in shelter? For access to more resources? For convenience? Or is the entire act of remaking a landscape in the image of human design basic to the human being itself? In the reading of the primary document—the cultural landscape—that is the result of this process and the action of the third theme, we see the most powerful of all human intersections with the earth.

In the eyes of author Pollan, Grandpa read the changing landscape as part of a natural spatial development. People would, of course, want to leave the city. They would, of course, want to maintain some link with it for its conveniences and social and economic benefits, but they would, at the same time, want to be closer to the nature that the vanishing potato farmlands represented. It need not be Long Island that we study to see evidence of this interaction with the environment. We can consider the farmlands that surround virtually every metropolitan settlement on the face of the earth. Cities grow, populations expand, land must be sought for such expansion, and farmland is inevitably replaced with blacktop, commerce, housing tracts, and roadways.

For the geographer this theme, and this particular urban expansion scenario, is elemental to the discovery process. Why are the new American urban neighborhoods to the west of the city center so often made up of the homes of the more wealthy? Why has the placement of satellite shopping centers in the suburbs so completely meant the near abandonment of the central city in this growth process? What are the social and demographic shifts that seem to flow in concurrence with these land use changes at the edges of our cities?

This theme of human-environment interaction is fundamental to all that the geographer attempts to discover. What forces have driven us to create golf courses in the desert? How can we explain the oil derricks on the state capitol grounds in Oklahoma? How can we justify the pattern of abandoning solid building stock in central cities even while we have countless homeless hanging around the first floors of these empty buildings? The question, then, is not simply one of making observations about the nature of such human modifications of the natural landscape; it also involves assessing the benefit of these changes. To put it in the scheme of O, SAE, Can You See, we need to evaluate the outcome of these changes. Are they working? If so, for whom? Could they work for more? If so, how?

To achieve discovery in geography, we must understand the cultural landscape. Analysis through the use of the five themes is one approach that leads to the necessary observations and the right questions. Let us carry that one step further by looking at the world through the fourth of the five fundamental themes, movement.

MOVEMENT

Home in Missoula,
Home in Truckee,
Home in Opelousas,
Ain't no home for me.
Home in old Medora,
Home in Wounded Knee,
Home in Ogallala,
Home I'll never be.

I took the Washington bus; wasted some time there wandering around; went out of my way to see the Blue Ridge, heard the bird of Shenandoah and visited Stonewall Jackson's grave; at dusk stood expectorating in the Kanawha River and walked the hillbilly night of Charleston, West Virginia; at midnight Ashland, Kentucky, and a lonely girl under the marquee of a closed-up show. The dark and mysterious Ohio, and Cincinnati at dawn. Then Indiana fields again, and St. Louis as ever in the great valley clouds of afternoon. The muddy cobbles and the Montana logs, the broken steamboats, the ancient signs, the grass and the ropes by the river. The endless poem. By night Missouri, Kansas fields, Kansas night-cows in the secret wides, crackerbox towns with a sea for the end of every street; dawn in Abilene. East Kansas grasses become West Kansas rangelands that climb up to the hill of the Western night. (Kerouac 1957, 225)

Geography's fundamental focus is space. All societies have a body of attitudes toward space, just as do all individuals. In the American culture, one of the most geographic definitions of our society is the capacity we have to overcome space, or more accurately, to be mobile. We give great energy and considerable resources to overcoming the tyranny of space or place. We move, we travel, we roam, we look ahead at goal areas, and we look back at places left behind. For the geographer, charting this movement is very useful in discovering the meaning of the cultural landscape.

As Jack Kerouac's character Sal Paradise recounts one of his trips (above), he provides one window on this theme of movement. He is in flow. The worlds that he sees become part of his mental map of the world. The ways in which he sees them and brings them to his readers affords them—us—a window on that map. The sense of flight (or is it approach?) in this excerpt reminds us that each scene is both a part of its own reality and a part of the observer's mental map. Each encounter with a person, a setting, or an event in such travel adds a new layer of understanding or impression to the repository that grows within our heads as we move through the cultural landscape.

To the geographer this theme of movement has a number of critical dimensions. For Kerouac it was human movement, human travel. We can dissect those scenes and gain at least partial understanding of the highways; the nature of some parts of some cities; and the sense of emptiness, oldness, openness, and unknownness that clutter together to contribute to this theme of movement as seen by one writer. Any one of us required to chart his or her movement for some experiment would no doubt be surprised at all that could be observed through such a demand. The geography of place, identity, anticipation, and regret would all well up from such pages. The richness of such observations becomes, then, part of the way in which we read the cultural landscape. They are essential building blocks in our capacity to discover meaning.

The theme of movement also embraces the physical elements of such geography. The road networks, the rail lines, the rutted farm roads, and the stark runways of unused airports—all

...ndscape features are part of what must be ... place in the geographic analysis of the movement theme. What decisions lead to the exact placement of a cloverleaf interchange on a federal highway? What impact do such cloverleafs have on the world on which they are overlain? What decisions lead to the construction of a train station on a rail line? Does it matter to a community that a decision is made not to have a train stop there or to remove a station that once functioned actively? Or do these transportation networks have significance only for those in motion?

At the same time, the movement of ideas, fads, technology, and information is also subsumed under this fourth theme. It is, then, the power of movement that continually introduces new influences in the creation of the cultural landscape. If a major television news or sports personality wears an unusual pair of glasses or necktie, all across the country people begin to search for the same fashion statement. When a successful movie features a style of clothing, stores from Florida to California to Minnesota find questions directed to them about the availability of exactly the same style.

Whether it is people, information, or grain moving across the landscape, there is inherent in this theme of movement a process of change underway. And the force of such change not only manifests itself in the way the affected landscapes appear but also causes people to think, to consider something new even while they reevaluate something traditional. This theme, then, is at the very heart of the reading of the primary document we call the cultural landscape. How is the theme of movement changing this setting?

REGIONS

She had grown up in a comfortable Queensland country town where the hills along the coastal range captured plentiful rain, the gardens were lush, and the rich soil suited small-scale agriculture. Until her marriage to my father at the age of twenty-eight, she had lived by choice in cities. . . . [Their married life] had begun in considerable style on the rich and well-established sheep station my father managed for one of Australia's great landholders. That homestead was situated on a river and overlooked a lake. . . . [They were now travelling to their own homestead.] The eighteen thousand acres they rattled across in their T-model Ford had no surface water, and only a few isolated and scraggy clumps of eucalyptus trees. It seemed flatter and more barren than any land [mother] had ever seen. She saw no landmarks to identify directions, only emptiness. My father saw strong fertile soil, indication of grazed-out salt-bush, dips and changes in the contours of the land and its soils, landmarks of all kinds. The contours of the isolated trees indicated the prevailing winds. The sand drifts told him the path of the dust storms which boiled out of the inland desert in a drought. In his mind's eye he had already taken possession of the earth and it was already blooming after the next rain. My mother, nursing her infant son, felt the flying sand become grit in her mouth and eyes and was temporarily daunted. (Conway 1989, 18–19)

The language of this passage from Jill Ker Conway's book about growing up in Australia shows us that the concept of region not only differentiates one place from another but also distinguishes one person's perception of a place from another's. The landscape begins to assume its character not only from the physical attributes it possesses but also from the inclinations already lodged in the minds of those who view it and describe it.

A region is a spatial construct created by geographers to enable them to focus on discrete units for consideration and analysis. It is given character by internal cohesion and reasonably clear borders. Region is one of the few universals that people associate with geography. As in the case of spatial arrangement as a singular geographic perspective on the world, the region is a domain that marks out the margins, the core, the meaning, and the significance of a geographic assessment. Realizing that regions are human constructs—that is, they are given meaning more by human assessment than by natural conditions—helps one to see how enormously flexible they can be. The concept of region is simply a tool for bringing the scale of analysis to a dimension that is relatively more manageable for description and analysis.

There are, for example, regions of commerce

or fear in neighborhoods. There are regions of higher rent and lower rent in shopping malls. There are regions of language, food preferences, religious custom, vegetation, or economic conditions at all scales and all over the world. The geographer's region is a marker that helps discovery in geography because it represents a world within a world. Sometimes that world is clearly seen, and sometimes only a few people see the nature of that special world. In the Conway excerpt above, the landscape that the father saw was very distinct from the same place as seen by the mother. The landscape was the same in objective terms, but when seen through personal filters of experience and responsibility, it became two different worlds, two distinct regions.

The act of discovery, then, includes not only sensing what the borders and characteristics of the region are but also seeing how widely perceived are those qualities that make that place a region.

Thus, by considering the five fundamental themes in geography—location, place, human-environment interaction, movement, and region—one is equipped to read the cultural landscape in a somewhat orderly fashion. Admittedly, we can read a scene without ever having heard of such organizers, but having these particular perspectives at the ready provides a structure from which pieces of observation and speculation can be hung as one ponders what additional data are necessary to promote analysis and suggest an evaluation of the utility and the appropriateness of the scene.

The five themes, then, plus the O, SAE, Can You See mechanisms are tools that the geographer uses to discover meaning on the horizon. Viewing an intersection, a pedestrian walking from one side of a familiar city to the other can determine the architectural elements of the place. The nature of the transportation network consisting of the streets and perhaps old trolley lines or the "one way" signs and traffic movement all help the reader to assess vitality—in terms of both the past and the present. The people who are crossing the streets, looking in the store windows, or looking out of the quiet stores are all markers that have to be considered as one attempts to discover meaning in even a mundane intersection. All the data are there—

it is up to the geographer to give them meaning and fit them into a mosaic that leads to understanding.

The same exercise of observation, speculation, and questioning can be worked while looking at an abandoned farmhouse and outbuildings along a gravel country road. The specific landscape elements are different, but the sense of inherent order in the initial human dedication to that locale, to that specific plot for a home or farm, and the potential basis for family life and securing a productive niche in the local community all swirl around the scene you look at from the broken gateway or even from your car window as you decide whether to explore and discover more completely what the deserted landscape is waiting to tell you.

If you want one more set of guidelines to help organize your reading of this primary document we call the cultural landscape, consider these final five filters that geographers now posit as essential to all geographic understanding (Downs 1992): pattern, scale, change, system, and perception. They constitute geographic filters of meaning that are vital to the ways in which geographers make sense of the world.

Patterns are the evidence of order in both the natural and the cultural world. They represent arrangements in climate, land use, population distribution, or attitudes toward suburbia that help to give geographic meaning to the landscape. Scale is the way the geographer brings spatial laws to assist in the analysis of everything from a small dooryard garden to the wide-open spaces of the Great Plains. Patterns, for example, occur at all scales. The geographer makes an effort to observe and understand patterns at the widest possible range of scales—from a city block to an entire continent.

Change is the dynamic that keeps geography interesting and the cultural landscape in flux. Human migration brings a continual suggestion of new customs, new land uses, new languages, and possibly new tensions to any given setting. Every time a new phenomenon is introduced into a given landscape, not only must the people exposed to this innovation decide whether to accept it, but they must also reconsider their own competing cultural pattern. And, of course, change is also a continual agent of influence on physical systems in terms of weather, climate, vegetation, fauna, and even topography.

System is the orderly and often predictable way in which change is introduced into the landscape. There are natural laws that manage the flow of forces of water and erosion, but there are also systematic forces in human migration, environmental perception, land use, and countless other cultural phenomena. As chaotic, for example, as an urban scene may appear on a Wednesday afternoon at rush hour, there are fundamental systems at work in the depopulating of the central city at that time on a daily basis. Determining the systems that operate in such a scene is another example of discovery in geography.

Finally, perception takes us right back to where we began. Each of us has a personal geography. We all have mental maps (not just one) of all sorts of worlds. We associate cultural qualities with physical landscapes (tropical islands or harsh, rocky coastal settings), just as we anticipate somewhat specific human responses to an ocean sunset or a mountain dawn. We sometimes even allow that there may be no objective reality at all, only individual perception. Whatever the ultimate reality of perception, it must be seen as one of the five filters of geographic understanding that can be applied to any scene, any landscape, as one tries to uncover meaning in the setting being discovered.

CONCLUSIONS

I am a patriot of a singular geography on the planet. I am proud of its landscape. I walk through the traffic of cities cautiously, always nimble and on the alert, because my heart belongs in the marshlands. (Conroy 1986, 5)

We are the children of our landscape; it dictates behavior and even thought in the measure to which we are responsive to it. I think of no better identification. (Durrell 1957, 41)

This is the bottom line. Each of us has in our souls some link to place, some identification with geography. As geographers attempting to re-read cultural geography, we can determine no better starting point than to discover our own sense of place. If we are searching for meaning to education, let us perhaps tell others about the significance of land use and environmental attitudes, but let us know that the real core of our search for meaning is to locate ourselves.

If we see the reading of the cultural landscape as an act of discovery illustrating the patterns, systems, and human-environmental interactions that characterize human effort, then we can see how central such activity is to all meaning. If we can determine—by landscape analysis and the reading of this primary landscape document that we have shaped over millennia and remake daily—what decisions have led people to do what they have done to their environmental settings, then we have a good approach to their whole being. And understanding such an essence, for individuals as well as cultural groups, is one of the very real benefits of education, of looking toward the horizon, and of discovering the dynamics of people and place.

And if all the prose exhortation in these pages seems too academic or too prescriptive for your particular interests, then go back to my opening line: throw out the books. Get out into the landscape and read it as a primary document that is being created even as we consider it. For in reading that record, you will find the real discovery in geography.

MARVIN W. MIKESELL **31**

AFTERWORD: NEW INTERESTS, UNSOLVED PROBLEMS, AND PERSISTING TASKS

There may still be human communities that are so isolated and immobile that their curiosity about the areal variation of behavior has been totally eclipsed. Nonetheless, most people are exposed to cultural difference and so have some interest, however naive and prejudiced, in what we call cultural geography. We should not forget that the enduring appeal of our small profession derives from the fact that it reflects a basic aspect of human curiosity. The status of cultural geography as a scholarly enterprise depends on how convincingly we can claim to have a discipline that permits us to see what others do not see or see with less clarity.

Many attempts have been made to defend this claim. *Re-reading Cultural Geography* is yet another one. The chief virtue of this new effort is that it presents a rich array of illustrative studies and informed commentary that provides the basis for assessing what cultural geographers, or more precisely, some American and British cultural geographers, have been trying to accomplish in recent years. I see and think others will also see in this welcome volume, evidence of both continuity and change, which is what we should expect in an intellectual endeavor that has persisting value and yet is always in need of renovation. Having offered well-deserved praise, I can now also offer some unbridled comments on issues that may not have been addressed adequately or may have been overlooked by the present generation of cultural geographers.

INHERENT DIFFICULTIES

Whether we admit it or not, commitment to cultural studies is an act of faith. We have to believe that culture is an operational rather than a heuristic concept. We also have to believe that we can overcome a formidable array of inherent difficulties. For example, although there are many universal elements of culture (language, religion, social organization, livelihood, entertainment, and so on), each local manifestation of these elements is unique. We are obliged, therefore, to see or at least try to see the generality in specific studies and the specificity in general studies. Again, culture is stable and yet dynamic. Examples of stagnation are hard to find, and continuity is evident even in cases of rapid evolution or assimilation. The study of culture also requires us to distinguish between what is invented or imported and between what is local or more widespread. Understanding culture always presupposes an awareness of scale and the complication produced by changes of scale. Regardless of scale, culture exhibits manifestations of both convergence and divergence. Finally, if we borrow Clifford Geertz's (1973, 5) wonderfully apt phrase and define culture as webs of meaning, then we must accept that we are trying to explain meanings that may not be comprehensible to the people entangled in the webs and that cannot be comprehended fully by those who are not.

The rewards of cultural study do not include prophetic certainty or grand simplification. Generalizations about culture are at best fragile works of synthesis that must be constructed and dismantled repeatedly. Needless to say, any author obsessed by fear of these difficulties would probably suffer from a terminal case of writer's block. This is not, of course, a message any friend of cultural geography should want to convey. Appreciation of difficulty, as opposed to fear or denial of it, is a prerequisite for overcoming difficulty. And professional morale is sustained by appreciation of collective as well as personal accomplishment. Occasionally, an individual scholar may complete a task that has eluded a battalion of scholars. Clarence Glacken's *Traces on the Rhodian Shore* (1967) and Eric Wolf's *Europe and the People without History* (1982) can be cited as notable examples of professionally enriching solo accomplishments. Progress is more likely to be revealed in a complicated series of such accomplishments. A bibliography that would document fully the long progression from *Grundlagen der Landschaftskunde* (Passarge 1919–21) to some influential recent work, for example, *Iconography of Landscape* (Cosgrove and Daniels 1988), would have hundreds of entries.

In cultural geography cumulative rather than additive growth is achieved primarily by cross-cultural comparison, historical verification, and expansion of inquiry from smaller to larger areas. We also depend on a dynamic according to which authors of case studies are challenged to expand their interest and authors of generalizations are confronted with specific exceptions. In addition to the criticism that may be directed to individual authors or several authors devoted to a common or related topic, cultural geographers also have a more general concern. Our field may be too large or too sparsely populated. Our literature may be alarmingly disparate. Personal isolation combined with remarkably varied interests could mean that we are capable of only sporadic and uncoordinated accomplishment. Variety may be the spice of life, but we might be better off if we could agree to concentrate our effort.

THE SEARCH FOR DEFINITION

It is still useful to recall a statement made by Edward Price (1968, 129): "Cultural geography is not a self-sufficient field of study that produces all of its own data and examines them as part of a closed system; it is rather an exchange in which data and interpretations from many sources are examined from one general point of view." The first part of this statement has such obvious merit that it can probably be accepted by all cultural geographers. I doubt, however, that the literature of cultural geography reveals any consensus on what might constitute "one general point of view." Many cultural geographers have struggled to solve this problem. I have tried elsewhere

(1992) to explain the background and context of the effort that Philip Wagner and I made in 1962. We asserted then that cultural geographers should be identified not by the phenomena they study but rather by the integrating concepts and processes that they stress. We also indicated that the literature we reviewed revealed preoccupation with five research themes: culture, culture area, culture history, cultural landscape, and cultural ecology. In a passage that was more wishful than realistic, we added that the definitive cultural geographer would be someone who thought automatically about all these themes regardless of initial preoccupation with any one of them.

The idea that cultural geography might be defined in reference to overlapping or convergent research themes was also presented in the very successful textbook of Terry Jordan and Lester Rowntree (1976 et seq.), but they endorsed a somewhat different set of themes: culture region, cultural diffusion, cultural ecology, cultural integration, and cultural landscape. The editors of the present volume indicate that they have detected no less than fourteen "distinct research themes," which they have grouped under three bold headings: "How the World Looks," "How the World Works," and "What the World Means." I believe this conception of cultural geography's mission can be expressed even more boldly: appearance, function, and meaning. These three words give us a "very big tent." Is it big enough to provide room for all cultural geographers? I think the answer to this question may have to be no, because the structure of the book seems to reflect the interests of scholars who are devoted to material rather than nonmaterial culture, and more specifically, those geographers whose primary concern is the appearance, function, and meaning of landscapes.

Words derived from the Germanic *land* (e.g., landscape, *Landschaft*, *landskap*) and the Romanic *pays* (e.g., *paysage*, *paisaje*, *paesaggio*) figure prominently in the vocabulary of geography. Understanding landscapes can be regarded as an important task for cultural geography, but this is not to say that such understanding is our only task. However we choose to define a culture area, it must include some pattern of coextensive communication, and the most effective means

of communication is language. In most of the world, cultural-geographic inquiry presupposes awareness of the separation or mingling of languages and dialects. The same can be said about religion. Unlike language, religion may have a prominent, visible manifestation in landscapes, but this is not the only reason why religion is important to us. Religion, like language, is a system of communication and a mechanism that promotes integration when it is not promoting conflict. The distribution of any faith poses questions about its origin, propagation, and frontiers. Religion is a value system that fosters and inhibits human activity and so should be a major concern of human geographers.

I have suggested elsewhere and should repeat here that one of our essential challenges is to seek understanding of the discordant relationship between the world political map and more complicated patterns of linguistic and religious distribution (Mikesell and Murphy 1991). I also believe that we should participate in the effort being made by scholars from many disciplines to understand the tension that exists in most of the world between subnational identity and national affiliation. Add the vast array of research problems implicit in the symbiotic relationship between community poverty or national debt and environmental degradation, and we have a rich program that extends far beyond any artifactual or landscape conception of cultural geography. The phrase that David Sopher (1973) selected to capture the essence of our field—"the spatial patterning of culture"—offers the benefit of maximum inclusion. Perhaps the same can be said of the title *Person, Place, and Thing* (Wong 1992). Landscape in all its various and ambiguous meanings is a very big word, but it is not big enough to be a synonym for cultural geography.

CONTINUITY AND CHANGE

Looking backward in 1978, it seemed to me that cultural geographers had exhibited several preferences: (1) a historical orientation, (2) a stress on human-induced environmental modifications, (3) a preoccupation with material culture, (4) a bias in favor of rural areas in this country and non-Western or preindustrial societies abroad, (5) a tendency to seek support from anthropology, (6) a commitment to substantive research and a consequent attitude of extreme individualism, and (7) a preference for fieldwork rather than "armchair geography."

Whether these retrospective generalizations were valid in 1978 is debatable. In any case, the assessment offered by the editors of the present volume demonstrates convincingly that we now have several alternative or complementary preferences, for example, urban areas, Western societies, and modern time. Continuing interests also reveal change. Current work on material culture often has a semiotic rather than a taxonomic rationale. Cultural geographers are now more inclined than previously to employ deductive reasoning and so can claim that they are, or at least hope to be, theoretical rather than "merely empirical." Because these preferences are well described in the introduction to this volume, it is not necessary for me to try to add qualification or elaboration.

It is necessary, however, to point to the tension that is always evident when there is competition between alternative scholarly preferences. Tension is exacerbated notably when advocates of an alternative preference adopt a deficit model of behavior and so are unable to appreciate the distinction between what is different and what is "inferior." Anyone who experienced the epic struggle in the 1960s between "number-crunching space cadets" and "old-fashioned merely descriptive regional geographers" will have some understanding of the communication problems created by deficit modeling. Among contending cultural geographers, invidious distinctions have been or might be phrased differently: "antiquarian elitists" versus "ultrarelevant postmodernists." Since we are all in the communications business, it ought to be self-evident that labels of this character generate distracting noise.

The tension produced by our situation of continuity and change would be reduced if we could agree that some of our traditional tasks have been completed and offer a "golden parachute," or at least a gold watch, to anyone who has been so engaged. Unfortunately, it does not seem that any of our tasks has been completed. Our oldest and perhaps most successful endeavor, cultural ecology, still offers an awesome array of

intellectually challenging and ultrarelevant research opportunities (Turner et al. 1990). Even culture history, now the least fashionable theme of cultural geography, offers a large set of unsolved problems. In spite of considerable effort, we must still struggle with the perennial problem of whether a given trait is sufficiently complex to suggest origin in only one area or sufficiently simple to have evolved spontaneously in several areas (Jett 1971). Many of the inherent difficulties of culture history seemed to have been dispelled when Julian Steward (1955) offered "multilinear evolution" as an alternative to "unilinear evolution." Debate was renewed when Elman Service (1960) suggested that it might still be possible to speak of a unilinear evolutionary law, that is, that specific evolutionary progress is inversely related to general evolutionary potential. How this law might be applied in studies of the transition from premodernity through modernity to postmodernity is an issue that cultural geographers have not yet addressed.

A host of unsolved problems are also evident in landscape study. The transition from morphological description to symbolic interpretation can probably be heralded as progress, but the now-fashionable idea that landscapes can be read as texts leaves us in a quandary, for the number of plausible readings is limited only by the number of potential readers, and any landscape is a composite, multilayered text. To shift from the text analogy to a more venerable idea, it is probably fair to say that landscape study has been inspired by a variant of the Cartesian principle: I see it, therefore it is. But if you do not see what I see, how can we agree on what "it" means? Landscape research inspired by the thought that superstructure reflects infrastructure presents us with another perplexity, because this vaguely Marxian notion can be applied so widely (e.g., posh suburbs, squalid slums, retirement communities) that it should probably be regarded as an axiomatic truth rather than a theory to be tested.

I think attention also should be directed to the problems that are entailed when attempts are made to isolate subcultures or countercultures in Western societies. The alienation or marginalization of our minority groups is usually defined in reference to the perceived hostility or indifference of governments that cater to majority-group sentiments. If so, it follows that rejection of "bourgeois epistemes" or disdain of official or elite culture can lead only to partial or distorted understanding. Such rejection or disdain requires us to endorse two implausible notions: that majority-minority roles are separable rather than reciprocal and that progress in cultural studies can be achieved by an exercise of subtraction.

Perhaps the most important "new" challenge for cultural geographers has to do with the function and status of women in both Western and non-Western societies. In most of our previous literature, it would be fair to say that half of the population has been ignored. This deficiency can be overcome by both male and female researchers in many or at least most Western countries. In many non-Western societies, and especially Islamic societies, sexual segregation may be so emphatic and ideas of honor and shame so well established that only female fieldworkers can have any real chance of gaining the knowledge that is needed for cross-cultural comparison. The feminist critique of the canons of cultural study requires more than verbal communication. An immense amount of difficult fieldwork needs to be done.

SAUER AND THE BERKELEY SCHOOL

Most commentators on the history or current orientation of cultural geography feel obliged to say something about Carl Sauer and the Berkeley school. As a student of Sauer and, consequently, a card-carrying member of his school, I am pleased that he has attracted so much attention. I suspect, however, that his early programmatic writing, which has been the main focus of this attention, has no direct bearing on the cultural geography that has been practiced or promoted in recent years. I also suspect that it is misleading to label Sauer as a cultural geographer. He can also be described as a biogeographer, historical geographer, prehistorical geographer, Latin American geographer, and, as the person who knew him best suggested (Leighly 1963), a land-and-life geographer. Some of these interests are evident in the work of his students; others are not. And many, perhaps most, of Sauer's students have pursued interests that are

not conspicuous in his writings (e.g., Spencer 1966; Sopher 1967; Zelinsky 1973). We should hope that his fascinating personality, provocative opinions, and remarkable accomplishment will continue to attract the attention of historians of geography and biographers. For most cultural geographers, however, "Sauerology" is a peripheral concern and maybe a distraction.

As for the Berkeley school and its alleged character as the central place of traditional cultural geography, I have to point to some discouraging realities. There has been only one attempt to elicit comments from graduates of this school on what may have been its distinguishing qualities (Speth 1988), only one responsible external review of the strengths and weaknesses of the school (Brookfield 1964), and only one critical analysis of traditional cultural geographers' use of the culture concept (Duncan 1980). Most of what has been written by self-styled radical, new, or social-cum-cultural geographers is superficial or worse: deconstruction without the benefit of a text. No critic of the Berkeley school has been sufficiently well informed to proclaim its persistent mission, which was to seek evidence of logic and pathology revealed in the record of the human use and misuse of the earth. That mission set the agenda for a wide array of field studies and more than a hundred book-length publications. Needless to say, there were and are other agendas for cultural geography and equally wide-ranging interests that were only latent or implicit in the program of the Berkeley school.

It is still useful to see cultural geography as a venerable enterprise and to focus attention on the work of notable pioneers. To understand where we might be going, it helps to know where we have been. But when interests are genuinely new, it serves no useful purpose to deflect attention to what an earlier generation did not do or to be preoccupied with the "deficiencies" of irrelevant literature. It is only entertaining, not enlightening, to imagine what might have happened if Sauer had been able to accompany a new cultural geographer on a tour of Latino communities in Los Angeles. Anyone blessed with this degree of imagination should also be able to appreciate the benefit of the latter following Sauer (1932) along the route to the legendary cities of Cíbola.

EVERYTHING IS IN ENGLISH?

Thanks to Ron Johnston (1979), an entire generation has been encouraged to believe in the existence of "Anglo-American human geography." This belief may have been reinforced by the U.S.-U.K. focus and English-only documentation of two recent attempts to clarify the objectives of cultural geography (P. Jackson 1989; W. Norton 1989). Interest in the origin and early development of cultural geography usually results in a different perspective: German and French literature is as prominent as American literature, and British authors are seldom mentioned. *Readings in Cultural Geography* had an international cast, with contributions from Austria, Brazil, Britain, France, Germany, Israel, Italy, Sweden, Switzerland, and the United States. The present volume, in contrast, offers evidence only of the cultural component of Anglo-American human geography.

My personal view is that cultural geography should still be regarded as an international venture. I have to concede, however, that scholarly innovations, regardless of their national origins, usually manage to cross political and linguistic boundaries. It is sufficient to recall that Karl Marx, Sigmund Freud, Emile Durkheim, and Max Weber composed their works in languages other than English and yet became dominating authorities of "our social sciences." Among the celebrities of recent metaphilosophical critique (Jürgen Habermas, Michel Foucault, Jacques Derrida, Henri Lefebvre, and Anthony Giddens), only Giddens initially published his work in English. So the question posed above may have a reassuring answer: everything may not be written first in English, but anything important eventually appears in English. The recent publication in English of an excellent review of the work of Japanese cultural geographers (Hisatake 1989) can be offered as evidence in support of this principle.

On the other hand, foreign work of potential use to us may not be sufficiently marketable (or metaphilosophical) to justify the translation and republication costs. Loss of significant information or delay in its diffusion into our linguistic domain is therefore a distinct possibility. For ex-

ample, the development of American cultural geography would have been enhanced in many ways if the remarkably comprehensive work of Maximilien Sorre (1943–1952) had been widely known and could have served as a complement or challenge to more narrowly defined authority.

The problem created by national-linguistic barriers is especially acute for scholars devoted to landscape study. Several of the articles in this volume establish conclusively that important work is being published in English, but the same can be said of work in French and German. Augustin Berque has written several books and numerous articles that offer fresh thinking and useful advice on landscape interpretation. It is unfortunate that *Le sauvage et l'artifice* (Berque 1986) and several programmatic statements (e.g., 1984; 1987) cannot as of now be required reading. This comment also applies to Gerhard Hard's *Die "Landschaft" der Sprache und die "Landschaft" der Geographen* (1970). And we now have a new quarterly journal, *Géographie et Cultures,* that could serve as the headquarters for an ecumenical movement among cultural geographers. In the inaugural issue, Paul Claval (1992) offers a well-balanced and appropriately international assessment of recent accomplishments and unfinished tasks.

Unless cultural geography is redefined as a study of our culture rather than of cultures, I do not see how the communications problems created by Anglo-American linguistic chauvinism can be denied. To be sure, anyone claiming now, as Carl Sauer did in 1956, that "a monolingual Ph.D. is a contradiction in terms" would probably be charged immediately with the heinous crime of "anti-modern elitism" (Sauer 1956b). The concern he expressed can be rephrased in words that may be more acceptable in our time: Is monolingual multiculturalism a contradiction in terms?

PERSISTENT PLURALISM

The word that best describes the intellectual affiliation of cultural geographers might be *confederation.* The looseness that this term suggests may inspire feelings of regret or misplaced nostalgia. I believe we should welcome the prospect of new and renewed efforts that are neither promoted nor restrained by any central authority. Does endorsing this idea require us to speak of cultural geographies rather than of cultural geography? I doubt that this is desirable or necessary. The difficulty we experience in describing common interests is experienced by all geographers and, whether admitted or not, by all or at least most social scientists. Pluralism is not a problem to be overcome. It is an inherent and persisting reality that we should try to understand and, in so doing, learn to accept.

The pluralism of cultural geography has several clear manifestations. Much effort is directed to understanding the appearance, function, and meaning of built environments. Much effort is also directed to understanding the processes (deforestation, erosion, reclamation, etc.) that result in modifications of natural environments. Other interests pursued vigorously or at least sporadically by cultural geographers (e.g., geolinguistics, dietary preferences, population movements, minority-group aspirations) may have no clear connection with natural or artificial environments. As a priori world citizens, we may also be concerned about the causes and consequences of language riots, "ethnic cleansing," and holy wars. Moreover, since our research must have a territorial and temporal focus, the number of cells in the matrix of cultural-geographic interests has no inherent limit.

Pluralism is also revealed in our external affiliations. The contributors to *Readings in Cultural Geography* included, in addition to geographers, an ethnozoologist, a linguist, three botanists, an archaeologist, a cultural cartographer, a historian, several anthropologists, and a "free-lance scholar." All but one of the contributors to the present volume are geographers, yet the literature cited here, and especially in the editors' wide-ranging introductory essay, is no less interdisciplinary. Biology and ecology are less conspicuous, but anthropology is still prominent, and other orientations not evident in the previous work, such as art history and semiotics, suggest new reading habits. Cultural geography also had or now seems to have extradisciplinary or post-disciplinary aspirations, as well as interdisciplinary ones. Political economy, which transcends

traditional disciplines, is a pervasive influence. The same can be said of the various incarnations and reincarnations of Marxism. We can now detect evidence of the growing popularity of other transcending interests, for example, cultural politics and political ecology.

Cultural geographers will never be able to agree on what should be required reading. Two recent works not cited in the introduction to this volume would be at the top of my list: *The City in Cultural Context* (Agnew, Mercer, and Sopher 1984) and *The Invention of Tradition* (Hobsbawm and Ranger 1983). On the other hand, many other works, unread by me, are cited and are placed in contexts that expose substantial gaps in my education. The education of a cultural geographer—or at least this cultural geographer—always entails remedial accomplishment. The fate of our pluralistic enterprise depends on how effectively we can pursue personal commitments while trying simultaneously to appreciate what others want to do. We all have convictions about research needs and educational objectives. "Come on in, the water is fine" is a suggestion any of us should be willing to entertain. "Drop everything and follow me" is a different kind of message that should not be heeded or even heard in a confederation.

SUMMARY THOUGHTS

This volume is a welcome and long-overdue successor to the work Philip Wagner and I accomplished thirty years ago, which now has only historical interest. It would, of course, be a sad commentary on the vitality of cultural geography if a work published so long ago had more than historical interest. The evidence offered here of new and renewed interests is refreshing and reassuring.

My one major concern is inspired by fear or at least suspicion that cultural geographers are inclined increasingly to deny the value of historical and international perspectives. The world we must try to understand is still marked for the most part by postcolonial rather than postmodern cultural indicators. The manifest disorder in our "new world order" invites us to consider not only contemporary transforming processes but also reactionary fundamentalism and the many cultural-geographic realities that were ignored or merely masked when the Hapsburg and Ottoman empires were dismembered after World War I and the British and French empires dissolved after World War II. The recent transformation of the Soviet Union into a conjugation of nations has exposed other problems of obvious interest. Our richly varied and troubled world presents us with countless examples of human conflict and accommodation, cultural survival dilemmas, and environmental management options that should encourage us to look far beyond the Western urban settings that are now attracting most of the attention of American cultural geographers. Fieldwork in non-Western countries has always been difficult and is now often dangerous, especially for Americans, yet it is impossible to imagine how the necessity of such effort can be denied. It would be ironic if scholars inspired by the thought that they are contributing to an enlarged mission for cultural geography were to adopt the motto of Disneyland and tell us that "it's a small world after all."

REFERENCES

Abler, Ronald F. 1987. What shall we say? To whom shall we speak? *Annals of the Association of American Geographers* 77:511–24.

Abu-Lughod, Janet L. 1989. *Before European hegemony: The world system A.D. 1250–1350.* New York: Oxford University Press.

Acrelius, Israel. 1874. *A history of New Sweden.* Trans. W. M. Reynolds. Philadelphia: Historical Society of Pennsylvania.

Adams, Edward D. 1927. *Niagara power.* 2 vols. Niagara Falls, N.Y.: Niagara Falls Power Co.

Adams, Paul C. 1992. Television as gathering place. *Annals of the Association of American Geographers* 82:117–35.

Adams, Richard. 1974. *Watership down.* Harmondsworth: Penguin.

———. 1978. *The plague dogs.* Harmondsworth: Penguin.

Adams, Richard N. 1988. *The eighth day: Social organization as the self-organization of energy.* Austin: University of Texas Press.

Adams, Thomas, Harold M. Lewis, and Theodore T. McCrosky. 1929. *Population, land values and government.* New York: Regional Plan of New York and Its Environs, Regional Survey of New York and Its Environs No. 2.

Adams, W., D. Van Gerven, and R. Levy. 1978. The retreat from migrationism. *Annual Review of Anthropology* 7:483–532.

African slavery adapted to the North and Northwest. 1858. *DeBow's Review* 25:378–95.

Agassiz, G. 1912. Niagara—the "mighty thunderer." *National Magazine,* September.

Agnew, John A. 1987b. *Place and politics: The geographical mediation of state and society.* Boston: Allen & Unwin.

———. 1987a. *The United States in the world economy: A regional geography.* Cambridge: Cambridge University Press.

Agnew, John A., and James S. Duncan, eds. 1989. *The power of place: Bringing together geographical and sociological imaginations.* New York: Unwin Hyman.

Agnew, John A., John Mercer, and David Sopher, eds. 1984. *The city in cultural context.* Boston: Allen & Unwin.

Agrarian Reform Archive (Cuzco). 1985. Resumen de precios agricolas, Cuzco.

Aguirre Beltrán, Gonzalo. 1979. *Regions of refuge.* Washington, D.C.: Society for Applied Anthropology.

Aiken, Charles S. 1977. Faulkner's Yoknapatawpha County: Geographical fact into fiction. *Geographical Review* 67:1–21.

———. 1979. Faulkner's Yoknapatawpha County: A place in the American South. *Geographical Review* 79: 331–48.

Aitken, Stuart C. 1991. A transactional geography of the image-event: The films of Scottish director, Bill Forsyth. *Transactions of the Institute of British Geographers,* n.s. 16:105–18.

Aitken, Stuart, Susan Cutter, Kenneth Foote, and James Sell. 1989. Environmental perception and behavioral geography. In *Geography in America,* ed. Gary L. Gaile and Cort J. Willmott, 218–38. Columbus, Ohio: Merrill Publishing Co.

Aladdin quite outdone: Giant palace to span the mighty Niagara cataract. 1896. *New York World,* 9 Feb.

Alcorn, John. 1977. *The nature novel from Hardy to Lawrence.* London: Macmillan.

Allen, Catherine J. 1988. *The hold life has: Coca and cultural identity in an Andean community.* Washington: Smithsonian Institution Press.

Allen, James P., and Eugene J. Turner. 1988. *We the people: An atlas of America's ethnic diversity.* New York: Macmillan.

Almonte, Juan N. 1925. Statistical report on Texas. Trans. Carlos E. Castañeda. *Southwestern Historical Quarterly* 28:177–222.

Altieri, Miguel, and Susanna Hecht, eds. 1989. *Agroecology and small farm development.* Boca Raton, Fla.: CRC.

Alvarez, José H. 1966. A demographic profile of the Mexican immigration to the United States, 1910–1950. *Journal of Inter-American Studies* 8:471–96.

Amin, Samir. 1973. *Neo-colonialism in West Africa.* New York: Monthly Review Press.

———. 1989. *Eurocentrism.* Trans. Russell Moore. New York: Monthly Review Press.

Andrew, Laurel B. 1978. *The early temples of the Mormons: The architecture of the Millennial Kingdom in the American West.* Albany: State University of New York Press.

Appleyard, Donald. 1979. The environment as a social symbol. *Journal of the American Planning Association* 45:143–53.

Ariès, Philippe. 1974. *Western attitudes toward death: From the Middle Ages to the present.* Trans. P. M. Ranum. Baltimore: Johns Hopkins University Press.

Arreola, Daniel D. 1981. Fences as landscape taste: Tucson's *barrios. Journal of Cultural Geography* 2:96–105.

———. 1984. Mexican American exterior murals. *Geographical Review* 74: 409–24.

———. 1987. Mexican American cultural capital. *Geographical Review* 77:17–34.

———. 1988. Mexican American housescapes. *Geographical Review* 78:299–315.

———. 1992. Plaza towns of south Texas. *Geographical Review* 82: 56–73.

Asad, Talal, ed. 1973. *Anthropology and the colonial encounter.* New York: Humanities.

Asante, Molefi K., and Mark T. Mattson. 1991. *Historical and cultural atlas of African Americans.* New York: Macmillan.

Association of American Geographers. 1984. *Guidelines for geographic education: Elementary and secondary education.* Washington, D.C.: Association of American Geographers.

Atack, Jeremy, and Fred Bateman. 1987. *To their own soil: Agriculture in the antebellum North.* Ames: Iowa State University Press.

Augelli, John P. 1962. The rimland-mainland concept of culture areas in Middle America. *Annals of the Association of American Geographers* 52:119–29.

Austen, Jane. 1948. *Sense and sensibility.* London: Allan Wingate.

Auster, Henry. 1970. *Local habitations: Regionalism in the early novels of George Eliot.* Cambridge: Harvard University Press.

Baker, John A. 1990. Biblical views of nature. In *Liberating life: Contemporary approaches to ecological theology,* ed. Charles Birch, William Eakin, and Jay B. Mc-Daniel, 9–26. Maryknoll, N.Y.: Orbis.

Baker, V. R., and C. R. Twidale. 1991. The reenchantment of geomorphology. *Geomorphology* 4:73–100.

Baldwin, James A. 1987. Research themes in the cultural geography of domesticated animals, 1974–1987. *Journal of Cultural Geography* 7:3–18.

Baldwin, Robert. 1956. Patterns of development in newly settled regions. *Manchester School of Economic and Social Studies* 24:161–79.

Balibar, Etienne, and Immanuel Wallerstein. 1991. *Race, nation, class: Ambiguous identities.* New York: Verso.

Baltzell, Edward Digby. 1979. *Puritan Boston and Quaker Philadelphia: Two Protestant ethics and the spirit of class authority and leadership.* New York: Free Press.

Bancroft, Hubert H. 1893. *The book of the fair.* Chicago: The Bancroft Co.

Banham, Reyner. 1971. *Los Angeles: The architecture of four ecologies.* Harmondsworth: Penguin.

Barbour, Ian G. 1990. *Religion in an age of science.* San Francisco: Harper & Row.

Barnes, Trevor J., and James S. Duncan, eds. 1992. *Writing worlds: Discourse, text and metaphor in the representation of landscape.* London: Routledge.

Barnouw, Erik. 1974. *Documentary: A history of the non-fictional film.* New York: Oxford University Press.

Barr, Alwyn. 1971. Occupational and geographic mobility in San Antonio, 1870–1900. *Social Science Quarterly* 51:396–403.

Barrell, John. 1982. Geographies of Hardy's Wessex. *Journal of Historical Geography* 8:347–61.

Barrett, Walter H. 1963. *Tales from the fens.* London: Routledge and Kegan Paul.

———. 1965. *A fenman's story.* London: Routledge and Kegan Paul.

Barrows, Harlan H. 1923. Geography as human ecology. *Annals of the Association of American Geographers* 13:1–14.

Barry, Richard H. 1901. *Snap shots on the midway of the Pan-American Exposition.* Buffalo: R.A. Reid.

Barth, Gunther. 1980. *City people: The rise of modern city culture in nineteenth-century America.* New York: Oxford University Press.

Barthes, Roland. 1972. *Mythologies.* Trans. Annette Lavers. London: Jonathan Cape.

———. 1979. *The Eiffel Tower and other mythologies.* Trans. Richard Howard. New York: Hill and Wang.

Bassett, Thomas J. 1988. The political ecology of peasant-herder conflicts in Northern Ivory Coast. *Annals of the Association of American Geographers* 78:453–72.

Bates, Herbert E. 1969. *An autobiography.* 3 vols. Vol. 1: *The vanished world.* London: Michael Joseph.

Baudrillard, Jean. 1988. *America.* Trans. Chris Turner. London: Verso.

Baumann, Duane D., and John H. Sims. 1974. Human response to the hurricane. In *Natural hazards: Local, national, global,* ed. Gilbert White, 25–30. New York: Oxford University Press.

Bausman, R. O., and J. A. Munroe. 1946. James Tilton's notes on the agriculture of Delaware in 1788. *Agricultural History* 20:176–87.

Bean, Frank D., and Benjamin S. Bradshaw. 1970. Intermarriage between persons of Spanish and non-Spanish surname: Changes from the mid-nineteenth to the mid-twentieth century. *Social Science Quarterly* 51:389–95.

Bellamy, Edward. 1888. *Looking backward, 2000–1887.* Boston: Ticknor.

Belloc, Hilaire. 1906. *Hills and the sea.* London: Methuen.

Bennett, Charles F. 1968. *Human influences on the zoogeography of Panama.* Ibero-Americana 51. Berkeley: University of California Press.

Bennett, John W., and Kenneth A. Dahlberg. 1990. Institutions, social organization, and cultural values. In *The earth as transformed by human action: Global and regional changes in the biosphere over the past 300 years,* ed. B. L. Turner II et al., 69–86. New York: Cambridge University Press.

Benson, Lee. 1972. *Toward the scientific study of history: Selected essays of Lee Benson.* Philadelphia: J.B. Lippincott Company.

Bentley, Phyllis E. 1932. *Inheritance.* New York: Macmillan.

———. 1941. *The English regional novel.* London: George Allen & Unwin.

Berenson, Bernard. 1953. *Seeing and knowing.* London: Chapin and Hall.

Berger, Meyer. 1951. *The story of the* New York Times. New York: Simon and Schuster.

Berlin, Ira. 1974. *Slaves without masters: The free Negro in the antebellum South.* New York: Vintage.

Bernal, Martin. 1987. *Black Athena: The Afroasiatic roots of classical civilization.* 2 vols. Vol. 1: *The fabrication of ancient Greece, 1785–1985.* Vol. 2: *The archeological and documentary evidence.* London: Free Association.

Berque, Augustin. 1984. Paysage-empreinte, paysage-matrice: élements de problématique pour une géographie culturelle. *L'Espace Géographique* 13:33–34.

———. 1986. *Le sauvage et l'artifice: Les Japonais devant la nature.* Paris: Gallimard.

———. 1987. Milieu et motivation paysagère. *L'Espace Géographique* 16:241–51.

Berry, Brian J. L. 1963. *Commercial structure and commercial blight.* University of Chicago Department of Geography Research Paper no. 85. Chicago: University of Chicago, Department of Geography.

———. 1967. *Geography of market centers and retail distribution.* Englewood Cliffs, N.J.: Prentice-Hall.

———. 1980. Creating future geographies. *Annals of the Association of American Geographers* 70:449–58.

———. 1991. *Long-wave rhythms in economic development and political behavior.* Baltimore: Johns Hopkins University Press.

Berry, Thomas. 1990. The spirituality of the earth. In *Liberating life: Contemporary approaches to ecological theology,* ed. Charles Birch, William Eakin, and Jay B. McDaniel, 151–58. Maryknoll, N.Y.: Orbis.

Berry, Wendell. 1985. *Collected poems.* San Francisco: North Point.

Bertelson, David. 1967. *The lazy South.* New York: Oxford University Press.

Berwanger, Eugene H. 1967. *The frontier against slavery: Western anti-Negro prejudice and the slavery extension controversy.* Urbana: University of Illinois Press.

Bhatia, B. M. 1967. *Famines in India.* Bombay: Asia Publishing House.

Bidwell, Percy W., and John I. Falconer. 1941. *History of agriculture in the northern United States, 1620–1860.* New York: Peter Smith.

Billinge, Mark. 1982. Reconstructing societies in the past: The collective biography of local communities. In *In period and place: Research methods in historical geography,* ed. Alan R. H. Baker and Mark Billinge, 19–32. Cambridge: Cambridge University Press.

Billinge, Mark, Derek Gregory, and Ron Martin, eds. 1984. *Recollections of a revolution: Geography as spatial science.* London: Macmillan.

Birch, Charles, and John B. Cobb. 1981. *The liberation of life: From the cell to the community.* Cambridge: Cambridge University Press.

Birks, Hilary H., H. J. B. Birks, Peter E. Kaland, and Dagfinn Moe, eds. 1988. *The cultural landscape: Past, present and future.* Cambridge: Cambridge University Press.

Black, J. N. 1970. *Dominion of man: Search for ecological responsibility.* Edinburgh: Edinburgh University Press.

Blaikie, Piers. 1978. The theory of the spatial diffusion of innovations: A spacious cul-de-sac. *Progress in Human Geography* 2:268–95.

———. 1985. *The political economy of soil erosion in developing countries*. London: Longman.

Blaikie, Piers, and Harold C. Brookfield. 1987. *Land degradation and society*. London: Methuen.

Blake, Peter. 1964. *God's own junkyard*. New York: Holt, Rinehart and Winston.

Blashfield, Edwin H. 1899. A word for municipal art. *Municipal Affairs* 3:582–93.

Blaut, James M. 1970. Geographic models of imperialism. *Antipode* 2 (1): 65–85.

———. 1973. The theory of development. *Antipode* 5 (2): 22–26.

———. 1976. Where was capitalism born? *Antipode* 8 (2): 1–11.

———. 1977. Two views of diffusion. *Annals of the Association of American Geographers* 67:343–49.

———. 1979. Some principles of ethnogeography. In *Philosophy in geography*, ed. S. Gale and G. Olson, 1–7. Dordrecht: Reidel.

———. 1980. Nairn on nationalism. *Antipode* 12 (3): 1–17.

———. 1982. Nationalism as an autonomous force. *Science and Society* 46:1–23.

———. 1984. Modesty and the movement. In *Environmental perception and behavior: An inventory and prospect*, ed. T. Saarinen, D. Seaman, and J. Sell, 149–63. University of Chicago Department of Geography Research Paper no. 209. Chicago: University of Chicago, Department of Geography.

———. 1987a. Diffusionism: A uniformitarian critique. *Annals of the Association of American Geographers* 77: 30–47.

———. 1987b. *The national question: Decolonising the theory of nationalism*. London: ZED.

———, ed. 1992. *Fourteen ninety-two: The debate on colonialism, Eurocentrism, and history*. Trenton, N.J.: Africa World.

———. 1993. *Diffusionism: Or history inside out*. New York: Guilford.

Blaut, James M., and Antonio Ríos-Bustamante. 1984. Commentary on Nostrand's "Hispanos" and their "Homeland." *Annals of the Association of American Geographers* 74:157–64.

Bleyer, Willard G. 1927. *Main currents in the history of American journalism*. New York: Houghton Mifflin.

Bloom, Alan. 1944. *The farm in the fen*. London: Faber and Faber.

———. 1953. *The fens*. London: Robert Hale.

Boal, Frederick W., and David N. Livingstone, eds. 1989. *The behavioural environment: Essays in reflection, application, and re-evaluation*. London: Routledge.

Boas, Max, and Steve Chain. 1977. *Big mac: The unauthorized story of McDonald's*. New York: New American Library.

Bock, Philip K. 1980. *Continuities in psychological anthropology*. San Francisco: W.H. Freeman.

Bogue, Allan G. 1968. *From prairie to cornbelt: Farming on the Illinois and Iowa prairies in the nineteenth century*. Chicago: Quadrangle.

Bolton, Herbert E. 1915. *Texas in the middle eighteenth century: Studies in Spanish colonial history and administration*. University of California Publications in History, vol. 3. Berkeley: University of California.

Boserup, Ester. 1965. *The conditions of agricultural growth: The economics of agrarian change under population pressure*. Chicago: Aldine.

Bourdieu, Pierre. 1977. *Outline of a theory of practice*. Cambridge: Cambridge University Press.

Bourke, John G. 1895. The folk-foods of the Rio Grande valley and of northern Mexico. *Journal of American Folk-Lore* 8 (28): 41–71.

Bovy, Piet H. L., and Eliahu Stern. 1990. *Route choice: Wayfinding in transportation networks*. Dordrecht: Kluwer.

Bowen-Jones, H. 1981. Technology and the Third World. In *The Third World: Problems and perspectives*, ed. A. Montfort, 76–83. London: Macmillan.

Bragg, Melvyn. 1977. *Speak for England: An oral history of England: 1900–1975*. New York: Knopf.

Brand, Stewart. 1976a. Editor's note to "Carl Ortwin Sauer, 1889–1975," by James J. Parsons. *CoEvolution Quarterly* 10 (Summer): 45.

———. 1976b. Editor's note to "The theme of plant and animal destruction in economic history," by Carl O. Sauer. *CoEvolution Quarterly* 10 (Summer): 48.

Bratton, Susan P. 1984. Christian ecotheology and the Old Testament. *Environmental Ethics* 6:195–209.

———. 1986. Christian ecotheology and the Old Testament. In *Religion and Environmental Crisis*, ed. Eugene C. Hargrove, 53–75. Athens: University of Georgia Press.

Braudel, Fernand. 1981-1984. *Civilization and capitalism, 15th to 18th century*. 3 vols. Vol. 3: *The perspective of the world*. Trans. Sian Reynolds. New York: Harper and Row.

Brewster, J. M. 1950. The machine process in agriculture and industry. *Journal of Farm Economics* 32: 69–81.

Brookfield, Harold C. 1964. Questions on the human frontiers of geography. *Economic Geography* 40: 283–303.

———. 1968. New directions in the study of agricultural systems in tropical areas. In *Evolution and Environment*, ed. E. T. Drake, 413–39. New Haven, Conn.: Yale University Press.

———. 1972. Intensification and disintensification in Pacific agriculture: A theoretical approach. *Pacific Viewpoint* 13:30–48.

———. 1973. *The Pacific in transition: Geographical perspectives on adaptation and change*. London: Arnold.

———. 1975. *Interdependent development*. Pittsburgh, Penn.: University of Pittsburgh Press.

———. 1984. Intensification revisited. *Pacific Viewpoint* 25:15–24.

———. 1988. Sustainable development and the environment. *Journal of Development Studies* 25:126–35.

Browett, John. 1980. Development, the diffusionist paradigm and geography. *Progress in Human Geography* 4: 56–79.

Brown, Lawrence A. 1981. *Innovation diffusion: A new perspective.* London: Methuen.

Brown, Marilyn A. 1981. Behavioral approaches to the geographic study of innovation diffusion: Problems and prospects. In *Behavioral problems in geography revisited,* ed. Kevin Cox and Reginald G. Golledge, 123–44. New York: Methuen.

Brown, Michael H. 1979. *Laying waste: The poisoning of America by toxic chemicals.* New York: Pantheon.

Brown, Ralph. 1943. *Mirror for Americans: Likeness of the Eastern Seaboard, 1810.* New York: American Geographical Society.

———. 1948. *Historical geography of the United States.* New York: Harcourt Brace and World.

Bruner, Jerome S. 1990. *Acts of meaning.* Cambridge: Harvard University Press.

Brush, Stephen B. 1987. The nature of farming systems and views of their change. In *Comparative farming systems,* ed. B. L. Turner II and Stephen B. Brush, 11–48. New York: Guilford.

Buber, Martin. 1937. *I and thou.* Trans. R. Gregor. Edinburgh: Clark.

Buley, R. Carlyle. 1959. *The Equitable Life Assurance Society of the United States.* New York: Appleton-Century-Crofts.

Bultmann, Rudolf. 1984. *New Testament and mythology and other basic writings.* Trans. and ed. by Schubert M. Ogden. Philadelphia: Fortress.

Bump, Jerome. 1974. Hopkins, the humanities, and the environment. *The Georgia Review* 28:227–44.

Bunge, William. 1962. *Theoretical geography.* Lund, Sweden: University of Lund, Department of Geography, Lund Studies in Geography, Series C, No. 1.

Bunge, William. 1971. *Fitzgerald: A geography of revolution.* Cambridge, Mass.: Schenkman.

Bunkse, Edmunds V. 1978. Commoner attitudes toward landscape and nature. *Annals of the Association of American Geographers* 68:551–66.

———. 1981. Humboldt and an aesthetic tradition in geography. *Geographical Review* 71:127–47.

Burck, Gilbert. 1959. How American taste is changing. *Fortune* 60 (July): 196.

Burgess, Jacquelin. 1982. Filming the Fens: A visual interpretation of regional character. In *Valued Environments,* ed. Jacquelin Burgess and John R. Gold, 35–54. London: Allen & Unwin.

———. 1990. The production and consumption of environmental meanings in the mass media: A research agenda for the 1990s. *Transactions of the Institute of British Geographers,* n.s. 15:139–61.

Burgess, Jacquelin, and John Gold, eds. 1985. *Geography, the media, and popular culture.* London: Croom Helm.

Burgess, Jacquelin, Carolyn M. Harrison, and Paul Maiteny. 1991. Contested meanings: The consumption of news about nature conservation. *Media, Culture and Society* 13:499–519.

Burns, Elizabeth K. 1980. The enduring affluent suburb. *Landscape* 24 (1): 33–41.

Burton, Ian. 1963. The quantitative revolution and theoretical geography. *Canadian Geographer* 7:151–62.

Burton, Ian, Robert Kates, and Gilbert White. 1978. *The environment as hazard.* New York: Oxford University Press.

Bury, John B. 1955. *The idea of progress: An inquiry into its origin and growth.* New York: Dover.

Butlin, Noel. 1983. *Our original aggression.* Sydney: Allen & Unwin.

Butterick, Charles. 1980. *Charles Olson and Robert Creeley: The complete correspondence,* vol. 5. Santa Barbara, Calif.: Black Arrow.

Buttimer, Anne. 1974. *Values in geography.* Association of American Geographers, Commission on College Geography, Resource Paper no. 24. Washington, D.C.: Association of American Geographers.

———. 1980. Home, reach and the sense of place. In *The human experience of space and place,* ed. Anne Buttimer and David Seamon, 166–87. London: Croom Helm.

Buttimer, Anne, and David Seamon, eds. 1980. *The human experience of space and place.* London: Croom Helm.

Butzer, Karl W. 1976. *Early hydraulic civilization in Egypt: A study in cultural ecology.* Chicago: University of Chicago Press.

———. 1980. Civilizations: Organisms or systems? *American Scientist* 68:517–23.

———. 1982. *Archaeology as human ecology: Theory and method for a contextual approach.* New York: Cambridge University Press.

———. 1984. Long-term Nile flood variation and political discontinuities in Pharaonic Egypt. In *From hunters to farmers,* ed. J. Desmond Clark and Steven A. Brandt, 102–12. Berkeley: University of California Press.

———. 1988a. Cattle and sheep from Old to New Spain: Historical antecedents. *Annals of the Association of American Geographers* 78:29–56.

———. 1988b. Diffusion, adaptation, and evolution of the Spanish agrosystem. In *The transfer and transformation of ideas and material culture,* ed. P. J. Hugill and D. B. Dickson, 91–109. College Station: Texas A & M University Press.

———. 1989. Cultural ecology. In *Geography in America,* ed. Gary L. Gaile and Cort J. Willmott, 192–208. Columbus, Ohio: Merrill.

———. 1990a. A human ecosystem framework for archaeology. In *The ecosystem approach in anthropology: From concept to practice,* ed. E. F. Moran, 91–130. Ann Arbor: University of Michigan Press.

———. 1990b. The realm of cultural-human ecology: Adaptation and change in historical perspective. In *The earth as transformed by human action: Global and regional changes in the biosphere over the past 300 years,* ed. B. L. Turner II et al., 685–701. Cambridge: Cambridge University Press.

———, ed. 1992a. *The Americas before and after 1492:*

Current geographical research. Special edition of *Annals of the Association of American Geographers* 82 (3).

———. 1992b. Judgment or understanding: Reflections on 1492. *Queen's Quarterly* 99 (Fall): 581–600.

———. 1992c. Spanish conquest society in the New World: Ecological readaptation and cultural transformation. In *Person, place, thing: Interpretive and empirical essays in cultural geography,* ed. Shue Tuck Wong, 211–42. Geoscience and Man 31. Baton Rouge: Louisiana State University, Department of Geography and Anthropology.

Byrne, Roger, and Mark Blumler. 1991. The ecological genetics of domestication and the origin of agriculture. *Current Anthropology* 32:23–54.

Camarillo, Albert. 1979. *Chicanos in a changing society: From Mexican pueblos to American barrios in Santa Barbara and southern California, 1848–1930.* Cambridge, Mass.: Harvard University Press.

Canales, Isidro V. 1971. *Los orígenes de la industrialización de Monterrey: Una historica economica y social desde la caida del segundo imperio hasta el fin de la revolución (1867–1920).* Monterrey: Librería Technológica.

Carlson, Alvar W. 1990. *The Spanish American homeland: Four centuries in New Mexico's Rio Arriba.* Baltimore: Johns Hopkins University Press.

Carlstein, Tommy. 1982. *Time resources, society and ecology: On the capacity for human interaction in space and time.* Vol. 1: *Preindustrial societies.* London: Allen & Unwin.

Carlstein, Tommy, Don Parkes, and Nigel Thrift. 1978. *Timing space and spacing time.* 3 vols. New York: Wiley.

Carlyle, T. 1867. *Shooting Niagara: And after?* London: Chapman and Hall.

Carman, Harry J., ed. 1964. *American husbandry.* Port Washington, N.Y.: Kennikat.

Carmody, John. 1980. *Theology for the 1980s.* Philadelphia: Westminster.

Carr, Archie. 1956. *The windward road.* New York: Knopf.

———. 1962. Foreword to *The green turtle and man,* by James J. Parsons. Gainesville: University of Florida Press.

Carr, Archie, Marjorie H. Carr, and Anne B. Meylan. 1978. The ecology and migrations of sea turtles, 7. The west Caribbean green turtle colony. *Bulletin of the American Museum of Natural History* 162 (1).

Carroll, John A, ed. 1969. Seminar on the teaching of Western history. In *Reflections of Western historians,* ed. John A. Carroll, 265–99. Tucson: University of Arizona Press.

Carroll, Kenneth L. 1950. Maryland Quakers and slavery. *Maryland Historical Magazine* 45:215–25.

———. 1961. Religious influences on the manumission of slaves in Caroline, Dorchester, and Talbot counties. *Maryland Historical Magazine* 56:176–97.

Carter, George. 1968. *Man and the land: A cultural geography.* New York: Holt, Rinehart and Winston.

———. 1977. A hypothesis suggesting a single origin of agriculture. In *Origins of Agriculture,* ed. C. A. Reed, 89–133. The Hague: Mouton.

Cary, Joyce. 1981. *Mister Johnson.* Alexandria, Va.: Time-Life.

Cawelti, John C. 1968. America on display: The world's fairs of 1876, 1893, 1933. In *The age of industrialism in America,* ed. Frederic C. Jaher, 317–63. New York: Free Press.

Césaire, Aimé. 1972. *Discourse on colonialism.* New York: Monthly Review Press.

Chamberlain, M. 1975. *Fenwomen: A portrait of women in an English village.* London: Virago.

Chamberlin, Thomas C. 1890. The method of multiple working hypotheses. *Science,* o.s. 15:92; reprint *Science,* n.s. 148 (1965): 754–59.

Chapin, Mac, ed. 1992. The co-existence of indigenous peoples in the natural environments of Central America. *Research and Exploration* 8 (2): map supplement.

Chapman, John. 1977. Los Angeles is just too much. *Los Angeles Times,* 28 June, Part II, 7.

Chilcote, Ronald H. 1984. *Theories of development and underdevelopment.* Boulder: Westview.

Childe, V. Gordon. 1951. *Social evolution.* New York: Henry Schuman.

Chisholm, Michael. 1982. *Modern world development.* Totowa, N.J.: Barnes and Noble.

Chorley, Richard J., and Peter Haggett, eds. 1967. *Models in geography.* London: Methuen.

Churchill, Allen. 1958. *Park Row.* New York: Rinehart.

Chute, Carolyn. 1985. *The beans of Egypt, Maine.* New York: Ticknor & Fields.

———. 1988. *Le Tourneau's used auto parts.* New York: Ticknor & Fields.

Clark, John G. 1966. *The grain trade in the Old Northwest.* Urbana: University of Illinois Press.

Clark, Kenneth. 1969. *Civilisation: A personal view.* London: British Broadcasting Corporation and John Murray.

Clarke, Ignatius F. 1979. *The pattern of expectation, 1644–2001.* New York: Basic.

Clarke, William C. 1966. *Place and people: An ecology of a New Guinea community.* Berkeley: University of California Press.

———. 1990. Learning from the past: Traditional knowledge and sustainable development. *Contemporary Pacific* 2:233–53.

Claval, Paul. 1992. Champ et perspectives de la géographie culturelle. *Géographie et Cultures* 1:7–38.

Clay, Grady. 1971. Swarming. *Landscape Architecture,* April: insert, "Scope III."

———. 1980. *Close-up: How to read the American city.* Chicago: University of Chicago Press.

Clayre, Alasdair, ed. 1977. *Nature and industrialisation: An anthology.* Oxford: Oxford University Press.

Clayton, W. W. 1878. *History of Onondaga County, New York.* Syracuse, N.Y.: D. Mason.

Cleary, M. C., and F. J. Lian. 1991. On the geography of Borneo. *Progress in Human Geography* 15:163–77.

Clemens, Paul G. E. 1974. From tobacco to grain: Economic development on Maryland's eastern shore, 1660–1750. Ph.D. diss., University of Wisconsin, Madison.

Clough, Shepard B. 1946. *A century of American life insurance.* New York: Columbia University Press.

Coatsworth, John H. 1981. *Growth against development: The economic impact of railroads in Porfirian Mexico.* DeKalb: Northern Illinois University Press.

Cochran, Thomas C. 1981. *Frontiers of change: Early industrialism in America.* New York: Oxford University Press.

Coelho, Philip P., and James F. Shepherd. 1976. Regional differences in real wages: The United States, 1851–1880. *Explorations in Economic History* 13:203–30.

Cohen, D., K. Warner Schaie, and K. Gribben. 1977. The organization of spatial abilities in older men and women. *Journal of Gerontology* 32 (5): 578–85.

Cohen, Mark N. 1977. *The food crisis in prehistory.* New Haven, Conn.: Yale University Press.

Cole, Arthur C. 1919. *The era of the Civil War, 1848–1870.* Springfield: Illinois Centennial Commission.

———. 1923. *Lincoln's "House Divided" speech: Did it reflect a doctrine of class struggle?* Chicago: University of Chicago Press.

Coles, William A., and Henry Hope Reed, Jr. 1961. *Architecture in America: A battle of styles.* New York: Appleton-Century Crofts.

Collins, Bruce. 1986. The Lincoln-Douglas contest of 1858 and the Illinois electorate. *Journal of American Studies* 20:391–420.

Collver, O. Andrew. 1965. *Birth rates in Latin America.* Berkeley: Institute of International Studies, University of California at Berkeley.

The color scheme at the Panama-Pacific International Exposition—a new departure. 1914. *Scribner's Magazine* 56 (Sept.): 277.

Comstock, Sara. 1928. The great American mirror: Reflections from Los Angeles. *Harper's Monthly,* May, 715–23.

Condit, Carl. 1960. *American building art: The nineteenth century.* New York: Oxford University Press.

Conklin, Harold C. 1954. An ethnoecological approach to shifting agriculture. *Transactions of the New York Academy of Science,* series 2, 17:133–42.

Conrad, Alfred H., and John R. Meyer. 1971. The economics of slavery in the ante-bellum South. In *The reinterpretation of American economic history,* ed. Robert W. Fogel and Stanley L. Engerman, 342–61. New York: Harper & Row.

Conrad, Peter. 1980. *Imagining America.* New York: Avon.

Conroy, Pat. 1986. *The prince of tides.* Boston: Houghton Mifflin.

Conway, Jill Ker. 1989. *The road from Coorain.* New York: Random House/Vintage.

Conzen, Michael P. 1990. Ethnicity on the land. In *The making of the American landscape,* ed. Michael P. Conzen, 221–48. Boston: Unwin Hyman.

Coombs, Albert E. 1930. *History of the Niagara Peninsula and the new Welland Canal.* Toronto: Historical Publications Association.

Coones, Paul, and John Patten. 1986. *The Penguin guide to the landscape of England and Wales.* Harmondsworth: Penguin.

Copeland, B. 1904. Niagara. In *Niagara and other poems,* 11–12. Buffalo: Matthews-Northrup.

Corn, Joseph C., ed. 1986. *Imagining tomorrow: History, technology and the American future.* Cambridge, Mass.: MIT Press.

Cornish, Vaughan. 1943. *The beauties of scenery.* London: Muller.

Cortés, Enrique. 1979. Mexican colonies during the Porfiriato. *Aztlán* 10:1–14.

Cosgrove, Denis. 1978. Place, landscape and the dialectics of cultural geography. *The Canadian Geographer* 22 (1): 66–72.

———. 1979. John Ruskin and the geographical imagination. *Geographical Review* 69:43–62.

———. 1983. Towards a radical cultural geography: Problems of theory. *Antipode* 15:1–11.

———. 1984. *Social formation and symbolic landscape.* London: Croom Helm.

———. 1985. Prospect, perspective, and the evolution of the landscape idea. *Transactions of the Institute of British Geographers* 10:45–62.

———. 1989. Geography is everywhere: Culture and symbolism in human landscapes. In *Horizons in human geography,* ed. Derek Gregory and Rex Walford, 118–35. London: Macmillan.

———. 1990. Environmental thought and action: Premodern and post-modern. *Transactions of the Institute of British Geographers,* n.s. 15:344–58.

———. 1992. *The Palladian landscape: Environmental transformation and its cultural representation in Renaissance Italy.* Leicester: Leicester University Press.

Cosgrove, Denis E., and Stephen Daniels, eds. 1988. *The iconography of landscape: Essays on the symbolic representation, design, and use of past environments.* Cambridge: Cambridge University Press.

Cosgrove, Denis E., and Peter Jackson. 1987. New directions in cultural geography. *Area* 19:95–101.

Cowardin, Lewis M., Virginia Carter, Francis C. Golet, and Edward T. LaRoe. 1979. *Classification of wetlands and deepwater habitats of the United States.* Washington: Office of Biological Services, Fish and Wildlife Services, U.S. Department of the Interior.

Cowgill, George L. 1988. Onward and upward with collapse. In *The collapse of ancient states and civilizations,* ed. N. Yoffee and G. L. Cowgill, 244–76. Tucson: University of Arizona Press.

Craig, Lois A. 1978. *The federal presence: Architecture, politics, and symbols in United States government building.* Cambridge, Mass.: MIT Press.

Craik, Fergus I. M. 1977. Age differences in human memory. In *Handbook of the psychology of aging,* ed. James E. Birren and K. Warner Schaie, 384–420. New York: Van Nostrand Reinhold.

Craik, Kenneth. 1986. Psychological reflections on landscape. In *Landscape meanings and values,* ed. C. Penning-Rowsell and D. Lowenthal, 48–64. London: Allen & Unwin.

Craven, Avery. 1964. *An historian and the Civil War.* Chicago: University of Chicago Press.

Cronon, William. 1983. *Changes in the land: Indians, colo-*

nists, and the ecology of New England. New York: Hill and Wang.

Crosby, Alfred W. 1972. *The Columbian exchange: Biological and cultural consequences of 1492.* Westport, Conn.: Greenwood.

———. 1978. Ecological imperialism: The overseas migration of western Europeans as a biological phenomenon. *The Texas Quarterly* 21 (1): 10–22.

———. 1986. *Ecological imperialism: The biological expansion of Europe, 900–1900.* New York: Cambridge University Press.

———. 1991. Infectious disease and the demography of the Atlantic peoples. *Journal of World History* 2: 119–33.

Cross, Whitney. 1950. *The burned-over district: The social and intellectual history of enthusiastic religion in western New York, 1800–1850.* Ithaca, N.Y.: Cornell University Press.

Crouthamel, James L. 1964. The newspaper revolution in New York, 1830–1860. *New York History* 45: 91–113.

Cumberland, Charles C. 1969. *Mexican revolution: Genesis under Madero.* Westport, Conn.: Greenwood.

Curti, Merle. 1959. *The making of an American community: A case study of democracy in a frontier county.* Stanford, Calif.: Stanford University Press.

Curtis, James R. 1980. Miami's Little Havana: Yard shrines, cult religion and landscape. *Journal of Cultural Geography* 11: 1–15.

Dampier, William. 1968 [1697]. *A new voyage round the world.* Reprint ed. New York: Dover.

Danhof, Clarence H. 1969. *Change in agriculture: The northern United States, 1820–1870.* Cambridge: Harvard University Press.

Daniels, Stephen. 1987. The implications of industry: Turner and Leeds. *Turner Studies* 9: 10–17.

Darby, H. Clifford. 1956. *The draining of the fens.* Cambridge: Cambridge University Press.

David, Paul A. 1966. The mechanization of reaping in the ante-bellum Midwest. In *Industrialization in two systems: Essays in honor of Alexander Gerschenkron by a group of his students,* ed. Henry Rosovsky, 3–39. New York: Wiley.

David, Paul A., and Peter Temin. 1976. Slavery: The progressive institution? In Paul A. David, Herbert G. Gutman, Richard Sutch, Peter Temin, and Gavin Wright, *Reckoning with slavery: A critical study in the quantitative history of American Negro slavery,* 165–230. New York: Oxford University Press.

Davidson, William V. 1974. *Historical geography of the Bay Islands, Honduras.* Birmingham, Ala.: Southern University Press.

———. 1984. The Garifuna in Central America: Ethnohistorical and geographical foundations. In *Black Caribs: A case study in biocultural adaptations,* ed. M. Crawford, 13–35. New York: Plenum.

Davis, Edward E. 1940. *The White Scourge.* San Antonio: Naylor.

Davis, Elmer. 1921. *History of the New York Times.* New York: The New York Times.

Davis, Fred. 1977. Nostalgia, identity and the current nostalgia wave. *Journal of Popular Culture* 11: 414–24.

Davis, Mike. 1990. *City of quartz: Excavating the future in Los Angeles.* London: Verso.

Davis, Richard H. 1891. Broadway. *Scribner's Magazine* 9: 585–604.

Dean, Thomas. 1975. *Post-theistic thinking.* Philadelphia: Temple University Press.

DeCelles, C. 1974. Ecology: A theological perspective. *American Benedictine Review* 25: 75–95.

Defoe, Daniel. 1724. *A tour thro' the whole island of Great Britain, divided into circuits or journies,* vol. 1. London: G. Strahan, W. Mears, R. Franklin, S. Chapman, R. Stagg, and J. Graves.

De Janvry, Alain. 1981. *The agrarian question and reformism in Latin America.* Baltimore: Johns Hopkins University Press.

De Janvry, Alain, Elisabeth Sadoulet, and L. W. Young. 1989. Land and labour in Latin American agriculture from the 1950s to the 1980s. *Journal of Peasant Studies* 16: 396–424.

De Laguna, Frederica. 1960. *The story of a Tlingit community: A problem in the relationship between archeological, ethnological and historical methods.* Smithsonian Institution, Bureau of American Ethnology, bulletin 172. Washington, D.C.: Smithsonian Institution, Bureau of American Ethnology.

De la Teja, Jesús F., and John Wheat. 1985. Bexar: Profile of a Tejano community, 1820–1832. *Southwestern Historical Quarterly* 89: 7–34.

De León, Arnoldo. 1982. *The Tejano community, 1836–1900.* Albuquerque: University of New Mexico Press.

De León, Arnoldo, and Kenneth L. Stewart. 1983. Lost dreams and found fortunes: Mexican and Anglo immigrants in south Texas, 1850–1900. *Western Historical Quarterly* 14: 291–310.

Denevan, William M. 1966a. A cultural-ecological view of the former aboriginal settlement in the Amazon basin. *The Professional Geographer* 18: 346–51.

———. 1966b. *The aboriginal cultural geography of the Llanos de Mojos, Bolivia.* Ibero-Americana 48. Berkeley: University of California Press.

———. 1970. Aboriginal drained-field cultivation in the Americas. *Science* 169: 647–54.

———. 1976. Introduction. In *The native population of the Americas in 1492,* ed. William M. Denevan, 1–12. Madison: University of Wisconsin Press.

———. 1980. Latin America. In *World systems of traditional resource management,* ed. Gary A. Klee, 217–44. New York: Wiley.

———. 1982. Hydraulic agriculture in the Americas: Forms, measures, and recent research. In *Maya subsistence,* ed. Kent V. Flannery, 181–203. New York: Academic.

———. 1983. Adaptation, variation, and cultural geography. *Professional Geographer* 35: 399–407.

———. 1992a. *The native population of the Americas in 1492.* 2d. ed. Madison: University of Wisconsin Press.

———. 1992b. The pristine myth: The landscape of the

Americas in 1492. In *The Americas before and after 1492: Current geographical research,* ed. Karl W. Butzer, 369–85. Special edition of *Annals of the Association of American Geographers* 82 (3).

Denevan, William M., Kent Mathewson, and Gregory Knapp, eds. 1987. *Pre-Hispanic agricultural fields in the Andean region.* 2 vols. British Archaeological Reports, Agricultural Series, no. 359. Oxford: BAR.

Denevan, William M., and B. L. Turner, II. 1974. Forms, functions, and associations of raised fields in the Old World tropics. *Journal of Tropical Geography* 39: 24–33.

Denevan, William M., and A. Zucchi. 1978. Ridged field excavations in the Central Orinoco Llanos, Venezuela. In *Advances in Andean Archaeology,* ed. D. L. Browman, 235–46. The Hague: Mouton.

Denievelle, Paul E. 1915. Texture and color at the Panama-Pacific Exposition. *The Architectural Record* 38 (November): 563–70.

De Renzi, Ennio, Pietro Faglioni, and Paolo Villa. 1977. Topographical amnesia. *Journal of Neurology, Neurosurgery, and Psychiatry* 40: 498–505.

Devall, Bill, and George Sessions. 1985. *Deep ecology: Living as if nature mattered.* Salt Lake City: Peregrine Smith.

Diamond, Irene, and Gloria F. Orenstein, eds. 1990. *Reweaving the world: The emergence of ecofeminism.* San Francisco: Sierra Club.

Dickens, Charles. 1895. *Little Dorrit.* New York: Macmillan.

Dickson, D. Bruce. 1988. Anthropological utopias and geographical epidemics: Competing models of social change and the problem of the origins of agriculture. In *The transfer and transformation of ideas and material culture,* ed. Peter J. Hugill and D. Bruce Dickson, 45–74. College Station: Texas A & M University Press.

Didion, Joan. 1992. Sentimental journeys. In *After Henry,* 253–319. New York: Simon and Schuster.

Dillard, Annie. 1987. *An American childhood.* New York: Harper & Row.

Dille, Robert C. 1962. *The collected works of Buck Rogers in the 25th century.* New York: Chelsea House.

Dirección Nacional de Estadística y Censos. 1966. *Centros Poblados. Tomo II.* Lima: Dirección Nacional de Estadística y Censos.

Dixon, James. 1849. *Personal narrative of a tour through a part of the United States and Canada.* New York: Lane & Scott.

Doddridge, Joseph. 1824. *Notes on the settlement and Indian wars of the western parts of Virginia and Pennsylvania.* Wellsburgh, Va.: The Gazette.

Dodge, Stanley D. 1937. Round table on problems in cultural geography. *Annals of the Association of American Geographers* 27:155–75.

Domar, Evsey. 1970. The causes of slavery or serfdom: A hypothesis. *Journal of Economic History* 30:18–32.

Domosh, Mona. 1985. Scrapers of the sky: The symbolic and functional structures of lower Manhattan. Ph.D. diss., Clark University, Worcester, Mass.

———. 1987. Imagining New York's first skyscrapers. *Journal of Historical Geography* 13:233–48.

———. 1988. The symbolism of the skyscraper: Case studies of New York's first tall buildings. *Journal of Urban History* 14:321–45.

———. 1989. New York's first skyscrapers: Conflict in the design of the American commercial landscape. *Landscape* 30 (2): 34–38.

———. 1990. Shaping the commercial city: Retail districts in nineteenth-century New York and Boston. *Annals of the Association of American Geographers* 80: 268–84.

———. 1992. Controlling urban form: The development of Boston's Back Bay. *Journal of Historical Geography* 18:288–306.

Donkin, Robin A. 1979. *Agricultural terracing in the aboriginal New World.* Viking Fund Publication in Anthropology no. 56. Tucson: University of Arizona Press.

Doolittle, William E. 1980. Aboriginal agricultural development in the Valley of Sonora, Mexico. *Geographical Review* 70:328–42.

———. 1984. Agricultural change as an incremental process. *Annals of the Association of American Geographers* 74:124–37.

———. 1985. The use of check dams for protecting downstream agricultural lands in the prehistoric Southwest: A contextual analysis. *Journal of Anthropological Research* 41:279–305.

———. 1988a. Intermittent use and agricultural change on marginal lands: The case of smallholders in eastern Sonora, Mexico. *Geografiska Annaler,* series B 70: 255–66.

———. 1988b. *Pre-Hispanic occupance in the Valley of Sonora, Mexico: Archaeological confirmation of early Spanish reports.* University of Arizona Anthropological Paper no. 48. Tucson: University of Arizona.

———. 1990. *Canal irrigation in prehistoric Mexico.* Austin: University of Texas Press.

Doran, Edwin, Jr. 1971. The sailing raft as a great tradition. In *Man across the sea: Problems with pre-Columbian contacts,* ed. Carroll L. Riley, J. Charles Kelley, Campbell W. Pennington, and Robert L. Rands, 115–38. Austin: University of Texas Press.

Doughty, Robin W. 1981. Environmental theology: Trends and prospects in Christian thought. *Progress in Human Geography* 5:234–48.

———. 1987. *At home in Texas: Early views of the land.* College Station: Texas A & M University Press.

Downs, Roger. 1992. [World class standards in geography.] Personal communication with C. L. Salter.

Downs, Roger M., and David Stea. 1977. *Maps in minds.* New York: Harper and Row.

Drabble, Margaret. 1979. *A writer's Britain: Landscape in literature.* London: Thames and Hudson.

Drengson, Alan R. 1988. Review of *Deep ecology,* by Bill Devall and George Sessions. *Environmental Ethics* 10: 83–89.

Driver, Felix. 1992. Geography's empire: Histories of geographical knowledge. *Environment and Planning D: Society and Space* 10 (1): 23–40.

Dryzek, John S. 1987. *Rational ecology: Environment and political economy.* Oxford: Blackwell.

Dublin, Louis I. 1943. *A family of thirty million: The story of the Metropolitan Life Insurance Company.* New York: Metropolitan Life Insurance Co.

Dubos, Rene. 1969. *A theology of the earth.* Washington, D.C.: Smithsonian Institution Press.

Dugdale, William. 1662. *The history of imbanking and drayning of divers Fenns and marshes, both in foreign parts, and in this kingdom, and of the improvements thereby extracted from records, manuscripts, and other authentick testimonies.* London: Alice Warren.

Duncan, James S. 1973. Landscape taste as a symbol of group identity: A Westchester County village. *Geographical Review* 63:334–55.

———. 1980. The superorganic in American cultural geography. *Annals of the Association of American Geographers* 70:181–98.

———, ed. 1982. *Housing and identity: Cross cultural perspectives.* New York: Holmes and Meier.

———. 1990. *The city as text: The politics of landscape interpretation in the Kandyan Kingdom.* Cambridge: Cambridge University Press.

Duncan, James S., and Nancy Duncan. 1984. A cultural analysis of urban residential landscapes in North America: The case of the anglophile elite. In *The city in cultural context,* ed. J. Agnew, J. Mercer, and D. Sopher, 255–76. Boston: Allen & Unwin.

———. 1988. (Re)reading the landscape. *Environment and Planning D: Society and Space* 6:117–26.

Dunn, Jacob P. 1888. *Indiana: A redemption from slavery.* Boston: Houghton Mifflin.

Dupree, H., and Wolf Roder. 1974. Coping with drought in a preindustrial, preliterate farming society. In *Natural hazards: Local, national, global,* ed. Gilbert White, 115–19. New York: Oxford University Press.

Durant, Samuel. 1878. *History of Oneida County, New York.* Philadelphia: Everts & Fariss.

Durant, Samuel W., and H. B. Peirce. 1878. *History of St. Lawrence County, New York.* Philadelphia: L.H. Everts.

Durrell, Lawrence G. 1957. *Justine.* London: Dutton.

———. 1969. *Spirit of place.* Ed. Alan G. Thomas. London: Faber and Faber.

Dysart, Jane. 1976. Mexican women in San Antonio, 1830–1860: The assimilation process. *Western Historical Quarterly* 7:365–75.

Earle, Carville V. 1975. *The evolution of a tidewater settlement system: All Hallow's Parish, Maryland, 1650–1783.* University of Chicago Department of Geography Research Paper no. 170. Chicago: University of Chicago, Department of Geography.

———. 1978. A staple interpretation of slavery and free labor. *Geographical Review* 68:51–65.

———. 1992. *Geographical inquiry and American historical problems.* Stanford, Calif.: Stanford University Press.

Earle, Carville V., and Ronald Hoffman. 1976. Staple

crops and urban development in the eighteenth-century South. *Perspectives in American History* 10: 7–78.

Eckel, Malcolm D. 1987. Perspectives on the Buddhist-Christian dialogue. In *Christ and the Bodhisattva,* ed. D. S. Lopez and S. C. Rockefeller, 43–64. Albany: State University of New York Press.

Edmonson, Munro S. 1961. Neolithic diffusion rates. *Current Anthropology* 2 (2): 71–86.

Edwards, Clinton R. 1965. *Aboriginal watercraft on the Pacific coast of South America.* Ibero-Americana 47. Berkeley: University of California Press.

Ehrenfeld, David, and Philip J. Bentley. 1985. Judaism and the practice of stewardship. *Judaism* 34:301–11.

Eichrodt, Walther. 1967. *Theology of the Old Testament.* 2 vols. Philadelphia: Westminster.

Eidt, Robert C. 1959. Aboriginal Chibcha settlement in Colombia. *Annals of the Association of American Geographers* 49:374–92.

Elazar, Daniel J. 1966. *American federalism: A view from the states.* New York: Thomas Y. Crowell.

Eliade, Mircea. 1959. *The sacred and the profane: The nature of religion.* Trans. Willard R. Trask. New York: Harper and Row.

Eliot, George. 1907. *Scenes of clerical life.* Boston: Houghton Mifflin.

———. 1982. *Middlemarch.* London: Zodiac.

Ellen, Roy. 1982. *Environment, subsistence and system: The ecology of small-scale social formations.* Cambridge: Cambridge University Press.

Emel, Jacques L., and Richard Peet. 1989. Resource management and natural hazards. In *New models in geography: The political economy perspective,* vol. 1, ed. R. Peet and N. Thrift, 49–76. London: Unwin Hyman.

Emerson, Ralph Waldo. 1904. *The complete works of Ralph Waldo Emerson.* Vol. 12: *Natural history of intellect and other papers.* Boston: Houghton Mifflin.

Engerman, Stanley L. 1973. Some considerations relating to property rights in man. *Journal of Economic History* 33:43–65.

English, Paul W., and James Miller. 1989. *World regional geography: A question of place.* New York: Wiley.

Ensminger, Robert F. 1992. *The Pennsylvania barn: Its origins, evolution, and distribution in North America.* Baltimore: Johns Hopkins University Press.

Entrikin, J. Nicholas. 1976. Contemporary humanism in geography. *Annals of the Association of American Geographers* 66:615–32.

———. 1984. Carl Sauer: Philosopher in spite of himself. *Geographical Review* 74:387–408.

———. 1991. *The betweenness of place: Towards a geography of modernity.* Baltimore: Johns Hopkins University Press.

Erickson, Clark. 1985. Applications of prehistoric Andean technology: Experiments in raised field agriculture, Huatta, Lake Titicaca, 1983. In *Prehistoric intensive agriculture in the tropics,* ed. I. S. Farrington, 209–32. British Archaeological Reports, International Series, no. 232. Oxford: BAR.

Evans, E. Estyn. 1973. *The personality of Ireland.* Cambridge: Cambridge University Press.

Everett, Donald E. 1961. San Antonio welcomes the "Sunset"—1877. *Southwestern Historical Quarterly* 65:47–60.

———. 1975. *San Antonio: The flavor of its past, 1845–1898.* San Antonio: Trinity University Press.

Eyre, S. R., and G. R. Jones, eds. 1966. *Geography as human ecology: Methodology by example.* New York: St. Martin's.

Faris, Gerald. 1974. Santa Monica Boulevard: The grotesque and the sublime. *Los Angeles Times,* 17 February, Part XI, 1.

Fawcett, W. 1902. The new Niagara. *American Manufacturing and Iron World,* 25 December, 717–20.

Federal Writer's Project. 1938. *Texas, San Antonio: An authoritative guide to the city and its environs.* San Antonio: Clegg.

Fehrenbach, T. R. 1978. *The San Antonio story.* Tulsa, Okla.: Continental Heritage.

Ferleger, Lou, ed. 1990. *Agriculture and national development: Views on the nineteenth century.* Ames: Iowa State University Press.

Feynman, Richard. 1988. *"What do you care what other people think?" Further adventures of a curious character.* New York: W.W. Norton.

Fine, David M. 1977. L.A. architecture as a blueprint for fiction. *Los Angeles Times Calendar,* 11 December, 20–21.

Finkelman, Paul. 1986. Slavery and the Northwest Ordinance. *Journal of the Early Republic* 6:743–70.

———. 1987. Slavery, "the more perfect union," and the prairie state. *Illinois Historical Journal* 80:248–69.

Fischer, David H. 1989. *Albion's seed: Four British folkways in America.* New York: Oxford University Press.

Fishman, Robert. 1977. *Urban utopias in the twentieth century: Ebenezer Howard, Frank Lloyd Wright, and Le Corbusier.* New York: Basic.

Fiske, John, and John Hartley. 1978. *Reading television.* London: Methuen.

Fitch, James M. 1948. *American building.* Boston: Houghton Mifflin.

Fitzgerald, F. Scott. 1954. *The great Gatsby.* Harmondsworth: Penguin.

Flannery, Kent V. 1982. The golden Marshalltown: A parable for archeology of the 1980s. *American Anthropologist* 84 (2): 265–78.

Flores Ochoa, Jorge A., and M. P. Paz Flores. 1983. La agricultura en lagunas del Altiplano. *Ñawpa Pacha* 21: 127–52.

Floyd, B. N. 1961. Toward a more literary geography. *The Professional Geographer* 13 (4): 7–11.

———. 1962. The pleasures ahead: A geographic meditation. *The Professional Geographer* 14 (5): 1–4.

Floyd, Troy W. 1967. *The Anglo-Spanish struggle for Mosquitia.* Albuquerque: University of New Mexico Press.

Foner, Eric. 1970. *Free soil, free labor, free men: The ideology of the Republican party before the Civil War.* New York: Oxford University Press.

Fonseca Martel, C., and E. Mayer. 1988. De hacienda a comunidad: El impacto de la Reforma Agraria en la provincia de Paucartambo, Cuzco. In *Sociedad andina, pasado y presente: Contribuciones en homenaje a la memoria de César Fonseca Martel,* ed. R. Matos Mendieta, 59–100. Lima: FOMENCIAS.

Foote, Kenneth E. 1983. *Color in public spaces: Toward a communication-based theory of the urban built environment.* University of Chicago Department of Geography Research Paper no. 205. Chicago: University of Chicago, Department of Geography.

———. 1985. Space, territory, and landscape: The borderlands of geography and semiotics. *Recherche Semiotique/Semiotic Inquiry* 5:158–75.

———. 1987. Relics of old London: Photographs of a changing Victorian city. *History of Photography* 11: 133–53.

———. 1988. Object as memory: The material foundations of human semiosis. *Semiotica* 69:243–68.

———. 1992. Stigmata of national identity: Exploring the cosmography of America's civil religion. In *Person, place, and thing: Interpretive and empirical essays in cultural geography,* ed. Shue Tuck Wong, 379–402. Geoscience and Man 31. Baton Rouge: Louisiana State University, Department of Geography and Anthropology.

Ford, Larry R. 1979. Urban preservation and the geography of the city in the U.S.A. *Progress in Historical Geography* 3:211–38.

Ford, Larry R., and Ernst Griffin. 1981. Chicano Park: Personalizing an institutional landscape. *Landscape* 25 (2): 42–48.

Forrester, G. C. 1976. *Niagara Falls and the glacier.* Hicksville, N.Y.: Exposition.

Forster, E. M. 1975a. *Howard's end.* Harmondsworth: Penguin.

———. 1975b. *Where angels fear to tread.* London: Edward Arnold.

———. 1976. *Aspects of the novel.* Harmondsworth: Penguin.

Fosberg, F. Raymond. 1976. Geography, ecology, and biogeography. *Annals of the Association of American Geographers* 66:117–28.

Foster, George M. 1962. *Traditional cultures, and the impact of technological change.* New York: Harper and Row.

Foucault, Michel. 1986. Of other spaces. *Diacritics* 16 (Spring): 22–27.

Francaviglia, Richard V. 1978. *The Mormon landscape: Existence, creation, and perception of a unique image in the American West.* New York: AMS.

Franchised Distribution. 1972. New York: The Conference Board.

Frank, Andre G. 1969. The sociology of development and the underdevelopment of sociology. In *Latin America: Underdevelopment or revolution, essays on the development of underdevelopment and the immediate enemy,* 21–94. New York: Monthly Review Press.

Frank, Andre G., and Barry Gills. 1992. The five thousand year world system: An interdisciplinary introduction. *Humboldt Journal of Social Relations* 18 (1): 1–79.

Freire, Paulo. 1972. *Pedagogy of the oppressed.* New York: Herder and Herder.

French, Karen E., and William R. Stanley. 1974. A game of European colonization in Africa. *Journal of Geography* 73 (7): 44–48.

Friedmann, John. 1987. *Planning in the public domain.* Princeton, N.J.: Princeton University Press.

Frucht, R. 1968. Emigration, remittances and social change aspects of the social field of Nevis, West Indies. *Anthropologica,* n.s. 10 (2): 193–208.

Frye, Northrop. 1976. *The sacred scripture: A study of the structure of romance.* Cambridge: Harvard University Press.

————. 1982. *The great code: The Bible and literature.* London: Routledge and Kegan Paul.

Fuller, R. Buckminster. 1970. Education for comprehensivity. In *Approaching the benign environment: The Franklin lectures in the sciences and humanities, first series,* by R. Buckminster Fuller, Eric A. Walker, and James R. Killian, Jr., 3–77. Auburn, Ala.: University of Alabama Press for Auburn University.

Fuson, Robert H. 1969. The orientation of Mayan ceremonial centers. *Annals of the Association of American Geographers* 59:494–511.

Fyle, C. Magbaily. 1981. *The history of Sierra Leone.* London: Evans Brothers.

Gade, Daniel W. 1975. *Plants, man and the land in the Vilcanota Valley of Peru.* Biogeographica No. 6. The Hague: W. Junk B. V.

————. 1976. L'optique culturelle dans la géographie américaine. *Annales de Géographie* 85 (472): 672–93.

————. 1989. Cultural geography, its idiosyncracies and possibilities. In *Applied geography: Issues, questions and concerns,* ed. Martin Kenzer, 135–50. Dordrecht: Kluwer.

Gade, Daniel, and M. Escobar. 1982. Village settlement and the colonial legacy in southern Peru. *Geographical Review* 72:430–49.

Gale, Stephen. 1977. Ideological man in a nonideological society. *Annals of the Association of American Geographers* 67:267–72.

Galeano, Eduardo. 1973. *The open veins of Latin America.* New York: Monthly Review Press.

Galloway, J. H. 1989. *The sugar cane industry: An historical geography from its origins to 1914.* Cambridge: Cambridge University Press.

Gara, Larry. 1975. Slavery and the slave power: A critical distinction. In *Beyond the Civil War synthesis: Political essays of the Civil War era,* ed. Robert P. Swierenga, 295–308. Contributions in American History no. 44. Westport, Conn.: Greenwood.

Garcia, Richard A. 1978. Class consciousness and ideology: The Mexican community of San Antonio, Texas: 1930–1940. *Aztlán* 9:23–70.

Gardner, Howard. 1983. *Frames of mind.* New York: Basic.

Garreau, Joel. 1981. *The nine nations of North America.*

Boston: Houghton Mifflin.

————. 1991. *Edge city: Life on the new frontier.* New York: Doubleday.

Garvan, Anthony. 1951. *Architecture and town planning in Colonial Connecticut.* New Haven, Conn.: Yale University Press.

Garvey, Anne. 1977. The fen tigers. *New Society* 41 (1 September): 429–30.

Gates, Paul W. 1957. Frontier estate builders and farm laborers. In *The frontier in perspective,* ed. Walker D. Wyman and Clifton B. Kroeber, 143–64. Madison: University of Wisconsin Press.

————. 1960. *The farmer's age: Agriculture, 1815–1860.* New York: Harper & Row.

Geertz, Clifford. 1963. *Agricultural involution: The process of ecological change in Indonesia.* Berkeley: University of California Press.

————. 1973. *The interpretation of cultures.* New York: Basic.

————. 1983. *Local knowledge: Further essays in interpretive anthropology.* New York: Basic.

Geffre, Claude, and M. Dhavamony. 1979. *Buddhism and Christianity.* New York: Seabury.

Genovese, Eugene D., and Leonard Hochberg, eds. 1989. *Geographic perspectives in history.* New York: Basil Blackwell.

Gibson, James R., ed. 1978. *European settlement and development in North America: Essays in geographical change.* Toronto: University of Toronto Press.

Giddens, Anthony. 1979. *Central problems in social theory: Action, structure, and contradiction in social analysis.* Berkeley: University of California Press.

Giedion, Sigfried. 1967. *Space, time and architecture: The growth of a new tradition,* 5th ed. Cambridge: Harvard University Press.

Gilbert, Anne. 1988. The new regional geography in English and French-speaking countries. *Progress in Human Geography* 12:208–20.

Gilbert, James B. 1991. *Perfect cities: Chicago's utopias of 1893.* Chicago: University of Chicago Press.

Gillette, King C. 1894. *The human drift.* Boston: New Era Publishing Co.; reprint 1976, Delmar, N.Y.: Scholar's Facsimiles and Reprints.

————. 1910. *World corporation.* Boston: New England News.

————. 1924. *The people's corporation.* New York: Boni and Liveright.

Gillmartin, Patricia P., and Jeffrey C. Patton. 1984. Comparing the sexes on spatial abilities: Map use skills. *Annals of the Association of American Geographers* 74: 605–19.

Gilpin, Robert. 1987. *The political economy of international relations.* Princeton, N.J.: Princeton University Press.

Giroux, Henry A. 1981. *Ideology, culture, and the process of schooling.* Philadelphia: Temple University Press.

Glaab, Charles N., and A. T. Brown. 1967. *The emergence of metropolis: A history of urban America.* London: Macmillan.

Glacken, Clarence. 1967. *Traces on the Rhodian shore: Nature and culture in Western thought from ancient times to the end of the eighteenth century.* Berkeley: University of California Press.

Glassie, Henry. 1968. *Pattern in the material folk culture of the eastern United States.* Philadelphia: University of Pennsylvania Press.

———. 1975. *Folk housing in middle Virginia: A structural analysis of historic artifacts.* Knoxville: The University of Tennessee Press.

———. 1982. *Passing the time in Ballymenone: Culture and history of an Ulster community.* Philadelphia: University of Pennsylvania Press.

Glazer, Nathan, and Daniel Moynihan. 1970. *Beyond the melting pot.* Cambridge, Mass.: MIT Press.

Godwin, Harry. 1978. *Fenland: Its ancient past and uncertain future.* Cambridge: Cambridge University Press.

Goetzmann, William H., and William N. Goetzmann. 1986. *The West of the imagination.* New York: Norton.

Gold, Herbert. 1975. Finding the times in offramp city. *New Republic,* 8 February.

Gold, John, and Jacquelin Burgess, eds. 1982. *Valued environments.* London: Allen & Unwin.

Goldberger, Paul. 1981. *The skyscraper.* New York: Knopf.

Goldman, H. L. 1971. Nikola Tesla's bold adventure. *The American West,* March, 4–9.

Golledge, Reginald G., and Robert J. Stimson. 1987. *Analytical behavioral geography.* London: Croom Helm.

Golson, Jack. 1977. No room at the top: Agricultural intensification in the New Guinea Highlands. In *Sunda and Sahul: Prehistoric studies in Southeast Asia, Melanesia and Australia,* ed. J. Allen, J. Golson, and R. Jones, 601–38. London: Academic.

Gonzalez, Nancie L. S. 1969. *Black Carib household structure: A study of migration and modernization.* Seattle: University of Washington Press.

Gorman, Chester. 1977. *A priori* models and Thai prehistory: A reconsideration of the beginnings of agriculture in Southeastern Asia. In *Origins of agriculture,* ed. Charles A. Reed, 321–56. The Hague: Mouton.

Gottmann, Jean. 1966. Why the skyscraper? *Geographical Review* 56:190–212.

Goudie, Andrew. 1990. *The human impact on the natural environment.* 3d ed. Cambridge, Mass.: MIT Press.

Gould, Peter. 1969. *Spatial diffusion.* Association of American Geographers, Commission on College Geography, Resource Paper no. 4. Washington, D.C.: Association of American Geographers.

———. 1970. Tanzania 1920–1963: The spatial impress of the modernization process. *World Politics* 22:149–70.

Gowans, Alan. 1986. *The comfortable house: North American suburban architecture, 1890–1930.* Cambridge, Mass.: MIT Press.

———. 1992. *Styles and types of North American architecture: Social function and cultural expression.* New York: Icon Editions.

Granberg-Michaelson, Wesley. 1990. Covenant and creation. In *Liberating life: Contemporary approaches to ecological theology,* ed. Charles Birch, William Eakin, and Jay B. McDaniel, 27–36. Maryknoll, N.Y.: Orbis.

Grau, Joseph A. 1976. *Morality and the human future in the thought of Teilhard de Chardin.* Rutherford: Fairleigh Dickinson University Press.

Gray, Lewis C. 1958. *History of agriculture in the southern United States to 1860.* 2 vols. Gloucester, Mass.: Peter Smith.

The great International Pon-Pacific Exposition. 1915. *Scientific American* 112 (27 Feb.): 194–95.

Grebler, Leo. 1965. *Mexican immigration to the United States: The record and its implications.* University of California, Graduate School of Business, Division of Research, Mexican-American Study Project, Advance Report no. 2. Los Angeles: University of California, Graduate School of Business.

Grebler, Leo, Joan W. Moore, and Ralph Guzman. 1970. *The Mexican-American people: The nation's second largest minority.* New York: Free Press.

Greenberger, Allen J. 1969. *The British image of India: A study in the literature of imperialism, 1880–1960.* Oxford: Oxford University Press.

Greene, Graham. 1978. Introduction to *The bachelor of arts,* by R. K. Narayan. Chicago: University of Chicago Press.

Gregory, Derek. 1978. *Ideology, science, and human geography.* London: Hutchinson.

———. 1981. Human agency and human geography. *Transactions of the Institute of British Geographers,* n.s. 6:1–18.

Griffin, David Ray. 1989. *God and religion in the postmodern world.* Albany: State University of New York Press.

Grigg, David G. 1980. *Population growth and agrarian change: An historical perspective.* Cambridge: Cambridge University Press.

Grigson, Geoffrey, ed. 1980. *The Faber book of poems and places.* Boston: Faber and Faber.

Griswold del Castillo, Richard. 1984. *La familia: Chicano families in the urban Southwest, 1848 to the present.* Notre Dame, Ind.: University of Notre Dame Press.

Grossman, Lawrence S. 1984. *Peasants, subsistence ecology, and development in the highlands of Papua New Guinea.* Princeton, N.J.: Princeton University Press.

Guelke, Leonard. 1974. An idealist alternative in human geography. *Annals of the Association of American Geographers* 64:193–202.

———. 1976. Frontier settlement in early Dutch South Africa. *Annals of the Association of American Geographers* 66:25–42.

Gunderson, Gerald. 1974. The origin of the American Civil War. *Journal of Economic History* 34:915–50.

Gutierrez, Félix F., and Jorge R. Schement. 1979. *Spanish-language radio in the southwestern United States.* University of Texas, Center for Mexican American Studies, Mexican American Monographs no. 5. Austin: University of Texas, Center for Mexican American Studies.

Gutkind, E. A. 1956. Our world from the air: Conflict

and adaptation. In *Man's role in changing the face of the earth,* ed. William L. Thomas, 1–44. Chicago: University of Chicago Press.

Habgood, John. 1990. A sacramental approach to environmental issues. In *Liberating life: Contemporary approaches to ecological theology,* ed. Charles Birch, William Eakin, and Jay B. McDaniel, 46–53. Maryknoll, N.Y.: Orbis.

Hagen, E. 1962. *The theory of social change: How economic growth begins.* Homewood, Ill.: Dorsey.

Hägerstrand, Torsten. 1962. The propagation of innovation waves. In *Readings in cultural geography,* ed. P. Wagner and M. Mikesell, 355–68. Chicago: University of Chicago Press.

———. 1967. *Innovation diffusion as a spatial process.* Trans. Allan R. Pred. Chicago: University of Chicago Press.

———. 1978. Survival and arena: On the life-history of individuals in relation to their geographical environment. In *Timing space and spacing time,* vol. 1: *Pre-industrial societies,* ed. T. Carlstein, D. Parkes, and N. Thrift, 122–45. London: Allen & Unwin.

———. 1988. Some unexplored problems in the modeling of culture change. In *The transfer and transformation of ideas and material culture,* ed. Peter J. Hugill and D. Bruce Dickson, 217–32. College Station: Texas A & M University Press.

Haggett, Peter. 1966. *Locational analysis in human geography.* New York: St. Martin's.

———. 1983. *Geography: A modern synthesis,* 3d ed. New York: Harper and Row.

Haggett, Peter, and Richard Chorley. 1969. *Network analysis in geography.* London: Edward Arnold.

Hahn, Steven, and Jonathan Prude, eds. 1985. *The countryside in the age of capitalist transformation: Essays on the social history of rural America.* Chapel Hill: University of North Carolina Press.

Haig, Robert M. 1927. *Major economic factors in metropolitan growth and arrangement.* New York: Regional Plan of New York and Its Environs, Regional Survey of New York and Its Environs No. 1.

Hales, Peter B. 1984. *Silver cities: The photography of American urbanization, 1839–1915.* Philadelphia: Temple University Press.

Haley, Alex. 1976. *Roots.* Garden City, N.Y.: Doubleday.

Halifax, Joan. 1990. The third body: Buddhism, shamanism and deep ecology. In *Dharma Gaia,* ed. Allan H. Badimer, 20–30. Berkeley: Parallax.

Hall, Peter. 1980. Review of *Geography and geographers: Anglo-American geography since 1945,* by R. J. Johnston. *Geographical Magazine* 52 (8): 593.

Hall, Peter, and Paschal Preston. 1988. *The carrier wave: New information technology and the geography of innovation.* London: Unwin Hyman.

Hall, Thomas D. 1989. *Social change in the Southwest, 1350–1880.* Lawrence: University Press of Kansas.

Hamlin, Talbot. 1953. *Architecture through the ages.* New York: G.P. Putnam's Sons.

Hammack, David. 1982. *Power and society: Greater New York at the turn of the century.* New York: Russell Sage Foundation.

Hammond, Kenneth A., George Macinko, and Wilma B. Fairchild, eds. 1978. *Sourcebook on the environment: A guide to the literature.* Chicago: University of Chicago Press.

Handlin, Oscar, and Mary F. Handlin. 1975. *The wealth of the American people.* New York: McGraw-Hill.

Handman, Max S. 1931. San Antonio: The old capital city of Mexican life and influence. *The Survey* 66:163–66.

Hansen, Barbara. 1985. Fajitas. *Los Angeles Times,* 9 May.

Hansis, R. 1976. Ethnogeography and science: Viticulture in Argentina. Ph.D. diss., Pennsylvania State University, University Park.

Hard, Gerhard. 1970. *Die "Landschaft" der Sprache und die "Landschaft" der Geographen.* Colloquium Geographicum 11. Bonn: Dümmlers.

Hardy, Thomas. 1888. The profitable reading of fiction. *Forum* 5 (March): 57–70.

———. 1912. *The Mayor of Casterbridge.* London: Macmillan.

———. 1974. *Jude the obscure.* London: Macmillan.

———. 1975. *Tess of the d'Urbervilles.* London: Macmillan.

———. 1976a. *Desperate remedies.* London: Macmillan.

———. 1976b. *A pair of blue eyes.* London: Macmillan.

———. 1978. After a journey. In *Selected poems,* ed. David Wright. Harmondsworth: Penguin.

Harewood, Jack. 1966. Population growth in Grenada. *Social and Economic Studies* 15:61–84.

Hargrove, Eugene. 1986. Religion and environmental ethics: Beyond the Lynn White Debate. In *Religion and environmental crisis,* ed. Eugene C. Hargrove, ix–xix. Athens: University of Georgia Press.

Harper's Weekly. 1880. 29:78.

Harpster, John W. 1938. *Pen pictures of early western Pennsylvania.* Pittsburgh: University of Pittsburgh Press.

Harrigan, Stephen. 1992. *Water and light: A diver's journey to a coral reef.* Boston: Houghton Mifflin.

Harrington, Michael. 1979. To the Disney station. *Harper's,* January.

Harris, David R. 1965. *Plants, animals, and man in the Outer Leeward Islands, West Indies.* University of California Publications in Geography 18. Berkeley: University of California Press.

———. 1990. Vavilov's concept of centers of origin of cultivated plants: Its genesis and its influence on the study of agricultural origins. *Biological Journal of the Linnean Society* 39:7–16.

Harris, David R., and Gordon C. Hillman, eds. 1989. *Foraging and farming: The evolution of plant exploitation.* London: Unwin Hyman.

Harris, L. J. 1978. Sex differences in spatial ability: Possible environmental, genetic, and neurological factors. In *Asymmetrical function of the brain,* ed. N. Kinsbourne, 405–52. New York: Cambridge University Press.

Harris, Marvin. 1968. *The rise of anthropological theory.* New York: Crowell.

Harris, N. Dwight. 1904. *The history of Negro servitude in Illinois and of the slavery agitation in that state, 1719–1864.* Chicago: A.C. McClurg.

Harris, R. Cole. 1977. The simplification of Europe overseas. *Annals of the Association of American Geographers* 67:469–83.

———. 1978. The historical mind and the practice of geography. In *Humanistic geography: Problems and prospects,* ed. D. Ley and M. S. Samuels, 123–37. Chicago: Maaroufa.

———. 1991. Power, modernity, and historical geography. *Annals of the Association of American Geographers* 81:671–83.

Hart, John Fraser. 1975. *The look of the land.* Englewood Cliffs, N.J.: Prentice-Hall.

———. 1982. The highest form of the geographer's art. *Annals of the Association of American Geographers* 72:1–29.

———. 1991. *The land that feeds us.* New York: W.W. Norton.

Hartshorne, Charles. 1948. *The divine relativity: A social conception of God.* New Haven, Conn.: Yale University Press.

———. 1967. *A natural theology for our time.* LaSalle, Ill.: Open Court.

———. 1971. Philosophical and religious uses of "God." In *Process theology,* ed. Evert H. Cousins, 101–18. New York: Newman.

Hartt, Mary B. 1901. The play-side of the fair. *The World's Work* 2:1097–1101.

Harvey, David. 1969. *Explanation in geography.* London: Edward Arnold.

———. 1979. Monument and myth. *Annals of the Association of American Geographers* 69:362–81.

———. 1985. *Consciousness and the urban experience: Studies in the history and theory of capitalist urbanization.* Baltimore: Johns Hopkins University Press.

———. 1989. *The condition of postmodernity: An enquiry into the origins of cultural change.* Oxford: Basil Blackwell.

———. 1990. Between space and time: Reflections on the geographical imagination. *Annals of the Association of American Geographers* 80:418–34.

Haught, John F. 1990. Religious and cosmic homelessness: Some environmental implications. In *Liberating life: Contemporary approaches to ecological theology,* ed. Charles Birch, William Eakin, and Jay B. McDaniel, 159–81. Maryknoll, N.Y.: Orbis.

Hayden, Dolores. 1976. *Seven American utopias: The architecture of communitarian socialism, 1790–1975.* Cambridge, Mass.: MIT Press.

———. 1981. *The grand domestic revolution: A history of feminist designs for American homes, neighborhoods, and cities.* Cambridge, Mass.: MIT Press.

Headrick, Daniel R. 1988. *The tentacles of progress: Technology transfer in the age of imperialism, 1850–1940.* New York: Oxford University Press.

Hebdige, Dick. 1979. *Subculture: The meaning of style.* London: Methuen.

Hecht, Susanna. 1982. Cattle ranching development in the eastern Amazon: Evaluation of a development policy. Ph.D. diss., Department of Geography, University of California, Berkeley.

Hecht, Susanna, and Alexander Cockburn. 1989. *The fate of the forest: Developers, destroyers, and defenders of the Amazon.* New York: Verso.

Heidegger, Martin. 1962. *Being and time.* Trans. John Macquarrie and Edward Robinson. New York: Harper and Row.

Helfand, Jonathan. 1986. The earth is the Lord's: Judaism and environmental ethics. In *Religion and environmental ethics,* ed. Eugene C. Hargrove, 38–52. Athens: University of Georgia Press.

Helms, Mary W. 1971. *Asang: Adaptations to culture contact in a Miskito community.* Gainesville: University of Florida Press.

Helms, Mary W., and Franklin O. Loveland, eds. 1976. *Frontier adaptations in lower Central America.* Philadelphia: Institute for the Study of Human Issues.

Henretta, James. 1978. Families and farms: Mentalité in preindustrial America. *William and Mary Quarterly,* 3d series, 35:3–32.

Hicks, John. 1969. *A theory of economic history.* Oxford: Clarendon.

Higham, John. 1965. *History: The development of historical studies in the United States.* Princeton: Princeton University Press.

Hill, Miriam H. 1985. Bound to the environment: Towards a phenomenology of sightlessness. In *Dwelling, place, and environment: Towards a phenomenology of person and world,* ed. David Seamon and Robert Mugerauer, 99–111. Dordrecht: Martinus Nijhoff.

Hilliard, Samuel B. 1972. *Hog meat and hoecakes: Food supply in the Old South, 1840–1860.* Carbondale: Southern Illinois University Press.

Hills, Richard L. 1967. *Machines, mills and uncountable costly necessities: A short history of the drainage of the fens.* Norwich: Goose & Sons.

Hilton, James. 1935. *Good-bye, Mr. Chips.* Boston: Little, Brown.

Hinojosa, Federico A. 1940. *El México de afuera.* San Antonio: Artes Gráficas.

Hipple, Walter J. 1957. *The beautiful, the sublime, and the picturesque in eighteenth-century British aesthetic theory.* Carbondale: Southern Illinois University Press.

Hirst, George S. S. 1910. *Notes on the history of the Cayman Islands.* Kingston: P.A. Benjamin Manufacturing Co.

Hisataki, Tetsuya. 1989. The development of cultural geography in Japan. In *Indigenous and foreign influences in the development of Japanese geographical thought,* ed. Hideki Nozawa, 15–41. Fukuoka: Institute of Geography, Kyushu University.

History of Greene County, New York. 1884. New York: J.B. Beers.

History of Herkimer County, New York. 1879. New York: F.W. Beers.

H.M.D. 1842. The falls of Niagara. *Western Literary Messenger,* 17 August, 56.

Ho, Ping-ti. 1977. The indigenous origins of Chinese agriculture. In *Origins of agriculture,* ed. Charles A. Reed, 413–84. The Hague: Mouton.

Hobsbawm, Eric J. 1992. *Nations and nationalism since 1780.* New York: Cambridge University Press.

Hobsbawm, Eric J., and Terence Ranger, eds. 1983. *The invention of tradition.* Cambridge: Cambridge University Press.

Holland, C. G., and R. O. Allen. 1975. The application of instrumental activation analysis to a study of prehistoric steatite artifacts and source material. *Archaeometry* 71 (1): 69–83.

Holland, Joe. 1989. The postmodern paradigm and contemporary Catholicism. In *Varieties of postmodern theology,* ed. David R. Griffin, William A. Beardslee, and Joe Holland, 9–27. Albany: State University of New York Press.

Holm, Thomas C. 1834. A short description of the province of New Sweden, now called by the English Pennsylvania, in America. *Memoirs of the Historical Society of Pennsylvania* 3:1–166.

Hooson, David. 1981. Carl O. Sauer. In *The origins of academic geography in the United States,* ed. Brian W. Blouet, 165–74. Hamden, Conn.: Archon.

Hopkins, Anthony G. 1973. *An economic history of West Africa.* New York: Columbia University Press.

Horowitz, Helen L. 1984. *Alma mater: Design and experience in the women's colleges from their nineteenth-century beginnings to the 1930s.* New York: Knopf.

Hoskins, W. G. 1955. *The making of the English landscape.* London: Hodder and Stoughton.

Howard, Allan. 1975. Pre-colonial centers and regional systems in Africa. *Pan-African Journal* 8 (3): 247–70.

Howard, Peter. 1991. *Landscapes: The artists' vision.* London: Routledge.

Howell, J. E. 1867. Niagara. In *Poems.* New York: J.E. Howell.

Howells, William D. 1971. *The selected edition of William Dean Howells.* Vol. 12: *The rise of Silas Lapham.* Bloomington: Indiana University Press.

Hoyle, B. S. 1974. *Spatial aspects of development.* London: Wiley.

Hubka, Thomas. 1984. *Big house, little house, back house, barn: The connected farm buildings of New England.* Hanover, N.H.: University Press of New England.

Hudson, Barbara Rubin. 1975. Monuments, magnets and pilgrimage sites: A genetic study in southern California. Ph.D. diss., University of California, Los Angeles.

———. 1976. The Forest Lawn aesthetic: A reappraisal. *Journal of the Los Angeles Institute of Contemporary Art* 9:10–15.

———. 1977. A chronology of architecture in Los Angeles. *Annals of the Association of American Geographers* 67:521–37.

———. 1979. Aesthetic ideology and urban design. *Annals of the Association of American Geographers* 69: 339–61.

Hudson, Brian. 1977. The new geography and the new imperialism: 1870–1918. *Antipode* 9 (1): 12–19.

Hudson, John C. 1988. North American origins of middlewestern frontier populations. *Annals of the Association of American Geographers* 78:395–413.

Hugill, Peter J. 1975. Social conduct on the Golden Mile. *Annals of the Association of American Geographers* 65: 214–28.

———. 1984. The landscape as a code for conduct: Reflections on its role in Walter Firey's "aesthetic-historical-genealogical complex." In *Place, experience, and symbol,* ed. Miles Richardson, 21–30. Geoscience and Man 24. Baton Rouge: Louisiana State University, Department of Geography and Anthropology.

———. 1986. English landscape tastes in the United States. *Geographical Review* 76:408–23.

Hugill, Peter J., and D. Bruce Dickson, eds. 1988. *The transfer and transformation of ideas and material culture.* College Station: Texas A&M University Press.

Humboldt, Alexander von. 1849. *Cosmos: A sketch of a physical description of the universe.* 2 vols. Trans. E. C. Otté. London: Henry G. Bohn.

Humphrey, N. K. 1976. The social function of intellect. In *Growing points in ethology,* ed. P. P. G. Bateson and R. A. Hinde, 303–17. Cambridge: Cambridge University Press.

Hurd, Richard M. 1903. *Principles of city land values.* New York: The Record and Guide.

Huxtable, Ada L. 1978. Architecture for a fast-food culture. *The New York Times Magazine,* 12 February, 23.

Innis, Donald Q. 1983. *Twenty-one days on spacecraft earth.* Geneseo, N.Y.: Intercropping.

Institute for Applied Geosciences. 1984. Mapa Planimétrico de Imagenes de Satelite (1:250,000), Cuzco, Peru, SD 19–5. Neu Isenberg, Germany.

Instituto Nacional de Estadística. 1983. *Censos Nacionales VIII de Población—III de Vivienda.* Lima: Instituto Nacional de Estadística.

International Committee to Promote Navy Island as Permanent Headquarters of the United Nations. 1945. Proposed United Nations headquarters: Navy Island, Niagara Falls. Niagara Falls, NY.

International Joint Commission on the Preservation and Enhancement of Niagara Falls. 1953. *Report of the International Joint Commission, United States and Canada, on the Preservation and Enhancement of Niagara Falls.* Washington, D.C., and Ottawa: Author.

Jackson, John B. 1953. The westward-moving house. *Landscape* 2 (3): 8–21.

———. 1970. *Landscapes: Selected writings of J. B. Jackson.* Ed. Ervin H. Zube. Amherst: University of Massachusetts Press.

———. 1972a. *American space: The centennial years, 1865–1876.* New York: Norton.

———. 1972b. Metamorphosis. *Annals of the Association of American Geographers* 62:155–58.

———. 1980. *The necessity for ruins, and other topics.* Amherst: University of Massachusetts Press.

———. 1984. *Discovering the vernacular landscape.* New Haven, Conn.: Yale University Press.

———. 1988. The accessible landscape. *Whole Earth* 58 (Spring): 4–9.

Jackson, Peter. 1989. *Maps of meaning: An introduction to cultural geography.* London: Unwin Hyman.

Jackson, Peter, and Susan J. Smith. 1984. *Exploring social geography.* London: Allen & Unwin.

Jackson, W. A. Douglas. 1985. *The shaping of our world: A human and cultural geography.* New York: Wiley.

Jaher, Frederic C. 1972. Nineteenth-century elites in Boston and New York. *Journal of Social History* 6:32–77.

———. 1973. Style and status: High society in late nineteenth-century New York. In *The rich, the well born, and the powerful,* ed. Frederic C. Jaher, 258–84. Urbana: University of Illinois Press.

———. 1982. *The urban establishment, upper strata in Boston, New York, Charleston, Chicago, and Los Angeles.* Urbana: University of Illinois Press.

Jakle, John. 1977. *Images of the Ohio Valley: A historical geography of travel.* New York: Oxford University Press.

———. 1982. *The American small town: Twentieth century place images.* Hamden, Conn.: Archon.

———. 1985. *The tourist: Travel in twentieth-century North America.* Lincoln: University of Nebraska Press.

———. 1987. *The visual elements of landscape.* Amherst: University of Massachusetts Press.

Jakle, John, Robert Bastian, and Douglas Meyer. 1989. *Common houses in America's small towns: The Atlantic Seaboard to the Mississippi Valley.* Athens: University of Georgia Press.

James, Marquis. 1947. *The Metropolitan Life.* New York: Viking.

James, Preston, and Geoffrey Martin. 1981. *All possible worlds: A history of geographical ideas.* New York: Wiley.

Jankowski, Martín S. 1986. *City bound: Urban life and political attitudes among Chicano youth.* Albuquerque: University of New Mexico Press.

Jeans, D. N. 1979. Some literary examples of humanistic descriptions of places. *Australian Geographer* 14:207–14.

Jencks, Charles. 1973. Ersatz in L.A. *Architectural Design* 43 (9): 596–601.

Jennings, Bruce. 1988. *Foundations of international agriculture research science and politics in Mexican agriculture.* Boulder, Col.: Westview.

Jett, Stephen C. 1971. Diffusion versus independent invention: The bases of controversy. In *Man across the sea: Problems of pre-Columbian contact,* ed. Carroll L. Riley, J. Charles Kelley, Campbell W. Pennington, and Robert L. Rands, 5–53. Austin: University of Texas Press.

———. 1991. Further information on the geography of the blowgun and its implication for early transoceanic contacts. *Annals of the Association of American Geographers* 81:89–102.

Jett, Stephen C., and Virginia E. Spencer. 1981. *Navajo architecture: Forms, history, distributions.* Tucson: University of Arizona Press.

Johannessen, Carl L. 1970. The domestication of maize: Process or event. *Geographical Review* 60:393–413.

Johannessen, Carl L., and Anne Z. Parker. 1988. American crop plants in Asia prior to European contact. *Yearbook of the Conference of Latin Americanist Geographers* 14:14–19.

Johnson, Allen W., and Timothy Earle. 1987. *The evolution of human societies: From foraging to agrarian state.* Stanford, Calif.: Stanford University Press.

Johnson, Kirsten. 1977. Do as the land bids: A study of Otomí resource use on the eve of irrigation. Ph.D. diss., Clark University, Worcester, Mass.

Johnston, Ronald J. 1979. *Geography and geographers: Anglo-American human geography since 1945.* London: Edward Arnold.

———. 1983. *Philosophy and human geography: An introduction to contemporary approaches.* London: Edward Arnold.

Jones, David R. W. 1970. The Caribbean coast of Central America: A case of multiple fragmentation. *Professional Geographer* 22:260–66.

Jones, E. L. 1974. Creative disruptions in American agriculture, 1620–1820. *Agricultural History* 48:510–28.

Jones, Oakah L. 1979. *Los paisanos: Spanish settlers on the northern frontier of New Spain.* Norman: University of Oklahoma Press.

Jones, Stephen B. 1952. The enjoyment of geography. *Geographical Review* 42:543–50.

Joranson, Philip, and Ken Butigan, eds. 1984. *Cry of the environment.* Santa Fe: Bear.

Jordan, Terry G. 1969. Population origins in Texas, 1850. *Geographical Review* 59:83–103.

———. 1978. *Texas log buildings: A folk architecture.* Austin: University of Texas Press.

———. 1982. *Texas graveyards: A cultural legacy.* Austin: University of Texas Press.

———. 1989a. New Sweden's role on the American frontier: A study of cultural preadaptation. *Geografiska Annaler* series B 71:71–83.

———. 1989b. Preadaptation and European colonization in rural North America. *Annals of the Association of American Geographers* 79:489–500.

Jordan, Terry G., and Matti Kaups. 1987. Folk architecture in cultural and ecological context. *Geographical Review* 77:52–75.

———. 1989. *The American backwoods frontier: An ethnic and ecological interpretation.* Baltimore: Johns Hopkins University Press.

Jordan, Terry G., Matti Kaups, and Richard M. Lieffort. 1986. New evidence on the European origin of Pennsylvanian V notching. *Pennsylvania Folklife* 36:20–31.

Jordan, Terry G., and Lester Rowntree. 1976. *The human mosaic: A thematic introduction to cultural geography.* San Francisco: Canfield Press; 5th ed., New York: Harper and Row, 1990.

Juergens, George. 1966. *Joseph Pulitzer and the New York World.* Princeton: Princeton University Press.

Jung, Carl G. 1968. *The archetypes and the collective unconscious.* 2d ed. London: Routledge.

Justim, Estelle, and Elizabeth Lindquist-Cook. 1985. *Landscape as Photograph.* New Haven, Conn.: Yale University Press.

Kabaker, Adina. 1977. A radiocarbon chronology relevant to the origins of agriculture. In *Origins of agriculture,* ed. Charles A. Reed, 957–80. The Hague: Mouton.

Kalm, Peter. 1972. *Travels into North America.* Barre, Mass.: Imprint Society.

Kates, Robert W. 1987. The human environment: The road not taken, the road still beckoning. *Annals of the Association of American Geographers* 77:525–34.

Kates, Robert W., and Ian Burton. 1986. *Geography, resources, and environment.* Vol. 2: *Themes from the work of Gilbert F. White.* Chicago: University of Chicago Press.

Katz, Cindi. 1991. Sow what you know: The struggle for social reproduction in rural Sudan. *Annals of the Association of American Geographers* 81:488–514.

Katz, Cindi, and Andrew Kirby. 1991. In the nature of things: The environment and everyday life. *Transactions of the Institute of British Geographers,* n.s. 16: 259–71.

Kay, Jeanne. 1985. Preconditions of natural resources conservation. *Agricultural History* 59:124–35.

———. 1988. Concepts of nature in the Hebrew Bible. *Environmental Ethics* 10:309–27.

Kazin, Alfred. 1988. *A writer's America: Landscape in literature.* New York: Knopf.

Kea, Ray. 1982. *Settlements, trade, and politics in the seventeenth-century Gold Coast.* Baltimore: Johns Hopkins University Press.

Kearney, Richard. 1991. *Poetics of imagining: From Husserl to Lyotard.* London: Harper Collins.

Keith, Thomas. 1983. *Man and the natural world: A history of the modern sensibility.* New York: Pantheon.

Keller, Morton. 1963. *The life insurance enterprise, 1885–1910.* Cambridge, Mass.: Belknap Press of Harvard University Press.

Kenzer, Martin, ed. 1987. *Carl O. Sauer: A tribute.* Corvallis: Oregon State University Press.

Kerouac, Jack. 1957. *On the road.* New York: Viking.

Kimber, Clarissa T. 1988. *Martinique revisited: The changing plant geographies of a West Indian island.* College Station: Texas A & M University Press.

Kinchen, David M. 1977. Indeterminate facade building opens. *Los Angeles Times,* 17 April, Part VIII, 5.

King, Anthony D. 1984. *The bungalow: The production of a global culture.* London: Routledge and Kegan Paul.

Kipling, Rudyard. 1933. The English flag. *Rudyard Kipling's verse: Inclusive edition 1885–1932.* London: Hodder and Stoughton.

Kirasic, K. C. 1988. Aging and spatial cognition: Current status and new directions for experimental researchers and cognitive neuropsychologists. In *Cognitive approaches to neuropsychology,* ed. J. M. Williams and C. J. Long, 83–100. New York: Plenum.

Kirk, William. 1952. Historical geography and the concept of the behavioral environment. *Indian Geographical Journal* Silver Jubilee Volume: 152–60.

Klauder, Francis J. 1971. *Aspects of the thought of Teilhard de Chardin.* North Quincy, Mass.: Christopher.

Klee, Gary A. 1980. Traditional wisdom and the modern resource manager. In *World systems of traditional resource management,* ed. G. A. Klee, 245–81. London: Edward Arnold.

Klein, Ira. 1973. Death in India. *Journal of Asian Studies* 32:639–59.

Klippart, John H. 1860. *The wheat plant: Its origin, culture, growth, development, composition, varieties, diseases, etc., etc. Together with a few remarks on Indian corn, its culture, etc.* Cincinnati: Moore, Wilstach, Keys.

Knapp, Gregory W. 1988. *Ecología cultural prehispánica del Ecuador.* Quito: Banco Central del Ecuador.

———. 1991. *Andean ecology: Adaptive dynamics in Ecuador.* Boulder, Colo.: Westview.

Knapp, Gregory W., and William M. Denevan. 1985. The use of wetlands in the prehistoric economy of the Northern Ecuadorian Highlands. In *Prehistoric intensive agriculture in the tropics,* ed. I. S. Farrington, 184–207. British Archaeological Reports, International Series, no. 232. Oxford: BAR.

Kniffen, Fred B. 1936. Louisiana house types. *Annals of the Association of American Geographers* 26:179–93.

———. 1965. Folk housing: Key to diffusion. *Annals of the Association of American Geographers* 55:549–77.

———. 1974. Material culture in the geographic interpretation of the landscape. In *The human mirror,* ed. Miles Richardson, 252–67. Baton Rouge: Louisiana State University Press.

———. 1976. Interview with Fred B. Kniffen, November 10, 1975. *Mississippi Geographer* 4 (Spring): 5–6.

———. 1990. *Cultural diffusion and landscapes: Selections by Fred B. Kniffen.* Ed. Jesse H. Walker and Randall A. Detro. Geoscience and Man 27. Baton Rouge: Louisiana State University, Department of Geography and Anthropology.

Kniffen, Fred B., and Henry Glassie. 1966. Building in wood in the eastern United States: A time-place perspective. *Geographical Review* 56:40–66.

Koepping, Klaus-Peter. 1983. *Adolf Bastian and the psychic unity of mankind.* St. Lucia, Australia: University of Queensland Press.

Koerner, Gustave. 1902. *Memoirs of Gustave Koerner, 1809–1896,* 2 vols. Ed. Thomas J. McCormack. Cedar Rapids, Iowa: Torch.

Kohak, Erazim V. 1984. *The embers and the stars: A philosophical inquiry into the moral sense of nature.* Chicago: University of Chicago Press.

Kohr, Leopold. 1986. *The breakdown of nations.* London: Routledge and Kegan Paul.

Kolata, Alan L. 1986. The agricultural foundations of the Tiwanaku State: A view from the heartland. *American Antiquity* 51 (4): 748–62.

Kong, Lily. 1990. Geography and religion: Trends and prospects. *Progress in Human Geography* 14:355–71.

Kowinski, William S. 1978. The malling of America. *New Times,* 1 May, 30–55.

———. 1985. *The malling of America: An inside look at the great consumer paradise.* New York: Morrow.

Krampen, Martin. 1979. *Meaning in the urban environment.* London: Pion.

Kriehn, George. 1899. The city beautiful. *Municipal Affairs* 3:594–601.

Kroc, Ray, with Robert Anderson. 1977. *Grinding it out: The making of McDonald's.*

Kroeber, Alfred L. 1937. Diffusionism. *Encyclopedia of the social sciences,* vol. 5, ed. Edwin R. A. Seligman, 139–42. New York: Macmillan.

Kroeber, Alfred L., and Clyde Kluckhohn. 1952. *Culture: A critical review of concepts and definitions.* Cambridge, Mass.: Harvard University, Papers of the Peabody Museum of Archaeology and Ethnology.

Kuhn, Thomas S. 1962. *The structure of scientific revolutions.* Chicago: University of Chicago Press.

Kulikoff, Allan. 1976. Tobacco and slaves: Population, economy and society in eighteenth-century Prince George's County Maryland. Ph.D. diss., Brandeis University, Waltham, Mass.

Kumar, Krishan. 1987. *Utopia and anti-utopia in modern times.* Oxford: Blackwell.

Kung, Hans, and Julia Ching. 1989. *Christianity and Chinese religions.* New York: Doubleday.

Kup, Alexander P. 1975. *Sierra Leone: A concise history.* New York: St. Martin's.

Lakeland, Paul. 1990. *Theology and critical theory.* Nashville: Abingdon.

Landau, Sarah B. 1986. Richard Morris Hunt: Architectural innovator and father of a "distinctive" American school. In *The architecture of Richard Morris Hunt,* ed. Susan R. Stein, 47–77. Chicago: University of Chicago Press.

Landolt, Robert G. 1976. *The Mexican-American workers of San Antonio, Texas.* New York: Arno.

Lane, Belden C. 1988. *Landscapes of the sacred: Geography and narrative in American spirituality.* New York: Paulist.

Lattimore, Owen. 1980. The periphery as locus of innovation. In *Centre and periphery: Spatial variation and politics,* ed. J. Gottmann, 205–9. Beverly Hills: Sage.

Lawrence, D. H. 1923. *Studies in classic American literature.* New York: Thomas Seltzer.

———. 1949. *The rainbow.* Harmondsworth: Penguin.

———. 1960. *Women in love.* Harmondsworth: Penguin.

Leaf, Murray J. 1979. *Man, mind, and science.* New York: Columbia University Press.

Lebergott, Stanley. 1964. *Manpower in economic growth: The American record since 1800.* New York: McGraw-Hill.

Leclaire, Lucien. 1954. *Le roman régionaliste dans les Isles Britanniques, 1800–1950.* Clermont-Ferrand: Bussac.

Leclerc, I. 1958. *Whitehead's metaphysics.* New York: Macmillan.

Lee, Laurie. 1956. *A rose for winter: Travels in Andalusia.* New York: Morrow.

Lee, Laurie. 1962. *Cider with Rosie.* Harmondsworth: Penguin.

Leeuwen, Thomas A. P. van. 1988. *The skyward trend of thought: The metaphysics of the American skyscraper.* Cambridge, Mass.: MIT Press.

Leighly, John. 1937. Some comments on contemporary geographical methods. *Annals of the Association of American Geographers* 27:125–41.

———, ed. 1963. *Land and life: A selection from the writings of Carl Ortwin Sauer.* Berkeley: University of California Press.

———. 1976. Carl Ortwin Sauer, 1989–1975. *Annals of the Association of American Geographers* 66:337–48.

———. 1978. Carl Ortwin Sauer, 1889–1975. In *Geographers: Bibliographic studies,* vol. 2, ed. T. W. Freeman and P. Pinchemel, 99–108. London: Mansell.

Lemon, James T. 1972. *The best poor man's country: A geographical study of early southeastern Pennsylvania.* Baltimore: Johns Hopkins University Press.

Lenin, Vladimir. 1976. *The agrarian question and the critics of Marx.* Moscow: Progress.

Lentnek, Barry. 1969. Economic transition from traditional to commercial agriculture: The case of El Llano, Mexico. *Annals of the Association of American Geographers* 59:65–84.

———. 1971. Latin American peasantry in transition to modern farming. *Proceedings, Conference of Latin Americanist Geographers* 1:161–66.

Leopold, Aldo. 1966. *A Sand County almanac.* New York: Ballantine.

Lessing, Doris. 1968. *Going home.* London: Panther.

Levander, Lars. 1943. *Övre Dalarnes bondekultur under 1800-talets förra hälft,* vol. 1. Stockholm: Jonson and Winter.

Levin, Harry. 1970. *The power of blackness: Hawthorne, Poe, Melville.* New York: Knopf.

Lévy-Bruhl, Lucien. 1966. *How natives think.* New York: Washington Square.

Lewandowski, Susan. 1984. The built environment and cultural symbolism in post-colonial Madras. In *The city in cultural context,* ed. J. Agnew, J. Mercer, and D. Sopher, 237–54. Boston: Allen & Unwin.

Lewin, Roger. 1989. *Human evolution,* 2d ed. Boston: Blackwell Scientific.

Lewis, Bernard C. 1940. The Cayman Islands and marine turtle. *Bulletin of the Institute of Jamaica Science,* series 2:Appendix, 56–65.

Lewis, Martin W. 1992. *Wagering the land: Ritual, capital, and environmental degradation in the Cordillera of northern Luzon, 1900–1986.* Berkeley: University of California Press.

Lewis, Peirce. 1972. Small town in Pennsylvania. *Annals of the Association of American Geographers* 62: 323–51.

———. 1975. Common houses, cultural spoor. *Landscape* 19 (2): 1–22.

———. 1976. *New Orleans: The making of an urban landscape.* Cambridge, Mass.: Ballinger.

———. 1979a. Axioms for reading the landscape. In *The interpretation of ordinary landscapes: Geographical essays,* ed. Donald W. Meinig, 11–32. New York: Oxford University Press.

———. 1979b. The unprecedented city. In *The American*

land, ed. Alexis Doster, Joe Goodwin, and Robert C. Post, 184–93. New York: Norton.

———. 1983. Learning from looking: Geographic and other writing about the American cultural landscape. *American Quarterly* 35:242–61.

———. 1985. Beyond description. *Annals of the Association of American Geographers* 75:465–78.

———. 1991. The urban invasion of the rural Northeast. In *National Rural Studies Committee: A proceedings,* ed. Emery Castle and Barbara Baldwin, 11–21. Corvallis: Oregon State University, Western Rural Development Center.

Ley, David. 1987. Styles of the times: Liberal and neoconservative landscapes in inner Vancouver. *Journal of Historical Geography* 13:40–56.

Ley, David, and Marwyn S. Samuels, eds. 1978. *Humanistic geography.* Chicago: Maaroufa.

Lich, Glen E., ed. 1992. *Regional studies: The interplay of land and people.* College Station: Texas A&M University Press.

Liebs, Chester H. 1978. Remember our not-so-distant past? *Historic Preservation* 30 (1): 30–35.

Limerick, Patricia N. 1987. *The legacy of conquest: The unbroken past of the American West.* New York: Norton.

Lincoln, Abraham. 1953. *The collected works of Abraham Lincoln, 1848–1858,* 8 vols. Ed. Roy P. Basler. New Brunswick, N.J.: Rutgers University Press.

Lincoln, Roger J., Geoffrey A. Boxshall, and P. F. Clark. 1982. *A dictionary of ecology, evolution and systematics.* Cambridge: Cambridge University Press.

Lindström, Peter. 1925. *Geographia Americae, with an account of the Delaware Indians.* Trans. and ed. Amandus Johnson. Philadelphia: Swedish Colonial Society.

Liston, J. K. 1843. *Niagara Falls: A poem in three cantos.* Toronto: Author; printed by J. H. Lawrence.

Litwak, Leon F. 1961. *North of slavery: The Negro in the free states, 1790–1860.* Chicago: University of Chicago Press.

Lockwood, Charles. 1976. *Manhattan moves uptown.* Boston: Houghton Mifflin.

Long, Edward. 1774. *The history of Jamaica . . . and account of the Mosquito Shore.* London: T. Lowndes.

Longmore, T. Wilson, and Homer L. Hitt. 1943. A demographic analysis of first and second generation Mexican population of the United States: 1930. *Southwestern Social Science Quarterly* 24:138–49.

Lopez, Barry. 1986. *Arctic dreams: Imagination and desire in a northern landscape.* New York: Scribner.

Lopez, David E. 1978. Chicano language loyalty in an urban setting. *Sociology and Social Research* 62:267–78.

Lord, J. C. 1869. The genius of Niagara. In *Occasional poems.* Buffalo: Breed and Lent.

Louv, Richard. 1983. *America II.* Boston: Houghton Mifflin.

Love, W. T. 1895. *Model City Bulletin* 1 (1) (10 August).

Lovell, W. George, and Noble David Cook. 1992. *"Secret judgments of God": Old World disease in colonial Spanish America.* Norman: University of Oklahoma Press.

Low camp—A kook's tour of southern California's fast-

disappearing unreal estate. 1965. *Los Angeles Magazine* 10 (November): 35–36.

Lowenthal, David. 1957. The population of Barbados. *Social and Economic Studies* 6:445–501.

———. 1961. Geography, experience, and imagination: Toward a geographical epistemology. *Annals of the Association of American Geographers* 51:241–60.

———, ed. 1967. *Environmental perception and behavior.* University of Chicago, Department of Geography, Research Paper no. 109. Chicago: University of Chicago, Department of Geography.

———. 1968. The American scene. *Geographical Review* 58:61–88.

———. 1972. *West Indian societies.* Oxford American Geographical Research Series no. 26. New York: Oxford University Press.

———. 1975. Past time, present place: Landscape and memory. *Geographical Review* 65:1–36.

———. 1985. *The past is a foreign country.* New York: Cambridge University Press.

Lowenthal, David, and Martyn J. Bowden, eds. 1976. *Geographies of the mind: Essays in historical geosophy.* New York: Oxford University Press.

Lowenthal, David, and Lambros Comitas. 1962. Emigration and depopulation: Some neglected aspects of population geography. *Geographical Review* 52:195–210.

Lowenthal, David, and Hugh C. Prince. 1965. English landscape tastes. *Geographical Review* 55:186–222.

Lowie, Robert H. 1937. *The history of ethnological theory.* New York: Holt, Rinehart and Winston.

Lowry, Bates. 1985. *Building a national image: Architectural drawings for the American democracy, 1789–1912.* Washington, D.C.: National Building Museum.

Lucas, C. 1930. *The fenman's world: Memories of a fenland physician.* Norwich: Jarrold.

Luten, Daniel B. 1980. *Progress against growth: Daniel B. Luten on the American landscape.* Ed. Thomas Vale. New York: Guilford.

———. 1991. Population and resources. *Population and Environment* 12:311–30.

Lutwack, Leonard. 1984. *The role of place in literature.* Syracuse, N.Y.: Syracuse University Press.

Lynes, Russell. 1954. *The taste-makers: The shaping of American popular taste.* New York: Harper.

MacMullin, R. B., F. L. Koethen, and C. N. Richardson. 1940. Chemical industry on the Niagara frontier. *Transactions of the American Institute of Chemical Engineers* 36:295–324.

Malinowski, B. 1927. The life of culture. In *Culture: The diffusion controversy,* ed. G. E. Smith. New York: Norton.

Mallory, William E., and Paul Simpson-Housley. 1987. *Geography and literature: A meeting of disciplines.* Syracuse, N.Y.: Syracuse University Press.

Marcus, Melvin G. 1979. Coming full circle: Physical geography in the twentieth century. *Annals of the Association of American Geographers* 69:521–32.

Markham, Beryl. 1983 [1942]. *West with the light.* San Francisco: North Point Press [Boston: Houghton Mifflin].

Marling, Karal A. 1984. *The colossus of roads: Myth and symbol along the American highway.* Minneapolis: University of Minnesota Press.

Marsh, George P. 1864. *Man and nature: Or physical geography as modified through human action.* New York: Charles Scribner.

Marshall, Lane. 1979. Agoramania: The influence of nostalgia on the contemporary American landscape. Unpublished paper, University of Illinois at Urbana, Department of Landscape Architecture.

Marshall, Sybil. 1967. *Fenland chronicle.* Cambridge: Cambridge University Press.

———. 1977. Fen tiger. *Vole* 3:46.

Martin, A. C., N. Hotchkiss, F. M. Uhler, and W. S. Bourn. 1953. *Classification of wetlands of the United States.* U.S. Fish and Wildlife Service, Special Scientific Report 20. Washington, D.C.: Supt. of Documents.

Martinez-Alier, Juan. 1992. Environmentalism and the poor: The ecology of survival. *Items* (Social Science Research Council) 46:1–5.

Marx, Karl, and Friedrich Engels. 1956. *The German ideology.* 3d ed. Moscow: Progress.

Marx, Leo. 1967. *The machine in the garden: Technology and the pastoral ideal in America.* New York: Oxford University Press.

Mascie-Taylor, C. G. N., and G. W. Lasker, eds. 1988. *Biological aspects of human migration.* Cambridge: Cambridge University Press.

Mather, John R., ed. 1991. *Global change: Geographic appraisals.* Tucson: University of Arizona Press.

Mathewson, Kent. 1984. *Irrigation horticulture in highland Guatemala.* Boulder, Colo.: Westview.

———. 1985. Taxonomy of raised and drained fields. A morphogenetic approach. In *Prehistoric intensive agriculture in the tropics,* ed. I. S. Farrington, 835–45. British Archaeological Reports, International Series, no. 232. Oxford: BAR.

———. 1987. Sauer south by southwest: Antimodernism and the austral impulse. In *Carl O. Sauer: A tribute,* ed. M. Kenzer, 90–111. Corvallis: Oregon State University Press.

———, ed. 1993. *Culture, form, and place: Essays in cultural and historical geography.* Geoscience and Man 32. Baton Rouge: Louisiana State University, Department of Geography and Anthropology.

Matthiessen, Peter. 1967. To the Miskito Bank. *The New Yorker,* 28 October, 120–64.

———. 1975. *Far Tortuga.* New York: Random House.

Maugham, W. Somerset. 1944. *The razor's edge.* Garden City, N.Y.: Doubleday, Duran.

Maverick, Augustus. 1970 [1870]. *Henry J. Raymond and the New York press.* Hartford, Conn.: A.S. Hale.

Maybury-Lewis, David. 1992. *Millennium: Tribal wisdom and the modern world.* New York: Viking.

Mayer, Enrique. 1985. Production zones. In *Andean ecology and civilization: An interdisciplinary perspective on Andean ecological complementarity,* ed. Shozo Masuda, Izumi Shimada, and Craig Morris, 45–84. Tokyo: University of Tokyo Press.

Mayo, James M. 1988. *War memorials as political landscape.* New York: Praeger.

Mayo, Morrow. 1933. *Los Angeles.* New York: Knopf.

McAlester, Virginia, and Lee McAlester. 1984. *A field guide to American houses.* New York: Knopf.

McCabe, James. 1872. *Lights and shadows of New York life.* Philadelphia: National.

McClelland, Daniel. 1961. *The achieving society.* Princeton: Van Nostrand.

McCullough, Edo. 1966. *World's fair midways.* New York: Exposition.

McDaniel, Jay B. 1988. Land ethics, animal rights, and process theology. *Process Studies* 17:88–102.

———. 1990. Revisioning God and the self: Lessons from Buddhism. In *Liberating life: Contemporary approaches to ecological theology,* ed. Charles Birch, William Eakin, and Jay B. McDaniel, 228–58. Maryknoll, N.Y.: Orbis.

McEvedy, Colin. 1980. *The Penguin atlas of African history.* London: Penguin.

McEvedy, Colin, and Richard Jones. 1978. *Atlas of world population history.* Harmondsworth: Penguin.

McGee, Mark G. 1979. Human spatial abilities: Psychometric studies and environmental, genetic, hormonal, and neurologic influences. *Psychological Bulletin* 86 (5): 889–918.

McGreevy, Patrick. 1984. Visions at the brink: Imagination and the geography of Niagara Falls. Ph.D. diss., University of Minnesota.

———. 1985a. Niagara as Jerusalem. *Landscape* 28 (2): 26–32.

———. 1985b. The wall of mirrors: Cultural reflections on the border landscape at Niagara Falls. Paper presented at the Annual Meeting of the Association for Canadian Studies in the United States. Philadelphia, 19–21 September.

———. 1987. Imagining the future at Niagara Falls. *Annals of the Association of American Geographers* 77: 48–62.

———. 1990. Place and the American Christmas. *Geographical Review* 80:32–42.

McIntosh, W. H. 1876. *History of Ontario County, New York.* Philadelphia: Everts, Ensign & Everts.

———. 1877. *History of Monroe County, New York.* Philadelphia: Everts, Ensign & Everts.

McKay, Donald V. 1943. Colonialism in the French geographical movement. *Geographical Review* 33:214–32.

McKinsey, Elizabeth. 1985. *Niagara Falls: Icon of the American sublime.* New York: Cambridge University Press.

McManis, Douglas R. 1972. *European impressions of the New England coast, 1497–1620.* University of Chicago Department of Geography Research Paper no. 139. Chicago: University of Chicago, Department of Geography.

McNeely, John H. 1964. *The railways of Mexico: A study in nationalization.* Southwestern Studies Monograph no. 5. El Paso: Texas Western College Press.

McWilliams, Carey. 1941. Mexicans to Michigan. *Common Ground* 2:5–17.

———. 1949. *North from Mexico: The Spanish-speaking people of the United States*. Philadelphia: Lippincott.

Mead, George H. 1938. *The philosophy of the act*. Chicago: University of Chicago Press.

Medeiros, Francine. 1980. *La Opinión*, A Mexican exile newspaper: A content analysis of its first years, 1926–1929. *Aztlán* 11:65–88.

Meier, Richard L. 1963. The organization of technological innovation in urban environments. In *The historian and the city*, ed. Oscar Handlin and John Burchard, 74–83. Cambridge, Mass.: MIT Press.

Meinig, Donald W. 1965. The Mormon culture region. *Annals of the Association of American Geographers* 55:191–220.

———. 1969a. *Imperial Texas*. Austin: University of Texas Press.

———. 1969b. A macrogeography of Western imperialism: Some morphologies of moving frontiers of political control. In *Settlement and encounter: Geographical studies presented to Sir Grenfell Price*, ed. F. Gale and G. H. Lawton, 213–40. Melbourne: Oxford University Press.

———. 1971a. Environmental appreciation: Localities as humane art. *The Western Humanities Review* 25:1–11.

———. 1971b. *Southwest: Three peoples in geographical change, 1600–1970*. New York: Oxford University Press.

———. 1972. American Wests: Preface to a geographical introduction. *Annals of the Association of American Geographers* 62:159–84.

———. 1978. The continuous shaping of America: A prospectus for geographers and historians. *American Historical Review* 83:1186–1205.

———. 1979a. The beholding eye: Ten versions of the same scene. In *The interpretation of ordinary landscapes*, ed. D. W. Meinig, 33–48. New York: Oxford University Press.

———, ed. 1979b. *The interpretation of ordinary landscapes: Geographical essays*. New York: Oxford University Press.

———. 1979c. Reading the landscape: An appreciation of W. G. Hoskins and J. B. Jackson. In *The interpretation of ordinary landscapes*, ed. Donald W. Meinig, 195–244. New York: Oxford University Press.

———. 1979d. Symbolic landscapes: Some idealizations of American communities. In *The interpretation of ordinary landscapes*, ed. Donald W. Meinig, 164–92. New York: Oxford University Press.

———. 1982. Geographical analysis of imperial expansion. In *Period and place: Research methods in historical geography*, ed. Alan R. H. Baker and Mark Billinge, 71–78. Cambridge: Cambridge University Press.

———. 1983. Geography as an art. *Transactions of the Institute of British Geographers*, n.s. 8:314–28.

———. 1986. *The shaping of America: A geographical perspective on 500 years of history*. Vol. 1: *Atlantic America, 1492–1800*. New Haven, Conn.: Yale University Press.

———. 1993. *The shaping of America: A geographical perspective on 500 years of history*. Vol. 2: *Continental America, 1800–1867*. New Haven, Conn.: Yale University Press.

Meir, Matt S., and Feliciano Rivera. 1981. *Dictionary of Mexican American history*. Westport, Conn.: Greenwood.

Meland, B. E. 1974. Grace: A dimension within nature. *Journal of Religion* 54:119–37.

Merchant, Carolyn. 1992. *Radical ecology: The search for a livable world*. London: Routledge.

The Metropolitan Life Building. c. 1910. New York: Metropolitan Life.

Meyer, Karl. 1970. Love thy city. *Saturday Review*, 28 April.

Meyrowitz, Joshua. 1985. *No sense of place: The impact of electronic media on social behavior*. New York: Oxford University Press.

Miele, F. 1979. Public preservation versus private development: Queen Victoria Park, Niagara Falls, Ontario. Senior Honors Essay, University of Waterloo, Department of Environmental Studies.

Mikesell, Marvin W. 1978. Tradition and innovation in cultural geography. *Annals of the Association of American Geographers* 68:1–16.

———. 1992. Reflections on a shared venture: Readings in cultural geography. In *Person, place, and thing: Interpretive and empirical essays in cultural geography*, ed. Shue Tuck Wong, 31–45. Geoscience and Man 31. Baton Rouge: Lousiana State University, Department of Geography and Anthropology.

Mikesell, Marvin W., and Alexander B. Murphy. 1991. A framework for comparative study of minority group aspirations. *Annals of the Association of American Geographers* 81:581–604.

Miller, Samuel H., and Sydney B. J. Skertchly. 1878. *The Fenland: Past and present*. Wisbech: n.p.

Mintz, Sidney. 1974. *Caribbean transformations*. Chicago: Aldine.

Mitchell, J. Kenneth. 1984. Hazard perception studies: Convergent concerns and divergent approaches during the past decade. In *Environmental perception and behavior: An inventory and prospect*, ed. T. Saarinen, D. Seamon, and J. Sell, 33–60. Chicago: University of Chicago Department of Geography Research Paper no. 209. Chicago: University of Chicago, Department of Geography.

Mitchell, Robert D. 1977. *Commercialism and frontier: Perspectives on the early Shenandoah Valley*. Charlottesville: University Press of Virginia.

Mitchell, William P. 1976. Irrigation and community in the Central Peruvian highlands. *American Anthropologist* 78:25–44.

Mizer, H. B. 1981. *Niagara Falls: A topical history*. Lockport, N.Y.: Niagara County Historical Society.

Moeschlin, Felix. 1931. *Amerika vom Auto aus*. Zurich: Erlenbach.

Moncrief, Lewis. 1970. The cultural basis for our environmental crisis. *Science* 170:508–12.

Monk, Janice. 1984. Approaches to the study of women and landscape. *Environmental Review* 8:23–33.

Monk, Samuel H. 1935. *The sublime: A study of critical theories in eighteenth-century England.* New York: Modern Language Association.

Montelius, Sigvard. 1960. Finn settlement in central Sweden. *Geografiska Annaler* 42:285–93.

Mooney, Christopher F. 1966. *Teilhard de Chardin and the mystery of Christ.* New York: Harper and Row.

Moore, Charles, Donlyn Lyndon, and Gerald Allen. 1974. *The place of houses.* New York: Holt, Rinehart and Winston.

Moore, Robert J. 1990. A new Christian reformation. In *Ethics of environment and development,* ed. J. R. Engel and Joan Engel, 104–13. Tucson: University of Arizona Press.

Moran, Emilio F., ed. 1990. *The ecosystem approach in anthropology: From concept to practice.* Ann Arbor: University of Michigan Press.

Morgan, Edmund S. 1975. *American slavery American freedom: The ordeal of colonial Virginia.* New York: Norton.

Morley, Joseph. 1906. Letters of Father Joseph Morley, S.J., and some extracts from his diary (1757–1786). *Records of the American Catholic Historical Society* 17: 180–210, 289–311.

Morrison, Hugh. 1952. *Early American architecture, from the first Colonial settlements to the National Period.* New York: Oxford University Press.

Moule, C. F. D. 1967. *Man and nature in the New Testament.* Philadelphia: Fortress.

Muir, Edward, and Ronald F. E. Weissman. 1989. Social and symbolic places in Renaissance Venice and Florence. In *The power of place: Bringing together the geographical and sociological imaginations,* ed. John A. Agnew and James S. Duncan, 81–104. London: Unwin Hyman.

Muller, Thomas, and Thomas J. Espenshade. 1985. *The fourth wave: California's newest immigrants.* Washington, D.C.: Urban Institute.

Mumford, Lewis. 1934. *Technics and civilization.* New York: Harcourt, Brace.

———. 1938. *The culture of cities.* New York: Harcourt, Brace.

———. 1944. *The condition of man.* New York: Harcourt, Brace.

———. 1961. *The city in history.* New York: Harcourt, Brace & World.

Munroe, Robert L., and Ruth H. Munroe. 1971. Effect of environmental experience on spatial ability in an East African society. *Journal of Social Psychology* 83:15–22.

Murguía, Edward. 1982. *Chicano intermarriage: A theoretical and empirical study.* San Antonio: Trinity University Press.

Murphy, Alexander B. 1988. Territorial policies in multiethnic states. *Geographical Review* 79:410–21.

———. 1991. Regions as social constructs: The gap between theory and practice. *Progress in Human Geography* 15:22–35.

Murray, John A., ed. 1991. *The islands and the sea: Five centuries of nature writing from the Caribbean.* New York: Oxford University Press.

Naess, Arne. 1984. A defence of the deep ecology movement. *Environmental Ethics* 6:265–70.

———. 1988. *Ecology, community and lifestyle: An outline of ecosophy.* Cambridge: Cambridge University Press.

Nag, Moni. 1980. How modernization can also increase fertility. *Current Anthropology* 21:571–88.

Nairn, Ian. 1965. *The American landscape: A critical view.* New York: Random House.

Nash, Manning. 1989. *The cauldron of ethnicity in the modern world.* Chicago: University of Chicago Press.

Nelson, Richard K. 1983. *Make prayers to the raven: A Koyukon view of the northern forest.* Chicago: University of Chicago Press.

Nerlove, Sara B., John M. Roberts, Robert E. Klein, Charles Yarbrough, and Jean-Pierre Habicht. 1974. Natural indicators of cognitive development: An observational study of rural Guatemalan children. *Ethos* 2 (3): 265–95.

Newbury, C. W. 1969. Trade and authority in West Africa from 1850 to 1880. In *Colonialism in Africa: 1870–1960,* ed. L. Gann and P. Duggan, 66–99. Cambridge: Cambridge University Press.

Newman, Lucile F., ed. 1990. *Hunger in history: Food shortage, poverty, and deprivation.* Oxford: Blackwell.

Newson, Linda A. 1976. Cultural evolution: A basic concept for human and historical geography. *Journal of Historical Geography* 2:239–55.

Newton, Milton B. 1974. Cultural preadaptation and the upland South. In *Man and cultural heritage,* ed. H. J. Walker and W. G. Haag, 143–54. Geoscience and Man 5. Baton Rouge: Louisiana State University, Department of Geography and Anthropology.

The new World Building. 1890. *Record and Guide,* 14 June.

The New York World, its history and new home. 1890. New York: n.p.

Nietschmann, Bernard Q. 1973. *Between land and water: The subsistence ecology of the Miskito Indians, eastern Nicaragua.* New York: Seminar.

———. 1974. When the turtle collapses, the world ends. *Natural History* 83:34–43.

———, ed. 1977. *Memorias de Arrecife Tortuga: Historia natural y económica de las Tortugas en el Caribe de América Central.* Managua: Colección Cultural, Banco de América.

———. 1979a. *The Caribbean edge: The coming of modern times to isolated people and wildlife.* Indianapolis: Bobbs-Merrill.

———. 1979b. Ecological change, inflation, and migration in the far western Caribbean. *Geographical Review* 69:1–24.

———. 1987. The third world war. *Cultural Survival Quarterly* 11 (3): 1–15.

———. 1989. *The unknown war: The Miskito nation, Nicaragua, and the United States.* New York: Freedom House.

———. 1990. Conservation by conflict. *Natural History,* November, 42–49.

———. 1991. The Miskito nation and the politics of self-determination. *Journal of Political Science* 19:18–40.

Nietschmann, Judith. 1975. *From subsistence to market: Changing social and economic relationships in a Miskito Indian Village.* Ph.D. diss., University of Michigan, Ann Arbor.

Noble, Allen G., ed. 1992. *To build in a new land: Ethnic landscapes in North America.* Baltimore: Johns Hopkins University Press.

Nolan, Mary L. 1983. Irish pilgrimage: The different tradition. *Annals of the Association of American Geographers* 73:421–38.

Norberg-Schultz, Christian. 1976. The phenomenon of place. *Architectural Association Quarterly* 8:3–10.

North, Douglass C. 1959. Agriculture in regional economic growth. *Journal of Farm Economics* 41:943–51.

North, Richard. 1977. Cycling without hills. *Vole* 3:47.

Norton, T. H. 1916. Niagara on tap. *Popular Science Monthly,* February.

Norton, William. 1989. *Explorations in the understanding of landscape: A cultural geography.* New York: Greenwood.

Norwood, Vera, and Janice Monk, eds. 1987. *The desert is no lady: Southwestern landscapes in women's writing and art.* New Haven, Conn.: Yale University Press.

Nostrand, Richard L. 1975. Mexican Americans circa 1850. *Annals of the Association of American Geographers* 65:378–90.

———. 1992. *The Hispano homeland.* Norman: University of Oklahoma Press.

Oberg, Kalervo. 1973. *The social economy of the Tlingit Indians.* The American Ethnology Society Monograph no. 55. Seattle: University of Washington Press.

Obiechina, Emmanuel N. 1975. *Culture, tradition and society in the West African novel.* Cambridge: Cambridge University Press.

Oelschlaeger, Max. 1991. *The idea of wilderness: From prehistory to the age of ecology.* New Haven, Conn.: Yale University Press.

———, ed. 1992. *The wilderness condition: Essays on environment and civilization.* San Francisco: Sierra Club.

Oliver, Paul. 1987. *Dwellings: The house across the world.* Austin: University of Texas Press.

Olmsted, Frederick L. 1978 [1857]. *A Journey through Texas; Or, a Saddle-Trip on the Southwestern Frontier.* Austin: University of Texas Press.

O'Riordan, Timothy. 1976. *Environmentalism.* London: Pion.

Orlove, Benjamin S., and Glynn Custred. 1980. The alternative model of agrarian society in the Andes: Households, networks, and corporate groups. In *Land and power in Latin America: Agrarian economies and social processes in the Andes,* ed. B. S. Orlove and G. Custred, 31–54. New York: Holmes and Meier.

Ortega Dueñas, Ramiro. 1987. Personal interview. Granja K'ayra, Universidad Nacional de San Antonio de Abad del Cuzco, 18 January.

Orwell, George. 1946. *Critical essays.* London: Secker & Warburg.

———. 1948. *Coming up for air.* London: Secker & Warburg.

Osae, T. A., S. N. Nwabara, and A. T. O. Odunsi. 1973. *A short history of West Africa.* New York: Hill and Wang.

O'Toole, James. 1977. *Work, learning and the American future.* San Francisco: Jossey-Bass.

The palace-building of the *New York Tribune.* 1875. *Potter's American Monthly* 5:538.

Palm, Risa. 1986. Coming home. *Annals of the Association of American Geographers* 76:469–79.

Panero, R., B. Candela, and W. McGuigan. 1968. Niagara Falls, New York: An appraisal of the city. Hudson Institute Paper H1-1099-p, 23 Sept. Croton-on-Hudson, N.Y.: Hudson Institute.

Panikkar, Kavalam M. 1959. *Asia and Western dominance.* London: Macmillan.

Parsons, James J. 1955. The Miskito pine savanna of Nicaragua and Honduras. *Annals of the Association of American Geographers* 45:36–63.

———. 1956. *San Andrés and Providencia, English-speaking islands in the western Caribbean.* University of California Publications in Geography 12 (1). Berkeley: University of California Press.

———. 1962. *The green turtle and man.* Gainesville: University of Florida Press.

———. 1969. Ridged fields in the Río Guayas Valley, Ecuador. *American Antiquity* 34:76–80.

———. 1970. The "Africanization" of the New World tropical grasslands. *Tübinger Geographische Studien* 34:141–53.

———. 1972. The spread of African pasture grasses to the American tropics. *Journal of Range Management* 25:13–17.

———. 1985. On "bioregionalism" and "watershed consciousness." *The Professional Geographer* 37:1–6.

———. 1986. A geographer looks at the San Joaquin Valley. *Geographical Review* 76:371–89.

———. Forthcoming. "Mr. Sauer" and the writers. In *The legacy of intellect: Carl O. Sauer and the Berkeley School,* ed. Martin Kenzer. Dordrecht: Kluwer.

Parsons, James J., and William A. Bowen. 1966. Ancient ridged fields of the San Jorge River floodplain, Colombia. *Geographical Review* 56:317–43.

Parsons, James J., and William M. Denevan. 1967. Pre-Columbian ridged fields. *Scientific American* 217:92–100.

Passarge, Siegfried. 1919–21. *Grundlagen der Landschaftskunde: Ein Lehrbuch und eine Anleitung zu landschaftskundlicher Forschung und Darstellung.* 3 vols. Hamburg: Friedrich.

Passmore, John A. 1974. *Man's responsibility for nature: Ecological problems and Western tradition.* New York: Scribner's.

Pasternak, Boris. 1961. *Dr. Zhivago.* Trans. Max Hayward and Manya Harari. London: Collins Fontana.

Patterson, Suzi. 1986. Cantu's Tex-Mex not playing fare. *San Antonio Light,* 1 June.

Paulin, Tom. 1975. *Thomas Hardy: The poetry of perception.* London: Macmillan.

Paullin, Charles O. 1932. *Atlas of the historical geography of the United States.* Ed. John K. Wright. Washington, D.C., and New York: Carnegie Institution of Washington and American Geographical Society of New York.

Pearse, Andrew. 1980. *Seeds of plenty, seeds of want: Social and economic implications of the green revolution.* Oxford: Clarendon.

Pease, Theodore C. 1925. *The story of Illinois.* Chicago: A.C. McClurg.

Pedersen, Paul O. 1970. Innovation diffusion within and between national urban systems. *Geographical Analysis* 2:203–54.

Peet, Richard, and Nigel Thrift, eds. 1989. *New models in geography: The political-economy perspective.* 2 vols. London: Unwin Hyman.

Peirce, H. B., and D. H. Hurd. 1879. *History of Tioga, Chemung, Tomkins and Schuyler Counties, New York.* Philadelphia: Everts & Ensign.

Peña, Manuel. 1985. *The Texas-Mexican conjunto: History of a working-class music.* University of Texas, Center for Mexican American Studies, Mexican American Monographs no. 9. Austin: University of Texas.

Penning-Rowsell, Edmund C., and David Lowenthal, eds. 1986. *Landscape meanings and values.* London: Allen & Unwin.

Peterson, R. A., and P. DiMaggio. 1975. From region to class, the changing locus of country music: A test of the massification hypothesis. *Social Forces* 53:497–505.

Peyton [Wertenbaker], Green. 1946. *San Antonio, city in the sun.* New York: McGraw-Hill.

Philo, C., ed. 1991. *New words, new worlds: Reconceptualising social and cultural geography.* Aberystwyth: Cambrian.

Pickett, C. E. 1877. The French Exposition of 1878. *San Francisco Examiner,* 26 October.

Pickles, John. 1985. *Phenomenology, science and geography: Spatiality and the human sciences.* Cambridge: Cambridge University Press.

Pinar, William, ed. 1974. *Heightened consciousness, cultural revolution, and curriculum theory.* Berkeley: McCutchan.

Pocock, Douglas C. D. 1978. *The novelist and the north.* University of Durham Department of Geography Occasional Publication no. 12. Durham, England: University of Durham, Department of Geography.

———, ed. 1981a. *Humanistic geography and literature: Essays on experience of place.* Totowa, N.J.: Barnes and Noble.

———. 1981b. Place and the novelist. *Transactions of the Institute of British Geographers,* n.s. 6:337–47.

———. 1988. Geography and literature. *Progress in Human Geography* 12:87–102.

Pollan, Michael. 1991. *Second nature: A gardener's education.* New York: Dell.

Popper, Frank. 1986. There's no place like home, baby. *American Land Forum* 6 (3): 8–10.

Porteous, J. Douglas. 1990. *Landscapes of the mind: Worlds of sense and metaphor.* Toronto: University of Toronto Press.

Porter, Enid. 1969. *Cambridgeshire customs and folklore.* London: Routledge and Kegan Paul.

Porter, Philip W. 1965. Environmental potentials and eco-nomic opportunities: A background for cultural adaptation. *American Anthropologist* 67:409–20.

———. 1978. Geography as human ecology. *American Behavioral Scientist* 22:15–39.

Pratt, Geraldine, and Susan Hanson. 1988. Gender, class and space. *Environment and Planning D: Society and Space* 6:15–35.

Pratt, Mary L. 1992. *Imperial eyes: Travel writing and transculturation.* London: Routledge.

Pred, Allan. 1982. Social reproduction and the time-geography of everyday life. In *A search for common ground,* ed. Peter Gould and Gunnar Olsson, 157–86. London: Pion.

———. 1984. Place as historically contingent process: Structuration and the time-geography of becoming places. *Annals of the Association of American Geographers* 74:279–97.

Price, Edward T. 1968. Cultural geography. In *International encyclopedia of the social sciences,* ed. David L. Sills, 6:129–34. New York: Macmillan and Free Press.

Price, Marie, and Martin Lewis. 1993. The reinvention of cultural geography. *Annals of the Association of American Geographers* 83 (1): 1–17.

Priestley, J. B., and Jacquetta Hawkes. 1955. *Journey down a rainbow.* New York: Harper.

Pringle, H. F., and K. Pringle. 1948. The cities of America: Niagara Falls. *Saturday Evening Post,* 30 October.

Pudup, Mary Beth. 1988. Arguments within regional geography. *Progress in Human Geography* 12:369–90.

The Pulitzer Building. 1890. *New York World,* 10 December.

Rad, Gerhard von. 1962. *Old Testament theology.* New York: Harper and Row.

———. 1964. *Prophets and the word of God.* Notre Dame: Fides.

———. 1980. *God at work in Israel.* Nashville: Abingdon.

Radin, Paul. 1933. *The method and theory of ethnology: An essay in criticism.* New York: McGraw-Hill.

Randell, Arthur R. 1969. *Fenland memories.* London: Routledge and Kegan Paul.

Raphael, Ray. 1985. *Cash crop: An American dream.* Mendocino, Calif.: Ridge Times.

———. 1986 [1976]. *Edges: Human ecology of the backcountry.* Lincoln: University of Nebraska Press [New York: Knopf].

Rapoport, Amos. 1969. *House form and culture.* Englewood Cliffs, N.J.: Prentice-Hall.

———. 1982. *The meaning of the built environment: A non-verbal communication approach.* Beverly Hills, Calif.: Sage.

Rasmussen, Steen Eiler. 1964. *Experiencing Architecture.* Cambridge, Mass.: MIT Press.

Ratzel, Friedrich. 1891. *Anthropogeographie.* Vol. 2: *Die Geographische Verbreitung des Menschen.* Stuttgart: J. Englehorn.

———. 1896. *The History of Mankind,* vol. 1. London: Macmillan.

Ray, Arthur. 1974. *Indians and the fur trade: Their role as trappers, hunters and middlemen in the lands southwest of Hudson Bay.* Toronto: University of Toronto Press.

Reed, Charles A., ed. 1977. *Origins of agriculture.* The Hague: Mouton.

Reed, Peter. 1989. Man apart: An alternative to the self-realization approach. *Environmental Ethics* 11:53–69.

Reed, S. G. 1941. *A history of the Texas railroads.* Houston: St. Clair.

Rees, Ronald. 1975. The scenery cult: Changing landscape tastes over three centuries. *Landscape* 19 (3): 39–47.

———. 1976. John Constable and the art of geography. *Geographical Review* 66:59–71.

———. 1978. Landscape in art. In *Dimensions of human geography: Essays on some familiar and neglected themes,* ed. Karl W. Butzer, 48–68. University of Chicago Department of Geography Research Paper no. 186. Chicago: University of Chicago, Department of Geography.

Reichman, Shalom, and Shlomo Hasson. 1984. A cross-cultural diffusion of colonization: From Posen to Palestine. *Annals of the Association of American Geographers* 74:57–70.

Reinhardt, Nola. 1988. *Our daily bread: The peasant question and family farming in the Colombian Andes.* Berkeley: University of California Press.

Reisler, Mark. 1976. *By the sweat of their brow: Mexican immigrant labor in the United States, 1900–1940.* Westport, Conn.: Greenwood.

Relph, Edward. 1970. An inquiry into the relations between phenomenology and geography. *Canadian Geographer* 14: 193–201.

———. 1976. *Place and placelessness.* London: Pion.

———. 1981. *Rational landscapes and humanistic geography.* London: Croom Helm.

———. 1987. *The modern urban landscape.* Baltimore: Johns Hopkins University Press.

Remy, Caroline. 1968. Hispanic-Mexican San Antonio: 1836–1861. *Southwestern Historical Quarterly* 71: 564–70.

Report of the debates and proceedings of the convention for the revision of the constitution of the state of Indiana, 1850. 2 vols. 1850. Indianapolis: A.H. Brown.

Return of the whole number of persons within the several districts of the United States, according to "an act providing for the enumeration of the inhabitants of the United States," passed March the first, one thousand seven hundred and ninety-one. 1791. Philadelphia: Childs and Swain.

Reyna, Jose R. 1982. Notes on Tejano music. *Aztlán* 13 (1–2): 81–94.

Richardson, Bonham C. 1975. *The overdevelopment of Carriacou. Geographical. Review* 65:390–99.

———. 1983. *Caribbean migrants: Environment and human survival on St. Kitts and Nevis.* Knoxville: University of Tennessee Press.

———. 1992. *The Caribbean in the wider world, 1492–1992: A regional geography.* Cambridge: Cambridge University Press.

Richardson, Miles, ed. 1974. *The human mirror: Material and spatial images of man.* Baton Rouge: Louisiana State University Press.

———. 1981. Commentary on "The Superorganic in American Cultural Geography." *Annals of the Association of American Geographers* 71:284–87.

———, ed. 1984. *Place, experience, and symbol.* Geoscience and Man 24. Baton Rouge: Louisiana State University, Department of Geography and Anthropology.

———. 1989. Place and culture: Two disciplines, two concepts, two images of Christ, and a single goal. In *The power of place: Bringing together geographical and sociological imaginations,* ed. John A. Agnew and James S. Duncan, 140–56. Boston: Unwin Hyman.

Richardson, Miles, and Robert Dunton. 1989. Culture in its places: A humanistic presentation. In *The relevance of culture,* ed. Morris Freilich, 75–90. New York: Bergin and Garvey.

Ricouer, Paul. 1979. The model of the text: Meaningful action considered as a text. In *Interpretive social science,* ed. Paul Rabinow and William M. Sullivan, 73–102. Berkeley: University of California Press.

Riddell, Barry. 1970. *The spatial dynamics of modernization in Sierra Leone.* Evanston: Northwestern University Press.

Riesman, David, with Nathan Glazer and Reuel Denney. 1950. *The lonely crowd: A study of the changing American character.* New Haven, Conn.: Yale University Press.

Riley, Carroll L., J. Charles Kelley, Campbell W. Pennington, and Robert L. Rands, eds. 1971. *Man across the sea: Problems of pre-Columbian contact.* Austin: University of Texas Press.

Riley, Robert B. 1980. Speculations on the new American landscapes. *Landscape* 24 (3): 1–9.

Riley, Robert B. Forthcoming. Notes on the new rural landscape. *Places.*

Rindos, David. 1984. *The origins of agriculture: An evolutionary perspective.* Orlando: Academic.

Roberts, Marion. 1991. *Living in a man-made world: Gender assumptions in modern housing design.* London: Routledge.

Robinson, Charles M. 1899. Improvement in city life. *Atlantic Monthly* 83:771–85.

———. 1901. *Modern civic art.* New York: Putnam's.

Robinson, Solon. 1936. Negro slavery at the South. In *Solon Robinson: Pioneer and agriculturalist,* 2 vols., ed. Herbert Anthony Kellar, 2:253–307. Indianapolis: Indiana Historical Bureau.

Rodney, Walter. 1972. *How Europe underdeveloped Africa.* London: Bogle L'Ouverture; Dar es Salaam: Tanzania Publishing House.

Rodríguez, José M. 1913. *Rodríguez Memoirs of Early Texas.* San Antonio: Passing Show.

Roemer, Kenneth M. 1976. *The obsolete necessity: America in utopian writings, 1888–1900.* Kent, Ohio: Kent State University Press.

Rogers, Everett. 1962. *Diffusion of innovations.* New York: Free Press.

Rogers, Everett, and F. Shoemaker. 1971. *Communication of innovations: A cross-cultural approach.* New York: Free Press.

Rogin, Leo. 1931. *The introduction of farm machinery in its relation to the productivity of labor in the agriculture of the United States during the nineteenth century.* Berkeley: University of California Press.

Rooney, John F., Wilbur Zelinsky, and Dean R. Lowder, eds. 1982. *This remarkable continent: An atlas of United States and Canadian society and culture.* College Station: Texas A&M University Press.

Rosales, Francisco A. 1976. The regional origins of Mexicano immigrants to Chicago during the 1920s. *Aztlán* 7:187–201.

Rosenberg, Robert, with Madelon Bedell. 1969. *Profits from franchising.* New York: McGraw-Hill.

Ross, Stanley R. 1955. *Francisco I. Madero, Apostle of Mexican Democracy.* New York: Columbia University Press.

Rotberg, Robert L., and Theodore K. Raab, eds. 1985. *Hunger and history: The impact of changing food production and consumption patterns on society.* New York: Cambridge University Press.

Rouse, Irving. 1961. Comments on Edmonson's "Neolithic Diffusion Rates." *Current Anthropology* 2:96.

Rowell, Geoffrey. 1974. *Hell and the Victorians.* Oxford: Clarendon.

Rowles, Graham D. 1978. *Prisoners of space?: Exploring the geographical experience of older people.* Boulder, Colo.: Westview.

Rowley, Charles D. 1972. *The destruction of aboriginal society.* Harmondsworth: Penguin.

Rowley, Gwyn. 1983. Space, territory and competition—Israel and the West Bank. In *Pluralism and political geography: People, territory and state,* ed. Nurit Kliot and Stanley Waterman, 187–200. London: Croom Helm.

Rowntree, Lester, and Margaret Conkey. 1980. Symbolism and the cultural landscape. *Annals of the Association of American Geographers* 70:459–74.

Rowntree, Lester, Kenneth E. Foote, and Mona Domosh. 1989. Cultural geography. In *Geography in America,* ed. G. Gaile and C. Willmott, 209–17. Columbus, Ohio: Merrill.

Rozett, John M. 1976. Racism and republican emergence in Illinois, 1848–1860: A re-evaluation of republican negrophobia. *Civil War History* 22:101–15.

Rue, Loyal D. 1989. *Amythia: Crisis in the natural history of Western culture.* Tuscaloosa: University of Alabama Press.

Rundstrom, Robert A., and Martin Kenzer. 1989. The decline of fieldwork in human geography. *Professional Geographer* 41:294–303.

Russell, Robert. 1857. *North America, its agriculture and climate; Containing observations on the agriculture and climate of Canada, the United States, and the island of Cuba.* Edinburgh: A. and C. Black.

Saarinen, Thomas, David Seamon, and James Sell, eds. 1984. *Environmental perception and behavior: An inventory and prospect.* University of Chicago Department of Geography Research Paper no. 209. Chicago: University of Chicago, Department of Geography.

Sack, Robert. 1980. *Conceptions of space in social thought.* London: Macmillan.

Sahlins, Marshall. 1976. *Culture and practical reason.* Chicago: University of Chicago Press.

———. 1977. *The use and abuse of biology: An anthropological critique of sociology.* Ann Arbor: University of Michigan Press.

Said, Edward W. 1978. *Orientalism.* New York: Pantheon.

Saladino, Gaspar J. 1960. The Maryland and Virginia wheat trade from its beginnings to the American Revolution. M.A. thesis, University of Wisconsin, Madison.

Sale, Kirkpatrick. 1985. *Dwellers on the land: The bioregional vision.* San Francisco: Sierra Club.

———. 1988. Deep ecology and its critics. *The Nation* 246:670–75.

Salter, Christopher L. 1978. Signatures and settings: One approach to landscape in literature. In *Dimensions of human geography: Essays on some familiar and neglected themes,* ed. Karl W. Butzer, 69–83. Chicago: University of Chicago Department of Geography Research Paper no. 186. Chicago: University of Chicago, Department of Geography.

———. 1987. *Geographic themes in United States and world history.* Washington, D.C.: National Geographic Society.

Salter, Christopher L., and William J. Lloyd. 1977. *Landscape and literature.* Association of American Geographers Resources Papers for College Geography no. 76-3. Washington, D.C.: Association of American Geographers.

Samuels, Marwyn S. 1979. The biography of landscape. In *The interpretation of ordinary landscapes,* ed. Donald W. Meinig, 51–88. New York: Oxford University Press.

Sánchez, José M. 1926. A trip to Texas in 1828. Trans. Carlos E. Castañeda. *Southwestern Historical Quarterly* 29:249–88.

Sánchez, Ramón. 1898. *Un viaje de maravatio a San Antonio de Bejar (Texas).* Zamora: Tip. Moderna.

Sánchez-Albornoz, Nicolas. 1974. *The population of Latin America: A history.* Trans. W. A. R. Richardson. Berkeley: University of California Press.

Sánchez Farfan, Jorge. 1983. Evolución y tecnología de la agricultura andina. Cuzco: Proyecto Investigación de los Sistemas Agrícolas Andinos (IICA/CIID).

Santibañez, Enrique. 1930. *Ensayo acerca de la inmigración mexicana en los Estados Unidos.* San Antonio: Clegg.

Santmire, H. Paul. 1968. I-thou, I-it, I-ens. *Journal of Religion* 48:260–73.

———. 1975. Reflections on the alleged ecological bankruptcy of Western theology. *Anglican Theological Review* 57:131–52.

———. 1985. *The travail of nature: The ambiguous ecological promise of Christian theology.* Philadelphia: Fortress.

Sauer, Carl O. 1925. The morphology of landscape. *University of California Publications in Geography* 2:19–54.

———. 1927. Recent developments in cultural geography. In *Recent developments in the social sciences,* ed. E. C. Hayes, 154–212. New York: J.B. Lippincott.

———. 1932. *The road to Cíbola.* Ibero-Americana 5. Berkeley: University of California Press.

———. 1938a. Destructive exploitation in modern colonial expansion. *Comptes Rendus du Congres International de Géographie, Amsterdam* 2 (3c): 494–99.

———. 1938b. The theme of plant and animal destruction in economic history. *Journal of Farm Economics* 20:765–75.

———. 1941a. Forward to historical geography. *Annals of the Association of American Geographers* 31:1–24.

———. 1941b. The personality of Mexico. *Geographical Review* 31:353–64.

———. 1950. Cultivated plants of South and Central America. In *Handbook of South American Indians,* ed. J. H. Steward, 6:487–543. Bureau of American Ethnology Bulletin 143. Washington, D.C.: Smithsonian Institution.

———. 1952. *Agricultural origins and dispersals.* New York: American Geographical Society.

———. 1956a. The agency of man on earth. In *Man's role in changing the face of the earth,* ed. William L. Thomas, 46–49. Chicago: University of Chicago Press.

———. 1956b. The education of a geographer. *Annals of the Association of American Geographers* 46:287–99.

———. 1962. Cultural geography. In *Readings in cultural geography,* ed. Philip Wagner and Marvin Mikesell, 30–34. Chicago: University of Chicago Press.

———. 1966. *The early Spanish Main: The land, nature, and people Columbus encountered in the Americas.* Berkeley: University of California Press.

———. 1971. *Sixteenth century North America: The land and the peoples seen by the explorers.* Berkeley: University of California Press.

Schement, Jorge R., and Ricardo Flores. 1977. The origins of Spanish-language radio: The case of San Antonio, Texas. *Journalism History* 4 (2): 56–58, 61.

Schleier, Merrill. 1986. *The skyscraper in American art, 1890–1931.* Ann Arbor, Mich.: UMI Research.

Schmink, Marianne, and Charles H. Wood. 1987. The "political ecology" of Amazonia. In *Lands at risk in the Third World: Local-level perspectives,* ed. P. D. Little, M. H. Horowitz, and A. E. Nyerges, 38–57. Boulder, Colo.: Westview.

Schob, David E. 1975. *Hired hands and plowboys: Farm labor in the Midwest, 1815–1860.* Urbana: University of Illinois Press.

Schoonmaker, Peter K., and David R. Foster. 1991. Some implications of paleoecology for contemporary ecology. *The Botanic Review* 57:204–45.

Schorske, Carl. 1981. *Fin-de-siècle Vienna: Politics and culture.* New York: Vintage.

Schultz, Theodore W. 1964. *Transforming traditional agriculture.* New Haven, Conn.: Yale University Press.

Schumm, Stanley A. 1991. *To interpret the earth: Ten ways to be wrong.* Cambridge: Cambridge University Press.

Schuyler, David. 1986. *The new urban landscape: The redefinition of city form in nineteenth-century America.* Baltimore: Johns Hopkins University Press.

Schuyler, Montgomery. 1894. Last words about the World's Fair. *Architectural Record* 3 (January-March): 291–301.

———. 1907. Some recent skyscrapers. *The Architectural Record* 22:161–76.

Schwarzbach, F. S. 1979. *Dickens and the city.* London: Athlone Press, University of London.

Scott, Gregory J. 1986. *Mercados, mitos, e intermediarios.* Lima: Universidad del Pacífico.

Scott, James C. 1985. *Weapons of the weak: Everyday forms of peasant resistance.* New Haven, Conn.: Yale University Press.

Scott, Jamie, and Paul Simpson-Housley, eds. 1991. *Sacred places and profane spaces: Essays in the geographics of Judaism, Christianity, and Islam.* New York: Greenwood.

Scott, Mel. 1969. *American city planning since 1890.* Berkeley: University of California Press.

Scott, N. A. 1974. The poetry and theology of earth: Reflections on the testimony of Joseph Sittler and Gerard Manley Hopkins. *Journal of Religion* 54: 102–18.

Scully, Vincent. 1979. *The earth, the temple, and the gods: Greek sacred architecture.* Rev. ed. New Haven, Conn.: Yale University Press.

Seamon, David. 1979. *The geography of lifeworld: Movement, rest, and encounter.* New York: St. Martin's.

Seamon, David, and Robert Mugerauer, eds. 1985. *Dwelling, place and environment: Towards a phenomenology of person and world.* Dordrecht: Nijhoff.

Segal, A. 1968. *The politics of Caribbean economic integration.* Río Piedras: University of Puerto Rico.

Seidenbaum, Art. 1976. A new kind of amusement park. *Los Angeles Times,* 9 May, Part VII, 1.

Sekul, Joseph D. 1983. Communities organized for public service: Citizen power and public policy in San Antonio. In *The politics of San Antonio: Community, progress, and power,* ed. D. R. Johnson, J. A. Booth, and R. J. Harris, 175–90. Lincoln: University of Nebraska Press.

Semple, Ellen C. 1903. *American history and its geographic conditions.* Boston and New York: Houghton Mifflin.

Service, Elman R. 1960. The law of evolutionary potential. In *Evolution and culture,* ed. Marshall D. Sahlins and Elman R. Service, 93–122. Ann Arbor: University of Michigan Press.

Shannon, Fred A. 1968. *The farmer's last frontier: Agriculture, 1860–1897.* New York: Harper & Row.

Shelley, Percy Bysshe. 1903. *Poems.* London: Blackie and Son.

Sherburne, D. W. 1966. *A key to Whitehead's "Process and Reality."* New York: Macmillan.

Sheridan, Thomas E. 1988. *Where the dove calls: The political ecology of a peasant corporate community in northwestern Mexico.* Tucson: University of Arizona Press.

Shields, Rob. 1991. *Places on the margin: Alternative geographies of modernity.* London: Routledge.

Shoard, Marion. 1982. The lure of the moors. In *Valued environments,* ed. John R. Gold and Jacquelin Burgess, 55–73. London: Allen & Unwin.

Short, John Rennie. 1991. *Imagined country: Environment, culture and society.* New York: Routledge, Chapman, and Hall.

Shortridge, James R. 1989. *The Middle West: Its meaning in American culture.* Lawrence: University Press of Kansas.

Shute, Nevil. 1955. *Requiem for a Wren.* London: Heinemann.

Sia, Santiago. 1985. *God in process thought: A study of Charles Hartshorne's concept of God.* Dordrecht: Nijhoff.

Siemens, Alfred H. 1983. Wetland agriculture in pre-Hispanic Mesoamerica. *Geographical Review* 73: 166–81.

———. 1989. *Tierra configurada.* Mexico: Consejo Nacional.

Sigmund, Paul E. 1990. *Liberation theology at the crossroads.* New York: Oxford University Press.

Sillitoe, Alan. 1975. *Mountains and caverns: Selected essays.* London: W.H. Allen.

Simmons, Ian G. 1989. *Changing the face of the earth: Culture, environment, history.* New York: Blackwell.

Simoons, Frederick. 1960. *Eat not this flesh: Food avoidances in the Old World.* Madison: University of Wisconsin Press.

———. 1981. Geographic patterns of lactose malabsorption. In *Lactose digestion: Climatic and nutritional consequences,* ed. David Paige and Theodore Bayless, 23–48. Baltimore: Johns Hopkins University Press.

———. 1991. *Food in China: A cultural and historical inquiry.* Boca Raton, Fla.: CRC Press.

Simpson-Housley, Paul, and G. Norcliffe, eds. 1992. *A few acres of snow: Literary and artistic images of Canada.* Toronto: Dundurn.

Sirelius, U. T. 1909. Über die primitiven Wohnungen der finnischen und ob-ugrischen Völker. *Finnisch-ugrische Forschungen* 9:17–113.

Sittler, Joseph. 1970. Ecological commitment as theological responsibility. *Zygon* 5:172–80.

Sitwell, O. F. G. 1981. Elements of the cultural landscape as figures of speech. *The Canadian Geographer* 25: 168–80.

———. 1990a. A human geographer looks at religion. *Religious Studies and Theology* 10 (2–3): 23–41.

———. 1990b. The expression of ideology in the cultural landscape: A statement of general principles illustrated with examples taken from Edmonton. In *A world of real places: Essays in honour of William C. Wonders,* ed. P. J. Smith and E. L. Jackson, 175–89. University of Alberta Department of Geography Studies in Geography. Edmonton: University of Alberta, Department of Geography.

Sitwell, O. F. G., and O. S. E. Bilash. 1986. Analysing the cultural landscape as a means of probing the non-material dimension of reality. *The Canadian Geographer* 30:132–45.

Skrabanek, R. L. 1970. Language maintenance among Mexican-Americans. *International Journal of Comparative Sociology* 11:272–82.

Slater, David. 1985. Social movements and a recasting of the political. In *New Social Movements and the state in Latin America,* ed. D. Slater, 1–26. Amsterdam: CED-LA.

Smith, Anthony. 1973. *The shadow in the cave.* London: Allen & Unwin.

Smith, Brent W. 1991. The late archaic Poverty Point trade network. In *The Poverty Point culture: Local manifestation, subsistence practices, and trade networks,* ed. Kathleen M. Byrd, 173–80. Louisiana State University Department of Geography and Anthropology Geoscience Publications. Baton Rouge: Louisiana State University, Department of Geography and Anthropology.

Smith, C. T., William M. Denevan, and P. Hamilton. 1968. Ancient ridged fields in the region of Lake Titicaca. *Geographical Journal* 134:353–67.

Smith, G. Eliot. 1971. *The diffusion of culture.* Port Washington, N.Y.: Kennikat.

Smith, Joseph. 1854. *Old Redstone, or historical sketches of western Presbyterianism.* Philadelphia: Lippincott, Grambo.

Smith, Page. 1966. *As a city upon a hill: The town in American history.* New York: Knopf.

Smith, Theodore C. 1967. *The Liberty and Free Soil parties in the Northwest.* New York: Russell & Russell.

Snider, Denton J. 1895. *World's Fair studies.* Chicago: Sigma.

Soininen, Arvo M. 1959. Burn-beating as the technical basis of colonisation in Finland in the sixteenth and seventeenth centuries. *Scandinavian Economic History Review* 7:150–66.

Soja, Edward. 1989. *Postmodern geographies: The reassertion of space in critical social theory.* London: Verso.

Sologiastoa, J. C., ed. 1924. *Guia general directorio Mexicano de San Antonio, Texas.* San Antonio: San Antonio Paper.

Sonnenfeld, Joseph. 1972. Geography, perception, and the behavioral environment. In *Man, space, and environment,* ed. Paul W. English and Robert C. Mayfield, 244–51. New York: Oxford University Press.

———. 1982. Egocentric perspectives on geographic orientation. *Annals of the Association of American Geographers* 72:68–76.

———. 1984a. Philosophical directions in environmental perception and behavioral geography: A commentary. In *Environmental perception and behavior: An inventory and prospect,* ed. Thomas F. Saarinen, David Seamon, and James L. Sell, 225–33. University of Chicago Department of Geography Research Paper no. 209. Chicago: University of Chicago, Department of Geography.

———. 1984b. Travel patterns: Waykeeping-wayfinding relationships. Paper presented at the Annual Meeting of the Association of American Geographers, Washington, D.C.

———. 1985. Tests of spatial skill: A validation problem. *Man-Environment Systems* 15 (3–4): 107–20.

———. 1988. Abilities, skills, competence: A search for alternatives to diffusion. In *The transfer and transformation of ideas and material culture*, ed. Peter J. Hugill and D. Bruce Dickson, 194–213. College Station: Texas A&M University Press.

———. 1991. Way-keeping, way-finding, way-losing: Disorientation in a complex environment. *National Geographical Journal of India* 37 (1–2): 147–60.

Sopher, David E. 1967. *The geography of religions.* Englewood Cliffs, N.J.: Prentice-Hall.

———. 1972. Place and location: Notes on the spatial patterning of culture. *Social Science Quarterly* 53: 321–37.

———. 1973. Place and location: Notes on the spatial patterning of culture. In *The idea of culture in the social sciences,* ed. Louis Schneider and Charles M. Bonjean, 101–17. Cambridge: Cambridge University Press.

Sorkin, Michael, ed. 1992. *Variations on a theme park: Scenes from the new American city and the end of public space.* New York: Hill and Wang/Noonday.

Sorre, Max. 1943–52. *Les fondements de la géographie humaine.* 3 vols. Paris: Armand Colin.

———. 1962. The geography of diet. In *Readings in cultural geography,* ed. Philip L. Wagner and Marvin Mikesell, 445–56. Chicago: University of Chicago Press.

Sorrell, Roger D. 1988. *St. Francis of Assisi and nature.* New York: Oxford University Press.

Soule, Judith D., and John K. Piper. 1992. *Farming in nature's image: An ecological approach to agriculture.* Washington, D.C.: Island.

Spann, Edward. 1981. *The new metropolis: New York City, 1840–1857.* New York: Columbia University Press.

Spate, O. H. K. 1988. *The Pacific since Magellan.* Vol. 3: *Paradise found and lost.* Minneapolis: University of Minnesota Press.

Special International Niagara Board. 1931. *Report of the Special International Niagara Board of the preservation and improvement of Niagara Falls and rapids.* Washington, D.C.: U.S. Government Printing Office.

Spencer, J. E. 1966. *Shifting cultivation in southeastern Asia.* University of California Publications in Geography no. 19. Berkeley: University of California Press.

Spencer, J. E., and Ronald J. Horvath. 1963. How does an agricultural region originate? *Annals of the Association of American Geographers* 53: 74–92.

Speth, William. 1977. Carl Ortwin Sauer on "destructive exploitation." *Biological Conservation* 11: 145–60.

———. 1981. Berkeley geography, 1923–33. In *The origins of academic geography in the United States,* ed. Brian W. Blouet, 221–244. Hamden, Conn.: Archon.

———. 1988. The "Berkeley School" questionnaire. *Proceedings of the New England–St. Lawrence Valley Geographical Society* 18: 26–30.

Spofford, Harriet P. 1877. San Antonio de Bexar. *Harper's New Monthly Magazine* 55: 831–50.

Squire, Shelagh J. 1988. Wordsworth and Lake District tourism: Romantic reshaping of landscape. *Canadian Geographer* 32: 237–47.

Starr, Roger. 1966. *The living end: The city and its critics.* New York: Coward-McCann.

Stea, David. 1980. Toward a cross-cultural environmental psychology. *Proceedings, 17th Interamerican Congress of Psychology,* Lima, Peru.

Stein, Howard. 1987. *Developmental time, cultural space: Studies in psychogeography.* Norman: University of Oklahoma Press.

Stein, Howard F., and William G. Niederland, eds. 1989. *Maps from the mind: Readings in psychogeography.* Norman: University of Oklahoma Press.

Steinbeck, John. 1951. *The grapes of wrath.* Harmondsworth: Penguin.

Steiner, Michael, and Clarence Mondale. 1988. *Region and regionalism in the United States: A source book for the humanities and social sciences.* New York: Garland.

Steinfeldt, Cecelia. 1978. *San Antonio was: Seen through a magic lantern; Views from the slide collection of Albert Steves, Sr.* San Antonio: San Antonio Museum Association.

Stern, Robert A. M., Gregory Gilmartin, and John M. Massengale. 1983. *New York 1900.* New York: Rizzoli.

Stern, Steve J. 1987. *Resistance, rebellion, and consciousness in the Andean peasant world, 18th to 20th centuries.* Madison: University of Wisconsin Press.

Stevens, Richard, and Yuk Lee. 1979. A spatial analysis of agricultural intensity in a Basotho village of southern Africa. *The Professional Geographer* 31: 177–83.

Steward, Julian H. 1955. *Theory of culture change.* Urbana: University of Illinois Press.

Stilgoe, John R. 1982. *Common landscape of America, 1580–1845.* New Haven, Conn.: Yale University Press.

Stoddart, David. 1986. *On geography and its history.* New York: Basil Blackwell.

Stokols, Daniel, and Irwin Altman, eds. 1987. *Handbook of environmental psychology.* New York: Wiley.

Storey, David. 1976. *Saville.* London: B.J. Cape.

Stott, Rebecca. 1989. The dark continent: Africa as female body in Haggard's adventure fiction. *Feminist Review* 32: 69–89.

Stott, William. 1973. *Documentary expression in thirties America.* New York: Oxford University Press.

Stout, Peter. 1859. *Nicaragua: Past, present and future.* Philadelphia: John E. Potter.

Strickland, William. 1971. *Journal of a tour in the United States of America, 1794–1795, with a facsimile edition of William Strickland's "Observations on the agriculture of the United States of America."* Ed. J. E. Strickland. New York: New-York Historical Society.

Suedfeld, Peter, and Jane S. P. Mocellin. 1987. The sensed presence in unusual environments. *Environment and Behavior* 19: 33–52.

Sulzinger, Richard. 1979. Will there be any truck stops in heaven? Images of the landscape in country and western music. Unpublished paper, University of Illinois at Urbana, Department of Landscape Architecture.

Summerson, John. 1963. Heavenly mansions: An interpretation of gothic. In *Heavenly mansions, and other essays on architecture,* 1–28. New York: Norton.

Sussex, Elizabeth, ed. 1975. *The rise and fall of the British documentary.* Berkeley: University of California Press.

Sutch, Richard. 1965. The profitability of ante-bellum slavery—revisited. *Southern Economic Journal* 31: 365–77.

Swallow, Norman. 1965. *Factual television.* London: Focal.

Taaffe, Edward J., Richard L. Morrill, and Peter R. Gould. 1963. Transport expansion in underdeveloped countries: A comparative analysis. *Geographical Review* 53: 503–39.

Tainter, Joseph A. 1988. *The collapse of complex societies.* New York: Cambridge University Press.

Talk of the town. 1989. *New Yorker,* 21 Aug.

Tarde, Gabriel. 1903. *The laws of imitation.* New York: Henry Holt.

Tawney, Richard H. 1936. *Religion and the rise of capitalism.* London: Murray.

Taylor, Paul S. 1933. *Mexican labor in the United States, migration statistics II.* University of California, Publications in Economics no. 12, 1:1–10. Berkeley: University of California Press.

Taylor, Robert R. 1974. *The word in stone: The role of architecture in the National Socialist ideology.* Berkeley: University of California Press.

Thomas, William L., Jr., ed. 1956. *Man's role in changing the face of the earth.* Chicago: University of Chicago Press.

Thompson, Edward P. 1978. *The poverty of theory and other essays.* New York: Monthly Review.

Thompson, Gary R., ed. 1974. *The Gothic imagination: Essays in dark romanticism.* Pullman: Washington State University Press.

Thonhoff, Robert H. 1971. *San Antonio stage lines 1847–1881.* Southwestern Studies Monograph no. 29. El Paso: Texas Western Press.

Thoreau, Henry David. 1862. Walking. *Atlantic Monthly,* June.

Thornbrough, Emma Lou. 1957. *The Negro in Indiana: A study of a minority.* Indianapolis: Indiana Historical Bureau.

Thornthwaite, C. W. 1961. The task ahead. *Annals of the Association of American Geographers* 51:345–56.

Thornton, Russell. 1987. *American Indian holocaust and survival: A population history since 1492.* Norman: University of Oklahoma Press.

Thorp, Rosemary, and Geoffrey Bertram. 1978. *Peru 1890–1977: Growth and policy in an open economy.* New York: Columbia University Press.

Thrift, Nigel. 1990. For a new regional geography I. *Progress in Human Geography* 14:272–79.

———. 1991. For a new regional geography II. *Progress in Human Geography* 15:256–65.

Tiedemann, Clifford, and Carlton S. Van Doren. 1964. *The diffusion of hybrid seed corn in Iowa: A spatial diffusion study.* Michigan State University Institute for Community Development and Services Bulletin B-44. East Lansing: Michigan State University, Institute for Community Development and Services.

Tijerina, Andrew A. 1977. Tejanos and Texans: The native Mexicans of Texas, 1820–1850. Ph.D. diss., University of Texas at Austin.

Tillich, Paul. 1952. *The courage to be.* New Haven, Conn.: Yale University Press.

Tillotson, Kathleen M. 1954. *Novels of the eighteen-forties.* London: Oxford University Press.

Tjarks, Alicia V. 1974. Comparative demographic analysis of Texas, 1777–1793. *Southwestern Historical Quarterly* 77:291–338.

Tobias, Michael, ed. 1985. *Deep ecology.* San Diego: Avant.

Todd, Frank M. 1921. *The story of the exposition.* New York: Putnam's.

Trillin, Calvin. 1977. Thoughts brought on by prolonged exposure to exposed brick. *New Yorker,* 16 May, 101–7.

Trinder, Barrie. 1982. *The making of the industrial landscape.* London: Dent and Sons.

Tuan, Yi-Fu. 1970. Treatment of the environment in ideal and actuality. *American Scientist* 58:244–49.

———. 1971. Geography, phenomenology, and the study of human nature. *Geographical Review* 68:1–12.

———. 1974a. Space and place: A humanistic perspective. *Progress in Geography* 6:211–52.

———. 1974b. *Topophilia: A study of environmental perception, attitudes, and values.* Englewood Cliffs, N.J.: Prentice-Hall.

———. 1975. Place: A humanistic perspective. *Geographical Review* 65:151–65.

———. 1976a. Geopiety: A theme in man's attachment to nature and to place. In *Geographies of the mind: Essays in historical geosophy in honor of John Kirtland Wright,* ed. David Lowenthal and Martyn J. Bowden, 11–39. New York: Oxford University Press.

———. 1976b. Humanistic geography. *Annals of the Association of American Geographers* 66:266–76.

———. 1977. *Space and place: The perspective of experience.* Minneapolis: University of Minnesota Press.

———. 1979a. *Landscapes of fear.* Minneapolis: University of Minnesota Press.

———. 1979b. Thought and landscape: The eye and the mind's eye. In *The interpretation of ordinary landscapes,* ed. D. W. Meinig, 89–102. New York: Oxford University Press.

———. 1984. *Dominance and affection: The making of pets.* New Haven, Conn.: Yale University Press.

———. 1986. *The good life.* Madison: University of Wisconsin Press.

———. 1989. *Morality and imagination: Paradoxes of progress.* Madison: University of Wisconsin Press.

———. 1990. Realism and fantasy in art, history, and geography. *Annals of the Association of American Geographers* 80:435–46.

———. 1991. Language and the making of place: A narrative-descriptive approach. *Annals of the Association of American Geographers* 81:684–96.

Tudor, Henry. 1834. *Narrative of a tour in North America.* London: James Duncan.

Turner, B. L., II. 1974. Prehistoric intensive agriculture in the Mayan lowlands. *Science* 195:118–24.

———. 1983. *Once beneath the forest: Prehistoric terracing in the Rio Bec region of the Maya lowlands.* Boulder, Colo.: Westview.

———. 1989. The specialist-synthesis approach to the revival of geography: The case of cultural ecology. *Annals of the Association of American Geographers* 79: 88–100.

Turner, B. L., II, and Stephen B. Brush, eds. 1987. *Comparative farming systems.* New York: Guilford.

Turner, B. L., II, and Karl W. Butzer. 1992. The Columbian encounter and land use change. *Environment* 34 (9): 16–20, 37–44.

Turner, B. L., II, William C. Clark, Robert W. Kates, John F. Richards, Jessica J. Mathews, and William B. Meyer, eds. 1990. *The earth as transformed by human action: Global and regional changes in the biosphere over the past 300 years.* New York: Cambridge University Press.

Turner, B. L., II, and William M. Denevan. 1985. Prehistoric manipulation of wetlands in the Americas: A raised field perspective. In *Prehistoric intensive agriculture in the tropics,* ed. I. S. Farrington, 11–30. British Archaeological Reports, International Series, no. 232. Oxford: BAR.

Turner, B. L., II, Robert Q. Hanham, and Anthony V. Portararo. 1977. Population pressure and agricultural intensity. *Annals of the Association of American Geographers* 67:384–97.

Turner, B. L., II, and Peter D. Harrison, eds. 1983. *Pulltrouser Swamp: Ancient Maya habitat, agriculture, and settlement in northern Belize.* Austin: University of Texas Press.

Turner, Bryan. 1978. *Marx and the end of Orientalism.* London: Allen & Unwin.

Turner, Frederick. 1980. *Beyond geography: The western spirit against the wilderness.* New York: Viking.

———. 1989. *Spirit of place: The making of an American literary landscape.* San Francisco: Sierra Club.

Turner, Paul V. 1984. *Campus: An American planning tradition.* Cambridge, Mass.: MIT Press.

Twain, Mark. 1885. *The Adventures of Huckleberry Finn.* New York: Charles L. Webster.

Union Carbide and Carbon Corporation. 1954. Chemical progress in Niagara Falls. 1954. *The Tapping Pot* 23:9. Niagara Falls, N.Y.: Union Carbide and Carbon Corporation, Electro Metallurgical Company.

U.S. Bureau of the Census. 1975. *Historical statistics of the United States, colonial times to 1970.* 2 vols. Washington, D.C.: Superintendent of Documents.

U.S. Department of the Interior, United States Geological Survey. 1970. *The National Atlas of the United States.* Washington, D.C.: U.S. Government Printing Office.

Upton, Dell. 1983. The power of things: Recent studies in American vernacular architecture. *American Quarterly* 35:262–79.

Urteaga Villanueva, Horacio. 1982. *Cuzco 1689, Economía*

y sociedad en el sur andino. Cuzco, Peru: Centro de Estudios Rurales "Bartolomé de las Casas."

Vale, Lawrence J. 1992. *Architecture, power, and national identity.* New Haven, Conn.: Yale University Press.

Vale, Thomas R., and Geraldine R. Vale. 1989. *Western images, western landscapes: Travels along U.S. 89.* Tucson: University of Arizona Press.

Vance, James E., Jr. 1977. *This scene of man.* New York: Harper's College.

Van Cleve, A. H. 1903. Utilization of water power at Niagara. *Bulletin of the Buffalo Society of Natural Science* 8 (1).

Vaughn, Charles L. 1974. *Franchising, its nature, scope, advantages, and development.* Lexington, Mass.: Lexington.

Vavilov, Nikolai I. 1951. *The origin, variation, immunity, and breeding of cultivated plants.* New York: Ronald.

Veblen, Thomas T. 1989. Biogeography. In *Geography in America,* ed. Cort Willmott and Gary Gaile, 28–46. Columbus, Ohio: Merrill.

Venturi, Franco. 1963. The history of the concept of "oriental despotism" in Europe. *The Journal of the History of Ideas* 24:133–43.

Venturi, Robert, and Denise S. Brown. 1971. Ugly and ordinary architecture of the decorated shed. *Architectural Forum* 135 (November): 64–67.

Venturi, Robert, Denise S. Brown, and Stephen Izenour. 1972. *Learning From Las Vegas.* Cambridge, Mass.: MIT Press.

Verano, John W., and Douglas H. Ubelaker, eds. 1992. *Disease and demography in the Americas.* Washington, D.C.: Smithsonian Institution.

Vernacular Architecture Forum. 1982, 1986, 1989, 1991. *Perspectives in Vernacular Architecture* 1–4. Columbia: University of Missouri Press.

Verne, Jules. 1863. *Five weeks in a balloon.* Paris: Hetzel.

———. 1911. *Robur, the conquerer.* In *Works of Jules Verne,* ed. Charles F. Horne, vol. 14. London: Vincent Park and Co.

———. 1911. *The master of the world.* In *Works of Jules Verne,* ed. Charles F. Horne, vol. 14. London: Vincent Park and Co.

Vicero, Ralph. 1976. Doctoral dissertations at the University of California, Berkeley, supervised by Carl O. Sauer and doctoral dissertations at the University of Wisconsin–Madison supervised by Andrew H. Clark. *Historical Geography Newsletter* 6 (1): 78–81.

Vidaurreta, Alicia. 1973–74. Evolución urbana de Texas durante el siglo XVIII. *Revista de Indias* 34–35 (131–38): 605–36.

Villasante Ortiz, Segundo. 1975. *Paucartambo: Vision monográfico. Tomo I.* Cuzco, Peru: Editorial Leon.

Vishnu-Mittre. 1978. Origin and history of agriculture in the Indian Subcontinent. *Journal of Human Evolution* 7:31–36.

Vlach, John M. 1976. The shotgun house: An African architectural legacy. *Pioneer America* 8 (1, 2): 47–56, 57–70.

Voget, Fred W. 1975. *A history of ethnology.* New York: Holt, Rinehart and Winston.

Von Eckardt, Wolf. 1977. The huckster peril on main street, U.S.A. *Los Angeles Times,* 5 December, Part II, 11.

Wacker, Peter O. 1975. *Land and people: A cultural geography of preindustrial New Jersey origins and settlement patterns.* New Brunswick, N.J.: Rutgers University Press.

Waddell, Eric. 1972. *The Mound Builders: Agricultural practices, environment, and society in the central highlands of New Guinea.* Seattle: University of Washington Press.

———. 1977. The hazards of scientism: A review article. *Human Ecology* 5:69–76.

Wagner, Philip L. 1972. *Environments and peoples.* Englewood Cliffs, N.J.: Prentice-Hall.

———. 1975. The themes of cultural geography rethought. *Yearbook of the Association of Pacific Coast Geographers* 37:7–14.

———. 1977. The concept of environmental determinism in cultural evolution. In *Origins of agriculture,* ed. Charles A. Reed, 49–74. The Hague: Mouton.

Wagner, Philip L., and Marvin Mikesell, eds. 1962. *Readings in cultural geography.* Chicago: University of Chicago Press.

Waldrop, M. Mitchell. 1988. Seeing all there is to see in the universe. *Science* 241:418–19.

Walker, J. K. 1984. The boll weevil in Texas and the cultural strategy. *Southwestern Entomologist* 9:444–63.

Walker, R. B. J. 1988. *State sovereignty, global civilization, and the rearticulation of political space.* Center of International Studies World Order Studies Occasional Paper no. 18. Princeton, N.J.: Center of International Studies.

Wallach, Bret. 1980. Logging in Maine's empty quarter. *Annals of the Association of American Geographers* 70:542–52.

———. 1981. Sheep ranching in the dry corner of Wyoming. *Geographical Review* 71:51–63.

———. 1991. *At odds with progress: Americans and conservation.* Tucson: University of Arizona Press.

Wallerstein, Immanuel. 1974. *The modern world-system: Capitalist agriculture and the origins of the European world-economy in the sixteenth century.* New York: Academic.

———. 1984. *The politics of the world-economy: The states, the movements and the civilizations.* New York: Cambridge University Press.

Warf, Barney. 1988. The resurrection of local uniqueness. In *A ground for common search,* ed. R. G. Golledge, H. Couclelis, and P. Gould, 50–62. Goleta, Calif.: Santa Barbara Geographical Press.

Warner, John D. 1900. Advertising run mad. *Municipal Affairs* 4:267–93.

Washington, George. 1925. *The diaries of George Washington, 1748–1799.* 4 vols. Ed. J. C. Fitzpatrick. Boston: Houghton Mifflin.

Watts, David. 1987. *The West Indies: Patterns of development, culture, and environmental change since 1492.* Cambridge: Cambridge University Press.

Watts, Michael J. 1983a. On the poverty of theory: Natural hazards research in context. In *Interpreting calamity from the viewpoint of human ecology,* ed. Kenneth Hewitt, 232–62. Boston: Allen & Unwin.

———. 1983b. *Silent violence: Food, famine, and peasantry in northern Nigeria.* Berkeley: University of California Press.

———. 1988. Struggles over land, struggles over meaning: Some thoughts on naming, peasant resistance and the politics of place. In *A ground for common search,* ed. Reginald G. Golledge, Helen Couclelis, and Peter Gould, 31–50. Goleta, Calif.: Santa Barbara Geographical Press.

Weber, Max. 1951. *The religion of China.* New York: Free Press.

———. 1958. *The Protestant ethic and the spirit of capitalism.* Trans. Talcott Parsons. New York: Scribner's.

Webster, J. Carson. 1959. The skyscraper: Logical and historical considerations. *Journal of the Society of Architectural Historians* 18:126–39.

Wedgewood, Iris V. 1936. *Fenland rivers: Impressions of the fen counties.* London: Rich and Cowan.

Weeks, O. Douglas. 1929. The League of United Latin-American Citizens: A Texas-Mexican civic organization. *Southwestern Political and Social Science Quarterly* 10:257–78.

Weightman, Barbara A. 1980. Gay bars as private places. *Landscape* 24 (1): 9–16.

Weisman, Leslie K. 1992. *Discrimination by design: A feminist critique of the man-made environment.* Urbana: University of Illinois Press.

Weisman, Winston. 1954. Commercial palaces of New York: 1845–1875. *Art Bulletin* 36:285–302.

———. 1970. A new view of skyscraper history. In *The rise of an American architecture,* ed. Edgar Kaufman, 115–62. New York: Praeger.

Weiss, Brian. 1974. Economía del Tortuguero: En cada venta una pérdida. In *Memorias de Arrecife Tortuga: Historia natural y económica de las Tortugas en el Caribe de América Central,* ed. Bernard Nietschmann, 161–79. Managua: Colección Cultural, Banco de América.

Wells, H. G. 1908. *The war in the air.* London: Bell and Sons.

Wendorf, Fred, and Romvald Schild. 1980. *Prehistory of the Eastern Sahara.* New York: Academic.

West, H. G. 1951. The house is a compass. *Landscape: Human Geography of the Southwest* 1 (2): 24–27.

West, Richard. 1977. From Texas with love. *Texas Monthly* 5 (6): 90–97.

West, Robert C. 1959. Ridge or "era" agriculture in the Colombian Andes. *Actas del XXXIII Congreso Internacional de Americanistas* 1:279–82.

———. 1979. *Carl Sauer's fieldwork in Latin America.* Ann Arbor, Mich.: University Microfilms.

————, ed. 1982. *Andean reflections: Letters from Carl O. Sauer.* Boulder, Colo.: Westview.

West, Robert C., and John P. Augelli. 1989. *Middle America: Its lands and peoples.* 3d ed. Englewood Cliffs, N.J.: Prentice-Hall.

Westermann, Claus. 1974. *Creation.* Philadelphia: Fortress.

————. 1982. *Elements of Old Testament theology.* Atlanta, Ga.: John Knox.

Westermann, J. H. 1952. *Conservation in the Caribbean.* Foundation for Scientific Research in Surinam and the Netherland Antilles Publication no. 7. Utrecht: Foundation for Scientific Research in Surinam and the Netherland Antilles.

————. 1953. *Nature preservation in the Caribbean.* Foundation for Scientific Research in Surinam and the Netherland Antilles Publication no. 9. Utrecht: Foundation for Scientific Research in Surinam and the Netherland Antilles.

Wheatley, Paul. 1971. *The pivot of the Four Quarters: A preliminary enquiry into the origins and character of the ancient Chinese city.* Chicago: Aldine.

————. 1983. *Nagara and Commandery: Origins of the Southeast Asian urban traditions.* University of Chicago Department of Geography Research Papers nos. 207–8. Chicago: University of Chicago, Department of Geography.

White, Gilbert, ed. 1974. *Natural hazards: Local, national, global.* New York: Oxford University Press.

White, Lynn. 1962. *Medieval technology and social change.* Oxford: Oxford University Press.

————. 1967. The historical roots of our ecologic crisis. *Science* 155:1203–1207.

————. 1968. *Machina ex Deo: Essays in the dynamism of Western culture.* Cambridge, Mass.: MIT Press.

Whitehead, Alfred N. 1920. *The concept of nature.* Cambridge: Cambridge University Press.

————. 1925. *Science and the modern world.* New York: Macmillan.

————. 1927. *Process and reality.* New York: Macmillan.

Whitmore, Thomas M., B. L. Turner II, D. L. Johnson, R. W. Kates, and T. R. Gottschang. 1990. Long-term population change. In *The earth as transformed by human action: Global and regional changes in the biosphere over the past 300 years,* ed. B. L. Turner II et al., 25–40. New York: Cambridge University Press.

Wilbanks, Thomas J. 1972. Accessibility and technical change in northern India. *Annals of the Association of American Geographers* 62:427–36.

Wilken, Gene. 1987. *Good farmers: Traditional agriculture in Mexico and Central America.* Berkeley: University of California Press.

Williams, Lynden S. 1990. Agricultural terrace evolution in Latin America. *Yearbook of the Conference of Latin Americanist Geographers* 16:82–93.

Williams, Michael. 1983. "The apple of my eye": Carl Sauer and historical geography. *Journal of Historical Geography* 9:1–28.

————. 1991. The human use of wetlands. *Progress in Human Geography* 15:1–22.

Williams, Raymond. 1961. *Culture and society.* Harmondsworth: Penguin.

————. 1965. *The long rebellion.* Harmondsworth: Penguin.

————. 1973. *The country and the city.* London: Chatto and Windus.

————. 1976. *Keywords: A vocabulary of culture and society.* Oxford: Oxford University Press.

Wilson, Alexander. 1992. *The culture of nature: North American landscape from Disney to the Exxon Valdez.* Cambridge, Mass.: Blackwell.

Wines, James. 1972. Case for the big duck. *Architectural Forum* 136 (April): 60–61. Chicago: Regnery.

Wishart, David J. 1979. *The fur trade of the American West, 1807–1840: A geographical synthesis.* Lincoln: University of Nebraska Press.

Wisner, B. 1977. Man-made drought in Eastern Kenya. In *Land-use and development,* ed. P. O'Keefe and B. Wisner. London: International African Institute.

Wittfogel, Karl. 1957. *Oriental despotism.* New Haven, Conn.: Yale University Press.

Wohlwill, Joachim F. 1973. The environment is not in the head! In *Environmental Design Research,* vol. 2: *Symposia and Workshops of the Fourth International EDRA Conference,* ed. Wolfgang F. E. Preiser, 166–81. Stroudsburg, Penn.: Dowden, Hutchinson, and Ross.

Wolf, Eric R. 1966. *Peasants.* Englewood Cliffs, N.J.: Prentice-Hall.

————. 1972. Ownership and political ecology. *Anthropological Quarterly* 45:201–5.

————. 1982. *Europe and the people without history.* Berkeley: University of California Press.

Wong, Shue Tuck, ed. 1992. *Person, place, thing: Interpretive and empirical essays in cultural geography.* Geoscience and Man 31. Baton Rouge: Louisiana State University, Department of Geography and Anthropology.

Wood, Theodore E. B. 1972. *The word "sublime" and its context: 1650–1760.* The Hague: Mouton.

Woodruff, William. 1966. *Impact of Western man: A study of Europe's role in the world economy, 1750–1960.* New York: St. Martin's.

Woods, Frances J. 1949. *Mexican ethnic leadership in San Antonio, Texas.* Washington, D.C.: Catholic University of America Press.

Woodward, Kenneth. 1985. In old San Antonio, *mestizaje* nurtures new American way. *Smithsonian* 16 (9): 115–27.

Wordsworth, William, and Samuel T. Coleridge. 1968. *Lyrical ballads 1805.* Ed. Derek Roper. London: Collins.

The World's Fair balance sheet. 1893. *Review of Reviews* 8 (Nov.): 522–23.

Worster, Donald. 1988. Doing environmental history. In *The ends of the earth: Perspectives on modern environmental history,* ed. Donald Worster, 289–307. New York: Cambridge University Press.

Wright, Angus. 1984. Innocence abroad: American agricultural research in Mexico. In *Meeting the expectations of the land,* ed. Wes Jackson, Wendell Berry, and Bruce Colman, 135–51. San Francisco: North Point.

Wright, Gwendolyn. 1991. *The politics of urban design in French colonial urbanism.* Chicago: University of Chicago Press.

Wright, John K. 1947. *Terrae incognitae:* The place of imagination in geography. *Annals of the Association of American Geographers* 37:1–15.

———. 1966a. *Human nature in geography.* Cambridge: Harvard University Press.

———. 1966b. Notes on early American geopiety. In *Human nature in geography,* 250–85. Cambridge: Harvard University Press.

Wright, Martin. 1958. The antecedents of the double-pen house type. *Annals of the Association of American Geographers* 48:109–17.

Wyckoff, William. 1979. *On the Louisiana school of cultural geography and the case of the Upland South.* Syracuse University Department of Geography Discussion Paper no. 54. Syracuse, N.Y.: Syracuse University, Department of Geography.

Yapa, Lakshman. 1977. The Green Revolution: A diffusion model. *Annals of the Association of American Geographers* 67:350–59.

———. 1980. Diffusion, development, and ecopolitical economy. In *Innovation research and public policy,* ed. John A. Agnew, 101–41. Syracuse, N.Y.: Syracuse University, Department of Geography.

Yapa, Lakshman, and Robert Mayfield. 1978. Nonadoption of innovations: Evidence from discriminant analysis. *Economic Geography* 54:145–56.

Yasuba, Yasukichi. 1961. The profitability and viability of plantation slavery in the United States. *Economic Studies Quarterly* 12:60–67.

Yeates, Maurice, and Barry Garner. 1976. *The North American city.* New York: Harper & Row.

Zelinsky, Wilbur. 1951. Where the South begins: The northern limit of the cis-Appalachian South in terms of settlement landscape. *Social Forces* 30:172–78.

———. 1955. Some problems in the distribution of generic terms in the place-names of the northeastern United States. *Annals of the Association of American Geographers* 45:319–49.

———. 1961. An approach to the religious geography of the United States: Patterns of church membership in 1952. *Annals of the Association of American Geographers* 51:139–93.

———. 1967. Classical town names in the United States: The historical geography of an American idea. *Geographical Review* 57:463–95.

———. 1970a. Beyond the exponentials: The role of geography in the great transition. *Economic Geography* 46:499–535.

———. 1970b. Cultural variation in personal name patterns in the eastern United States. *Annals of the Association of American Geographers* 60:743–69.

———. 1973. *The cultural geography of the United States.* Englewood Cliffs, N.J.: Prentice-Hall.

———. 1975. The demigod's dilemma. *Annals of the Association of American Geographers* 65:123–43.

———. 1980. Lasting impact of the prestigious gentry. *Geographical Magazine* 52 (12): 817–24.

Zilversmit, Arthur. 1967. *The first emancipation: The abolition of slavery in the North.* Chicago: University of Chicago Press.

Zimmerer, Karl S. 1991. Wetland production and smallholder persistence: Agricultural change in a highland Peruvian region. *Annals of the Association of American Geographers* 81:443–63.

Zimmerman, Michael E. 1988. Quantum theory, intrinsic value, and panentheism. *Environmental Ethics* 10:3–30.

Zonn, Leo, ed. 1990. *Place images in media: Portrayal, experience, and meaning.* Savage, Md.: Rowman and Littlefield.

Zube, Ervin H., and Margaret J. Zube, eds. 1977. *Changing rural landscapes.* Amherst: University of Massachusetts Press.

Zukin, Sharon. 1991. *Landscapes of power: From Detroit to Disney World.* Berkeley: University of California Press.

EDITORS AND CONTRIBUTORS

Daniel D. Arreola is associate professor of geography at Arizona State University, Tempe, Arizona 85287-0104.

James M. Blaut is professor of geography at the University of Illinois at Chicago, Chicago, Illinois 60680.

Jacquelin Burgess is a reader in the Department of Geography, University College, 26 Bedford Way, London WC1H 0AP, United Kingdom.

Karl W. Butzer holds the Raymond C. Dickson Centennial Professorship of Liberal Arts in the Department of Geography at the University of Texas at Austin, Austin, Texas 78712-1098.

Denis E. Cosgrove is a reader in cultural geography in the Department of Geography at the Loughborough University of Technology, Loughborough, Leicestershire LE11 3TU, United Kingdom.

Alfred W. Crosby is professor of geography and American studies at the University of Texas at Austin, Austin, Texas 78712-1098.

Mona Domosh is associate professor of geography in the College of Liberal Arts at Florida Atlantic University, Davie, Florida 33314.

Robin W. Doughty is professor of geography at the University of Texas at Austin, Austin, Texas 78712-1098.

James S. Duncan is professor of geography at Syracuse University, Syracuse, New York 13244-1160.

Carville Earle is professor and chair of the Department of Geography and Anthropology at the Louisiana State University, Baton Rouge, Louisiana 70803-4105.

Kenneth E. Foote is associate professor of geography at the University of Texas at Austin, Austin, Texas 78712-1098.

Peter J. Hugill is professor of geography at Texas A&M University, College Station, Texas 77843.

Barbara Rubin Hudson received her Ph.D. in geography from the University of California, Los Angeles, and her J.D. from the Illinois Institute of Technology. She is currently engaged in the private practice of law. Her address is P.O. Box 94, Danville, Virginia 24543.

John Brinckerhoff Jackson, founder and editor (1951–1969) of *Landscape* magazine, has retired to the Southwest. His address is Route 14, Box 26, Santa Fe, New Mexico 87505.

Terry G. Jordan holds the Walter Prescott Webb Chair in History and Ideas in the Department of Geography at the University of Texas at Austin, Austin, Texas 78712-1098.

Peirce F. Lewis is professor of geography at Pennsylvania State University, University Park, Pennsylvania 16802.

Patrick V. McGreevy is professor in the Department of Geography and Earth Science at Clarion University of Pennsylvania, Clarion, Pennsylvania 16214.

Kent Mathewson is associate professor of geography and anthropology at Louisiana State University, Baton Rouge, Louisiana 70803-4105.

Donald W. Meinig is professor of geography at Syracuse University, Syracuse, New York 13244-1160.

Marvin W. Mikesell is professor of geography at the University of Chicago, Chicago, Illinois 60637.

Bernard Q. Nietschmann is professor of geography at the University of California, Berkeley, California 94720.

James J. Parsons is professor emeritus in the Department of Geography at the University of California at Berkeley, Berkeley, California 94720.

Douglas C. D. Pocock is a reader in geography at the University of Durham, Durham DHI 3LE, United Kingdom.

Miles E. Richardson holds the Fred B. Kniffen professorship in the Department of Geography and Anthropology at Louisiana State University, Baton Rouge, Louisiana 70803-4105.

Robert B. Riley is editor of *Landscape Journal* and professor of landscape architecture and architecture at the University of Illinois at Urbana-Champaign, Urbana, Illinois 61801.

Christopher L. Salter is professor and chair in the Department of Geography at the University of Missouri at Columbia, Columbia, Missouri 65211.

Jonathan M. Smith is assistant professor of geography at Texas A&M University, College Station, Texas 77843.

Joseph Sonnenfeld is professor emeritus of geography at Texas A&M University, College Station, Texas 77843.

Philip L. Wagner is professor emeritus in the Department of Geography at Simon Fraser University, Burnaby, British Columbia V5A 1S6, Canada.

Karl S. Zimmerer is associate professor in the Department of Geography at the University of Wisconsin at Madison, Madison, Wisconsin 53706.

INDEX

Adams, Richard (writer), 365

adaptation, 6, 150, 169, 171–172, 236–237, 239, 412; architectural, 338; behavioral, 284, 288, 414; biological, 172, 258, 414; to changing environmental conditions, 283–284, 255, 257; cultural, 168, 171–172, 227, 230, 232, 279, 413–416; diffusion of, 179; to disorientation in environment, 379–382; and innovation, 21, 169, 171–172; institutional, 425; of Miskito Indians, 237, 239, 255, 257; primate, 158; processes of, 413–416; strategies of, 227–232, 379–381

adaptive strategies. *See* adaptation, strategies of

aesthetics, 288, 346, 430; of high culture, 326; and landscape appreciation, 288; legislated, 327; of Midwestern landscapes, 154; of skyscrapers, 161; urban, 329–330, 341–344. *See also* ideology, aesthetic

agency. *See* human agency

agency and institution (theme), 21, 169–170

agricultural intensification. *See* agriculture, intensification of

Agricultural Origins and Dispersals (Carl O. Sauer), 12–13, 285

agriculture, 279–280, 284–285; in Andean wetland, 260–278; in antebellum U.S., antebellum, 201–212; Boserup's theory of intensification for, 171, 285; capitalist, 21; in colonial Chesapeake, 205–207; commercialization of, 417; diffusion of, 12, 28, 173; drained-field, 184, 189, 280; dry-field, 184; ethnoagriculture, 422; European, 183, 229; European, in seventeenth century, 228; farming systems, 406; impact on landscape, 423; intensification of, 168, 171–172, 244, 246, 269, 285, 416; and irrigation, 116, 118, 184, 262, 416; market, 249, 252; in midwestern U.S., 112; among Miskito Indians, 251; of Mormons, 47, 116; in New Sweden, 227–228; nonmechanized, 274, 276; in northern U.S., 212; origins of, 12, 173, 184, 189;